Cyprus

THE ROUGH GUIDE

Rough Guide credits

Text editor:	Paul Gray
Series editor:	Mark Ellingham
Editorial:	Martin Dunford, Jonathan Buckley, Jo Mead, Samantha Cook, Alison Cowan, Amanda Tomlin, Annie Shaw, Vivienne Heller, Sarah Dallas, Chris Schüler, Helena Smith, Kirk Marlowe
Production:	Susanne Hillen, Andy Hilliard, Judy Pang, Link Hall, Nicola Williamson, Helen Ostick
Cartography:	Melissa Flack, David Callier
Online Editors:	Alan Spicer (UK), Andrew Rosenberg (US)
Finance:	John Fisher, Celia Crowley, Catherine Gillespie
Marketing & Publicity:	Richard Trillo, Simon Carloss, Niki Smith (UK), Jean-Marie Kelly, (US)
Administration:	Tania Hummel, Mark Rogers

ACKNOWLEDGEMENTS

The author would like to acknowledge, on the ground in the South, Christofis Kykas in Nicosia (again); Lefkos Christodoulou, Agros enthusiast; Yiannis Christofides, for correcting errors in Plátres listings; Walter Pouder, for opening my eyes to scuba possibilities around the Akámas; and **Adrian Akers-Douglas**, for gracious hospitality and stimulating conversations. In the North, continued thanks to **Küfi Birinci** for nocturnal tours and his usual forthright views, Ahmet Dervi for frank talks, and Peter Personn and Brigitte Wieschollek for inside tips around Kyrenia.

In the writing phase of this project, **Tanya Colebourne-Tsikas** and Jenny Colbourne provided masses of supplementary information on Nicosia, Limassol, and Páfos districts, Stephanie Ferguson forwarded Limassol taverna tips, and Penny Michael did the same for Larnaca. **Lance Chilton** and **David Whaley** provided invaluable contributions on wildlife, while **David Pearlman**, naturalized Cypriot and Páfos enthusiast, fact-checked the entire book to detect various lapses in archeological terminology, taste and historical accuracy. Back in the UK, Jenny Turner of the *Guardian* provided supplementary snippets on the North, David Barchard, former Ankara correspondent of the *Financial Times*, explained the finer points of the Asil Nadir scandal, and Clement Dodd furnished complementary bibliographic material. Continued thanks also to everyone who helped with the first edition.

At Rough Guides, **Paul Gray** meticulously edited the text, and hearty thanks are also due to Jennifer Speake for proofreading and Mick Bohoslawec for map-making. Many thanks, too, for readers' contributions – the roll of honour appears on p.379.

Published June 1996 by Rough Guides Ltd, 1 Mercer Street, London WC2H 9QJ.
Distributed by the Penguin Group:

Penguin Books Ltd, 27 Wrights Lane, London W8 5TZ
Penguin Books USA Inc., 375 Hudson Street, New York 10014, USA
Penguin Books Australia Ltd, 487 Maroondah Highway, PO Box 257, Ringwood, Victoria 3134, Australia
Penguin Books Canada Ltd, 10 Alcorn Avenue, Toronto, Ontario, Canada M4V 1E4
Penguin Books (NZ) Ltd, 182–190 Wairau Road, Auckland 10, New Zealand

Typeset in Linotron Univers and Century Old Style to an original design by Andrew Oliver.
Printed in the United Kingdom by Cox and Wyman Ltd (Reading).
Illustrations on p.1 and p.303 by Henry Iles.

400pp. includes index

A catalogue record for this book is available from the British Library.

ISBN 1-85828-182-2

Cyprus

THE ROUGH GUIDE

Written and researched by
Marc Dubin

THE ROUGH GUIDES

LIST OF MAPS

Cyprus	vi–vii
The South	47
Larnaca and Around	54–55
Larnaca	57
Limassol and Around	80–81
Limassol	84–85
Ancient Kourion	99
Páfos and the West	106–107
Káto Páfos	111
Ktíma Páfos	117
Akámas Peninsula	140
The High Tróödhos	156–157
Tróödhos Summit	161

South Nicosia and Around	188
South Nicosia	192–193
The North	215
North Nicosia and Around	220–221
North Nicosia	222–223
Kyrenia and the North Coast	240–241
Kyrenia	244
Central Kyrenia	247
Famagusta and	
the Kárpas Peninsula	272–273
Famagusta	274
Famagusta: Walled City	278–279
Ancient Salamis	285

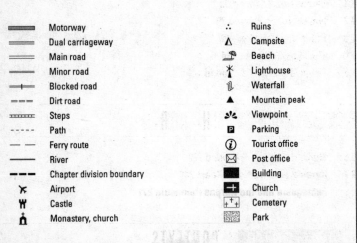

MAP SYMBOLS

▬▬	Motorway	∴	Ruins
══	Dual carriageway	Δ	Campsite
══	Main road	🏖	Beach
──	Minor road	⚡	Lighthouse
╫	Blocked road	🜄	Waterfall
═══	Dirt road	▲	Mountain peak
▭▭▭	Steps	🏔	Viewpoint
-----	Path	🅿	Parking
─ ─	Ferry route	ⓘ	Tourist office
～～	River	⊠	Post office
▬ ▬	Chapter division boundary	■	Building
✈	Airport	⊞	Church
♜	Castle	✚	Cemetery
♙	Monastery, church	▨	Park

CONTENTS

Introduction viii

PART ONE   BASICS   1

Getting There from Britain 3
Getting There from North America 8
Getting There from Australasia 10
Red Tape and Visas 12
Health and Insurance 12
Information and Maps 14
Money and Banks 18
Costs 19
Getting Around 20
Accommodation 25

Eating and Drinking 27
Communications: Post and Phones 34
The Media 36
Opening Hours, Holidays and Festivals 38
Sites, Churches, Museums and Mosques 40
Police, Trouble and Harassment 42
Sports and Outdoor Activities 43
Shopping 44
Directory 44

PART TWO   THE SOUTH   47

■ 1   **Larnaca and Around 53**
■ 2   **Limassol and Around 79**
■ 3   **Páfos and the West 105**
■ 4   **The High Tróödhos 154**
■ 5   **South Nicosia and Around 187**

PART THREE   THE NORTH   215

■ 6   **North Nicosia and Around 220**
■ 7   **Kyrenia and the North Coast 240**
■ 8   **Famagusta and the Kárpas Peninsula 271**

PART FOUR   CONTEXTS   303

The Historical Framework 305
Summer 1974: Personal Accounts 334
Wildlife 340

Books 359
Language 363
Glossary 372

Index 375

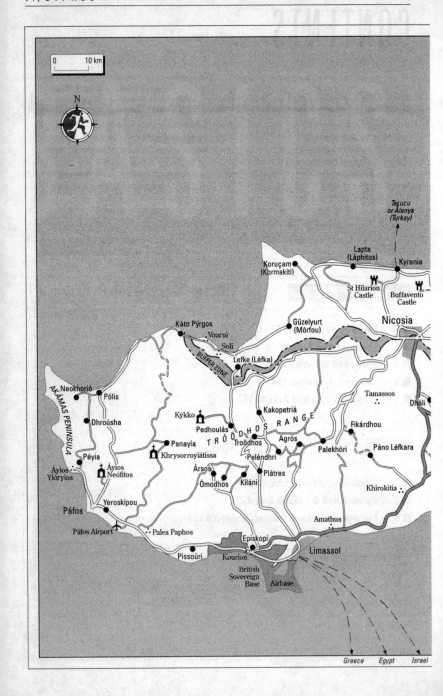

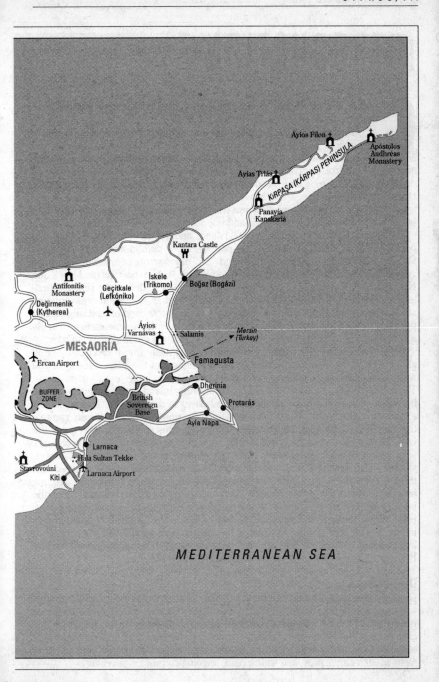

INTRODUCTION

Cyprus, the Mediterranean's third largest island after Sicily and Sardinia, defers only to Malta as the newest state in the region, having come into existence on August 16, 1960. For the first time, following centuries of domination by whatever empire or nation held sway in the eastern Mediterranean – including, from 1878 to 1960, **Great Britain** – the islanders seemed to control their own destiny. Such empowerment proved illusory: no distinctly Cypriot **national identity** was permitted to evolve by the island's Orthodox Christian Greek and Muslim Turkish communities. Within four years, tension between these two groups rent the society asunder, followed in 1974 by a political and ethnic division of the island imposed by the mainland Turkish army.

However, **calm** now reigns on the island, and for British visitors there's a persistent sense of déjà vu to Cyprus, perhaps more than in any other ex-Crown Colony. Pillar boxes still display "GR" and "ER" monograms near zebra crossings; grandiose colonial public buildings jostle for space with vernacular mud-brick and Neoclassical houses; and of course driving is on the left. Before the recent founding of universities in both South and North, higher education was pursued abroad, preferably in the UK, and **English** – virtually a second official language in the South – is widely spoken. Despite the bitterness of the independence struggle against the UK, all is forgiven (if not exactly forgotten) a generation or so later.

Even the most ardent Cyprus enthusiast will concede that it can't compete in allure with more exotic, airline-poster destinations, yet the place grows on you with prolonged acquaintance (as evidenced by the huge expat population). There's certainly enough to hold your interest inland once you tire of the **beaches**, which tend to be small, scattered coves in the South, or longer, dunier expanses in the North. Horizons are defined by one of **two mountain ranges**: the convoluted massif of the Tróödhos, with numerous spurs and valleys, and the wall-like escarpment of the Kyrenia hills, seemingly sculpted of papier-mâché.

In terms of **special-interest** visits, archeology buffs, wine-drinkers, flower-sniffers, bird-watchers and mountain-bikers are particularly well catered for, though state-of-the-art nightlife and cultural diversions can be thin on the ground, in keeping with the predominantly forty- and fifty-something clientele and the island's provincialism. This has a natural consequence in the overwhelming presence of the **package industry**, supported by law in the South, by unwritten rule in the North, and placing several of the bigger resorts effectively off-limits to independent travellers. But for an undemanding, reasonably priced **family holiday** most months of the year, Cyprus is still a good bet.

Divided Cyprus

Long-dormant rivalry and resentment between Cyprus' two principal ethnic groups was reawakened late in the 1950s by the Greek Cypriot campaign for *énosis* or **union with Greece**. Following independence, disputes over the proper respective civic roles of the Greek and Turkish Cypriot communities, and lingering advocacy of *énosis*, or *taksim* (**partition of the island** between Greece and Turkey) by extremists in each camp, provoked widespread, ongoing communal violence.

Abetted by interested outsiders, these incidents – and a CIA-backed coup against the elected government – culminated in the 1974 operation by the Turkish army which effectively **partitioned** the island, with both Greek and Turkish Cypriots on the "wrong" side of the ceasefire line compelled to leave their homes. Nicosia, the capital, approximately at the centre of Cyprus, was divided like Berlin, and remains so at present; much of Famagusta, formerly home to about eight percent of the island's population, lies abandoned. If this all sounds eye-rollingly familiar in the wake of events in former Yugoslavia and the Russian Federation, there was during the 1960s and 1970s a relative novelty to the crises that repeatedly convulsed Cyprus.

In the **aftermath** of 1974, the two zones of Cyprus nurse grievances against each other that are difficult for many outsiders to fathom, and North and South remain mutually isolated, having developed over time into parallel societies, destined, perhaps, never to converge again. The island's division is comparable to that of Germany, though as Cyprus is a far more intimate place the scale of human tragedy has been more visible. **Reunification**, if and when it comes, is bound to be hedged with conditions, and fraught with pitfalls similar to the German experience: while South and North are both avowedly capitalist, the linguistic and religious gulf separating the two communities, compounded by nearly three decades of enforced segregation, may prove impossible to bridge.

Where to go

Because of the mutual hostility of South and North, you'll have to **choose** which side of Cyprus to visit on any given trip: except for heavily restricted day trips from the South into the North, you are not allowed to move from one side of the island to the other. If you go to the South after having been to the North, keep evidence of such a journey out of your passport (see "Visas and Red Tape" in *Basics* for a full explanation).

Yet either portion of the island has plenty to keep you busy for the typical one-, two- or three-week duration of package deals. When the **South's** busiest beaches east of **Larnaca** pall, there's the popular hill village of **Páno Léfkara**, unique sacred art at Byzantine **Angelóktisti church** and nearby Lusignan "**Chapelle Royale**", or the atmospheric Muslim shrine of **Hala Sultan** to the west. Beyond functional **Limassol**, the Crusader tower of **Kolossi** guards vineyards as it always has, while extensive ancient **Kourion** sprawls nearby atop seaside cliffs.

Of the three main south coast resorts, **Páfos** has most recently awoken to tourism, but with its spectacular Roman mosaics and early Christian relics has perhaps the most to offer. The hinterland of Páfos district belies its initial bleak appearance to reveal fertile valleys furrowing ridges sprinkled with brown-stone villages and, to either side of the **Akámas Peninsula**, the last unspoiled stretches of coast in the South. If you don't require lively nightlife, then **Pólis** or **Latchí** make good, comfortable overnight bases in this area, serving too as springboards into the foothills of the Tróödhos mountains.

Inland from Páfos or Limassol, the **mountains** themselves beckon, covered in well-groomed forest, lovingly resuscitated from a nadir last century. **Plátres**, the original Cypriot "hill station", makes a logical base on the south side of the range; to the north, more authentic village character asserts itself at **Pedhoulás** or **Kakopetriá**. Scattered across several valleys, a dozen or so magnificently **frescoed late-Byzantine chapels** provide an additional focus to itineraries here if the scenery and walking opportunities aren't enough.

Southern **Nicosia** – the Greek Cypriot portion of the divided capital – while not immediately appealing, can boast an idiosyncratic old town in the throes of revitalization, and, in the Cyprus Museum, one of the finest archeological collections in the Middle East. North Nicosia, on the other side of the nearly impervious 1974 ceasefire line, is graced with most of the island's Ottoman monuments – and also introduces the Frenchified ecclesiastical architecture bequeathed by the Lusignan dynasty.

For the majority of tourists in the **North**, however, **Kyrenia** is very much the main event, its old harbour the most sheltered and charming on Cyprus. Some resort development straggles to either side of town, but this coast is still light-years behind the South in that respect. The shaggy hills looming above support three medieval **castles** – **St Hilarion**, **Buffavento** and **Kantara** – whose views and architecture rarely disappoint. Add villages in picturesque settings below the ridgeline, and it's little wonder that outsiders have been gravitating here longer than anywhere else on the island.

The **beaches** north of Famagusta are Kyrenia's only serious rival for tourist custom, and hard to resist in tandem with **Salamis**, the largest ancient site on Cyprus. **Famagusta** itself is remarkable, another Lusignan church-fantasy wrapped in some of the most imposing Venetian walls in the world – though churches and ramparts aside there's little else to see or do, the town having lain devastated since the Ottoman conquest. North of the beach strip, the **Kırpaşa (Kárpas) Peninsula** points finger-like towards Syria, its fine beaches and generous complement of early churches – most notably at **Áyios Fílon** and **Ayía Triás** – little frequented.

When to go

Because of a situation as much **Middle Eastern** as Mediterranean, Cyprus repays a visit in almost any month; the overall mildness of the **climate** allows citrus to grow at altitudes of 450 metres, grapevines to flourish up to 1000 metres and frost-tender cedars to sprout at 1500-metre elevations in the Tróödhos. Such plant-zone limits would be unthinkable even on nearby Crete, despite an identical latitude of 34 degrees north.

If you're coming for the **flora and birdlife** – as more and more people do – then **winter and spring**, beginning early December and late February respectively, are for you. Rain falls in sporadic bursts throughout this period and into March, leaving the rare spectacle of a green, prairie-like Mesaoría, the central plain which most tourists only know as a parched, stubbly dustbowl. You'll also **cut costs** significantly by showing up in the off-season.

As the months progress and the mercury climbs, you can either brave the multitudes at the seashore – considerable in the South – or follow the wildflowers inland and up the slopes of the Tróödhos mountains, veritable havens of **coolness** and relative solitude. In the coastal South, **mid-summer** is a bit too hot for comfort, and of course incurs **high-season** prices (June–Sept). During July or August you're probably better off in the **North**, where the seaward, damper slope of the Kyrenia hills especially offers a refuge both from crowds and extreme temperatures.

Autumn is delightful, with the sea at its warmest, forays into the hills benefiting from **stable weather**, and the air (around Limassol or Páfos especially) heavy with the fumes of fermenting grapes. And if it's **resort life** you're after, the coastal strips don't completely wind down until after New Year.

AVERAGE TEMPERATURES AND RAINFALL					
	Jan	March	May	July	Sept	Nov
Nicosia						
Max °F	59	66	85	98	92	72
Min °F	42	44	58	70	65	51
Days of rain	14	8	3	0	1	6
Kyrenia						
Max °F	62	65	78	91	87	73
Min °F	48	49	60	72	69	58
Days of rain	13	7	2	0	1	7
Tróödhos foothills						
Max °F	47	54	70	84	77	60
Min °F	36	39	52	64	59	46
Days of rain	14	9	3	1	1	6

[The Cypriot] is entering in thousands that trough – of how many generations? – between peasant honesty and urban refinement. "To be civilised," a Nicosia friend told me, "our people must first be vulgar. It is the bridge between simplicity and culture."

Colin Thubron

THE
BASICS

GETTING THERE FROM BRITAIN

The majority of visitors arrive in Cyprus, South or North, by air as part of an all-inclusive package; from the UK there are frequent scheduled or chartered year-round flights from London and several regional airports. The South is also easy to reach from most neighbouring countries except Turkey, from where you can fly only to the North. Coming to the island-nation by boat, you can choose from among several embarcation points in Greece, Israel and Egypt (for the South) and Turkey (for the North).

BY PLANE TO THE SOUTH

Scheduled flights to either part of Cyprus are somewhat overpriced for the number of air-miles involved; except in winter you'll often get better value from a charter, though see the warning under "Packages" in this section.

SCHEDULED FLIGHTS
Larnaca and **Páfos** on the coast are the southern Republic's two international airports. **Cyprus Airways**, the national carrier, offers summer service to Larnaca from London Heathrow (2 daily), London Gatwick (several weekly), Birmingham (3 weekly) and Manchester (3 weekly). Winter schedules shrink to 1 daily from Heathrow, 3 weekly from Gatwick, twice weekly from Manchester and twice weekly from Birmingham. Summer frequencies to Páfos are somewhat less: 2 to 3 weekly from London Heathrow; 2 to 3 weekly from Gatwick; and 1 weekly each from Manchester and Birmingham. In winter departures decrease to just twice weekly

from Heathrow, once or twice weekly from Gatwick, and 1 weekly each from Manchester and Birmingham. Owing to successful competition from *Air 2000* (see below), it's anticipated that *Cyprus Airways* will axe some of its Birmingham and Manchester flights in 1996 or 1997.

British Airways offers five weekly flights from Heathrow to Larnaca in winter, though these tend to arrive in the small hours; summertime sees daily departures, with more civilized arrival hours for weekend services.

Lately, some of the most convenient and frequent services are those offered by **Air 2000**, which flies to Larnaca from Gatwick 6 times weekly, from Birmingham 3 times weekly, and from Manchester once weekly; and to Páfos from Gatwick 4 times weekly (on 2 days), and from Manchester or Birmingham once or twice weekly. In winter scheduled departures drop to once weekly on all these routes.

Cyprus Airways and *British Airways* services are common-rated; **fares** from Heathrow to either Cypriot airport range from £210 to £280 for a 6- to 60-day APEX return, depending on whether or not you fly on holidays or at weekends. Summertime (1 May–28 Oct) APEX tickets with identical conditions will set you back £300–350, depending on the day of travel. *Air 2000* tickets are significantly cheaper at £185–270 for a 3- to 45-day winter APEX fare, rising to £220–300 in summer (reckoned as 1 April–31 Oct by this company).

CHARTER FLIGHTS
Charter companies such as *Eurocypria, Monarch, Caledonian, All Leisure, Airworld* and *Air 2000* also provide air links from Britain, but owing to Cypriot law (see "Packages") seats are difficult to get on a flight-only basis. When available they tend to be for periods of only one or two weeks. Regional UK airports of origination include Bristol, East Midlands, Edinburgh, Exeter, Glasgow and Newcastle for Larnaca, and Bristol, Cardiff, East Midlands, Glasgow and Newcastle for Páfos.

FLIGHTS FROM NEIGHBOURING COUNTRIES
Larnaca can also be easily reached from most **neighbouring countries** by plane, with flights on *Cyprus Airways* from Athens (3–4 daily, 2–3 in winter), Cairo (3 weekly, 2 in winter), Heraklion, Crete (3 weekly, summer only), Rhodes (4 weekly, summer only) and Tel Aviv (4 weekly, 3 in winter).

AIRLINES AND TRAVEL AGENTS

AIRLINES SERVING THE SOUTH

Air 2000 ☎0161/745 4644.

British Airways 156 Regent St, London W1R 5TA (☎0345/222111).

Cyprus Airways Euston Centre, 29–31 Hampstead Rd, London NW1 (☎0171/388 5411); c/o Midland Airport Service, ☎0121/767 7702; Manchester Airport, Terminal 1 (☎0161/489 3177).

AIRLINES SERVING THE NORTH

Akdeniz Airlines c/o *TK Air Travel*, 46 Newington Green, London N16 9PX (☎0171/359 9214).

Cyprus Turkish Airlines c/o *CTA Holidays*, 41 Pall Mall, London SW1Y 5JG (☎0171/930 4851).

Istanbul Airlines c/o *President Holidays*, 542 Kingsland Rd, London E8 4AH (☎0171 249 4002).

DISCOUNT FLIGHT AGENTS

Campus Travel, 52 Grosvenor Gardens, London SW1W 0AG (☎0171/730 3402); 541 Bristol Rd, Selly Oak, Birmingham B29 6AU (☎0121/414 1848); 61 Ditchling Rd, Brighton BN1 4SD (☎01273/570226); 39 Queen's Rd, Clifton, Bristol BS8 1QE (☎0117/929 2494); 5 Emmanuel St, Cambridge CB1 1NE (☎01223/324283); 53 Forest Rd, Edinburgh EH1 2QP (☎0131/668 3303); 166 Deansgate, Manchester M3 3FE (☎0161/833 2046); 105–106 St Aldates, Oxford OX1 1DD (☎01865/242067). Student/youth travel specialists, with branches also in YHA shops and on university campuses all over Britain.

Council Travel, 28a Poland St, London W1V 3DB (☎0171/437 7767). Flights and student discounts.

STA Travel, 86 Old Brompton Rd, London SW7 3LH; 117 Euston Rd, London NW1 2SX; 38 Store St, London WC1 (☎0171/ 361 6161); 25 Queens Rd, Bristol BS8 1QE (☎0117/929 4399); 38 Sidney St, Cambridge CB2 3HX (☎01223/366966); 88 Vicar Lane, Leeds LS1 7JH (☎0113/244 9212); 75

Deansgate, Manchester M3 2BW (☎0161/834 0668); 36 George St, Oxford OX1 2OJ (☎01865/ 792800); and branches in Birmingham, Canterbury, Cardiff, Coventry, Durham, Glasgow, Loughborough, Nottingham, Warwick and Sheffield. Worldwide specialists in low-cost flights and tours for students and under-26s.

Trailfinders, 42–50 Earls Court Rd, London W8 6FT (☎0171/938 3366); 194 Kensington High St, London W8 7RG (☎0171/938 3939); 22–24 The Priory, Queensway, Birmingham B4 6BS (☎0121/ 236 1234); 48 Corn St, Bristol BS1 1HQ (☎0117/ 929 9000); 254–284 Sauchiehall St, Glasgow G2 3EH (☎0141/353 2224); 58 Deansgate, Manchester M3 2FF (☎0161/839 6969). One of the best-informed and most efficient agents.

Travel Bug, 597 Cheetham Hill Rd, Manchester M8 5EJ (☎0161/721 4000). Large range of discounted tickets.

Union Travel, 93 Piccadilly, London W1 (☎0171/ 493 4343). Competitive airfares.

Olympic Airways also flies into Larnaca from Athens at least twice daily. Páfos is also served from Athens (2–3 weekly in summer, 1 weekly in winter) and Heraklion (1 weekly, summer only). It's worth asking for student discounts if eligible; otherwise, you'll pay about £180 equivalent return from Athens, the longest haul in.

BY PLANE TO THE NORTH

Because of the IATA boycott of north Nicosia's "black" airport at **Ercan**, North Cyprus has direct air links only with Turkey, where northern European planes must first touch down (usually at Istanbul, Izmir or Antalya). Despite this, reasonably frequent scheduled flights start from several UK airports,

and even a number of charter lines extend from Turkey into the North. Almost without exception they tend to arrive between 10pm and midnight.

SCHEDULED FLIGHTS

Istanbul Airlines (*İstanbul Hava Yolları*) flies into Ercan throughout the year twice a week from London Heathrow, once from Manchester (via Stansted in the summer) and once from Gatwick. In summer there is usually an extra weekly flight from Gatwick, as well as a route from Cardiff. **Akdeniz Airlines** offers four weekly flights in summer, two from Stansted and one apiece from Heathrow and Manchester; only the Stansted service persists during the winter. **Cyprus Turkish Airways**, a

TOUR OPERATORS

GENERAL OPERATORS TO THE SOUTH

Amathus Holidays 51 Tottenham Court Rd, London W1P 0HS (☎0171/636 9873). Four- and five-star hotels, no villas or village accommodation.

Argo Holidays 100 Wigmore St, London W1H 9DR (☎0171/331 7070). Top-end hotels and apartments at the major resorts, plus Voúni and Vássa village houses.

Cyprair Holidays 23 Hampstead Rd, London NW1 3JA (☎0171/388 7515). Subsidiary of *Cyprus Airways*, concentrating on luxury hotels and fancier apartments.

Cyprosun Holidays 163 Sutton Rd, Wylde Green, Birmingham B23 5TN (☎0121/382 6611). Good for flight-only and fly-drive holidays, or flexible-duration packages.

First Choice First Choice House, Peel Cross Rd, Salford, Manchester M5 2AN (☎0161/742 2262).

Another sizable general tour operator, also offering a range of self-catering villas in Ómodhos.

Inspirations Victoria House, Victoria Rd, Horley, Surrey RH6 7AD (☎01293/822244). More extensive than usual range of departures from regional UK airports, plus imaginative fly-drive itineraries and a full village accommodation programme.

Libra Holidays 343 Ballards Lane, London N12 8LJ (☎0181/446 8231). Luxury hotels and Ómodhos village houses, through one of the longest-established operators.

Magnum Travel 747 Green Lanes, Winchmore Hill, London N21 3SA (☎0181/360 5353). Upscale hotels in the major resorts, plus Ómodhos village houses.

Sunworld 71 Hough Side Rd, Pudsey LS28 9BR (☎0113/255 5222). Mostly mid-range hotels, plus village accommodation at Ómodhos and Kalavassós.

SPECIALIZED OPERATORS TO THE SOUTH

Exalt PO Box 337, Káto Páfos, Cyprus (☎06/243803). Jeep, canyoning and walking safaris to remote, unspoiled parts of Páfos district.

Marengo Publications Guided Walks 22 River View, Retford, Notts DN22 7UL (☎01777/705588). Week-long, March-only botanical tours near Pólis, led by accomplished botanist Lance Chilton.

Ornitholidays (☎0243/821230). Long-established bird-watching tour specialist.

Platinum Golf Holidays Georgian House, 5 Pavilion Parade, Brighton, East Sussex BN2 1RA (☎01273/622622). Golf packages for the Tsádha course, based in Páfos area hotels.

Sunvil Travel Sunvil House, 7–8 Upper Square, Old Isleworth, Middlesex TW7 7BJ (☎0181/568 4499). Quality villas and restored village houses throughout Páfos district, as well as selected hotels.

Waymark Holidays 44 Windsor Rd, Slough SL1 2EJ (☎01753/516477). Walking holidays in Páfos district and the Tróödhos.

GENERAL AND SPECIALIZED OPERATORS TO THE NORTH

Anatolian Sky Holidays Imex House, 52 Blucher St, Birmingham B1 1QU (☎0121/633 4018). Emphasis on high-quality bungalow complexes around Kyrenia and Famagusta.

Cyprus Paradise 689 High Rd, Finchley, London N12 0DA (☎0181/343 8000). Excellent range of character villas at Kármi, Kyrenia and Béllapais, plus the better self-contained resorts around Kyrenia.

Mosaic Holidays Patman House, George Lane, South Woodford, London E18 2LS (☎0181/532 9050) or in Manchester (☎0161/236 2353). Stress on high-end properties owned and managed by itself, plus a few seafront villas.

President Holidays 542 Kingsland Rd, London E8 4AH (☎071/249 4002). Represents most hotels and bungalow complexes in Kyrenia and Famagusta.

Regent Holidays Regent House, 31A High St, Shanklin, Isle of Wight PO37 6JW (☎01983/864212). Better than many for self-catering villas and flight-only deals.

Scuba Cyprus 533A Kingsland Rd, London E8 4AZ (☎0171/923 2085). Scuba packages, based at 3 hotels just inland from the usual dive venue.

Sunquest Holidays 23 Princes St, London W1R 7RG (☎0181/499 9991). Veteran Turkey specialist, recently expanded into the Kyrenia area.

Tapestry Holidays 24 Chiswick High Rd, London W4 1TE (☎0181/742 0077). Good range of cottages and villas at Kármi and several other spots, plus most of the best Kyrenia and Famagusta bungalow resorts.

subsidiary of state-run *Turkish Airways*, offers three weekly winter flights from Heathrow to Ercan, dropping to two in summer. Extra summertime load is handled out of Stansted, where the two weekly winter services (construed as 1 Nov–28 March) jump to five weekly in summer. **Fares** tend to start at just under £200 return during winter, with substantial hikes in summer.

OTHER FLIGHTS FROM TURKEY

From Turkey itself, you can choose from a number of scheduled airlines. *Cyprus Turkish Airways (Kıbrıs Türk Hava Yolları* in Turkish) flies in from Adana (3 weekly), Ankara (daily), Istanbul (2 daily), and Izmir (2 weekly). *İstanbul Hava Yolları* offers three weekly services from Istanbul, plus less frequent flights from Izmir, Ankara and Antalya, while *Akdeniz* and *Sunex* each chip in one weekly service from Istanbul and Antalya. Return fares from the Turkish mainland to the North are periodically offloaded for as little as £40 equivalent round trip – if you don't have a car, a far better option than the ferry from southern Turkey (see below).

PACKAGES

Cyprus ranks as the most packaged destination in the Mediterranean after Malta, a status mandated by law in the **South**. Current regulations stipulate that only holidaymakers on fully inclusive packages may board charter craft flying out of Luton, Birmingham and Manchester, while at other UK airports, only fifteen percent of charter seat capacity is allowed to be sold on a seat-only basis – offending airlines are heavily fined. The message is clear – budget travellers need not apply – and has been reiterated by stiff hikes in package **prices** since 1993. Expect to pay £580 to £650, flight inclusive, for a two-week high-season package in a three-star hotel or detached villa, £520 for a two-star hotel or more modest village house, and a minimum of £440 for a self-catering tower-block flat; peak season is reckoned as July through September.

Prices in the **North** are much the same for equivalent facilities, with somewhat less fluctuation between low- and high-season prices. Again, high season is nominally rated as July to September. **Two-centre holidays** – a week in Turkey plus a week on Cyprus – are popular, and make a virtue of the necessity of stopping over in Turkey.

BY BOAT TO THE SOUTH

Despite the fact that Cyprus is an island, sailing there is not a conspicuously popular option except

for ex-kibbutz volunteers taking it in as a stopover on the way back from Israel. Much of the fleet operating out of the South is devoted to (not particularly recommendable) 48-hour cruises taking in Egypt and the "Holy Land", pitched at package customers with a spare weekend.

You can reach **Limassol**, the South's main port, from Piraeus, Heraklion and Rhodes in Greece, Haifa (Israel), and Port Said (Egypt). Frequency of departure per shipping company tends to be once a week in season, and service never completely stops in winter with certain shipping lines. Summarized following are the current offerings of various shipping companies. Student/youth, railpass and return-ticket discounts are usually available, as are stopovers.

All **fares** should be taken merely as guideline estimates only. In any case, sailing isn't a conspicuously economical way to reach the island unless you happen already to be in Israel, Rhodes or Crete and decide to tack Cyprus on to your travel plans. A cabin from Rhodes or Crete (Heraklion) to Limassol, for instance, costs a significant fraction of a student/youth flight from either place to Larnaca; Haifa–Limassol is comparatively a better deal. Bringing a vehicle is such an expensive proposition that it usually works out cheaper to leave your car behind and hire one in Cyprus (see p.23).

SHIPPING COMPANIES, ROUTES AND FARES

Poseidon Lines runs its craft the *Sea Harmony* or *Sea Wave* all year between Piraeus–Rhodes–Limassol–Haifa and back via the same ports; Piraeus departure is early Monday evening, with arrival in Limassol Wednesday morning or noontime. Return from Haifa is Thursday evening, with arrival in Limassol the next morning. During July and August an extra stop is made in Heraklion, Crete, in both directions.

Vergina Lines runs its *Vergina* from the beginning of April to the end of October, between Piraeus–Rhodes–Limassol–Haifa and back via the same ports; Piraeus departure is early Thursday evening, with arrival in Limassol Saturday morning. Return from Haifa is on Sunday evening, arriving in Limassol the next morning.

Salamis Lines operates the *Nissos Kypros* year-round between the ports of Piraeus, Rhodes, Limassol and Haifa; this departs Piraeus Thursday evening, reaching Limassol Saturday morning, and returning from Haifa Sunday evening.

Most of the vessels belonging to **Louis Cruise Lines** do just that, with the exception of the

SHIPPING LINE AGENTS FOR THE SOUTH

Louis Cruise Lines port agents

Haifa *Dolphin Shipping Agency*, 104 HaAtzma'ut Rd (☎04/523953).

Port Said *Mena Tours*, El Gomhoria St (☎66/225742).

Poseidon Lines port agents

Kavoúri Voúlas (near Athens) Alkyonídhon 32 (☎01/96 58 300).

Rhodes *Kouros Travel*, Karpáthou 34 (☎0241/22 400).

Haifa *Jacob Caspi*, 76 HaAtzma'ut Rd, cnr Natan St (☎04/674444).

Salamis Lines port agents

Piraeus Filellínon 9 (☎01/42 94 325).

Rhodes *Kydon Tourist Agency*, Ethelondhón Dhodhekanisíon 14 (☎0241/27 900).

Haifa *Allalouf Shipping*, 40 HaNamal St (☎04/671743).

Vergina Lines port agents

Piraeus Aktí Sakhtoúri 11 (☎01/41 32 392).

Rhodes *Kouros Travel*, Karpáthou 34 (☎0241/22 400).

Haifa *Jacob Caspi*, 76 HaAtzma'ut Rd (☎04/674444).

Princessa Cypria, which runs a regular, bona fide ferry service between Limassol, Haifa and Port Said. Departures from Egypt, the service's only really unique feature, are Thursday and Sunday evenings.

For exact, current **fares**, consult the agencies above. As a general guideline, count on £31–36 deck class, depending on season, from Haifa to Limassol, increasing to £60–70 for the cheapest inside cabin with shower and toilet; from Rhodes reckon on £36–41 for deck class, rising to £70–90 for a cabin with private facilities. The smallest car brought over from Israel will cost £47–55 to transport, from Rhodes £55–66. Greek port taxes weigh in at £15 per person and £31 per vehicle.

BY BOAT TO THE NORTH

Since only Turkey recognizes the Turkish Republic of Northern Cyprus, the only way to reach the North by boat is to leave from one of three Turkish ports, Taşucu, Alanya or Mersin. **Fares**, currently subsidized by the Turkish government, are relatively reasonable. This may change, of course, in the wake of any peace settlement, with free movement to the South for foreigners and a sharp hike in ferry tariffs equally likely possibilities. Again, sample figures are converted from Turkish lira and are intended only as guidelines. Note that in all cases service in either direction on **weekends** is extremely limited.

SHIPPING COMPANIES, ROUTES AND FARES
Mersin–Famagusta is the most reliable, weather-proof crossing owing to the large size of the ships, and is favoured by many locals despite its relatively long duration and higher cost compared to Kyrenia-based routes (see below). The only company on this route is the Turkish state-run *TML*, represented by *KTDI* in Famagusta; for some years now its sailing pattern has featured Mersin departures at 10pm on Monday, Wednesday and Thursday, with arrival the next day in Famagusta at 8am. Tuesday, and Friday the boat returns from Famagusta at 1pm, docking in Mersin at 10pm the same day. Only one class of passenger fare is cited, at £33 in pullman seats (including port tax). Transporting a car costs £27, including tax. It may be worth asking for a ten percent student discount or return-passage discount.

Taşucu–Kyrenia looks temptingly short on a map, but the standard of craft in service can be pretty poor, and a nominal four-hour trip easily becomes an eight-hour ordeal in case of storms in the straits, or malfunctioning engines. No cabins are available on the **overnight ferries**, another reason to recommend the **daytime catamaran** or **hydrofoil** services.

There are currently four **companies** – TML plus three private outfits – serving this route; only two of the boats carry vehicles. **Prices** are similar for all of them, but standards of service vary. Single passenger fares range from £13 to £16, less any applicable discounts such as return passage or student status. A medium-sized car costs £40 to ferry, campers £60. There are in addition assorted annoying taxes and chits of formalized *baksheesh* totalling about £4 for passengers and roughly the same for vehicles.

Fergün's broken-down tub the *Fatih* (cars carried) is worth avoiding if you have the choice; it leaves Taşucu Sunday through Thursday at midnight, arriving in Kyrenia the next morning (that is, Mon–Fri mornings). By contrast, their summertime-only "Express" catamaran (foot passengers only) leaves every day at 11am and 2.30pm, taking just two hours for the journey. *Ertürk*'s namesake boat (cars carried) is smaller and faster than the *Fatih*, keeping much the same schedule, and has slightly cheaper fares than *TML* or *Fergün*. From

March to September, *TML* runs a small passenger-only ferry at midnight Sunday through Thursday, arriving in Kyrenia at dawn Monday–Friday. During peak season only, *Sidereal Lines* has swift daily hydrofoil services on the Taşucu–Kyrenia route.

Three times weekly during summer, *Fergün* provides evening "Express" service to the Turkish resort of **Alanya**, returning to **Kyrenia** at dawn the following day.

GETTING THERE FROM NORTH AMERICA

There are at present just two weekly direct air links between North America and Southern Cyprus (none to the North), and as yet very few package tours. Thus getting to Cyprus is best considered as an adjunct to a wider European or Mediterranean tour. Throughout North America, "low season" to Cyprus means October 1–May 14, "high season" May 15–September 30. Fares quoted below, with a price range from low to high season, include applicable taxes. Virtually all of the tickets discussed are APEX fares, booked at least 14 days in advance and good for 6 to 60 days.

TO THE SOUTH

From the USA, common-rated carriers *Gulf Air* or *Cyprus Airways* run **non-stop flights** twice weekly from Houston and New York JFK to Larnaca (currently Thurs & Sun) for about $US730

for a 90-day APEX ticket in May, $900 in high summer. This is by far the least expensive air link from North America to the South.

Next best alternative might be the **one-stop flight** on *Olympic Airways*, which covers the route New York JFK–Larnaca via Athens five days weekly (connection from Boston twice weekly) for $1240–1370 depending on season; from September until June, *Olympic* often has special promotions which match the *Cyprus Airways/Gulf Air* ticket prices cited above.

British Airways offers daily service from most major US and Canadian gateway cities to Larnaca via London, but be careful how you purchase tickets: oddly, a single itinerary booked as (for example) New York JFK–London–Larnaca and back, at $1540, costs far more than the price of separate JFK–London–JFK and London–Larnaca–London tickets. Unless you want to stopover in London, pay attention to onward flight times out of Heathrow, which are currently in the evening on weekdays, mid-morning at weekends (summer only).

Other reasonable one-stop solutions include *KLM*, which flies twice weekly from New York JFK, Houston or Los Angeles to Larnaca via Amsterdam for $1224–1370. Note that *KLM* and *Cyprus Airways* have recently concluded a route-sharing agreement between Amsterdam and Larnaca, so that in effect frequencies on this corridor may soon be daily. *Swissair* flies from New York JFK four times weekly to Larnaca via Zurich; fares are the same as on *KLM*.

Only if these alternatives don't pan out might you consider the no-frills flights of Romania's *TAROM*, flying New York JFK–Bucharest–Larnaca twice weekly, for about US$1245 for a 60-day ticket in May. If planning your return leg separately, note that *TAROM* tickets are considerably cheaper when bought within Cyprus.

From Canada, options are pretty well limited to *Swissair*'s four weekly services from Montreal to Larnaca via Zurich – APEX tickets cost CDN$1632–1842 – or *KLM*'s three weekly runs from Toronto to Larnaca via Amsterdam, weighing in at CDN$1821–1982.

TO THE NORTH

Because of the international air boycott of the North, getting there from North America means just one route: a flight to Istanbul, either direct or via a European city, with onward connection to Ercan (north Nicosia) airport.

From the US, *THY*, the Turkish state carrier, has daily, usually direct, services from New York to Istanbul, from where its subsidiary *Cyprus Turkish Airways* flies to Ercan at least once daily. Best APEX fares (7- to 30-day stay, tax included) are $745–1340, depending on season. Reckon on another $278, year round, for the add-on leg from Istanbul to Ercan, but you will do much better purchasing this final sector of the journey in Istanbul itself – have a two-day stopover with the money you save. *Delta Airlines* offers daily, semi-direct service from New York JFK to Istanbul (fuel stop in Frankfurt, no change of plane) for a more economical $758–1098, while *Lufthansa* flies from most major US cities to Frankfurt, and then on to Istanbul on a different aircraft, for similar prices.

From Canada, there is currently no direct service even to Turkey – choose between *Swissair*'s four weekly Montreal–Zurich flights, with onward conections to Istanbul (CDN\$1431–1631), or *KLM*'s daily Toronto–Istanbul flights via Amsterdam (CDN\$1433–1708). *KLM* also offers a connecting service out of Vancouver for CDN\$2010.

SPECIALIST AGENTS

THE SOUTH

Amelia Tours (☎1-800/742 4591). Nine-day, spring and autumn package tours of the South; plus independent accommodation and car rental arrangements.

Amphitrion Holidays (☎1-800/424 2471). General Hellenic package arranger.

Cyprus Tours (☎1-800/221 8899). Good for airfares, and travel within the South.

Cyprus Trade & Tours (☎1-800/338 3855). Tailor-made, special-interest itineraries, plus

hotel, cruise, airfare particulars to and within Southern Cyprus.

Great Escapes Travel (☎1-800/278 8721). Two-week guided tours, based in Larnaca, to Tróödhos, Páfos and Nicosia.

Homeric Tours (☎1-800/223 5570). General Hellenic specialist with a small Cyprus programme.

THE NORTH

Club America 61 East 52nd Street, New York NY 10017 (☎212/972 2865). Air tickets to the North on *THY/CTHY*, hotel accommodation and airport transfers.

Esplanade Tours (☎1-800/426 5492). Eight-day tours of the castles and ancient sites of the North in spring and autumn.

GETTING THERE FROM AUSTRALASIA

There are no direct air links between Australia or New Zealand and any part of Cyprus, despite the sizable expatriate Cypriot community in Australia. The most cost-effective strategy will usually be to get a good deal on a ticket to Athens, Istanbul or London, and have an "add-on" fare written

from there. In the fare discussions following, for most airlines "low season" means January 16–February 28, and October 1–November 30, while "high season" means May 16–31, June 1–August 31, and December 1–January 15. Round-trip fares are quoted in the dollars of the originating country, ie AUS\$ or NZ\$.

To the South, the shortest one-stop services from Australia are on *Gulf Air*, thrice weekly Sydney–Larnaca via Bahrain (\$1835–2270), and *Olympic Airways*, twice weekly Sydney–Larnaca via Athens (\$2230–2430). You won't save much money by flying *KLM* or *Aeroflot* to Athens (\$1700–2400), and then taking an add-on flight on *Cyprus Airways* or *Olympic* to Larnaca (another \$300, plus about \$32 for Athens airport tax); it's better to go to London on *Philippine Airlines* or *Garuda* from Brisbane, Sydney or Melbourne (several times weekly; \$1550–2000), and then on from there. During their charter season, *Britannia* flies from Sydney to London for \$1200–1800, from where you can take advantage of frequent scheduled links and the well-developed package industry down to Cyprus South or North (see "Getting there from Britain").

From New Zealand, *Alitalia* flies several times weekly Auckland–Larnaca via Rome ($2250–2850); your next best bet is on common-rated *Qantas*, *Singapore Airlines* and *Thai* to Athens at $2300–2900. To London, *Garuda* flies

twice weekly from Auckland ($2110–2420), as does *Britannia* from November to March ($1415–2119).

Options to Istanbul, for access **to the North**, are limited to the thrice-weekly Singapore–Istanbul service on *THY* – which means first getting from Australasia to Singapore on *Qantas*; total costs will be $1750–2100, plus about $256 for the final leg to Ercan in North Cyprus.

AIRLINES

Aeroflot 388 George St, Sydney (☎02/9233 7911). No NZ office.

Alitalia Orient Overseas Building, 32 Bridge St, Sydney (☎02/9247 1308); 6th Floor, Trustbank Building, 229 Queen St, Auckland (☎09/379 4457).

Britannia Airways Aus-Extras Level 6, 210 George St, Sydney (☎02/9251 1299). No NZ office.

Garuda 175 Clarence St, Sydney (☎02/334 9900); 120 Albert St, Auckland (☎09/366 1855).

Gulf Air 403 George St, Sydney (☎02/9321 9199). No NZ office.

KLM 5 Elizabeth St, Sydney (☎02/9231 6333; toll-free 1800/505 747). No NZ office.

Olympic Airways Floor 3, 37–49 Pitt St, Sydney (☎02/9251 2044). No NZ office.

Philippine Airlines 49 York St, Sydney (☎02/9262 3333). No NZ office.

Qantas Chifley Square, cnr Hunter and Phillip streets, Sydney (☎02/957 0111); Qantas House, 154 Queen St, Auckland (☎09/357 8900).

Singapore Airlines 17–19 Bridge St, Sydney (☎02/9236 0144; local-call rate 13 1011); Lower Ground Floor, West Plaza Building, cnr Customs and Albert streets, Auckland (☎09/379 3209).

Thai Airways 75–77 Pitt St, Sydney (☎02/844 0999; toll-free 1800/422 020); Kensington Swan Building, 22 Fanshawe St, Auckland (☎09/377 3886).

Turkish Airways c/o Level 16, 388 George Street, Sydney (☎02/9221 1711). No NZ office.

TRAVEL AGENTS

Brisbane Discount Travel 360 Queen St, Brisbane (☎07/3229 9211).

Budget Travel 16 Fort St, Auckland; other branches around the city (☎09/309 4313; toll-free 0800/808 040).

Destinations Unlimited 3 Milford Rd, Milford, Auckland (☎09/486 1303).

Flight Centres Australia: Circular Quay, Sydney (☎02/9241 2422); Bourke St, Melbourne (☎03/650 2899); plus other branches nationwide. New Zealand: National Bank Towers, 205–225 Queen St, Auckland (☎09/309 6171); Shop 1M, National Mutual Arcade, 152 Hereford St, Christchurch (☎09/379 7145); 50–52 Willis St, Wellington (☎04/472 8101); other branches countrywide.

Harvey World Travel Princess Highway, Kogarah, Sydney (☎02/567 099); branches nationwide.

STA Travel Australia: 732 Harris St, Ultimo, Sydney (☎02/9212 1255; toll-free 1800/637 444); 256 Flinders St, Melbourne (☎03/9347 4711); other offices in Townsville, state capitals and major universities. New Zealand: Travellers' Centre, 10 High St, Auckland (☎09/366 6673); 233 Cuba St, Wellington (☎04/385 0561); 223 High St, Christchurch (☎03/379 9098); other offices in Dunedin, Palmerston North, Hamilton and major universities.

Thomas Cook 96 Anzac Ave, Auckland (☎09/379 3920); branches throughout NZ.

UTAG Travel 122 Walker St, North Sydney (☎02/956 8399); branches throughout Australia.

SPECIALIST AGENTS

Grecian Tours Travel 237a Lonsdale St, Melbourne (☎03/9663 3711). Accommodation and car rental.

Greek Tours Floor 2, 243 Edward St, Brisbane (☎07/3221 9700). Accommodation and tours in Southern Cyprus.

Sun Island Tours 92 Goulburn St, Sydney (☎02/9983 2144). Accommodation, car rental and cruises out of Southern Cyprus.

RED TAPE AND VISAS

British, EU, Canadian, Australasian and US nationals require only a valid passport for entry into either the south or the north sectors of Cyprus, and both sets of authorities routinely stamp you with a three-month tourist visa on arrival. However, you must choose which portion you will visit on any given trip – until and unless any peace settlement takes effect, there is no possibil-ity of foreign tourists moving from the North to the South, and severely limited provision in the opposite direction.

Furthermore, the southern Republic has declared all seaports and airports in the North "prohibited ports of entry and exit"; this means that if there's any evidence in your passport of such a visit to North Cyprus, you will be subse-quently denied entry to the South – and occasion-ally, depending on the immigration officials you encounter there, to Greece as well. So upon arri-val in the North, be sure to ask for the visa to be stamped on a separate, loose slip of paper; vehi-cles can also be entered on the same detachable visa. Most Turkish Cypriot customs officials speak good English, but if in doubt the Turkish for "On a loose sheet, please" is *Lütfen gevşek kağıtda*. Staff at Ercan airport are fairly used to such requests and keep a stack of loose visa slips handy next to the computer used for logging in your passport data.

The other potential sticking point on entry to the South is the ban on any imported **perish-ables**; eat those apples on the boat or plane in, or the customs officers will eat them for you.

HEALTH AND INSURANCE

In general, Cyprus is a healthy place, and you're unlikely to experience any problems other than a spell of constipation brought on by initial contact with the rather heavy food. Water is fit to drink almost everywhere except Famagusta (where the sea has invaded well bore-holes), though not always so tasty; bottle water is widely available. No inoculations are required for any part of Cyprus, though as ever it's wise to keep your tetanus booster up to date.

HEALTH HAZARDS

Most routine threats to your health have to do with overexposure, the sea and flying insects. Wear a hat and drink plenty of fluids during the hot months to avoid the danger of **sunstroke**. **Jellyfish** are rare, **sea urchins** more common; their presence on rocky coasts indicates a mild pollution problem as well. If you are unlucky enough to tread on, or graze, one, a sterilized sewing needle, scalpel and olive oil are effective aids to removing spines; left unextracted, they will fester. A pair of swim goggles and footwear for walking over tidal rocks should help you avoid both.

The worst maritime danger – fortunately quite rare – is the **weever fish**, which buries itself in tidal sand with just its poisonous dorsal and gill spines protruding. If you step on one the sudden pain is unmistakably excruciating and the venom exceptionally potent. Consequences range up to permanent paralysis of the affected area, so the imperative first aid before rushing to a doctor is to immerse your foot in water as hot as you can stand. This degrades the toxin as well as relieving the swelling of the joints and attendant pain.

In terms of dry-land beasties, there are **scorpions** about – tap out your shoes in the morning – and one stubby, mottled species of **viper**; antivenins for it are available at local pharmacies. Those enormous, two-metre-long black **whip** or **Montpellier snakes** which you'll see on the road are usually harmless to humans, and in fact were imported to hunt both rodents and other venomous serpents. **Mosquitos** (*kounoúpia* in Greek, *sivrisinek* in Turkish) can be troublesome in summer, especially between Famagusta and the Kırpaşa (Kárpas) peninsula; solutions offered by hotels include pyrethrum incense coils, electrified vapour pads, or air-conditioned rooms with closed windows.

There are few stray animals on Cyprus and thus (uniquely for this part of the world) **rabies** is not much of a danger. Indeed one of the few things the Greek and Turkish Cypriot communities agreed on before 1974 was to round up and put down most stray dogs, since many carried **echinococcosis**, a debilitating liver fluke which could spread to humans. Adherence to the practice is laxer now in the North, but overall the canine population is still not up to previous levels.

MEDICAL ATTENTION

The standard of health care is relatively high in Cyprus, with many English-speaking and -trained doctors; indeed health care for residents of surrounding Middle Eastern nations has recently become a highly successful hard-currency earner. The fancier hotels can generally make recommendations of local practitioners, and may even post lists of them. General **hospitals** in both sectors of the island have walk-in casualty wards where foreigners can have cuts sewn up and broken bones set at no cost.

Minor ailments can be dealt with at **chemists** (*farmakío* in Greek, *eczane* in Turkish); pharmacists are well trained and can often dispense medicines which in Britain would only be available on prescription. In the South, you can dial the operator on ☎192 to ask for the rota of night-duty chemists; in both North and South, this is also published regularly in the English-language newspapers (see "The Media", below).

TRAVEL INSURANCE COMPANIES

UK

Columbus Travel Insurance 17 Devonshire Square, London EC2M 4SQ (☎0171/375 0011).

Endsleigh Insurance 97–107 Southampton Row, London WC1B 4AG (☎0171/436 4451).

Frizzell Insurance Frizzell House, County Gates, Bournemouth, Dorset BH1 2NF (☎01202/292333).

THE US AND CANADA

Access America ☎1-800/284-8300.

Carefree Travel Insurance ☎1-800/323-3149.

International Student Insurance Service

(**ISIS**) – sold by *STA Travel* (☎1-800/777-0112).

Travel Guard ☎1-800/826-1300.

AUSTRALIA AND NZ

Ready Plan 141–147 Walker St, Dandenong, Victoria (toll-free ☎1800/337 462); 10th Floor, 63 Albert St, Auckland (☎09/379 3208).

UTAG 347 Kent St, Sydney (☎02/9819 6855; toll-free 1800/809 462).

INSURANCE

In neither South nor North Cyprus does the social insurance system extend to visitors. While the surplus of doctors drives down private clinic consultation fees to about C£10, and virtually halves the cost of even fairly major surgical procedures compared to northern Europe or the US, it's still a good idea to take out some form of **travel insurance** policy. Just about any travel agent, bank or insurance broker will sell you comprehensive cover which includes not only medical expenses but also loss or theft of belongings.

If you intend to hire an off-road vehicle or motorbike, or engage in **special activities** such as para-sailing, horse-riding or scuba-diving, you may need a more specialized policy: be sure to check with your insurers when getting cover.

To make a **claim**, you'll need documentation of all expenses, including pharmacy receipts. If you have anything stolen, go to the nearest police station, report the theft and get a copy of the report or the identification number under which it has been filed: you will need this when making a claim back home. In the South, the Cyprus Tourism Organisation has a special corps of "Tourist Assistants" to act as trouble-shooters in the event of mishaps.

INFORMATION AND MAPS

Before leaving home it's worth stopping in at the tourist office of whichever part of Cyprus you intend to visit, since their stock of brochures and maps is invariably better than what's to be found once you're on the island. The Cyprus Tourism Organisation (CTO) of the internationally recognized Republic of Cyprus, with longer experience of such things, not surprisingly showers you with an avalanche of professionally presented and often useful material on every conceivable topic; the North Cyprus Tourist Office's offerings, while both less slick and less substantial, are recommended mainly because they include the only existing town plans with current Turkified street names.

USEFUL FREE PUBLICATIONS: SOUTH

Among the **CTO titles** to look out for include the *Guide to Hotels, Travel Agencies and other Tourist Services*, a massive but often elusive compendium of virtually every licensed lodging in the South, plus car-rental firms, supposedly published each May but always delayed; *Cyprus, 9000 Years of History and Civilisation*, summarizing points of interest; *Cyprus Travellers Handbook*, containing nuts-and-bolts facts, rules, handy addresses and (fairly up-to-date) site and museum opening hours; a *Diary of Events*, a yearly calendar which should be supplemented by a more current and detailed monthly cyclostyle available in Cyprus; *Cyprus Domestic Transportation Services, Itineraries and Tariffs*, a complete tally of bus and taxi schedules and fares between the major towns and resorts; the *Timetable of Boat Services between Cyprus, Greece and the Middle East*, finalized by the end of May each year; and *Urban Bus Routes*, foldout maps/schedules for Limassol and Nicosia.

The CTO has **offices** in the Republic of Cyprus at Nicosia, Limassol, Larnaca, Páfos, Ayía Nápa, and (April–Oct) Plátres. Hours are typically Monday to Saturday 8.15am–1.45pm, plus late Monday and Thursday afternoon hours (4–6.15pm summer, 3–5.30pm winter), with small local variations; exact addresses are given in the text of the *Guide*.

USEFUL FREE PUBLICATIONS: NORTH

Essential **North Cyprus publications** are the *North Cyprus Tourist Map*, which in addition to being virtually the only printed source of villages as renamed in North Cyprus, also shows most of the southern villages from which the refugee Turkish Cypriots came; the *City Plans* for Girne, Lefkoşa and Gazimağusa, as Kyrenia, Nicosia and Famagusta are called in Turkish; and a glossy pamphlet entitled *Hotels of North Cyprus*, with photos and descriptions of amenities (as well as car-rental franchises), which could be useful if found in the UK.

North Cypriot **tourist offices** are found only in Famagusta and Nicosia; theoretical hours are given in the *Guide*, but especially in the off-season experience has proven them to be shut when they shouldn't be. If you want to take advantage of their services, it's therefore essential to call their closest overseas branch before departure.

MAPS – AND PLACE NAME PROBLEMS

There are vast numbers of complimentary and commercial maps available for Cyprus, but no single one of them is entirely satisfactory – you'll probably want at least two – and most handle the fact of the island's division awkwardly.

SUGGESTED ROAD MAPS

It's wisest to get an overall touring map of the island, as well as any topographical maps, before leaving home, since some of the better ones are banned in the South for political reasons. The best **small-scale road maps** are the *Freytag*

Berndt 1:250,000 folding map the *Bartholomew Clyde Leisure Map* at 1:300,000 and the *AA-Macmillan* at 1:275,000. The *FB* has place names with Greek lettering and accentuation, and its depiction of minor roads is accurate; *BC* has better town plans included on the back, with accented Roman-alphabet renditions of villages on the main map; while the recently improved *AA* map's main strengths lie in its ease of reading, a 1:80,000 Tróödhos detail map on the verso, and its being the only commercial map showing the new Turkish village names in the North.

The *Cyprus Road & Touring Map* (1:275,000), jointly published by Interworld/HDA, is the only commercial map showing the current motorway network in the South, complete with exit numbers, but otherwise offers nothing special. *GeoCenter*'s 1:200,000 offering is excellent for geographical features and roads, but has adopted the official transliteration scheme of the southern Republic (see box on p.17), which may be a transient phenomenon. The official *Survey of Cyprus Administration & Road Map* (1:250,000) dates from 1985, but it does show contours, district boundaries and the ethnic composition of each village on Independence; road tracings are fairly accurate, though in many cases surfaces have been improved in the interim.

The CTO gives out a number of **free maps**: *A Visitor's Map of Cyprus*, the entire island at 1:400,000; Nicosia city centre and suburbs; Limassol town and environs; Larnaca town and environs; Ayía Nápa and environs; Páfos and

THE UK

Daunt Books 83 Marylebone High St, London W1 (☎0171/224 2295).

National Map Centre 22–24 Caxton St, London SW1 (☎0171/222 4945).

John Smith and Sons 57–61 St Vincent St, Glasgow G2 5TB (☎0141/221 7472).

Stanfords 12–14 Long Acre, WC2 (☎0171/836 1321); 52 Grosvenor Gardens, London SW1W 0AG; 156 Regent St, London W1R 5TA.

The Travel Bookshop 13–15 Blenheim Crescent, London W11 2EE (☎0171/229 5260).

Maps by **mail or phone order** are available from *Stanfords*, ☎0171/836 1321.

USA

The Complete Traveler Bookstore 199 Madison Ave, New York, NY 10016 (☎212/685 9007); 3207 Fillmore St, San Francisco, CA 92123 (☎415/923 1511).

Rand McNally* 444 N Michigan Ave, Chicago, IL 60611 (☎312/321 1751); 150 E 52nd St, New York, NY 10022 (☎212/758 7488); 595 Market St, San Francisco, CA 94105 (☎415/777 3131); 1201 Connecticut Ave NW, Washington, DC 20003 (☎202/223 6751).

Sierra Club Bookstore 730 Polk St, San Francisco, CA 94109 (☎415/923 5500).

Traveler's Bookstore 22 W 52nd St, New York, NY 10019 (☎212/664 0995).

*Note: For other locations, or for maps by mail order, call ☎1-800/333 0136 (ext 2111).

CANADA

Open Air Books and Maps 25 Toronto St, Toronto, ON M5R 2C1 (☎416/363 0719).

Ulysses Travel Bookshop 4176 St-Denis, Montréal (☎514/289 0993).

World Wide Books and Maps,1247 Granville St, Vancouver, BC V6Z 1E4 (☎604/687 3320).

AUSTRALIA

Bowyangs 372 Little Burke St, Melbourne (☎03/9670 4383).

The Map Shop 16a Peel St, Adelaide (☎08/8231 2033).

Perth Map Centre 891 Hay St, Perth (☎09/322 5733).

Travel Bookshop 20 Bridge St, Sydney (☎02/9241 3554).

NEW ZEALAND

Specialty Maps 58 Albert St, Auckland (☎09/307 2217).

environs; and the Tróödhos. These are all reasonably accurate, especially the new Nicosia and Páfos sheets, but others – particularly the Tróödhos and Ayía Nápa maps – are ten years old and more, so that errors and obsolescences have inevitably crept in.

TOPOGRAPHICAL MAPS

Unless you plan to do some hard-core, cross-country exploration, the walking maps in this book are adequate to take you around safely. Otherwise, **topographical maps** are prepared by the Department of Lands and Surveys. The forty sheets of the 1:50,000 series are classified, and available only through special petition to the DLS in south Nicosia (☎02/304120), and only certain sheets of the 1:25,000 series, mostly of the southwest and southeast corners of the island, are still available under the same conditions. Fortunately the popular Tróödhos area is still covered, but maps date from 1960 and, as with all the DLS maps, are lettered in

Roman alphabet only, in the pre-1995 transliteration system.

Not surprisingly the Turkish military occupying the North do not make available to the public anything they have prepared.

PROBLEMS WITH BOUNDARIES

All existing island-wide maps have **limitations** to usefulness owing to international non-recognition of the **Turkish Republic of Northern Cyprus** (TRNC) – and poor documentation of the **Attila/Green Line**, the ceasefire line marking the Turkish Army's furthest advance in August 1974, and the attendant **buffer zone** to either side of it. This zone, also called the "dead zone" or No-Man's Land, is off-limits to everyone except UN personnel or local farmers, and varies in width from a few paces in Nicosia to a few kilometres at the old Nicosia airport and the Nicosia–Larnaca expressway. Greek Cypriot depictions of the Attila Line tend to be optimistic, placing it at the limit of the Turkish advance rather than at the southern Republic's edge of the buffer zone; all maps in this guide show the correct extent of the buffer zone, into which you should not venture unless accompanied by authorized military personnel.

PLACE NAMES IN THE NORTH

A major problem in the North is that all maps except the TRNC's tourist handout, and the *AA-Macmillan* product, continue to show **only Greek place names** in the North as it existed pre-1974, despite the fact that all Greek sign-posts have long since vanished there. The southern Republic considers this Turkification just one aspect of the "cultural vandalism and falsification of history", as they put it, which has taken place in the North since 1974. Even the Turkish Cypriots in the North, whether native or resettled refugees, are often nonplussed by the official village names imposed on them, since virtually every place had a Turkish Cypriot form – often phonetically related to the Greek rendition – which is still used in conversation in preference to the often clumsy official name. Only certain villages and towns which had always had Turkish names were exempted from the Turkification campaign.

In "The North" section of **this guide**, first the "new" name as it appears on road signs is cited, followed by the pre-1974 Greek name. and finally (if known) Turkish Cypriot names **in brackets**. Maps also show first the post-1974 name, and then the internationally recognized name in brackets.

Throughout the book the **internationally accepted forms** for the five largest towns – Nicosia, Limassol, Larnaca, Famagusta and Kyrenia – are used in preference to the vernacular renditions, which are given just once for reference at the beginning of accounts.

POLITICALLY CORRECT NOMENCLATURE: THE SOUTH

Considerable dismay was prompted, both in South Cyprus and abroad, in late 1994 by the sudden and arbitrary introduction of a new nomenclature and Greek-transliteration system for all place names in the South. Despite the misgivings of mayor Lelos Demetriades, the name "Nicosia" was officially abolished by a vote of councillors, replaced by Lefkosia even in English literature; those concerned believed that Nicosia was a colonial imposition of the British, though in fact the word dates to Lusignan times. Similarly, Larnaca became Larnaka, Limassol woke up to Lemesos, and Paphos ended up as Páfos (the only instance this book conforms to, to distinguish it from ancient Paphos). Street names were also re-transliterated, wholesale, and in some cases renamed for EOKA heroes.

The person behind the new spellings is a single ultra-nationalist, Menelaos Christodhoulou, who speaks an impenetrable form of *katharévoussa* (artificially "purified" Greek), a former roadworks employee now posted to the Ministry of Education and Culture, who is supported by Klaire Angelidhou, Minister of Education and Culture. In their eyes, the campaign was justified by the Cypriot dialect's manifest inferiority to the language of "mother Greece", although Cypriot is actually more venerable and truly "Greek" in retaining extensive vocabulary and pronunciation unchanged since the Bronze Age.

Most foreign residents and native islanders alike strongly object to the new rules, not least because the old system gave non-Greek speakers a reasonably phonetic rendition for pronunciation. Organizations opting out of the new scheme include Friends of the Earth, the Laona Project, most wildlife conservation bodies, several municipalities (including Nicosia borough Eylenjá, which refused to be rechristened "Aglangiá"),and most international map and book publishers – including Rough Guides. Given its massive unpopularity, the scheme will hopefully not survive the next elections, though you should prepare yourself during the interim for some bizarre roadsigns not matching any available maps. If the intent was to increase the "Hellenic dignity" of place names, the move has had precisely the opposite effect; flippant souls quickly dubbed "Germasogia" (ex-Yermasóyia) "Germy-Soggy", and pointed out that "Choirokoitia" (previously Khirokitiá) sounded like an orgy within a music group. It seems ironic that the Southern government should, on the one hand, castigate Turkish Cypriots for their forcible change of names in the North, and then engage in a similar mutilation of cultural heritage on their own turf.

MONEY AND BANKS

Unusually among travel destinations, Cyprus' low crime rate – South or North – and British affiliations make pounds sterling notes, plastic and sometimes even an ordinary bank chequebook preferable to travellers' cheques as a way of carrying your money. In general the Southern banking system is more efficient, but by way of compensation you can pay for many things in the North directly with foreign cash.

THE SOUTH

The currency of the southern Republic of Cyprus is the **Cyprus pound** (C£), which though not traded internationally is a strong, stable currency with a current unit value equal to roughly £1.25 sterling or $1.90. You may import travellers' cheques without **restrictions**, but cash amounts in excess of £650/$1000 should be declared if you intend to re-export a significant portion of it. You are officially allowed to import or export only C£50, but checks on this are rare. If you're heading to Greece, for instance, you can easily exchange any excess Cypriot pounds for Greek drachmas at a good rate.

CURRENCY

The Cyprus pound is divided into 100 cents (*sent* in Cypriot Greek): there are coins of 1, 2, 5, 10, 20 and 50 cents, and paper notes of 1, 5, 10 and 20 pounds (only banks or post offices stock, and bother much with, 1- or 2-cent coins). Before 1983 the pound was divided into 20 shillings; it was also divided into 1000 mils. You still hear people referring habitually to a sum of 50 *sents* as *dhéka shillingia* (ten shillings) or *pendakósia mil* (500 mils), so be prepared for such idioms.

BANKS AND EXCHANGE FACILITIES

Southern **banks** are open 8.15am–12.30pm, Monday to Friday, with many branches in well-touristed areas offering a supplemental afternoon service, Tuesday to Friday, from 3.30 or 4–6.30pm. Banking and exchange facilities in the two airport arrival lounges are open for all flights. Almost any **monetary device** is easily exchanged: cash (with no commission), travellers' cheques and Eurocheques (subject to standard fees). However, it's worth noting that Thomas Cook travellers' cheques can be exchanged commission-free at any branch of the *Bank of Cyprus*. If you have an account with *Barclays* you can withdraw cash using a personal cheque (supported by a guarantee card or a Barclaycard Visa), at *Barclays* branches in the South only. **Plastic** is also useful: the widespread cashpoint machines of *Barclays* and the *Popular Bank* (*Laïki Trapeza*) will accept overseas *Visa* cards, provided you know your PIN number. *Access/Mastercard* holders can obtain cash advances from autotellers of the *National Bank of Greece*. *American Express* has offices offering the usual facilities to its card holders in Limassol, Larnaca and Nicosia; addresses are in the *Guide*.

THE NORTH

Since 1983, legal tender in the Turkish Republic of Northern Cyprus is the **Turkish lira** (TL) – a decision taken more for ideological posture than sound economic reasons, and one with which few inhabitants are happy, given its current devaluation/inflation rate of close to seventy percent yearly. As a result of this imported hyperinflation, prices quoted in TL are fairly meaningless, so in the *Guide* all northern rates are given in pounds sterling. You can in fact still use the C£ in many hotels, but it's treated like any other foreign note and change given in TL. Rumour has it that, with any durable settlement, the Cypriot pound will be reintroduced as the uniform currency throughout the island, regardless of what the details of territorial jurisdiction are.

CURRENCY

The Turkish lira comes in coins of 2500, 5000 and 10,000 denomination, and paper notes of 10,000, 20,000, 50,000, 100,000, 250,000, 500,000 and 1 million. Coins of less than 2500TL still theoretically exist, but are inadequate even to pay for a pee in a public convenience.

At present there are no strict **controls** on the amount of cash or travellers' cheques imported into the North, but you should leave with as few TL as possible – for the simple reason that they're worthless outside of Turkey or North Cyprus.

BANKS AND EXCHANGE FACILITIES

The several **banks** operating in North Cyprus are fairly inconvenient as tourist facilities for two reasons: the red tape involved in exchange is fairly off-putting, and most foreign tills keep inconveniently short working hours (8.30am–noon Mon–Fri), the main exceptions being the *Türk Bankası*, which stays open until 1 or 2pm and also has a 3.30–6pm shift on Monday, and the *Tuncabank* in Kyrenia. With typical late-evening arrival times at the North's two airports, the banks there – which keep no special after-hours – are similarly useless. A much better bet are the **money exchange houses**, at least one of which functions in each of the major towns. Open from 8am to 6pm Monday to Friday except for a possible lunch break, plus Saturday morning, they give speedy service and top rates for foreign cash and travellers' cheques without taking commission.

Foreign-currency **notes** are in many ways the best form in which to bring funds, the chance of

theft being very slim. You can often pay directly for hotel bills, souvenir purchases, restaurant meals and hotel extras such as sauna or phone fees with overseas cash – and you may well *have* to pay the airport cabbie in sterling. Even UK one-pound, and sometimes even fifty-pence, coins are widely accepted at exchange houses, as well as at many shops and hotel receptions. At least one of the exchange houses (in northern Nicosia; see p.234) accepts **personal cheques** drawn on a British bank and supported by a guarantee card – though you should certainly not rely on this as a sole method of getting cash. Finally, **plastic** is very handy, both for large transactions such as car rental, and for use in the handful of cashpoint machines scattered across the North – they accept both *Visa* and (with some coaxing) *Access/Mastercard*, upon entry of the proper PIN number. Locations are detailed in the *Guide*.

COSTS

The main Cyprus travel season begins early in spring and extends well into autumn, with July/August visits fairly unappealing for a number of reasons. Obviously you'll save a lot on accommodation tariffs in either part of Cyprus if you're willing to go outside of mid-summer, a sensible strategy whatever your budget. Some form of student identification is useful for discounted admission to arche-ological sites and museums, whose fees in any case are modest throughout the island.

THE SOUTH

The southern **Republic of Cyprus** has a some-what unfair reputation for being nightmarishly

expensive. This is a leftover from the days when it *was* pricier than almost any other nearby coun-try, but with soaring prices the rule in both Greece and Turkey, costs in the South's well-regulated economy are beginning to seem rela-tively reasonable.

Historically, costs have run between 15 and 20 percent higher than in Spain, for example, but that much less so than in France. In the wake of Britain's departure from the ERM, however, southern Cyprus seems rather closer to French levels of expense, as the pound has yet to recover its pre-1992 value. For North Americans, Cyprus is not a conspicuously cheap country – the French comparison will seem valid for the forsee-able future.

Travelling independently in the South, you should budget a **minimum** of around C£17 per person a day. This assumes, however, exclusive reliance on bicycles, or **public transport** at C£1–2 a go, staying in one of the limited number of basic village pensions or no-star hotels at C£5–8 per person a night, and only one modest meal out for about C£5, with the balance of food bought from shops.

To travel in some degree of **comfort** and style, though, you'll want at least C£34 disposable per person, which should let you book a modest but acceptable hotel on double occupancy basis and share the cost of a **rental car** (and petrol – slightly less than in Britain), as well as two full main meals. **Beer and wine** are good, and cheapish at C£0.70 and C£2.50 per large bottle respectively; village wine from the barrel goes for as little as C£1.50, while brandy sours run under a pound. If you're not too fussy about what you drink, you can find wine in shops for as little as C£0.80 a litre, and brandy at C£2 per litre.

Winter travel – or even extended residence, a popular strategy with British OAPs – offers considerable savings. Car rental can be fifty percent cheaper, and hotels nearly as much. Full English breakfast at coastal resorts can be had for about C£1, while a three-course set meal with wine can go for as little as C£3.50. If you wear out your wardrobe, February sales for shoes and clothing take place as in northern Europe.

THE NORTH

The economy of **Northern Cyprus**, both before and since it adopted the Turkish lira as official currency in 1983, has lagged behind that of the South, and consequently it is significantly cheaper – except in the confines of a three- or four-star resort. You'll even find certain items less expensive than in Turkey, owing to a combination of subsidies, local production and judicious direct imports from Britain.

For various reasons it's paradoxically much harder to travel independently in the North despite its lower costs at street level. You're at a considerable disadvantage given the very limited number of hotels geared to a walk-in trade; at package-oriented hotels theoretical over-the-counter prices are considerably higher than those granted to advance bookings and agencies. Owing to the unstable nature of the Turkish lira, accommodation rates are invariably quoted in hard currency, usually pounds sterling, and the *Guide* follows this example. There are a handful of small **pensions and hotels** in Kyrenia, for example, poised between Turkish mainland clientele on a shopping spree and the bottom end of the package trade, charging £6–10/$10–16 per person a night; elsewhere in the North you can count the number of such places on one hand.

Eating out can sometimes be cheaper than in Turkey, for example; even in the Kyrenia area or at major hotels it's difficult to spend more than £7/$11 per person on a meal, plus a pound or less for imported Turkish booze. **Car rental** is inexpensive, starting at about £11/$18 a day all-in during the off-season, and petrol is also fairly cheap at 37p/$0.57 a litre. **Overall**, budget about **£32/$50** a day per person (including accommodation) to live quite well.

GETTING AROUND

Cyprus has decent bus services throughout the island, and in the South the useful institution of the service (shared) taxi makes getting around straightforward and cheap.

Private taxis are relatively expensive; there has been no train service since the early 1950s. Car rental is reasonable by European standards, making it a hugely popular option for visitors to either side of the island – and something you should seriously consider, as the best way to reach isolated points of interest.

LOCAL BUSES IN THE SOUTH

The most important **inter-urban routes** in the **South** are served by a number of private companies, whose terminals tend to be clustered at various points in the main towns: there's never really anything that could be singled out as a central bus station. Except on Sundays, when services can be skeletal, departures are fairly frequent during daylight hours – up to six times a day between Nicosia and Limassol, or nine times from Larnaca to Ayía Nápa. **Fares**, sold at kerbside offices or on board, are reasonable; crossing the island from Nicosia to Páfos, for example, won't set you back much over C£3. If you make forays into the Tróödhos, however, you'll find frequencies dropping sharply, with the need to plan an overnight in the hills; to explore up there it's far simpler to have a car, using the coastal towns as jump-off points.

Worth just a mention are the villagers' **market buses** – essentially Bedford truck chassis with a sort of multi-coloured charabanc mounted on top. These mostly South Cypriot institutions are marvellously photogenic, but with their typical once-daily, 6am-out-2pm-back schedules – plus school-bus seating – they're unlikely to be of much practical use.

LOCAL BUSES IN THE NORTH

In the **North**, local buses are more consciously modelled on the Turkish system, with coaches gathered at a single vehicle park and a ticket-sales/waiting building adjacent. With fewer cars in the poorer economy, locals are more dependent on buses and accordingly departures are more frequent – as much as quarter-hourly between north Nicosia and Kyrenia. **Fares** are also lower than in the South, but once again you'll find public buses inconvenient to do much adventuring. Often your fellow passengers will not be native Cypriots, but Anatolian settlers and soldiers returning to postings. Walking along roads, you may be "tooted" at by the drivers of oncoming buses in a bid to get your custom; wave them down if you want to ride.

URBAN BUSES

Of all the island cities, only Nicosia and Limassol are really big enough to make **urban buses** an absolute necessity. With very few exceptions, however, these run only from about 6am to 6pm (7pm in summer). Fares cost between C£0.30 and C£0.40, and route maps – worth snagging if you're staying a long time – are available from the pertinent tourist office. In and around Larnaca and Páfos, a few routes are of interest to visitors, and detailed in the town accounts.

SERVICE TAXIS AND DOLMUŞES

One of Cyprus' more useful ways of getting about is the shared taxi or minibus, called a **service**

taxi in the South or a **dolmuş** in the North. Service taxis carry four to seven passengers, can be booked by phone, and will pick up and drop off at any reasonable point (eg a hotel or private house). Price-wise they are extremely reasonable – little more than double the bus fare for the same route – and journey times are quick, though sometimes drivers' style may have you fearing for your life. Local women scream at the drivers when they overtake on blind, hairpin curves; you'll be too petrified.

In the South, some of the so-called scheduled **minibus services** up to the Tróödhos resorts or out to the lonely northern beaches near Pólis seem to straddle categories a bit; they may offer pick-up service and/or refuse to depart at all without a certain quota of passengers. Strictly speaking, there are no shared saloon cars in the North, but rather minibuses which dawdle, engines idling, in bus parks until they are full or nearly so, thus meeting the definition of *dolmuş* – "stuffed".

TAXIS

Privately hired **taxis** within urban areas in the **South** have rigidly controlled fares, not exorbitant by British standards. The meter starts at C£0.55, with a minimum charge of C£0.75. The meter ticks over at the rate of C£0.21 per kilometre on a single trip, C£0.15 per kilometre on an out-and-back journey. Between 11pm and 6am a night supplement of thirty percent on the taximeter amount is applicable, with a minimum charge of C£1. The first piece of luggage per person is carried free, with each additional item accruing a twenty-cent charge.

There also exist numbers of **rural taxis** providing service between Tróödhos resorts or foothill villages and nearby towns; for these trips you should know the going rate as meters will not be used. As guidelines, Nicosia to Plátres will cost about C£20 per carful; from Limassol to the same place slightly less; from Larnaca to Páno Léfkara about C£12.

In the relatively small towns of the **North**, there's less need for urban taxis; moving between population centres, fares for the same distance are comparable to those in the South, for example £15 from Ercan airport to Kyrenia.

HITCHING

With public transport costs reasonable, **hitch-hiking** is not conspicuously popular in the

Republic of Cyprus, among either locals or tourists, and would not be pleasant in the blisteringly hot months of summer. But there are no laws against it, the CTO even recognizes it as an option in their pamphlets, and in the rural areas it's an excellent way to meet people. However, it's probably best to reserve hitching as a strategy for getting between isolated villages in the Tróödhos or the Páfos hills. In the North it would be slow work indeed, given the limited number of private cars (less than 20,000).

DRIVING

Well on three-quarters of visitors to either part of Cyprus end up driving themselves around at some time during their stay, and this is really the best way to see the country. Either a licence from your home country or an International Driving Permit is acceptable throughout the island.

ROAD RULES AND CONDITIONS

Traffic moves **on the left** throughout the island, as in the UK and most Commonwealth nations. **Front-seatbelt** use is mandatory on the open road but discretionary in towns; children under five years of age may not occupy the front seats, and kids five to ten only if wearing seatbelts. **Drunk-driving** laws are nearly as strict as in the UK or North America: 39mg of alcohol allowed per 100ml of breath, 90mg alcohol per 100 ml of blood.

Speed limits in the South are 100km/hr (minimum 65km/hr) on dual carriageways, 80km/hr on other rural roads, and 50km/hr in towns. Entry into urban zones is announced by big signs reading "*Katikómeni Periokhí*" (Built-up Area). In the North, limits are roughly the same but often posted in miles per hour: 60mph on the Kyrenia–Nicosia–Famagusta highway, 40mph on smaller backroads, and 30mph in built-up areas. Urban boundaries aren't explicitly signposted but there are remarkable numbers of khaki-drill-clad policemen maintaining speed traps with hand-held radar devices at town outskirts.

In the larger Southern towns, use the designated lots for **parking**; they're not expensive – C£0.40 or C£0.50 for half-day use is the norm. Meters on some commercial streets take twenty-cent coins for each hour, and yellow lines at kerbsides mean the same thing as in Britain: single, no parking during business hours; double, no parking *or* stopping. No-parking zones are poorly indicated in the North, though a policeman may appear and politely tell you if you're being blatantly illegal.

Roads themselves range from the excellent dual carriageways linking Nicosia with Kyrenia, Limassol and Larnaca to unspeakable hill tracks fit only for jeep or mountain bike. The Limassol–Páfos road in particular, not yet replaced by an expressway, is inadequate for the traffic load it has to carry and easily rates as the most dangerous road in southern Cyprus; relief will only come after 1999, when extension of the existing motorway beyond Episkopí is completed. On the other side of the Green Line, the presence of unlit military lorries, lumbering along the Nicosia–Famagusta highway in particular, makes night driving in the North most inadvisable; there have been numerous fatalities, including that of one of the president's sons, from drivers rear-ending such poorly visible hazards. Many secondary roads throughout the island, while usually paved, are single-lane colonial relics with merely a thin layer of asphalt strewn over cobbles. This makes them extremely bumpy, with very sharp edges over which you're forced to put two wheels by oncoming traffic.

Signposting varies, too; village exits are usually not obvious, so you'll get acquainted with the boys in the central café asking directions; otherwise you may well end up caught at the bottom of a steep cul-de-sac, with reversing the only way out. By contrast, the Tróödhos and Kyrenia range forestry roads, despite their often horrific condition, are almost always admirably marked. However, in North Cyprus, many rural signs are badly faded, not having been repainted at all since 1974.

All **road distances** are marked in kilometres in the South; accordingly, all rental car speedometers there indicate kilometres, as do internationally sold maps. In the North, a transitional state exists: kilometres are signposted along major highways, but distances appear – if at all – in miles on secondary roads or forest tracks, where you might have to keep a sharp look-out for old colonial milestones. A good rental car speedometer in the North will show distances in both miles and kilometres.

FUEL

In the **South**, either premium or unleaded fuel varies in cost from about C£0.35 to C£0.38 a litre, VAT inclusive, slightly less than in the UK, though a good deal more than in North America. Stations are normally open Monday to Friday 6am to 6pm (sometimes 7pm), with Saturday and Sunday closure at 4pm. On Sundays and holidays only about ten percent of the South's stations are open, on a rota basis; it's fairly easy to run out if you're not careful, so plan ahead. To address this problem, large numbers of automatic, 24-hour stations have begun operation in all the major towns, with a consequent reduction in staffed stations; at these you feed C£1, C£5 or C£10 notes into a machine which then shunts that amount's worth of gas to your pump. They can be unnerving at first, but generally work well. However, the machines don't actually make change; if your banknote exceeds the value of your fuel needs, hit the button marked "Receipt"; you'll get a sales slip showing actual sale, which you can exchange for a refund of the difference at the same station during daylight staffing hours.

Owing to the phasing out of various subsidies, fuel costs in **North Cyprus** have jumped 35 percent in recent years, averaging about 37p/$0.57 per litre; unleaded fuel is not yet available. Stations, especially in the Kyrenia area, tend to be open until 9 or even 10pm, with near-normal service on Sunday.

CAR RENTAL

It's worth stressing that the **condition** of rental cars on either side of the Line can be appalling, with bad brakes the most common fault; if at all possible, take the candidate car for a spin around the block before accepting it. Reputable chains in the South will furnish you with a list of their branches Republic-wide, which should be contacted in event of a breakdown. Rental cars in both South and North have distinctive red **number plates** beginning with "Z", and their drivers are usually accorded every consideration by police – for example, a warning instead of a ticket for not buckling up, However, visitors usually may not cross the Green/Attila Line in either direction with rental (or indeed their own) cars; even when allowed, you may find that the insurance has been voided by such a journey.

In the **South**, numerous agencies, including all international and several local chains, offer primarily A- and B-group Japanese compacts both at airports and in towns. If you have a choice, prefer the Subaru M80 or the Suzuki Marutti to the underpowered Suzuki Alto. Summer rates start at C£11 a day, unlimited mileage and most insurance included, but VAT exclusive, a figure which should be kept in mind as a yardstick when pre-booking an A-group vehicle from overseas. In or near high season you should reserve in advance, not difficult since so many fly-drive packages are offered. You are virtually obligated to accept the additional daily fee of C£3 for Collision Damage Waiver (CDW); remember also that venturing onto dirt tracks with a non-4WD vehicle will usually void your insurance coverage if you

---

INTERNATIONAL CAR-RENTAL CHAINS

UK

Avis ☎0181/848 8733.
Budget ☎0800/181181.
Europcar/InterRent ☎01345/222525.
Hertz ☎0345/555888.
Holiday Autos ☎0990 300400 (invariably comes up with advantageous deals in Southern Cyprus, arranged through local chains).

NORTH AMERICA

Avis ☎1-800/331 1084.
Budget ☎1-800/527 0700.
Hertz in the US, ☎1-800/654 3001; in Canada, ☎1-800/263 0600.
Holiday Autos ☎1-800/422 7737.
Thrifty ☎1-800/367 2277.

AUSTRALIA

Avis Level 2, 15 Bourke Rd, Mascot, NSW (toll-free ☎1800/225 533).

Budget central reservations, local-call rate ☎13 2848.

Hertz 10 Dorcas St, South Melbourne (local-call rate ☎13 1918).

NEW ZEALAND

Avis Building 4, 666 Great South Rd, Penrose, Auckland (☎09/525 1982).

Budget central reservations ☎09/275 2222.

Hertz 154 Victoria St West, Auckland (☎09/309 0989).

Local chain outlets and one-offs are given in "Listings" of each major town account.

damage the undercarriage. During winter, rates drop to as little as C£7 per day, all inclusive (even the VAT).

Minimum hiring age is generally 21; credit cards are the preferred method of payment. An unusual quirk of Southern rentals is that you may be asked to deposit a sum (eg C£12 for a 40-litre tank), in cash or with credit card, covering the cost of a **full tank** of petrol; the idea is to return the car as empty as possible, rather than full as in other countries. If you return the car to a staffed office, rather than leaving it in the airport parking lot upon departure (more likely), the company is supposed to refund the value of the fuel remaining in the tank.

Because the **North** is unrecognized internationally, none of the overseas chains are represented there, leaving the field clear for local entrepreneurs. There are no longer any car-rental booths at Ercan Airport, so you'll be stranded unless you've pre-arranged to have a car meeting your flight arrival. Arrange a fly-drive package through a tour operator, or contact the agencies noted in Kyrenia, north Nicosia or Famagusta from overseas.

Left-hand-drive cars made in Turkey are invariably cheaper to rent than rarer right-hand-drive vehicles. **Rates** for a bottom-end Renault 12 start at about £15.50 per day, including CDW, in high summer; expect to pay 25 percent less out of season. Credit cards or foreign cash are preferred payment methods, though be aware that most companies slap a seven-percent surcharge on the card bookings to cover the devaluation of the Turkish lira between time of rental and presentation of the slip, and an equal number require full advance payment of the estimated rental price in cash.

BRINGING YOUR OWN CAR

Like their owners, cars brought over on boats to either side of Cyprus are allowed to stay for three months, and may not move over the Attila/Green Line. In the event of any formal settlement between the Greek and Turkish zones, this will probably change, with all sorts of new regulations pertaining. In neither the southern Republic nor in the North are **Green Cards** of foreign insurance valid; you will be insured on the spot as you roll off the boat, for a fee roughly proportional to your intended length of stay; as an example, £9/$14 will get you two weeks of basic, third-party cover in the North.

Mechanics in the South are largely geared to the Japanese models which have virtually captured the market there, but other European makes are represented. Try very hard not to have a breakdown in the North; owing to the small internal market and international boycott, it can take days if not weeks to find parts, either new or scoured from the limited number of junkyards.

MOPEDS AND CYCLES

In the coastal resorts of the South, you can rent small **mopeds** for about C£4 a day; few people will want to take them further than the beach, as you will get scant respect from four-wheeled motorists on curvy mountain roads. Rental motorbikes have yet to appear in the North. Crash helmets are supposedly compulsory in the South.

By contrast, the uplands of either South or North are ideal for **mountain biking**. Both the Tróödhos range and the Kyrenia hills are laced with a network of dirt forest tracks which would be extremely tedious for hiking but constitute a mountain-biker's dream. With some planning or guidance (group bike tours are beginning to be advertised) you could cover either range from end to end in a matter of a few days. Mountain bikes are for sale in south Nicosia and Limassol (see "Listings" for those cities), and for rent in the main Tróödhos resort of Plátres. Incidentally, few rented bikes are supplied with pumps or tyre repair kits.

Additionally there are less specialized, general bike sales and repairs shops in most of the South's larger towns, which you will almost certainly take advantage of, if only to buy patches or replace a pump worn out from constantly pumping up flat tyres. Plentiful thorns on the road ensure a steady incidence of punctures, and there's the usual hot-country problem of the sun melting the rubber solution, so repair jobs won't last if you leave the bike in full sun. Cypriot car drivers tend to regard bicyclists as some lower form of life – on a par with the snakes found deliberately run over everywhere – and can be very aggressive, so pedal defensively.

ACCOMMODATION

The majority of visitors to Cyprus arrive on some sort of package that includes accommodation. That's not to say that independent travel is impossible: most of the Southern hotel listings in the *Guide* are for establishments that are more geared for walk-in trade, and not block-booked by foreign operators.

Despite the literally hundreds of thousands of beds, overbooking in the South has historically been a serious problem, except during the recent slack summers of 1993 and 1995. The limited number of pensions and rooms in private houses are mostly in the South, in the Tróödhos or Páfos district, often occupied by Cypriot holiday-makers.

Northern Cyprus, on the other hand, has scarcely fifty resort-standard hotels or self-catering establishments, rarely if ever full – not too surprising when you consider that scarcely thirty thousand English-speaking tourists show up in a typical year. Much of the tourist industry in the North is carried on in hotels abandoned by Greek Cypriots and let out on a concession basis by the government, and such establishments are often

inefficiently run. Only since the late 1980s have numbers of privately funded, purpose-built and professionally managed resorts sprung up. Our accommodations listings show a preference for these, and it is worth making an effort to book into them.

HOTELS, GUEST HOUSES AND PRIVATE ROOMS IN THE SOUTH

The CTO grades and oversees most accommodation outfits in the South, be they hotels of zero to five stars, guest houses or self-catering units. Their names, locations and current prices are shown in the *Guide to Hotels* issued yearly, but this can be hard to find, and does not distinguish between the relatively few establishments which welcome independent travellers and the vast majority which is pitched at package bookings. Neither does it distinguish between those among the bottom-end listings which are geared for conventional tourist trade, and some which double up as brothels.

HOTELS

All **hotels** of one star or over, and some of the unstarred ones, have en-suite baths. Hotel rooms are most frequently offered on a bed-and-(continental) breakfast basis; charged separately, breakfast rarely exceeds C£2, but frankly if you're having to pay extra, it's better to go out and find a full English breakfast for roughly the same price.

Single occupancy **prices** tend to be well over half the double rate, and maximum rates must be posted either in the room itself or over the reception desk on a CTO-validated placard. Generally there won't be any fiddling in this regard, and except between June and August you may have some scope for bargaining, again stipulated by

CTO rules. Travelling **independently** outside peak season, it's usually possible to find comfortable if modest hotel rooms vacant for less than C£20 double; if you insist on arriving in summer, then you're probably wisest to book in advance from Britain on a package basis.

GUEST HOUSES AND PRIVATE ROOMS

Guest houses, typically charging C£5–9 per person, are a feature of life in the centres of the larger Southern towns and certain Tróödhos resorts. Some, as in Páfos and Larnaca, are reasonably reputable; others (in Limassol and Nicosia especially) are pretty grim or dodgy in some respect. We've made distinctions clear in the town accounts.

The CTO disavows all knowledge of, or responsibility for, **unlicensed rooms** in private rural houses, but they do exist, particularly in the villages of Páfos district and the Tróödhos foothills, both north and south slopes. The going rate currently is about C£5 per person, and this often includes some sort of breakfast. They can offer quite a good look at country domestic life, and are recommended at least once – particularly welcoming families may lay on an evening meal at little or no extra cost, feeding you far better than at the nearest tourist grill. If there are no advertising signs out, the best strategy is to contact the *múkhtar* (village headman) and have him arrange something.

HOTELS IN THE NORTH

Choice is more limited in **Northern Cyprus**: the broad middle ground between luxury compounds and soldiers' dosshouses is thinly inhabited, and many establishments are block-booked by the operators of package-tours, making just showing up on the off-chance a risky endeavour. The North's tourism authority nominally exercises some control over hotel standards and prices, though in practice things tend to be a bit more free-wheeling.

"APART-HOTELS", VILLAS AND LONGER STAYS

An increasing percentage of Cypriot accommodation, in both the South and the North, is **self-catering** in so-called tourist apartments or **"apart-hotels"**, or the more appealing semi-detached **villas**. In the southern Republic the best of these tend to be concentrated in Páfos district, with more scattered around Larnaca and Ayía Nápa; in Northern Cyprus they are almost exclusively in and around Kyrenia. The majority of villas have good amenities and are well maintained by Mediterranean standards, the odd water shortage or power cut aside. See the "Getting There" sections above for specialists offering something out of the ordinary.

If you intend to **stay longer** in the South it's worth scanning adverts in travel or estate agency windows and in the back pages of the two English-language newspapers. Rents for one-bedroom furnished flats start at about C£140 a month; two-bedrooms fall in the C£180–230 range. In Northern Cyprus such lettings are done almost exclusively through agencies, with rents beginning to climb lately to somewhere near levels in the South.

BUDGET OPTIONS: HOSTELS, MONASTERIES AND CAMPSITES

Neither the South or the North is on the backpackers' trail, and what few independent travellers they get tend to be impecunious kibbutz workers just off the boat from Israel. Yet a number of official YHA and private hostels are worth mentioning, plus (in the South) some attractive campsites.

ACCOMMODATION PRICES IN THE NORTH

The hotels and apartment-hotels in the North which can offer rooms to independent travellers (ie those which are not monopolized by package-tour operators) have been categorized according to the price codes given below. These categories represent the minimum you can expect to pay in the high season for a double room or a two-person self-catering unit. As prices quoted in the unstable Turkish lira are fairly meaningless, the codes are based on the pound sterling, the most widely recognized foreign currency in the North, which can often be used to pay hotel bills.

① £10–15   ③ £20–25   ⑤ over £30

② £15–20   ④ £25–30

HOSTELS

In the **South**, there are simple but clean **hostels** in Nicosia, Larnaca, Páfos and on Mount Olympus in the Tróödhos; a YHA card is generally not required, and bunk charges won't exceed C£3, plus another pound for sheets if needed. There is also the extremely popular forestry lodge at Stavrós tis Psókas in the Tillyrian hills. Full details for all of these are given in the *Guide*.

In the **North**, you'll find a number of workmen's and soldiers' dosshouses in Kyrenia, Famagusta and (especially) Nicosia, but these are in general pretty unsavoury and only for desperate males. The Alevkaya (Halévga) forestry refuge in the Kyrenia hills, still shown on many maps, closed some years ago and is now a botanical museum and herbarium.

MONASTERIES

Because hospitality at the various **monasteries** of the South has been so abused in recent years, and the hotels which claimed to lose business were so vociferous in their complaints, several large monasteries in the South are now extremely reluctant to give overnight shelter to the non-Orthodox. In any case they are prevented by law from doing so in summer; virtually the only exception is Stavrovoúni near Larnaca, but you had better display a sincere interest in Orthodox Christianity.

CAMPSITES

The South of the country has six official **campsites**, at Ayía Nápa, Tróödhos resort, Governor's Beach (near Limassol), Coral Bay and Yeroskípou (both near Páfos), and Pólis; most of them are open March to October inclusive, with fees ranging from C£1 to C£1.50 daily per person, with similar charges per tent or caravan. In addition, the forestry department runs 25 more or less amenitied **picnic sites**, mostly in the Tróödhos, where you could probably get away with a discreet overnight in a caravan – any more than that and the rangers would move you on.

The North can muster just two established campsites – one west of Kyrenia, the other near Salamis – and a bare handful of picnic areas, for example at ancient Salamis and in the Kyrenia hills.

EATING AND DRINKING

Food throughout Cyprus is generally hearty rather than refined, and on the tourist circuit at least can seem monotonous after a few days. In many respects resort food is the unfortunate offspring of generic Middle Eastern, and British, cooking at its least imaginative; the fried potato is the tyrant of the kitchen, resulting in a "chips with everything" style of cuisine. If all else fails you can seek solace in the excellent beer and wine of the South. Restaurant fare in the North is a bit lighter and more open to outside influences, especially mainland Turkish, but still heavily Anglicized.

All this is unfortunate, since once off the beaten track, or in a private home, meals are consistently interesting and appetizing, even if they'll never get three stars from Michelin. Less obvious, vegetable-based delights derived from such home cooking are featured in the following food lists.

BREAKFAST

In the **South**, the **breakfast** (*próyevma*) offered through less expensive hotels tends to be minimum-effort continental, with tea/coffee, orange juice and slices of white toast with pats of foil-wrapped butter, jam and (if you're lucky) a slice of processed cheese or *halloúmi*. If you crave more, you'll have to pay extra for bacon-and-eggs-type English breakfasts, either at the hotels or at special breakfast bars in town. More comfortable hotels above two stars will generally provide a more substantial buffet breakfast.

Northern Cyprus has embraced the mainland Turkish breakfast, which means untoasted bread, *beyaz peynir* or white cheese, *kaşar* (kasseri) cheese, olives and either tea or coffee. In the better hotels, these will be presented as a buffet with cold meats and fresh fruit as well.

SNACKS

Cypriots are not as prone to eating on the hoof as Greeks or Turks. On both sides of the Line small British-style cafes sell sandwiches and drinks, but local solutions are less numerous.

Stuffed baked goods in the **South** include *eliópitta*, olive-turnover; *takhinópitta*, a pastry with sesame paste; and *kolokótes*, a triangular pastry stuffed with pumpkin, cracked wheat and raisins. *Aïráni* (*ayran* on the Turkish side) is a refreshing street-cart drink made of diluted yoghurt flavoured with dried mint or oregano and salt, though the dwindling number of vendors seem restricted to Larnaca and Nicosia. *Soudzoúkou*, a confection of almonds strung together and then dipped like candle wicks in a vat of grape molasses and rosewater, are sold everywhere in the South for about C£4 a kilo and make an excellent food for the trail; so does *pastelláki*, a seasame, peanut and syrup bar costing about the same. Other less elaborate dried seeds and nuts are easily available in markets.

In the **North**, street vendors also offer *börek*, a rich, flaky layered pastry containing bits of meat or cheese. You'll have to sit down in a *pideci* or "pizza parlour" for a *pide* (Turkish pizza); usual toppings are *peynirli* (with cheese), *yumurtalı* (with egg), *kıymalı* (with mince), *sucuklu* (with sausage) or combinations of the above. Usually a small bowl of *çorba* (soup) is ordered with a *pide*.

FRUIT AND FOOD SHOPPING

Cypriot **fruit**, especially from the South, has a well-deserved reputation. Because of the long growing season, varieties tend to appear well before their counterparts in Europe – for example strawberries in April, watermelons in June. Everything is grown locally in the South, since the government bans imported products – ostensibly to keep the island pest-free but also to protect the local farmers and specifically exclude sales from the North.

Froutaría is Greek for a roadside fruit-and-vegetable stall, *manav* the Turkish word. The central covered bazaars of all the major towns also usually have a good selection, though in the North much comes from Turkey, since the orchard potential of the Kyrenia hills and the Mórfou plain is limited.

Strawberries are available in the South all year round. Medlars and loquats ripen in mid-spring; their large pips and papery husks may have you wondering why people bother until you taste them. Apricots are next up, followed by peaches, imported from Turkey into the North. Watermelons grown in Páfos district and around Nicosia are on sale everywhere from June on, followed by dessert melons. Plums are also excellent in early summer; cherries, solely from the Tróödhos villages of the South, are delicious in their several varieties.

Towards autumn prickly pear fruit constitutes an exotic challenge, tasting like watermelon once you penetrate its defences. Table grapes of marketable quality are confined to the South, an adjunct of the wine industry. Citrus, specifically oranges, mandarins and grapefruit, is ready in winter. The best oranges are called "Jaffa", something of a misnomer as they're elongated rather than round, juicy and almost seedless. Recently exotics such as avocadoes, bananas, guavas, kiwis and starfruit have also been introduced in the warmer corners of Páfos district, and mangos will probably soon follow.

FOOD SHOPPING
Shopping for yourself in the South, supermarkets and corner stores are easy to find your way around. Labelling is always in English as well as Greek. Local dairy products in all flavours and sizes are conspicuous, as are smoked breakfast and picnic meats; the best are listed below. In all of the major towns of the South, central market halls are excellent sources of farm produce and meat; additionally there are often lively street markets immediately around them, for example in Páfos on Saturdays.

In the North things aren't so self-explanatory, nor abundant, but you certainly won't starve if self-catering. There are central market halls for produce in Kyrenia and north Nicosia.

RESTAURANTS

It takes some diligence to avoid the bland, over-fried stodge dished out to undiscriminating tourists at most restaurants. Generally this means going upmarket, to (often) expat-run restaurants with more imaginative menus; to a remote village setting (in the South), especially to the *exokhiká kéndra* or country tavernas which cater to locals but only serve lunch except in summer; or to a mid-town *ouzerí* (Greek; sometimes referred to as a *mezé*-house) or *meyhane* (Turkish), where local delicacies are served to accompany drink. A watered-down, taverna version of this is the *mezé*, a succession of up to twenty small plates served in succession until you're sated. This is usually very good value, though in the South there is a minimum party of two, often four, persons.

As a rule main-dish portions are generous (if a bit too heavy on the chips), somewhat offsetting the apparent highness of the **prices**. Entrees cost between C£3 and C£5, with menu prices usually including a ten-percent service charge and VAT (currently eight percent).

MEAT AND FISH

Meat dishes tend to predominate, both on and off resort menus. *Kleftikó* (Gr) or *küp kebap* (Trk) is arguably the national dish, a greasy, gristly slab of lamb or goat roasted with vegetables until tender in an outside oven – you see them next to virtually every farmhouse. Lamb chops – *payidhákia* (Gr) or *pırzola* (Trk) – are small by English or North American standards but tasty; *souvláki* or *şiş* is pork arrayed in chunks on a skewer and grilled. The Venetians introduced pigeons to the island and they're much tastier than you'd imagine; quail is the gamier alternative, and both seem much more common than chicken. *Afélia* means pork chunks in red wine and coriander seed sauce and not surprisingly is found only in the non-Muslim Greek community; *sheftália/şeftalya* are small rissoles of mince, onion and spices wrapped in gut, found all over the island. *Moussakás/musaka*, aubergine and potato slabs overlaid with mince and white sauce in its truest form, is better on the Greek side; *karnıyarık* is a meatier Turkish eggplant dish without the potato or sauce.

Fish is not as plentiful as you'd think around the island, and not as cheap. The best places to get it are around Pólis in the South and on the Kırpaşa (Kárpas) peninsula, or at Boğaz, in the

North; otherwise you can safely assume that all seafood has been flash-frozen and shipped in from elsewhere. *Marídhes*, the least expensive fish in the South, are traditionally sprinkled with lemon slices, rolled in salt and then eaten whole, head and all. Barracuda and *sokan* are best grilled, and either grouper or *lágos*, usually batter-fried, must be well done to be appetizing. In North Cyprus, *sokan*, *mercan*, *karagöz* and *barbun* are the best-value species. Across the island, squid and octopus are also standard budget seafood options.

VEGETARIAN FOOD

Vegetarians may have more limited options at times, especially in the South, where some restaurateurs think that offering overpriced plates of chips and tomatoes justifies claims of catering to meat-avoiders. *Mezé*, fortunately, is largely meat-free, consisting principally of *húmmos/humus* (chickpea paté), *tahíni/tahın* (sesame puree), olives, fried *halloúmi/helim* cheese and other titbits. Salads are offered with all entrees, usually a seasonal medley of whatever's to hand: lettuce, tomatoes, parsley, cucumbers, cheese and onions (the latter served on a separate plate). Chefs who try harder may treat you with *rokka* (rocket) greens with their pleasant peppery taste, coriander sprigs or purslane weed – this last much tastier than it sounds. Caper plants are served pickled whole, thorns and all. In the South, fava beans are pureed into *louvána* soup, not to be confused with *louviá* (black-eyed peas); *óspria* is the general term for any pulse dish. In winter especially *trakhanás/tarhana*, a soup of grain soaked in yoghurt, is prepared, though it is often made with chicken stock. Healthier starch sources than the potato include mild-flavoured *kolokássia* (chunks of taro root, a relative of the yam introduced by the British) and *pourgoúri* (cracked or bulgur wheat).

DESSERTS AND SWEETS

Ice cream is everywhere, made by small local dairies, and far more prominent than the traditional Levantine sweets; Turkish or Italian style is invariably better than imitation British. In the South, *P&P* (*Papaphillipou & Patisserie Panayiotis*) is generally accepted as the best local ice cream brand. Creme caramel and European-style pastries are also well represented. Among oriental **sticky cakes**, you'll most often find *baklavás/baklava*, phyllo pastry layers alternating

A GLOSSARY OF FOOD TERMS

In the following lists, the Greek term precedes the Turkish, finally the English. If there is no Greek or Turkish equivalent, a dash is shown.

Basics

neró/su	water	*elióti/–*	olive bread	*gála/süt*	milk
eliés/zeytin	olives	*piláfi /pilav*	cooked rice	*méli /bal*	honey
pítta/pita	flat Arab bread	*pourgoúri /bulgur*	cracked wheat	*voútiro/*	butter
psomí/ekmek	bread	*yiaoúrti /yoğurt*	yogurt	*tereyağ*	

Appetisers (Mezé) and Picnic Items

talatoúra/cacık	yogurt, cucumber and herb dip	*anári/lor*	soft, crumbly sweet cheese, byproduct of above
taramás /tarama	pink fish roe paté		
húmmos/humus	chickpea mash	*fétta/beyaz peynir*	white goat's or ewe's cheese
tahíni /tahın	sesame seed paste		
loúntza/–	smoked pork loin slabs	*kasséri/kaşar*	kasseri cheese
hirómeri/–	cured local ham	*moúgra/–*	pickled cauliflower
tsamarélla/–	lamb- or goat-based salami	*tsakistés/–*	split olives marinated in coriander seed, lemon and garlic
halloúmi /hellim	minty ewe's cheese, often fried		

Meat and Game Entrees

kleftikó/küp kebap	lamb baked in an outdoor oven	*zalatína/–*	brawn
		kotópoulo/piliç	chicken
souvláki/şiş kebap	meat chunks grilled on a skewer	*peristéri/güverçin*	pigeon
		kounélli/tavşan	rabbit
rífi/–	whole lamb on a spit	*ortíkia/bıldiırçıvn*	quail
sheftália/şeftalya	grilled mince-and-onion pellets in gut casings	*ambelopoúlia/–*	pickled songbirds trapped in snares
keftédhes/köfte	meatballs	*karaóles/salyangoz*	snails
pastirmás /pastırma	greasy sausage *or* cured dry meat	*loukániko/bumbar*	skinny home-made sausages
glikádhia/–	sweetbreads		

Soups

avgolémono/düğün	egg-lemon	*patsás/iskembe*	tripe
trakhanás/tarhana	grain, yogurt, spices		

Preparation Terms

tis óras, sta kárvouna/komurde, ızgarada	grilled
tiganitó/yağda	fried
stifádho/yahni	stewed in a sweet onion and tomato sauce
parayemistá/dolması	stuffed
plakí /pılakı	vinaigrette, marinated
oftó	baked, warmed

Fish and Seafood

péstrofa/–	trout (farmed)	*fangrí/mercan*	common bream
parpoúni/barbun	red mullet	*spáros/karagöz*	two-banded or ringed bream
koutsomoúra /tekir	goatfish (like mullet)		
sorkós/sargoz	bream	*skathári/sarıgöz*	black bream
marídhes/–	whitebait	*tsipoúra /çıpura*	gilt-head bream
wópes/küpes	bogue	*sinagrídha/sinagrit*	dentex
parakoúdha/–	barracuda	*hános/asil hanı*	comber
lagós/lagos	a rich cod-like fish	*smérna/merina*	moray eel
rofós/orfoz	grouper, rather boney	*garídhes/karides*	small prawns
–/sokan	cheapish medium-size fish	*khtapódhi /ahtapod*	octopus
		kalamarákia/kalamar	small squid

Vegetables

saláta/salata	any salad	*kírtamo/–*	rock samphire
maroúli/marul	lettuce	*agrioaspáragos/–*	wild asparagus
rókka/rokka	rocket greens	*kapária/gebre*	pickled caper plants
koliándhros/kolandro	coriander	*anginátes/enginar*	artichokes
maídhanos/maydanos	parsley	*spanáki/ıspanak*	spinach
glistirídha/semiz otu	purslane	*patátes/patates*	potatoes
lákhano/lahana	cabbage	*kolokássia/yer elması*	taro root
domátes/domates	tomatoes	*kolokithákia/kabak , bules, or kolokas*	courgettes
kremídhi/soğan	onion		
skórdho/sarmısak	garlic	*bámies/bamya*	okra
repánia/turp	radish	*bezélia/bezelye*	peas
(kafteró) pipéri/ (acı) biber	(hot) pepper	*fasólia/fasulye*	beans
		koukiá/bakla	broad beans
manitária/mantar	mushrooms	*kounoupídhi/ karnabahar*	cauliflower
molehíya/molehiya	a mint-like leaf used as flavouring, or served steamed on its own	*louviá/burulce*	black-eyed peas
		óspria/–	generic for any pulse

Typical Dishes

távas/tava	sweetish stew with onions	*–/karnıyarık*	similar to preceding but no sauce or potato
moussakás/musaka	aubergine and potato slabs overlaid with mince and white sauce	*koupépia/yaprak dolması*	vine leaves filled with rice
kolokótes/–	turnovers stuffed with pumpkin, raisins and bulgur	*bourékia/börek*	turnovers filled with meat or cream cheese
		–/lazböreği	meat-filled crêpes topped with yogurt

Nutty Snacks

soudzoúkou/–	almond string dipped in rosewater and grape molasses	*pastelláki/–*	sesame, peanut and syrup bar
		halepianá/şam fıstığı	pistachios
fistíkia /fıstık	peanuts	*amígdhala/badem*	almonds

DESSERTS, SWEETS AND FRUIT

In the following lists, the Greek term precedes the Turkish, finally the English. If there is no Greek or Turkish equivalent, a dash is shown.

Desserts and Sweets

pagotó/dondurma	ice cream	muhallebí /mahallebi	rice-flour and rosewater pudding
baklavás/baklava	phyllo pastry layers with nut-honey filling	glyká/reçel	preserved candied fruit
kataïfi/kadayıf	same as above but with "shredded wheat" instead of pastry sheets	Types of glyká in the South include:	
		vissino	sour morello cherry
loukoumádhes/lokma	deep-fried batter rings	kerási	Queen Anne-type cherry
halvás/helva	grainy paste of semolina or tahini	petrokéraso	dark red cherry
		kitrómilo	Seville orange
krem karamel/krem karamel	creme caramel	vazanáki	baby aubergines
		síko	fig

Fruit

fráoules /çilek	strawberries	síka/incir	figs
moúsmoule/muşmula	medlars	stafília/üzüm	grapes
méspila/yeni dunya	loquats	míla/elma	apples
kaïsha, khrisómila/kayısı	apricots	akhládhia/armut	pears
rodhákina/şeftali	peaches	portokália/portakal	oranges
karpoúzi/karpuz	watermelon	lemónia/limon	lemons
pepóni /kavun	dessert melon	mandarínia/mandalin	mandarins
paraméles/erik	plums	gréypfrout/grepfrut	grapefruit
kerásia/kiraz	cherries	banánes/muz	banana
papoutsósiko/frenk inciri	prickly pear		

with honey and nuts; galaktopoúreko/su böreği; phyllo pastry filled with custard; and kataïfi/kadayıf, similar to baklava but in a "shredded wheat"-type winding. There are in addition a number of pancake-and-filled-crêpe sweets which you are unlikely to encounter except in a village-festival setting. Glyká, preserved candied fruit (and vegetables) of assorted types, is another village speciality but one occasionally sold to outsiders.

DRINKING

Traditionally Cypriots drink only as accompaniment to food, and prefer nothing stronger than brandy or raki; inebriated north European louts staggering down the streets are apt to offend local sensibilities in either community.

WINE

Owing to near-ideal climate and soils, Cypriot experience in wine-making stretches far back in antiquity, and the tradition has been carried on

with excellence – indeed **wine-drinking** can be one of the highlights of a vacation here. The industry is based almost entirely in the South, and largely dominated by four vintner-owned co-operatives, KEO, ETKO, LOEL and SODAP. However, there are also a number of independent micro-wineries whose products are superior – examples are listed below.

A Cyprus Trade Centre booklet has listed close on forty labels of wine, sherry and brandy, quite a total for a medium-sized island, with more being added slowly as the result of research and new varietal planting. You would have to be a pretty dedicated toper to get through all of them during a short stay, so the evaluations below should give you a head start.

Arsinoë is a very dry **white** offering from SODAP, while LOEL's Palomino is a dry white, smoky in colour and taste; both are available in small, tenth-of-a-gallon bottles. ETKO's White Lady is another contender in the dry-white market. Bellapais (KEO), a medium dry sparkling wine a bit like Portuguese vinho verde, comes in

DRINKS

In the following list, the Greek term precedes the Turkish, finally the English. If there is no Greek or Turkish equivalent, a dash is shown.

kafés/kahve	Oriental coffee, served:	krasí/şarap	wine
		áspro/beyaz	white
pikrós/sade	unsweetened	mávro/kırmızı	red
métrios/orta	medium sweet	kokkinélli/roze	rosé
glikós/şekerli	very sweet	aïráni/ayran	diluted yoghurt with herbs
tsáï/çay	tea		
bíra/bira	beer	himós/meyva suyu	fruit juice

white and **rosé** versions. Afrodhite (*KEO*), an acceptable medium dry cheap white, or *LOEL*'s Saint Hilarion, are about as sweet as you'd want to drink with food; Saint Panteleimon (*KEO*), essentially a dessert or mixer white, is too sugary for most tastes. *Sódha* is the lingua franca for plain soda water – useful for making wine spritzers of those sweeter varieties.

KEO's Rosella is a very dry, dark rosé; the same company makes Othello, a full-bodied **red** not unlike a Cabernet Sauvignon. Hermes is for those who like a a rough, dry red. Every major vintner has a version of Commandaria, a red dessert wine related to Madeira, with an interesting pedigree going back at least ten centuries. After ageing in barrels, some residue is left in before filling the next batch, so theoretically every bottle contains a trace of that long-ago original vintage. Each major vintner produces dry, medium and sweet cream **sherries**, most famous of these being *ETKO*'s Emva line.

In the Tróödhos foothill villages, it's worth asking for the local **barrel wine**: cheaper, often very good and sold in half- or full-litre measures. The Khrysorroyiátissa monastery bottles a reputedly excellent dry white, Ayios Andronicos, and a pale red, Ayios Elias. Current **micro-winery** goodies include Anassa and Ambelidha, two from *Ayios Amvrosios*; Cava Rotaki, from the *Linos* winery; Salera red or white from *Olympus* in Ómodhos, though this can be uneven; the "Kilani Village" red or white, from *Ayia Mavri* winery; and *Laona*, from the namesake vintners in Ársos village, although this last was bought in 1995 by ETKO.

BEER

KEO **beer** is a pleasant pilsener, in small 325-ml or deceptively large 645-ml bottles; you'll drink it all easily in summer conditions, though it's also

sneakily strong – 4.5 percent alcohol. By comparison, the draught version is insipid and watery. *Carlsberg* is the "other" beer, available in the same sizes; the same brewery now makes an "Ice" variety, worth getting at supermarkets only. In North Cyprus, your choices are the Turkish mainland *Efes* label or *Gold Fassl*, an Austrian lager made locally under licence.

SPIRITS

Stronger local **firewater** includes *zivanía*, nearly pure grape alcohol produced greatly in excess of local requirements. Some is flavoured with botanical agents for home use; the rest is sold to the Southern government or exported to fortify weak drink as far away as Russia. *KEO* also makes a range of **hard liquor**, though imported booze is easily available. As for **brandy**, *Peristiani* "31" is fine, though locals both sides of the Line prefer to tipple either *KEO*'s Three Kings (the best, and more expensive), or *Hadjipavlu Anglias*, both smuggled into the North. "Brandy sour", brandy spiked with lime or lemon juice and Angostura bitters, is effectively the national aperitif and beloved of holidaymakers; unfortunately use of premixed citrus base, which can't really substitute for fresh ingredients, is on the increase.

WINES AND SPIRITS IN THE NORTH

In **North Cyprus**, one lonely distillery near Famagusta makes *raki* – an aperitif similar to *ouzo* – and a decent brandy, but *Aphrodite*, the single red/white wine from straggly grapes in the Kyrenia hills and the Kárpas, is laughable. Most wine at restaurants in North Cyprus, red or white, is imported from Turkey; *Turasan* and *Peribacası*, two quality labels from Cappadocia, are about the best, edging out *Kavaklıdere*'s rougher, more acid Yakut red.

TEA, COFFEE AND SOFT DRINKS

Tea in both communities comes in somewhat expensive packs of bags, though in the North Anatolian settlers have introduced, in the villages at least, the practice of brewing loose tea in a double-boiler apparatus known as a *çaydanlık*. *Rombouts* instant **coffee** may be preferable to *Nescafé*. Traditional Middle Eastern coffee, fine-ground, boiled without filtration and served in small cups, comes in three grades: plain, medium sweet, and very sweet. **Juices** throughout the island come in a rainbow of flavours and are excellent, available at markets in either litre cartons or bottles. Fresh citrus juice goes briskly at most resort bars. Among brands of **mineral water** in the South, *Montano* has an edge, if only because of its packaging in two-third litre glass bottles.

COMMUNICATIONS: POST AND PHONES

Both the postal and phone systems of post-independence Cyprus were modelled on those of Britain, but since the events of 1974 these facilities have diverged considerably in North and South. Both offer fairly reliable services (the South, as ever, more efficient), though outgoing mail is invariably quicker than incoming.

POST

Post offices in the **South** are generally open Monday to Friday 7.30am to 1pm (1.30pm in the cooler months) plus Thursday 3 to 6pm; in the four largest towns, a limited number of branches, listed in the *Guide*, are open every weekday afternoon from 3 to 6pm (4–7pm May–Sept), as well as Saturday 9 to 11am. **Outgoing mail** is reliable, though not especially cheap at C£0.35 for a 20-gramme letter to the EU, C£0.21 for a postcard, C£0.36 and C£0.26 respectively to North America, and C£0.41 and C£0.31 to Australasia. Stamps can also be purchased from newsagents, but they may not know the exact rates for your destination.

Numbers of quaint colonial **pillar-boxes** survive, the royal monograms "GR" and "ER" still visible through coats of fresh yellow paint. The same central post offices which have afternoon services also have **poste restante** and **parcel** facilities.

In **Northern Cyprus**, post offices are open 7.30am to 2pm and 4pm to 6pm Monday to Friday, 9am to noon Saturday. **Outgoing mail** is tolerably quick, considering that it has to be shuffled through Turkey to get around the international postal union boycott; despite this, North Cyprus issues its own stamps, with a postcard rate to the UK of about 29p, 36p for a letter. As in the South, look for kerbside pillar-boxes, now a distinctly faded yellow. Parcels are easily sent from Nicosia, Famagusta or Kyrenia. **Poste restante** service is theoretically available in these three towns.

PHONES

Cyprus has a fair-to-good phone service, though call boxes are fewer than in the UK or North America throughout the island, verging on non-existent in the North. Southern services are modelled on UK prototypes, right down to the model of phoneboxes used; those in the North (not surprisingly) are an extension of the mainland Turkish system.

THE SOUTH

Phones in the Republic of Cyprus are administered by the Cyprus Telecommunications Authority, **CYTA** for short. Town- and village-centre **call boxes**, while not as common as they should be, usually work, and take coins or telecards.

Booths with **coin-operated** phones are an endangered species, found principally in isolated areas, and accepting 10-cent coins as a minimum. Counter-top coin-op phones in hotel lobbies and

SENDING MAIL TO NORTH CYPRUS

Because of the international postal union boycott of North Cyprus, both incoming and outgoing mail is initially routed through Turkey. When writing to anyone in North Cyprus, you must add a special post code – **Mersin 10, Turkey** – to the last line of the address (this designates the tenth county of Mersin province – further support to the contention that North Cyprus is being subject to creeping annexation by Turkey). If you fail to do so, the letter may be misdirected to the South or more likely to the "addressee unknown" bin.

restaurants are identical to such in the UK, and take 5-, 10- or 20-cent coins; push the "Drop" button when your party answers.

For **overseas calls**, a better bet are the ubiquitous, if somewhat noisy, **telecard phones**; often you have to keep your thumb on the back end of the card to keep it from popping out. You can purchase C£3, C£5 and C£10 telecards from CYTA offices, certain banks, post offices, corner kiosks and wherever you see the telecard logo displayed. The C£10 cards permit about twenty minutes of chat to the UK, less than half that to North America. **Cheap rates** apply within the South between 8pm and 7am daily, for overseas calls between 10pm and 8am Monday to Saturday, and all day on Sunday.

All call booths should have detailed calling instructions in English, but if not, to phone overseas from Cyprus, dial ☎00 – waiting for changes in tone – and then the country code (posted in all booths), national code and subscriber number. The quality of connections is usually very good. There are automatic direct-dial connections with virtually everywhere except North Cyprus and Turkey –

INTERNATIONAL PHONE CODES FROM CYPRUS

International operator (for reverse-charges calls) ☎198. This service is available from private or hotel phones in the South only.

UK ☎00 44
Republic of Ireland ☎00 353
Netherlands ☎00 31
USA & Canada ☎00 1
Australia ☎00 61
New Zealand ☎00 64
South Africa ☎00 27

with whom the Republic is still technically in a state of belligerence and mutual non-recognition.

However, despite propaganda to the contrary it is possible – just – to make calls **to the North**, using the UN operator based at Nicosia airport; dial ☎02/359703 or 359704 to be connected. In theory you'll get six minutes of conversation free, but in practice the line is often engaged, necessitating up to an hour of persistent trying to get through.

All Southern phones have six-digit numbers and two-digit area codes, the first digit of which is always zero. Dialling the Republic of Cyprus from overseas, the **country code is ☎357**, followed by the area code minus its initial zero.

Except in Nicosia and Pedhoulás, there are no longer any call booths at the various CYTA branches in the major towns – you'd only really go there to buy telecards. Calls from your hotel room may be worth considering for the quiet surroundings alone, though ask about surcharges so that you're not stuck with an outrageous bill.

THE NORTH

Phones in the Turkish Republic of Northern Cyprus are handled by the *Telekomünikasyon Dairesi* or Telecom Division. The pre-1974 network has been completely replaced by an imported Turkish system, which features orange **call boxes** accepting either tokens (*jetons*) or *telekarts*, both available only from the *Telekomünikasyon* offices. Tokens come in three sizes – small, medium and large – and you'd need stacks of the largest ones to make an international call; cards are preferable. However, call boxes of either sort are so exceedingly rare that we've located and counted them in the *Guide*. Many seem to be following their 1960s predecessors into dereliction and disconnection; when you do find a working one it invariably has a long queue of students and soldiers.

You may get more joy from the bare handful of **Telekomünikasyon offices** themselves, where you pay after completing your call from peaceful booths or counter phones.

All in all, it's best to place any calls from your **hotel room**; the admittedly outrageous surcharge (100 percent on the already steep basic rate of £1.50 a minute to the UK) is more than worth the extra convenience and privacy, and occasionally the front desk forgets to charge you upon departure. Once clear of the hotel circuitry, dial ☎00 to get an **international line**, followed by the usual repertoire of country and area codes. As in the South, calls **across the Attila Line** are normally

---

USEFUL TELEPHONE NUMBERS AND CODES

The South

Inland directory assistance ☎192	Larnaca district ☎04
Overseas directory assistance ☎194	Limassol district ☎05
Police, fire and ambulance ☎199	Páfos district ☎06
Nicosia district ☎02	Mobile phones ☎09
Ayía Nápa district ☎03	

The North

Directory assistance ☎118	International operator ☎115

---

blocked, but again you can use a UN number (in this case ☎228 3963) to get through, subject to the same conditions and caveats as going in the reverse direction.

In 1993, North Cyprus went over to the ten-digit Turkish phone number convention: a three-digit code, **☎392**, which applies to the entire country, followed by a seven-digit subscriber number. When ringing from overseas, you must preface these ten digits with the international code for Turkey, **☎90**; as in matters postal, Turkey effectively "fronts" for North Cyprus in the international arena.

THE MEDIA

For a modest-sized island, Cyprus is served by a disproportionately large number of printed publications and TV or radio channels. Part of this is a result of non-market factors, such as sponsorship of print media by political groups on both sides of the Line, and also to its critical position in the east Mediterranean, enabling the island both to tap the airwaves from, and to beam to, neighbouring countries.

NEWSPAPERS AND MAGAZINES

While the vernacular-language print media will be inaccessible to most visitors, there are a number of informative, locally produced English-language publications aimed primarily at expats. A very few foreign newspapers are available – at a price.

THE SOUTH

Nearly a dozen Greek-language newspapers, many toeing a particular party line, cater to native readers in the South. Among **English-language papers**, the *Cyprus Weekly* (C£0.40, Fridays) has in recent years become progressively more downmarket and anti-Turkish, while its rival

the daily (except Mon) *Cyprus Mail* (C£0.30), has under new management become one of the better papers on the island, worth a read for its "Tales from the Coffee Shop" column alone. Editorial content aside, both have news, extensive small ads and daily/weekly programmes for most radio and TV stations. The *Mail* features brief weekday sections for movies and exhibits, and chemist rotas, though the Sunday edition is particularly valuable for its "What's On" section giving the week's listings of film, TV, radio and live events. Chemist and Sunday petrol station schedules appear in the *Weekly*, along with a more extensive, pull-out arts-review section called "Lifestyle", plus a separate "TV Weekly". **Foreign newspapers** are pricy: C£1.20 for *The Times* or the *International Herald Tribune* and C£0.90 for the *Guardian*.

THE NORTH

You'll see only the very occasional *Financial Times* in the North, the rather turgid *Turkish Daily News* from the mainland, plus the Asil-Nadir-owned weekly *Cyprus Today* (Saturday, 40p) in English; this has radio and TV listings, plus the rota of late-night chemists and complete Ercan airport flight info. There are also a half-dozen Turkish-language papers, nearly all affiliated with a political party.

RADIO, TV AND CINEMA

The advantages of having your own electronic media for propaganda purposes are not lost on either of Cyprus' two main communities, so that there's an ongoing "battle of the transmitters". *Bayrak*, the North's radio voice, dangles lengthy Greek-music and -language programming to reel in Southern listeners, as prelude to news broadcasts presenting the South in a bad light, overrun with mafiosi, graft and terrorism; for its part, Southern station *CyBC* (*Cyprus Broadcasting Corporation*), even in its Turkish-language programming, studiously refers to the North as "Turkish-occupied territory", and Denktaş as "leader of the Turkish Cypriot community". In recent years, programming hours have lengthened and a number of private stations have emerged to challenge the government monopoly, a sharp break from the past where meagre advertising revenues and a limited audience dictated just a few hours' broadcasting per day.

RADIO

On the **radio**, *CyBC*'s strictly Greek Programme 1 can be found at 96.4 FM, 6am to midnight. *CyBC*'s Programme 2, at 91.1 and 92.4 FM during the same time slot, has a more cosmopolitan lineup with news in English at 10am, 2pm and 8pm, and all English programming from 8pm to midnight. The *BBC World Service* broadcasts at 1323 AM from 6am to 3am except from 10.30 to noon when it goes to 639 AM; reception is usually very strong, since the transmitter for the whole Middle East sits on the coast between Larnaca and Limassol. The British Sovereign Bases operate the *British Forces Broadcasting Service* (*BFBS*), in English with Western programming, on Programme 1 (24hr) at 91.9 and 99.6 FM and the better Programme 2 (6am to 1.30am) at 89.9 and 95.3 FM. Skipping along

the dial you'll also find several private, local stations.

In **the North**, the official *Bayrak Radyo* (87.8 and 105 FM, 1494 AM) functions most of the afternoon and early evening.

TV

CyBC 1 and *2* beam **TV** from **the South** daily from about 3pm to midnight and from 7am to 3am respectively; programming is a lively mix of soaps, films, music, talk shows and documentaries. There's a lot of foreign material with its original soundtrack, and even the Greek transmissions have English and Turkish subtitles. Otherwise people tune in to the Greek stations *ET1* and *Antenna* from Rhodes, or independent stations *Logos*, *Sigma*, *LTV*, *METV*; or *BBC* affiliates *BBC Prime* and *SSVC*. Satellite dishes pick up *Star Plus* and *CNN*.

In **the North**, *Bayrak Televizyon* broadcasts Monday to Friday from 6.30pm to about 10.30pm, with English news at opening time. Otherwise people make do with *TRT* from Turkey.

CINEMA

In terms of **cinema**, there are nine regularly functioning movie-houses in south Nicosia, four in Limassol, and two in Larnaca; the British, French and Russian cultural centres in south Nicosia also screen their share of films. Fare at the commercial cinemas, except for the art-house *Cine Studio* in south Nicosia, tends to be first-run but somewhat gormless caper/action releases, while the cultural centres predictably feature more art films and retrospective series. Prints are generally in the original language, with Greek subtitles. Screening times and addresses are not given in the foreign-language press, so you must phone or walk by the cinema for details.

At the moment there is just one international-standard cinema operating in the **North**, the *Mızırlızade* in north Nicosia (☎22 89 698), though at last glance fare was of the *Full Metal Jacket* and *Species* variety.

OPENING HOURS, HOLIDAYS AND FESTIVALS

Business hours throughout the island are scheduled around the typical Mediterr-anean mid-day siesta. Generally the South's public holidays have a religious focus, reflecting the Greek Orthodox Church's pre-eminent position in the culture, while the North – technically a secular society – has more commemorations of salient events in Turkish communal history. In recent years many special events have been developed by the Southern tourism authorities, with a view to a foreign audience, to supp-lement the bedrock of traditional religious festivals.

OPENING HOURS

Town shops in **the South** are meant to be open daily in summer 8am to 1pm and again from 4 to 7pm, except for Wednesday and Saturday when there are no afternoon hours. Summer is construed as May 1 to September 30. Winter hours are 8.30am to 1pm and again from 2.30 to 5.30pm (3 to 6pm for offices), with the same Wednesday and Saturday afternoon closures.

Both mountain village stores and establishments in tourist resorts are likely to keep longer hours. Food shops along roads leading to dormitory/suburb villages around major towns will be open beyond 7pm, often until 9.30pm.

In **the North**, summer hours are supposedly 7.30am to 1.30pm and 4 to 6pm Monday to Friday, plus a morning session on Saturday. In winter shops are meant to be open 8am to 5.30pm Monday to Saturday. Observance of schedules may be haphazard, with 2 to 3.30pm a common period of summer closure.

PUBLIC HOLIDAYS IN THE SOUTH

In the South, there is near-complete overlap between religious and bank **holidays**, so of the dates below official business is only conducted (after a fashion) on *Kataklismós*. When these dates fall on a Sunday, the subsequent Monday is usually a public holiday – in the case of Easter, the following Tuesday is also a bank holiday, though shops will be open.

RELIGIOUS HOLIDAYS IN THE SOUTH

New Year's Day in Cyprus is the feast day of **Áyios Vasílios** (St Basil), and the evening before, most homes bake a *vasilópitta* or cake containing a coin bringing good luck to the one finding it in their slice. The saint is also the Cypriot equivalent of Santa Claus, and gifts are exchanged on this day, not at Christmas.

In the Orthodox Church, **Epiphany** marks the baptism of Christ in the Jordan, and the conjunction of the Holy Trinity; the Greek name *Fóta* or "Lights" refers to the resulting inner illumination. Holy water fonts in churches are blessed to banish the *kalikándzari* demons said to run amok on earth since Christmas. As a finale at seaside locations, a local bishop hurls a crucifix out over the water, and young men swim for the honour of recovering it.

Green Monday comes at the end of the ten days of **Carnival**, the occasion for fancy-dress balls and parades, most notably at Limassol. In rural areas, the day also signals the beginning of a strict meatless fast of seven weeks for the devout. March 25 is usually billed as "Greek National Day", but is more properly the feast of *Evangelismós* or the **Annunciation**.

Observance of **Easter** starts early in **Holy Week**, and the island's small Catholic and Armenian communities celebrate in tandem with the Orthodox majority. The most conspicuous customs are the dyeing red of hard-boiled eggs on Maundy Thursday, the baking of special holiday cakes such as *flaoúnes*, and on Good Friday the solemn procession of the *Epitáfios* or Christ's funeral bier in each parish, whose women provide its elaborate floral decoration.

On Saturday evening, huge bonfires (*lambrádjia*) are set – giving rise to the word **Lambrí**, the alias for Easter in Cypriot dialect –

HOLIDAYS IN SOUTH CYPRUS			
1996	**1997**	**1998**	
1 January	same	same	Áyios Vasílios (New Year's Day)
6 January	same	same	*Fóta* (Epiphany)
26 Feb	10 March	2 March	Green (Lent) Monday
25 March	same	same	Annunciation
1 April	same	same	Southern Republic Day
12 April	25 April	17 April	Orthodox Good Friday
14 April	27 April	19 April	Orthodox Easter Sunday
1 May	same	same	Labour Day
3 June	16 June	8 June	*Kataklismós* (Flood Feast)
15 August	same	same	Assumption of the Virgin
1 October	same	same	Cyprus Independence Day
28 October	same	same	Greek National Day
25, 26 December	same	same	Christmas, Boxing Day

before the spectacular midnight *Anástasi* or Resurrection mass. Not everyone will fit into the confines of a typical village church, so crowds gather in the courtyard, around the embers of the fire. Observance is pretty casual, even by Greek rural standards; the noise of high-decibel fireworks set off by teenagers – everything from Roman candles to dynamite left over from the Limnítis mine (in Tillyría) – all but drowns out the liturgy, such that in one recent year the priest at Neokhorió village on the Akámas peninsula refused to proceed with the service.

Things calm down temporarily at midnight, when the officiating priest appears from behind the altar screen bearing a lighted candle and the news of eternal life for believers, and soon church interiors and courtyards are ablaze with the flame passed from worshipper to worshipper. It is considered good luck to get your candle home still alight, to trace a soot-cross over the door lintel; then the Lenten fast is broken with *avgolémono* soup, and family members crack their red-dyed eggs against each other (owner of the last unbroken egg "wins").

Kataklismós or the **Festival of the Flood**, seven weeks after Easter, is unique to Cyprus; elsewhere in the Orthodox world it is merely Pentecost or the Feast of the Holy Spirit, but here it's a pretext for a week or so of popular events. At all coastal towns people crowd into the sea and sprinkle each other with water; the festival ostensibly commemorates the salvation of Noah and his family from the Flood, but it's likely a vestige of a much older pagan rite in honour of Aphrodite's birth, or perhaps her purification after sleeping with Adonis.

Christmas (*Khristoúyenna*) is relatively subdued in Cyprus, though inevitably European-style commercialization has made inroads. The most durable old custom is that of the *kálanda* or carols, sung by children going door-to-door accompanying themselves on a triangle. It's worth noting that many establishments (restaurants and KEO brewery tours, for example) seem to shut down between Christmas and New Year, opening only sporadically between January 1 and 6.

OTHER EVENTS IN THE SOUTH

In addition to the strictly ecclesiastical holidays, municipalities and tourist boards lay on a number of other events, with a steady eye on the foreign audience. The most reliable of these include the May *Anthistíria* or **Flower Festivals**, best in early May at Larnaca, and mid-May at Páfos; the Limassol and Larnaca municipal festivals in July; the **Páfos festival** of music, theatre and dance staged in the ancient odeion and medieval castle from June to September; and the **Limassol Wine Festival**, with free tasting sessions in the central park, during the first week of September. If you're determined to coincide with any or all of these, get a copy of the CTO's annual "Diary of Events" or the monthly cyclo-styled update produced at each local tourist office.

PUBLIC HOLIDAYS IN THE NORTH

In the **North**, the holiday calendar is again a mix of religious holidays – all receding eleven days yearly because of the lunar Muslim calendar – and official commemorations, many imported from Turkey. Unlike in the South, there's just not the budget or inclination for laying on big theme bashes. The most extravagant are occasional folkloric performances at the castles of Famagusta and Kyrenia, and unpredictably dated harvest festivals on the Mesarya (Mesaoría) for the cherished orange, strawberry and watermelon crops.

The official holidays of the North are fairly self-explanatory, though a word on the movable religious feasts is in order. *Şeker Bayramı* marks the end of the fasting month of Ramazan, and is celebrated with family get-togethers and the distribution of presents and sweets to children. *Kurban* commemorates the thwarted sacrifice of Ishmael by Abraham – a Koranic version of the Abraham and Isaac story – and used to be distinguished by the dispatch and roasting of vast numbers of sheep; the custom is now on the wane in Cyprus.

PUBLIC HOLIDAYS IN THE NORTH

1996	1997	1998	
1 January	same	same	New Year's Day (*Yılbaşı*)
20–22 Feb	9–11 Feb	29–31 Jan	Şeker Bayramı
23 April	same	same	Turkish National Sovereignty and Children's Day
1 May	same	same	Labour Day
19 May	same	same	Youth and Sports Day
29 April–1 May	18–21 April	7–10 May	*Kurban Bayramı*
20 July	same	same	Peace Operation Day
1 August	same	same	TMT Day
30 August	same	same	*Zafer Bayramı* (Victory Day)
6 August	27 July	16 July	*Mevlûd* (Muhammad's Birthday)
29 October	same	same	Turkish Republic Day
15 November	same	same	TRNC Foundation Day

SITES, MUSEUMS, CHURCHES AND MOSQUES

Archeological sites and museums throughout the island have user-friendly opening times, though you may find certain Northern museums and monuments shut without explanation owing to staffing problems. Admission fees are modest, especially compared to neighbouring countries, and in the South at least polite signs instructing you to "Please ask for your ticket" are a far cry from the typically growling human Cerberus blocking the way in Greece or Egypt. Churches and mosques of interest to visitors have less established visiting hours and operate on a "donation" basis.

OPENING TIMES AND ADMISSION FEES

The more popular ancient sites in the **South** are fenced but accessible from roughly 7.30am to near sunset all year, though even during long-day months they're rarely open past 7.30pm. Most museums shut for lunch for some time between 1.30 or 2.30 pm and 3 or 4pm, with finally evening closure usually at 6pm, never later than 7pm. On public holidays (see previous section) most outdoor sites are unaffected, but many museums keep short – or no – hours, and everything shuts on Easter Sunday. Exact details for each establishment are given in the text of the *Guide*. No entrance fee exceeds C£1, and most are currently C£0.50; children under 10 usually get in free.

Operating hours at the limited number of museums and sites in **Northern Cyprus** are vaguely similar; admission fees cost 40p–£1, depending on the attraction.

CHURCHES

Most of the famous **frescoed churches** of the **South** are still used in some sacred capacity, and kept locked to protect them from thieves and the elements; accordingly they often don't have set visiting hours. Part of the experience is locating the key-keeper, not always a priest, who may live or work some distance away. A donation to the collection box, if not the person himself, is required; complete instructions are given for each monument described in the *High Tróödhos*. Since all but a few churches are still consecrated, men may not usually enter in shorts, nor women in pants of any sort, and neither sex in sleeveless tops – wraps are not provided, so bring suitable garb. Photos, especially with flash, are simply not allowed.

MOSQUES

Most **mosques** in the South are now kept locked, presumably awaiting the hypothetical return of their Turkish Cypriot users. One apiece still functions in south Nicosia, Limassol and Larnaca, meeting the needs of the Republic's sizable population of Arabs and Iranians – as well as the handful of remaining Turkish Cypriots in the South. The *tekke* of Hala Sultan near Larnaca is also still an active place of pilgrimage for island and foreign Muslims, as well as a tourist attraction.

Some rules of **etiquette** apply to any mosque throughout the island. Contrary to what you may read in other sources, shoes must be removed at the entrance, and one does not enter scantily clad – this in effect means the same guidelines as for churches, above. Native Cypriot Muslims are remarkably easy-going (eg their tolerant attitudes towards drinking and dogs) and flattered at any attention to their places of worship, so you would have to do something fairly insensitive to irk them. As a minimum, don't enter mosques when a service is in progress, and try not to walk in front of a praying person.

CHURCHES IN THE NORTH

Since the events of 1974 only a bare handful of **churches in the North** (detailed in the *Guide*) continue to function as houses of Christian worship. The rest have been either converted into mosques or museums, or desecrated in various ways, mostly by the Turkish army but occasionally by Anatolian settlers or Turkish Cypriots.

This behaviour is naturally seized on by the outraged Greek Cypriots as further proof of (mainland) Turkish barbarism, and used to good effect in their sophisticated "public relations" efforts – one particularly graphic publication is entitled *Flagellum Dei* (The Scourge of God), referring to Attila the Hun, lately reincarnated in the Greeks' view. The Southern government pointedly contrasts the treatment of these buildings with the relative consideration accorded to mosques in the South, which are held in trust by a Religious Affairs Department, provided with a tiny budget to maintain the buildings.

For their part, the Northerners either tend not even to acknowledge that an injury has been done, or justify it as the understandable venting of frustrations and aggressions on the most tangible, helpless reminders of the atrocities perpetrated on the Turkish Cypriots by EOKA. Specifically, it is claimed that the ringing of church bells often signalled the start of an anti-Turkish-Cypriot pogrom in formerly mixed villages.

What this means to a visitor is that the Northerners are touchy about requests to visit churches not specifically prepared for public use. You will often find abandoned churches off-limits as military depots, and/or appallingly vandalized, sometimes with their entrances bricked up to prevent further damage. In any case it's a depressing exercise visiting these battered buildings, empty of the devotion which the Greek Cypriots lavished on them, and something most people will only do once or twice.

POLICE, TROUBLE AND HARASSMENT

In general, Cyprus has to be one of the safest Mediterranean travel destinations: assault and burglary are almost unknown, and the atmosphere is so unthreatening that you catch yourself feeling silly for locking a rental car. What little crime there is tends to be overwhelmingly of the fraud-and-smuggling variety, leavened of late by a series of eight grisly killings inside the Cypriot underworld.

Authorities and police in both communities go out of their way to make tourists, so vital to the island economy, feel welcome, and the most likely occasion for misunderstandings will be the various **military zones** – far more numerous in the North than in the South. Unless you are actually visiting someone living in the buffer (demilitarized, "dead") zone, or are escorted by authorized UN or Cypriot military personnel, you'll at least raise an eyebrow or two by driving into it – certainly in the North – and could provoke an international incident by using any roads marked as blocked-off on our maps. **Border violations**, especially going from North to South, are taken very seriously indeed, with the standard penalty three months' imprisonment. A rather clueless tourist did three weeks in the South for this late in 1995; he got off so lightly only because it was shown that, for inexplicable reasons, guards on either side of the Line waved him through, and in the latter case even helped him find a hotel room in Larnaca – where the police picked him up that night.

Do heed the **"no photography"** signs near military bases throughout the island, as well as along the Attila Line (the Green Line in Nicosia). If you are caught photographing, even inadvertently, a military installation anywhere in Cyprus, your film may be confiscated – politely, and possibly returned after processing and screening, in the South; more brusquely by the Turkish Army in the North. In the southern Republic some or all of certain monasteries are now off-limits to cameras, since the monks grew tired of being zoo-animal-type attractions. Similarly, don't sneak snaps of the interiors of the South's frescoed churches – caretakers accompany you inside to prevent this, among other reasons.

Casual visitors have until now been unlikely to see much evidence of the more unsavoury, organized crime on the island. But late in 1995, a spectacular scandal broke, implicating the higher ranks of the South's police force in a spate of gangland shootings, car bombings, apartment arson and torture of suspects in detention. President Clerides himself announced that significant numbers of the police force were involved in battles for control of the South's lucrative gambling, drug-smuggling and prostitution rackets. Though it all sounds lurid, as long as you avoid cabarets, massage parlours, gambling dens and unwise purchases of controlled substances, you should avoid being caught in crossfire or getting on the wrong end of police batons in custody (several young Britons arrested on drug charges were among those allegedly mistreated).

If you have anything **stolen**, it is still worthwhile – despite all the foregoing – to report the theft at the nearest police station and get a copy of the report or the identification number under which your report is filed: you will need this if you intend to make an insurance claim once you get back home (see "Health and Insurance").

SEXUAL HARASSMENT AND PROSTITUTION

Both Greek and Turkish Cypriot men are more reserved than their mainland counterparts, though as throughout the Mediterranean, resort areas support numbers of underemployed Romeos. Limited instances of north European women arriving specifically to look for adventure fuel the myth of the "easy", available blond Nordic type and do not make life simpler for foreign women uninterested in such attention. Told to desist in no uncertain terms, the lechers usually will. In the more traditional inland areas, unescorted women will generally be accorded village courtesy.

Foreign men who stumble on the **red-light districts** of Limassol and Nicosia in the **South** will probably find invitations from open doorways and bar-fronts more ridiculous than threatening; unaccompanied foreign women should avoid these areas. Nearly two hundred prostitutes(about 1 for every 300 adult males), mostly Romanian and Russian, work assorted brothels and nightclubs in the **North**; indulging would be foolhardy, to put it mildly, since they've toured most of Turkey on their backs before arriving here, and HIV infection is rife among them.

SPORTS AND OUTDOOR ACTIVITIES

Because of its mild climate, Cyprus is a good place to indulge in assorted open-air athletic activities. The CTO even devotes an entire six-page, large-format leaflet to the subject, detailing indoor facilities as well. In terms of spectating, football and tennis – for which the South hosts several major international tournaments yearly – are the big events.

WATER SPORTS

Virtually all resorts in the South cater well to any water sport you could mention, from kayaking to para-sailing by way of water-skiing. **Windsurfers** are available everywhere, but you only get strong breezes around the island's capes: in the far southeast, between Ayía Nápa and Protarás; around Páfos; and occasionally on the exposed coast west of Pólis. Small sailcraft can be rented from the marinas at Larnaca, Limassol and Páfos. In North Cyprus, windsurfing and sailing facilities concentrate west of Kyrenia, and at the luxury hotels near ancient Salamis.

Perhaps the biggest attraction is underwater; unusually for the east Mediterranean where submerged antiquities are prone to theft, **scuba** is encouraged by the tourism authorities and actively promoted by numerous dive operators –

we've listed at least one in each major resort – and it's worth taking advantage. In the North, a scuba school operates both out of Kyrenia's old harbour, and from Alsancak.

ON LAND

Cypriots are big **tennis** buffs, participatory as well as watching, and most hotels over three stars in either the North or the South will have their own courts. Otherwise, courts are open to the public in all the big Southern towns.

Mountain-biking has already been noted as a possibility in "Getting Around", but there are also some bona fide marked trails – as opposed to vehicle tracks – in the Southern hills, prepared expressly for **hiking** by the CTO in conjunction with the forestry division. The *Guide* covers all of them, though the longest itinerary will fill just a single day; there are as yet no long-distance routes the length of the Tróödhos. It's more difficult, but still possible, to walk in the steeper Kyrenia hills as long as you steer clear of military areas, though a recent, catastrophic fire has detracted considerably from the appeal of the countryside.

Southern Cyprus can boast the exotic attraction, for the Middle East, of a **ski** resort. There's a single complex of four lifts on the northeast face of Mount Olympus, the island's summit. The season lasts approximately from January to early April; don't come specially.

Since 1995 **golf**, focused on the new golf course at Tsádha in Páfos district (with two others under construction), has been heavily promoted to visitors (see box on p.133 for some background). Most package-tour operators offer the option of pre-booking greens fees, which depending on the company vary from C£22–24 per day, up to C£120–130 per week.

For some arcane reason the Turkish Cypriots are very keen on **tae kwan do**, and despite the North's recognition problems, international competitions have been held there.

SHOPPING

Cyprus, North or South, is not a souvenir hunter's paradise, but while you're travelling around there are certain items worth looking out for. See also the note on Bargaining in the "Directory", following.

THE SOUTH

The South is most famous for **lacework**, produced principally at Páno Léfkara, equidistant from the three largest towns, though beware of imported Irish lace. Arguably more attractive, colourful, loom-woven items, rather more likely to be indigenous, are available at Fíti in Páfos district. Reed **basketry** is another distinctive product, especially in Páfos district; of particular interest are the almost Amerindian-looking, bi- or tri-colour circular **mats** (called *tséstos* in Greek, *tsesta* or *paneri* in Turkish), which adorn the walls of many tavernas. You can find reed products at the central covered markets of Nicosia, Páfos, Limassol and Larnaca, as well as at Yeroskípou and Liopétri villages.

Another taverna-decor staple which can still be purchased are *kolókia* or **etched gourds**, embossed with designs either painted or burned on.

More urban specialities include **shoes**, **silver jewellery** and **optical goods**. High-quality sunglasses at the numerous opticians cost about the same (less VAT) as in North America, owing to direct importation, and thus much less than in Britain. The much-vaunted stock of contact lenses seems limited to Bausch and Lomb products.

The government-run **Cyprus Handicraft Service** has several fixed-price retail outlets, which gather together under one roof "approved" examples of each craft. It's worth stopping in to gauge quality and cost at the very least; addresses are given in the box.

THE NORTH

There is rather less on offer in the **North**, though the basketry products seem more refined, and comparatively expensive; you can find very strong, large **baskets** suitable for clothes hampers in north Nicosia and the village of Edremit, though as in the South the items tend to be made elsewhere, in remote villages with no sales facilities. Junk and antique dealers in Nicosia and Famagusta have a limited and expensive stock of **old copper** and **household implements**.

Otherwise you are faced with the task of sifting through a fair amount of second-rate kitsch (garish backgammon sets, thin-gauge copper lanterns, onyx eggs, ceramic ashtrays), offloaded from Syria and Turkey, lying in wait for tourists insisting on something "Oriental".

CYPRUS HANDICRAFT CENTRES

South Nicosia Athalássas 186 (☎02/305024); Laïkí Yitoniá (☎02/303065)

Larnaca Kosmá Lysióti 6 (☎04/630327)

Limassol Themídhos 25 (☎05/330118)

Páfos Apostólou Pávlou 64 (☎06/240243)

DIRECTORY

ADDRESSES In the Greek Cypriot sector, addresses are written either in Greek or in English. When in Greek, the number follows the street name, for example "Leofóros Faneroménis 27". The same place in English is still usually cited, despite the recent Hellenization campaign, as "27, Faneromenis Avenue". Post codes exist but are not yet used much; more often a district within the municipality is cited.

In Northern Cyprus, addresses can be somewhat vaguer. They are generally given bilingually

(Turkish/English) on visiting cards and bumph, but if not, *Caddesi*, abbreviated Cad, means avenue; *Bulvarı* (Bul) is boulevard; *Meydan/Meydanı* (Meyd) is plaza; *Sokak/Sokağı* (Sok) means street; and *Çıkmazı* (Çık) is a dead-end alley. *Karşısı* means "opposite from", as in *PTT karşısı*, "opposite the post office".

BARGAINING Not a regular feature of Cypriot life, except in the case of any souvenir purchase where price is not marked. Don't expect the vendor to come down more than twenty percent, however. Hotels and pensions in the South have prices prominently displayed, and there is generally no upward fiddling in this respect. At slow times you can get rooms for twenty percent less than posted rates; the same applies to car rental. In the North things are more flexible; written rates and prices are not so conspicuous, but again expect only small discounts.

BRING... a water container for hot-weather ruin-tramping; a torch for dark corners of same, and for outlasting power cuts in Northern Cyprus; bath/sink plugs (rarely supplied) for washing clothes, 37mm and 44mm diameter best; a line and clips for hanging said clothes; a small alarm clock; some form of flying-bug repellent (sold in the South, though) or netting; and sunscreen cream with a protection factor of over 15 (difficult to find). In the North you'll want all of the above, plus slide photo film and contact lens solutions from home; in the South these can be found with some diligence.

CAMPING GAS In the South, 190-ml canisters for Bluet stoves are commonly available from scuba and sports shops, plus selected appliance shops; in the North they are harder to find, but begin by asking at hardware stores and service stations. 250-gramme cylinders are also available throughout Cyprus. If you're showing up with a big stove in a yacht or a camper van, be aware that the nipple fittings at the crown of the standard ten-kilo bottles on Cyprus match those of continental Europe, not (curiously) neighbouring Greece or Turkey, so don't import cylinders from either country. Ten-kilo refills are widely sold at filling stations and grocery shops.

CHILDREN AND BABIES They are sacred in both communities, and should present few problems travelling; in most resorts geared for the package trade on either side of the island, family-sized suites are easy to come by. Baby formulas and nappies are available in pharmacies or supermarkets everywhere.

CIGARETTES AND SMOKING In the South there is a small homegrown tobacco industry, plus hoard-ings and ashtrays everywhere, but despite this locals are light puffers compared to all the surrounding countries, and non-smoking areas and campaigns are gaining ground. Nicotine habits are a bit more pronounced in Northern Cyprus, based almost entirely on rough Anatolian brands, but again you won't die of asphyxiation if you're a non-smoker.

CONTRACEPTIVES Throughout the island condoms are sold in pharmacies; the Greek for them is *profilaktiká*, the Turkish is *preservatif*. Users of other methods should come prepared from home.

DEPARTURE TAX Included in the price of air and ferry tickets in the southern Republic; in the North, various annoying chits are dispensed upon check-in at either ferry harbour and either airport, whose total cost (payable in Turkish lira) equals £4–5.

ELECTRIC CURRENT Throughout the island, this is 220–240 volts AC, with triple, rectangular-pin plugs as in Britain: hence you don't need any sort of adaptor to run electrical appliances. In very old buildings, however, you may still encounter double, round-pin, Chelsea-system sockets. Two-to-three pin adaptors are often furnished in better hotels and villas for use by continental customers; if not, they are easily purchased in corner shops.

Visitors from mainland Europe or North America may well want to come equipped with a two-to-three adaptor suitable for hair dryers, as they are expensive and not as easily found. You can easily and cheaply prepare one by replacing the 1-amp fuse in a unit marked "for shaver only" with a 5-amp fuse.

EMERGENCIES In the South, dial ☎199 for Police/Fire/Ambulance; ☎192 for information on night-duty chemists. In the North, emergency numbers are peculiar to each of the largest towns, but good luck finding a working public phone – better to flag down a taxi and take victim(s) to the hospital.

GAY LIFE This is virtually non-existent, at least above ground, in the tight-knit, family-orientated Cypriot society – in either community. In the South all homosexual acts between men are illegal, with offenders liable in theory to five years in prison; even "attempts to commit" homosexual acts (that is, propositioning somebody) potentially face a sentence of three years. In the run-up to full EU membership, various European authorities have pointed out that this is at major variance with standards in other member countries; thus far the South has only undertaken not to prosecute "overt" acts, rather than decriminalizing homosexual behaviour on the statute books. The North, while having no specific legislation, shares the same attitude, and both communities will be hostile to any open display of gay affection between foreigners. Contact is thus subtle: the few bars in Limassol and Nicosia that have reputations as gay meeting places are mentioned in the text.

LAUNDRY Most major towns in the South have at least one laundrette; otherwise do your own.

NATURISM Unisex topless is the rule in the busier resorts of the South, and with some discretion in North Cyprus. And that's about as far as you'll prudently go.

TIME Two hours ahead of GMT, and seven hours ahead of EST. Clocks go forward for summer time the last weekend in March and back again the last Sunday morning in September, so for most of October the whole island is only one hour ahead of Britain, and in April, eight hours ahead of New York. A recorded time message can be heard by dialling ☎195 in the South.

TIPPING Since a ten-percent charge is included on virtually all restaurant bills in the South, no extra amount need be left unless table-waiting was exceptional; in the North, where only the fancier places will tack on an identical fee, use your discretion. Taxi-drivers, especially in the South, expect a gratuity.

TOILETS In the South, these tend to be found in parks, on coastal esplanades, etc; sometimes there's a five- or ten-cent fee. They tend to close by 5pm from October to April. In the North, pay toilets are well signed in strategic crannies of Kyrenia harbour, Famagusta old town and Nicosia, but you're more likely to be using restaurant and hotel loos. When present, bowl-side baskets are for collecting paper which would block temperamental drains.

VAT Since July 1, 1992, an eight-percent VAT (Value Added Tax) has prevailed in the southern Republic, which is scheduled to rise in stages to fifteen per cent, in preparation for membership of the European Union. VAT will be introduced in the North at some time during 1996 (postponed from September 1995), exact percentage to be determined.

WEIGHTS AND MEASURES The southern Republic went completely metric in 1987, while North Cyprus clings stubbornly to many Imperial units, most obviously the mile, though this has recently disappeared from signposting along the main highways (though not from many minor roads). There are two Ottoman holdovers on both sides of the Line: the *dönüm*, a measure of land equal to about a third of an acre, and the *oka*, equal to 2.8 pounds and still occasionally met with in food markets.

WORK Despite a growing labour shortage in the tourism and agricultural sectors of the **southern Republic**, a job there is only strictly legal if arranged before you leave home. Your prospective employer will apply on your behalf for either a three- or six-month permit, though positions in hotels sometimes merit a two-year permit.

In recent years many of these jobs were taken by hungry Bulgarians, Romanians, Russians, Egyptians, Lebanese and Sri Lankans. Other foreigners you see at work in resorts are invariably tour-group couriers recruited and paid from abroad. Native teachers of English are of a sufficiently high standard that you are unlikely to land an ESL/TEFL-type job. Unions are well organized and aggressive in looking after their own; employers can only hire foreigners after having satisfied the authorities that the help cannot be recruited locally. Indeed, at the end of 1995 it was reported that the unions had finally succeeded in having all foreign hotel workers sacked and deported, though only time will tell if this measure has teeth. So it's best, if showing up on spec straight off the boat from Israel or Egypt, not to bank on anything other than an informal spell of picking grapes for a rural family.

Opportunities for work in **Northern Cyprus** are even more limited; your only chance is to start a business with imported capital, such as a windsurfing school, which stakes out a patch in which locals can't or won't compete. Economic stagnation is the overriding issue here, and a likely consequence of any peace settlement is the repatriation of as many Anatolian settlers as possible and a general consolidation by the North Cypriot authorities to protect the locals in their jobs.

THE SOUTH

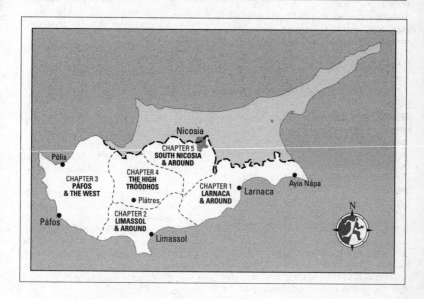

INTRODUCTION

Foundation of the island-wide **Republic of Cyprus** in 1960 was a compromise solution to a Gordian knot of imperial, regional and ethnic problems. Independence was the middle way between remaining a British colony, union (*énosis*) with Greece or a double partition between Greece and Turkey reflecting the **mixed Greek and Turkish population**. Like most compromises it left few happy, in particular the Turkish Cypriot minority community – and the more intransigent pro-*énosis* guerrillas in **EOKA** (*Ethnikí Orgánosis Kypríon Agonistón* or "National Organization of Cypriot Fighters"). Tragedy was almost inevitable, and by 1974 control of the northern 38 percent of the island had passed to the Turkish Cypriots and the Turkish Army. Yet for most of the world, Cyprus still means the Greek-Cypriot-inhabited, southern Republic of Cyprus.

If you're used to Greece, you'll find South Cyprus more **civilized**: things work better; administratively, there's less wasted motion; drivers are marginally more courteous to pedestrians and each other. People in general – often educated abroad and multi-lingual – seem relatively cosmopolitan, a useful trait when hosting thousands of tourists.

Scratch this veneer, though, and island society proves paradoxically more **traditional** than Greece: the social scale is cosy, with much of the population acquainted on sight if not exactly on first-name basis. Until recently the village was the core social unit; women – despite public presence – are still expected to "know their place"; and the Orthodox Church remains enormously influential, tapping a vein of uncomplicated, fervent faith co-existing with the worldliness.

Despite a recent, politically motivated Hellenization campaign mounted in the South, there is in fact little love lost between Greek Cypriots and continental Greeks. The latter are generally referred to in Cyprus as *kalamarádhes*, and the mainland dialect as *kalamarístika*. These terms first arose nearly two centuries ago, when schoolmasters from peninsular Greece first introduced "proper" Greek to the island; these purveyors of linguistic rectitude were dubbed *kalamarádhes* (quill-wielders), after the main tool of their trade. Over time, the word came to apply, in a mixture of opprobrium and affection, to all mainlanders, especially the corps of Greek army officers on the island during the 1960s. Some – specifically keepers of Páfos and London tavernas revelling in the name *O Kalamaras* – wear the label as a badge of honour, but it's most often prefixed indivisably by *poústi* (sodomite).

The troubled republic

Both parochialism and internationalism were exhibited to destructive effect over the **fourteen turbulent years** between independence in 1960 and the catastrophe of 1974. Power-sharing between the two communities, regulated by a meticulously detailed constitution, had by 1964 collapsed in an orgy of recriminations and violence orchestrated by EOKA and its Turkish counterpart **TMT** (*Türk Müdafaa Teskilati* or "Turkish Defence Organization"). The island was further destabilized through meddling by "mother" countries Greece and Turkey; soon the superpowers and the UN were inextricably involved.

Cyprus limped along as a unitary state for ten more years, albeit with a thoroughly poisoned civic life: Turkish Cypriots withdrew from the mainstream into a series of TMT-defended **enclaves**, while the Greek Cypriots retaliated by severely restricting traffic in goods or persons across their boundaries. Feeble intercommunal overtures alternated with fresh incidents, but Cypriot society was already split, with Turkish Cypriots relegated to second-class citizenship in their laagers.

When all-out war erupted in July 1974, only the exact timing and details came as a surprise. **EOKA-B**, successor to EOKA, staged a **coup** aimed at effecting *énosis*; in response the Turkish army, technically acting as guarantor of the island's independence, **landed** on the north coast and instead presided over de facto partition. The Greek Cypriots fled, or were expelled from, the North, the population of the scattered Turkish Cypriot enclaves soon replacing them.

In the immediate **aftermath** of the war, all Cyprus was prostrate, with both ethnic communities demoralized and fearful, the economy in tatters. The South was particularly hard hit: 165,000 Greek Cypriots had immediately fled the North, to be followed within a few years by 15,000 more. The Turkish army held the most productive portions of the island, assiduously developed since 1960: the Greek Cypriots lost the fertile citrus groves around Mórfou, the busy port of Famagusta with its bulging warehouses, and lucrative tourist facilities in Kyrenia and Varósha. Southern unemployment stood at forty percent until 1976, with the added burden of providing emergency shelter for the refugees.

South Cyprus today

Since 1974, the South has wrought an **economic miracle** – but at a price. Developing the hitherto untouched southern coast for tourism, with few zoning restraints and maximum financial incentives, was seen as the quickest fix for a dire predicament. More than two decades later, with **tourism** the country's biggest foreign-currency earner, the results are all too plain: hideous strips of uninterrupted tower blocks on the coast around Larnaca, Limassol, Ayía Nápa and Páfos.

Inland, crash programmes rehoused the refugees in often shoddily built **housing estates**, whose grimness has never diminished the appeal of a return to the North. The relocation of nearly a third of Cyprus' population has meant overcrowding (artificial, given the relative emptiness of North Cyprus) and inflated property prices. Private, speculative development has taken too much precedence over delayed and underfunded public works.

All this threatened not only the visual **environment** but the ecological one, too: on an island permanently short of water, with most of it trapped in the North, supplies barely sufficed for the hotels which continued to sprout uncontrollably. Lately there have been signs of a rethink, as conservationists organize to protect remaining unspoiled landscapes, and to promote human-scale tourism. The government has provided muddled direction: while one agency proposed national parks, the tourism authority long adhered to a policy of encouraging five-star, high-impact tourist installations. In May 1995, a moratorium was declared on new construction of all types of accommodation, both on the coast and inland, essentially freezing the number of licensed tourist beds in the South at just over 80,000. Cut-rate package tourism is seen as damaging to the social and environmental fabric, but mid-recession there have not been enough customers at luxury facilities to justify their multiplication. The compromise – Green **"agro-tourism"** in Páfos district – is still in its infancy, so gauging effectiveness seems premature.

By way of balance to this dependency on volatile tourism patterns, the demise of nearby Beirut as a business centre came as a welcome windfall for Cyprus. The South is now established as a popular venue for **international conferences**, and – thanks to its taxation policies and reliable infrastructure – as a base for **offshore companies**. Liaisons begun in the heyday of the non-aligned movement, and the traditional importance of the local Communist Party, continue to pay dividends in trade relations with eastern Europe, Africa and the Middle East. Since 1993, Russian investment in particular – much of it money in need of laundering – has flooded into the country, something reflected in a rash of restaurant menus, estate agent signs and tourist literature printed in Cyrillic. For the most part Cypriots welcome these big spenders, not looking too closely at the source of their wealth.

Light industrialization resumed after 1976, much of it geared towards export markets. High-quality medical care at the main hospitals, though not literally an exportable commodity, is successfully pitched to immediately neighbouring countries as a hard-currency earner. Labour-intensive handicraft cooperatives set up in 1975 preserve skills particular to the lost northern homelands. Spurred by well-trained and -paid workers, **economic growth** since 1977 has been impressive, producing, of late, an unskilled labour shortage. Until late 1995 large numbers of Asian and eastern European guest-workers staffed various hotels, restaurants and brothels, saving for down-payments on property back home, but in the former two types of venue their days seem numbered, as the powerful local unions have demanded a crackdown on importation of labour. While all credit is due to the Greek Cypriots for reviving their part of the island, there's no denying that much of the recovery has been subsidized by **foreign aid**. Only the southern Republic has membership in such international bodies as UNESCO and the World Bank, and has thus been eligible for assistance from those organizations.

Despite retaining its original name, the contemporary Republic of Cyprus is a fundamentally different country: all but mono-ethnic, yet with *énosis* buried as a realistic option; its 1960 constitution a dead letter; and public life preoccupied with *Tóh Kypriakó* (**National Question**) – the imposed partition of the island.

Everywhere posters and graffiti refer to the events of 1974, as do periodic heartfelt demonstrations, with little need of stage-managing. The right of Greek Cypriots to **return** to their homes and properties in the North is the most emotionally charged issue: nostalgically named refugee clubs attempt to link the generation born in exile with ancestral towns, and maintain community solidarity for a possible day of repatriation. Telephone directories still list numbers in the North as they were before July 1974, and the offical hotel guide pointedly cites Famagusta and Kyrenia resorts as named before the Turkish intervention, without, however, giving any practical details.

Strategies for reconciliation

Without the military means to expel the Turkish army, the South has instead exploited its monopoly of world forums to mount a relentless propaganda campaign against, and **boycott** of, the Turkish Republic of Northern Cyprus (TRNC) in an attempt to bring it to heel. Ire is directed at Turkey too, in overseas court cases demanding that vanished property or persons be accounted for.

When advised that this is unlikely to create a favourable climate for reconciliation, the South retorts that giving North Cyprus more breathing space would remove any incentive for it to come to a federal agreement.

With the benefit of **hindsight**, some Greek Cypriots have assimilated bitter political lessons, and recognize the wisdom of contrite gestures towards the Turkish Cypriots, initiatives unthinkable before 1974. Despite the official campaign against the TRNC, many willingly admit past errors: in particular there's widespread revulsion at the activities of EOKA-B, who during their short-lived 1974 reign killed more Greek Cypriots than Turkish Cypriots. A retrospectively rosy view of intercommunal relations before 1960 prevails in the South; but whether this is genuine or promulgated to counter Northern pessimism is debatable.

Officially the southern Republic is still **bi-communal**, though barely 3000 island-born Turks – less than half a percent of the population – continue to live there. Banknotes and many public signs remain trilingual in Greek, Turkish and English; radio and TV broadcast Turkish-language programmes; the 80-seat parliament currently functions with only 56 deputies, the balance reserved for hypothetical Turkish representatives. In its propaganda and negotiating position the government woos the North, offering generous constitutional concessions if Turkish Cypriots would abandon their insistence on separate states.

The Southern government tried to prevent the 45,000 **Turkish Cypriots in the South** from departing – voluntarily or otherwise – to the North in early 1975, correctly fearing that the Turkish side would deem this a quid pro quo for the involuntary expulsion of Northern Greeks. Prodigal-son-type publicity greets the rare Turkish Cypriot returning to the South, as they represent a tiny reversal of the island's apartheid. All property of Southern Turkish Cypriots is technically held in trust by the government, current Greek Cypriot occupiers having only rental agreements with their departed true owners.

After the repeated failure of UN-sponsored intercommunal negotiating sessions, the Southern government is determined to carry on as the sole "legitimate representative of Cyprus", with or without the consent of the Turkish Cypriots. Since 1990 the Republic of Cyprus has actively pursued membership in the EU, scheduled to occur before the end of the century. Predictably enough the Turkish Cypriots have objected that the South has once again presumed to speak for the whole island – a fairly typical example of the long-running gap in understanding as to what the appropriate roles of communities and central government are on Cyprus.

CHAPTER ONE

LARNACA AND AROUND

The southeast flank of Cyprus, centred around **Larnaca**, is the most tourised portion of the island – a consequence of the 1974 Turkish invasion, and the subsequent conversion of hitherto sleepy Larnaca airfield into the southern republic's main international airport. Except for its hilly western part, the district can't be reckoned very alluring scenically – not that this is likely to bother many of the patrons of the burgeoning resorts, who seldom venture far from a clear, warm sea and their self-contained hotels.

Despite being a moderate distance from the mega-resorts at the tip of the island, historic **Larnaca** is still a popular base for the area, and just large enough to retain – for the moment – some character independent of tourism. Southwest of the town are two of the most appealing, and most easily accessible, monuments in the area: the Muslim shrine of **Hala Sultan** by Larnaca's salt lake, and the mosaic-graced Byzantine church of **Angelóktisti** at Kíti. **Perivólia**, on the approach to **Cape Kíti**, is perhaps the last human-scale resort in this part of the island, but the coast beyond will reward only the most determined explorers, preferably kitted out with a jeep. The little port of **Zíyi** with its many fish tavernas is more easily reached from the main Nicosia–Limassol expressway.

Inland, a number of attractions are scattered to either side of this expressway. Neolithic **Khirokitiá** is one of the oldest known habitations on the island, and a visit can be easily twinned with one to **Páno Léfkara**, a picturesque village in the Troödhos foothills renowned for its handicrafts. More directly approached from Larnaca along a secondary road, the **"Chapelle Royale"** at **Pýrga** is a rare example of Lusignan sacred mural art, and nearby **Stavrovoúni** an equally unusual instance of a strictly penitential Cypriot Orthodox monastery. To the west of Pýrga, **Kórnos** village has a reputation as a pottery centre, as does **Kofínou**, next settlement down the highway, though the latter is more famous for a particularly ugly intercommunal incident during the days of the unitary republic.

East of Larnaca, there is little to specifically recommend: the sandy crescent of Larnaca Bay, the British Sovereign Base Area of Dhekélia and the slender

---

ACCOMMODATION PRICES IN THE SOUTH

All hotel and apartment-hotel prices in the South have been categorized according to the price codes given below. These categories represent the minimum you can expect to pay in the high season for a double room or a two-person self-catering unit. Single rooms will normally cost 50–80 percent of the rates quoted for a double room. Rates for dorm beds in hostels, where guests are charged per person, are given in Cyprus pounds, instead of being indicated by price code. For further details, see p.25.

① under C£12	④ C£20–25	⑦ C£35–40
② C£12–16	⑤ C£25–30	⑧ C£40–50
③ C£16–20	⑥ C£30–35	⑨ over C£50

beaches to either side of Cape Gréko are each blighted in their own way. **Ayía Nápa**, though by no means the largest permanent community, mushrooms in season to become the busiest downmarket resort in the area, while the strip at **Protarás** on the northeast coast is newer and more exclusive.

LARNACA (LÁRNAKA)

LARNACA has little tangible evidence of its eventful history, and is today a tourist centre and minor port forgetful of its past; yachts in its marina far outnumber freighters in the adjacent commercial harbour. Gone is the romantic town of eighteenth-century engravings, with only horrific summer heat, an adjacent salt lake and palm trees to impart a nostalgic Levantine touch. With a permanent population struggling to crest 100,000, Larnaca is barely half the size of Limassol, and more encroached upon by (mostly Scandinavian) tourism. The shore esplanade is touted as an echo of the French Riviera, and the hotel "ghetto" to the north of town is correspondingly less important. Amidst the holiday-making it's sobering to consider that much of the recent growth is due to regional catastrophe. Numbers were first swelled by Greek refugees from Famagusta in 1974,

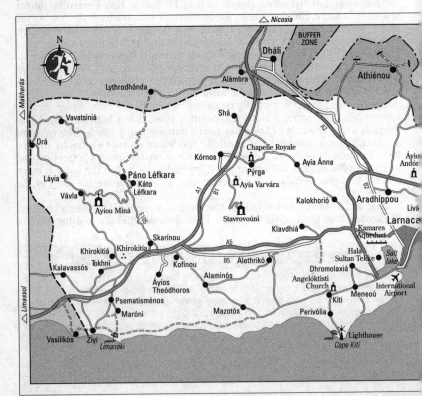

and a year or two later by Christians from Lebanon – for whose benefit the occasional passenger ferry to and from Jounieh operates.

Some history

The site of Larnaca was originally colonized by Mycenaeans in the thirteenth century BC but had declined, like many other Mediterranean towns, by about 1000 BC. It emerged again as **Kition** two centuries later, re-established by the Phoenicians, and resumed its role as the port exporting copper from rich deposits at Tamassos and elsewhere in the eastern Tróödhos. A subsequent period of great prosperity was complicated by the city's staunch championing of the Persian cause on Cyprus: Kimon of Athens, heading a fleet sent in 450 BC to reduce Kition, died outside the wall in the hour of what proved to be a fleeting victory. Persian influence only ended with the Hellenistic takeover of the whole island a century later, a period which also saw the birth of **Zeno**, Kition's most famous son (and a Phoenician), expounder of the Stoic philosophy in his adopted home town of Athens.

Christianity came early to Kition, traditionally in the person of **Lazarus**, the man resurrected by Christ at Bethany. Cast adrift in a leaky boat by irate Pharisees not wanting evidence of miracles, Lazarus supposedly landed here to

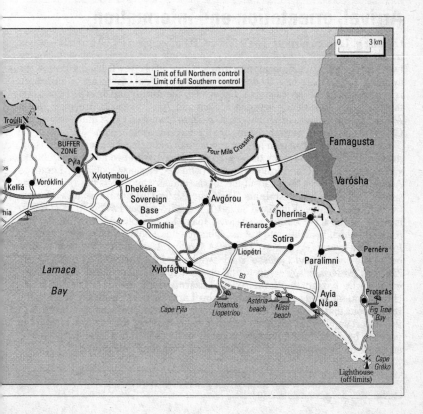

become the city's first bishop and, following his (definitive) death, patron saint. After an otherwise uneventful passage through the Roman and early Byzantine eras, Kition suffered the same seventh-century Arab raids as other Cypriot coastal settlements. It didn't really recover until the end of the Lusignan era, when the Genoese appropriation of nearby Famagusta prompted merchants to move here to take advantage of the small port; by now the anchorage was called **Salina**, after the salt lake just inland.

The name **Larnaca**, derived from *larnax* (a sarcophagus or urn, of which there were plenty to hand from various periods of the town's past), only gained wide currency at the start of Ottoman rule. By the eighteenth century its new status as the premier port and trade centre of the island – it briefly eclipsed Nicosia in population – saw numerous foreign consuls take up residence at Larnaca. Britain's consul often simultaneously administered the English Levant Company, a trading organization analogous to the British East India Company. Around the consuls gathered the largest foreign community on the island, leading lives of elegant and eccentric provinciality, the inspiration for reams of travel accounts of the time. In 1878 the British landed here to take over administration of Cyprus, and it was not until after World War II that Larnaca again fell behind Famagusta and Limassol in importance.

Arrival, orientation and information

Landing at Larnaca **airport**, you'll find a **CTO** office open for all arrivals – which means pretty much around the clock – and ample exchange facilities, including two *Visa*-accepting **cashpoint machines**. Quite likely you'll have a rented car awaiting you as part of a fly-drive arrangement; if not, there are a half-dozen rental booths in the arrivals area. Otherwise, the **municipal bus** #19 goes into town up to 17 times daily between 6.30am and 7pm in season, dropping you at Ayíou Lazárou Square. Alternatively, a taxi into town won't cost much more than C£2.50 at day rates – as ever, make sure the meter is switched on.

Larnaca's street plan, with its numerous jinks and name-changes, is confusing, made only slightly less so by the sea being due east, with two north–south boulevards paralleling it. The **Finikoúdhes** or palm-tree esplanade, officially **Leofóros Athinón**, constitutes the heart of the tourist industry and, at its north end, hosts several important **bus terminals**. The large **Platía Dhimokratías** (often known by its English name, "King Paul Square", and still Vasiléos Pávlou on most maps) is home to the **CTO office** (Mon–Sat 8.15am–1.45pm, plus Mon & Thurs 3.45–6.15pm), which in addition to the usual bumph has a noticeboard worth checking for coming events. From here, **Leofóros Grigóri Afxendíou** is the main avenue out to the Nicosia and Limassol roads, while the inland parallel of the sea front, **Zínonos Kitiéos**, leads south to the covered central market and, via the alleyways of the bazaar, to **Platía Ayíou Lazárou**, home to its ornate namesake church and more bus stops. **Odhós Ayíou Lazárou**, later **Stadhíou**, reaches the roundabout that gives onto both the Nicosia road and **Leofóros Artemídhos** to the airport and beyond along the coast. If you're **driving**, the one-way system can prove to be a nightmare; **parking** is pretty well confined to a large purpose-built structure on Faneroménis, about 200m inland from the Finikoúdhes.

The Larnaca area phone code is ☎04.

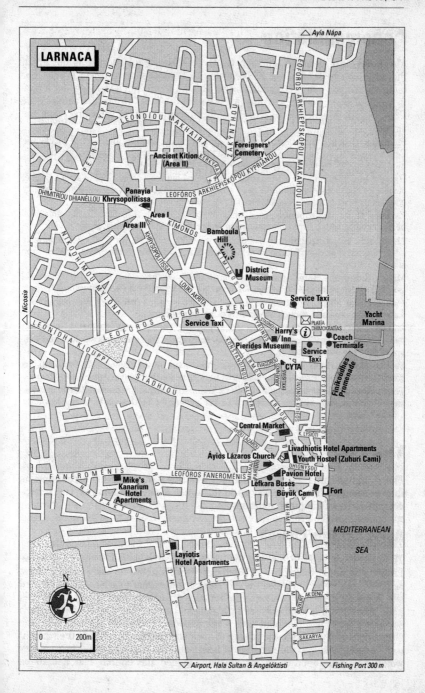

LARNACA

△ Ayía Nápa

△ Nicosia

LEONDÍOU MAKHAIRA

PETROU KYPRIANOU

DHIMITRÍOU DHIANÉLLOU

Ancient Kition
(Area II)

Foreigners'
Cemetery

KERKYRAS

ZAKYNTHOU

LEOFÓROS ARKHIEPISKÓPOU MAKARÍOU III

LEOFÓROS ARKHIEPISKÓPOU KYPRIANOÚ

Panayia
Khrysopolítissa

Area I

Area III

KIMONOS

KILKIS

Bamboula
Hill

District
Museum

NIKODÍMOU MYLONA

KHRYSOPOLÍTISSAS

KOURÍ AKRÍTA

ZINONOS

LEONIDHA KIOUPPI

LEOFÓROS GRIGÓRI AFXENDÍOU

Service Taxi

Service Taxi

Harry's
Inn

Pierides Museum

STASÍNOU

KYRIAKOÚ

KONSTANDÍNOU

EVAGÓROU

ARMENIKÍS

EKKLISÍAS

CYTA

✉ PLATÍA
DHIMOKRATÍAS

(i)

Service
Taxi

Coach
Terminals

Yacht
Marina

Finikoúdhes Promenade

STADHIOU

LEOFÓROS ATHINÓN

ERMOU

ZINONOS KITÍOU

Central Market

AYÍOU LAZÁROU

FANEROMÉNIS

NAFPÁKTOU

LEOFÓROS ARTÉMIDHOS

LEOFÓROS FANEROMÉNIS

Áyios Lázaros Church

MIKHAÍL KAROLÍDHI

K. LYSIÓTI

Livadhiotis Hotel Apartments

Youth Hostel (Zuhuri Cami)

DHIONYSOU

Pavion Hotel

Léfkara Buses

Büyük Cami

□ Fort

Mike's
Kanarium
Hotel
Apartments

OKULTAR

STANILI

MIKHAÍL AIL

PIYALÉ PASHA

MEDITERRANEAN

SEA

Layiotis
Hotel Apartments

SOCA

BÜZÜM

AK DENIZ

SAKARYA

N

0   200m

▽ Airport, Hala Sultan & Angelóktisti   ▽ Fishing Port 300 m

Accommodation

The **hotel and pension** situation for those showing up on spec is not great, though much better than in Páfos, owing to Larnaca's more urban profile. For budget rates you can pretty much forget about a room with a sea view; for a relatively quiet sleep, you're best off some ways south of the town centre along Piyale Paşa towards Mackenzie Beach, the rather meagre strip of sand preceding the airport.

Flamingo Beach, Piyale Paşa, past the fishing port, just opposite the start of Mackenzie Beach (☎650621, fax 656732). One of Larnaca's top hotels: there's a rooftop pool and all other mod cons, and all rooms have an oblique balcony view of the sea. ⑥.

Harry's Inn, Thermopýlon 2 (☎654453). Very central but reasonably quiet (it's not a brothel despite its ramshackle appearance), with sympathetic management and a small garden. Only one "luxury" room has its own bathroom. Price includes continental breakfast. ②.

Layiotis Hotel Apartments, Artemídhos 31 (☎624700, fax 626152). Comfortable one-bedroom units, with comparable facilities to *Mike's*, inland in a residential area. ③.

Livadhiotis Hotel Apartments, Nikoláou Róssou 50 (☎626222, fax 626406). Comfortable one-bedroom short-stay flats in a modern block opposite the youth hostel; prices drop sharply in winter. ④.

Mike's Kanarium Hotel Apartments, Faneroménis 60 (☎625340). Built in 1993 and still looking new, these units with air-con, kitchenette and TV represent excellent value. ③.

Pavion Hotel, Platía Ayíou Lazárou 11, overlooking the church (☎656688). Well-placed hotel with all rooms en suite, though breakfast is rather perfunctory. ③.

Sandbeach Castle, Piyale Paşa, past the fishing port (☎655437, fax 659804). Virtually the only Larnaca hotel with its feet in the sea, this mock-castle construction is smallish and well-priced for its two-star rating. ④.

Sveltos Beach Hotel Apartments, Piyale Paşa, south of the fishing port (☎657240, fax 657254). Beachfront hotel apartments within the city limits. ③ studios, ④ one-bedroom units.

Youth Hostel, Nikoláou Róssou 27 (☎621188). Housed partly in the disused Zuhuri mosque; passably clean, with kitchen facilities. C£3 per person for IYHF members, non-members C£3.50.

The City

The sights of Larnaca can be seen in a leisurely day, preferably a cool one, as they're scattered in such a way as to make use of the minimal city bus service difficult and a walking tour appealing.

Áyios Lázaros church

The most obvious place to start a tour of the city is the landmark church of **Áyios Lázaros** (summer daily 8am–12.30pm & 3.30–6.30pm; winter daily 8am–12.30pm & 2.30–5pm). Poised between the old Turkish and bazaar quarters, it was erected late in the ninth century to house the remains of Lazarus, fortuitously discovered here. The church is distinguished by a graceful Latinate belfry, part of a thorough seventeenth-century overhaul and a miraculous survival of Turkish rule; the Ottomans usually forbade the raising of such structures, considering their height a challenging insult to the minarets of Islam, and (more realistically) fearing they would be used to proclaim insurrection. Indeed the church had had to be ransomed from the Turks in 1589, and was used for joint worship by Roman Catholics and Orthodox for two centuries after – as evidenced by Greek, Latin and French inscriptions in the Gothic-influenced portico, in addition to the earlier Byzantine and Lusignan coats of arms near the main south door.

The spare stone interior (consequence of a fire in 1970) is a relief after the busy decoration of many Cypriot churches. Three small domes are supported on four pillars slit into doublets, with narrow arches springing from wedged-in Corinthian capitals. The celebrated carved *témblon* (altar screen), partly restored after the fire, and a Rococo pulpit on one pillar (for Latin use) are some three hundred years old; on another pillar hangs a filigreed icon of Lazarus emerging from his tomb, an image reverently paraded in the presence of the bishop of Kition every Easter Saturday evening.

The musty-smelling crypt under the altar supposedly housed the relics of Lazarus only very briefly – they were taken to Constantinople by Leo in 901, whence they were stolen, turning up later in Marseilles. But his purported tomb eventually formed part of a catacomb of general use, as witness several sarcophagi lying about here. In the northeast corner of the outside compound are more graves in a locked enclosure – this time of British consuls, merchants and family members who died in Larnaca's unhealthy climate during the sixteenth to nineteenth centuries.

The former Turkish quarter

Stretching from Áyios Lázaros almost to the fishing port, the extensive Turkish quarter has retained its old street names, but is now home to Greek refugees from Famagusta and the Kárpas villages. Judging from some impressive houses and bungalows, the Turks here seem to have been wealthier than in Páfos – but there are "chicken shacks" as well. Originally the late medieval church of the Holy Cross, the porticoed, flying-buttressed **Büyük Cami** (Cami Kebir), at the north end of quarter, now sees use by the local Egyptian/Lebanese/Iranian population. Bowing to the demands of tourism, the mosque is now open in daylight hours, except during services; for an extra "donation" it's possible to climb the minaret as well. The nearby **fort** (Mon–Wed & Fri 7.30am–5pm, Thurs 7.30am–6pm; C£0.50), a 1625 Turkish refurbishment of a Lusignan castle, stands mostly empty at the south end of the Finikoúdhes, but its upper storey hosts a small museum of oddments from Hala Sultan Tekke and Kition. The place is also the occasional venue for evening functions, when you can inspect the courtyard, and reflect on the fact that before World War II the British used this as a prison.

The beach and bazaar area

Immediately north of the fort stretches the **Finikoúdhes** promenade, recently redesigned as a pedestrian-only zone, with vending stalls and car park banished. This in turn is fronted by the town beach – some 800 mediocre metres of gritty, hard-packed sand, well patronized despite its condition. If it's not to your taste, there are somewhat better beaches to either side of town (see pp.66 & 73).

The bulk of the bazaar sprawls north of Áyios Lázaros; at its heart stands the covered central market, similar to a French *halle*, a good place for fruit and veg or reed-woven souvenirs (more shopping options are discussed on p.63). Even if you're not staying at the youth hostel, stop in a moment to examine the mosque that houses it, the unusual nineteenth-century **Zuhuri Cami** (literally, "Clown Mosque") with its double dome.

The Pierides Museum

Conveniently situated on the way to various tourist facilities on Platía Dhimokratías, the **Pierides Museum** shares an old wooden house at Zínonos Kitiéos 4 with the Swedish consulate, and was renovated to good effect in late 1994 (Mon–Fri 9am–1pm & 3–6pm, Sat 9am–1pm, Sun 10am–1pm; C£1). The building was the home of Dhimitrios Pierides, who began his conservation efforts in 1839, using his wealth to discreetly salvage what archeological treasures he could from tomb-plunderers, including the infamous Luigi Palma di Cesnola, first US consul at Larnaca. Unlike state-run archeological museums, the collection, which was expanded by Pierides' descendants, ranges across the whole island; it's strongest on Archaic terracottas, plus other unusual small objects that have escaped the attention of official museums.

The collection

Among the oldest items in the four small exhibit rooms are some greenish picrolite idols from the Chalcolithic period (*c.* 3000 BC), and the famous **"Howling Man"** of the same era from Souskiou, featured on the museum poster. He could be filled with liquid through his hollow head, to "pee" out of a prominent member as he sits on a stool; the mechanics give little clue as to whether he had a religious or secular function. Numerous examples of painted **Archaic pottery** are notable, especially one decorated with a so-called "astronaut" figure (beloved of Erich von Daniken and other extraterrestrial-visitation nutters), bouncing on what appear to be springs or other mechanical devices. Among the imported painted Attic ware, you'll find Theseus about to run the Minotaur through with his sword, while on another pot two centaurs, emblems of lust, flank a courting couple.

The collection of relatively rare Classical and Hellenistic **terracottas** includes a funerary reclining man from Marion, in perfect condition down to the fingers, and a model sarcophagus with three pull-out drawers. Other oddities include a surprisingly delicate spoon among a trove of Early Bronze Age black incised ware; a Classical baby's bottle; plus a glass fish, a glass pig, and a variegated bird from the Roman era. Less unexpected are the Archaic female statuettes brandishing drums and other votive offerings, which were left in shrines as "permanent worshippers".

The Archeological Museum

Larnaca's other significant collection, the **Archeological Museum**, stands a ten-minute walk away, north of Grigóri Afxendíou (Mon–Fri 7.30am–2.30pm, plus Sept–June Thurs 3–6pm; C£0.50). It's purpose-built and so better laid out and lit than the Pierides, with excellent labelling and explanatory panels, but there's a feel of pickings and leavings compared to Nicosia's Cyprus Museum or the Pierides itself. The management has been reduced to displaying, in the entry hall, copies of a famous statue of Artemis and funerary stele (the originals in Vienna and Berlin respectively).

The collection

Pre-eminent in the early part of the collection is a reconstruction of a **Neolithic tomb** from Khirokhitía, complete with a stone atop the corpse's chest indicating a fear of its returning from the dead. Later exhibits clearly illustrate how Late Bronze Age pottery, especially the so-called "white slip ware", prefigured the decorated dishes of the Geometric era. The fact that the latter were painted only on the outside (discounting the possibility that any inside designs were worn off by use) may indicate that they were meant to be hung up by their handles as decoration, like the woven trivets of today.

Vast amounts of **Mycenaean pottery** in the so-called "Rude" (ie rustic) Style, dug up at adjacent Kition, demonstrate Argolid settlement around 1200 BC; the prize exhibit is a fish *kratir* (large wine goblet) from Áyios Dhimítrios near Kalavassós. Cypriot literacy dates to at least two centuries earlier, as evidenced by a display of Cypro-Minoan inscriptions (so far undeciphered), while a case of items imported towards the end of the Bronze Age demonstrates trade links at the same time; notice an ivory lamp in the shape of a fish. Back among indigenous ware, there's an unusual clay torch from Pyla, and a clay brazier-pan from Athiénou – perhaps meant to heat bedclothes or a small room. Terracotta highlights in the Archaic section include a horse and rider with emphasized eyes, plus a couple – possibly royal or divine – in a horse-drawn chariot.

Ancient Kition

Most of ancient Kition lies under modern Larnaca, and thus cannot be excavated, though the Swedes under Einar Gjerstad began to make attempts during the 1920s. The British made matters worse in 1879 by carting off much of what had survived above ground to fill malarial marshes with "rubble". Their depredations were severest at the ancient acropolis on Bamboúla hill, directly behind the Archeological Museum in a fenced-off parkland; consequently there's little to see except for a nearby dig site – possibly the Phoenician port, far inland from today's shoreline – next to the municipal tennis courts on Kilkís Street. So-called Areas I and III, at the north end of Kímonos opposite the weird, top-heavy belfry of Panayía Khrysopolítissa church, are Late Bronze Age holes in the ground of essentially specialist interest now that they have disgorged their treasures.

Area II

The one exception to this inaccessibility is the so-called **Area II**, beyond Arkhiepiskópou Kypriánou, from which you turn up Kérkyras to reach the gate at the northwest corner of the site (Mon–Fri 7.30am–2.30pm, plus Thurs 3–6pm; C£0.50). A wooden catwalk is provided for an overview of ongoing excavations, though until these are completed, the site is not as well labelled or as edifying as it might be. The Phoenician resettlement sits atop Late Bronze Age foundations, abutting the mixed mud-brick and stone wall which bounded Kition to the north. The main structures are a large ashlar-based shrine, rededicated to the fertility goddess Astarte in Phoenician times, and four smaller earlier temples, one of them linked to the smelting workshops found here, suggesting, if not worship of a copper deity, then at least a priestly interest in its production. In another of the shrines, thought to be that of a masculine seafaring god, a pipe for the ritual smoking of opium was discovered. Few Hellenistic or Roman artefacts were found here, making the site unusual and archeologically important – as well as politically touchy, as the Greek Cypriots are often less than enthusiastic about remains indicating Asiatic cultural origins.

Eating, drinking and nightlife

It doesn't take much nous to work out that you're going to get ripped off at the glittery purveyors of "international" stodge along the Finikoúdhes. However, a little foraging about away from the obvious will turn up numerous good, reasonably priced eating and drinking venues in Larnaca.

Seafront

Afrouyia Paximadhia, Mikrís Apouáthras 9. Small bakery offering olive bread and Armenian mini-pizzas.

Arax, Kosmá Lysióti 3, just behind the Finikoúdhes. Small but tasty portions of Lebanese and Armenian specialities.

Koullis, Piyale Paşa 5, and **Vassos Varoshiotis**, Piyale Paşa 7, corner of Sakarya. Adjacent, rival tavernas specializing in fish and catering to a local clientele; recent reports differ but suggest that the latter may have a slight edge.

Megalos Pefkos, right beside the fort on Leofóros Athinón. If you insist on eating on the Finikoúdhes, this is the least expensive spot here.

Militzis, Piyale Paşa 42, 300m south of the fort. Limited menu, but what they do – meat, cheese, casserole dishes – they do well, generously and without grease.

Inland

Belle Helene, Artemídhos 69. Sweet and savoury baked snacks; open daily.

Ilocanda, at the roundabout at the north end of Arkhiepiskópou Makaríou, intersection Giáni Timáyia. Filipino and Chinese food, next to the *Dandela* cabaret. Closed Sun.

Iy Mavri Helona (The Black Turtle), Mehmet Ali 11, near the *Pavion Hotel*. In the wake of recent expansion, some of the rough edges of this endearing little *ouzerí* have been filed smooth, but it's still a source of abundant, unusual *mezédhes* (crabs, snails, beets, mushrooms) that won't set you back much more than C£7 for two. Popular with locals and tourists alike. Loud, live music Wed, Fri & Sat; closed Sun.

1900 Art Café, Stasínou 6. Housed in a turn-of-the-century mansion, as the name suggests, and run by a local radio-journalist and an artist. The downstairs bar-café, which doubles as a gallery, serves snacks, including vegetarian ones; a more elaborate restaurant upstairs offers home-style cooking and selected village wines. Open daily except Tues.

Vassos, in the Sunbag Building, Evagórou. Limited, Greek-only menu, but a source of sustaining traditional recipes for tradesmen and nightclub staff. Point to the stewpot of your choice and confirm prices. Open for lunch and 5pm–5am.

Outlying districts

Flamingoes, adjacent to Hala Sultan Tekke, 3km out of town. Slightly pricy, but good, original Cypriot and international recipes; as a rule, go for the day's specials. Wonderfully atmospheric setting, marred only by nocturnal mosquitoes.

Taste of Paradise Steak House, on the road southwest from Hala Sultan Tekke to Meneoú village (☎424148 if you get lost). Never mind the silly name, this popular place offers very good and abundant *mezé* for under C£4.

Nightlife and entertainment

Watch the hoardings of the municipality for details of events, especially during **Kataklismós**, the five-day Festival of the Flood, usually held in June (see p.40). Most years, one of the commercial sponsors or the *Cyprus Weekly* publishes a full programme of events; the evening singing, dancing and verse competitions are heavily subscribed. Vendors' stalls, normally forbidden on the Finikoúdhes, return at this time to sell everything from canaries to plastic toys.

There are three **cinemas** in town, showing first-run "family entertainment": *Attikon* (☎652873), *Othellos* (☎657970), and *Rex* (☎652223).

Shopping

In the former Turkish quarter, just inland from Piyale Paşa and five blocks south of the fort, are the studios of five leading Cypriot **ceramicists**, all of Famagusta origin. On the adjoining lanes called Ak Deniz and Bozkurt, the workshops of *Efthymios Symeou, Stavros Stavrou, Fotini Kourti-Khristou, Fotos Demetriou* and *Elena* turn out a wide variety of thin stoneware and raku ware, either practical or decorative, in both traditional and innovative motifs.

Closer to the town centre at Stadhíou 5, *Ekfrasi*, a **gallery** managed by the co-owner of the *1900 Art Café*, features the works of contemporary Cypriot and foreign artists; it's open evenings only from 5 to 8pm, and is shut during August.

Connoisseurs of second-hand items should gravitate towards the Sunday **open-air market** and car-boot sale, next to the Atlantis funfair on the main Larnaca–Dhekélia road. In-town possibilities include *Larnaca Thrift Shop*, Prótis Avrilíou 67 (Mon–Thurs 8.30am–1pm, all day Fri), or another shop at Mikhaïl Parídhi 7.

Listings

Airport information ☎643300.

American Express c/o *Mantovani Travel Plan*, Platía Dhimokratías (across from the tourist office; ☎465 2024).

Bookstore *Academic & General*, Ermoú 41.

Bus companies Principal outfits include *Kallenos*, to Nicosia, Limassol, Ayía Nápa and Protarás, and *EMAN*, to Ayía Nápa, from the terminal opposite *Four Lanterns Hotel* on the Finikoúdhes; and *Lefkara*, to the village of the same name, from Platía Ayíou Lazárou.

Car rental Many firms are along Leofóros Arkhiepiskópou Makaríou, north of the CTO, so comparison shopping is often just a matter of a short stroll. Only the big international chains, plus *Thames* (mobile ☎09/515157), maintain booths at the airport. Outlets include: *Andy Spirou/Europcar*, JGL Building, Dhekélia road (☎645590); *Astra/Eurodollar*, Artemídhos 3 (☎624422); *Budget/Petsas*, Karydes Court, Leofóros Afxendíou (☎623033); *Champion*, Arkhiepiskópou Makaríou 62 (☎655504); *Hertz*, Arkhiepiskópou Kyprianoú 3 (☎655145); *Phoenix*, Arkhiepiskópou Makaríou 65 (☎623407); *Thames*, Platía Dhimokratías 13 (☎656333); *Theodoulou Self Drive*, Leonídha Kiouppí 13 (☎627411).

Exchange Most convenient bank branches are immediately around the CTO office (*Visa*-accepting cashpoint machines, too), with a few more on Ayíou Lazárou. *Access/Mastercard* machine at *Ethniki Trapeza/National Bank* on Zínonos Kitiéos.

Laundrettes *Artemis*, Armenikís Ekklisías 12; Mon–Fri 8am–6pm (until 8pm in summer), Sat 8am–3pm; service wash C£3.50, including drying. Also *New London*, Nikodhímou Mylóna 34.

Post offices The main branch, next to the CTO on Platía Dhimokratías, keeps short afternoon and Saturday morning hours; a small branch opposite Áyios Lázaros church is open Mon–Fri mornings only.

Scuba schools *Louis Loizou*, Evanthías Pierídhou 33D (☎627091); *Octopus Diving Centre*, opposite *Palm Beach Hotel* (☎635571).

Service taxis *Acropolis* (☎655555), corner Grigóri Afxendíou and Arkhiepiskópou Makaríou, to Limassol and Nicosia; *Makris* (☎652929), on Platía Dhimokratías, same destinations; *Kyriakos* (☎655100), Ermoú 2C, corner Afxendíou, Nicosia only.

AROUND LARNACA

Larnaca is conveniently situated at the centre of its administrative district, with a number of archeological sites, handicraft villages and rather less traditional resorts scattered in a broad arc all around. With the city as a base, it's easy to make several full- or half-day trips to the surrounding attractions. To do this with any degree of flexibility, you'll need a car – although public transport links the city with the majority of the sites detailed, there are few connections between them. Outside of Larnaca itself, **accommodation** can be found only at Perivólia, Kalavassós and the overgrown resorts around Ayía Nápa.

Southwest from Larnaca: the coastal route

The main expressways to Limassol and Nicosia take off well inland west of the city, leaving the **coastal plain** to the southwest relatively untravelled except for local village traffic. This is one patch of Cyprus, though, where the best bits are the easiest of access.

Hala Sultan (Umm Haram) Tekke

The mosque or **Tekke of Hala Sultan (Umm Haram)**, 5km southwest of Larnaca just past the airport, is quite possibly the first thing of note that you'll see in Cyprus, since it's clearly visible from jets coming in to land on the nearby runway. According to the foundation legend, Muhammad's maternal aunt, accompanying her husband on an Arab raid of Cyprus in 649, was attacked by Genoese forces here, fell from her mule, broke her neck and was buried on the spot. A shrine grew up around the grave on the west shore of a salt lake, surrounded today by an odd mix of date palms, cypress and olives. Rain permitting, a tank and a series of channels water the grove, adding to the oasis feeling of this peaceful, bird-filled place.

Tekke literally means a dervish convent, but this was always merely a *marabout* or saint's tomb. Despite the events of 1974, it's still a popular excursion target for Greek Cypriots and **place of pilgrimage** for Cypriot and foreign Muslims, for Hala Sultan ranks as one of the holiest spots of Islam, after Mecca, Medina, Kairouan and Jerusalem. The twin name is Turkish/Arabic: *Hala Sultan* means the "the Ruler's paternal aunt", while *Umm Haram* or "Sacred Mother" seems an echo of the old Aphrodite worship.

The site and environs

Having left your shoes at the door, you're ushered inside the present nineteenth-century mosque (daily, nominally 7.30am–sunset; donation) to the **tomb recess** at the rear, on one side of the mihrab. Beside the presumed sarcophagus of the Prophet's aunt, there's a recent tomb of the Turkish wife of King Hussein of the Hejaz. Above the graves you'll see three slabs of rock forming the dolmen that probably marked the grave until the mosque was built. The horizontal slab, a fifteen-ton meteorite chunk, is said to have been suspended miraculously in mid-air for centuries, before being forcibly lowered into its present position to avoid frightening the faithful who prayed underneath.

The dolmen and the mosque were by no means the first permanent structures here; remains of a **Late Bronze Age town**, west of the access road and car park, have been excavated since the late 1970s, yielding various treasures (many, appropriately enough, from Egypt).

Flamingoes and other migratory birds stop over at the **lake** during winter and early spring (see "Wildlife" in *Contexts*), hence *Flamingoes*, the excellent adjacent taverna, reviewed on p.62. Salt is still mined commercially here in late summer, the season of the lake's greatest shrinkage, though the turnover doesn't remotely approach the export trade that thrived here until Ottoman times. Like the *tekke*, the lake has a foundation legend, too: lately resuscitated Bishop Lazarus, passing by, asked a woman carrying some grapes for a bunch; upon her rude refusal, he retaliated by turning her vineyard into the salty lagoon, now three metres below sea level.

The *tekke* can almost be reached by **public transport** on the #6 municipal bus from Platía Ayíou Lazárou in Larnaca; have the driver set you down at the signposted one-kilometre side road, just the far side of the causeway over the salt lake.

On the north shore of the lake near the Limassol-bound road is the so-called **Kamares aqueduct**, built in 1747 at his own expense by Abu Bekir, the only popular Ottoman governor of the island. The 75 surviving arches were in use as recently as 1939.

Angelóktisti church

The #6 bus continues, a dozen times daily during daylight hours, to **KÍTI**, 11km from Larnaca. At a prominent three-way junction in the village, where roads head shoreward for Perivólia or on to Mazotós, stands the Byzantine **church of Angelóktisti** (Mon–Sat 8am–4pm, Sun 9am–noon & 2–4pm; donation). If necessary, the key can be fetched from the nearby snack bar, and smocks are provided for the scandalously dressed; since this is still Kíti's main church, making visits during Sunday morning liturgy is in fact problematic. The exterior, with its many curved surfaces, is pleasing; most of the church dates from the eleventh and twelfth centuries, having replaced an original fifth-century sanctuary destroyed by the Arabs. What today serves as a narthex and display area for old icons (signs in Greek warn the faithful not to kiss them if wearing lipstick) began life as an apsed and groin-vaulted Latin chapel in the thirteenth or fourteenth century. The main nave has three aisles, a single apse and no true narthex, though there's a large *yinaikonítis*, and all-seeing eyes to either side of the *témblon*.

The mosaic

The highlight of Angelóktisti is the **mosaic** (illuminated on request) in the conch of the apse, probably the last surviving section of the original building. Inside a floral/vegetal border, the Virgin lightly balances a doll-like infant on her left arm as she gazes sternly and unwaveringly to a point just left of the viewer. The pair is attended by two dissimilar archangels with fish-scale wings – Gabriel on the right is fleshier, more masculine – proffering celestial orbs and sceptres in the direction of the Infant. The age of the mosaic is controversial, but the Ravenna-esque artistic conventions, especially Mary's stance on a jewelled pedestal and inclination to left, would suggest the sixth century. Yet it is far more refined than the purportedly contemporaneous mosaic in the North Cyprus' church of Kanakariá, which was the only other Cypriot mosaic *in situ* until its desecration (see p.296).

Perivólia, Cape Kíti and beyond

Just 2km southeast of Kíti, **PERIVÓLIA** is developing as a resort because of its proximity to the **beaches** on Cape Kíti, 3km further in the same direction. These beaches, to either side of the lighthouse, are mostly scrappy, narrow and sharply shelving, with large pebbles on a sand base. Nonetheless, self-catering hotel apartments are springing up on the outskirts and "Flats to Let" signs abound in the village, an indication of just how desperate for fresh shorefront resorts the South is. If you have a rented car, Perivólia could be a good, relatively quiet base as it's not too tatty yet. Numerous **tavernas** in the village centre also make it a good destination for a night out from Larnaca.

A restored sixteenth-century **Venetian watchtower** looms conspicuously on a knoll just over a kilometre north of the modern lighthouse. Dirt tracks converge there from all directions, and it's always in sight – though not especially compelling when you get there.

Westwards to Maróni

Returning to Kíti village, it's possible to to follow the coast **westwards** by taking first a paved road, then turning onto a badly signposted dirt track 2km before Mazotós. The track is fairly rough, more so if you make a wrong turn, when it would be easy for a saloon car to founder in a deep rut or sand pit. The shore here is little developed except for farms and Cypriots' weekend villas, and frankly there's not much to justify any exploitation; the few beaches are rocky and difficult to reach, though once you are in the water the seabed is sandy enough.

If you persevere along the rough coastal track, you eventually return to civilization at either Zíyi or Maróni, though either is, in fact, simpler to reach along the old, inland trunk road or the newer, parallel expressway. Spread appealingly over several hills, **MARÓNI** is a major hothouse-vegetable centre. Its atmospheric old town, like that of Psematisménos 2km north, is home to numerous, mainly British expatriates, and quite a few properties are still for sale or being renovated. Despite (or perhaps because of) its status as a mixed village before 1974, its Greek Cypriot inhabitants were claimed to be among the most virulently nationalist in the district, and, in the words of one resident, "made Nikos Sampson look like a Communist supporter". When the Turkish Cypriots left in late 1974, the remaining villagers bulldozed their houses and claimed their fields, rather than distribute them to refugees from the North.

Zíyi

ZÍYI, 3km southeast of Maróni, sprang up in the last century as the first Cypriot port dedicated to shipping out carob pods; the Greek name, as does the Turkish moniker *Terazi*, means "weighing scales". The Cypriot republic inherited two military bases here from the British, their radar masts overshadowing the regional BBC transmitter. Today this identity sits incongruously with Zíyi's newer role as a minor resort, with no fewer than eight fish **tavernas** drawing in crowds from as far away as Nicosia. Of these, *Iy Apovathra*, in the old customs house at the base of the jetty, has long been considered the best, while the *Lapithos Fish Taverna* is a good second choice; *Santa Elena*, a few paces inland in a converted, vaulted carob warehouse, is less seafood-orientated and thus a bit cheaper.

The lack of beaches in the area doesn't seem to deter local day-trippers and weekend flat-owners. The nearest approximation is at **Limanáki**, about 2km east of Zíyi, though there's no sign: look for a side track to seaward just west of the turn-off for Maróni, beside an enormous and unmissable beached wooden caïque. This little bay has the only patch of sand for miles around, but the cove is jetsam-prone, and the taverna behind has been derelict for some time.

Kalavassós

If you're seized by an urge to **stay** in the area – and it does have the virtue of rough equidistance from Nicosia, Larnaca and Limassol – cross the expressway from either Maróni or Zíyi to **KALAVASSÓS**, where frogs croaking in the nearby riverbed offer the only nocturnal disturbance. Restored village houses or individual rooms can be rented at fairly reasonable daily rates (from around C£6 per person) by contacting Sofronis Potamitis (☎333180, fax 332295) or the village's gregarious butcher, Stavros (☎332244), who serves up excellent *mezédhes* at the *Tenta Café*, at the north end of Kalavassós. The *Bridge House Tavern* at the village entrance also arranges rooms (☎332501), as well as providing unexceptional but cheap and cheerful meals. Two important nearby excavated sites – the Neolithic town of Tenta, roughly contemporary with Khirokitiá (see below), and Áyios Dhimítrios, a large Late Bronze Age town with ashlar buildings and gravel-paved streets – are not yet open to the general public.

Western Larnaca district

Compared to the parched, apparent wastelands around Nicosia or Larnaca and the low-rise excesses of outer Limassol, the gently rolling country at the western end of Larnaca district presents a welcome change, with trees, streams, and a hint of the Tróödhos foothills further west. Several points of interest flank the Limassol–Nicosia expressway, suitably provided with exit roads across and onto the old highway, which in many respects is better for short distances here.

Khirokhitiá

Some of the earliest traces of human settlement in Cyprus, around 6800 BC, are found at Neolithic **KHIROKITIÁ**, roughly halfway between Larnaca and Limassol on the modern expressway. The proper name of the site is Khirokitiá-Vouni, but it's most often called simply Khirokitiá after the modern village to the northwest.

The excavated area forms a long ribbon on a southeast-facing slope dominating a pass on the age-old highway from the coast to Nicosia. It's supposedly open Mon–Fri 7.30am–5pm, Sat & Sun 9am–5pm (C£0.50; an explanatory pamphlet is available at the ticket booth for C£0.35), but at weekends at least it's unwise to show up after 1pm. The site is not well fenced, however, and can be easily entered along the well-trodden path beginning behind the booth. Despite noisy distraction from the motorway, Khirokitiá ranks among the most rewarding of Cypriot ruins. The only nearby amenity is a taverna on the access road from the main highway, on the east side of the bridge over the Maróni creek.

The site

The combination of arable land below and an easily defensible position was irresistible for the settlement's founders, thought to have come from the Levantine coast or Anatolia. Archeological investigations are continuing in the earliest inhabited sector, a saddle between the two knolls at the top of the slope; despite the limited area uncovered to date, it seems certain that most of the hillside was inhabited.

What's visible thus far are housing foundations – most substantial and recent at the bottom of the slope – and a maze of lanes, dictated more by the placement of dwellings than any deliberate planning. You walk up on what appears to be the main street, but is in fact a defensive **perimeter wall**, something which becomes more obvious at the top of the hill; the very few houses that were built outside it were later enclosed by a secondary outer wall.

The sixty-odd circular **dwellings** exposed to date, all of the *tholos* or beehive type, are single-storeyed structures that probably had flat roofs. Interior walls were lined with stone benches doubling as sleeping platforms, with scanty illumination provided through slit windows. The largest dwelling, an egg-shaped chieftain's **"mansion"** with an inner diameter of just under six metres, had two rectangular piers supporting a loft. As the structures deteriorated, they were flattened into rubble and built over by the next generation (it was this practice that prompted the now-discarded theory that the perimeter wall was in fact the main street, its elevation constantly raised to keep pace with the level of the new houses). This "urban-renewal" method has greatly complicated modern excavations, which began in 1936, two years after the site's discovery; these have yielded vast troves of small Neolithic objects, undisturbed by vandals and now to be seen at the Cyprus Museum in Nicosia (see p.204).

Estimates for the maximum **population** of Khirokitiá run as high as 2000, an astounding figure for the time. Wheel-less pottery techniques were known only in the **local culture**'s latter phases; during the so-called Aceramic period, the inhabitants worked strictly in stone, turning out, for example, relief-patterned grey andesite bowls and rather schematic idols. Flint sickle blades, grinders hollowed out of river boulders and preserved cereal grains provide proof of the community's largely agricultural basis, though hunting, particularly for deer, was important too.

The Khirokitians **buried their dead** in the fetal position under the earth floor, or just outside the entrance, of some of the round-houses – a rather convenient, if unhygienic form of ancestor reverence; beneath one dwelling, twenty-six graves on eight superimposed levels were discovered. The deceased were surrounded by offerings and personal belongings, exquisite stone-and-shell necklaces being found in female graves; more ominously, the corpses usually had their chests crushed with a grinding quern to prevent the dead returning. Infant mortality was high, and adult skulls show evidence of ritual deformation – surviving infants would have been tightly bound on a cradle-board to flatten the back of the head.

Hill villages: the long way to Páno Léfkara

Rather than proceed from ancient Khirokitiá along the expressway to the most direct side road for Páno Léfkara, a rewarding detour can be made through some little-visited hill villages. Khirokitiá village straddles a ridge 2km west of the ruins and offers a foretaste of **VÁVLA**'s array of beautiful old houses, which are slowly being bought up and restored; at weekends snacks are offered at the lone *kafenío* here. Vávla marks the turnoff for **Ayíou Miná**, one of several functioning convents in the South, but so far the least touristed despite its proximity (7km) to Páno Léfkara. The Byzantine-Gothic church, probably founded by the Dominicans during the fifteenth century, provides the main focus of interest; the friendly nuns produce icons and honey, both offered for sale.

The main valley road from Vávla continues up through less distinguished Láyia and Orá, beyond which the surface abruptly deteriorates as you crawl over a saddle towards **VAVATSINIÁ**, nestling in a fold of Mount Kiónia at the top of the valley that drains towards Ayíou Miná. Above the central church, an *ayíasma* (holy spring with curative powers) issues from a deep shaft; below the church, a taverna, packed out at weekends, looks across the gorge towards a typical peaked-roof hill-country chapel: fresco-less but with a carved-wood interior. As you leave the village in the direction of Páno Léfkara, you pass another enormous taverna on the outskirts, also jammed on holidays with Cypriot trippers.

Páno and Káto Léfkara

The next junction on the main highway to the east of Khirokitiá is the turning for **PÁNO LÉFKARA**, 700m above sea level on the fringes of the Troödhos and reached along an easy climb on the well-made E105 road. Approaching, it's best not to take the first signposted turn-off into the village – there's no parking on this side and it leaves you with a bit of a hike into town.

In Lusignan times a retreat of the Orthodox clergy, Páno Léfkara is now almost a small town, a very handsome one to boot, and should be visited for that reason alone: arches make veritable tunnels in the streets, and fine door frames and balconies complete the picture. Many of the old houses are being restored by Cypriots and foreigners, though prices are high owing to equidistance from the South's three largest towns. There was a small Turkish quarter here, too, down at the low end of the village by the mosque.

The usual reason for visiting is to sample the **lace and silver** for which the place is famous; it is claimed, somewhat apocryphally, that Leonardo da Vinci purchased a needlepoint altarcloth for Milan cathedral when he came to Cyprus in 1481. The silver jewellery and ware, men's work, seems more reasonably priced than the women's lace, and both are sold in over half a dozen shops, mostly along the main commercial street – though the villagers all have an eye for the main chance, and everyone from petrol pump attendant to café owner will happily trot out the work of relatives at the first opportunity. It's as well to know that the "lace" to be embroidered is actually imported Irish linen. On the whole, prices are inflated in Páno Léfkara, so bargain hard, or seek out better deals in surrounding villages. The **Patsalos Folklore Museum** (Mon–Sat 10am–4pm; C£0.50), devoted largely to the two crafts, might be a useful first stop before going on a shopping spree. Páno Léfkara is also noted for its Turkish delight (*loukoúmia*), and if you're lucky you can catch a demonstration of its manufacture.

Practicalities

It's easiest to leave a vehicle at the northeast end of the village, where a line of arched, wooden-floored *kafenía* and a take-away kebab stall or two opposite the school offer a marvellous tableau of the village elders playing at cards and dice. Páno Léfkara has two **hotels**: the appealing *Lefkarama* (☎/fax 342000; ③), built partly around a tenth-century chapel, which offers advantageous half-board rates; and the pricier, newly constructed *Agora* (☎342901, fax 342095; ⑥). At lunchtime, the *Lefkarama*'s **restaurant**, with indoor and courtyard seating, has much the most complete menu around; try the quails if they're available. On the main market street, *Lemonies* serves good kebabs in its garden but isn't especially inexpensive.

Káto Léfkara

Páno Léfkara's lower neighbour, **KÁTO LÉFKARA**, is also architecturally of a piece, but much less frequented – here too, however, there is a snack bar and several trinket shops. The real sight in Káto is the largely twelfth-century **church of the Arkhángelos** (always unlocked), by itself in a field to the south-west of the village car park. Although the preservation and quantity of its **interior frescoes** cannot rank it with the best examples of painted churches in the High Troödhos, what remains is well worth the slight detour. The oldest and best surviving images decorate the apse, with *Christ's Communion with the Apostles* (six of whom are missing) above five early Fathers of the Church. Over the south door, *The Holy Handkerchief* is essentially a *Pandokrátor* superimposed on a shawl, just below a badly deteriorated *Baptism*. A much later (fifteenth-century) *Resurrection* in the arch of the west vault looks suspiciously like *The Healing of the Leper*.

Pottery villages: Kofínou and Kórnos

Back on the route towards Nicosia, you'd detour almost immediately for **KOFÍNOU**, which has just a single pottery workshop, *Skutari Craft Pottery*, near the ugly prefab church. The present villagers are refugees from the North; this was among the largest, nearly all-Muslim villages in the South, attacked on scanty pretext by EOKA on November 15, 1967. Before a truce was arranged two days later, 25 local Turkish Cypriots had died, and the incident nearly precipitated a Greek–Turkish war. Scars of the battle are still evident in the old Turkish quarter, now abandoned, boarded up and signposted as "Government Property". The incoming Greek Cypriots were housed in a grid-plan prefabricated development to the west. Kofínou is well known locally for its **kléftiko** houses: if you're in the mood for a stodgy but good-value lunch of oven-roasted lamb and potatoes, check out the *Pentadaktylos Kleftiko House*, or any one of the other half-dozen that lie adjacent to the Larnaca-bound motorway.

KÓRNOS, 11km north on the other side of the highway, is a more cheerful place, set in a tree-lined stream valley, and also occupies itself with pottery (*kórnos* means "clay" in Cypriot dialect). Signs point you to the main works (shut Sunday) at the northeast edge of town, where you'll see large piles of unsifted, coarse clay, mixing pits and a pair of kilns. If you want large *kioupiá* or plant-pots for a villa terrace, this is the place, though transporting them overseas would be another matter.

Stavrovoúni monastery

Proportionate to its population, Cyprus contributes more monks to the monastic enclave of Mount Áthos in northern Greece than any other Orthodox country. You can get a glimpse of the reasons why at the **monastery of Stavrovoúni**, perched atop an isolated, 689-metre crag that dominates this corner of the island.

Its foundation legend places it as the oldest religious community on Cyprus: St Helena, mother of Roman Emperor Constantine, supposedly came through here in 327 on her way back from Jerusalem, leaving a fragment of the True Cross (plus the entire cross of the Penitent Thief). Previously home to a temple of Aphrodite, the peak took its modern name from this (*Stavrovoúni* means "Cross Mountain"), and a religious community quickly sprang up around the holy relics.

In Lusignan times Benedictine monks displaced Orthodox ones, but despite an imposing fortified design, both monastery and revered objects were destroyed after the 1426 rout of King Janus nearby (see below). Today's silver reliquary crucifix, which supposedly encases the venerated sliver of the True Cross, dates only from the late fifteenth century; perhaps the contents are identical with the purported Cross of the Penitent Thief which a wandering Dominican friar claimed to have seen here, still intact, by the altar in 1486.

After the Turkish conquest the monastery was burned again, and only in the last century was Stavrovoúni rebuilt, on the old foundations, and repopulated – by both monks and dozens of cats, the latter a scourge of snakes here as at the Cape Gáta nunnery at Akrotíri. But by the late 1970s the place was in decline once more, with just two elderly monks besides the abbot (who is still here, in his fifty-third year of residence). Stavrovoúni had given up its once-extensive holdings to surrounding villages, a process doubtless completed by the pressure of refugees from the 1974 invasion, though it retained the nunnery of Ayía Varvára at the base of the hill as a dependency.

Monastery life

Today about twenty very committed, mostly young monks perform a rota: six or seven up in the citadel, the rest down at Ayía Varvára at any given time. They are on an **Athos-type regimen**, strictest on the island, which entails a day divided into roughly equal thirds of prayer and study, physical labour and rest. "Rest" means only two frugal, meat-less meals, just before midday and an hour or so before sunset, taken together in the tiny refectory, plus sleep interspersed between the nocturnal devotional periods. As a minimum there are four communal liturgies each day in the courtyard church: matins before dawn, the main liturgy after sunrise, vespers before the evening meal, and compline afterwards.

Life has been eased somewhat by the recent paving of the steep, twisty road up and provision of mains water and electricity, but winters on top are severe, and the monks still do a full day's work on the surrounding agricultural terraces in addition to their devotions. Honey and sultanas, the latter legendarily having their first Cypriot cultivation here, make up some of the harvest. The icon-painting studio of Father Kallinikos at Ayía Varvára is well signposted; he is considered one of the finest living practitioners of the art, and his work is accordingly expensive.

Visits

Equally strict conditions apply for **visiting** the upper monastery. In accordance with Athonite rules, no women are currently admitted at all, even female infants; no entry is allowed from noon to 3pm (11am–2pm in summer – the monks don't keep summer time); and photos are forbidden – cameras must be left at the guard house at the foot of the long stairway up from the car park. In sum, you don't come here to gawp – except perhaps at the amazing views, since there's little remaining of artistic or architectural merit after the pillaging and fires – but on pilgrimage, possibly to stay the night on invitation.

A Greek sign in the entry hall sums up the monastic creed: "If you die before you die, then when you die you won't die." In other words, he who has renounced the world gains eternal life. When a monk *does* die bodily, he is interred for the prescribed three years of Orthodoxy and then exhumed for display in the ossuary, his religious name emblazoned across the forehead of his skull.

Pýrga: the "Chapelle Royale"

Near the centre of **PÝRGA** village, just 3km from Kórnos and east of the expressway, stands the **"Chapelle Royale"**, a small, frescoed Lusignan shrine actually dedicated to St Catherine (daylight hours according to keeper's whim; C£0.50). It owes its alias to a fine wall-painting of **King Janus**, who, together with his queen, Charlotte of Bourbon, built the chapel in 1421. "Good King Janus" was among the last of Cyprus' Crusader monarchs, as respected as he was ineffective; just a few kilometres south, below Khirokitiá, runs the Maróni stream where his armies were defeated by the Mamelukes in 1426. Janus was held prisoner in Cairo for two years before being ransomed, and this little church is his only surviving legacy.

The building itself is quite plain, merely a single-vaulted structure with three doorways. By 1426 all the inside surfaces had been decorated by a Greek Cypriot painter effecting a unique synthesis of Byzantine and Latin iconographic elements; unhappily only a small fraction of the paintings survive. Janus appears, along with Queen Charlotte, as a tiny, kneeling figure at the foot of a fragmentary *Crucifixion* on the east wall. On the northeast ceiling you can make out *The Raising of Lazarus* and a *Last Supper*, the latter the best-preserved image here and – unusually in Cyprus – identified in French. Opposite these frescoes, also tagged by French inscriptions, *The Ascension* and *The Pentecost* are just recognizable.

Kelliá: the church of Áyios Andónios

Though not strictly speaking in the west of Larnaca district, the Byzantine **church of Áyios Andónios**, a mere 5km north of Larnaca via Livádhia, makes a satisfying complement to the two preceding sites. Commanding a hillock just west of the formerly wholly Turkish Cypriot village of **KELLIÁ**, it was originally erected in the ninth century, though what you see now is an engaging medley of eleventh- to fifteenth-century styles, plus an eighteenth-century west arcade.

Since whitewash and extraneous buttressing were removed, the value of Áyios Andónios' Byzantine **frescoes** has been recognized and the church is now kept scrupulously locked; to visit the interior, you must track down the caretaker, most likely at the bus-stop *kafenío* down in the village. The murals exposed thus far decorate four interior pillars and the west wall. Most notable are two versions of *The Sacrifice of Isaac*, and a rudimentary ninth-century *Crucifixion* on the southeast pier.

East of Larnaca: the resort coast

As you head out of the city, the bight of Larnaca Bay bends initially north. It takes nearly 5km to outrun the oil refineries and tankers at anchor; paragliders and clusters of hotels, neither yet so densely packed as at Limassol or Káto Páfos, indicate that you have at last done so. The **beach** here is acceptable for a dip, but

---

SPECIAL USES FOR THE DHEKÉLIA SOVEREIGN BASE

The existence of the **Dhekélia Sovereign Base** (see box on p.96), and its inviolability even in the wake of the 1974 invasion, has given rise to some anomalies in the supposedly hermetic separation of Cyprus North and South. Both Turkish and Greek Cypriots continue to hold jobs on the base; access from the South is unrestricted, and with the right paperwork Northerners can enter along the so-called "Four Mile Crossing" from Famagusta, and at two or three other points. Turkish Cypriots wishing to make clandestine visits to the South, especially for nightlife, need only leave their Northern numberplate cars in the base, and have Greek friends with suitable cars waiting for them (Northerners with a business or relatives in Pýla are entitled to visit).

PÝLA, entirely within the buffer zone near a point where the boundaries of the North, the South and the Dhekélia base meet, has acquired special notoriety as one of only two remaining bi-ethnic villages in the southern Republic (the other is Potamiá, near Nicosia, though there the two ethnic communities are kept physically segregated). Preserved here is an approximate microcosm of island life between 1963 and 1974: Greek (67 percent) and Turkish (33 percent) Cypriots live in proximity but not together, with two opposing coffee-houses (one – guess which – emblazoned with a prominent "Macedonia is Greek" banner) and separate communal schools. Disputes over Turkish-Cypriot-owned property boundaries often require the mediation of the local UN post, currently manned by civilian Irish policemen. A medieval tower, bespattered with pigeon droppings, looms beyond the minaret, both overawed by a ring of modern Turkish army watchtowers on the crags just above – hence no photos anywhere in the village.

The only tacit intercommunal cooperation involves the **smuggling** of vast amounts of goods from the North, just 5km away across Sovereign Base territory at Pérgamos (Beyarmudu). This loophole makes a mockery of the Republic of Cyprus' prohibition on "foreign" agricultural produce, with even fruit from hated Turkey entering via this corridor. Particularly on the access road in from Larnaca, numerous shops long did a roaring trade in "duty-free" jewellery and designer clothing, though lately most of these have been driven out of business by harassment from the authorities and price-cutting elsewhere. Greek Cypriot police may still periodically set up roadblocks in the area to search for such contraband, so shopping here is probably a poor idea, especially if receipts show that you've purchased from a Turkish-Cypriot-owned enterprise. One establishment that can be more wholeheartedly recommended is the Turkish-Cypriot-managed taverna *Golden Barrel* on the road in, which (by UN personnel accounts) hosts fairly wild Friday and Saturday night revels.

nothing to scream about: the tidal zone is reefy, the water interrupted by rock jetties and breakwaters. Beyond the strip of hotels, there's even less to stop for as the route curls east, and halting is awkward once inside the Dhekélia Sovereign Base – home to an enormous and ugly power station, between the highway and the sea, in addition to British Forces.

Once outside the Sovereign Base, your first detour might be to **Potamós Liopetríou**, a long, narrow creek-inlet that's a genuine, rare fishing anchorage. The only facilities are two tavernas, though the fish in particular is not cheap, and the northerly one is quite unwelcoming. This is a shame, as the place is attractive – if beachless, though some sand has been hopefully strewn at a suitable bathing spot near the mouth of the inlet. It appears that the French poet Rimbaud stopped in, too, working as a quarry foreman in 1879 before supervising the construction of the governor's residence in the Tróödhos.

Ayía Nápa

In his book *Journey into Cyprus*, Colin Thubron describes cooking a fish, in the summer of 1972, on the empty beach below the then-fishing village of **AYÍA NÁPA**, and later being awoken by sandflies. Were he today to find an unpoliced stretch of sand, he would be lucky to sleep at all over the din of nearby clubs and discos. Any local identity has been utterly swept aside since Thubron's visit, with Ayía Nápa press-ganged into service as one of the South's largest package resorts, replacing the lost paradises around Famagusta. You don't really need a guidebook to find your way about here – all is pretty self-explanatory – but rather a fat wallet, and a large liver capacity.

The beach is still obvious enough, but packed out, a crescent swathe extending east hundreds of metres from the fishing harbour whose tavernas are among the most expensive on the island. Ayía Nápa also has a reputation for (by Cypriot standards) hard nocturnal living, with well over a dozen bars and discos, thronged by a rowdy, largely working-class clientele from various points in northern Europe. Above Platía Seféri, nominal centre of the old village, anything not a pub is likely to be a clothes shop or an overpriced restaurant: striking out in virtually any direction, you can pick up a copy of many English newspapers (though these are far outnumbered by Swedish tabloids), or tank up on Woodpecker cider and beans on toast.

The monastery of Ayía Nápa

Amidst all this, the Venetian-style **monastery of Ayía Nápa** comes as a beautiful, peaceful shock, with its arched cloister enclosing an irregularly shaped, flower-decked courtyard. In the middle spurts an octagonal **fountain**, its sides decorated with reliefs and the whole surmounted by a dome on four pillars. Across the way burbles a boar's-head spout, the terminus of a Roman **aqueduct** whose spring-fed waters were the impetus for sporadic settlement here since Hellenistic times – and the focus of the monastery's foundation legend.

During the sixteenth-century Venetian heyday in Cyprus, some hunters had a mangy dog whose coat improved markedly after visits to a hidden spring. Curious, the hunters followed the wet dog, finding not only the source of the abandoned aqueduct but also an icon of the Virgin hidden here for 700 years since the Iconoclast crisis, when Byzantine zealots briefly outlawed the adoration of such images. News of the waters spread, with humans availing themselves of its healing powers, and soon a monastery was founded around the lower end of the refurbished aqueduct. Work was completed just in time for the Turkish conquest, after which the Catholics were expelled from the complex and replaced with more tractable Greek Orthodox monks; they too soon departed but a village sprang up around the abandoned monastery, attracted by the flow of water.

The **church**, off to the right (west) of the sloping courtyard, is partly subterranean and has a magnificent fanlight-cum-rose window over the door. In the gloom at the base of the stairs down, you'll find a supplementary Latin chapel, from the time of the monastery's original dedication, though the miraculous icon has long since vanished. Back outside you can clamber up onto part of the **perimeter wall**, looking towards the sea over a cistern and two giant sycamore figs, said to be six centuries old. The Venetian designers built the wall to keep pirates at bay but it now has the unforeseen but happy effect of cordoning off the place from the new Viking barbarians. Immediately around it, a half-dozen of the louder pubs must test the resolve of ecclesiastical conference delegates, who are the only people allowed to stay as guests in the nominally still-functioning monastery, restored during the early 1970s and made available to the World Council of Churches.

The Marine Life Museum

Besides the monastery, the only other real "sight" in Ayía Nápa is the **Marine Life Museum**, housed in the municipality at Ayías Mávris 25 (May–Sept Mon–Sat 9am–2pm, plus Mon & Thurs 4–6.30pm; Oct–Apr Mon–Sat 9am–2pm, plus Mon & Thurs 3–5.30pm; C£0.50). Funded, like the eponymous museum in Larnaca, by the Pierides Foundation, it consists largely of the seashell and fossil collection of naturalist George Tornaritis, plus stuffed or preserved specimens in dioramas.

> The phone code for Ayía Nápa and environs, officially known as "Free Famagusta" district, is ☎03.

Practicalities

Orientation is straightforward: **Nissí** is the initial name of the main road west to Nissí and Larnaca, 39km distant; **Arkhiepiskópou Makaríou** descends from the central square, **Platía Seféri**, to the harbour; and **Krýou Neroú** heads out east towards Cape Gréko. Above Platía Seféri, the trunk routes dissolve into a welter of narrower streets on the hillside. *EMAN* **buses** will drop you either down at the main ticket office near the base of Makaríou, or up at stops near the none-too-enthusiastic **CTO** at the corner of Krýou Neroú and Makaríou (Mon–Sat 8.30am–1.45pm, plus Mon & Thurs 4–6.15pm), next to the *Cyprus Airways* office.

If you're **staying** here, it's 98 percent certain that you've come on a package. Even the most rock-bottom hotel, the one-star *Napa Sol*, Nissí 79 (☎722044; ⑥), is firmly on the tour operators' lists. The only other comparable hotel option is the somewhat better-positioned *Leros* (☎721126; ⑤), opposite *EMAN* on Makaríou, recently overhauled and pitching itself of late to non-package guests. Most other affordable accommodation in Ayía Nápa is self-catering, with studios suitable for two starting at about C£16, two-bedroom units at roughly double that figure.

Don't expect much Cypriot character when **eating out**, though *Markos* near the monastery is acceptable. Aside from the manifold bars, more "wholesome"

entertainment is laid on in the last week of September as part of the Ayía Nápa **festival**: several days of folkloric displays, music, dance, theatre and other events in and around Platía Seféri, by the monastery.

Rounding out amenities, the **post office** keeps limited afternoon and Saturday morning hours. The numerous **banks** are liberally sown with *Visa*-accepting cashpoint machines. **Car rental** franchises cluster near the start of Nissí avenue, with several more in nearby Protarás (see below).

West of Ayía Nápa

Some 2km west of central Ayía Nápa on its namesake avenue, **Nissí beach** is for once as attractive as touted – but in high season it's hopelessly crowded as the four or five hotels here, a discreet distance behind, disgorge their occupants onto the few hundred metres of sand, or into the handful of snack kiosks above the tidemark. At such times especially you can retreat by wading out to the islet which lends the beach definition, and its name (*nissí* means "island").

The local **campsite** is nearby to the west, between Nissí and the turnoff for **Astéria beach** on the Makrónissos peninsula; it's open March to October, charging C£1.50 a day per tent or caravan plus C£1.25 per person.

Inland: the Kokkinokhoriá

Away from the south coast, the gently undulating terrain is dotted with the **Kokkinokhoriá** or "Red Villages", so called after the local soil, tinged red by large amounts of iron and other metallic oxides. This is the island's main potato-growing region, the little spuds irrigated by water drawn up by the dozens of windmills, and harvested in May to appear subsequently in British corner shops. (Lately the overdrawn aquifer has been invaded by the sea, and fresh water must be brought in from the Tróödhos.) Less salutary is the area's reputation for the trapping of songbirds for food (see p.356), particularly at Paralímni; *ambelopoúlia* are small fig-eating blackcaps (often known by their Italian name, *beccafico*), pickled whole and exported to the Middle East.

Other than this, there is little to be said for the hinterland, and even the CTO admits as much in its earnest, rather desperate promotion of the handful of unheralded late medieval churches scattered in and around the various relentlessly modern villages. Despite their inland location, however, they are too close to the seashore fleshpots to have escaped notice from tourists and expatriates, so at Dherínia and Paralímni in particular there are various facilities.

Dherínia

In **DHERÍNIA**, expensive but tasty *Taylor's* on the Sotíra road is just one of several **tavernas** – the others are on the Frénaros road – which attract foreigners. Dherínia is most visited, however, for its hilltop setting virtually on the Attila Line and the resulting overlook of the "dead zone" towards Famagusta and its modern suburb Varósha. Disconnected windmills spin aimlessly, or stand devaned and idle in the abandoned fields to the north. Two view-cafés charge C£0.50 for the privilege of using their binoculars to take in the sad tableau of Varósha crumbling away, its rusty construction cranes frozen in their positions of August 1974.

Paralímni

In the wake of the invasion, **PARALÍMNI**, a few kilometres south of Dherínia, became the administrative capital of "Free Famagusta" district, and as such has a concentration of banks, petrol pumps, shops and venues for cultural events – as well as the most northerly access to the strip of Greek-Cypriot-controlled coast below Famagusta. Beachfront development extends to just a bit north of Ayía Triás cove; working your way south on the still-narrow road to the minuscule beach at **PERNÉRA**, you can eat at *Taverna Onasis*, which is where the numerous building-site crews in the area go for a no-nonsense feed; until the next tower block rears up, it even has a sea view of sorts. If you fancy staying, there are numbers of self-catering **apartments** that could be had early or late in the year on a walk-in basis, both along the Paralímni–Ayía Triás road and immediately around Pernéra.

East of Ayía Napá: Protarás and Cape Gréko

Pernéra merges south into the formerly pristine stretches of **PROTARÁS**, aka "Fig Tree Bay", a developmental disaster of some twenty wall-to-wall hotels, packed out from mid-May onwards with relatively well-behaved Scandinavian families. The famous but rather narrow sandy beach is not even indicated from the inland bypass road, lined by a dozen restaurants – only the hotels themselves are signposted. Thus if you don't know that the *Sunrise Beach Hotel* marks the north end of the bay, and the *Nausicaa Beach Hotel Apartments* the southern extreme, it's quite easy to drive right past Protarás resort without ever seeing the sea. Once you do figure it out, you'll find that big shoreline lawns and swimming pools, substantial enough to accommodate the crowds, supplement the lack of sands – conveying a clear message that, unless you're actually staying at one of the behemoths or using their manifold recreational facilities (water-skiing, paragliding and so on), you're not welcome here. It's difficult to imagine a setting less appropriate for non-package visitors. At least the sea, if you do manage to reach it, is as clear and warm as you'd hope for.

Cape Gréko

Chances for a quiet swim are better south of Protarás, where the road along the mostly rocky shoreline passes through a brief patch of forest en route to **Cape Gréko**, Land's End for this corner of the island. Tiny beaches offer good snorkelling in the vicinity of Kónos bay, though even here excursion boats tend to arrive by noon. Despite the area's status as a national reserve, the tip of the cape remains off-limits owing to a lighthouse, military installation and the Radio Monte Carlo relay station. Reefy coves to either side of the final isthmus see some yacht traffic, though swimming is difficult if the wind is up, as it frequently is.

A favourite landlubbers' activity in the area is to **hike the coastline** from Protarás to Ayía Nápa (or vice versa), following a dirt track that runs parallel to the shore; this three-to-four-hour outing will take you past impressive cliffscapes, sea caves, a natural rock arch and a Roman quarry. All told, however, the area's intrinsic merits are sufficiently limited to make you wonder how much it would have been developed for tourism, had the much better beaches from Famagusta northwards remained under Greek Cypriot control.

travel details

Buses

From **Larnaca** to: Ayía Nápa (7 daily Mon–Sat, 4 on Sun in season, 5 daily out of season, on *EMAN*; 6–8 daily Mon–Sat on *Kallenos*; 45min); Limassol (2–4 daily Mon–Sat on *Kallenos*; 1hr 15min); Nicosia (6–7 daily Mon–Sat on *Kallenos*; 1hr); Páno Léfkara (1 daily, at 1pm, on the village bus; 45min); Paralímni via Protarás on *Kallenos* (8 daily Mon–Sat; 1hr); via the Kokkinokhoriá on *Paralímni Bus* (6–7 daily Mon–Sat; 45min).

From **Ayía Nápa** to: Nicosia (1 daily, early morning, on *EMAN*; 1hr 30min); Paralímni via Protarás (9 daily Mon–Sat, 5 on Sun in season, 3–4 daily Mon–Sat out of season; 20min).

Angelóktisti	Αγγελόκτιστη	ΑΓΓΕΛΟΚΤΙΣΤΗ
Ayía Nápa	Αγία Νάπα	ΑΓΙΑ ΝΑΠΑ
Áyios Lázaros	Αγιος Λάζαρος	ΑΓΙΟΣ ΛΑΖΑΡΟΣ
Ayíou Miná	Αγίου Μηνά	ΑΓΙΟΥ ΜΗΝΑ
Cape Gréko	Ακρωτήρι Γρέκο	ΑΚΡΩΤΗΡΙ ΓΡΕΚΟ
Dherínia	Δερύνεια	ΔΕΡΥΝΕΙΑ
Hala Sultan	Χάλα Σουλτάν	ΧΑΛΑ ΣΟΥΛΤΑΝ
Kalavassós	Καλαβασός	ΚΑΛΑΒΑΣΟΣ
Káto Léfkara	Κάτω Λεύκαρα	ΚΑΤΩ ΛΕΥΚΑΡΑ
Khirokitiá	Χοιροκοιτιά	ΧΟΙΡΟΚΟΙΤΙΑ
Kíti	Κίτι	ΚΙΤΙ
Kofínou	Κοφίνου	ΚΟΦΙΝΟΥ
Kórnos	Κόρνος	ΚΟΡΝΟΣ
Larnaca (Lárnaka)	Λάρνακα	ΛΑΡΝΑΚΑ
Maróni	Μαρώνι	ΜΑΡΩΝΙ
Páno Léfkara	Πάνω Λεύκαρα	ΠΑΝΩ ΛΕΥΚΑΡΑ
Paralímni	Παραλίμνι	ΠΑΡΑΛΙΜΝΙ
Perivólia	Περιβόλια	ΠΕΡΙΒΟΛΙΑ
Pernéra	Περνέρα	ΠΕΡΝΕΡΑ
Protarás	Πρωταράς	ΠΡΩΤΑΡΑΣ
Pýla	Πύλα	ΠΥΛΑ
Pýrga	Πύργα	ΠΥΡΓΑ
Stavrovoúni monastery	Μονή Σταυροβούνι	ΜΟΝΗ ΣΤΑΥΡΟΒΟΥΝΙ
Vavatsiniá	Βαβατσινιά	ΒΑΒΑΤΣΙΝΙΑ
Vávla	Βάβλα	ΒΑΒΛΑ
Zíyi	Ζύγι	ΖΥΓΙ

CHAPTER TWO

LIMASSOL AND AROUND

Limassol (*Lemessós* in Greek), the island's second largest town, will be your introduction to the Republic of Cyprus if you arrive by sea. It's a brash, functional place, with little to recommend it, even as a base for touring, other than gritty authenticity. More than anywhere else in the South, the city has acted as a magnet for extensive and debilitating urban drift from the poor, low-altitude hill villages just north.

In those foothills, whose nearer settlements are now little better than commuter bedrooms for the big city, the most interesting spots, such as **Potamioú**, **Ómodhos** and **Vouní**, might not rate a special detour, but are easily visited en route to the high Tróödhos. Other half-inhabited hill hamlets, such as **Akapnoú** and **Odhoú**, see few outsiders, despite CTO promotion as centres of "agro-tourism", and require considerable energy to reach.

Along the coast east of Limassol, you have to outrun sixteen kilometres of fairly horrific hotel development, some of the worst in the Mediterranean, before the tower blocks halt just past ancient **Amathus**, a small but evocative site. Just before the coast road veers inland towards Nicosia, there's access to **Governor's Beach**, virtually the last remaining unspoiled stretch of sand in the district.

Heading out of Limassol in the opposite direction holds more promise. A long if unscenic beach fringing the **Akrotíri peninsula**, home to one of the island's three British bases, ends near the legend-draped convent of **Ayíou Nikoláou tón Gáton**. On the far side of the lagoon, orange and eucalyptus groves soften the landscape en route to the atmospheric crusader castle of **Kolossi** and the clifftop ruins of **Kourion**, together with its associated **sanctuary of Apollo Hylates**, one of the most impressive ancient sites in the South. You can swim at the beach below the palisades, but it's probably better to wait until reaching the more secluded bays near **Pissoúri**, a favourite hideout of British expats and squaddies.

ACCOMMODATION PRICES IN THE SOUTH

All hotel and apartment-hotel prices in the South have been categorized according to the price codes given below. These categories represent the minimum you can expect to pay in the high season for a double room or a two-person self-catering unit. Single rooms will normally cost 50–80 percent of the rates quoted for a double room. Rates for dorm beds in hostels, where guests are charged per person, are given in Cyprus pounds, instead of being indicated by price code. For further details, see p.25.

① under C£12	④ C£20–25	⑦ C£35–40
② C£12–16	⑤ C£25–30	⑧ C£40–50
③ C£16–20	⑥ C£30–35	⑨ over C£50

Limassol (Lemessós)

Although not without charm in its old centre of Levantine stone buildings and alleyways, **LIMASSOL (LEMESSÓS)** is primarily the industrial and commercial capital of the southern coast, specializing in wine-making, citrus processing and canning. Since 1974 and the loss of Famagusta, it is also the South's largest port, with container ships at anchor near the seafront esplanade throughout the year. The transient presence of sailors, and off-duty Brits from the nearby base, may also account for the largest red-light district in the island. With close to 200,000 more ordinary inhabitants, Limassol basks in its reputation as a mini-Texas of conspicuously consuming, gregarious *nouveaux riches*. Money is frittered away at "exclusive" nightclubs, just off the expressway to Larnaca, which supposedly never close; even receipts in modest town restau-

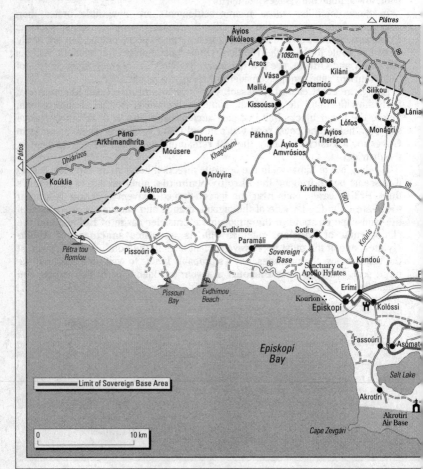

rants are apt to be A5-size computer printouts more appropriate to a warehousing business.

Most of the tourist industry hereabouts is ghettoized in a long, unsightly ribbon of development east of the town, leaving the workaday atmosphere of the centre relatively unscathed. But after looking in at the several museums and the winery, and perhaps taking a stroll around the bazaar, you'll probably be ready to move on.

Some history

A near-complete lack of significant monuments attests to the relative youth of the town. Limassol hardly existed before the Christian era, being for centuries overshadowed by Amathus to the east and Kourion to the west. It burst into prominence in 1191, when the fiancée and sister of the crusading English king

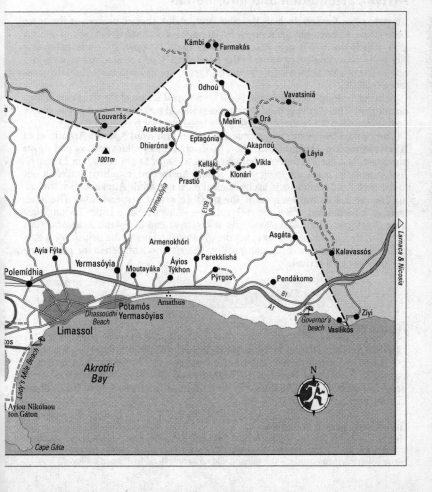

Richard the Lionheart were nearly shipwrecked just offshore, and subsequently ill-treated by Isaac Komnenos, self-styled ruler of the island. Upon appearing a few days later and hearing of this insult to his women, Richard landed nearby in force, married Berengaria of Navarre on the site of the present-day castle, and went on to claim the island after defeating Isaac in battle.

There followed two centuries of prosperity, with both the Hospitallers and Templars having extensive holdings around Limassol after the loss of the Holy Land. But then an earthquake and devastating raids by the Genoese, Mamelukes and finally the Turks, combined to level the settlement by the beginning of the Ottoman era. It's only since the end of the last century that the town has grown again, and squalidly at that.

Arrival, orientation and information

All passenger **ferries** dock at the new port, about 4km southwest of the town centre; bus #1 runs into town every 15–20 minutes, but only from 6am to sunset, after which the half-hourly #30 takes over until 11.30pm, its route extending along the coast boulevard down to the hotel strip. If you're in a hurry, jump into one of the private taxis waiting by the port gate; the trip into town shouldn't cost more than C£2.

Arriving by **long-distance bus**, you'll be dropped at one of the terminals shown on our map. Those driving their own vehicles should make for the public **car parks** on the seafront promenade, or privately operated ones inland along Elládhos.

The coastal boulevard, whose name changes first from **Spýrou Araoúzou** to **Khristodhoúlou Hadjipávlou**, then to Ikostiogdhóïs Oktovríou as you move northeast, is a fair fraction of what you need to know to get around in Limassol. Just inland, the main shopping street, **Ayíou Andhréou**, roughly parallels it out to the municipal gardens and archeological museum, while **Anexartisías**, threading the central downtown area, is the most important perpendicular. The main **tourist information** office (Mon–Fri 8.15am–2.30pm, Sat 8.15am–1.30pm, plus Mon 3–6.15pm, Thurs 3–6.30pm) sits at the west end of Spýrou Araoúzou (bus #15), but their stock of leaflets is not the greatest – owing to the British presence, material in English can disappear quickly. There's also a branch in the port terminal, open for boat arrivals.

The Limassol area phone code is ☎05.

Accommodation

Low-cost accommodation in Limassol is scarce, with little in between the funky guest houses of the bazaar, catering to refugees and those awaiting ferries to Israel or Greece, and the pricy package digs of the resort strip. Certain no- or one-star hotels, like the *Metropole* in the bazaar, or the *Panorama* in the red-light district, are worth avoiding.

Guest houses and pensions

Hellas, Zik Zak 9, just off Angíras behind the Cami Kabir (☎363841). Best placed and least weird of Limassol's ultra-budget accommodation, in a sparse but clean, old stone building. Some bathless rooms overlook the minaret and an atmospheric tradesmen's alley. ①.

Luxor Guest House, Ayíou Andhréou 101 (☎362265). On the pedestrianized portion of the shopping street, which is barred to night-time traffic, so quiet – though singles are dingy. ①.

Old Port Rooms to Let, Dhimitríou Mitropoúlou 7 (☎362447). Opened in 1995, excellently sited near the castle and the best value of this bunch; en-suite rooms, with attached café-restaurant providing snacks and breakfast. ①.

Moderately priced hotels

Aquarius, Potamós Yermasóyias district, just past the turning for Moutayáka village (☎322042, fax 312030). The only human-scale beachfront development along Limassol's "Riviera", this smallish, modest hotel has a pool, attractive rear gardens, its own patch of beach and a loyal return clientele. Also an affiliated scuba school (see p.88). ⑥.

Chez Nous Sunotel, Potamós Yermasóyias, roughly halfway between *Sunny Beach* and *Aquarius* (☎323033, fax 321228). Another smallish hotel, slightly inland but with a pool, available at even more advantageous rates if pre-booked as part of a package. ⑥.

Continental, Spýrou Araoúzou 137 (☎362530, fax 373030). Atmospheric two-star relic that's deservedly popular with the business trade; also a recommended restaurant (see p.87). ⑤.

Sunny Beach, Ikostiogdhóïs Oktovríou, at its extreme east end by the town limits (☎324626, fax 324606). Unmissable round structure, well placed across from the start of Dhassoúdhi beach and well priced for a two-star hotel. ⑤.

The City

Limassol presents a number of isolated points of interest rather than a town personality to savour: believe it or not, from 1974 to 1994 this was, numerically speaking, the number one tourist base in the South, but it won't take more than a full day, sandwiched between two overnights, to take in all there is to see.

The castle

Unassuming from the outside, **Limassol castle** stands in a pleasant garden immediately north of the old port. What you see today is a careful restoration of Byzantine foundations, Venetian vandalism, Turkish adaptation for military purposes and British justice (it was a jail during the colonial period). Tradition places, on May 12, 1191, the marriage of Richard the Lionheart and Berengaria in the long-vanished Byzantine chapel of St George, somewhere under the existing walls; anticipating his rout of Isaac, Richard also had himself crowned King of Cyprus and his bride Queen of England, in the presence of assorted Latin clerics and nobility.

Currently the castle houses the **Cyprus Medieval Museum** (Mon–Fri 7.30am–5pm, Sat 9am–5pm; C£0.50), though the building, with its musty, echoing vaults, air shafts and masonry groins, is as interesting as any of the exhibits, most of which are on the upper floor. The stress is on metalware, heraldry and sacred art, including bas-reliefs and pottery with Christian designs; the best bits are silver Byzantine plates showing events in the life of David, part of the Lambousa Treasure (see p.255), and two sets of armour from the Lusignan period (twelfth–fifteenth century). You can climb to the roof terrace, and then up the secondary tower, for excellent views over the town.

The bazaar

The neighbourhood surrounding the castle was once the Turkish commercial district, as street names will tell you, and its lanes are still worth a brief wander.

The **Cami** (pronounced "Jami") **Kabir**, its minaret visible from the castle roof, is still used by Limassol's Arab and remaining Turkish Cypriot population, though the **Cami Jedid** (also known as the Köprülü Hacı İbrahim Ağa mosque), at the far end of Angíras nearer the former Turkish residential quarter, is firmly locked. Also on Angíras, identifiable by a huge, fragrant eucalyptus in the yard, is a café that's much more genuine than the fast-food joints immediately around the castle. The latter alternate with tacky souvenir stalls; the **covered central market** may appeal more. A few minutes' walk past the Cami Kabir, beyond the hideous turn-of-the-century cathedral of Ayía Nápa, the old *mitrópolis* of **Áyios Andhrónikos**, built in mock-Byzantine style during the 1870s, hides in a cul-de-sac accessible only by a single alley from the waterfront.

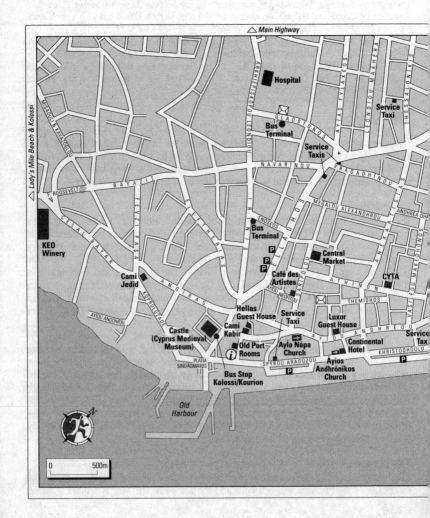

Winery tours

The city's four distilleries are strung in a row along Franklin Roosevelt, south-west of the old harbour; the regular morning tour laid on by *KEO*, the largest booze outfit on the island, is currently your only chance to visit this industry. Some parking in front of the plants is available, but it's a brief walk from the castle area, or a #19, #30, or #22 bus ride along Roosevelt – perhaps better options after the final tasting session.

To join the daily 10am tour at *KEO*, just show up at 9.50am (except in summer when you should book on ☎362053) in the reception area of the administration building, just behind the parking lot. In the space of about half an hour you're rather perfunctorily shown the cellars for the heavy, sweet Commandaria (see

p.33), where a third of each barrelful is retained as the *mána* or "mother" ferment for the next cycle; the distillery for *zivanía* (grape-mash spirit), used to fortify *KEO*'s line of hard liquor; the 40,000-litre oak ageing barrels for brandy; and barrels of sweet and cream sherry ageing out in the sun (the dry stuff stays in a dark cellar). The primarily middle-aged, British patrons barely suppress their eagerness for the tour to end at the tasting session, a wonderful excuse to get as pissed as you like for free, and before noon to boot (though you're encouraged to buy bottles from a sale counter). It is, in fact, a good opportunity to familiarize yourself with Cypriot wine types, to lessen the likelihood of getting stuck with an unlovely vintage in a taverna.

The Folk Art Museum

At the opposite end of Ayíou Andhréou, near the corner of Óthonos keh Amalías at no. 253, the **Folk Art Museum** has filled a grand old mansion with rural and domestic knick-knacks, woodwork, traditional dresses and jewellery (June–Sept Mon–Fri 8.30am–1.30pm & 4–6.30pm; Oct–May Mon–Wed & Fri 8.30am–1.30pm & 3–5.30pm, Thurs 8.30am–1.30pm; C£0.30). The lighting and labelling aren't good, however, and you're virtually obliged to buy the guide booklet to make much sense of the exhibits.

A short stroll northwest along Zínonos from Ayíou Andhréou will bring you to Platía Iróön, the heart of Limassol's **red-light district**, consisting of a dozen or so cabarets and a smaller number of inconspicuous one-storey brothels and divey, two-storey "pensions" in the narrow streets around. Of late the Thai and Filipino "artistes" of old have been replaced with Romanians and Russians, part of the tide of eastern Europeans from all walks of life to wash over the island in recent years.

The municipal gardens and the archeological museum

Beyond the Folk Art Museum sprawl the **municipal gardens**, a couple of acres of well-tended greenery fronting the sea, with a café offering good sandwiches. The gardens are the venue for the **September Wine Festival** (first half of the month) and at other times are an excellent place to wait for a ferry boat. There's also a **mini-zoo** (daily 9am–noon & 3–7pm; C£0.50), really mostly an aviary.

The district **archeological museum** is strongest on Archaic, Geometric and Bronze Age artefacts (Mon–Fri 7.30am–5pm, Sat 9am–5pm, Sun 10am–1pm; C£0.50). The left-hand gallery is ninety percent pottery, best of which are the Geometric-era dishes – an obvious inspiration for the modern woven circular wall-hangings you see everywhere in tavernas. Archaic terracotta figurines also abound, with what are thought to be toys scattered amongst the animal-drawn chariots and other votive offerings. Highlights include a *rhyton* in the form of a bull, and a headless torso with unusually detailed hands holding a bird to its chest. Female figures, possibly offerings for fertility, clasp their breasts or a mirror (a symbol of Aphrodite/Astarte), and one plays a frame-drum. A column capital in the guise of Hathor demonstrates the introduction of Egyptian gods to the island; bird-necked zoomorphic Bronze Age pots with vestigial noses and ears round out the hall's exhibits.

The smaller, central Classical room is sparsely stocked except for some gold and precious-stone jewellery; there's also a curious anthropomorphic lamp-stand, with ears for an oil wick and the head hollowed to accommodate a candle or incense. The Roman section on the right contains the usual painted and multi-coloured glass; incidentally, ancient glass was little different from modern products – the rainbow/oil-slick effect is the result of sodium and potassium ions leaching into the alkaline soils in which the objects were embedded before discovery.

Eating, drinking and nightlife

As with Larnaca, so with Limassol: the plastic-fantastic, steak-and-chips eateries along the waterfront are dismissable, but a bit of resourcefulness and expenditure of gasoline or shoe leather are well rewarded.

Seafront

Continental Hotel Restaurant, Spýrou Araoúzou 137. Good-value, three-course Cypriot meal for C£4, served 10.30am–10.30pm.

Glaros, 700m west of the old harbour at the end of Ayíou Andoníou. Fish restaurants – especially close to the old port – are generally overpriced in Limassol; this one, perched above the sea and favoured by locals, is one of the more reasonable, but still works out at about C£10 per person with drink. Open evenings and weekend lunchtimes only; ☎357046 for evening reservations.

Nityayia Far East Restaurant, at the entrance to the old harbour. Wrap-around aquarium decor to distract you from the relatively authentic Chinese, Japanese and Thai dishes. Count on about C£15 for two.

Seamen's Club, Spýrou Araoúzou, directly opposite the CTO. The canteen of the seamen's union, open to the public, is not nearly as grim as it sounds: straight-ahead Cypriot standards in fair-sized, moderately priced portions, with terrace seating towards the seafront (weather permitting).

Slow Boat, Khristodhoúlou Hadjipávlou 173. Despite (or perhaps because of) being largely staffed by returned London Cypriots, this is reckoned the best of Limassol's several Chinese eateries.

Old town and market area

Mikri Maria, Angíras 3, near corner Irínis. Characterful hole-in-the wall offering inexpensive Cypriot fare, most reliably at night; unfortunately "Little Mary" of the name has been unwell lately, so this restaurant's future is in doubt.

Le Petit Paris, Gládstonos, near corner Anexartisías. One of the few cake shops that offers seating and coffee as well.

Toh Sokaki, Irínis 80. Joint Israeli and Cypriot management offer good cooking and congenial atmosphere. Evenings only.

O Vasilikos, Ayíou Andhréou 252. Popular, slightly ritzy restaurant, lodged upstairs in an old house, with no menu, just several daily specials plus *mezé*. Live music at weekends may bump the price up even more.

Yermasóyia area

Lefteris, two-thirds of the way up the through road on the left, Yermasóyia village. The oldest, most characterful and still the best of the many tavernas here, which have made this dormitory village *the* evening place to eat near Limassol. Visually startling, with rural impedimenta worthy of a museum tucked in alcoves around the staggered flagstone seating terraces, and hundreds of customers' mementos pinned on the walls. If success has spoiled the cuisine a bit, the *mezé*-format meals are still excellent value at about C£5 per head. Reservations advised on ☎325211. Closed Sun.

Sole Mio, Yioryíou tou Prótou 7, Potamós Yermasóyias, 100m west of Dhassoúdhi beach entrance. A good Italian splurge, with dishes other than the usual pizza, but not cheap at about C£26 per couple for the works.

Drinking and nightlife

Name **musical acts** often perform at the *Pattikhio Theatre* on Ayías Zonís; watch
hoardings for details. Limassol can muster four **cinemas**: *Othellos*, Thessaloníkis
19 (☎352232); *Oscar* (☎374306); *Pallas* (☎362324); and *Hollywood* (☎362436). The
town centre also has a number of reasonable bars and music bars, mostly concentrated along or just off the west end of Ayíou Andhréou.

Alaloum, Ayíou Andhréou 216. One of the more lasting music bars in this area, which has
endured several closures in recent years.

Cafe des Artistes et Galerie, corner Ayíou Neofítou and Saripólou, between Ayíou
Andhréou and the central market. Courtyard restaurant and bar, with live music nightly; also
an upstairs gallery with frequently changing exhibits by foreign and Cypriot artists.

Ikho Evdhomindapende Boite, Ayíou Andhréou 259. Pub-like atmosphere, enhanced by a
pool table. The place also does duty as the headquarters of the local Green movement, as
distinct from Friends of the Earth. Occasional live music; open 6pm to midnight.

Irodhio, Ayíou Andhréou 238. "Bar-café-crêperie" in an old mansion.

Listings

Bookstores *Ioannidhes*, Athinón 30, is best for books on Cyprus and also for Department of
Lands and Surveys maps; *Kyriakou* is a more English-orientated general-purpose bookstore
at Gríva Dhiyení 3; *Tereza's Book Swop*, Athinón 14–18, features a large stock of secondhand
paperbacks.

Bus companies Useful outfits include *KEMEK/Kallenos*, to Larnaca, Nicosia, Páfos and
select Tróödhos villages, corner Irínis and Enóseos (☎363241); *Costas Bus*, Thessaloníkis
9B, to Nicosia and Páfos (☎354394); *Platres*, Eleftherías 50 (☎362907); and *Agros Bus*, at the
KEMEK terminal.

Car rental *Andy Spyrou/Europcar*, Omonías 38–40 (☎371441); *Astra/Eurodollar*, Yioryíou
tou Prótou, Seagate Block 1, Potamós Yermasóyias (☎323365); *Leo's* (reckoned the least
expensive), Yioryíou tou Prótou, River Plaza Complex, Block 1, Suite 7, Potamós
Yermasóyias (☎321271); *Petsas/Budget*, Yioryíou tou Prótou, Sea Breeze Block 1, Potamós
Yermasóyias; *Rent-a-Reliable*, Yioryíou tou Prótou, Belmar Complex C, Shop 5C, Potamós
Yermasóyias (☎312345); *Sea Island*, Neapolis Centre G1–3, Ithákis (☎374728).

Exchange There are plenty of banks in the bazaar. *Barclays* on Spýrou Araoúzou, near the
tourist office, has the most convenient of several ATMs for *Visa* cardholders; *Access/
Mastercard*-accepting machines are at the *Ethniki Trapeza/National Bank* branches opposite
the central post office branch off Athinón, and 400m west of Dhassoúdhi beach gate.

Ferry agents *Salamis Tours*, Salamis House, Khristodhoúlou Hadjipávlou 179, corner
Katsounótou (☎355555), for the *Nissos Kypros*; *Oriana Cruise Lines* (no address available;
☎340111), for the *Vergina* or *Queen Vergina*; *Amathus Navigation*, Sindágmatos 2, entrance
to the old harbour (☎341043), for *Poseidon Lines* ships such as the *Sea Harmony*, *Sea Wave*
and *Sea Serenade*. For a description of routes and prices, see p.6.

Laundry Anastási Shoúkri 20 (formerly Kánningos), near the archeological museum (Mon–
Fri during normal shopping hours; service wash only, for C£3).

Bicycles *Micromania*, Kránou 15, Potamós Yermasóyias, for mountain bikes; *Kostakis
Aristidhou* on Irínis does reasonable and quick repairs and servicing.

Post offices Main branch, with late afternoon hours and parcel/poste restante service,
somewhat inconveniently located on Gládstonos; more central branch for outbound letters
just off Athinón in the bazaar.

Scuba schools *Aquarius*, attached to the namesake hotel in Potamós Yermasóyias
(☎326652); *Nikos*, Spýrou Araoúzou 47 (☎372667); *PADI*, 12km east of town at the yacht
marina gate (☎326576).

Service taxis *Makris*, Elládhos 166 (☎365550), goes to Nicosia, Larnaca and Páfos; *Kyriakos/Karydas*, Thessaloníkis 21 (☎364114), has services to Nicosia and Páfos; *Kypros*, Hadjipávlou 193 (☎363979), goes only to Nicosia; *Acropolis*, Spýrou Araoúzou 49 (☎366766), serves only Larnaca; and *Nea Pafos*, Vragadhínou 1 (☎355355), is, predictably, devoted to Páfos.

Shopping *Cyprus Handicraft Service*, Themídhos 25, off Anexartisías, which carries government-vetted and fixed-priced stock of typical crafts is worth stopping in to get an idea of the range of products available. *Skaraveos*, Ayíou Andhréou 236, sells unusual, though not cheap, glass and ceramic souvenirs and *objets d'art*. At the *Workshop of Ceramic Art*, Khrístou Sózou, between Ayíou Andhréou and Spýrou Araoúzou, you'll find highly idiosyncratic, often eerie, work by Pambos Mikhlis, displayed in an old house just behind the seafront.

Telephones CYTA is at the corner of Athinón and Márkou Bótsari (daily 7am–7pm).

Yacht trips *Sail Fascination* (PO Box 257; ☎364200, fax 352657) offers a selection of day and overnight sailing trips out of Limassol old port.

The Limassol foothills

Inland from Limassol, the foothills of the Tróödhos range are home to a substantial fraction of Cyprus' commercial **vineyards**; otherwise there's little other significant economic activity as far as the outside world is concerned. Many of the villages, set amidst poor terrain covered in maquis vegetation, are dying, with futures only as weekend retreats for city-dwellers, holiday homes for foreigners, or artists' colonies.

The rise to the highest peaks of the Tróödhos is not straightforward: roads going inland rollercoaster past the first set of barrier ridges into hollows and hidden valleys that contain most of the places described below. Outsiders are most likely to pass through the various settlements just off the two main highways up towards the Tróödhos, the **E601** and the **B8**, which begin at **Erími** and **Polemídhia** respectively on the Limassol coastal plain. At one time or another most of these places were fiefs of the Hospitallers or other Lusignan nobility; they are mostly between 600 and 800 metres above sea level, which results in a pleasant climate even in high summer.

The westerly Tróödhos approach: the Krassokhoriá

The large villages clustered near the top of the westerly route towards the Tróödhos are collectively labelled the **Krassokhoriá** (wine villages) in CTO promotion, and whether or not anyone else calls them by this name, they are indeed renowned for their dry wine. At vintage time in autumn, huge lorries groaning with grapes lumber along the mostly narrow roads, and signs warn of grape-juice slicks on the pavement.

Vouní

Your first likely detour from the E601 is just past Áyios Amvrósios, a seven-kilometre drive towards mostly abandoned but highly picturesque **VOUNÍ**, where the remaining elders sit at a few *kafenía* on the *Paliostráta*, the old high street. The village has recently been listed as a protected architectural showcase, and the few ongoing renovations are to be carried out with traditional materials and methods. But so far there's little other evidence of gentrification, and the only tourist amenity is the British-run *Vouni Tavern*, on the main bypass road towards Kiláni (☎323601 to verify meal hours).

Kiláni and Ayía Mávra

KILÁNI, 5km northeast along a much better road than maps imply, is architecturally less of a piece but more lively; there's an artist's studio here and a pedestrianized area with several *kafenía*, one of which serves *muhalebí* (rose-water flavoured jelly) as a sweet, a disappearing recipe remembered nostalgically by any Cypriot over thirty. Behind the ugly modern church of Panayía Eleoússa, the Limassol archbishopric has set up an **ecclesiastical museum** of items scoured from crumbling churches roundabout. It's a better-than-average collection, with a stress on intricately crafted sacred objects as well as icons. Hang purposefully about the church square and a rather demented old man will accost you, admit you to the two-room exhibit and thrust an informative leaflet in your hands. Evidently Kiláni was chosen as the venue for its past importance in church affairs; nearly a half-dozen bishops of the sixteenth to eighteenth centuries hailed from here, and indeed the archbishopric of Limassol itself was based here for some years during the seventeenth century, when Limassol was at its nadir.

Continuing a kilometre up the valley of the Krýos stream from Kiláni, you can't possibly miss the twelfth-century chapel of **Ayía Mávra**, set in the river gorge by some trees and a handful of *exokhiká kéndra* or rural weekenders' tavernas. The little church is all that remains of a much larger monastery, and a spring still burbles from the apse; according to legend the water flows from a cleft in the rock created when Mávra, pursued against her will by her father and proposed fiancé, appealed to the Virgin to preserve her vow of chastity – and was promptly swallowed by the low cliff. This tale, told with variations around the Greek Orthodox world, is a revamping of the pagan legend of Daphne pursued by Apollo; in fact, the historical Mávra supposedly married St Timothy. Inside are some smudged fifteenth-century frescoes, but *Ayios Timotheos* (St Timothy) and *Mávra* herself have been cleaned, and face you as you enter (the key is always in the door); a rendition of *The Virgin Enthroned* graces the conch of the apse.

Potamioú and Vássa

At Kissoúsa a right turn off the E601, followed by another at the next junction, leads up to **POTAMIOÚ**, arguably more beautiful than Vouní and graced by the sixteenth-century Ayía Marína church, plus the ruins of Byzantine Áyios Mnáson outside the village, in the streambed of the Khapótami.

Bearing left instead at the second junction brings you to **VÁSSA**, 35km from Limassol and focus of one of the better-executed **restored accommodation** schemes. George Argyrides manages *Village Houses*, five premises of different sizes (☎364718 or 243863, fax 346333), beginning at C£20 each per day from March through November. You needn't be running downhill for everything, as there are sufficient facilities in Vássa, including the hilltop view **taverna** in the old schoolhouse, serving excellent country cooking among the trees.

Ómodhos

Three kilometres beyond either Potamioú or Vássa brings you to the more heavily promoted **ÓMODHOS**, unusually laid out around its **monastery of Timíou Stavroú** (the Holy Cross), with a vast cobbled square leading up to it – probably an instance of Lusignan town planning, since rarely in the Greek world is a monastery the core of a settlement. Although of Byzantine foundation, what you see now dates entirely from the early and mid-nineteenth century. Dositheos and

Khryssanthos, sponsors and abbots of the monastery during its late medieval revival, were hanged by the Ottoman authorities with various others in 1821 when news of the mainland Greek rebellion reached the island. Since 1917 the monastery has been empty of monks, and Orthodox pilgrims visit principally for the sake of purported Crucifixion relics kept inside the otherwise undistinguished church. The gallery of the upper storey is sporadically open, and worth the climb up for its intricate woodwork. This includes carved lattice railings along the walkway past wooden cell doors; at the northeast corner of the enclosure, wood ornamentation reaches new heights in the fantastic bishop's room, with its carved ceiling and cabinets lining the east wall.

The village itself is pleasant enough, despite written and verbal blandishments to visit rather bogus traditional houses and an alarming concentration of *Visa* and *Access* signs. Best souvenir buys might be bottles of the red and white local wine – *Gerolemo* is particularly recommended – or *loukoúmia* (Turkish delight); only some of the basketry and lace displayed here are locally crafted. A number of simple restaurants and cafés alternate with the souvenir displays on the field-stoned plaza that slopes down to the monastery's portal. The liveliest time to visit would probably be September 14, when the monastery church functions as the focus of the festival of the Holy Cross, which spills out onto the square outside.

Malliá, Ársos and the ridge route to Páfos

MALLIÁ, overlooking a major junction near the end of the E601 with bearings for Vássa, Ársos and Dhorá, was the largest Turkish Cypriot village in the Limassol hills; since 1974 it has been barely occupied by Greek Cypriot refugees, and its western, clifftop neighbourhood, tipped with minarets, stands desolate.

ÁRSOS, 3km north, is much the largest of the *Krassokhoriá*, and while it's an attractive, stone-built village, there's nothing in particular to see other than the **Laona winery** (☎243200 for arranging visits). This was long reckoned one of the best small vintners on the island, but recently it was bought up by major player *ETKO*, so continued quality can no longer be automatically assumed.

From Ársos you can easily carry on to Áyios Nikólaos, near the head of the Dhiárizos valley (see p.150), or backtrack slightly to follow an interesting ridge route into Páfos district, following the east flank of the valley, with spectacular views west to the Páfos hills. **DHORÁ**, the remotest of the *Krassokhoriá*, is an attractive place on the brow of a ridge whose narrow lanes may repay parking your vehicle and exploring on foot. The authorities are currently extending the paved surface 2km southwest to the district boundary at tiny **MOÚSERE** hamlet, half-abandoned in the greenery hiding it and doubtless the next target for artist-restorers. You then face five rough, unpaved kilometres before asphalt resumes at Arkhimandhríta, from where it's plain sailing down to Koúklia (see p.122).

The easterly Tróödhos approach: artists' colonies

The more heavily used of the two main highways to the Tróödhos, the B8 up from Exit 28 of the coastal expressway, is also the duller route; there's little to prompt a halt until the short turning left to **MONÁGRI**, about 20km out of Limassol. Here the **monastery of Arkhángelos**, founded in the twelfth century, overlooks vineyards and the Koúris river valley. The eighteenth-century church and the grounds have recently been restored by the Monagri Foundation, headed by Richard and Judy Sale, to serve as a gallery and artists' studios and accommodation, with the full cooperation of the Bishop of Limassol and the Department of Antiquities. The twelfth-century monastic church of **Panayía Amasgoú**, 3km downriver from the village on the west bank, has fine frescoes from four periods up to the sixteenth century; the nuns of the surrounding convent will show you around.

A little further up the B8 on the right is the one-kilometre sideroad to **LÁNIA**, an entire village which some years ago was bought up and tastefully renovated as an artists' colony. Saturday is open-house day for the various studios, when the incongruously hideous **taverna** on Lánia's outskirts also does a thriving trade.

Eastern hill villages

Perhaps the most isolated and forlorn of the villages in the Limassol foothills are a cluster near the border of Larnaca district, described in a deceptively well-written CTO pamphlet entitled "Remote Villages of Cyprus". While the text doesn't quite make the area out to be some miniature version of Tuscany, you do need to take the descriptions with a grain of salt.

Easiest access to this area is via either the Yermasóyia or Parekklishá exits of the Limassol–Nicosia expressway. The former side road is a bit better, running 22km out of Yermasóyia to Dhieróna and **ARAKAPÁS**, with its much-restored Latin church of **Panayía Iamatikí** on the outskirts as the road turns east towards Eptagónia. The two latter villages are the closest things to going concerns here-abouts, with olive and mandarin orchards providing a precarious living.

The twistier road in from Parekklishá emerges after 16km on a knoll at **KELLÁKI**, with a grand view of the ridges of Pitsiliá on the far side of the valley. But otherwise neither Kelláki nor its neighbour Prastío, downhill to the west, are up to much, despite a hopeful sign "Area Tourist Information Here" at the Kelláki *kafenío*. The main problem, from a tourist-development point of view, is that just enough money has trickled in to finance a certain amount of unsightly improvements and ruin the architectural homogeneity of the places.

You may get a better idea of local vernacular architecture by following the tourist board's suggested detour east of Kelláki. **KLONÁRI** hamlet, some 6km east, has a fine church of Áyios Nikólaos, bare inside though built in the standard Tróödhos style (see p.166), but the tenants of the smelly dovecotes far outnumber the remaining humans. The dozen houses of **VÍKLA**, a couple of dirt-road kilometres further, are completely abandoned despite a fine setting; the best road on to Akapnoú takes off from Klonári, not from here as most maps indicate. **AKAPNOÚ**, to the north on a hillock surrounded by relatively fertile and well-watered land, has retained about thirty inhabitants and some attractive houses; though the people are friendly enough, the place is visibly poor, with next to nothing on offer at the *kafenío* by the square, with its recent but appealing church of Áyios Yióryios. West of the village, in the fields, the small chapel of **Panayía tou Kámbou** boasts some sixteenth- and seventeenth-century frescoes.

You return to the main road at **EPTAGÓNIA**, like Arakapás a relatively busy place; west, on the road between the two, a new purpose-built primary school serves the region's children, the individual village schools long since having closed down. **MELÍNI**, 4km north, has another standard-issue gabled church and marks the start of the impressive climb up to **ODHOÚ**, at the edge of the high Tróödhos and actually just over the border into Larnaca district. Marvellously set amidst 850-metre crags overlooking the canyon up which you've come, the village itself is again an unhappy architectural hotch-potch, modest prosperity having prompted some cheap and easy renovations; it enjoys some summer day-trip trade owing to its cool climate.

Beyond Odhoú an extremely steep dirt road climbs to an 1100-metre pass in the Pitsilian ridges; once over the watershed, paved road appears simultaneously with a view down onto handsomely spread-out Farmakás and Kámbi (see p.183), your reward for getting a car this far.

East of Limassol: the coast

The town beach at Limassol, stony and flanked by intermittent breakwaters, is pretty forgettable; recognizing this, the CTO has improved a beach at **Dhassoúdhi**, about 4km east of town near the edge of Potamós Yermasóyias. But you really need to travel further towards Larnaca before reaching any monuments of interest, or patches of fairly natural coastline.

Amathus (Amathoúnda)

Some 13km east of Limassol town centre, just before the end of the resort strip, **ancient Amathus** (fenced but gate unlocked, no fee) is signposted just inland from the coast road. Limassol city **buses** #6 and #30 pass the site.

Some history
Amathus is among the oldest of Cyprus' city-kingdoms, with a purported foundation by a son of Hercules, who was revered as a god here. The legend seems to indicate settlement by the original island colonists, with a later Phoenician religious and racial overlay. In some versions of the myth Ariadne, fleeing from the labyrinth on Crete, was abandoned here and not on Aegean Naxos by Theseus; she died here in childbirth, and was buried in a sacred grove, where her cult melded easily with that of Aphrodite. Lightly Hellenized, and prone to worshipping Egyptian gods as well as Asiatic ones, Amathus sided with Persia against Salamis and the other Cypriot kingdoms during the fifth- and fourth-century BC revolts, though it later declared for Alexander the Great.

The Romans made it capital of one of the four administrative districts of the island; this anticipated a bishopric in Byzantine times, when it was the birthplace of St John the Almoner, patron of the Order of the Knights Hospitaller. But decline and destruction ensued after the seventh century, and the city was largely forgotten until the nineteenth century, when its tombs to the west were looted and much of its dressed stone taken to Egypt to line the locks of the new Suez Canal.

The site
Of the place itself, you see mostly a vast paved **agora**, studded with a dozen restored and re-erected columns, including three spiral-fluted and two square ones. In the middle of the area, a square foundation filled with rubble and masonry fragments had an uncertain function – either an altar base, or the centre of a stoa. Under a corrugated-roof shelter are more column chunks and pediments which await final disposition, all found since excavations resumed in 1975.

Backed into the bluff at the northwest end of the marketplace is what appears to be an elaborate **waterworks system**: the flow of a niche-spring was diverted through tunnels to sluices, feeding a small basin at the head of more channels running to a pair of large cisterns. Some water appears to have run through open gutters, but you can still see a conspicuous large water-main which, exposed, leads some way out into the marketplace. A stepped street leads up the partly excavated slope past rows of Hellenistic-era **houses**.

At the seaward end of the agora, the symbolism in some pebbled floor mosaics suggests that a round precinct containing them may be the foundations of a **Christian basilica**. The site is still unlabelled and thus less rewarding than it might be; a raised viewing dais near the presumed basilica will hopefully get a site plan installed on it soon.

Up on the bluff is the ancient acropolis, with stretches of defensive **walls** and the remains of a **temple** jointly dedicated to Aphrodite and Hercules. Across the road, towards the sea, are more sections of wall and traces of the ancient port, now submerged to a distance of several hundred yards from the shoreline; earthquake and subsidence have laid them low. It is claimed that Richard the Lionheart landed at this particular bay in May 1191, to begin his march on Limassol.

Governor's Beach (Aktí Kivernítou)

Something resembling undeveloped beaches can be found 29km east of Limassol at **Governor's Beach**, right on the district border and just a few kilometres off the expressway at Exit 16. Despite the singular name, this is not one but several coves at the base of the low chalk cliffs here, endowed with fine, contrastingly dark sand that fills quickly on warm weekends. Each cove is lorded over by rustic **tavernas**, each of these claiming to be at the "real" beach.

The road from the expressway forks almost immediately, and the left-hand turning splits again, each junction festooned with contradictory signs. The right-hand option leads to the *Adamos* taverna, overlooking the broadest, cleanest stretch of sand and sunbeds, with *Sofroniou* nearby; *Faros*, as the name (Lighthouse) implies, is out on a rocky cape beyond, looking towards the ugly cement plant at Vasilikós which mars the area. The coves on the far left are narrower and cliff-girt, served by the cheap, cheerful and mildly eccentric *Panayiotis* and overlooked by the adjacent *Kalymnos* **campsite**; this is rather bleak and shadeless, popular with caravans which seem to be semi-permanently installed here but not really suitable for tents.

The Akrotíri peninsula

At the southwest end of Limassol, near the entrance to the new port, you're presented with a choice of means for leaving the city: along the minor, eventually unpaved road paralleling the Akrotíri peninsula's east shore, or roughly west across the base of the peninsula to the Fassoúri plantations.

Lady's Mile Beach

Known as **Lady's Mile Beach** in honour of a mare named Lady that a British officer used to exercise here, the east shore is, in fact, closer to four miles of grey, hardpacked sand. Little development has taken place because it's the property of the British Ministry of Defence and also because, with a mosquito-ridden salt lake behind, it's not very good as a beach (though the bird life in the lake is rewarding; see "Wildlife" in *Contexts*). The barely sloping tidal flats are better for jogging (and dune-buggying, as dozens of locals do) than sunbathing. Every few hundred metres there's an impermanent-looking café or taverna catering for the weekend crowds of city people, but camping is not allowed as, surprisingly, parts of the beach are supposedly a turtle-nesting area. Occasional summer **buses** venture beyond the #1 and #30 terminus at Limassol's new harbour.

Ayíou Nikoláou ton Gáton and Akrotíri

At the south end of Lady's Mile, the dirt track takes a bend inland to follow the south shore of the salt lagoon; after less than a kilometre an unsigned driveway on the left wiggles through a gap in the fence and past hedgerows to the grounds of the convent of **Ayíou Nikoláou ton Gáton** (St Nicholas of the Cats).

The peculiar name springs from a wonderful Byzantine **legend**, according to which St Helena imported hundreds of cats from Egypt or Palestine, at the time of St Nicholas' fourth-century foundation, to control the population of poisonous snakes which infested the place. The monks at what was originally a monastery would summon their moggies to meals by the tolling of a bell, and another bell would send them out into the surrounding fields to battle the serpents, so that "nearly all were maimed [in the words of a visiting Venetian monk of 1484]: one has lost a nose, another an ear; the skin of one is torn, another is lame; one is blind of one eye, another of both."

The habit of keeping cats to battle the island's numerous snakes spread quickly to most of the other Cypriot monasteries, and also to Rhodes; when the Knights Hospitaller of St John moved there, they are said to have taken a whole shipload of cats with them. More recently, the Greek Nobel laureate George Seferis used the inter-species struggle as a metaphor for opposition to the dictatorship then in power in Greece, in virtually his last published poem "The Cats of St Nicholas":

> *Wildly obstinate, always wounded,*
> *They annihilated the snakes, but in the end they were lost,*
> *They just couldn't endure so much poison . . .*

The contemporary reality of Ayíou Nikoláou is not so lofty: a working cloister, recently remodelled and of little architectural interest other than a fine coat of arms over the door of the thirteenth-century church. Today the convent is home to a handful of aged nuns and – still – dozens of cats, many as ragged-looking as those seen by the Venetian. They stalk about like the denizens of a temple to the Egyptian cat-god which may once have stood here, and Cape Gáta (She-Cat), out past the runway of the Akrotíri airfield, is named for them, too.

Akrotíri

The main dirt access road heads west back to asphalt at the village of **AKROTÍRI**, distinguished mainly by the privilege of dual nationality for its inhabitants – it is the only Cypriot village not excluded from Sovereign Base territory – and the improbable number of tavernas, aimed at the dependants of Her Majesty's Finest. They are stationed beyond the checkpoint to the south, in a no-go area; you have to turn northwest towards Fassoúri and Kolossi, passing close by a forest of listening and transmitting devices.

THE BRITISH SOVEREIGN BASES

One of the conditions of Cypriot independence in 1960 was the setting aside of a certain percentage of the island's area as British military bases, known as the **Sovereign Base Areas** or SBAs for short. In fact, the date of nationhood was delayed by disputes over the exact size of the SBAs, which eventually resulted in a figure of about 99 square miles. Most of this area consists of the Episkopí Garrison, around the village of that name; the adjoining Akrotíri Air Field; and the Dhekélia Base between Larnaca and Ayía Nápa. The borders of the bases were drawn in such a way as to exclude almost all private land and villages – the only exception being Akrotíri village. In addition to these main bases, fifteen so-called "retained sites" or annexes are scattered across the South; the most conspicuous of these include the RAF radar domes on Mount Olympus, the BBC transmitters at Zíyi, and the posted artillery range on the Akámas Peninsula.

Technically the bases form British Dependent Territories administered by a military governor, though the population of about 9000 (roughly half servicemen, the rest their dependants and other civilians) is subject to a civil legal system based closely on Cypriot law. Justice is dispensed at a courthouse and jail, which in 1992 held two British airmen accused of espionage; after considerable expenditure of taxpayers' money, the prosecutor's case collapsed in an ignominy of poor documentation. The highly publicized 1995–96 trial of three squaddies, accused of raping and murdering a Danish tour courier near Ayía Nápa, was conducted in a Cypriot court, because the offence occurred outside base territory. As a result of this crime, British forces are now unwelcome at many resorts; perhaps not coincidentally, security is now quite tight within the SBAs, with all vehicles liable to be stopped and checked by the distinct SBA police force, and photography strictly forbidden. Relatives of service personnel, and ex-servicemen who have served with the British Army or with the UN, might wish to write to the Commanding Officer before leaving the UK to arrange for a base pass to spare embarrassment and inconvenience. Otherwise, there is no formal border control: the main indications that you've entered a base are a sudden outbreak of UK-style street signs, with names like Pembridge Housing Estate or Yorkshire Road, and Cat's-eye reflectors in the middle of the road. South Cypriots as well as foreigners circulate freely across SBA boundaries, and some 2300 Greek Cypriots have jobs on the two largest bases.

Strangely, about 300 Turkish Cypriots also continue to work at the Dhekélia base; they enter via the "Four Mile Crossing", a thin sliver of British territory abutting the outskirts of Famagusta, and the Attila Line. With the proper identification, British forces and their families can also cross in the other direction. After August 1974, almost 10,000 Turkish Cypriots from the Limassol area, escaping reprisal attacks by EOKA-B, sought shelter in the Episkopí base for six months, until they were airlifted out to Turkey – and from there to the North.

The official rationale for the bases' 1960 establishment and continued existence asserts their vital importance to British strategic interests as listening posts, east Mediterranean airfields, and warm-winter training areas. Indeed Britain's 1878 acquisition of Cyprus as a complement to Malta and Gibraltar, and stubborn retention of the island in the face of nationalist agitation, was premised on such logic. But it is more an irony of history than a demonstration of accidental foresight that only since the late 1950s, with the winding up of empire and successive Middle Eastern crises, have the SBAs come to play the role originally envisioned for the whole island.

West to Kolossi and Kourion

The good road west from near the Limassol new harbour, signed towards Asómatos and Fassoúri, is the most scenic route to Kolossi and Kourion, far less dangerous and no longer than the main inland highway. Giant cypresses, planted long ago as windbreaks, have grown up to form lofty tunnels over the road; eucalyptus clumps drained the swamps here and allowed extensive orange groves to flourish. At roadside stalls near the *Red Seal Plantation*, you can buy giant sacks of the fruit, the cheapest in the South.

Kolossi

Long before citrus, sugar cane and grapes were cultivated in this area; the **castle of Kolossi** (June–Sept daily 7.30am–7.30pm; Oct–May daily 7.30am–5pm; C£0.50; frequent #16 or #17 **bus** from Limassol, Mon–Fri only), just south of the village of that name, still stands evocatively amid the vineyards that helped make it famous. Its story is also linked inextricably with the Hospitallers, whose *commanderie* it was, the name later bestowed on the rich dessert wine, Commandaria.

The Knights were first granted land here in 1210 by the Lusignans, and the castle that grew up became their headquarters after the Crusaders' final loss of the Holy Land. Even after the Order shifted to Rhodes exactly a century later, the Knights kept Kolossi as the headquarters of their local fiefs, which included dozens of foothill villages. Mameluke raids of the fifteenth century virtually levelled the original castle, later rebuilt on a smaller scale; in 1488 the Venetians appropriated it, along with the Order's other holdings. The Ottomans allowed the place to fall slowly into disrepair until the British restoration of 1933.

Today's three-storey, keep-style structure stands among the ruins of a much larger castle; from the **coat of arms** of the Grand Master Louis de Magnac, set into the east wall, a date of approximately 1450 has been deduced for the earlier restoration. Modern stairs have replaced a defensive retractable ramp up to the first-floor door; the ground floor with its vital well, in effect a three-chambered storage basement, originally had no entrance from outside. In the left-hand, vaulted room of the middle storey, probably the kitchen, you'll see the first of several huge **fireplaces**, more appropriate to northern European chateaux and not equalled on the island since. By the spiral stairway in the other room, a glass plate protects a damaged **fresco** of *The Crucifixion*. The upper storey has thinner walls, and two grand halls perpendicular to those below – presumably the quarters of de Magnac, as his heraldry again appears on one of the two back-to-back fireplaces. Benches flanking most of the window niches add a homely touch. Steps continue to the flat roof-terrace, where machicolations over the gate permitted the pouring of noxious substances onto uninvited guests.

The other roofed building in the precinct is the **sugar factory**, a barn-like vaulted structure also buttressed externally; first the Knights, and later the Venetians produced sugar locally, though the establishment of slave-worked plantations in the Caribbean put paid to the Cypriot industry early in the Ottoman occupation. The still-visible cane-crushing millstone outside was watered by sluices fed in turn by a huge aqueduct, now shaded by a giant pepper tree, at the northeast corner of the grounds. Evidently the springs still ran until recently, as modern, metal-sheathed extensions of the spillways snake through burgeoning flower gardens. Within sight of the castle, to the northeast, the usually locked twelfth-century church of **Áyios Efstáthios** was the Knights' place of worship.

If you crave a meal after your visit, the *Kolossi Steak House* in the adjacent village is recommended not only for tender steaks, but also seafood. A bill for two won't exceed C£16 with drink.

Kourion (Curium)

Perched dramatically on a sheer bluff overlooking the sea, **Kourion** is easily the most spectacular of the South's archeological sites – even though close up some of its individual attractions may be out of bounds or incoherent while excavations continue. Kourion consists of two sites, entirely contained within the Episkopí Sovereign Base: the ancient city, closer to Kolossi, and the sanctuary of Apollo Hylates, a few kilometres west – you'll want half a day to see them both. The ruins lie about 5km west of Kolossi, and benefit from the same bus service. The **site museum** is some distance away from the old city, in the large village of **EPISKOPÍ**, and easier visited in tandem with Kolossi. Follow signs through Episkopí to the church of Ayía Paraskeví; the museum (Mon–Fri 7.30am–2pm, plus Sept–June Thurs 3–6pm; C£0.50), in the old rambling house once lived in by archeologist George McFadden, stands opposite. The collection, occupying two wings, consists largely of terracotta objects from Kourion, the sanctuary of Apollo and two minor sites nearby. While in Episkopí, you might lunch at the *Episkopi Village Inn*, centrally located opposite the *Bank of Cyprus*.

Some history

Despite discouraging water-supply problems, this easily defensible clifftop may have been first settled in Neolithic times, but a recognizable city only got underway following Mycenaean colonization between the fourteenth and twelfth centuries BC. Kourion played a leading – negative – role in the **Cypriot rebellion against Persia**; at a critical moment its king Stesenor defected to the enemy with a considerable body of troops, guaranteeing the island's re-subjugation. Like Amathus, however, it later championed Alexander against the Persians, and remained an important town throughout the Roman and early Byzantine periods; indeed, most of what can be seen today dates about evenly from those two eras. Following a cataclysmic earthquake in 365 AD, the city was utterly destroyed, and only tentatively rebuilt and resettled over the next few decades. After the seventh-century Arab raids, Kourion, like many other coastal settlements on Cyprus, was abandoned for good, and its bishop moved to nearby Episkopí.

The notorious American consul-turned-antiquarian **Luigi Palma di Cesnola** began excavating (or rather plundering) in 1865, and eleven years later claimed to have chanced on several untouched hoards of gold, silver, bronze and objects inlaid with precious stones, suggesting that Kourion had been far wealthier than anyone imagined. Even at the time many doubted his story, accusing him of doctoring the evidence and assembling the collection from his activities at various sites scattered across the island. Whatever, the troves were shortly sold en bloc to the New York Metropolitan Museum and came to be known as the **Curium Treasure**.

Between 1933 and 1954, George McFadden of the University of Pennsylvania carried out rather desultory **archeological excavations** at both the ancient city

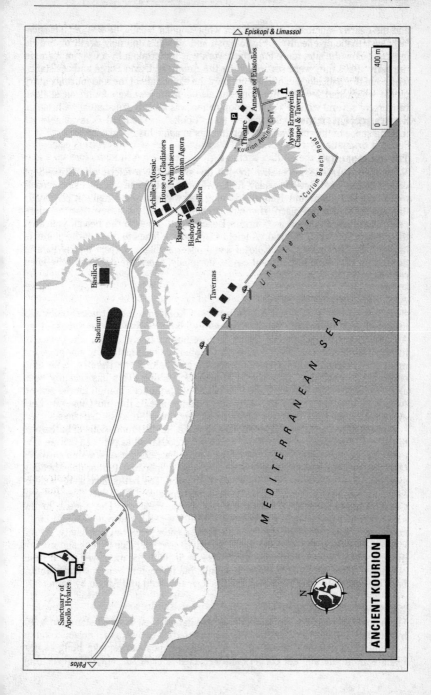

ANCIENT KOURION

△ Episkopí & Limassol

Baths
Annexe of Eustolios
Ayios Ermoyénis Chapel & Taverna
Theatre
Kourion Ancient City
Achilles Mosaic
House of Gladiators
Nymphaeum
Roman Agora
Baptistry
Bishop's Palace
Basilica
Curium Beach Road
Unsafe area
Basilica
Tavernas
Stadium
Sanctuary of Apollo Hylates
△ Pátos

MEDITERRANEAN SEA

400 m
0

N

and the nearby sanctuary of Apollo. But while popular locally, he was not a particularly systematic or effective archaeologist, and after his untimely death by drowning just below the site, more important work was undertaken by a Cypriot team. In the early 1980s they were succeeded by the American David Soren and assistants, who soon dramatically established not only the exact date of the mid-fourth-century quake which had levelled Kourion, but also – from jewellery found on skeletal remains of several victims – that its population was already substantially Christian. Soren's account of these discoveries (see "Books" in *Contexts*) is invaluable for making sense of the ruins, and placing the city in some historical context.

The ancient city

More than usual, it's imperative to visit the site of the **ancient city** (June–Sept daily 7.30am–7pm; Oct–May daily 7.30am–5pm; C£0.50) early or late, since coach tours between 10am and 1pm utterly clog the walkways and make it physically impossible to see the place. If you're driving yourself, be aware that the more prominent turnoff signed as "Curium Beach Road" goes to the beach; you want the next turnoff west, "Kourion Ancient City", which leads to most of the points of interest. **Public buses**, via Kolossi and Episkopí village, depart hourly 9am to noon from just outside Limassol castle; curiously, there are only two scheduled returns, at 11.50am and 2.50pm.

EASTERN HIGHLIGHTS

"Kourion Ancient City" road passes traces of Kourion's ancient **necropolis** and the medieval chapel of **Áyios Ermoyénis**, built to house the relics of an Anatolian martyr whose coffin floated ashore here; a lively festival takes place in the surrounding eucalyptus grove each October 5. Once inside the site gate, the main car park and bus turn-around area is just behind the **theatre**, a second-century AD reworking of an earlier Hellenistic version. This has recently been again brashly restored, and is used for performances in high tourist season (watch for posters locally with acts and ticket venues); the most famous, held every year since 1961, are the mid-June and September Shakespeare plays.

Immediately northeast, under sheltering roofs, lie the foundations of **baths** and the so-called **annexe of Eustolios**, which were both built as part of a private villa in the late fourth century AD, and later donated for public use. Wooden catwalks take you around and above the baths' intricate hypocaust (under-floor heating system), plus the celebrated fifth-century **mosaics**. The baths have as their highlight, in the central room, mosaics of a partridge and of Ktisis, the spirit of Creation personified as a woman holding a rule measure. The annexe to the south features on its atrium pavement a beautiful panel showing fish and birds, commonly used decorative symbols during the early years of Christianity. A long inscription reflects the establishment of Christianity: "In place of rock and iron, or gleaming bronze and diamonds, this house is girt with the much-venerated signs of Christ." Two others, at the west vestibule, bid the visitor welcome and mention both the original owner Eustolios and the former patron god Apollo by name.

WESTERN HIGHLIGHTS

From the car park the track continues hesitantly west some distance to a 70-metre-long fifth-century **basilica**, once supported by two sets of a dozen columns but now quite ruinous. Working with straitened, post-earthquake budgets, the bishops quite literally cut corners and recycled ancient masonry wherever they could. At the southwest, narthex end you can admire the view over the sea and also an unusual, deep hexagonal **fountain**.

Next door the smaller **baptistry**, of a slightly later date, is in better condition, with more complete geometric floor mosaics and the odd standing column. In the middle is another hexagonal pool for holy water, and on the south side of the nave a marble-lined, cruciform font which shows signs of having been modified for infant baptism once the entire adult population of Kourion had been converted. At the seaward end of the building, some surviving arches are thought to be part of a **bishop's palace**.

All of the monuments north and east of the basilica, baptistry and bishop's palace have been off-limits since 1975 owing to ongoing excavations. Moreover, in 1994 the supplementary north entrance to the ancient city off the Limassol–Páfos road was blocked off, and a disused CTO pavilion and site ticket office next to the baptistry demolished. Descriptions of the following sites are included in hopes that they will soon be opened to the public.

The Roman **agora**, with its stretch of re-erected second-century colonnade, is flanked by the **nymphaeum** (fountain-house), once fed by an aqueduct which also must have supplied some conspicuous baths. Excavation barriers may or may not permit an on-tiptoe glimpse of the late Roman "**House of Gladiators**" and the **Achilles Mosaic**. The former takes its name from a floor mosaic of two gladiators in combat, attended by a referee; all the figures are named with inscriptions, and presumably were stalwarts of contests in the nearby theatre. The badly damaged Achilles Mosaic shows Odysseus detecting Achilles disguised as a maiden; the same building, possibly used for public functions, has a panel of Ganymede being kidnapped by Zeus disguised as an eagle.

The beach

The **beach** southwest of the ruins is reachable by one of two roads past Áyios Ermoyénis and its attendant *exokhiko kéndro*. Once you're clear of the prominently marked unsafe area, the water is cleaner and deeper (beyond the pink buoys) than the 800m of hard-packed sand suggests. The swimmable end of the beach is dotted with a number of impromptu **tavernas**, their minimalist construction, like the ones at Lady's Mile, owed to short-term concessions from the British; the *Sunshine Tavern*, with such delicacies as grilled pigeon, is perhaps the best of the bunch.

The sanctuary of Apollo Hylates

At the large sacred complex surrounding the sanctuary of Apollo Hylates (same hours as Kourion; C£0.50), about 2km west of Kourion proper, Apollo was worshipped as the god of the surrounding woodland and as protector of the pre-Christian city. Today a huge RAF antenna farm west of the sanctuary distracts somewhat from the atmosphere, but it is still an attractive archeological site.

The sacred precinct was consecrated during the eighth century BC, but the present buildings are early Roman, flattened by the great earthquake of 365 AD. The two ancient **gates**, that of Paphos on the west and of Kourion on the east, are no longer intact, though the path from the ticket office passes the stumps of the former. On the right, before reaching the Kourion gate, you'll see the **palaestra** area, in one corner of which still stands a large water jug, used by athletes to cool off. Beyond, to the northeast, the **baths** sprawl under a tin shelter protecting piles of hypocaust stones.

The **processional way** starts at the extensive **xenon** or inn for pilgrims, with its restored Doric colonnade, and passes the presumed **priests' quarters** and precinct walls as it climbs a slight slope to the partly restored **temple of Apollo**. Two columns, a wall corner, and an angle of the pediment enclose the altar area, open to the sky even in its day, and most holy; unauthorized individuals profaning it even with an inadvertent touch were hurled off the Kourion cliffs to appease the god's wrath. On the west side of the grounds, near the site of the Paphos gate, are the foundations of the **display hall** for votive offerings; between it and the processional way hides a curious round structure or **vothros**, not yet completely excavated, where it is surmised the priests discreetly disposed of old and surplus gifts to the god.

A curious and ubiquitous feature of the sanctuary are series of broad **stone channels** hacked out of the strata. Once thought to be aqueducts, current theory identifies them as planter boxes used by the priests of Apollo for landscaping the grounds in a manner fitting for a woodland god.

Not much is left of the imperial Roman **stadium** (access unrestricted), 500m to the east; it once seated six thousand, but now just a few rows of seats, and three gaps where the gates were, can be distinguished. On a knoll still further east, fenced but with its gate always open, a sixth-century **basilica** has a huge well in the floor, and traces of floor mosaic in the altar area. Much of the flooring, however, was found in 1974 to be marble plaques pilfered from the nymphaeum in the city, laid face down so that bas-reliefs of pagan mythological scenes would not offend Christian sensibilities.

West towards Páfos: beaches

The limits of the Episkopí Sovereign Base extend almost to the boundary of Páfos district, again having the happy side effect (whatever you think of its political wisdom) of protecting the local coast from gross despoliation. Some 27km west of Limassol, watch for a sign to seaward pointing to "**Evdhímou jetty**", not to be confused with the inland village of Evdhímou (Avdhímou), which like its three western neighbours was Turkish-Cypriot-inhabited before 1974. What's actually indicated is a decent shingle and coarse sand beach alongside the mooring facility; a single restaurant serves fish on occasion.

Pissoúri

The only really sizable coastal settlement between Episkopí village and the Páfos border is **PISSOÚRI**, draped appealingly over a ridge a bit south of the highway, though disfigured with too many new buildings to be really attractive close up. Owing to a relative calm and proximity to the Episkopí Sovereign Base, it's a favourite of service families, with a half-dozen places to **stay** and **eat**. Among these, the *Victoria Hotel*, just off the main square (☎221182; ②), is newish, reasonably priced and has an attached snack bar. Occupying a converted, century-old farmhouse, the long-established and rather snooty *Bunch of Grapes Inn* is a firm favourite of the post-imperial set, where reservations are usually necessary (☎221275, fax 222510; ⑤). Among the four **tavernas** in the village centre not attached to hotels, the *Stani* gets high marks.

Pissoúri's **beach**, 3km below the village along a good but twisty road, is a lot longer (nearly a kilometre) than it appears from above, well protected and sandy.

You could do worse than base yourself here, with thus far just a handful of tavernas, villa developments and hotel-apartments. *Kotzias Apartments* (☎221014, fax 222449; ⑤) are attractively set in well-maintained gardens and available through *Survil*. The *Monte Beach* restaurant at the strand's west end, despite a mega-casino appearance, is not at all bad and is reasonably priced at under C£4 a head.

Pétra toú Romíou

Beyond Pissoúri, the coast road is desolate until, just over the boundary in Páfos province, the imposing shoreline monolith of **Pétra toú Romíou** invariably prompts drivers to slam on their brakes at a strategic viewpoint and fish for the camera. (You can admire the view at more leisure from the CTO food/drink/souvenir pavilion here, just inland and up the hill.) In legend this was the spot where Aphrodite, ancient patron goddess of Cyprus, emerged from the sea foam, though the formation actually takes its name (Rock of Romios) from the Byzantine folk-hero Dhiyenis Akritas, aka Romios, who used this and other boulders as missiles against pirates.

A longish beach of pebbles and coarse sand extends mostly to the west of the largest rock and its satellites, though it must be said that its popularity is due mostly to its mythic associations and ease of access; the high-speed traffic whizzing by just overhead hardly makes it alluring. The ocean here is also prone to murkiness at most seasons – were Aphrodite to repeat her performance today, she would most likely emerge draped in seaweed, not foam.

travel details

Buses

From **Limassol** to: Agrós (1 daily Mon–Fri at 11.45 am with *Agros Bus*; 1hr 30min); Kourion (5 daily on Episkopí village bus; 20min); Larnaca (4 daily Mon–Fri, 2 on Sat with *Kallenos*; 1hr); Nicosia (6 daily Mon–Fri with *KEMEK*, 1–2 daily Mon–Sat with *Costas*; 1hr 15min); Páfos (1 daily Mon–Sat with *KEMEK*, 1–2 daily Mon–Sat with *Costas*; 1hr 15min); Plátres (1 daily Mon–Fri at about noon with *Karydas*, 3 a day in August; 1 daily at 2pm with *Platres Bus*; 1hr 30min).

International ferries

Two to three weekly, depending on season, from **Limassol** to Haifa (Israel), Rhodes and Piraeus (Greece); one or two weekly to Heraklion (Greece), summer only; one weekly to Ancona (Italy) and Port Said (Egypt), summer only. See p.6 for a detailed summary of ferry routes.

Akapnoú	Ακαπνού	ΑΚΑΠΝΟΥ
Akrotíri	Ακρωτήρι	ΑΚΡΩΤΗΡΙ
Aktí Kivernítou	Ακτή Κυβερνήτου	ΑΚΤΗ ΚΥΒΕΡΝΗΤΟΥ
(Governor's Beach)		
Amathoúnda	Αμαθούντα	ΑΜΑΘΟΥΝΤΑ
Amathus	Αμάθους	ΑΜΑΘΟΥΣ
Arakapás	Αρακαπάς	ΑΡΑΚΑΠΑΣ
Ársos	Άρσος	ΑΡΣΟΣ
Ayíou Nikoláou	Αγίου Νικολάου	ΑΓΙΟΥ ΝΙΚΟΛΑΟΥ
tón Gáton	τών Γάτων	ΤΩΝ ΓΑΤΩΝ
Dhorá	Δορά	ΔΟΡΑ
Episkopí	Επισκοπή	ΕΠΙΣΚΟΠΗ
Eptagónia	Επταγώνια	ΕΠΤΑΓΩΝΙΑ
Evdhímou	Αυδήμου	ΑΥΔΗΜΟΥ
Kelláki	Κελλάκι	ΚΕΛΛΑΚΙ
Kiláni	Κοιλάνι	ΚΟΙΛΑΝΙ
Klonári	Κλωνάρι	ΚΛΩΝΑΡΙ
Kolossi	Κολόσσι	ΚΟΛΟΣΣΙ
Kourion (Curium)	Κούριον	ΚΟΥΡΙΟΝ
Lánia	Λάνια	ΛΑΝΙΑ
Limassol (Lemessós)	Λεμεσός	ΛΕΜΕΣΟΣ
Malliá	Μαλλιά	ΜΑΛΛΙΑ
Melíni	Μελίνη	ΜΕΛΙΝΗ
Monágri	Μονάγρι	ΜΟΝΑΓΡΙ
Moúsere	Μούσερε	ΜΟΥΣΕΡΕ
Odhoú	Οδού	ΟΔΟΥ
Ómodhos	Όμοδος	ΟΜΟΔΟΣ
Pétra toú Romíou	Πέτρα τού Ρωμίου	ΠΕΤΡΑ ΤΟΥ ΡΩΜΙΟΥ
Pissoúri	Πισσούρι	ΠΙΣΣΟΥΡΙ
Potamioú	Ποταμιού	ΠΟΤΑΜΙΟΥ
Potamós Yermasóyias	Ποταμός	ΠΟΤΑΜΟΣ
	Γερμασόγειας	ΓΕΡΜΑΣΟΓΕΙΑΣ
Vássa	Βάσα	ΒΑΣΑ
Víkla	Βίκλα	ΒΙΚΛΑ
Vouní	Βουνί	ΒΟΥΝΙ

CHAPTER THREE

PÁFOS AND THE WEST

S ince the final collapse of the Byzantine empire in the fifteenth century, the western end of Cyprus has traditionally been the island's remotest and least-developed portion. Following the Ottoman conquest, the district of Páfos also became the most Turkified part of the island, with close to a third of the population being Turkish Cypriot before the events of 1974. These conditions inevitably had a profound effect on local customs and speech, with the accent and dialect of both communities strongly influencing each other – and virtually incomprehensible to outsiders. Another result of the area's relative isolation was the Greek community's retention of a large vocabulary of Homeric Greek, a heritage of the original Mycenaean colonization that further complicated the linguistic profile. Other Cypriots labelled the Pafiots as backward, mongrel bumpkins and told (and still tell) scurrilous jokes about them; the Pafiots retorted that this was simply jealousy at work, since they were more intelligent than the other islanders.

With the departure of the Turkish commmunity in 1975, and the opening of the Páfos international airport in 1983, local idiosyncracies have inevitably diminished, and the level of touristic development is rapidly coming to match that of the other coastal districts. But big chunks of Páfos are still exhilaratingly wild, villages characterful, and the beaches arguably the best in the South. Towards off-islanders, the Pafiots continue to display an extroverted bluntness, which might cause offence if you didn't realize they generally mean well.

The town of **Páfos** is showing all the signs of too-rapid growth, but it still makes for a comfortable overnight stay and has much to offer in the way of antiquities, as does its predecessor **Palea Paphos**, at the modern village of **Koúklia**. Middle and late Byzantine monuments await you at **Yeroskípou**, **Émba** and the **monastery of Áyios Neófitos**, and near handsome villages such as **Péyia** and **Dhroúsha** at the base of the Akámas peninsula. The coast itself improves as you head north from Páfos, with the beaches around **Lára** in particular still the focus of battles between developers and conservationists, the latter for the moment prevailing.

ACCOMMODATION PRICES IN THE SOUTH

All hotel and apartment-hotel prices in the South have been categorized according to the price codes given below. These categories represent the minimum you can expect to pay in the high season for a double room or a two-person self-catering unit. Single rooms will normally cost 50–80 percent of the rates quoted for a double room. Rates for dorm beds in hostels, where guests are charged per person, are given in Cyprus pounds, instead of being indicated by price code. For further details, see p.25.

① under C£12	④ C£20–25	⑦ C£35–40
② C£12–16	⑤ C£25–30	⑧ C£40–50
③ C£16–20	⑥ C£30–35	⑨ over C£50

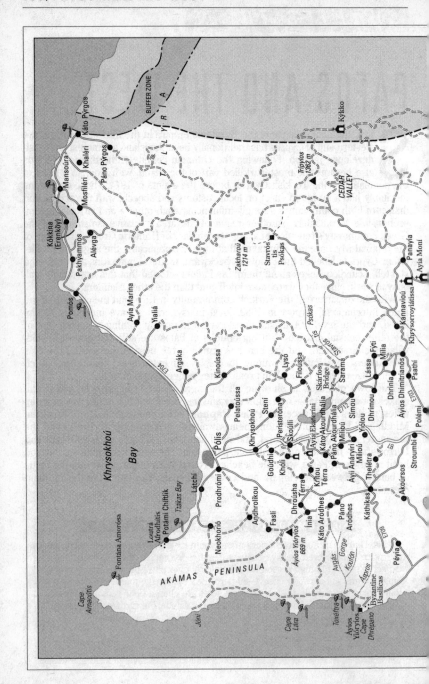

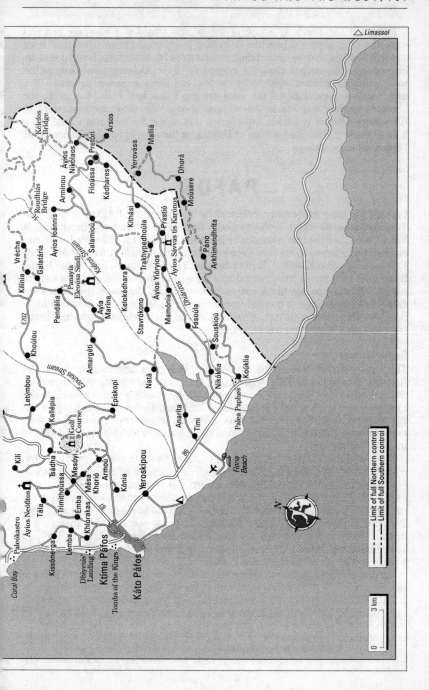

Pólis, on the northerly shore of the island, provides a blissfully peaceful retreat, with uncluttered beaches stretching in either direction. The small town and a limited number of surrounding resorts form bases for jeep, boat, mountain-bike or foot explorations along the rugged tip of the **Akámas peninsula** to the west – thinly vegetated, slashed by ravines, and lately proposed as the South's only national park. East of the road linking Páfos and Pólis, the landscape becomes gentler and life in the villages around the showcase monastery of **Khrysorroyiátissa** is easier, but there's still scope for adventure (and good hiking) in the uninhabited forests of **Tillyría**, or the equally isolated **Kséros and Dhiárizos river valleys**.

PÁFOS

Perhaps the most noteworthy feature of the district capital **PÁFOS** is its layout. Two distinct settlements – the harbour, archeological zone and hotel strip at **Káto Páfos**, and the true town centre of **Ktíma**, 3km up the hill – are jointly and confusingly referred to as Néa (New) Páfos, to distinguish it from Palea (Old) Paphos, now called Koúklia, 16km to the east. The upper town, first settled by the Byzantines as a haven from coastal attacks, seems in some danger of losing its separate identity, as the blank spaces between it and the lower resort area are slowly but surely filled in by ready-mix concrete lorries and their offspring high-rises. For the moment, though, it's still a pleasant if unremarkable provincial capital of less than 30,000 permanent inhabitants.

Some history

The foundations of **Néa Páfos** are obscure; in legend Agapenor, leader of the Arcadian contingent to Troy, was shipwrecked near here in the twelfth century BC and decided to stay. But it seems to have been only a minor annexe to the sanctuary and town at old Páphos (see p.122) until Hellenistic times, when the last independent Pafiot king, **Nikoklis**, laid out a proper city. Its perimeter walls enclosed much of the headland behind the harbour, which shipped out timber from the hill forests.

The Ptolemies made Páfos the island's rather decadent administrative centre, which it remained during the Roman period, when it rejoiced in the pompous title of **Augusta Claudia Flavia Paphos**. Cicero was proconsul here for two years, as was one **Sergius Paulus**, the first recorded official convert to Christianity, at the behest of apostles Paul and Barnabas. Acts 13:6–12 records the event, with (for good measure) the incidental blinding of a pagan sorcerer who attempted to distract the new believer. Despite this success Paul seems to have had a hard time combating Aphrodite's love-cult here, and was reputedly scourged for his trouble on the site of the Byzantine basilica.

Successive earthquakes, including two in the fourth century, relegated Páfos to the status of a backwater, and the Cypriot capital reverted to Salamis (Constantia), though Páfos was designated – and has since remained – an important bishopric. The **Arab raids** of the seventh century completed the process of

The telephone code for the entire Páfos district is ☎06.

desolation, however, and for more than a millennium afterwards visitors were unanimous in characterizing the shabby port as a hole – that is, if they were lucky enough to survive its endemic diseases and write about it.

Under **British administration** Páfos' fortunes perked up: the harbour was dredged and the population began to climb from a low point of less than 2000 to about 9000 at independence. During the late 1950s, when Páfos district was a hotbed of EOKA activity, the British had a major interrogation and confinement centre in the town. But when in 1974 **Archbishop Makarios** took refuge here following the EOKA-B coup, it was the British who saved his bacon by airlifting him out by helicopter to the Akrotíri air base (see p.147).

Arrival and information

Taxis from the 15-kilometre-distant **airport** (there is no bus service) shouldn't set you back more than C£5 to Ktíma, perhaps C£6 to Káto Páfos; strenuously resist those drivers who demand up to C£8. If you haven't arranged fly-drive or a coach transfer to your accommodation, you'll have to submit yourself to the taxi-drivers' attentions, as there are only a pair of relatively pricy car-hire booths, as well as a part-time tourist info booth, at the arrival lounge at present. However, Páfos Airport is slated to undergo a massive overhaul, including the addition of a second terminal, between now and 1999, so expect the place to be a building site until further notice.

Driving into Káto Páfos from elsewhere, if you're not booked into accommodation with parking space, you'll probably end up in the enormous, apparently free, dirt lot behind the waterfront – in high season the narrow streets of the hotel "ghetto" will be out of the question. Up in Ktíma you're best off using the enormous pay car park at the foot of the bluff on which the bazaar and old Turkish quarter of Moúttalos is built.

Páfos' **tourist information office**, which has an unusually complete stock of maps and handouts (Mon–Sat 8.15am–1.30pm, plus Mon & Thurs 3–6.15pm), can be found in Ktíma on Pávlou Melá, still cited as Gládstonos on many maps and home to most tourist services.

MUNICIPAL BUS SERVICES

Near the main car park in Ktíma is the central stop for *ALEPA* **municipal bus services**, with several useful lines along the main drags: Káto Páfos and Ktíma (often cited as "Agorá" on bus schedules) are linked every 15–30 minutes during daylight hours by bus #11, which plies Leofóros Apostólou Pávlou, connecting the two districts, and Posidhónos, the shorefront road of Káto's southerly hotel ghetto. The #10 bus – which actually stops down in the car park – goes further afield, diverging from Apostólou Pávlou at Leofóros Táfon ton Vasiléon and heading out past the northwesterly resort strip en route to Coral Bay; the #15 plies a similar route, beginning from Káto Páfos.

Numbered ALEPA routes to the **suburb villages** of Yeroskípou, Lémba, Kissónerga, Émba, Tála, and Trimithoússa begin at the Karavélla parking lot off Andhréa Yeroúdhi in Ktíma. Ask at the central kiosk there for your bus, as they tend not to have their route numbers or destinations prominently displayed.

Accommodation

In Páfos, upper and lower, there are now about 15,000 guest beds, the town recently having overtaken Limassol as the South's largest resort. Since the recent wave of gentrification and development, little decent accommodation remains, especially in Káto Páfos, that is not part of the pre-booked package scene. Many of the places below are no exception, but at least are used to being approached individually.

Axiothea, Ívis Malióti 2, a stair-street off Apostólou Pávlou, Ktíma (☎232866, fax 245790). Strategically located on Moussalás hill, the ancient acropolis, the bar and terrace of this congenially run medium-sized hotel have unbeatable views over the town and coast; no pool. ⑥ (substantial long-stay discounts). *Ambassador Hotel Apartments*, across the way at no. 1, are co-managed (④); both premises are available through *Sunvil*.

Kinyras Hotel, Arkhiepiskópou Makaríou 91, Ktíma (☎241604, fax 242176). Small hotel in a restored 1920s building near the bazaar, with its own bar and garden-restaurant. ⑤.

New Olympus, Výronos 12, near the archeological museum (☎232020, fax 232031). This unmistakable grey, three-storey Art-Deco/Neoclassical hybrid has an exceptionally quiet location at the east edge of town, with sea views from some rooms, and a pool. Often booked out by tour operators. ⑤.

The Park Mansion, Pávlou Melá (Gládstonos), below the tourist office (☎245645, fax 246415). Rambling, renovated 200-year-old building overlooking Páfos' central park, with a variety of tile-floored rooms, a characterful arcaded dining room, and a small but well-attended pool. ⑤ (advantageous half-board rates available).

Pyramos Hotel, Ayías Anastasías 4, Káto Páfos (☎235161, fax 242939). The least expensive hotel, and virtually the only walk-in option, in the main resort area; pleasant enough, with its own inexpensive bar, near several medieval monuments and a number of recommended restaurants. ④.

Trianon Guest House, Arkhiepiskópou Makaríou 99 (☎232193). A bit noisy, and over-heated by the laundry downstairs, but fairly clean and central, with kitchen facilities. ①.

Youth Hostel, Eleftheríou Venizélou 37, Ktíma (☎232588). Fifteen minutes' walk northeast of the town centre, but clean and quiet enough. C£2.50 per person in one of three six-bed rooms.

Káto Páfos

The main resort strip in **Káto Páfos**, east of Apostólou Pávlou and the harbour, constitutes a repertory of opticians, estate agents, indistinguishable restaurants, clothes shops, souvenir kiosks, banks and travel agencies with little character, the pattern repeating itself every couple of hundred metres along **Leofóros Posidhónos**, the shoreline boulevard. It's a fairly lacklustre sequence, and to begin a tour of the lower town you're better off heading straight for the harbour, roughly equidistant from most points of interest. Immediately around, or just inland from the harbour are traces of the ancient and medieval town, as so often in Cyprus placed cheek-by-jowl or converted for use by later occupiers. The harbour-mouth **fort** and its inland counterpart **Saránda Kolónes** are both originally Lusignan, while the early churches of **Ayía Kyriakí** and **Ayía Solomóni** both show signs of previous use. The Hellenistic **Tombs of the Kings** eventually saw service as Christian catacombs. But the glory of Káto Páfos, and the chief motive for a visit if you're not actually staying here, is the series of **Roman mosaics** found northwest of the harbour; having been buried and forgotten over centuries, they were never subsequently modified or adapted.

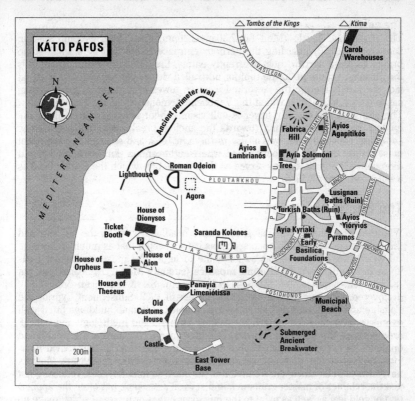

Local **beaches** extend east of the little port, fronting the row of mega-hotels which have sprung up here since 1983; they are serviceable at best and, like the municipal beach at the east edge of our map, have to be artificially supplemented with sand from elsewhere.

The harbour

The harbour area was "improved" between 1992 and 1995, with the quay re-masoned and pedestrianized, and the old customs house restored; however the effect was largely spoiled by a hideous concrete superstructure, and it seems the refurbishing will not continue, as the local authorities refuse to cooperate with the CTO, who were behind the plan. Thus far the quay esplanade consists of a half-dozen indifferent patisseries and tavernas trading largely on their position.

The foundations of the Byzantine church **Panayía Limeniótissa**, destroyed like so much else during the seventh century, can be seen a few paces inland from the suspended project; the Danish crusader Eric the Good, one of many who died here, was supposedly buried inside the ruins. On the waterfront, **cruises** in glass-bottomed boats are on offer: C£5 for a short hop to a wreck, C£8 up to Lára Bay, or C£15 all the way around the Akámas peninsula.

The castle

The diminutive **castle** (Mon–Fri 7.30am–2.30pm, plus Thurs 3–6pm, Sat–Sun 9am–5pm; C£0.50) guarding the harbour entrance is reached by a small stone bridge across a narrow moat. Currently empty, the building's main attraction is the chance to climb up to the roof for unrivalled views over the port and town. In fact the fort is merely the reworked western tower of a much larger Lusignan castle dating from 1391, which the Venetians demolished nearly a century later. The stump of the easterly tower is still visible about seventy metres along the modern mole, itself pointing towards the ancient breakwater, half awash. The Ottomans repaired what was of use to them in 1592, and seemed to have spent most of their time on the roof terrace, where eight cannon slots are angled in odd directions. The ground floor served as their dungeons, which the British used as a salt warehouse till 1935.

The Paphos mosaics

Whatever else happens in Páfos, the entire headland between the harbour and the lighthouse will remain open space, as it's suspected that as much archeological wealth lies buried as has so far come to light. The most spectacular finds unearthed to date are the **Roman mosaics** (summer Mon–Fri 7.30am–7pm, Sat & Sun 9am–5pm; winter Mon–Fri 8.30am–5pm, Sat & Sun 9am–5pm; C£1), discovered accidentally by a ploughing farmer in 1962. Subsequent Cypriot and Polish excavations revealed an extensive complex of Roman buildings fitted with exquisite floor mosaics, showing episodes from ancient mythology and considered perhaps the best in the eastern Mediterranean. Nowhere is the wealth and opulence of imperial Roman Paphos better suggested than in these vivid floorings, new stretches of which seem to be discovered every few years. Mosaics have always been an expensive medium, far more so than frescoes, requiring not just the retainer of master craftsmen and several assistants, but often the application of gold leaf as well as paint to the tiny glass cubes or tesserae which make up the images. Other, less costly, tesserae were chipped from stones of the appropriate colour. Modern shelters protecting the mosaics are naturally lit and provided with ample catwalks for viewing – though often the colours are far from dazzling, since the tesserae are not kept polished as they were in their day.

The House of Dionysos

The largest building in the mosaics complex, next to the ticket booth, is the **House of Dionysos**, so called because of repeated representations of the god, and probably built in the late second or early third century AD as the villa of a wealthy merchant. However a much earlier Hellenistic pebble-mosaic, showing the monster Scylla, has been relocated to a previously undecorated floor, and is the first thing you see on entering. Towards the rear of the building Zeus as an eagle abducts Ganymede, while Dionysos frolics with Ariadne, attended by Cupid and a hunting dog.

But the most famous panels ring the main atrium, on the west side of which Apollo pursues Daphne, while her father the river-god reclines below; in a nearby panel Poseidon chases after the nymph Amymone with more success, as evidenced by Cupid hovering over the sea-god's quarry. The *Triumph of Dionysos*, with the god riding in a chariot pulled by two she-leopards and flanked by satyrs, slaves and bacchantes, reflects the decadence of the Roman town.

Another long panel, familiar to any London underground rider who has read a Cyprus Wine Board advert, shows first Dionysos proffering a bunch of grapes to the nymph Akme – as her name implies, the personification of perfection (in this case a good vintage). Next King Ikarios, legendary first manufacturer of wine, with a bullock-drawn cart of the new elixir; and on the far right, two lolling, inebriated shepherds rather redundantly labelled "The First Wine-Drinkers". The first piss-up apparently ended badly – in the unshown sequel, friends of the shepherds, thinking them poisoned, murdered Ikarios. To the left of this group the tragedy of Pyramus and Thisbe unfolds, the lion escaping with Thisbe's mantle, and Pyramus shown erroneously as the god of the eponymous river in Anatolia.

Around the other three sides of this atrium, there is fine animal detail in a series of hunting scenes; elsewhere a peacock dominates the central square of one of several excellent geometrical floors. At the edge of several panels, visitors are exhorted to "Rejoice" (*Khairei*), presumably with liberal quantities of wine – from these inscriptions it's deduced that these panels formed the floor of a banqueting hall or a reception room.

The House of Aion
In the **House of Aion**, uncovered in 1983, the mosaics are later (mid-fourth century) and more sophisticated in theme and execution. In the lower right panel, Apollo sentences the silenus Marsyas, who dared challenge him to a musical contest, to his fate of being flayed. In the next scene above, the result of a beauty contest between Cassiopeia and several nereids is depicted; the latter, losers, ride sulkily away on an assortment of sea monsters. Still on the right, the topmost frame shows Hermes offering baby Dionysos to the centaur Trofeus for rearing, surrounded by nymphs preparing a bath. The left-hand scenes are less intact; of the god Aion, from whom the building takes its name, only the head is visible, and a version of Leda preparing to meet the Swan is somewhat damaged. Except for the statue niche in the west wall, the building itself is a purpose-built reconstruction, though of old masonry.

The House of Theseus
The next precinct, the **House of Theseus**, takes its name from a round mosaic of coarse tesserae that portrays Theseus brandishing a club against the (vanished) Minotaur, while Ariadne and personifications of Crete and the Labryrinth look on. Under the same sheltering roof, in the next room, a very late (fifth-century) mosaic, *The First Bath of Achilles*, is shown: a nursemaid carries him firmly in the presence of the Three Fates and his parents. Its arrangement strongly prefigures the iconography of early Christian portrayals of the Nativity, wherein the Virgin reclines in the same way as the nymph Thetis, and the three Magi replace the Fates. It is speculated that this building, or a vanished adjacent one, was the location of Sergius Paulus' interviews with the apostles.

The House of Orpheus and House of the Four Seasons
At present the **House of Orpheus** is closed to the public, but should it have opened by the time you visit you'll be treated to the sight of Orpheus charming a naturalistic bestiary with his lyre, in an exceptionally large floor panel. A smaller panel shows a naked Hercules about to strangle the charging Lion of Nemea with his bare hands.

The **House of the Four Seasons**, a new area discovered early in 1992 and still closed to the public, was provisionally named for personifications of the seasons, though only Autumn has survived. Most of the images in what was evidently another sumptuous mansion are engagingly realistic hunting scenes: a tiger claws the haunches of a wild ass, and a hunter faces off with a marauding lion, while a deer runs away from the melee. On the floor of what was possibly the banqueting hall are more animal portraits, including a dog chasing a hare, and a goat shown, unusually, full-face – in both pagan and Christian mosaic and fresco imagery, animals are usually depicted only in profile (later to be joined by non-Christians and the wicked), with the frontal view reserved for humans.

Other Roman and Byzantine sites

From the northerly access road to the mosaics, which has been officially renamed Sofías Vémbou in honour of a patriotic 1940s Greek torch singer, a short lane leads up to the **Roman odeion** (gate open dawn to dusk; free), a workmanlike 1970s restoration of the theatre and not very compelling unless there's an event on. Of the contemporary agora, beyond the stage to the east, there's virtually nothing to see at the moment except weeds. From the *odeion* parking lot a passable dirt track leads northwest to the picturesque **lighthouse**, beyond which are the most intact stretches of the city's **perimeter wall**.

Saránda Kolónes

Right beside Sofías Vémbou, the fortress of **Saránda Kolónes**, signposted as Byzantine, is actually a Lusignan structure built atop its predecessor (unrestricted access). Almost as soon as it was completed, it was destroyed by an earth tremor in 1222, and before excavations undertaken between 1957 and 1983, the only objects visible above ground were numerous tumbled columns – hence the Greek name which means "Forty Columns".

It's still a confusing jumble of moat-ringed masonry; some well-worn latrines, near the remaining arches, are the only obvious items – they were fitted with doors, in deference to Christian modesty. The pavement is riddled with sewer tunnels, vaults and stables, some interconnecting and offering rather claustrophobic touring. For a supposed stronghold, an improbable number of sally ports fitted with stairs breach the roughly square walls. The ramparts were originally entered by a gateway on the east, and sported eight mismatched towers.

Ayía Kyriakí (Khrysopolítissa)

Crossing busy Apostólou Pávlou, you can find the hotel-obscured start of pedestrianized Stassándhrou, which leads directly to **Ayía Kyriakí (Khrysopolítissa)**. This late (eleventh- or twelfth-century) Byzantine church, with a later belfry, is dwarfed by the vast foundations of an earlier, seven-aisled basilica and an archiepiscopal palace, both destroyed by the all-scouring Arab raids. What's left are extensive fourth-century floor mosaics and a scattering of probably contemporary columns, including one dubbed "St Paul's Pillar" after the apocryphal tradition that the apostle was tied to it and scourged. Since it's still being excavated, the fourth-century zone, considerably below modern ground level, is currently off-limits. Access to Ayía Kyriakí itself is via a catwalk. The small church is bare of any decoration inside, and has recently been ceded by the Orthodox bishop of Páfos to the Catholic and Anglican expatriate communities – perhaps the first time heterodox rites have been celebrated here since the Lusignans displaced the Orthodox with a Catholic diocese in 1220. To the north are scattered the domed Ottoman baths and the Lusignan baths, which the Turks heavily modified, as well as a Byzantine church converted to a mosque and a tiny, cottage-like modern mosque used by local Turks until 1975.

The catacombs of Ayía Solomóni and Fabrica hill

Ayía Kyriakí lies near the easternmost circuit of ancient walls, and other points of historical interest lie up Apostólou Pávlou. The **catacombs of Ayía Solomóni**, just east of the pavement, are overshadowed by a huge terebinth tree festooned with knotted-together kerchiefs, a practice common to both Christians and Muslims throughout the Middle East and similar in efficacy to the prayer flags of the Buddhists. Steps lead down to a multi-chambered, sunken sanctuary honouring one of those obscure, weirdly named saints in which Cyprus seems to specialize – in this case a Jewish woman whose seven children were martyred by one of the Seleucid kings of Palestine. It's thought that the subterranean complex was once the synagogue of Roman Paphos, and doubtless a pagan shrine before that. The frescoes in the small chapel are a mess, first vandalized by the Crusaders; more curious is a sacred well, accessed by a separate flight of stairs, with water so clear that you'll step into it unintentionally even though you've been warned. Directly across Apostólou Pávlou is the similar catacomb-shrine of Áyios Lambrianós.

The rock outcrop just north, known as **Fabrica hill**, contains more tunnelled-out tombs and churches, including those of Áyios Agapitikós and Áyios Misitikós. These two shrines honour saints even more shadowy than usual, and pointedly unrecognized by the Orthodox Church. According to legend, dust gathered from the floor of the former can be used as a love-charm (*agápi* means "love" in Greek), but from the latter has the opposite effect (*misós* means "hate"): useful magic that presumably ensures the saints' long-running veneration. Australian excavations since 1995 on the south slope of Fabrica hill are bringing to light remains of a Classical amphitheatre.

The Tombs of the Kings

From the vicinity of Fabrica hill, a well-signed major road, Leofóros Táfon ton Vasiléon, leads 2km northwest to more rock-cuttings, the so-called **Tombs of the Kings** (summer Mon–Fri 7.30am–7pm, Sat & Sun 9am–7pm; winter Mon–Fri 7.30am–5pm, Sat & Sun 9am–5pm; C£0.50). Rock outcrops near the shore – called *Paleokástra* ("Old Citadels") for their similarity to castles – conceal dozens of tombs hacked out of the soft strata, since this was a permissible distance outside the city walls. There's no evidence of royal use, merely that of the local privileged classes, starting in the third century BC. Their design, curiously, is not strictly indigenous but heavily indebted to Macedonian prototypes, passed on from Alexander's legions to the Ptolemies who ruled Cyprus.

Eight complexes of tombs are singled out for you by number, and include several reached by stairs down to sunken courts, ringed by peristyles of rough square, or round fluted, Doric columns carved from the living rock. Beyond the colonnades, passages lead to rooms with alcoves or niches provided for each corpse. At anniversaries of the death of the deceased, relatives would troop out to the tomb for a *nekródhipno* or ceremonial meal, with the leftovers deposited near the actual sepulchre; variants of this custom still prevail in Greek Orthodox observance. Carved crosses and traces of fresco pigment in a few tombs suggest their use as catacombs in early Christian times. Later they were systematically looted (have no fear of encountering skeletons, or hopes of artefacts) and scholarly excavations only began in 1977. Today it's still an eerie place, the drumming of the distant sea and chirps of nesting birds the only sounds.

Ktíma

Looking down from the edge of the escarpment on which **Ktíma** is built, you can appreciate the Byzantines' defensive reasoning: it's nearly a sixty-metre drop in elevation to the coastal plain, with the harbour fort assuming toy-like dimensions at this distance. The main thoroughfares of Pávlou Melá and Pallikarídhi subdivide the upper town: to the east a dull cantonment of broader avenues lined by the courts, police station, archbishop's house, the park, tourist facilities and museums, while on the west the more vernacular neighbourhood forms a warren of narrower, denser-gridded streets encompassing the bazaar and the old Turkish quarter.

The market and Moúttalos

Heading west on Agorás, the continuation of Makaríou, you quickly reach a relatively ornate, turn-of-the-century building, the **covered market**, which has a good selection of local souvenirs as well as fresh produce. South of this, over the edge of the palisade, you'll spy a medieval **"Turkish" hamam** down by the car park, recently restored but kept firmly locked; in fact it appears to have originally been a Latin, or even Byzantine church.

Continuing northwest, the alleys of the former Turkish quarter of **Moúttalos** narrow in, and you can reflect on the fact that before 1974 this was a guarded enclave, with many refugees from outlying Pafiot villages. The sole architectural monument here is the **Cami Kebir** or "Great Mosque", once the Byzantine church of Ayía Sofía and still a handsome building.

Finally, near the end of the clifftop neighbourhood, there's a plaza dotted with kebab houses and clubs used by the locals, all Greek refugees from the North. Overhead a metal archway reads *Ne Mutlu Türküm Diyene* ("How fortunate for him who can say 'I am a Turk' "). The Greek Cypriots have not defaced or changed this or any of the numerous surviving Turkish street signs, but merely edited it with an addition of their own. Dangling below, it says: "We do not forget the enslaved territories" (ie the North). After the often conspicuous wealth of urban Greek Cyprus, the meanness of the bungalows here may come as a shock – you are not merely looking back twenty years in time, but also at the consequences of government measures against the enclaves, whereby a long list of materials deemed "militarily strategic" were forbidden to be brought in.

The museums

The southeastern cantonment of Ktíma is home to the three most important museums of Páfos district, collectively worth a half-day of your time.

The Ethnographical Museum

First stop might be the privately run **Ethnographical Museum** at Éxo Vrýsis 1, south of the park, occupying two floors of the Eliades family mansion (summer Mon–Fri 9am–1pm & 3–7pm, Sat 9am–1pm, Sun 10am–1pm; winter Mon–Fri

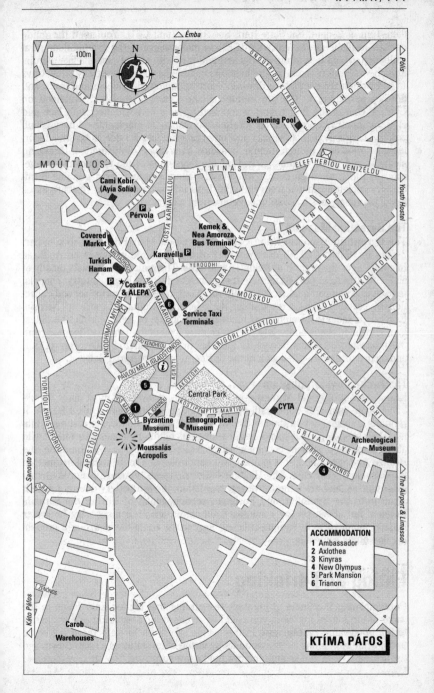

KTÍMA PÁFOS

ACCOMMODATION
1 Ambassador
2 Axlothea
3 Kinyras
4 New Olympus
5 Park Mansion
6 Trianon

9am–1pm & 2–5pm, Sat 9am–1pm, Sun 10am–1pm; C£1). You need the guide booklet available at the entrance (C£3) to make sense of the ground-floor rural collection, which intermingles priceless antiques with recent cast-offs like aluminium cheese-graters. Some of the best bits include basketry, especially straw trays (*tsésti*), which are mandatory viewing before shopping trips; sieves and irons; and devices pertaining to the processing of cotton, now a vanished livelihood on Cyprus. One of the four rooms is mocked up as a bed-chamber, with lace and clothing; another contains a comprehensive display of nineteenth-century island pottery. Larger items, of the sort now often pressed into service as taverna decor, include *pinakótes* (dough mould boards), *dhoukánes* (flint-studded threshing sledges) and three wagons parked on the flagstones of the cruciform passageway. In the sunken garden, a wood-fired bakery stands near a genuine third-century rock-tomb hewn from the cliff. Less interesting are four upstairs cases full of jewellery, fossils, coins and pottery from all eras.

The Byzantine Museum

The **Byzantine Museum** (Mon–Sat 9am–1pm, plus Mon–Fri 2–6pm in summer, 2–5pm in winter; C£0.50) occupies part of the bishopric premises on Andhréa Ioánnou, near the church of Áyios Theódhoros. The collection consists mostly of sixteenth-century, post-Byzantine **icons** rescued from local country chapels; though of a uniform quality, few really stand out in what is Cyprus' second collection of portable icons after that in the Makarios Cultural Centre in Nicosia. Exceptions include an eighth- or ninth-century image of Ayía Marína, the oldest icon known on the island; a late twelfth-century icon of the Panayía Eleoússa from the monastery of Áyios Sávvas tis Karónos in the Dhiárizos valley (see p.150); and a curious double-sided icon of the thirteenth century from Filoússa.

The Archeological Museum

Ktíma's **Archeological Museum** is well east out of town, off most maps (Mon–Fri 7.30am–2pm & 3–5pm, until 6pm Thurs, Sat & Sun 10am–1pm; C£0.50). It requires a special detour, and sufficient time for the extensive, interesting exhibits. The chronological displays begin with Chalcolithic figurines and rather wild abstract pottery, which becomes recognizably zoomorphic by the time the Bronze Age is reached; this exotic trend continues, in a more refined manner, in the Archaic display case. The Hellenistic-Roman room, as usual, features myriad glass objects, and more figurative representation, though pottery does not appear again until the Byzantine and Lusignan section, much of it from the Saránda Kolónes fort. Perhaps the strangest later items are Hellenistic clay hot-water bottles, moulded to fit various afflicted body parts, and a finely wrought crouching lion of the same age.

Eating and drinking

Contemplating the knots of identikit restaurants that clutter Káto Páfos in the wake of the tourist invasion, you could be excused for despairing of any characterful, good-value **restaurants** in the region. Yet even in Káto there are some finds, while Ktíma has a few standouts by virtue of its status as a "real" town, and the areas between and around the two hold a few surprises.

Ktíma

Acropolis Moussalas, cul-de-sac of Andhréa Ioánnou, in open space next to *Axiothea Hotel*. Mostly grills, but also large salads and portions of vegetables; tasty and reasonable at about C£4.50 per person with wine. Often shuts Easter week.

Fettas Corner, corner Ioánni Metaxá and Makaríou, opposite the fountain roundabout. Evening-only eatery offering a range of meat and veg dishes, with limited outdoor seating by the park.

Sovvos, Petrákis Miltiádhous 15, market area. Friendly, lunch-only *sheftália* and kebab joint, with soups and vegetables too, and a view from the rear outdoor seating only partly sullied by the car park below. Mixed clientele of tourists and tradesmen.

Stavros, Platía Mouttálou. Best of a handful of grill houses here, not least because they also do cheap, abundant, largely vegetarian *mezé*: caper greens, beets, mushrooms, *koupépia*, coriandered pancetta, stews. Very "local" atmosphere; tourists so far a rarity.

Káto

Avgerinos, Minóön 4, near Ayía Kyriakí. Inexpensive and atmospheric place (doubly surprising considering its location), serving up grilled meat, all sorts of fresh fish (notably swordfish) and village wine.

Gorgona, Lédhas 10, near Leptos Basilica Gardens. Not your best bet for local food, but you'll find big, reasonably priced steaks (speciality flambé) and European desserts.

Hondhros, Apostólou Pávlou 96, at the edge of the archeological zone. Well-executed, moderately priced Cypriot standards; pleasant outdoor seating, especially at lunch, but please do not feed the numerous cats.

In between Ktíma and Káto

Nicos Tyrimos, Agapinóros 75, behind the old carob warehouses on Apostólou Pávlou (☎242846). Arguably Páfos' best fish restaurant, with a wide, fresh selection, preceded in spring by unusual, abundant *mezédhes* like *agrioaspáragos* (wild aspragus), *kírtamo* (rock samphire), and fried baby crabs. About C£10 per head with wine and service charge. Shut Mon; reservations advisable.

Sanouto's Meze House, Ayías Théklas, between Koráï and Theodhórou Zenónos, Káto Pervólia district (☎241528). A Scots-Cypriot duo do unusual, well-presented *mezédhes*, mostly vegetarian with a strong herbal flavouring (Chef "Ali" is a botanical expert); also wine from the barrel. The portions aren't huge, and prices aren't rock-bottom at about C£6 for the twelve-plate works, but worth it. The convivial old house has only twenty seats, so reservations are essential in the cooler months; there's more capacious garden seating in summer. Supper only (after 9.45pm); closed Sun.

Vesuvio's, Agapinóros 31, 300m above *Nicos Tyrimos*. Very popular amongst locals in the know and a good bet for a snack at the sidewalk seats or a quick take-away: kebabs, T-bone steaks and swordfish.

Suburb villages

Akis Tavern, Kósta Partasídhi 3, Yeroskípou, west edge of village (☎241665). Copious plates of such delicacies as *eliés óftes* (baked olives), baby crabs, chicken livers. About C£5, with booze extra. Closed Tues; reservations advisable.

Apothiki/The Barn, west side of the village just south of the through road, Kissónerga. This converted carob warehouse was the first in the wave of "*mezé*" houses which has become a Pafiot trend. Ample choice for vegetarians, and a large open fire in the middle during winter.

Pitsillas, north of the through highway, Yeroskípou. If greasy goat *kleftikó* and nothing but is your thing, this is the unpretentious place for it. Lunch and dinner.

Drinking and nightlife

Local **nightlife** – such as it is – is concentrated down in the hotel district of Káto Páfos, along Posidhónos or just inland.

California Beach Bar, near the intersection of Ayíou Andoníou and Konstandínas, Káto Páfos. A likely choice from among the cluster of music bars and clubs in this area; happy hour 7–10pm.

La Boite 67, harbour, Káto Páfos. Students from the Lemba art school and Páfos trendies tend to be found drinking between or after meals at Andreas and Athina Haralambidhis' pub. Athina often sings at the live music sessions on Wed, Fri, Sat and Sun nights.

Rainbow Disco, opposite the *California*. The largest and oldest disco in Páfos, a pick-up joint for local lads on the make; C£3 admission includes one drink.

Listings

Animal welfare To report abuses, ring the expatriate-run hotline on ☎234203, 235759 or 235018.

Bookstore *Axel*, Arkhiepiskópou Makaríou 66, Ktíma.

Bus companies The most useful companies include, in Ktíma, *KEMEK*, on Leondíou, just off Thermopýlon, opposite the Pérvola car park (☎234255), whose buses run to Limassol; *Costas*, at Nikodhímou Mylóna 2B, near the old central post office (☎241717), which has services to Limassol and Nicosia; and *Nea Amoroza*, Evagóra Pallikarídhi 79 (☎236740), to Pólis and Pomós.

Car rental *Andy Spyrou/Europcar*, corner Posidhónos and Natalías (☎241850); *Astra/ Eurodollar*, Apostólou Pávlou, Marina Court (☎242252); *Budget/Petsas*, Apostólou Pávlou 86, Green Court (☎235522); *Geko*, Dhionýsou 8 (☎232848); and *Sea Island*, Apostólou Pávlou, Antigoni Konstantinou Shopping Centre G8/G9 (☎231365).

Exchange Most banks are up around Platía Kennedy in Ktíma, including *Barclays*, right on the square, with a *Visa*-accepting cashpoint machine. The *Ethniki Trapeza/National Bank* at Arkhiepiskópou Makaríou 108A has an *Access/Mastercard* autoteller, while the *Laiki Trapeza*, a bit further down, has another *Visa*-compatible machine. The *Lombard Nat West* branch in the bazaar is open through the afternoon.

Laundrette Near the corner of Posidhónos and Alkmínis in Káto Páfos.

Post offices The nominal main branch, in an old colonial building on Nikodhímou Mylóna (Mon–Fri 7.30am–1pm, plus Thurs 3–6pm), has been effectively supplanted for things like parcels and poste restante by the new district sorting office on the corner of Eleftheríou Venizélou and Vasiléos Konstandínou. The Káto Páfos branch on Ayíou Andoníou sometimes has afternoon service.

Scuba diving *Cydive*, Posidhónos 1, Káto Páfos (☎234271, fax 235307), British-run and the longest-established school in the district, is well thought-of locally.

Service taxis *Karydas/Kyriakos* at Evagóra Pallikarídhi 9 in the very centre of Ktíma (☎232459), *Nea Páfos/Makris* on the same street at no. 19 (☎332132), and *Kypros* at Arkhiepiskópou Makaríou 134 (☎237722). All offer direct service to Limassol only; service to anywhere else is via Limassol.

Shopping The *Cyprus Handicraft Service* showroom is at Apostólou Pávlou 64, Ktíma. *Mikis Antiques*, Fellahoglou 6, Ktíma, has some wonderful Belle Epoque phonographs and furniture, as well as the more usual rural artefacts.

Swimming pool If for any reason the sea doesn't appeal, there's a good public pool on the corner of Elládhos (the continuation of Pallikarídhi) and Onoúfriou Klirídhi: open-air, heated and open at least 9am–4pm daily.

Travel agencies *Exalt*, PO Box 337, or Ayías Kyriakís 24, Káto Páfos (☎243803), does unusual jeep or trek day excursions across Páfos district; choose from among a traverse of the Avgás gorge, a jeep safari though Akámas, exploring the lower reaches of several river valleys, or canyoning further upstream near the Tróödhos foothills. Prices are C£22 for treks, C£25 for jeep itineraries, VAT included; enthusiastic, knowledgeable leadership and often lunchtime catering by the management of *Sanouto's* (see "Eating and drinking", above). *Iris Travel*, Pávlou Melá 10, across from the CTO, is recommended for reasonable international air tickets.

BEYOND PÁFOS

Leaving Páfos behind in almost any direction, rolling, well-tended hills and deep river valleys provide relief from the occasional tattiness of the town. The sudden, recent growth of tourism on the coast halted the depopulation of the closer hill villages, but chances of traditional livelihoods surviving in the remoter settlements are pretty slim; accordingly the rural areas are a favourite target for foreign second-home hunters.

To the southeast, there is little beyond what meets the eye from the Páfos–Limassol highway, unless you bother to drive a considerable way up the Kséros and Dhiárizos river valleys. Northwest of town, the coast is surprisingly deserted once past the last gasp of resort development. Head north by a choice of routes towards Pólis, second town of the district, and you're seemingly on a different island, while east of the main Pólis-bound road lies some of the emptiest country on Cyprus, essentially abandoned after 1975 or relegated to backwater status by the proximity of the Attila Line.

Southeast from Páfos

The hopelessly overcrowded main road **southeast from Páfos** passes over a trio of rivers, the lower reaches of streams beginning far up in the Pafiot corner of the Tróödhos range (exploring the Kséros and Dhiárizos valleys is described on p.149). The resulting fertility (notably in melons) softens the usual mineral, parched yellowness of the south Cypriot coast, and seems to be in sympathy with the age-old worship of the island's patron goddess, Aphrodite, at Yeroskípou and Palea Paphos. Little tangible remains of her shrines, but her worship continues faintly in Christianized forms.

Eastern beaches

The Páfos town beaches, specifically those fringing the eastern hotels, aren't up to much; to reach anything moderately attractive you have to get some way out of town. The first substantial strip is the maintained and improved **CTO beach** along the shore below Yeroskípou, near the *Zenon Gardens Campsite* (C£1 per site, plus C£1 per person) which tends to get buzzed by low-flying aircraft and run out of mains water. The other is **Flória beach**, seaward of Tími village, about halfway along the airport spur road – follow signs pointing to the dirt drive that leads to some ramshackle tavernas and the first hints of development. There's also an official picnic ground in a eucalyptus grove nearby.

Yeroskípou (Yeroskípos)

YEROSKÍPOU village ("Yerostchípou" in dialect) has lately become virtually a suburb of Páfos, beginning just a kilometre or so beyond the district archeological museum, and linked with Ktíma (Karavélla parking lot) by the regular *ALEPA* **buses** #1 and #2–1. The name is a modern rendition of the ancient *Hieros Kipos* or "Sacred Garden and Grove", consecrated to Aphrodite, which grew in the fertile plain below towards the sea.

These days Yeroskípou has a couple of decent eateries (see p.119), and a reputation as a crafts centre, as reflected by numerous stalls on the main road peddling basketry and Turkish delight, and by the Yeroskípou **Folk Art Museum** (Mon–Fri 7.30am–2.30pm, plus Sept–June Thurs 3–6pm; C£0.50). This, on Leondíou just south of the through road, is lodged in the former house of a certain Andreas Zoumboulakis, British vice-consul here in the early nineteenth century, and better known as Hadji Smith, having adopted his sponsor's surname. The museum, on two storeys, is probably the best of its kind on the island, emphasizing domestic implements on the ground floor, local costumes upstairs, plus decorated gourds, including one fashioned into a stringed instrument.

Ayía Paraskeví church

Nothwithstanding its name, the village proper is probably of Byzantine origin, and the best demonstration of this is the renowned church of **Ayía Paraskeví** bang in the middle (key at house opposite if locked).

Damaged aniconic frescoes in the altar dome date construction to the ninth century, and the church is unique on the island in having six domes, including that of the reliquary under the nineteenth-century belfry. Most of the surviving frescoes, recently cleaned to good effect, date from the fifteenth century. Up in the central cupola hides a crude but engaging *Virgin Orans*; opposite the south door are *The Last Supper, The Washing of the Feet, The Betrayal* – where figures in Lusignan armour date the images – and *Pilate Washing his Hands*. Across from these you see *The Birth and Presentation of the Virgin*. Further up towards the altar screen, there's an unusual representation of *Simon carrying the Cross for Christ*, with a *Nativity* and *Baptism* opposite. The church itself was originally cruciform with a single nave, but had an ungainly narthex added to the south side last century, and also at some point a *yinaikonítis* or women's gallery in the rear. July 25–26 marks the **feast** of the patron saint; this is also a good spot to participate in the Greek Easter Resurrection Mass.

Palea Paphos and Koúklia

Approaching the boundary of Limassol district, some 11km east of Yeroskípou, you can't help noticing a large, solidly built structure on a prominent rise. This is **La Cavocle**, a fourteenth-century manor that's the inevitable marker-cairn and introduction to both the ancient city of **Palea Paphos**, and the large village of **KOÚKLIA** just to the north. Once an ethnically mixed community, Koúklia remains a pleasant if unremarkable place of low houses, whose meandering lanes converge on a small *platía* with a church and some coffee-shops. Indifferent to the trickle of tourists visiting the nearby ruins, it has changed little – except for the departure of its Turkish Cypriots – since independence. One post-1975 development here is the outstanding *Dhiarizos* **taverna**, opposite the central church, open for lunch and supper. This specializes in rural, often wild, food such as *ambelopoúlia* (songbirds), snails, *bourékia* (sweet cream cheese turnovers), livestock testicles, and *tchakistés* (warm split olives in lemon, garlic and coriander), but also caters well for vegetarians. In summer, there's extra seating outdoors, though in any season reservations (☎432243) are a good idea. There's a decent hotel nearby at Nikóklia, a short way up the Dhiárizos valley (see p.150).

The site

The ancient temple stood on a knoll about 2km inland, overlooking the sea but probably not the orchards and gently sloping fields which have appeared since. Despite the hoariness of the cult here, there's little above-ground evidence of it or of the city which grew up around, and the archeological site itself is really of specialist interest. The courtyard-type **sanctuary of Aphrodite** (summer daily 7.30am–7pm; winter daily 7.30am–sunset; C£0.50), with rustic, relatively impermanent buildings, was common in the pre-Hellenic Middle East; thus little has survived other than low foundations to the north as you enter. Matters were made worse for posterity when a wealthy Roman chose to build a private villa, bits of its mosaic floor still visible, next to the archaic shrine in its last years, and the medieval placement of sugar-milling machinery atop the convenient stone foundations was extremely destructive to anything remaining above knee level. Finally, the nearby villagers, from Byzantine times onwards, treated the ruins as a quarry – virtually every old building in Koúklia incorporates a cut stone or two from the shrine area.

In one corner of the precinct a sign points along the short path to the "**Leda Mosaic House**", but fails to mention that the central figure, Leda baring her behind to the lustful Zeus-swan, is a copy. The replica was installed here after the

---

THE PAPHIOT CULT OF APHRODITE

The cult of the ancient Cypriot patron goddess Aphrodite is of considerable antiquity; it was already established in a hilltop temple at Palea Paphos in about 1500 BC, and a town sprang up around it, capital of one of the original island kingdoms. Foundation legends credit the hero Kinyras with being first king and consort of Aphrodite, who supposedly emerged from the sea nearby at Pétra toú Romíou. Their beautiful daughter Myrrha was turned into a fragrant bush by the jealous goddess, and Adonis, born of its wood, completed the cycle by becoming Aphrodite's lover.

All this reflects historical facts about the Kinyrid dynasty, who not only "wedded" the goddess through the temple prostitutes, but married their own daughters upon the death of their wives – royal descent was reckoned through the women of the line. Despite the incest it was a relatively civilized observance, considering that the Asiatic love goddesses, to whom Aphrodite owed much in pedigree and ritual, used to sacrifice their consorts after the rite of lovemaking.

The sacred prostitutes were apparently island matrons and damsels obliged by custom to give themselves at least once to strangers in the temple precincts. The business of prostitution was invariably brisker at the spring festivals for Aphrodite and Adonis, when separate processions of garlanded men and women made their way from Nea Paphos to the shrine via Yeroskípou. The ritual survives in the modern spring flower festival, the *Anthistíria*, which is celebrated with special enthusiasm in Ktíma, and in *Kataklismós*, the Flood Festival in June, where the obligatory sea-plunge seems to commemorate Aphrodite's emergence from the waves. Worship here continued until the fourth-century edict of Theodosius banning paganism, nearly eight hundred years after the foundation of Nea Paphos.

original was stolen by art thieves, then luckily recovered, to be lodged in the relative safety of Nicosia's Cyprus Museum.

Outside the sacred precinct, there's even less to see until the Swiss-sponsored excavations are completed. To the northeast, off the road towards Arkhimandhríta, are the remains of a **city gate**, and a **siege ramp** built by the Persians in 498 BC to breach the city walls. The defenders burrowed under the ramp in a vain attempt to collapse it and thus the Persian war-engines atop; two of the tunnels are now open for public inspection. The **necropolis** (still under investigation) lies to the southeast of the hill, and appears to have escaped the notice of tomb robbers.

Just east of the precinct stands the usually locked twelfth-to-sixteenth-century church of **Panayía Katholikí**, new goddess of the local cult. Should you gain admission, there are traces of fourteenth-century frescoes inside, the most curious being gargoyle-like personifications of the rivers Tigris and Euphrates on the west wall. Until recently Koúklia village women used to light candles nearby in honour of the Panayía Galaktariótissa – the Virgin-Who-Gives-Milk-to-Mothers.

La Cavocle and the local museum

The most obvious and worthwhile item in the main archeological zone is the four-square Lusignan manor of **La Cavocle**, whose name is a rendering of (take your pick) the Greek *kouvoúkli*, "canopy"; *kovoukuleris*, the royal bodyguard; or more likely the Latin *cubiculum*, "pavilion" – corrupted in whichever case to Koúklia, the name of the modern village. La Cavocle was headquarters of the Crusaders' surrounding sugar plantations, and continued to serve as the "big house" of a large farm in Ottoman times. Only the east wing survived the Mameluke raid of 1426; the rest, including a fine gate tower, is a Turkish reconstruction. Because the courtyard level has risen over the centuries, you descend slightly to the ground floor of the east wing, where a purported thirteenth-century banquet room has a groin-vaulted ceiling.

This fine specimen of domestic Crusader architecture is being prepared for use as part of an expanded **local museum** (same hours as the site), at present housed entirely upstairs. Among the few exhibits in Gallery I is one of several existing *betyls* or phallic cult monoliths (the biggest one is in Nicosia), which, not unlike Hindu Shiva *lingams*, used to be anointed with olive oil by local women well into modern times. Gallery II contains finds of all eras from the site, in chronological order. Best is the huge chalk bathtub of the eleventh century BC, complete with a soap dish. Most of the other items are painted pottery, with some bronze work, much of which was found in the rubble piled up by the Persians to support their attack ramp.

North from Páfos

North of Páfos the landscape is initially flat and uninspiring, dotted with large villages that are essentially dormitories for the district capital, and increasingly for long-term foreign residents. Only as the terrain begins tilting gently up at the first outriders of the Tróödhos mountains does development diminish and the mystique of the country reassert itself.

Most of the inland settlements immediately north from Páfos town can boast some late Byzantine church or remains, but with the exception of the following two monuments, all have had their appeal compromised by ill-advised additions or renovation.

Émba and Panayía Khryseléoussa

In the middle of ÉMBA, 3km north of Páfos, the twelfth-century church of **Panayía Khryseléoussa** sits in exalted isolation, though the parkland all around it burns to a crisp by June. A dome perches at each end of the double-cruciform ground plan, and the narthex with stairs up to vanished monks' cells on the mortared roof is an eighteenth-century addition. Loiter about purposefully and a guardian with the key will appear, but only if you're suitably dressed.

Inside, late fifteenth- or early sixteenth-century frescoes were recently cleaned, but they'd been badly retouched during the late nineteenth century, and some were damaged by the quake of 1953. However, anything that remained out of reach of the "restorer" is still worth scrutiny. A good example is the *Apocalypse* and *Second Coming* on the right of the main nave's vault, which is very fine high up but mauled below. Funds permitting, the cruder overpainting will eventually be removed by the archeological services, so visits should become even more rewarding with time.

The *témblon* (altar screen) dates from the sixteenth century, and just as the guard says, the eyes of St John the Divine (on the panel left of the main icon) seem to follow you around the room. The revered icon of the Virgin is unique in that both she and the Child are crowned; there is also a sixteenth-century icon of the apostles.

ALEPA urban **bus** #4 from Ktíma's Karavélla car park passes through Émba.

The monastery of Áyios Neófitos

Nine kilometres from Páfos and five from Émba, at the head of a wooded canyon, the **monastery of Áyios Neófitos** (Ayíou Neofítou) appears suddenly as you round a curve. Twice each weekday, the *ALEPA* #4 **bus** extends its route beyond Tála to call in here.

The hermit Neophytos, born in 1134 near Léfkara, moved here from the monastery of Khrysostómos near Nicosia at the age of 25, seeking solitude in this then-desolate region. His plan backfired badly; such was Neophytos' reputation that he became a guru of sorts to numerous disciples who gathered around his simple cave-hermitage, founding the monastery here long before his death in 1219 or 1220. Unusually for one of the desert saints, Neophytos was a scholar and commentator of some note, and a few of his manuscripts have survived. Among these are the *Ritual Ordinance*, a handbook for monastic life, and a historical essay on the acquisition of Cyprus by the Crusaders in 1191, deeply disparaging of the two protagonists Isaac Komnenos and Richard the Lionheart. That he could write this with impunity is perhaps a measure of the respect in which he was held during his lifetime.

The katholikón and the hermitage of Neophytos

The enormous monastery compound, home now to just seven monks, consists of a square perimeter cloister enclosing a garden-with-aviary, with the **katholikón** or central church on its own terrace. In the vault over the northernmost of three aisles, westernized, early sixteenth-century frescoes of events from the life of Christ face others portraying mystical aspects of Christ and the Virgin. A window in the apse splits the *Communion of the Apostles* into halves: Christ appears in each, bestowing the Eucharist on six disciples. But pleasant as they are, the *katholikón* and the monastery grounds are not the main reason visitors come up here.

On the far side of the car park with its café (lively during the feasts of January 24 and September 27), at the very head of the ravine, cave-niches form the **énkleistra** or **hermitage of Neophytos**. This has parallels most obviously with the roughly contemporary man-made cave-shrines of Cappadocia; here, too, the hermit supposedly dug many of the cavities himself, and it is conceivable that a few of the oldest frescoes are by Neophytos, though most were merely done under his supervision. At least two other painters, one signing his work as that of Theodore Apseudes, were involved.

Visits begin with stairs mounting to a pair of chambers on the left comprising a chapel, dedicated to the Holy Cross and completely decorated by 1196. These frescoes, of a "primitive" Syrian/Cappadocian style, were redone in 1503 and cleaned in 1992, so it's easy to make out scenes such as the *Last Supper* (complete with Judas reaching over the carrots and radishes of the Hebrew Passover to snatch the Fish of the Believer), the *Washing of the Feet*, and Roman soldiers portrayed as Crusaders, all culminating with the *Ascension* on the dome hacked from the soft rock. In the central altar chamber, two archangels seem like celestial policemen (as they indeed are in Orthodox belief), escorting Neophytos to the ranks of angels in a ceiling painting of the more fashionable Constantinopolitan school. The chamber furthest right was Neophytos' private quarters, with benches, niches and a desk carved for his use, as well as his sarcophagus – appropriately presided over by an image of the *Resurrection*, but prematurely emptied in 1756 so that Neophytos' bones might serve as relics. Today pilgrims to the *katholikón* kiss his skull in its silver reliquary.

The upper caves of the cliff-face are undecorated and currently inaccessible. Neophytos retreated there in 1197 after the lower levels became unbearably busy with his unintended followers; he is said to have ensured his privacy with a retractable ladder.

Northwest along the coast

Leaving Páfos towards the **northwest**, the road past the Tombs of the Kings continues as a broad avenue for some kilometres, passing phalanxes of new hotels and self-catering apartments, which are sprouting at an alarming rate regardless of the nature of the (often rocky) shore below. It's strange to reflect that in the 1950s this coast was so deserted that EOKA chose it as a landfall when smuggling in arms and men from Greece. Today, signs for Chinese and Indian restaurants lend the only exotic touches, along with the banana plantations inland that testify to the mildness of the climate. Overall, it is not a prospect that holds much promise for seclusion and beauty, but surprisingly you are heading towards one of the most unspoiled stretches of shoreline in the South. **Buses** run as far as Coral Bay, but there's no public transport to Áyios Yióryios, or any point beyond along the coast.

Lémba

An inland route from Ktíma, which joins up with the coast road beyond Kissonérga, brings you after 4km to **LÉMBA**, home to the **Cyprus College of**

Art; *ALEPA* **bus** #4 runs here ten times each weekday from Ktíma's Karavélla parking lot Outrageous roadside sculpture by the principal, Stass Paraskos, indicates your approach to the college, a fully accredited institution offering a three-year or post-graduate programme in fine art (for enrolment information abroad, contact the college at 23 Oakwood Road, Sturry, Canterbury, Kent CT2 0LU, UK). Visitors are welcome at the dozen or so studios, and there is a small gallery of finished work for sale. Two independent **potteries** within sight of the college, particularly the *Lemba Pottery* (☎243822), are also well worth calling in at.

Conspicuously signposted at the downhill end of town, the Lémba **prehistoric site** (entry unrestricted) was founded in about 3500 BC and flourished for over a thousand years, courtesy of the nearby spring and stream (not potable today, alas). The well-labelled **Lemba Experimental Village**, a thorough reconstruction of three Neolithic dwellings courtesy of a University of Edinburgh team, lends considerable interest, and in terms of architectural appeal compares rather favourably with the appalling tower blocks visible to seaward.

Dhiyenis' Landing: the Áyios Yióryios museum

A similar distance out of Páfos along the coast road, the site of George Dhiyenis Grivas' disembarkation on November 10, 1954 to begin coordination of the EOKA uprising is now prominently marked below the village of Khlórakas as **"Dhiyenis' Landing"**, one of the many manifestations of a recent upsurge in nationalist fervour in the South (for more information on Grivas, see p.200). Right by the sea, just south of the enormous *St George Hotel*, which was constructed by the bishopric of Páfos to commemorate the landing, a purpose-built **museum** houses the gun-running caique *Ayios Yioryios* (open daily; free). This was captured by the British along with its Greek crew of five, and eight local EOKA activists who had come to meet them, on January 25, 1955. On the walls are archival photos of the capture and trial of the thirteen, along with British testimonials to the bravery of many of these men during the recent world war – subtly reiterating the long-standing Greek Cypriot position that they were virtually owed independence in return for their faithful service to the Allies.

Coral Bay

With the coast hitherto inaccessible or overrun by hotels, the first place that might tempt you to stop is **"Coral Bay"** (officially Máa), 10km out of Páfos and blessed with a public-access beach: hotels do not quite monopolize it, and this is the end of the *ALEPA* #10 and #15 **bus** lines from town. A sandy, 600-metre crescent is hemmed in by a pair of headlands, with two snack bars and sunbed rental places behind. Atop the promontories and up on the access road, however, are a rash of hotels and a "village" of support services and summer homes for wealthy Nicosians and expats. If it weren't for the signs you probably wouldn't find the beach, which in fact has been diminished somewhat by spoil from the mammoth, self-contained *Leptos Coral Beach Hotel* and marina, a fairly good example of what has gone awry in local tourist development since the mid-1980s. On the north-westerly headland are traces of **Paleókastro**, a Bronze Age settlement excavated before 1985 but still fenced off. There's a **campsite** behind the beach, *Feggari Camping*, which, given the area's transport connections, would make a more practical base than the site near Yeroskípou.

Áyios Yióryios

Just past Coral Bay, developments cease fairly abruptly amid vineyards and grain fields; the road, while still asphalted, dwindles too. The Roman town on **Cape Dhrépano**, 8km beyond, has shrunk to a modern Christian church at **ÁYIOS YIÓRYIOS**, with a nearby offering-tree like that at Ayía Solomóni in Káto Páfos, next to a medieval chapel dedicated to St George. Prayers are still said here for the recovery of lost objects and people (hence the tree).

Some 200m southeast of the modern church – the path is distinct despite a lack of signs – sprawls an enormous Byzantine sixth-century **basilica complex,** with extensive panels of geometric and animal floor mosaics. In the northerly aisle of the nave, an octopus is surrounded by birds, fish and even a turtle; two panels right of this, a crustacean and a snail appear. Such bestiaries are common enough in pagan art, but rare in Christian iconography; it has been theorized that they refer to a pre-lapsarian Golden Age evoked in Isaiah 11:6–9. The most vivid geometric mosaics, a trellis pattern of interlocking curved squares, are at the southwest corner, in the elevated baptistry. Another later, smaller basilica lies to the south, with attractive column capitals but no mosaics. Although both enclosures are fenced off, both fences are badly holed enough to permit easy access.

Aside from the basilica mosaics, the headland has little allure other than spectacular sunsets, and a possible role as a base for exploring the Akámas peninsula. Don't bother following signs down to Moudhális harbour and beach – the anchorage is fine for the local fisherpeople, but the sand is artificially strewn and badly littered, the water hardly more salubrious. Better swimming alternatives are found by going south, beyond the basilica, where sculpted rock formations offer good sunbathing and conceal miniature sandy coves. It is also possible to walk back to Coral Bay, some 6km along the coast through fairly empty countryside.

Practicalities

Several **hotel-tavernas** are scattered about the cape within walking distance of each other. Of these the *Saint George* (☎621306; ②) is the sea-view establishment, while *Yeronisos* (☎621078; ②) is a one-star hotel, slightly inland by the access road. The adjacent *West End Rooms & Restaurant* is probably the best value here, with immaculate en suite doubles (☎621555; ②). One of the better **eateries** in the area is about 2km inland from the headland, before the turning for Cape Lára: the *Arizona Restaurant* serves simple but good-quality Cypriot food, with a stress on *kleftikó* and *soúvla*. The name, says the South African-Cypriot proprietor, comes of watching too many TV Westerns.

The Avgás gorge, Cape Lára and beyond

At the intersection 500m inland from Áyios Yióryios, the right-hand dirt track signposted "Akámas Peninsula, 18km" is perhaps more rewarding, taking you towards the finest canyons and beaches on this coast. The road, badly chewed up by British military vehicles, is passable with caution in a saloon car as far as the junction 8km beyond Cape Lára, but for any forays beyond you really need a four-wheel-drive vehicle to handle the sand bogs and ditch-sized ruts.

The Avgás (Avákas) and Koufón gorges

The first attractive sandy bay, signposted as "White River Beach", lies about a kilometre north of the junction, at the mouth of the Áspros gorge, but most drivers will press on another 1500m to **Toxéftra beach**, at the mouth of the **Avgás** ("Avákas" in dialect) **gorge** system.

With your own vehicle, you can bear right, following a wooden forestry department sign, then immediately left and up onto the driveway towards an odd hilltop compound ringed by palms and bananas; in season, this is the *Vaklarin* **café-tavern** run by the hospitable Savvas Symeon. About C£4 will see you through a meal of salad, grilled meat, chips and a beer. From the "observation deck", flanked by rock sculpture, you've comprehensive views over the beach below, the length of Akámas, and the gorge system just east and below, your probable immediate goal.

An ordinary car can continue down past *Vaklarin* to the point where the valley, initially given over to grapefruit and banana plantations, splits into the two notable ravines. After parking near the more spectacular left-hand (northerly) one, which is the Avgás gorge proper, you can start off on the **trail** which quickly appears. The canyon walls soar ever higher, and before June at least there's plenty of water, duly tapped by irrigation piping for the thirsty orchards downstream. Some fifteen minutes along, the gorge narrows into a spectacular gallery where the sun rarely penetrates, before opening again at the foot of a rather steep, scrambly pitch that becomes nearly impassable at the half-hour mark. Yet *Exalt* (see Páfos "Listings") leads trek groups through here, and you would, after another hour of uphill trekking, eventually emerge atop a cliff in the Péyia forest.

The right-hand (southerly) gorge of **Koufón** seems initially less impressive, but after about twenty minutes past weirdly eroded rocks you reach a point where rock-climbing and/or abseiling skills are required.

Cape Lára and beyond

The symmetrical cape at **Lára**, just over 5km north of Avgás and nearly 28km from Páfos, shelters large sandy beaches on either side, which you choose according to how the wind is blowing. The slightly overpriced but beautifully set *Kendron Lara* **café-snack bar** overlooking the kilometre-long southerly beach is so far the only facility (reliably open May–Sept).

The smaller northerly bay, signposted as **"Lara Turtle Station"**, is one of several local nesting grounds for green and loggerhead sea turtles. Gently shelving, and thus warm enough for dips early in spring, this is even more scenic than its neighbour, backed by low cliffs and buffeted by the surf which wafts the turtles in on midsummer nights to lay their eggs. Accordingly the whole area is fenced, with a gate which may be locked on nesting-season evenings (June–Sept), when the station at the far north end of the beach is staffed by volunteers. At other times access is uncontrolled, the only evidence of the midsummer activity being stacked wire-mesh cages used to protect the turtle nests from marauding foxes.

Beyond Lára, the coastal track continues past more tiny coves on its way to Jóni and the haphazardly controlled British Army firing range (see p.141). Aside from completely retracing steps to Páfos, there are three alternative ways out of the Lára area. The best, and the only route reliably practicable in an ordinary car, involves heading 8km north to **Koudhounás junction**, then climbing for 5km more through thick forest to the ridge track above the Smiyiés picnic grounds.

SEA TURTLES AND THEIR CONSERVATION

The western coast of Páfos district is one of the last Mediterranean nesting grounds of **green and loggerhead turtles**, both endangered species. Although oceangoing reptiles, the turtles require dry land to lay eggs, gravitating late at night towards long, fine-sand, protected beaches for the purpose.

In Cyprus, the turtles nest every two to four years from early June to mid-August, laying clutches of about a hundred round eggs at a depth of 50 to 70cm every two weeks during this period. The hatchlings emerge after dark some seven weeks later, instinctively making for the sea, which they recognize by reflected moon- or star-light. Thus any artificial light sources behind "turtle beaches", ie flashlights, tavernas or hotels, disorientate the baby turtles, who head in the wrong direction to die of dehydration. Similarly, if the females are disturbed by light or movement, they will return to the sea without depositing their eggs properly. Because of these factors, green turtles have ceased to breed at now-developed coasts near Coral Bay and around Ayía Nápa; loggerheads still attempt to nest on beaches fringed by light sources, which usually results in death for the hatchlings.

It is thought that sea turtles reach maturity between fifteen and thirty years after hatching, and by an imperfectly understood imprinting process return to the very beach of their birth to breed. Perhaps one in a thousand hatchlings survives to adulthood; predators, particularly foxes, dig up the eggs on land; a high surf can literally drown the eggs; and until they attain sufficient size at about ten years of age the juveniles are easy prey for sharks, seals, and large fish.

Surveys taken in 1976 and 1977 showed an alarming drop in Cypriot turtle populations, to barely a hundred green turtle females in the Lára region, and a slightly larger number of loggerheads (which also nest in the Pólis area). Accordingly, in 1978 the Lara Turtle Conservation Project and its field station were established in an attempt to reverse this decline. Each summer, volunteers search this and nearby beaches for the telltale tracks that females leave behind when returning to the sea; nests are assessed for viability, and if poorly sited, the eggs are dug up, transferred to Lára for reburial, and protected by wire anti-fox mesh. Turtle gender is determined by incubation temperature, which in turn is a function of nest depth: 29–30°C results in an even sex balance, lower temperatures in more males, higher temperatures in excess females. Since its inception, the Lára programme has resulted in a quadrupling of the yearly survival rate for hatchlings, and staff scientists have also begun experimenting with raising young turtles in tanks to further reduce mortality; such a tank is exhibited at Káto Páfos harbour.

Despite financial support by the government's Department of Fisheries since 1978 and (more recently) the EU, the turtle conservation project may ultimately be futile if development battles raging over this deceptively peaceful place go the wrong way. The designation of the entire coast from "White River Beach" to a point several kilometres north of Lára did not prevent 25 lorry-loads of sand from Toxéftra beach being illegally carted away by minions of the bishop of Páfos in early 1995, for use in the Tsádha golf course; the archdiocese also plans to put up a luxury resort within sight of Lára. Almost the only non-governmental groups opposing such schemes are Friends of the Earth, the management of *Exalt Travel*, and the Laona Project (see below for the latter).

Otherwise, the more northerly of two signposted dirt tracks heading inland from behind Lára south beach winds **up to Ínia village**. In dry weather you can just make the climb, a rise in altitude of 500m past the outcrops of Áyios Yióryios peak, in the lowest gear of an ordinary car; however recent reports indicate large rock-falls en route which are unlikely to have been bulldozed away, so enquire first at the *Kendron Lara*. The signposted track **up to Káto Aródhes**, a few hundred metres south of the Ínia-bound one, should only be attempted with a 4WD vehicle.

Villages of the Akámas heights

North of an imaginary line joining Áyios Yióryios and Péyia village, the **Akámas peninsula** begins. Named after a legendary lover of Aphrodite, this is the most desolate, and very nearly the most thinly populated, portion of Cyprus. An inclined plane of sparsely vegetated chalk and reef limestone atop sharp volcanic peaks, it drops off sharply to the east and north but falls more gradually west towards the sea, furrowed by ravines that hide precious water. At its centre the land climbs to a spine of hills nearly 700m high, now supporting the bulk of permanent habitation in the area, though in ancient times the coastline was more important.

Several of the villages here were partly or wholly Turkish Cypriot before 1974, and the subsequent exodus left them almost empty: their lands, however extensive, were generally too poor to attract refugees from the North. Other, wholly Greek Cypriot communities have shrunk as well – the usual emigration overseas or to Cypriot towns, often no further than the service jobs of the Páfos resorts. Mostly the old remain, some wondering why the "miracle" of Ayía Nápa shouldn't be repeated here.

Virtually the only organization to suggest otherwise is the **Laona Project**, a venture of the Cypriot chapter of Friends of the Earth, supported monetarily by the European Commission and the philanthropic Leventis Foundation. Theirs is a two-pronged programme: to secure protection for the natural environment of the wildest parts of the Akámas, and to revive the dying villages by introducing "sustainable tourism" – specifically the restoration of selected old properties for use as visitor accommodation, and the involvement of tourists in the day-to-day activities of the villages. So far *Sunvil Travel*, a quality British tour operator, has been the main taker, offering a variety of Laona-restored accommodation between Páfos and Pólis. For more information on the aims of the Laona Project, contact them at PO Box 257, Limassol (☎05/369475, fax 352657). You can also directly book the 26 properties available to date through this number (ask for Haris Karaian, Artemis Yiordamli, or their assistant), or make arrangements in person at the *Vrysi* cafe in Krítou Térra. The village houses, in Milioú, Páno and Káto Akourdhália, Krítou Térra and Káthikas, cost about C£20 per day for two.

Péyia and Káthikas

Some 4km above Coral Bay, along good roads shown incorrectly on most maps, the large village of **PÉYIA** tumbles down a hillside overlooking the sea. After the excesses of Káto Páfos, the place's very ordinariness counts as an asset, but already identity is shifting uneasily as it becomes a dormitory community for vast numbers of expats buying purpose-built villas or renovating old houses.

You can **stay** short-term at the *Christina* (☎233742, fax 235505; ②), or at a handful of other less formal establishments. It's worth coming up here just to eat at some of the half-dozen decidedly carniverous **tavernas** grouped around the fountain square; *Peyia* is one of the better ones, generous-portioned for the money. The adjacent *Kyrenia*, which serves a fixed *mezé* accompanied by good house red for about C£5 a head, is renowned for entertaining evenings of magic-trick cabaret and dance contests. Péyia is important enough to rate its own *ALEPA* **bus** connection on line #7, up to six times daily, fewer on Saturday.

The E709 road from Péyia curls west then east as it climbs scenically through dense pine forest on its way to **KÁTHIKAS**, up on the Akámas watershed at the very edge of the commercial grape-growing zone (try the local winery's Mosel-like Vasilikon). The Laona Project has an information centre here behind the church, but the main highlight is an excellent **taverna**, *Araouzos*, 150m west of the church on the through road. Open for lunch and dinner, it's famous for such home-style dishes as *kolokássi* (taro root) with pork, *domátes me avgá* (sun-dried tomatoes with egg), rabbit stew, *spanakórizo* (spinach pilaf) and of course their rendition of baked olives. The exact menu changes nightly, on a set-price basis of all you can eat and drink (of the excellent house red) for about C£6. Justly popular, *Araouzos* is packed with a mix of Cypriots and tourists on most weekend nights, when reservations are virtually mandatory (☎633035).

The ridge route to Pólis

At Káthikas the E709 turns north to track the spine of Akámas; it's a drive worth doing at least once for its own sake, as opposed to the quicker, main valley route.

All the villages along here require slight detours – bearing left initially takes you onto the parallel access road for the two Aródhes settlements, Ínia and Dhroúsha. **PÁNO ARÓDHES** is still mostly inhabited, but there are no amenities for outsiders, and it suffered severe damage from an earthquake on February 23, 1995; many buildings around the handsome square, including the church, are now unsound and await repairs. **KÁTO ARÓDHES** was also badly hit, but before that was a sad casualty of 1974, many cracked houses emblazoned with the Turkish star and crescent standing empty, the fields around largely abandoned. Humbler **ÍNIA**, in the shadow of craggy Áyios Yióryios peak, roof of the Akámas, can offer the *Panorama Taverna*, but most of the tourist activity hereabouts takes place in neighbouring Dhroúsha.

Dhroúsha

Despite incipient gentrification, courtesy of magnificent views and a growing community of foreigners, **DHROÚSHA**, with its fine stone dwellings and winding streets, is still perhaps the best single target along this ridge. There are just 400 current inhabitants, but it's claimed that fifty times that many loyal emigrants and descendants live abroad, whose simultaneous appearance at holiday times puts such a strain on resources that the locally funded and staffed *Dhrousha Heights* **hotel** (☎332351, fax 332353; ⑥) was the result. With sweeping views, plus a small pool and tennis court, it's now also popular with foreign walking groups. It's also possible to rustle up less expensive private **rooms** by asking around at the several **tavernas**. Of these, *Savvas Kapsalos* – which doubles as one of the *kafenía* and is signposted only in Greek – is the most reliably open, doing vegetarian *mezé*, a meat entree with seasonal vegetables and wine by the glass for under C£5. Slightly more elaborate (the tables actually have cloths) but more erratic in its opening hours, *Fanis*, 40m uphill, features vegetarian's nightmares like suckling pig on the spit, liver and lung stew or *arkhídhia* (sheep's balls), in addition to *mezé* dishes.

Beyond Dhroúsha, head north to rejoin the main ridge road, which brings you to Prodhrómi, just west of Pólis, without any complications. Alternatively, you could cut eastwards from Dhroúsha across the main ridge road, to reach Krítou Térra and its abandoned ex-Turkish neighbour, Térra, a kilometre north down the same valley.

Krítou Térra

KRÍTOU TÉRRA is a lot bigger and more handsome than initial impressions suggest, with old houses lining the lush, upper banks of the ravine and covering the ridge beyond. It supposedly dates from Roman times, and was the birthplace of Hadjiyiorgakis Kornesios (see p.199). Lately the Laona Project has restored the trough spring at the village entrance, and established just opposite a locally run café-taverna, *Vrysi*; unfortunately this is not geared up for serving substantial meals without advance arrangement (☎322576).

Krítou Térra also marks one possible approach to the late Byzantine church of Ayía Ekateríni (see p.134): pass the single central *kafenío* (beyond the *Vrysi*) and a signposted Laona/*Sunvil* property, and exit the village on a cement drive descending south into a canyon; follow this track as it bends north-northeast to reach the lonely church after 4km.

Along the Páfos–Pólis highway

The busier, **B7** route north out of Páfos to Pólis, the district's second town, climbs to a saddle near Tsádha and then rollercoasters through the gentle hills around Stroumbí and Yiólou, two of several local villages devoted to wine-grapes.

GOLF IN CYPRUS

In April 1994, Cyprus' first **golf course** (excluding the two reserved for British Forces, at Dhekélia and Episkopí) opened 1500m southeast of Tsádha village. It occupies land which formerly belonged to the late medieval **monastery of Stavrós tís Mýthas**, now marooned in the middle, and tenanted by one Father Varnavas, who is very welcoming (especially to lady visitors).

At first thought, a golf course might seem a strange idea for an island perennially short of water that ought perhaps to be reserved for agriculture. The new course has also depleted equally scarce local beaches; its traps were allegedly filled with sand stolen by night from the Toxéftra turtle-nesting area. The lorry contractor, working for the bishop of Páfos, was caught red-handed, and both men were fined wrist-slap amounts; subsequently the good bishop, who had authorized the alienation of monastic lands to lay out the course, announced that he considered his debt to society fully discharged.

For its part, the family now managing the golf course claims that their sand is *not* from Toxéftra, and that the lawns are irrigated with water unfit for other purposes. They also argue that, with EU membership for Cyprus pending and Europe avalanched with oranges and tomatoes, as well as drowning in a wine lake, the country has no choice but to opt for high-end tourism of this type. Already two other courses are planned, near Koúklia and behind Lady's Mile Beach in Limassol. But the pivotal issue in light of the recent slump in Cypriot tourism, as with the island's superfluous four- and five-star luxury complexes, is whether enough foreigners will pay the going rates to keep such outfits alive (see *Basics* for greens-fee information).

The hummocky terrain is softened, too, by fruit trees and the occasional hedge of artichokes, budding until May.

Áyii Anáryiri Milioú and the Akourdhália villages

Beginning the gradual descent to Pólis, you might detour 2km west to the calcium-sulphate spa of **ÁYII ANÁRYIRI MILIOÚ**, with its modest one-star **hotel** (☎632318; ④) and cool, mineral-water pool in a secluded, citrus-planted valley. **MILIOÚ** village itself, 1km further, was badly hit by the February 1995 quake (the two fatalities were recorded here) but still has an oasis feel; there's a coffee-shop for refreshment and a high-quality weaving studio, *Anthoulla's*.

A direct onward road from Milioú to Páno Akourdhália shown on most maps does not appear to exist. You actually emerge at **KÁTO AKOURDHÁLIA**, blessed with a "Folk Art Museum" in the former school, 300m west of the village centre (the headman Mr Sofokleous has the key and can often be found working in the dog-guarded farm a little way down the track to Ayía Paraskeví). Just before the folk museum, a signposted cement, then dirt, track leads west to reach after 1500m the jewelbox-like chapel of **Ayía Paraskeví**, perched opposite a ruined watermill on the flank of the Kyparísha gorge. Restored in 1991, its original construction date is uncertain – estimates vary by nearly a thousand years – but some time between the twelfth and fifteenth centuries inclusive seems likely. Though completely bare of decoration, it is well worth the special trip, not least for its magical setting above the ravine here. Káto also offers the newly restored, seven-room *Amarakos Inn*, complete with attached restaurant and set in a small orchard, available through the Laona Project (see p.131) or through *Sunvil* in Britain.

PÁNO AKOURDHÁLIA, when you finally reach it by continuing southwest on the main road through Káto, boasts a sixteenth-century church as attractive as its modern replacement is hideous, and a Laona-instigated herb centre in the old school.

Ayía Ekateríni

About 1km short of Skoúlli village on the B7, a standard-issue brown and white sign points the way towards **Ayía Ekateríni**, 1500m along a side road to the left, the best-preserved late Byzantine church in the Akámas. Set in the middle of vineyards, the church is unusual for its southwest-to-northeast orientation, its lofty central cupola and its arcaded, domed narthex of the sixteenth century betraying Lusignan influence. There was apparently once another structure similar to the narthex on the north side, also with three domes, hence Ayía Ekateríni's local nickname of "Seven-Domed" (counting the central one). Since the 1953 earthquake, only traces of frescoes remain (the interior is usually locked to protect them), but the masonry is largely intact, and the setting, looking across the Stávros tis Psókas stream valley to the Tillyrian Tróödhos, is enchanting – try to be here towards the end of the day, as the sun sets on the hills opposite.

Skoúlli, Khóli and Khrysokhoú

On the east side of the B7 outside **SKOÚLLI**, the Herpetological Society of Cyprus (effectively "Snake George" Wiedl, an Austrian ex-UN soldier) has set up a roadside **reptile exhibit**, which includes at least one specimen of every Cypriot endemic species, including the recently rediscovered grass snake, long feared extinct (March–Oct daily 9am–1pm & 3–7pm; C£0.50).

Just before the Skoúlli bridge, a narrow, inconspicuous road leads west towards **KHÓLI**, remarkable for an exceptional restored villa, *Ta Palatia* (available through *Sunvil*), and two beautiful post-Byzantine churches. The early sixteenth-century **Arkhángelos church** is actually predated by half a century by its belfry, which was built by James II as a watchtower to monitor the Ottoman threat. Inside the barrel-vaulted, single-ribbed church a number of frescoes survive, most notably a *Crucifixion* in the south vault of the curiously elevated west end. There are also some frescoes in the nearby fifteenth-century chapel of the **Panayía Odhiyítria**; the village priest has keys for both churches if necessary.

Approaching Pólis, you can't help but notice the forlorn mosque, once a Byzantine chapel, of **KHRYSOKHOÚ** village, abandoned like many other Turkish settlements to the south and east of Pólis in 1975. In this case the surrounding farmland was fertile enough to attract a full complement of Greek Cypriot refugees. The mosque, neglected though not actively desecrated, is open for visits to its plain interior.

Pólis and around

Set back slightly from the Stavrós tis Psókas stream as it enters Khrysokhoú bay, **PÓLIS** is the most easy-going of the island's coastal resorts, and the only one that makes much provision for independent travellers. The Berlin hippies who "discovered" the place in the early 1980s have since moved on, or gone upmarket, so that mild gentrification is beginning to set in. The small, linear town straggles along a ridge and the road down to the shore, with hotels only slowly displacing citrus on the the surrounding coastal plain. The scenery, whether looking west towards the tip of Akámas, or out to sea, is magnificent, and nearby beaches, if not always brilliant, are more than serviceable.

Pólis Khrysokhoú – to give the complete historical title – occupies the sites of ancient Marion and Arsinoë, the former a seventh-century BC foundation which grew wealthy from the nearby copper mines until being destroyed by Ptolemy I, leaving little evidence of its existence other than thousands of tombs. A later member of the dynasty founded the replacement town of Arsinoë slightly to the west, and it came to be called Pólis in Byzantine times. Recent years have not been as peaceful as present appearances suggest; Turkish villages on the coast and in the valleys to the northeast and southeast got on poorly with the pro-*énosis* Greeks of the town, with a UN post required to keep order until the evacuations of 1975.

There are few specific sights in Pólis other than its old downtown stone buildings, with their ornate doorways and interior arches; the outstanding exception is the late Byzantine church of **Áyios Andhrónikos** (not yet open to the public at the time of writing), northwest of the pedestrian zone by a car park. Long the central mosque for the Turkish community, since their departure it has been examined by archeologists, and cleaning of extensive, previously whitewashed sixteenth-century frescoes has been completed. Unhappily, the images revealed are in a rather unedifying condition; disgruntled locals claim that the eyes of the saints were deliberately gouged out, a fairly common sacrilege. (The small chapel of Áyios Andhréas, on the way to the campsite, is by contrast bare inside.)

Practicalities

Outside July and August, this is one place in the South where you could get away with driving up and finding **accommodation** on the spot; plenty of "rooms to let" signs line the highway, especially in the direction of Latchí, though it would seem that thus far many of these are unlicensed by the CTO. Within the town itself, choices range from the equally modest *Lemon Garden* (☎321443; ②), inland on the road to Káto Pýrgos, and *Sea View Apartments* (☎321276; ②), on a small turn-off from the access road to the campsite, to the fancy sea-view studio units of the *Bougenvilea* (☎322201, fax ☎322203; ⑤), also partway along the campsite road.

The **campsite** itself (March–Oct) is magically set in a jungle of eucalyptus and calamus 1500m north of town, at the east end of the long beach that stretches all the way from Latchí. At C£1.50 per tent/carvavan, and C£1 per person, it can't be faulted except for its relative remoteness, though the road back up to Pólis is lined with a few snack bars, grocers such as *Palm Supermarket*, the hospital and an excavated patch of ancient Arsinoë.

Other amenities in Pólis include a **post office**, four **banks** (including the *Laïki Trapeza/Popular Bank* with a *Visa*-compatible auto-teller), a rash of **moped rental** agencies, the *Nea Amoroza* **minibus** booking office (☎321114) and the municipal **market hall**, which is the best place to buy fruit and meat for miles around.

Eating and drinking are easily seen to in the compact town centre, though most restaurants are on the expensive side. The *Old Town Tavern* near the turning for Latchí offers a range of vegetarian plates; *Arsinoe*, closer to the centre, specializes in fish and homemade wine, and is always mobbed. Across the street and a bit south, *Charlies Mikis* has a wider-ranging menu, similar to the *Old Town* but slightly less pricy; the *Lemon Garden*, besides being a source of accommodation, also does good pizzas.

Most **nightlife** seems to revolve around a pedestrianized three-way junction, now the triangular central plaza, where a half-dozen self-styled "café-bar-snacks" vie for your attention; among these *Savvas* seems to have a slight edge. Elsewhere, several more pubs occupy old buildings, most enjoyable of them being the *Brunnen* in one of the many abandoned Turkish houses tucked below the summit ridge: garden seating around the fountain, and inexpensive *mezé* with your drinks.

Northeast of Pólis

There's relatively little traffic up the coast towards Káto Pýrgos, partly because its backwater status was reinforced in 1974 by the ceasefire line just beyond – the former direct route to Mórfou and Nicosia can no longer be used. The area only comes alive in summer, when it's a retreat of some importance for Cypriots who haven't the appetite or the wallet for the purpose-built hotel strips and restaurants elsewhere in the South. Public transport is rare along this stretch – at most two buses daily to Pomós – so you really need your own wheels, and a fair bit of spare time for the arduous detour around the Kókkina enclave.

Pomós and Pakhýammos

The first twenty-odd kilometres towards Pomós parallel the little-developed but exposed shoreline, though cement villas are already going up, perhaps to handle any future overflow from Páfos and Pólis. **POMÓS** itself has a few self-catering apartments, but the village is quite featureless, and the obvious main beach not much to scream about. The promisingly named "Paradise Beach" is well hidden and a considerable scramble downhill. The best pretext for a visit are two excellent, reasonable **fish tavernas** near the fishing anchorage, of which *Sea Cave* has the edge.

Things improve scenically as you round the prominent cape and bounce along the deteriorating road into aptly named **PAKHÝAMMOS** ("Broad Sand"); here the settlement tilts downhill towards the functional beach, with organized amenities limited to a taverna at the local pilgrimage shrine of Áyios Rafaélos, and a mini-market.

Around the Kókkina enclave

Beyond Pakhýammos the narrow road, barely maintained since 1974, climbs sharply inland through forested hills, a tedious twenty-kilometre, 45-minute detour to avoid the problematic enclave of **KÓKKINA** (Erenköy). The local administration hasn't bothered to improve the bypass, probably because it's assumed Kókkina and the old coast road will be ceded to the South in any settlement. Along the way, Greek Cypriot and Turkish Cypriot watchtowers face each other, a few hundred metres apart; the single UN post is currently manned by Argentines, often to be seen jogging along the road. You'll pass through long-abandoned Turkish hamlets such as Alévga and Áyios Theodhóros, and surviving Greek Mosfiléri, before reaching the coast again at **MANSOÚRA**, deserted except for a Greek Cypriot outpost, a small beach with taverna and the beautiful medieval bridge that carries the old road just upstream.

THE KÓKKINA ENCLAVE

The **Kókkina enclave** was off-limits to Greek Cypriots years before the Turkish Army made it a beach-head in 1974; Turkish Cypriot extremists used it as an off-loading port for supplies from Turkey, just as their EOKA counterparts used the then-empty westerly Páfos coast. Matters came to a head on August 3, 1964 when three thousand National Guard troops under the command of General George Grivas (see p.200) attempted to put a stop to this activity by attacking Kókkina and several surrounding Turkish hamlets. The outnumbered defenders were forced to fall back into Kókkina itself, at which point Turkish jets appeared from the mainland, bombing and strafing nearby Greek villages (including Pólis), with heavy casualties. Outright war between Greece and Turkey was only narrowly avoided through UN intervention, and the irreparable estrangement of the two island communities, which had begun the previous year, was now virtually complete. Until 1974, Turkish Cypriots from the hills around continued to enter the fortified enclave; after the invasion, all civilians were relocated to the Kárpas peninsula, and Kókkina became strictly a Turkish army base, which it remains.

Káto Pýrgos

Set amongst peach orchards beside the buffer zone, **KÁTO PÝRGOS** is a surprisingly large place, which, despite mediocre beaches to either side and a certain scruffiness, is well equipped for guests, with no fewer than three largish **hotels** and numerous self-catering units that cater largely for Nicosians. Among the hotels, *Tylo Beach* is the most central and comfortable (☎522348, fax 522136; ⑤). Other than going swimming, eating fish and watching Greek Cypriot or UN troops, however, there's little to do here and scant opportunity for excursions in any direction.

West of Pólis: Latchí, Neokhorió and beyond

Once clear of the "suburb" of **PRODHRÓMI**, with its extensive self-catering accommodation, the road west from Pólis hugs the so far little-developed but often windswept beach on its way to Latchi, often confusingly spelled "Latsi" in both Greek and English lettering.

Latchí

The most celebrated "fishing village" of Páfos district, **LATCHÍ** has lately acquired a rather tatty air, at least on its inland side, where a long succession of souvenir shops, groceries, banks, and a few small hotels and apartments mimic in miniature Káto Páfos' seafront boulevard. Latchí's seaward aspect is more appealing, where half a dozen fish tavernas jostle to be close to the picturesque anchorage inside the rubble breakwater.

The least expensive **accommodation** options in town are the *Latsi* (☎321411, fax 321468; ③), close to the harbour but hardly state-of-the-art lodging, and the one-star *Souli* (☎321088, fax 322474; ④), by itself well west of town. For a well-executed luxury complex, available through most package companies in advance, try the *Elia Latchi Village* (☎321011, fax 322024; ⑧); *Sunvil Travel* has exclusive control of a number of excellent villas a few kilometres inland. Although the waterfront promenade has been improved, most of the **restaurants** there are much of a muchness. *Yangos and Peter's*, the oldest one, still serves reasonable seafood, while *May Day* at the opposite end of things is a congenial bar that also offers light snacks.

At Latchí's good pebble **beach**, low-key water sports like windsurfing or canoeing are on offer; however, the beach itself improves as you head east towards the Pólis campground, or west towards Loutrá Afrodhítis. A real recreational find in town is *Atlantis Diving*, which offers a variety of **scuba outings** to underwater highlights along the northeast Akámas shore; the main sites are around Áyios Yióryios island, a protected marine reserve, and out towards Cape Arnaoútis. Even shallow beginner's dive classes are likely to see brilliant orange moray eels, groupers, octopi, and perhaps a ray. An intro dive for the unsure costs C£27, certification courses start at C£170, or you can dive twice daily over five days for C£120. Contact Walter Polder or his assistants directly on phone/fax ☎322096.

Neokhorió

At the junction 1500m beyond Latchí, the inland turning leads to **NEOKHORIÓ**, with a dramatic hillside setting for its stone houses. The place was moribund before 1985, but has lately been almost wholly renovated as the effects of tourism pulse uphill. There's a fair amount of self-catering **accommodation**, available through several package companies including *Sunvil*; barring that, you can make local arrangements for a room in a family's house. No need to eat at sea level either, as there are two restaurants, *Smiyies* and *The Stone Taverna*.

On the northwest outskirts of Neokhorió, you might seek out the *Triskelion Pottery* of Ara Nigogossian and Nancy Hocking, the only ceramicists on the island doing exact, high-quality Bronze and Iron Age replicas (it's probably best to call ☎322068 first to make sure they're not in Nicosia or England). Neokhorió is also known for its lively **Easter Sunday festival**, with traditional games such as tug-of-war, street snacks and evening live music.

Neokhorió overlooks the **Petrátis Gorge**, famous for its bat cave (one of two caverns here) filmed by David Attenborough in 1985. The lower reaches of the canyon, clogged by boulders and vegetation, are really too rough for casual trekking; if you're interested, *Exalt Travel* (see Páfos "Listings") occasionally organizes expeditions here.

Beyond Neokhorió: ghost hamlets and Smiyiés

Once clear of the village, if you bear left and down at the first junction, this scenic dirt track crosses the shallow top of the Petrátis Gorge before reaching the former Turkish villages of **ANDHROLÍKOU** and **FASLÍ**. These are now desolate except for one goatherd family in the former; notwithstanding a reasonable amount of water by Akámas standards, the poor soil and lack of electricity failed to attract fleeing northerners. A saloon car can just get through, but as always in the Akámas you'll feel more confident with a four-wheel-drive as you wind past the ghost hamlets and under the antenna-crowned crenellations of **Áyios Yióryios**, summit of the Akámas, en route to Ínia (see p.132).

The right-hand turning just outside Neokhorió leads, after 4.5km of occasionally very rutted track (just passable in a two-wheel-drive), to the prepared picnic grounds at **Smiyiés**, a pleasant, piney spot with a slightly sweet spring, at one end of the eponymous nature trail (see p.142). Another 500m of careful driving brings you out onto the summit ridge, covered with yellow gorse and white rock rose in spring. Turn left and go another 500m or so to the well-signed top of the five-kilometre link road down to Koudhounás and eventually Cape Lára (see p.129).

Ttákas Bay

Staying with the paved coast road below Neokhorió, you'll pass the turn-off for the friendly *Ttakkas Bay Restaurant*, which has a loyal return clientele. Of late it's become a bit pricy, probably as a result of being written up in numerous publications (as a sign boasts); the food's still okay, but you're definitely paying for the superb setting. The bay in question, just out front, has a good **beach** of coarse sand and pebbles, with showers and rental sunbeds; carry on east around some rocks and you'll find about a kilometre more of the same, undisturbed except for one motel-restaurant on a low bluff.

The Akámas wilderness

Neokhorió is the last bona fide village before the final, tapering tip of the Akámas peninsula. Except for dense pine groves along the summit ridge, the region is largely deforested, though there are springs and tiny streams tucked into relatively lush hollows and gorges. The coast drops off fairly sharply, especially on the northeast shore, and there's very little sandy shoreline anywhere. It's a severely impressive rather than calendar-page beautiful landscape, much of its appeal residing in the near-absence of human activity; in spring and autumn appearances of migrating cranes, herons and storks add to the allure.

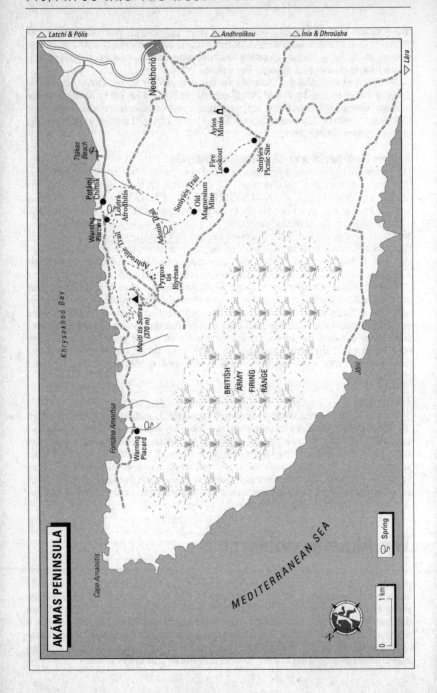

AKÁMAS PENINSULA

Latchí & Pólis

Andhrolíkou

Ínia & Dhroúsha

Lára

Neokhorió

Áyios Minás

Fire Lookout

Smiyiés Picnic Site

Tsákas Beach

Potámi Chiftlík

Smiyiés Trail

Warning Placard

Loúra Afrodhítis

Old Magnesium Mine

Adónis Trail

Aphrodíte Trail

Pýrgos tís Riyénas

Khrysokhoú Bay

Moúti tís Sotíras (370 m)

BRITISH ARMY FIRING RANGE

Jóni

Fontána Amorósa

Warning Placard

Cape Arnaoútis

MEDITERRANEAN SEA

Spring

1 km

0

N

THE AKÁMAS FIRING RANGE

One of the conditions of Cypriot independence was the reservation by the UK of various "retained sites" on the island other than the Sovereign Bases, and an extensive **artillery firing range** west of the Akámas watershed is one of them. Periodically the range is closed to the public for military exercises, and warning signs indicate when you are entering a potential zone of live firing. Given lingering resentment against British forces for failing to do more to stop the invasion of 1974, it's hardly surprising that the shellings are deeply unpopular locally; one warning placard recently sported the spray-painted graffito "Go Do Your Exercises in Hyde Park!".

Ironically, the British military presence has helped keep the area in a relatively pristine state, as several attempts since 1988 to have the Akámas region declared the first bona fide Cypriot national park have so far come to nothing. Hunters continue to shoot within the boundaries of the proposed park, and already the Carlsberg brewing magnate Fotos Fotiades has done some preliminary bulldozing for a holiday village at Vakhínes, near the edge of the firing range. Full protection for one of the island's last wilderness areas remains in doubt; those responsible for the dreariness of the major Miami-style strips on the southern coast will doubtless attempt to do the same here, if they're allowed to.

Yet, un-Green as this may sound, it's territory often best explored from a boat (*Exalt Travel* in Páfos or *Atlantis* in Pólis can help), or in a four-wheel-drive or on some sort of very sturdy two-wheeler. The few marked trails are summarized below, but a plethora of unmarked jeep tracks go virtually everywhere, and the often shadeless terrain will not conduce to aimless wanderings on foot, especially between June and September.

Loutrá Afrodhítis (Baths of Aphrodite)

The road along the northern side of the peninsula from Pólis and Latchí ends at a car park and **CTO pavilion** just past the few houses of Potámi Chíftlik hamlet. Here, the named "Aphrodite" nature trail, diverging from a rough coastal jeep track at a distinctive wooden canopy and archway, begins with a five-minute walk to **Loutrá Afrodhítis**, the "Baths of Aphrodite". In legend the goddess retired here to bathe before (and after) entertaining assorted lovers; today's reality is a flagstoned area beside an attractive pool about four metres across, the headspring of the irrigated oasis below, fed by drips off the rock face of a grotto smothered in wild fig trees. Signs forbid you to succumb to the temptation of bathing in the shallow water, drinking it, or climbing the trees.

Akámas trails and tracks

A combination of the "Aphrodite", "Adonis" and "Smiyiés" trails described below would give you the best possible transect of the Akámas watershed, though you'd encounter a small problem when you reached the Smiyiés picnic grounds – **getting to Neokhorió**, the closest habitation. The road there is quite rough – an ordinary car will just make it, but a taxi-driver would probably refuse the trip or charge you dearly. So whether starting or ending a trek here, you'd likely have to either shuttle between in a jeep, or count on walking the extra 4.5km to/from the village.

In order to make any sense of the "Aphrodite" or "Adonis" nature-trail labelling, you need the 28-page **key booklet** "Nature Trails of the Akamas", distributed free by the CTO and widely available both on the island and overseas. The Smiyiés trail is not as yet so documented.

To access the trails from the pool, proceed downstream on a narrower path to rejoin the coastal track, inland of which is a warning placard with this cheery notice from the UK Ministry of Defence: "Keep out when red flags are flying as (artillery) firing is then in progress. Do not touch any object on the ground as it may explode and kill you." It is wise to make enquiries at the nearby CTO pavilion before setting out.

The "Aphrodite" nature trail

Just before that MOD placard, you head up the continuation of the **"Aphrodite" nature trail**, climbing from carob, mastic and eucalyptus near sea level up to juniper, pine and other species labelled in Greek and Latin; in May, white *Cistus* (rock rose) is everywhere. At the top of the first hard climb you get good views east over the Pólis coastal plain and nearby offshore islets, before a straight-marching trail heads west through an old firebreak. There are some waymarks, plus lots of shotgun shell-casings: birds, especially quail, love the *frígana* (scrub biome), and Cypriots are keen (and in this case illegal) hunters. Somewhat under an hour above Aphrodite's baths you'll arrive at a picnic area in a hollow shaded by a gigantic oak tree; a spring here is unreliable. The adjacent **Pýrgos tis Riyénas** archeological site – apparently the remains of a Byzantine monastery or Lusignan fort – is self-explanatory.

Walk about five or ten minutes west-northwest along a dirt track from the ruins and oak tree, before bearing right onto the trail's continuation (marked by a cairn), and again right onto a dirt track. The path is finally subsumed into the narrow, sharply climbing track, which ends some twenty minutes above the oak with an opportunity to detour left on a path to the viewpoint atop the 370-metre summit known as **Moúti tis Sotíras**. There's a suicide leap out towards Cape Arnaoútis, the very end of Akámas, so you retrace your steps – all of a ten-minute detour – down to the signed junction for the descending, onward footpath to the coast.

Ingeniously engineered into the seaward-facing slopes of the mountain, this offers one more bush-shaded viewpoint before meeting up with the coastal track within around half an hour. You can avoid a fair amount of track-walking on the way back to the car park by keeping to the slightly higher path system until it ends a few minutes before some smelly goatpens to seaward. You'll need to budget approximately two and a half hours for the entire loop out of the CTO pavilion.

The "Adonis" and "Smiyiés" nature trails

From the oak-shaded picnic area by Pýrgos tis Riyénas, another nature trail, the **"Adonis"**, heads off south on a most interesting course. The path initially climbs for fifteen minutes over a saddle, then becomes a wider track heading southeast. After ten minutes on this, you bear left (east) again onto the resurgent trail, which in five more minutes reaches a reliable spring in a forested dell at the head of a canyon.

There's also an important marked junction here: northeast down the canyon back to Loutrá Afrodhítis along the Adonis trail, or south onto the **"Smiyiés"** path. Following the latter for just over five minutes brings you to the kiln stack and tunnels of a derelict magnesium mine, which is also accessible by jeep track along the ridge to the west. The path continues briefly east, then heads south again on a fairly level course before reaching the Smiyiés picnic site within another hour.

From the dell-spring, the continuation of the "Adonis" trail back towards the CTO pavilion descends northeast along the canyon, following a water pipe at first, before curling east. Next you bear north, away from the pipe, then east again across what is now a plateau along the much-widened track through the scrub. Rather suddenly there's a zigzag plunge down towards the coastal road, the route debouching under a now-familiar standard-issue nature trail canopy, about a kilometre southeast of the CTO parking lot. From the spring-junction down to the coast road, count on a good hour.

The Fontána Amorósa coastal track

The most straightforward – and arguably the least exciting – Akámas walk is the one leading to **Fontána Amorósa**, a popular excursion destination almost at Cape Arnaoútis. It's perhaps best done in conjunction with one of the inland nature trails, and is frankly more enjoyable on a mountain bike. If you intend to walk much of it, you'd do well to arrange a boat ride from Latchí to drop you off at Fontána Amorósa, and walk back along the route of your choice – it's very tedious both ways. A simple tramp back to the CTO pavilion takes about 90 minutes; just keep to seaward at every option. Some path shortcuts are possible, especially those mentioned above at the base of Moúti tis Sotíras. Vegetation en route is mostly juniper and mastic bush, with scattered pines. The coast itself, disappointingly, is not very usable; the sea is quite clear, but a northern exposure means lots of debris in the coves of mixed sand and pebbles (if it's beaches you're after, they're better, if less private, at Ttákkas and east of Latchí).

The celebrated **spring** at Fontána Amorósa is a crashing non-event – diligent combing of the bushes turns up nothing more substantial than a tiny, murky well on the cliff overlooking the protected bay. Mythological hype surrounding the "fountain of love" stems from the sixteenth-century Italian traveller and poet, Ludovico Ariosto, who confused it with Loutrá Afrodhítis, to the frustration of all who followed him. On the bright side, the best swimming along the route is just below, where a small sand and gravel beach at the base of the cliff lies out of the wind.

More marvellous than the *fontana* perhaps is the canyon track up behind the artillery-range warning sign just to the east; about four hundred metres along this, in a stream gully, **drinkable water** trickles amid the greenery.

Alternatively, it's possible to continue two-plus kilometres northwest along the track towards Cape Arnaoútis, lengthening the hike by about an hour. There's not much out here except for the wreck of a freighter which foundered some years ago, a popular venue for advanced scuba dives.

Eastern Páfos district: hill villages and monasteries

East of the main Páfos–Pólis road, the severity of the Akámas yields to more forgiving, stereotypically beautiful countryside, largely given over to vineyards and almond groves. The goal of most trippers here is the large village of **Panayía**, and the historic monastery of **Khrysorroyiátissa** just south, but there are a few worthwhile halting points before. Beyond Panayía, it's possible to strike out north into the Tillyrian wilderness (see p.148) and, with some hard driving, the coast northeast of Pólis; or, with greater facility, to turn south to explore the valleys of the Kséros and Dhiárizos rivers (see p.149).

You've a choice of **approach roads**. Coming from Páfos, the quickest route – on the broad E703 highway – passes through Polémi and descends to Kannavioú, negligible except for the chance to eat at tree-shaded tavernas, before the final climb to Panayía.

Starting at Pólis, the best road (officially E712) threads the villages of Símou, Dhrímou, Lássa and Dhrinía, all scattered on the south-bank ridge of the Stavrós tis Psókas stream canyon, before linking up with the E703 at Áyios Dhimitrianós, just below Kannavioú. From Símou, you can descend north for 2km to view the remains of the Lusignan **Skárfos bridge**, which carried the medieval Páfos–Pólis road just upstream from the modern road, below Saramá.

Fýti

At Lássa it's worth making a brief detour up to **FÝTI,** the most architecturally distinguished of this group, where locally woven **lacework** and **runner rugs** are sold both out of the old houses and at the restaurant on the main square. While there is little of the hustle that accompanies the trade in Páno Léfkara (see p.69), and it's commendable to see production (and buy) at source, you won't save over the prices at Páfos market. Next to the church, the *Fyti Taverna* is a restored coffee-shop and *mezé* house (☎732540), whose energetic young chef provides a full spectrum of dishes, including many vegetarian offerings and excellent home-made *loúntza* (smoked pork loin).

Panayía and around

Though shown on most maps as "Páno [ie Upper] Panayía", no Káto (Lower) is visible and the town limits sign merely announces **PANAYÍA**, the largest of several settlements near the headwaters of the Ézousas stream. Here, 750m up, you're at the fringes of the Tróödhos mountains, with walnut trees and tufts of forest visible on the ridge behind. The village is famous as the birthplace of the late Archbishop and President Makarios III, honoured by two small museums and an enormous statue in the main square. At the rear of the plaza sits the grandiosely named **Makarios Cultural Centre** (Tues–Sun 9am–1pm & 2–5pm; free), devoted to photos and paraphernalia of the great man's activities. While the mock-up of the radio set over which Makarios broadcast his defiance of the July 15, 1974 coup is of some interest, the displays are in general pretty feeble, padded out with such vaguely pertinent items as the slippers and alarm clock of a cousin, and rosters of the 1974 war dead from the village.

More atmospheric, perhaps, is **Makarios' Childhood House**, well signposted south of and below the central *kafenío* crossroads. If the gate's locked when it should be open (nominally daily 10am–1pm & 2–6pm; donation) try phoning ☎722858 for Maria the key-keeper. With its pleasant garden and two interior rooms, it seems surprisingly large for a peasant house of the early twentieth century – until you realize that the livestock occupied the back room, with two adults and four children up front. Photos of crucial moments in Makarios' life –

some duplicates of those in the Cultural Centre – and assorted household knick-knacks make up the exhibits.

Practicalities
There's a line of tavernas across the road from the statue *platía*, including one offering beds, though reports have been received of assorted rip-offs here, and the eateries all appear to be owned by the same family. Your best bets for **food** are the newly opened *Vouni Panayia Winery Restaurant*, where, as well as going on a free tour of the winery, you can enjoy a good lunch washed down by samples of vintages, and the *Kentron Avramis*, outside Asproyiá on the main road up from Kannavioú, which serves good salads and *halloúmi*. Several **buses** daily call in from the Pérvola car park terminal in Páfos.

Khrysorroyiátissa monastery
Just 3km south of, and slightly higher than Panayía, the **monastery of Khrysorroyiátissa** (in church Greek, "Khrysorroyiatíssis") stands at a shady bend in the road, gazing out over terraced valleys to the west. Revisionist derivation of the unusual name, "Our Lady of the Golden Pomegranate", from an epithet of the Virgin as Golden-Breasted, seems to point suspiciously back in time to Aphrodite's similar attribute. A twelfth-century foundation legend centres on the hermit Ignatius, who retrieved a glowing icon of the Virgin from the Pafiot shore and, as so often when miraculous images make their wishes known, heard a celestial voice advising him to build a home for her here. Over the years this particular manifestation of the Virgin became the patronness of criminals, who prayed to avoid arrest or for a light sentence – probably a holdover of the safe haven granted to fugitives in certain pagan temples. Dating like the rest of the structure from 1770, with 1967 repair of fire damage, the *katholikón* is plunked down in the middle of the triangular cloister dictated by the site. Its most interesting feature is not the *témblon* or the hidden icon, but the carved and painted wood-panel *yinaikonítis* in the rear of the nave.

Khrysorroyiátissa is ostensibly a working monastery – the reasonably priced products of the basement winery, including *zivanía*, are on sale in the shop, and the current abbot Dionysios is meticulously involved with icon restoration. But the few monks are shy of the tourist hordes, and the guest quarters are shut for repairs until 1997.

The courtyard seems open for visits all day, but the shop and *katholikón* close from noon to 2pm. Outside the walls a panoramic snack/drink bar is not grossly overpriced, and presumably comes alive at the local February 1–2 and August 14–15 festivals.

Ayía Moní monastery
In comparison, the small monastery of **Ayía Moní**, 1500m beyond Khrysorroyiátissa and mostly dating from the seventeenth and eighteenth centuries, has little to offer the casual tourist. Restoration has been done in such a way that the church, originally built in the sixth century atop a temple of Hera and thus one of the oldest in Cyprus, now appears to belong to no particular period. Of late, Ayía Moní has been reoccupied by shy nuns, who are especially uncomfortable in the presence of men; a message by the door reads "Not open to tourists [ie heterodox heathens]". If your Greek is up to it, you might get permission to make a brief and unobtrusive visit.

ARCHBISHOP MAKARIOS III (1913–77)

Makarios III, President-Archbishop of Cyprus and the dominant personality in post-independence Cyprus until 1974, was a contradictory figure. Both a secular and a religious leader, his undeniable charisma and authority were often diminished by alternating spells of arrogance and naivety, coupled with a debilitating tendency to surround himself with pliant yes-men. Many observers, not least Turks and Turkish Cypriots, found it difficult to understand the fusion of his two roles as spiritual and political leader of the Greek Cypriots, in what was nominally a secular republic; they failed to take into account the fact that such a strategy was institutionalized in Greek communal history since the fall of Byzantium. Cyprus is still ambivalent about him: officially revered in the South, detested in the North, a balanced, homegrown appraisal of his life – including his alleged numerous relationships with women – seems unlikely in the near future.

One among four children of Christodhoulos and Eleni Mouskos, he was born **Michael Mouskos** in Panayía on August 13, 1913. He herded sheep in the forest above the village before spending his adolescence as a novice at **Kýkko monastery** (see p.170) in the nearby mountains – where he made friendships and contacts later to prove invaluable. The monks paid his matriculation fees at the prestigious Pancyprian Gymnasium in Nicosia; after graduating in 1936, Mouskos proceeded to Greece, where he attended university and managed to survive World War II. Postgraduate work in Boston was interrupted in April 1948 by the news that he had been chosen Bishop of Kition (Larnaca).

Adopting the religious name **Makarios (Blessed)**, he also turned his attention to politics in his homeland. Soon after coordinating a plebiscite in early 1950 showing 96 percent support among the Greek Orthodox population for *énosis* or union with Greece, he was elected Archbishop of all Cyprus, which made him the chief Greek-Cypriot spokesman in future negotiations with the British colonial masters. With George Grivas, in 1952 he co-founded **EOKA** (Greek Organization of Cypriot Fighters) to struggle for *énosis*. But Makarios initially baulked at the violent methods proposed by Grivas, and for various reasons the rebellion did not begin until April 1955. Makarios' connections at Kýkko proved essential, as both he and Grivas used the monastery as a hideout, recruiting centre and bank.

It didn't take the British long to determine who was behind the revolt, and Makarios plus three other clerics were **deported** to the Seychelles, but released after a year of house arrest on condition they didn't return to Cyprus. So Makarios was able to continue his tactic, evolved since 1948, of travelling around world power centres watching the strategies of others and drumming up support for his cause – particularly among newly independent portions of colonial empires. Among tactics to be emulated were accepting help from whatever quarter offered – including AKEL (the Cypriot Communist Party) and the Soviet Union. In the short run this went some way towards uniting polarized Greek Cypriot society and much of world opinion behind *énosis*, but in the more distant future would generate accusations of unscrupulousness – and earn him the undying, and ultimately destructive, enmity of the overwhelmingly right-wing membership of EOKA.

The last straw, as far as most of EOKA was concerned, was his reluctant acceptance in 1959 of the British offer of **independence** for the island, rather than *énosis*. Grivas returned to Greece, soon to plot more mischief, while Makarios was elected first president of the new republic. He faced an unenviable task, not least convincing suspicious Turkish Cypriots that his departure from the cause of *énosis* was genuine. In this he failed, most signally in 1963 and 1964, by first showing considerable lack of tact in proposing crucial constitutional changes to the Turkish

Cypriot Vice-President, then by failing to decisively restrain EOKA appointees in his cabinet and EOKA gunmen in the streets, and finally by outright threats of violence against the Turkish Cypriot community during the Kókkina incident (see p.137).

It's conceivable that, during the early years of the Republic, Makarios was backpedalling towards *énosis*, but following the colonels' coup in Greece of April 1967, he again saw the advantages of non-aligned independence, especially if the alternative were union with a regime he openly detested – and his own relegation in status to that of a backwater bishop. By early 1968 he had publicly proclaimed the undesirability of *énosis* and began looking for ways out of the impasse, specifically by reopening negotiations with the Turkish Cypriots. But these talks, which continued intermittently until 1974, were never marked by any sufficiently conciliatory gestures – though admittedly such actions would have exposed him to danger from unreconstructed EOKA extremists, which shortly materialized anyway.

To these vacillations on the relative merits of *énosis* and independence, and Makarios' continued espousal of the non-aligned movement (not to mention his relations with communists at home and abroad) can be traced the roots of the growing **US opposition** to the archbishop. US President Richard Nixon vilified him as "Castro in a cassock", while Secretary of State Henry Kissinger openly sought a way to remove this obstacle to more malleable client-states in the Mediterranean. The Greek junta's views on Makarios matched his opinion of them, so they needed little encouragement to begin conspiring, through cadres planted in the National Guard and EOKA-B (a Grivas revival), for his overthrow. Despite repeated, unsuccessful **plots**, instigated by the junta and the CIA, to assassinate him between 1970 and 1974 – including the shooting down of his helicopter – Makarios unwisely vacillated on how to handle their proxies, EOKA-B; by the time the archbishop and his supporters decided on firm suppression, in April 1974, it was too late.

On **July 15, 1974**, the EOKA-B-infiltrated National Guard, commanded by Greek junta officers, stormed the archiepiscopal palace in Nicosia, Makarios' residence, inflicting such comprehensive damage that a clear intent to kill him was evident. Makarios miraculously escaped, however, being spirited by loyalists first to his old refuge at Kýkko and later to the archiepiscopal palace in Páfos, where he broadcast a message disproving announcements of his death. From there his old adversaries the British airlifted him onto the Akrotiri airfield and thence to London and exile. Neither the British nor the Americans initially bestirred themselves much to reinstate a leader whom they felt had received his just desserts for years of intriguing.

Yet Makarios' long practice as emissary to and of the Third World paid off, particularly at the UN, and late in 1974 he was able to **return to Cyprus**, addressing a huge rally in Nicosia with the consummate showmanship which came so naturally to him. He resumed office as president, but the multiple attempts on his life and the depressing fact of the island's continuing division must have weighed on him. On August 3, 1977 Makarios suffered a fatal heart attack, and five days later was buried in an artificial grotto on Throní hill, near Kýkko.

Controversy surrounded even the unseasonable downpour at the time of his funeral: the Greek Cypriot eulogists characterized the rain as the tears of God weeping for His servant, while the Turkish Cypriots – watching the proceedings on television to make sure their bogeyman was really dead – retorted with their folk belief that the sins of the wicked deceased were washed away by the rains before burial.

The Tillyrian wilderness

North of Panayía extends a vast, empty, wooded tract of hills, historically known as **Tillyría**, though strictly speaking the label doesn't apply until you're past the Stavrós tis Psókas forestry station. Unlike the highest stretches of the Tróödhos, the region is not and never has been appreciably settled, frequented in the past mainly for the sake of its rich copper mines (now worked out). If you're staying anywhere on the Pólis coast, a drive through here, and a ramble along the nature trails, satisfactorily completes a day begun in the Páfos hills.

"Cedar Valley"

Leaving Panayía on the route signposted for Kýkko monastery, follow the recently repaved road, always veering towards Kýkko at the well-marked junctions, for 22km until the paving ends abruptly upon arrival at "**Cedar Valley**". This is no more or less than that, a hidden gulch with thousands of specimens of *Cedrus brevifolia*, a type of aromatic cedar indigenous to Cyprus, first cousin to the more famous Lebanese variety and now principally found here. At a hairpin bend in the track, there's a picnic area and a spring, while a sign points to another track – wide but not suitable for vehicles – that leads 2.5km up to 1362-metre Trípylos peak. Strangely, the hike passes few of the handsome trees; they're mostly well downstream, and (perhaps intentionally) inaccessible.

Kýkko itself (see p.170), some 20km further along dirt roads, is much more easily approached from Pedhoulás in the Tróödhos. If you're heading on to Stavrós tis Psókas and the coast, backtrack 4km from the picnic site to the junction marked "Stavros". Follow the sign right and you'll pass, after 6km, a labelled jeep track coming down from the Trípylos summit.

Stavrós tis Psókas and beyond

Some 7km further, there's another important junction: right goes down and north to the coast, left and south descends 3km more to the colonial-era forestry station and rest house at **Stavrós tis Psókas**. The name is that of a monastery, abandoned last century, which once stood here, and is usually politely translated as "Cross of Measles"; it actually means "Cross of the Mange", and in the days before pesticide lotions a spontaneous cure of scabies must have seemed well-nigh miraculous.

The attractive **facilities** at Stavrós include a small café with snacks, the forestry headquarters for Páfos district, a petrol pump intended for staff, a **campsite**, and the extremely popular **hostel**, whose bunks must be reserved in advance from June to August (☎332144 or 722338): C£5 for a bunk in simple rooms with en suite bathrooms. The rangers will proudly assure you that this is the coolest spot in the district (850m up in deep shade, it's not hard to believe); most visitors drive up the easy way, on the wide, surfaced road taking off between Kannavioú and Panayía.

The nature trails

Forestry staff can point you in the direction, near the campsite, of an enclosure for Cyprus **mouflon**, only just saved from extinction – they're now the logo of

Cyprus Airways. Wild members of the small herd also roam the surrounding ridges, but you're exceedingly unlikely to see one running free while hiking one of the two surveyed **nature trails**. It's unhappily difficult to hike these as a loop, though you can just about do them back-to-back, making the most of a day sandwiched in between two nights here. The first, heralded by the same distinctive archway and canopy as used on the Akámas peninsula, begins about halfway along the seven-kilometre stretch of forestry track east of Stavrós towards Trípylos, and plunges off the ridge to end near the final side-turning into the station. The second one begins downstream from the campsite and climbs up the ridge towards Zakhárou peak (1212m), ending prominently in another archway up at the three-way saddle-junction where auto tracks go either to Trípylos, the coast or back down to the station.

Out to the coast

The route **to the coast** is well signposted, but it's slow going and requires stamina which may not be available at the end of a long day. Occasionally rally-style driving in an ordinary car will end you up in Pomós (29km from the junction; see p.137) in about an hour, Káto Pýrgos (37km; see p.137) or the inland salient of the Kókkina detour (25km) in just over an hour. En route you'll notice how the careful husbandry of the British and Republican forestry services was set back considerably by the Turkish Air Force, which set the trees alight with napalm during the summer of 1974; patterns of long reafforestation terraces are still some years from fully reversing this act of economic sabotage.

The Kséros and Dhiárizos valleys

The far southeast of Páfos district is taken up by two major river valleys, those of the **Kséros** and the **Dhiárizos**. They offer not only exciting landscapes and ample opportunities for walking, but monumental attractions in the form of abandoned monastic churches on the riverbanks, and two ancient bridges over the streams. The latter formed an integral part of the **Venetian camel-caravan route**, the beasts transporting copper ore from the Troödhos down to Páfos or Pólis. Not being as durable as the cobbled, round-island Roman road, the Venetian path can scarcely be traced any longer, but the bridges are still there to be enjoyed. If you don't trust your own route-finding abilities, *Exalt Travel* (see Páfos "Listings") is the principal operator organizing day expeditions to the valleys.

The upper Kséros valley

The upper reaches of the Kséros valley, which contain the more interesting monuments, are easily reached from the vicinity of Ayía Moní (see p.145), from where it's 8km via Kilínia to ex-Turkish **VRÉCHA**. Before 1974, this constituted a major enclave, something borne out by an empty UN post, and abundant graffiti in favour of "Taksim" (partition of Cyprus between Turkey and Greece) and "Volkan" (the Turkish Cypriot militants' organization); possibly in retaliation, the Republican administration never provided the place with electric current. Though it's one of the most beautiful spots in the district, with ample water and land, Vrécha remains abandoned except for a Greek Cypriot goatherd and his wife.

From the lower, southern end of Vrécha it's under an hour's descent on foot to a derelict, single-arched **watermill** near the banks of the Kséros River; as in most such structures, the valuable millstone has been filched, recycled for use in modern olive presses. The medieval **Roúdhias** (pronounced "Roothkias") **bridge**, a simple, round-arched span hidden by trees, lies a ten-minute walk upstream from here. It's also accessible by a more direct, but harder to find, jeep track from Vrécha, which crosses a modern bridge just above the older one. Once past this point, the track system can be followed east, then south, for about 20km to Áyios Nikólaos (see opposite).

Panayía Eleoússa Síndi

Heading back through Kilínia, you can proceed south via Galatária to Pendália, where a southeasterly dirt track of about 5km provides the usual approach point to the lonely monastery of **Panayía Eleoússa Síndi**, at the mouth of a side stream on the west bank of the Kséros valley, here considerably wider than at Roúdhias. The main watercourse here is flanked by defunct watermills, which once ground the monastery's corn. Síndi is currently being restored (hopefully with more sensitivity) by the same team that saw to Ayía Moní, who intend to reconstruct the cells around the courtyard with an eye toward monastic rehabitation. The most striking feature here, once inside the walled compound, is a wonderful fieldstoned courtyard; the very plain, high church with its octagonal lantern dome dates from the early sixteenth century.

The Dhiárizos valley

The Dhiárizos valley is in general very appealing, better watered than the Kséros, or the Ézousas further west. The easiest introduction to it, if you haven't got a jeep, is via the turning off the B6 southeast of Páfos for **NIKÓKLIA** (not to be confused with nearby Koúklia). Here, it's possible to **stay** at the *Vasilias Nikoklis Inn* (☎432211, fax 432467; ③), also called "The Old Country Inn", a restored medieval roadside hostelry with beamed ceilings and fairly modern rooms. The menu of the attached **restaurant** isn't very adventurous, but it's reasonable value, served in appealing surroundings and the last prepared food you'll see for a while.

Heading upstream, you wind past **MAMÓNIA**, which was virtually the only local Orthodox village at independence; the *Mylos* **tavern** on the roadside just north of the village serves good light lunches and dinners. Old **PRASTIÓ**, on the east slope of the increasingly sheer valley, was like Souskioú and Fasoúla downstream shattered by the quake of 1953; the replacement, roadside prefab grid opposite had hardly been occupied before communal troubles dictated its abandonment.

Áyios Sávvas tis Karónos

Prastió is the closest place to the intriguing monastic church of **Áyios Sávvas tis Karónos**, with the best access downstream via a dirt track which takes off across the river some 3km east of Áyios Yióryios; an ordinary car can make the side trip after some fifteen minutes of careful driving. Founded in 1120, this rectangular, gable-roofed church represents a mix of Frankish and Byzantine traits introduced at the two restorations of 1501 and 1742; the monastery outbuildings, in ruins since the last century, include an arcaded meeting hall.

Áyios Nikólaos and the Kélefos bridge

Beyond Kithási, the last valley-bottom settlement of what was a Turkish Cypriot enclave, the road crosses the Dhiárizos and skims the district border as it climbs through more prosperous Kédhares, Pretóri and Filoúsa, before reaching **ÁYIOS NIKÓLAOS**. This is one of the highest of the Dhiárizos villages, beautifully set amidst orchards and irrigation ditches, and boasts one of the few tavernas in the Dhiárizos valley. It is also the easiest access point for the graceful **Kélefos bridge** ("Tzílefos" in dialect), reached along a six-kilometre dirt track northwestwards, which, more photogenic than the Roudhiás bridge, spans the upper Dhiárizos with a pointed arch. From the Kélefos bridge, with a decent map to navigate by, you can either carry on east to the Élea bridge and Finí village in the Troödhos, or retrace your steps to Áyios Nikólaos and cross the district border to visit the *Krassokhoriá*.

travel details

Long-distance buses

From **Ktíma Páfos** to: Limassol (Mon–Fri 4–5 daily, 3 on Sat, on *KEMEK*; Mon–Sat 1–2 daily on *Costas*; 1hr 15min); Nicosia (Mon–Sat 1 daily on *KEMEK*; Mon–Sat 1–2 daily on *Costas*; 2hr 45min, via Limassol); Pólis (Mon–Fri 10–11 daily, 5 on Sat, with *Nea Amoroza;* 45min); Pomós (Mon–Fri 4 daily, 3 on Sat, with *Nea Amoroza*; 1hr 45min).

Local buses (*ALEPA*)

From **Ktíma Páfos (Karavélla parking lot)** to: Áyios Neófitos (Mon–Fri 2 daily; 20min); Émba (Mon–Fri 8 daily, 4 on Sat; 15min); Lémba (Mon–Fri 10 daily, 5 on Sat; 15min); Péyia (Mon–Fri 6 daily, 4 on Sat; 30min); Yeroskípou (Mon–Fri 13 daily, 6 on Sat; 10min).

From **Ktíma Páfos (Market parking lot)** to: Coral Bay (Mon–Fri 12 daily, 9 on Sat; 30min); Káto Páfos (summer Mon–Sat dawn–7.30pm every 15min, Sun dawn–6.30pm every 30min; winter Mon–Sat dawn–1pm every 15min, 1pm–6.30pm every 30min, Sun dawn–6.30pm every 30min; 20min).

From **Káto Páfos** to: Coral Bay (summer daily 8am–7pm every 20min, 7–11.30pm every 30min; winter daily 8.30am–6pm every 30min; 40min).

Agorá	Αγορά	ΑΓΟΡΑ
Akámas	Ακάμας	ΑΚΑΜΑΣ
Akourdhália,	Ακουρδάλια,	ΑΚΟΥΡΔΑΛΙΑ,
Páno/Káto	Πάνω/Κάτω	ΠΑΝΩ/ΚΑΤΩ
Aródhes, Páno/Káto	Αρόδες, Πάνω/Κάτω	ΑΡΟΔΕΣ, ΠΑΝΩ/ΚΑΤΩ
Avgás/Avákas Gorge	Αργάκι τής	ΑΡΓΑΚΙ ΤΗΣ
	Αβγάς/Αβάκας	ΑΒΓΑΣ/ΑΒΑΚΑΣ
Ayía Moní	Αγία Μονή	ΑΓΙΑ ΜΟΝΗ
Áyii Anáryiri Milioú	Άγιι Ανάργυροι Μηλιού	ΑΓΙΙ ΑΝΑΡΓΥΡΟΙ ΜΗΛΙΟΥ
Áyios Neófytos	Άγιος Νεόφυτος	ΑΓΙΟΣ ΝΕΟΦΥΤΟΣ
Áyios Nikólaos	Άγιος Νικόλαος	ΑΓΙΟΣ ΝΙΚΟΛΑΟΣ
Áyios Yióryios	Άγιος Γεώργιος	ΑΓΙΟΣ ΓΕΩΡΓΙΟΣ
Dhiárizos (valley)	Διάριζος	ΔΙΑΡΙΖΟΣ
Dhroúsha	Δρούσια	ΔΡΟΥΣΙΑ
Émba	Έμπα	ΕΜΠΑ
Fýti	Φύτι	ΦΥΤΙ
Ínia	Ίνια	ΙΝΙΑ
Kannavioú	Κανναβιού	ΚΑΝΝΑΒΙΟΥ
Káthikas	Κάθηκας	ΚΑΘΗΚΑΣ
Káto Páfos	Κάτω Πάφος	ΚΑΤΩ ΠΑΦΟΣ
Káto Pýrgos	Κάτω Πύργος	ΚΑΤΩ ΠΥΡΓΟΣ
Khóli	Χώλι	ΧΩΛΙ
Khrysokhoú	Χρυσοχού	ΧΡΥΣΟΧΟΥ
Khrysorroyiátissa	Μονή	ΜΟΝΗ
monastery	Χρυσορρωγιάτισσης	ΧΡΥΣΟΡΡΩΓΙΑΤΙΣΣΗΣ
Kilínia	Κοιλίνια	ΚΟΙΛΙΝΙΑ
Kissónerga	Κισσόνεργα	ΚΙΣΣΟΝΕΡΓΑ
Koufón Gorge	Αργάκι τών Κουφών	ΑΡΓΑΚΙ ΤΩΝ ΚΟΥΦΩΝ
Koúklia	Κούκλια	ΚΟΥΚΛΙΑ
Krítou Térra	Κρήτου Τέρρα	ΚΡΗΤΟΥ ΤΕΡΡΑ
Kséros (valley)	Ξέρος	ΞΕΡΟΣ
Ktíma	Κτήμα	ΚΤΗΜΑ
Lára	Λάρα	ΛΑΡΑ
Lássa	Λάσα	ΛΑΣΑ
Latchí	Λατσί	ΛΑΤΣΙ
Lémba	Λέμπα	ΛΕΜΠΑ
Loutrá Afrodhítis	Λουτρά Αφροδίτης	ΛΟΥΤΡΑ ΑΦΡΟΔΙΤΗΣ
Moútallos	Μούταλλος	ΜΟΥΤΑΛΛΟΣ
Neokhorió	Νεοχωριό	ΝΕΟΧΩΡΙΟ
Nikóklia	Νικόκλεια	ΝΙΚΟΚΛΕΙΑ
Páfos	Πάφος	ΠΑΦΟΣ
Pakhýammos	Παχύαμμος	ΠΑΧΥΑΜΜΟΣ
Panayía	Παναγία	ΠΑΝΑΓΙΑ

Pendália	Πεντάλια	ΠΕΝΤΑΛΙΑ
Péyia	Πέγεια	ΠΕΓΕΙΑ
Pólis	Πόλις	ΠΟΛΙΣ
Pomós	Πωμός	ΠΩΜΟΣ
Skoúlli	Σκούλλη	ΣΚΟΥΛΛΗ
Smiyiés	Σμιγιές	ΣΜΙΓΙΕΣ
Stavrós tís Psókas	Σταυρός τῆς Ψώκας	ΣΤΑΥΡΟΣ ΤΗΣ ΨΩΚΑΣ
Tála	Τάλα	ΤΑΛΑ
Trimithoússa	Τριμιθούσα	ΤΡΙΜΙΘΟΥΣΑ
Tsádha	Τσάδα	ΤΣΑΔΑ
Yeroskípou	Γεροσκήπου	ΓΕΡΟΣΚΗΠΟΥ

CHAPTER FOUR

THE HIGH TRÓÖDHOS

Rising to nearly 2000 metres, the Tróödhos (three syllables with stress on the first, pronounced "Tro-o-dhos" rather than "True-dhos") form the mountainous backbone of the southern Republic's territory. Geologically they are a volcanic mass, long extinct and well worn down, but with rich mineral or metallic deposits formerly (in some cases still) mined. Too low and hummocky to be stereotypically alpine, the Tróödhos still acquit themselves as a mountain resort area, and their western part supports what is boasted, with some justification, as the best-managed island forest in the Mediterranean.

In every era the range has been both a barrier and a resource, and later a refuge for Hellenic culture. Ancient miners clear-felled its trees to feed smelting furnaces, the forests growing conveniently close to the copper works of Tillyría. The devastating coastal raids of middle Byzantine times left the hills untouched, and during nearly four centuries of Lusignan rule, when the Orthodox Church was humiliatingly subordinated elsewhere, the Tróödhos provided a safe haven for a minor renaissance in its fortunes – most strikingly evidenced in the famous collection of **frescoed rural churches** here. The Ottomans didn't bother to settle the region, and when the mainland Turks returned in 1974, the obstacle the mountains represented, as much as any ceasefire agreement, may have deterred them from overrunning the entire island. Among foreign occupiers, only the British, homesick and sweltering down in the flatlands, realized the recreational potential of the mountains, with a lacework of roads and assorted architectural follies.

Uniquely in Cyprus, South or North, the independent traveller has a slight edge, or at least not a strong disadvantage, in the Tróödhos. While there certainly are package groups in the fancier **hotels**, more modest establishments – of which there are numbers – welcome walk-in business, geared as they are to a local clientele. The only catch is that much of the less expensive accommodation only opens during the height of summer, so outside that you may find yourself with a limited choice. Despite nominally short distances between points, **touring** here is time-consuming, and you'll be more comfortable changing your base of operations on

---

ACCOMMODATION PRICES IN THE SOUTH

All hotel and apartment-hotel prices in the South have been categorized according to the price codes given below. These categories represent the minimum you can expect to pay in the high season for a double room or a two-person self-catering unit. Single rooms will normally cost 50–80 percent of the rates quoted for a double room. Rates for dorm beds in hostels, where guests are charged per person, are given in Cyprus pounds, instead of being indicated by price code. For further details, see p.25.

① under C£12	④ C£20–25	⑦ C£35–40
② C£12–16	⑤ C£25–30	⑧ C£40–50
③ C£16–20	⑥ C£30–35	⑨ over C£50

occasion, moving on once the potential of a valley is exhausted, rather than pitting yourself and car against a hundred-odd kilometres of serpentine road on a daily basis. Reckon on a leisurely week to see all the Tróödhos have to offer, and don't expect much help from very infrequent bus connections to Limassol or Nicosia.

The functional, though beautifully set resort of **Plátres** is the usual gateway to the region from the south, with the largest concentration of hotels on that side of the watershed. Its higher neighbour **Tróödhos** has no village character to speak of but is the jump-off point for a day's walking around the highest summit, **Mount Olympus**. Good roads lead from either village to **Pedhoulás**, chief village and resort of the Marathássa valley – and also your introduction to the painted churches of the Tróödhos, both here and downstream at **Moutoullás** and **Kalopanayiótis**. Pedhoulás also offers the easiest access to **Kýkko monastery**, out by itself at the edge of the Tillyrian wilderness.

The next sub-region east of Marathássa, Soléa, has as its "capital" the resort of **Kakopetriá**, with its preserved old quarter and unusually accessible concentration of frescoed churches, up-valley at **Áyios Nikólaos tís Stéyis** and downstream at the adjacent village of **Galáta**. Slightly less convenient is the magnificent church of **Asínou**, arguably the finest in the Tróödhos.

East of Marathássa and Soléa lies the harsher terrain of Pitsiliá, largely bare of trees but in many ways more dramatic than its neighbours. From Kakopetriá you climb over the central ridge to the valleys where the fine churches of **Panayía tou Araká**, **Stavrós tou Ayiasmáti** and **Panayía Koúrdhali** are hidden.

The best overnight base in Pitsiliá is **Agrós**, from where you're poised to visit more churches at **Peléndhri** and **Louvarás** before beginning a descent to Limassol. Alternatively you can follow the Tróödhos peak line to its end, passing the lively, untouristed town of **Palekhóri** en route to the showcase village of **Fykárdhou** and the **monastery of Makherás**. From there, the most logical descent is to Nicosia, though it is fairly easy to reach Larnaca.

PLÁTRES AND AROUND

On the south-central flank of the Tróödhos, **Plátres** is the first taste of the range for many people, and easily – perhaps too easily – accessible from Limassol, 37km distant, by a pair of well-engineered roads. The quickest route, the B8, goes via Trimíklini; the other, more scenic option, described in *Limassol and around*, starts at Episkopí and heads north to either Perapedhí or Mandhría.

Above the lateral road linking these three, vineyards cease and cherry orchards and pines begin, signalling your arrival in the high Tróödhos. A tangle of major and minor roads converges on Plátres from every direction, reflecting its touristic importance – though not necessarily its intrinsic interest.

Plátres

At an altitude of 1150m, forest-swathed **PLÁTRES** stays cool and green most of the summer, courtesy of the Krýos stream rushing below. Indeed the town has been characterized as the "Cypriot Simla" for its role as the premier "hill station" in colonial days. Long after independence, it remains a big haunt of expats and enlisted men – you can watch footie in one of several pubs, and many tavernas

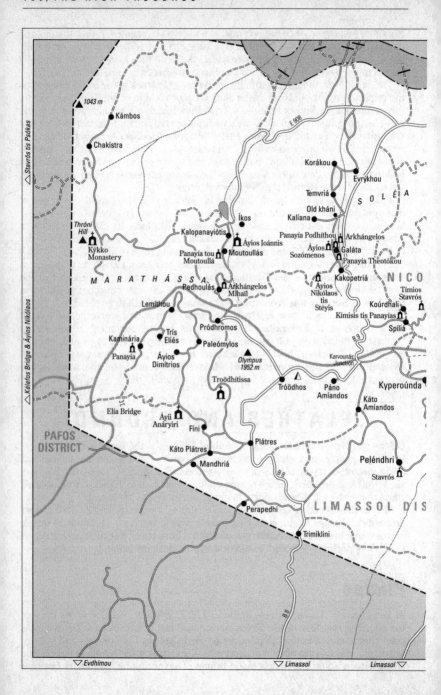

▲ 1043 m

Kámbos

Chakístra

Korákou

Evrýkhou

Temvriá

Old kháni

S O L É A

Kalíana

*Throní
Hill*

Íkos

Kalopanayiótis

Kýkko
Monastery

Áyios Ioánnis

Panayía Podhíthou

Arkhángelos

Panayía tou
Moutoullá

Moutoullás

Áyios
Sozómenos

Galáta

M A R A T H Á S S A

Pedhoulás

Arkhángelos
Mihaíl

Panayía Théotókou

N I C O

Kakopetriá

Lemíthou

Áyios
Nikólaos
tis
Stéyis

Tímios
Stavrós

Kamінária

Trís
Eliés

Pródhromos

Koúrdhali

Panayía

Áyios
Dimítrios

Paleómylos

Kímisis tis Panayías

Spíliá

▲
*Olympus
1952 m*

Karvounás
Junction

Troödhítissa

Tróödhos

△

Páno
Amíandos

Kyperoúnda

Elía Bridge

Áyii
Anáryiri

Fíni

Káto
Amíandos

Káto Plátres

Plátres

Peléndhri

Mandhriá

Stavrós

Perapedhí

L I M A S S O L D I S

Trimíklini

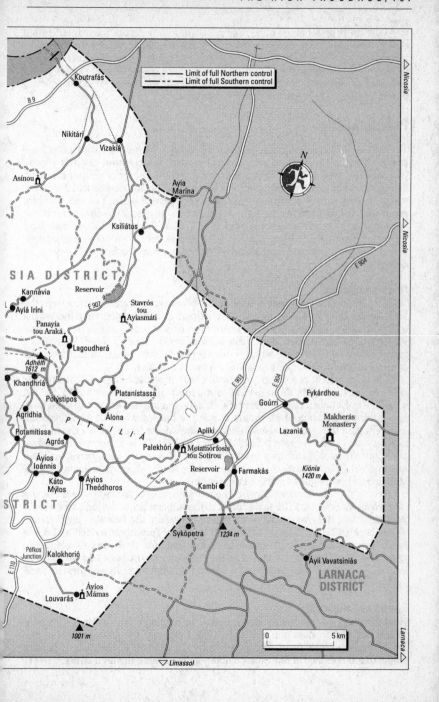

are tuned to British Forces radio. Comparisons with the more famous Indian hill station were doubtless partly inspired by a few remaining villas with whimsical turrets and rooflines, but a staggering quantity of modern development pitched at foreigners is dwarfing the "Raj days" architecture, especially at Plátres' south end, and in summer the main drag is an unenticing uproar of double-parked buses, strolling day-trippers and tacky souvenirs.

Practicalities

The extent of Plátres' commercial district is a single high street, with a combination **post/telephone office**, and adjacent **tourist information branch** (April–Oct Mon–Fri 9am–3.30pm, Sat 9am–2.30pm), behind the large central car park. From this same square daily market charabancs run to Nicosia and Limassol, while *Karydas* runs a **minibus** to Limassol on a service basis. You can also hire **mountain bikes** (look for the sign) to explore the myriad wide dirt tracks in the surrounding hills, and a **supermarket** (the *New*) at the lower junction sells food for hikes. The more villagey quarter, inhabited by locals and deceptively large, lies to the south, with a **filling station** – one of the very few in the Tróödhos, so take advantage.

Accommodation

Many of the dozen local **hotels and guest houses** are scattered away from the high street, their locations shown on a helpful placard posted near the tourist office. However, the majority of these are open only at peak summer season, have let their CTO certification lapse, have seen better days, or all three. Plátres as a resort has in fact lost caste with the islanders themselves and, all that new villa construction notwithstanding, is in something of a decline.

Pick of the hotels geared up for walk-in clientele would have to be the one-star *Minerva* on the upper through-road, open most of the year (☎05/421731, fax 421075; ④). Botanist Yiannis Christofides, an engaging and knowledgeable host, is the third generation of his family to run the hotel since 1947; breakfasts are excellent, and the rooms non-institutional in their decor. If this is full, the two-star *Edelweiss* across the street (☎05/421335, fax 422060; ⑤) is an acceptable alternative, centrally heated and open most of the year. The no-star *Lanterns* on the main lower street (☎05/421434; ③) is also one of the more reliably functioning hotels, and often drops its rates slightly out of season.

Among the hotels more usually booked as part of a package, the three-star *New Helvetia* (☎05/421348, fax 422148; ⑥) is a magnificent period piece (1929) perched above the river at the north end of the resort; the four-star, aptly named *Forest Park* (☎05/421751, fax 421875; ⑨) has been recently extended and offers every conceivable comfort, including indoor/outdoor pools, tennis court and gym. The *New Helvetia* is featured in the *Amathus*, *First Choice* and *Sunvil* catalogues, while the *Forest Park* can be booked through virtually any British package company.

Eating and nightlife

Restaurant prices are nearly identical and, for mediocre fare, inflated – it's hard to get out of the door for less than C£6. Currently the best food is at the Psilódhendhro **trout farm** (lunchtime only). In addition to the rash of pubs, a single **disco** operates in high season about halfway along the high street.

Around Plátres

Two popular excursions – one riding, the other mostly walking – start from Psilódhendhro, just north of Plátres. The remote **monastery of MESAPOTAMÓS** lies 7km east along a dirt track pelted hazardously by rock falls. Having been abandoned for some time, the monastery is now derelict and of little interest except as something to point your mountain bike towards; church-sponsored youth groups apparently unlock the courtyard gate for weekend outings. The streamside Arkolakhaniá picnic site about 1km before might be more compelling as a goal.

Caledonian falls

More absorbing is the drive-walk up to **Caledonian falls**, dubbed "Nature Trail number 3" by the CTO, also beginning (or ending) at Psilódhendhro. The first 45 minutes of climbing are along a car track, with one right fork, after which the route dwindles to a marked trail. The impressive, eleven-metre cascade, highest on the island, beckons a few minutes later, in a pleasantly wooded ravine. Lots of water crossings are involved in continuing upstream along the path; you'll get your feet wet in the springtime. Some 45 minutes beyond the falls you emerge at the opposite trailhead, marked by the familiar canopied noticeboard, about one kilometre from the Tróödhos resort (see below). If you do this walk in the opposite direction, the access slip road off the Tróödhos-bound highway, just below that serving the "*Katoikiai*/Residences" of the president, is also well signposted. Hiking downhill to the falls also takes about 45 minutes, owing to the roughness of the trail at some points – those with trainers beware.

The walk is short enough that retracing your steps is not so arduous; if you're vehicle-less and intent on leaving Plátres, it's worth noting that this trail, despite its steepness, is much the quickest way of getting up to the Tróödhos resort on foot.

Before British administration began in 1878, the area was little visited except for gatherers of snow (used for refrigeration), but shortly thereafter a military training camp was established near the site of present-day Tróödhos, and a **summer residence** built for the British High Commissioner. Now the retreat of the president of the southern Republic, this stands just above the high end of the Caledonian falls trail. Signs discourage entry at the start of the driveway, but you may want to stop in to read the rather startling plaque to one side of the door of what looks like an ordinary Highland shooting lodge. Written in French, it declares: "Arthur Rimbaud, French poet and genius, despite his fame contributed with his own hands to the construction of this house, 1881." Rimbaud's two visits to Cyprus were sandwiched between time with the Dutch colonial army in Java, recuperation from typhoid in France, and a stint in the Horn of Africa; he in fact merely supervised a work party here and did no actual manual labour – nor was he yet famous.

Mount Olympus

At 1952m (6404ft), the Khionístra peak of **MOUNT OLYMPUS** is the highest point on Cyprus. It does not rise particularly dramatically from the surrounding uplands, which are cloaked in typically dense and pampered forest of hardy black

and Calabrian pine, with a smattering of Cypriot cedar and junipers. The trees
keep things cool except perhaps in August, and provide much of the justification
for three marked nature trails. In winter, the northeast-facing slopes are host to
the island's only ski resort. The area is worth a visit at any time of year; however
the altitude and terrain can act as traps for sudden storms in most months, so
don't step off unprepared onto the paths. When you do, you'll find them refresh-
ingly empty.

The Tróödhos resort

The only thing resembling permanent habitation in the peak zone is a strip of
development, called **Tróödhos**, flanking the main road junction about 1700m
above sea level. By no stretch of the imagination is this a village, merely a resort
complex with a petrol pump and the opportunity for some very tame horse-
riding. All day long through much of the year it's beset by tour coaches whose
clients barely venture off the single parade with its handful of undistinguished
kebab houses. There seems little to recommend an overnight here other than
the piney air, with a limited choice of **hotels**: the recently revamped *Troodos
Sunotel* (☎05/421635, fax 422500; ⑧), and the more modest *Jubilee* (☎05/421647;
⑥). Just north of the major T-junction, the **youth hostel** asks a bit more than
usual at C£3 per person, plus a C£1 sheet fee; alternatively, the congenial, popular **campsite**, 1km northeast of the intersection on the road to Nicosia, charges
C£1.50 per tent and C£1 per person. The only public **bus** up here operates from
the Costanza bastion in Nicosia at noon from Monday to Saturday, returning the
next day at dawn.

A summit loop-hike

Perhaps the **best high Tróödhos hike** is the circuit made possible by combining nature trails #1 and #4. It can be done in half a day – slightly more if you make the detour to the actual summit – and in clear weather offers simply the best views of the island, as well as an attractive plant (and bird) community en route. The walk is most enjoyable in the springtime, when numerous streams (and the one improved spring) are still flowing.

Itineraries **begin** at the archwayed trailhead for nature route #1, at the north end of the resort parade, opposite the phone station. A signpost reading "Chromio 8km" is somewhat misleading: the labelled path is approximately that distance, but you never actually end up at the abandoned chromium mine in question. Your first fork is some twelve minutes out; go left for now, following red-dot waymarks. The proper trail skims the 1750-metre contour with little significant height change. Some forty minutes along, there's a three-way junction; ignore a wide track up the ridge to the right but not the onward trail taking off behind a wooden bench. Within ten more minutes there's a masonry fountain, running much of the year. An abandoned chromium mine shaft 1 hour 25 minutes out is often flooded and probably dangerous to explore; here shun wider tracks in favour of the

narrower path hairpinning back left along the far side of the creek valley. Just under two hours along, you've a first view of Pródhromos village far to the west, and its giant, empty Hotel Berengaria. Soon a TV tower looms overhead, then the trail becomes a track through mossy pines about ten minutes before ending, two-and-a-half hours into the hike, on the Tróödhos–Pródhromos road.

Rather than emerging onto the road, bear up and right along a **link trail** for just three minutes – worn yellow plastic discs on some trees serve as waymarks – to the intersection with Trail #4, a true loop closer to the summit. It's possible to follow it right (anti-clockwise), but for the quickest way back to the original trail-head, take a left, crossing the runs of two T-bar ski lifts. Once past the second lift, there's a fine view northeast over northern Cyprus, as you progress roughly parallel to the road back to Tróödhos. You soon meet the tarmacked side road up to Khionístra peak with its RAF radar domes – another retained site – and TV tower, and winter-only café; cross to the nature-trail canopy opposite to stay with the path. At the next track junction bear left, keeping to path surface; three minutes along this bear left again at trees tacked with a yellow arrow and a red dot, forsaking both a track ahead down the ridge and the onward nature trail in favour of an older track dropping down into the valley on your left.

Rocks here are splashed with a few **blue dots**; followed in reverse up the hill, this blue-marked route passes a giant, labelled black pine and the top of the "Sun Valley" lift on its route to the summit area. This is a better detour than following the previously encountered paved drive; in addition to the electronic installations, there is sparse evidence near the peak of a Venetian watchtower and an ancient temple of Aphrodite.

Resuming the descent, you drop through a defile, and then the narrowing track curls back to join Trail #1 just below the *Jubilee Hotel*. You should be back at the starting point roughly an hour and fifteen minutes from the "Chromio" end of the same path (not counting any detours to the peak), for a total walking time of 3 hours 45 minutes.

The Makriá Kondárka trail

This additional short walk is just the thing if you haven't had enough for the day. The path begins inconspicuously at the southeast end of the Tróödhos resort, beyond the police station; if you end up at an off-limits British base, you'll know you've missed the trailhead. At a moderate pace, the out-and-back route should take just over 90 minutes; the destination is the viewpoint of **Makriá Kondárka** at 1700 metres, allowing unobstructed views southeast over the Limassol foothills and coastal plain. On the way back you get to look at the incongruous radar "golf balls" and telecom tower on Khionístra, as well as the huge scar of the Amíandos open-pit asbestos mine, largest in the world, to the northeast.

West of Plátres and Tröödhos

Rather than proceeding directly from Plátres or Tröödhos resort to the Marathássa valley, it's worth detouring slightly along one of three more roundabout, westerly routes, which converge at the alpine settlement of **Pródhromos**. Venerable **Tröödhítissa monastery** is the most interesting sight on the quickest of the three options, a direct, entirely paved route from Plátres. Closer to Plátres lies workaday **Finí** village, with a crafts tradition and better eating than at the neighbouring resort. Rather than proceeding due north from Finí via the pleasant but nondescript hamlets of Áyios Dhimítrios and Paleómylos, veering west along partly dirt roads could be justified by a trio of **minor medieval monuments** along the way.

Tröödhítissa monastery

Nestled in orchards and pines 8km northwest of Plátres at about 1200m elevation, the **monastery of TRÖÖDHÍTISSA** (daily 6am–noon & 2–8pm) is the highest working monastery in the land. It owes its thirteenth-century foundation to a wonder-working icon which, as ever, floated mysteriously over from Asia Minor at the height of the eighth-century Iconoclast controversy. Two hermits guarded it in a nearby cave for some years; after they had died and the memory of the relic faded, an unearthly glow alerted a succeeding generation to its presence, and a suitable home was built for the image. A marked three-minute trail up to the hallowed **cave** begins 300m east of the turnoff for the monastery; a sign in Greek reads, "to the cave in which the icon of the Virgin Tröödhitíssas was found". On arrival, the diminutive grotto has little palpable air of mystery, though at least it's not tastelessly gaudy; in the cascade-lashed gorge below, British forces often hone their abseiling techniques.

The present monastery buildings date mostly from 1730, supplemented by a modern **hostelry**, off-limits from June 15 to September 15. Eight monks still live here, and the same austere regimen as at Stavrovoúni (see p.71) prevails, so frivolous requests to stay the night are not appreciated. In the **katholikón** it's traditional for monks to encircle young women with a medallion-studded girdle, said to induce fertility – in the old days any resulting boy-child had to be dedicated to the church as a monk, or "ransomed" with a generous donation. A marvellous icon, a silver-sheathed *Virgin Enthroned*, is displayed to the left of the Holy Door in the fine *témblon*. Adjacent to the monastery is an *exokhikó kéndro* for refreshments, at its busiest on the August 14–15 and November 20–21 festivals of the Virgin.

Finí

A recently opened, paved side road just 1km up the Tröödhítissa-bound highway provides easy, fairly direct access to **FINÍ**, just 4km from Plátres by this route. Unlike Plátres this is a working village with a functioning primary school, and attracts few visitors for the sake of its semi-arid landscape or domestic architecture. What mostly distinguishes the village is a surviving crafts heritage: there are still a few potteries turning out an assortment of practical and kitsch wares, a traditional chair-maker, and the privately run **Pivlakion Museum** (daily, reasonable daylight hours; donation). This, recently expanded into a medieval basement, is run by Theofanis Pivlakis, who personally escorts visitors through his collection of rural oddments. Though enormous *pithária* (olive-oil jars) are no longer made commercially here, a number of older specimens, with date stamps just above their middle, are on view. Fashioned by a wheel-less method, they were built upward from a knob at the base, like a swallow's nest.

The other reason to stop in at Finí is its **restaurants**. *A Taste of Village – Phini Tavern* is a wild misnomer; what's actually on offer is well-executed, reasonably priced European food, particularly fish and steaks; reservations in high season are virtually mandatory (☎05/421828). Just up the street, the locals frequent *Toh Iliovasilema*, which does all the standard grills.

Áyii Anáryiri and Kaminária

Some 2km west of Finí on the narrow paved road to Paleómylos, look out for a small cement wayside shrine dedicated to **Áyii Anáryiri**. This flanks the start of a dirt track down to the namesake fifteenth-century monastic church, in a lovely setting surrounded by orchards. An eerie legend attaches to the place, specifically that on Saturday at dusk a ghostly horseman emerges through the dog-toothed west portal, oldest surviving portion of the building. A new, locking door has been fitted, presumably resistant to spectral dashes, yet Áyii Anáryiri seems an altogether unlikely spot for hauntings. It is probably not worth hunting down the key to glimpse the few surviving, late medieval frescoes within.

Just past the Áyii Anáryiri shrine, bear left (west) onto a rough but passable dirt track; after just over 7km, you'll reach another junction. Hard by it is the single-arched **Elía bridge**, the easterly link in the Venetian caravan route (see p.149). Though smaller and less impressive than the Kélefos and Roúdhias bridges to the west, the little bridge enjoys a fine position amidst dense forest, with a perennial brook flowing underneath.

Kaminária: the chapel of Panayía
From the Elía bridge junction, the track system leads west towards Kélefos and Áyios Nikólaos village (see p.151), or north within 5km to the friendly, surprisingly large village of **KAMINÁRIA**. On a knoll west of the village stands the early sixteenth-century **chapel of Panayía**, with frescoes from the same era. Ask at the central *kafenío* for the priest with key, and expect to return there for a post-viewing coffee.

Although it cannot compare with the first-division painted churches of the Tróödhos, Panayía is compelling enough in its own right. The most interesting surviving frescoes include, on the north wall, the donor family in French-influenced period dress; the *Sacrifice of Isaac* inside the *ierón*; St Mamas on his lion on the west wall; and, as part of the *Crucifixion*, a weeping, crouching Virgin, with two friends standing behind, entirely western imagery imported into late Byzantine iconography.

Pródhromos

Along with Páno Amíandos, **PRÓDHROMOS** is the highest true village in the country at 1400m elevation. It's also noted for its apples, but unless you coincide with the season, the most interesting item here is the rambling, hilltop, chateau-like **Hotel Berengaria**, abandoned in 1980 – it couldn't compete with the luxurious *Churchill Pinewood Valley*, just downhill to the north. A foreign consortium briefly considered purchasing it for refurbishment, but the hotel's dereliction is rapidly approaching write-off status. The vandalized interior makes for oddly absorbing rummaging, scattered correspondence files providing a thumbnail social history of the British empire.

The village itself, a fairly desolate place with just one or two shops and a petrol pump at its top end, appears no longer to be an option as a fallback base, since its other hotel (the *Alps*) also appears to have closed down. Anyone staying in the immediate area does so at the lately remodelled, three-star *Churchill Pinewood Valley* (☎02/952211, fax 952439; ⑧), 3km north towards Pedhoulás, a self-contained luxury **resort** available through virtually every tour operator.

MARATHÁSSA

Directly north over the ridge from Pródhromos yawns the valley of **Marathássa**, an introspective, deep canyon of Asiatic grandeur. Like most watercourses on the north side of the Tróödhos, the Setrákhos stream draining it runs at present into North Cyprus, and a dam has been built to rescue the water that would otherwise go unharnessed into "enemy" territory. Marathássa is famous for its cherry orchards, from which it makes a partial living; tourism, while catered to, is not the be-all and end-all that it is at Plátres. The valley can boast a respectable concentration of frescoed churches, and while not strictly speaking within Marathássa, the prestigious monastery of Kýkko is easiest reached from here.

Pedhoulás

At the top of the Marathássa valley, 1100m up, **PEDHOULÁS** has a very different feel from Pródhromos: more compact and amphitheatrically laid out in tiers, though close up most of the buildings are not so attractive. As a base it's a viable alternative to Plátres, both for convenience to Marathassan sights and for the range of choice in eating and sleeping.

Arkhángelos Míhaïl church

The main sight, and quite possibly your first frescoed church of the Tróödhos, is **Arkhángelos Míhaïl**, in the lower quarter of the village. The warden, Panayiótis, lives in a house with pale green shutters and doors, 50m uphill on the same side of street; otherwise he can often be found at the junction of the Moutoullás road, 300m uphill, near a café and two stores.

The core of the church dates from 1474, so the style of its recently cleaned images is naturalistic and unaustere as befits the post-Byzantine revival. The archangel Michael himself looms left (north) of the minimalist *témblon*; beside him is shown the *Sacrifice of Abraham*, the usual signature-mark of Goul or an apprentice (see box), with the principals of the potentially gruesome drama radiating a hieratic serenity.

Starting on the south wall, there's a clockwise life-cycle of the Virgin and Christ: in *The Betrayal* a miniature Peter lops off the ear of a centurion in Crusader dress, while two apostles cense the Virgin's bier in the *Assumption*. Over the north door, donor Basil Khamadhes and his family, in noble costume of the period, hand a model of the church to the archangel, who emerges from a curtain-like fold of cloud next to the dedicatory inscription. Above the *Virgin Orans* in the apse looms a smudged *Ascension*, in lieu of the usual *Pandokrátor*.

Practicalities

Best value among inexpensive **accommodation** here are the newish, well-appointed rooms above the centrally located *Mountain Rose* restaurant (☎02/952727; ②), or failing that the year-round, no-star hotel *Christy's Palace* 150m east

---

FRESCOED CHURCHES OF THE TRÓÖDHOS

Indisputably the most remarkable monuments in the Tróödhos, if not the whole island, are a group of lavishly **frescoed Byzantine churches**, mostly on the north slopes of the range. The earliest of these date from the eleventh century, with construction continuing until the early 1500s; frescoes were applied sporadically over the whole period, so that they serve as a chronicle of changing dress styles and artistic tastes, often juxtaposed in the same building. The oldest frescoes were executed in what is termed the **hieratic or monastic style**, with roots in Syria and Cappadocia; later Byzantine work reflected the arrival of artisans from Constantinople in the twelfth and thirteenth centuries. As Lusignan rule advanced, the building and decorating of these chapels became of necessity a provincial, rearguard action, since the Orthodox were effectively banished from the larger towns. The so-called **post-Byzantine revival style** of the fifteenth and sixteenth centuries is at once more naive and naturalistic, with fascinating period details, humanistic liberties taken with Orthodox iconographic conventions, and in general echoes of Renaissance art.

Architecturally, most of these country churches were originally simple rectangular structures about the size of a small barn; later they often grew domes, less frequently narthexes. If it didn't originally exist, an all-encompassing, drastically pitched roof would be added at some point to shed dangerously heavy snow, with ample provision for domes if necessary. Most importantly, by extending down to the ground on one or both sides, they enclosed L- or U-shaped spaces which *de facto* served as narthexes, so that many frescoed exterior walls were now afforded some protection. It's worth saying that almost every Tróödhos village has such a pitched-roof church – but only a very few are still painted inside.

Certain departures from the usual **iconography** were caused by the many pitched, domeless roofs; there were often no cupola, squinches or vaults for the usual hierarchical placement of the *Pandokrátor* (Christ in Majesty), cherubim, evangelists and so on. However the cartoon-strip story-telling format, chosen to teach the Gospel to largely illiterate parishioners, was enhanced in small rectangular churches. The usual arrangement is a fairly complete life-cycle of the Virgin and

(☎02/952655; ③). Several other hotels and guest houses are open mid-summer only; most characterful and quietest of these is the two-star *Marangos* (☎02/952657; ④), a somewhat down-at-heel stone structure panoramically sited at the northwest edge of town.

When **eating out**, avoid the unseemly lunchtime scrums of the tour groups at *Mountain Rose* and its rival *Two Flowers* in favour of sixty-year-old *Toh Vrysi* (alias *Harry's*), a shady and authentic *exokhikó kéndro* on a minor road up to the main highway, open daily most of the year. This features Arsos red wine, home-style dishes such as pickled wild mushrooms, occasionally white-fleshed wild trout (as opposed to the pink farmed variety), and a full spectrum of candied fruits and vegetables – a possible consolation if you miss the local cherry season. It's not rock-bottom cheap, but portions are generous, so show up hungry. "Harry" also sells canned and bottled products to take away, including his own cherry brandy.

Rounding out the list of amenities are **banks**, a **CYTA** station and a minuscule **post office**. The once-daily market **bus** on the Nicosia–Plátres line passes through here early in the morning.

Jesus, with emphasis on the crucial dedications to God of both and various miracles and events of his ministry. Over the door, the donor/builder usually appears in a portrait, presenting the church in miniature to Christ or the Virgin, below an inscribed request for mercy at the Last Judgement.

Variations from the pattern – details such as shepherds playing rustic instruments of the time, period costumes and humorous touches – are what make each church interesting. Selected Old Testament personalities or episodes, rarely seen in Cyprus outside the Tróödhos, such as the *Sacrifice of Abraham*, recur particularly in late fifteenth-century churches, and act as the signature of a certain **Philip Goul**, presumably a Latinized Greek, or one of his apprentices.

Most of the churches are proudly proclaimed on their identifying plaques as being listed on the UNESCO World Cultural Heritage roster, and kept firmly **locked**, with no set opening hours. Thus hunting down the key is an integral part of your visit; instructions on how to find it are given in the account of each church. Sometimes the **caretaker** is a layman who lives nearby, otherwise a peripatetic priest who might not show up until the next day, as he could be responsible for conducting liturgies at several neighbourhood churches. Wardens vary in terms of knowledgeability (none are trained guides, though some have a basic grasp of the images if you understand Greek) and cordiality, the latter not surprisingly often a function of how many importunate foreigners they have to escort. While there is no set admission fee, a **donation** is expected, especially in cases where you've taken the key-keeper miles out of his daily routine. Usually a box is provided in the church; otherwise you should tip the responsible person at the conclusion of your visit. Fifty cents is sufficient for a small church where the guard lives next door; a pound for a large monument off in the woods.

Binding **recommendations** would be subjective; if you're keen, you can see all of the churches in a few days. If your interest is more casual, three or four will be enough – the most important are reckoned to be Asínou, Áyios Ioánnis Lambadhistís, Áyios Nikólaos tís Stéyis, Panayía toú Araká and Stavrós toú Ayiasmáti. If you develop a compulsive interest in the subject, a recommended specialist guide is *The Painted Churches of Cyprus*, by Andreas and Judith Stylianou (Trigraph, London, 1985), C£18 and easily available at good Cypriot bookshops.

Moutoullás: Panayía toú Moutoullá

The earliest surviving example of the Tróödhos pitched-roof church, **Panayía toú Moutoullá** (1280), stands next to the cemetery at the highest point of **MOUTOULLÁS** village, 3km below Pedhoúlas. A set of steps leads up from the road, above the sharp turn in the ravine, to a somewhat crotchety caretaker's house just below the church.

You enter via two sets of doors, the outer pair piercing the protective structure grown up around the original church, the inner ones (and the altar screen) very fine, carved antique pieces. The village is still renowned for its carved feed-troughs and other utilitarian objects, as well as its spring water, bottled way down in the canyon.

On the original exterior wall of the church, now within the L-shaped "narthex", Christ is enthroned over the inner doors, flanked by *Adam and Eve, Hell and Paradise* (with the saints marching in). Inside, the cycle of events is similar to that of Arkhángelos Míhaíl in Pedhoúlas, but less complete, and stopping with the *Assumption* rather than the *Ascension*; the caretakers claim that the British, while engaged in an anti-EOKA raid, damaged many scenes. An unusual *Nativity* on the south wall shows the Virgin rocking the Christ Child in his cradle (she's usually still reclining after having given birth), while Joseph sits on a wooden donkey saddle much like ones that were formerly produced in the village. An equally rare martial *Áyios Khristóforos* (St Christopher) stands opposite *Áyios Yióryios* (St George) on the north wall, slaying a dragon with the crowned head of a woman. On the west wall, *The Raising of Lazarus* includes the obligatory spectator holding his nose against the reek of the tomb; on the north wall, there's a rather stiff portrait of donor Ioannis Moutoullas and wife. Overall, the images don't rank among the most expressive or striking in the Tróödhos, but are the earliest, unretouched frescoes among the churches.

Kalopanayiótis

Just over a kilometre further down the Setrákhos valley from Moutoullás, **KALOPANAYIÓTIS** seems a bit less concrete than Pedhoúlas, more geared to tourists than facility-less Moutoullás, and the most compact of the three villages – though it has a suburb hamlet, Íkos (alias Níkos), downstream and across the river. Many old handsome houses have retained their tiled roofs, and there are fine views up-valley to Pedhoúlas. The village is thought to be the descendant of ancient Lampadhou, which produced the saints Iraklidhios and Ioannis (see below). There are also two fine old **bridges** in the area: one next to the local sulphur springs, the other just upstream from the local reservoir and below Íkos, still serving a little-used medieval trail descending from Íkos to the west bank of the valley.

Of the three no-star **hotels** here, all on the through road and all seemingly geared to the domestic spa trade, the sprucest is the *Kastalia* (☎02/952455, fax 02/457532; ③) near the middle of the village – though *Heliopoulis* (☎02/952451; ③) at the south end of Kalopanayiótis is currently being renovated. For **meals** out, you're restricted to your hotel's diner or two kebab houses.

The monastery of Áyios Ioánnis Lambadhistís

Plainly visible from Kalopanayiótis across the river, and accessible by a one-kilometre side road or a more direct footbridge (or by dirt track from Íkos), the rambling **monastery of Áyios Ioánnis Lambadhistís** (May–Sept daily 8am–noon & 1.30–6pm) is probably the successor to a pagan shrine, owing its foundation to some cold sulphur springs just upstream. The saint in question is not John the Evangelist, but a local ascetic who died young, to whose tomb were ascribed healing powers. This is one of the few early Tróödhos monasteries to have survived relatively intact from foundation days – many of the painted churches are lonely *katholiká* bereft of long-vanished cloisters, and those monasteries that still exist have been renovated beyond recognition over the centuries. If the courtyard and church doors are not open during the posted hours, enquire at the café adjacent for the (none too friendly or patient) caretaker-priest. From October to April, the café will probably not be operating, and you'll have to fetch the priest from his house in the village, on the east side of the through road, north of Ayía Marína church. The local **festival** takes place on October 3–4.

Huddled together under a single, huge, pitched roof are three **churches**, the whole wider from south to north than long, and built to an odd plan. The double main nave, one part dedicated to Iraklidhios during the eleventh century, the other to Ioannis a hundred years later (though redone in the mid-1700s), is entered from the south side; other doors lead to a later narthex and a Latin chapel added towards the end of the fifteenth century.

The frescoes

By virtue of the building's sheer size, there is room for nearly complete coverage of the synoptic gospels, and a number of duplications, stemming from the **frescoes** having been added in stages between the thirteenth and fifteenth centuries. The *Pandokrátor* in the dome of the nave dedicated to Iraklidhios, and panels over the side entrance, are the oldest frescoes.

The earlier subjects are the usual locally favoured ones, with slight variations: in the *Resurrection*, Christ only lifts Adam, and not Eve, from Hell, and the *Sacrifice of Abraham* is idiosyncratic in its position on the south wall rather than in the *ierón*. There are several versions of *Christ before Pilate*, and two *Raisings of Lazarus* from obviously different eras, both on the south side of the nave. As so frequently in Tróödhos frescoes, children – here wearing black gloves – shimmy up a date palm for a better view of the *Vaïofóros* or *Entry into Jerusalem*, where Christ rides side-saddle on a rather grouchy-looking ass.

The later frescoes of the northerly Latin chapel constitute the most complete Italo-Byzantine series on the island, and it seems almost certain that the native Cypriot painter had stayed for some time in Italy. Most panels take as their theme the *Akathistos* hymn in praise of the Virgin, with 24 stanzas (and thus 24 scenes) beginning each with a letter of the Greek alphabet. By the small apse, a natural-ized *Arrival of the Magi* shows the backs of all three galloping off, on horses turned to face you, as if part of the background to a Renaissance canvas, not the main subject. The Roman soldiery in several panels not only wear crusader armour, but fly pennants with a red crescent, apparently a Roman symbol before being adopted as an Islamic one. In *The Hospitality of Abraham*, one of a few exceptions here to the *Akathistos* theme, the patriarch washes the feet of three decidedly Florentine angels prior to having them at table.

Kýkko monastery and around

Nineteen paved but twisty kilometres west of Pedhoulás sits the enormous, fabulously wealthy **monastery of Kýkko** (Kýkkou), one of the most celebrated in the Orthodox world. Here Michael Mouskos, better known as Makarios III, began his secondary education, and later served as a novice monk, prior to using the monastery as a hideout during his EOKA days (when Grivas' headquarters were nearby). Thus Kýkko is inextricably linked with the Cypriot nationalist struggle.

Despite these hallowed associations, the place is of negligible artistic or architectural interest; the mosaics and frescoes lining the corridors and the *katholikón*, however well intentioned, are workmanlike and of recent vintage – some as new as 1987. Repeated fires since Kýkko's twelfth-century foundation by the hermit Isaiah have left nothing older than 1831. Isaiah had been given an **icon** of the Panayía Eleoússa, the Most Merciful Virgin, by the Byzantine emperor Alexios Komnenos in gratitude for curing the latter's daughter. The monastery grew up around this relic, claimed to have been painted by Luke the Evangelist, which now has pride of place in a rather gaudy shrine in front of the *témblon* or altar screen. Considered too holy for the casual glances of the possibly impious and unworthy, who would run the risk of a most unmerciful instantaneous blinding, the original image has been encased in silver for almost four centuries now. Nearby in the *katholikón* is a brass arm, said to be that of a blasphemous Turk who had it so rendered by the icon's power, when sacrilegiously attempting to light his cigarette from a lamp in the sanctuary.

On weekends Kýkko is to be avoided (or gravitated towards, according to your temperament), when thousands of Cypriots descend upon the place. A ban on photos in the church is cheerfully ignored by proud relatives video-ing and snapping the relay baptisms which take place then; lottery ticket-sellers circulate out in the courtyard as howling babies are plunged one after another, accompanied by a barrage of flashbulbs, into the steaming font. Monks at more austere monasteries ridicule the practice – what's the matter with one's local parish church for christening your child, they say – but this ignores the tremendous prestige of Kýkko, and the ease of access from Nicosia along recently improved roads.

Besides the pilgrimage activities, there's a **museum** of ecclesiastical treasures adjoining the inner courtyard (C£0.30). At Room 13, to the right of the main gate of the outer courtyard, you can request a room in the enormous *ksenónas* or guest quarters, though if you're not Orthodox you'll certainly be quizzed as to why you wish to stay overnight.

Throní

The longish, scenic trip in from Pedhoulás is much of the attraction; it can be prolonged by another 2km to a final car park below **Throní**, the hill atop which stands the **tomb of Makarios**. This is a bunker-like capsule, with the main opening to the west and a National Guardsman keeping a permanent vigil. A modern **shrine** just south adorns the true summit, which allows comprehensive views of the empty Tillyrian hills to the west, and Mount Olympus to the east; in many ways it's a better vantage point than the latter. On the yearly festival (September

7–8) the numinous icon of Kýkko is paraded at the shrine amid prayers for a rainy winter. The stark concrete design of the chapel is further offset by a wish-tree (more accurately, wish-bush) on which old ladies have tied votive hankies, tissues and streamers as petitions for more personal favours from the Virgin.

Kámbos

Just before Kýkko, signs beg you to head north 8km to visit **KÁMBOS**, the only substantial habitation in Tillyría, poised in isolation about halfway down the slope towards the Attila Line. There seems little reason to go, other than the appeal of a quite untouristed place; you may even **stay** at the *Kambos* guest house (☎02/942320; ②), with meals also offered.

SOLÉA

The region of Soléa, centred on the Karyótis stream valley, was the most important late Byzantine stronghold in the Tróödhos, as witnessed by its large concentration of churches. The terrain is much less precipitous than adjacent Marathássa on the west, from which Soléa is accessible by a steep but passable dirt road taking off from just above the *Churchill Pinewood Valley* resort between Pródhromos and Pedhoulás. Kakopetriá is Soléa's chief village and showcase, conveniently close to several frescoed churches, but nearly half a dozen small hamlets, in varying states of preservation, are scattered downstream and worth a visit, ideally on a bicycle.

Kakopetriá

KAKOPETRIÁ, "Wicked Rock-Fall", takes its name from a rash of boulders which originally studded the ridge on which the village was first built. Most were removed, but some had to stay, including **Pétra tou Andhroyínou** (Couple's Rock), a particular outcrop on which newly-weds used to clamber for good luck – until one day the monolith heaved itself up and crushed an unlucky pair to death.

Low enough at 660m elevation to be very warm in the summer, Kakopetriá was formerly a wine and silk-weaving centre, but is now a busy, trendy resort, the closest Tróödhos watering-hole to Nicosia. The village straddles the river, which lends some character, as does the officially protected (and not yet too twee) old quarter. This was built on a long ridge splitting the stream in two; a preservation order was slapped on it in 1976, but a few new buildings apparently got in after it went into effect. Derelict traditional dwellings have been bought up at premium prices and redone tastefully, mostly by Nicosians.

Down in the western stream, across an old bridge, hides an old water-powered grain mill, also refurbished, and bird houses for the ducks and pigeons that frequent the place. An adjacent drink stall has seats at the base of the towering *Maryland at the Mill* restaurant, a creation (in vernacular style) of John Aristidhes, one of the conservation advocates.

Practicalities

Many **hotels** are grouped around the telecommunications tower on the east bank of the river, on Gríva Dhiyení, but they're relatively expensive and have little character compared to establishments lining the river, some of which have water-front balconies. Such options there include the hotel-restaurants *Romios* (☎02/ 922456; ②) and adjacent *Zoumos* (☎02/922154; ②), plus the recently renovated one-star hotel *Kifissia* (☎02/922421; ④), all on the way to Áyios Nikólaos tís Stéyis (see below). Down past the bridge on the old road to Galáta – in fact near the edge of the latter – are two places renting **rooms**: *Kendro Dhilinia* (☎02/ 922455; ②), surprisingly comfortable for the price, with attached bathrooms; and the restaurant *Kouspes* next door. An excellent choice in the old quarter are the rooms under the *Kafenio Galini*, most of which overlook the stream ravine (☎02/ 922602 or 922810; ①).

Maryland at the Mill is certainly your best bet for **eating out**; the food, with trout featured, is abundant, well prepared and not vastly overpriced. Though there's some tour-bus clientele, seating on two levels accommodates crowds, and a summer-only waterside annexe – the *Mill Restaurant* – offers a slightly different menu. Other eating options are poor. You won't save much money or do your stomach any favours by dining in the noisy, car-plagued high street on the east bank, so you may as well enjoy the atmosphere in the old district for the same price. *Kendro Meteora* (food in summer only) perches above Pétra tou Andhroyínou, *The Village Pub* – with food as well as drink – just below. Kakopetriá has banking, post and phone amenities, and frequent **buses** to and from the Costanza bastion terminal in Nicosia.

Áyios Nikólaos tís Stéyis

The engaging church of **Áyios Nikólaos tís Stéyis** stands about 4km above Kakopetriá, on the west (river) side of the dirt road over to Marathássa. Once part of a monastery, it is now isolated at the edge of the archdiocese's YMCA-type camp and recreation centre. You cannot drive up to it, but must walk through a gate/turnstile and along a path skirting the playing pitch. When the church is open (Tues–Sat 9am–4pm, Sun 11am–4pm), an attendant can point out the salient features in English.

The core of the church, with some of the oldest frescoes in the Tróödhos, dates from the eleventh century. A dome and narthex were added a hundred years later, and during the fifteenth century an unusually extravagant protective roof (hence the name, *tís Stéyis* meaning "of the Roof") was superimposed on the earlier domed cross-in-square plan. As so often, the frescoes are attributable to a sequence of periods, from the eleventh century to (in the south transept) the fourteenth and fifteenth, thereby spanning all schools from the traditional to post-Byzantine revival.

The most unusual, later images are found in the transept: the north side has a *Crucifixion* with a personified sun and moon weeping, and an unusual *Myrrofóri* (*Spice-Bearers at the Sepulchre*), with the angel sitting atop Christ's empty tomb, proclaiming Christ's resurrection to the two Marys (Magdalene and the mother of James) and Martha.

The *Nativity* in the south transept vault shows the Virgin breast-feeding the Child with a symbolic, anatomically incorrect teat – icons of the subject (*Panayía Galaktotrofoússa*) abound but frescoes are rare, mostly confined to Coptic Egypt. Around her goats gambol and shepherds play bagpipe and flute, while a preco-ciously wizened duplicate infant Jesus is given a bath by two serving-maids. Similarly unusual is the *Archangel Holding the Child* in the same corner. Opposite the *Nativity* unfolds the locally more favoured ordeal of the *Forty Holy Martyrs*, Christian soldiers in the Roman army tortured by immersion in a freezing lake at Anatolian Sebastaea. One, weakening in resolve, heads for the shore where warm soup-kettles have been set up to tempt the condemned, but a Roman guard, overcome with admiration for the Christians, is seen shedding his tunic to join them. The tale of the Forty Martyrs, with its moral of solidarity, constancy and endurance of pain, was a favourite among the officers of the Byzantine army. The warrior saints Yióryios and Theódhoros (George and Theodore), in crusader dress, brandish their panoply of arms on one column of the nave.

Galáta

Around 1500m north of Kakopetriá, **GALÁTA** is a far more aesthetic village, the through road lined with handsome old buildings sporting second-storey balustrades. Just 2km further down the valley, the best example of these is an old **kháni** or wayfarers' inn, between the turnings for Kaliána and Temvriá. Keep an eye peeled for a modern *Khani Kafenio*; the old inn is two buildings beyond, on the same side of the road.

Galáta's notable churches are numerous, scattered and – as usual – locked. You'll need a vehicle, and some patience in tracking down the busy guardian-priest: he lives in a one-storey brick farmhouse at the end of the lane leading east from the school; a small sign on a power pole reads "*Ikía Iereá*" (priest's house). The school road is narrow and unmarked, taking off inconspicuously northeast, parallel to a cement retaining wall that shores up the main Galáta–Nicosia slip road.

Arkhángelos and Panayía Podhíthou

The road from the school leads north a few hundred metres to the adjacent sixteenth-century churches of Panayía Podhíthou and Arkhángelos, the most notable of several in and around Galáta. The former was once part of a monastery, but today both stand alone, awash in springtime beanfields, on the east bank of the river.

Arkhángelos (1514), the first and smaller church, is also known as Panayía Theotókou but described as such to avoid confusion with a nearby namesake church (see below). The interior adheres to local conventions as to style and choice of episodes, featuring an unusually complete life of Christ, with such scenes as *The Prayer in Gethsemane*, *The Washing of the Feet* and *Peter's Denial*, complete with crowing cock; fish peer out of the River Jordan in the *Baptism*. The chronological sequence begins with *The Prayer of Joachim* (the Virgin's father) near the door, finishing with *The Redemption of Adam*. Most unusually there's the signature of the painter, Simeon Axenti, in the panel depicting the donor Zacharia family, who were of Hellenized Venetian and Lusignan background, the women following the Catholic rite, the men adhering to Orthodoxy. Such arrangements were not uncommon in formerly Byzantine territories captured by the West.

The unusual shape of **Panayía Podíthou**, built in 1502, dictates an equally unconventional arrangement of the cartoon-like panels. Abbreviated lives of the Virgin and Christ are relegated to the *ierón* (the area beyond the altar screen). In the apse, Solomon and David stand to either side of the Italo-Byzantine

Communion of the Apostles; at the top of the pediment formed by the roofline, the Burning Bush is revealed to Moses. The walnut *témblon* itself, complete with gargoyles from which lamps are hung, is magnificent despite its icons having been stolen or taken to Nicosia for restoration.

Above the west entry door, its favoured position, there's a very detailed, Italianate *Crucifixion*, complete with the two thieves, the Virgin fainting, Mary Magdalene with loose hair at the foot of the cross and the soldier about to pierce Christ's side. Indeed the sense of tumult and vulgar spectacle is totally un-Byzantine; onlookers' dress, demeanour and facial features are highly differentiated, and approach caricature at times. Out in the U-shaped "narthex", created by the later addition of the peaked roof, the donor Dhimitrios de Coron and his wife appear on the left of the *Redemption*; above this the *Virgin Enthroned* appears in the company of various Old Testament prophets, rather than with the usual *Fathers of the Church* as at neighbouring Arkhángelos.

Áyios Sozómenos

If you wish, the same genial priest will accompany you to **Áyios Sozómenos**, 50m behind and uphill from Galáta's big modern church. Its iconography is very similar to that of Arkhángelos – hardly surprising since the artist (Axenti) and construction date are identical. The frescoes are numerous but relatively crude, and can't compare to those at Podhíthou or Arkhángelos.

However there are some wonderful touches: in the lower echelons of saints on the north wall, the dragon coils his tail around the hind legs of St George's charger as he's dispatched; a maiden chained at the lower right demonstrates how the tale is a reworking of the Perseus and Andromeda myth. On the south wall, St Mamas holds his lamb as he rides an anthropomorphized lion (see p.181 for an explanation). Overhead, the original painted wooden struts are still intact (they've rotted away in most other churches); behind the *témblon*, a *Pentecost* takes place on the left, in addition to the typical episodes of Abraham's life to either side of the apse. Out in the U-shaped narthex, there's a damaged *Apocalypse* left of the door, while various ecumenical councils (complete with heretics being banished) meet on the other side.

Panayía Theotókou and Ayía Paraskeví

Two more churches, one of essentially specialist interest, flank the road up to Kakopetriá. The early sixteenth-century **Panayía Theotókou** is next to the *BP* petrol station, where the key is kept; the interior preserves an unusually large panel of *The Assumption*, with Christ holding the Virgin's infant soul, plus *a Pentecost* and a fine *Angel at the Sepulchre*. Behind the handsome *témblon*, *The Hospitality of Abraham* is offered on the right, with his vivid attempted *Sacrifice* opposite. In the apse conch, the *Virgin Enthroned* reigns over the six *Ierárkhi* (*Fathers of the Church*) below, while over the entrance, the donors, Leontios and Loukretia, huddle with a half-dozen others.

Ayía Paraskeví, contemporary with Áyios Sozómenos and Arkhángelos, is a bit downhill on the opposite side of the pavement, next to a playground, but it's not worth the bother to fetch the key opposite as there's nothing inside but some fresco fragments in the apse and a faded painted *témblon*.

Asínou (Panayía Forviótissa)

Arguably the finest of the Tróödhos churches, **Asínou (Panayía Forviótissa)** lies out in the middle of nowhere, but emphatically justifies the detour off the B9 Kakopetriá–Nicosia road. The key-priest, rather formal but civil, lives in **Nikitári village**, reached via Koutrafás or Vizakiá; you ask after him in the café across from the modern church. Asínou gets some coach-tour attention, so he may already be up there, 4km above village, or at home for an undisturbable afternoon nap.

The popular, less formal name of the church stems from the ancient town of Asinou, founded by Greeks from Argolid Asine but long since vanished; the same fate has befallen any monastery which was once here, leaving only an *exokhikó kéndro* across the road, with the beautiful countryside an ideal place for a Sunday outing. *Panayía Forviótissa* may mean "Our Lady of the Pastures", though only the church-crowned hilltop is treeless, with forested river valley all around; another derivation has it as "Our Lady of the Milkwort", and it must be said that botanical epithets of the Virgin are common on Cyprus. A barrel-vaulted nave, remodelled during the fourteenth century, dates originally from 1105; an unusual narthex with dome and two bays was added a century later, giving the church a "backwards" orientation from the norm. Panayía Forviótissa's frescoes span several centuries from the construction date to the early 1500s, and were cleaned between 1965 and 1967.

The interior

Many of the myriad **panels** in the nave were skilfully redone in the fourteenth or fifteenth century. The vaulted **ceiling** of the nave is segmented into recesses by two arches: one at the apse, the other about two-thirds of the way west towards the narthex door. In the westernmost recess, the *Forty Martyrs of Sebastaea* on the north curve seem more natural than those at Áyios Nikólaos tís Stéyis, despite their crowns floating down from Heaven; the Holy Spirit also descends at *Pentecost* overhead, and Lazarus is raised on the south of the same curve. In the middle recess, the life of Christ from *Nativity* to *Resurrection* is related; here the *Crucifixion* is treated as just one panel of many, not as in higher, barn-like churches where it often dominates the triangular pediment over the door. Generally, the fresco style is highly sophisticated and vivid: *St Trifon* on one arch could be a portrait from life of a local shepherd; the three *Myrrofóri* (spice-bearing women at the sepulchre) recoil in visible alarm from the admonishing angel. In the **apse**, an almost imploring twelfth-century *Virgin* raises her hands in benediction, flanked by the two archangels, while to either side Christ offers the wine in the *Communion of the Apostles* (save for Judas, who slinks away). Over the south door, the builder Nikiforos Mayistros presents a model of the church to Christ in a panel dated 1105 by its dedicatory inscription, while a fine *Dormition of the Virgin* hovers over the west door of the nave.

The **narthex frescoes** are of the fourteenth century, with wonderful whimsical touches. On the arch of the door to the nave, a pair of hunting hounds tied to a stake and their moufflon quarry make an appearance, heralds of the Renaissance as Byzantine iconography has no place for dogs. In the shell of the north bay, Earth (riding on a lion) and Sea (upon a water monster) are personified; in the opposite bay, the donors appear again, praying in period dress before a naturalistic *Virgin and Child*, above an equestrian *St George* and the lion-mounted *Áyios Mamas*. Below the Earth and the Sea, St Peter advances to open the *Gates of Paradise*, while the patriarchs Abraham, Isaac, and Jacob wait to one side. In the cupola the *Pandokrátor* presides over the *Twelve Apostles*, with *The Blessed and the Damned* depicted on arches to either side.

PITSILIÁ

Southeast and uphill from the Soléa valleys, the region of **Pitsiliá** is a jumble of bare ridges and precipitous valleys forming the east end of the Tróödhos range. Instead of forests, groves of hazelnut and almonds grow, though there are pines on the north slopes. Grapevines flourish, too, but for local use, not the vintners' co-ops; in some villages they're guided on elaborate trellises over streets and houses.

Pitsiliá is noticeably less prosperous and less frequented than Marathássa or Soléa, though surprisingly three large villages – almost small towns – are strung along near the ridge line: Kyperoúnda, Agrós and Palekhóri. Roads, though recently improved, are still challenging and slow-going to say the least.

The easiest roads into Pitsiliá head east from Tróödhos resort or southeast from Kakopetriá, converging at the junction known as the Karvounás crossroads 1200m above sea level. From there you are within easy reach of Kyperoúnda and the ridge walk above it, or the historic church at Koúrdhali, actually a short way off the road up from Kakopetriá.

From Asínou, you're best off returning to Nikitári (you'll probably have to chauffeur the priest back anyway), then heading east to Vizakiá to adopt the road signed up to Kannávia – which eventually ends on the highway between Karvounás and Kyperoúnda, via Ayía Iríni and its noteworthy church. Alternatively, about 3km above Vizakiá, a passable dirt road veers east towards Ayía Marína (with an extremely rough option to Ksiliátos part way). You are now well placed to visit the two finest churches in Pitsiliá, Panayía tou Araká and Stavrós tou Ayiasmáti; the paved main road, signposted to Lagoudherá, climbs through a forested canyon, passing a dam that makes a tempting picnic spot.

Panayía tou Araká

The large, single-aisled church of **Panayía tou Araká** ("Our Lady of the Pea") enjoys a wonderful setting amid trees – and the wild peas of the name – on a terrace 500m northwest of **Lagoudherá village**, about halfway to Sarandí village (where a taverna operates seasonally). The caretaker priest lives in the large adjacent building, possibly a surviving portion of the monastery which was once attached. The local **festival** on September 7–8 celebrates the birth of the Virgin.

The **interior frescoes** of 1192 are not as numerous as they might be, since the original west wall, presumably with a *Crucifixion*, was removed when the existing narthex was built late in the seventeenth century. They are exceptionally clear, however, having been cleaned between 1968 and 1973, and include, unique in the Tróödhos, an undamaged *Pandokrátor* in the dome (which protrudes partially through the pitched roof). Below Christ, his eyes averted in the Hellenistic manner, Old Testament prophets, rather than the usual apostles, alternate with the twelve dome windows, each clutching a scroll with his prophecy anticipating the Saviour. Edging further down, the archangel Gabriel, wings and robes swept back by the force of his rapid descent, approaches the Virgin opposite for the *Annunciation*.

Above the *Virgin Enthroned* in the apse, strangely averting her eyes to the right, Christ ascends to heaven in a bull's-eye mandorla (an almond-shaped aura often used by painters to enliven the risen Lord), attended by four acrobatic angels. The *témblon* is intact, its Holy Gates (for the mysterious entries and exits of the priest during the liturgy) still in place. Instead of a true transept, there are two pairs of painted recesses on each of the side walls. Flanking the south door, *Zozimadhon Spoon-feeds Osia Maria (Mary the Beatified) of Egypt*; Mary was an Alexandrian courtesan who, repenting of her ways, retired to the desert to perform austere penances for forty years and was found, a withered crone on the point of death, by Zozimadhon, abbot of St Paul's monastery near the Red Sea. Above them there's a fine *Nativity*, with, as ever, a preternaturally aged Infant being bathed, while on the right the angel gives the good news to the shepherds, one of whom plays a pipe. In the north recess nearest the apse, reflecting the story told in Luke 2:25, Simeon lovingly holds Christ for his *Presentation in the Temple*, the child wearing a single earring in his left ear, as was the Byzantine custom for infant sons. The *Panayia Arakiotíssa*, in the opposite south-wall recess, is conceptually linked with the *Presentation*; having received back her son, the Virgin's expression is sorrowful in acknowledgement of the two flanking angels proffering the instruments of the Passion.

Stavrós tou Ayiasmáti

In the next valley east of Lagoudherá, **Stavrós tou Ayiasmáti** is an attractive basilica-church, again once part of a monastery. You need to stop first in **Platanístassa village**, where the key-keeper Vassilis Hadjiyeoryiou lives – he is most easily found by enquiring at Makis' café, or ring in advance (if your Greek is up to it) on ☎02/652562. The church itself, whose **festival** is on September 13– 14, is located 7km to the north: 3km down-valley on tarmac, the balance on a good dirt road. The setting is even better than at Panayía tou Araká, in an almond grove at the margin of the forest, with a patch of the Mesaoría visible to the northeast.

The church
The church is filled with recently cleaned, late fifteenth-century **frescoes** by Philip Goul; an inscription over the south door records both his artistry and the patronage of the priest Petros Peratis. The highlight is a **painted cross** in a niche on the north wall (the name *Stavrós* means "Holy Cross"), surrounded by small panels of episodes relating, however tenuously, to its power, sanctification and rediscovery, such as the Hebrews petitioning Pharaoh (top), or the vision of St Constantine in 312 AD (left).

Behind the *témblon*, and above an interesting Holy Table (for celebrating the Orthodox liturgy), the Virgin and Child both raise hands in blessing in the apse, flanked by Old Testament prophets David, Daniel, Solomon and Isaiah; nearby the *Communion of the Apostles* has a single figure of Christ (usually there were two) offering the Eucharist to six with his right hand, and the Communion wine to the other half-dozen with his left. The four evangelists are arranged in pairs to either side of the altar screen; the archangel Michael, in the arched recess to the right of *témblon*, holds not the usual opaque orb but a transparent "crystal ball" containing the Christ child.

Elsewhere along the vaults and walls of the nave there's a complete gospel cycle, including such arcane details as apostles with their backs to the viewer in the *Last Supper*, *Pilate Washing his Hands*, trumpeters in the panel of *The Mocking*, and *Doubting Thomas* probing Christ's lance wound. The crowing rooster in *Peter's Denial* is larger than any of the human figures, while in the otherwise serene *Assumption of the Virgin*, a miniature angel strikes off the hands of an impious Jew who attempted to knock over the Virgin's bier. On the pediment of the west wall, the *Ancient of Days* presides over the *Descent of the Holy Spirit*, above the *Crucifixion*. Christ's blood drips down into Adam's skull below, the key-warden will tell you, in order to revivify it for the *Redemption*, shown outside in a niche of the uncleaned narthex.

This and other exterior frescoes are thought not to be by Goul, and were repainted last century to detrimental effect. Right of the *Redemption* the *Last Judgement* unfolds, while on the left stand the three patriarchs Abraham, Isaac and Jacob. The U-shaped narthex, extending around the north and south sides of the church, was used by local shepherds as a sheep pen before the monument's importance was recognized.

The Madhári ridge walk

From either Lagoudherá or Platanístassa paved roads complete the climb to the Tróödhos summit ridge, where the vine-draped villages of Álona and Polýstipos huddle just under 1100 metres. The watershed is crossed a little higher, with a well-marked side road to the CYTA transmission station on the sides of 1612-metre **Mount Adhélfi**.

If you're interested in walking the **nature trail on Madhári ridge**, this is one possible starting point. Near the end of this side road, which is also signposted for the nature trail system, park opposite the CYTA towers, next to an abandoned military guardhouse. Here a standard-issue wooden sign announces "Circular Nature Trail *Teisia tis Madharis* 3 1/2 km". The path begins right behind the guardhouse, heading northwest on a course that roughly follows the contour through midget golden oaks and weird rock formations. After 45 minutes of rollercoastering along the north flank of Adhélfi peak, you'll emerge right under the fire tower capping Point 1612, having linked up with the longer, point-to-point trail from Kyperoúnda (see below). From this point it's less than fifteen minutes back east along the road to the old guardhouse.

On balance, this not-quite-circular walk is best viewed as an extension to the basic Madhári ridge walk, usually begun **from Kyperoúnda**, some 7km west via Khandhriá. At the western edge of Kyperoúnda, just beyond the Mitsubishi representative and the *Amazel Restaurant* on the bypass road, an unmarked dirt track heads north for 1800m to the saddle at about 1400m elevation. Just to one side stands the familiar wooden paraphernalia marking the start of such trails, with a sign proclaiming "Glory to You, Oh God" in New Testament Greek – plus the precise distance to be covered (3750m). Except for some clumps of man-high golden oak (*Quercus alnifolia*), there's little but low scrub en route, so the exposed ridge is best traversed early or late in the day during summer. Views of virtually half the island, from the Kyrenia hills to the Akrotíri salt lake, are the thing: you gaze over nearer valleys and villages both north and south of the ridge, with the sea on three sides of Cyprus visible in favourable conditions.

After some initial tangling with a more recently cleared firebreak track, the path settles into a rhythm of wobbling either side of the watershed (also the boundary between Limassol and Nicosia districts) as it meanders through scrub and thin forest. Some 45 minutes along, you reach the 1500-metre saddle between Madhári ridge and Adhélfi peak, with another half-hour's hiking bringing you to the fire tower atop Point 1612 – a bit more if you detour to the modestly described "Excellent Viewpoint" part way. The service road past the CYTA station continues to the very base of Adhélfi, where a group could perhaps be picked up by a non-walker's car without having to retrace their steps.

Minor churches: Tímios Stavrós and Kímisis tís Panayías

Immediately north of Madhári ridge, in the vicinity of Spiliá village, nestle two relatively minor but enjoyable painted churches, both dating from the first quarter of the sixteenth century. The dirt track to the western trailhead of the Madhári nature path continues 2km to a junction, and the resumption of asphalt: left leads within 500m to Spiliá and thence Koúrdhali hamlet; straight descends 2km in tight curves to Ayía Iríni village, just before Kannávia.

The diminutive church of **Tímios Stavrós** at Ayía Iríni, just north of and above the village on a hillock, had its frescoes cleaned and masonry consolidated throughout 1995, so the key/admission policy is uncertain at the time of writing. Should you gain entry, you'll see a rustic *Nativity* over the south door, with the *Convention of the Archangels* just east. The conch of the apse is devoted to the iconographic convention known as the *Deësis*, the only such depiction on Cyprus: the Virgin and John the Baptist flank a seated Christ, who proffers with his left hand a text proclaiming him to be the prophesied Christ and Judge of the Last Day. To the left of the apse, an angel lifts Christ from the sepulchre, an artistic convention combining the so-called "Utter Humiliation" variation of Byzantine *Depositions* and the western *Pietà*. In the triangular pediment above the apsidal vault, there's an unusual, westernized *Holy Trinity*, with the enthroned Father upholding the crucified Son, appropriately enough for a shrine of the Holy Cross (*Tímios Stavrós* in Greek).

Koúrdhali: Kímisis tís Panayías

The three-aisled basilica of **Kímisis tís Panayías** in Koúrdhali lies just under 2km below the central junction in Spiliá, on the bank of a stream crossed by a tiny humpback bridge built entirely of roof-tiles. It was founded in the sixteenth century as the *katholikón* of a (long-vanished) monastery by the deacon Kourdhalis, for whom the hamlet is named. The bulk of the surviving frescoes are on the west wall, surmounted by a naturalistic, Italo-Byzantine *Crucifixion* featuring, as to be expected from a sixteenth-century church, notables in

Venetian apparel – including a rather scandalously attired Virgin in a low-cut dress, fainting into the arms of her friends. Subsequent episodes include a dramatic *Doubting Thomas*, at the far upper right of the panels here, with Christ all but daring the apostle to touch his wound. Right of the west door, in the *Dormition of the Virgin* above the donor portraits, a rather piratical-looking, long-fingered St Paul crouches at the foot of the bier. The eastern apse is taken up by a fine *Virgin Orans*, attended by archangels in Byzantine noble costume.

The guardian is a certain Ayisilaos, who lives in the house beside the little bridge which links the church to the main road; he can be difficult, and the key is sometimes left in the door, but the light switches inside are hard to find without his help. The local festival is August 14–15.

Agrós and around

The only feasible overnight option in Pitsiliá is **AGRÓS**, a surprisingly large village more or less at the top (1000m elevation) of Limassol district's commercial wine-grape region. Also known for its sausage, ham and rose-water extraction industries, Agrós won't win many beauty contests but it's well placed for two days' forays to nearby sights, as it lies roughly equidistant from several post-Byzantine frescoed churches. Being less frequented than the monuments of Marathássa and Soléa, these give more sense of personal discovery, and their surrounding villages deserve a brief stroll-through as well. In Agrós proper, there are no historic churches, despite its role as refuge for two venerable twelfth-century icons of Christ and the Virgin; the villagers themselves pulled down the 800-year-old, frescoed monastery housing them in 1894, during a protracted land-ownership dispute with the local bishop.

The relatively recent appearance of Agrós on the tourism map is due almost entirely to the efforts of Lefkos Christodoulou, enthusiastic booster of the area's merits and manager of the enormous, communally-owned **hotel**, the *Rodon*, 1km south of the village on the Potamítissa road (☎05/521201, fax 521235; ⑦). Substantial discounts apply off-season, and also to bookings through *Amathus*, *Sunworld* or *Sunvil*. The hotel has a well-regarded restaurant, a pool and a tennis court, and Lefkos hands out a 1:25,000 photostat map detailing walks around Agrós, in addition to arranging group hikes.

In the village itself, the one-star *Vlachos Hotel* (☎05/521330, fax 521890; ③), despite an indifferent position on the high street, represents excellent value at C£13 per person half-board, with supper a groaning *table d'hôte*; otherwise *Iy Kiladha*, a taverna just north of the *Vlachos* in a tree-shaded kink of the through road, offers some vegetarian fare. Agrós also has the only **petrol pump** for some way around, so fill up before a day's touring.

Peléndhri: the church of Stavrós

Of the villages with frescoed churches around Agrós, **PELÉNDHRI** (sometimes rendered "Peléndhria") is the easiest to reach, accessed initially on the direct, paved Agrós–Potamítissa road, which as yet does not appear accurately on any commercial map. The main attraction here is the fourteenth-century painted **church of Stavrós**, isolated at the south edge of Peléndhri, overlooking a reservoir; the friendly key-keeping priest lives 200m up the road towards Káto

Amíandos. A square ground plan divided into three aisles, unique in Cyprus, is capped by a very narrow, high dome supported by four columns; for once there is no narthex.

On your right as you enter, there's a *Tree of Jesse*, showing the genealogy of Jesus. Straight ahead on a column, the two donors of the church are shown below a *Doubting Thomas*; just to the left is a Lusignan coat of arms. At the rear of the central aisle, above the wooden lattice of the deacon's pulpit, are scenes from the life of the Virgin, the best-preserved (or at least the cleanest) frescoes in the entire building. Opposite this, a *Nativity* tells much about Lusignan domestic life, and Joachim and Anna present the infant Mary for blessing by the high priests, the most vivid of fourteen panels on the life of the Virgin. A multi-coloured *témblon* is in good condition, and to its left the enshrined cross for which the church is named stands encased in silver near a representation of the *Epitáfios* (the Dead Christ), next to a fresco of three *Ierárkhi* (Church Fathers) in the left-hand apse.

Louvarás: the chapel of Áyios Mámas

The main Limassól-bound E110 road from Agrós via Káto Mýlos descends to Péfkos junction above **KALOKHORIÓ**, where there's the only food and petrol for quite some distance around. Meals are to be had up at the café on the south side of the crossroads, and the fuel is sold from jerry cans at the postal agency across from the irrigation pool in the village centre.

A four-kilometre side road takes off southeast from the crossroads, ending at **LOUVARÁS**, whose dishearteningly modern outskirts give no hint of the traditional village core to the east, nor of the tiny but exquisitely painted **chapel of Áyios Mámas**, hidden on the edge of the old quarter, at the very end of the paved road in. Don't confuse it with the bigger, newer church of Pródhromos nearby, across from which lives Grigoris the key-keeper, in the house with a front garden. He speaks some English, learned (he claims) during five years as an aide to General Montgomery.

The little chapel, with frescoes dating from 1495, features Philip Goul at perhaps his most idiosyncratic. On the south wall, Christ heals the paralytic and the blind man, teaches, and meets the Samaritan woman at the well; the three sleeping guards at the *Resurrection* wear Lusignan armour. Also on the south

---

SAINT MAMAS AND HIS LION

Prominent on the north wall of the Louvarás church is a panel of the church's dedicatory saint, **Mamas**, cradling a lamb as he rides a rather bemused, anthropomorphized lion. The legend behind this peculiar iconography, found in many Cypriot churches, runs as follows: Mamas was a devout Byzantine hermit who refused to pay income tax since, as he logically pointed out, he had no income other than alms. The local governor ordered him arrested, but as he was being escorted into custody a lion – unknown on Cyprus – leapt from a roadside bush onto a lamb grazing peacefully nearby. The saint commanded the lion to stop his attack, picked up the lamb, and completed his journey into the capital riding on the chastened lion. Sufficiently impressed, the governor exempted Mamas from taxes thereafter, and ever since the saint has enjoyed fervent worship as the patron of tax-evaders (a highly developed cult in the Hellenic world).

wall, closer to the *témblon*, is an exceptionally expressive *John the Baptist*, clutching a staff which ends in a cross-and-anchor motif. Beside the west door, the Gadarene swine leap over the brink – you can see the demons entering them; above the door appear the donors of the church, two couples in late Lusignan dress. In the *Last Supper* on the same surface, Christ does not (as in other local murals) attempt to prevent Judas from reaching for the fish. At the very top of the apsidal pediment on the east side, the *Ancient of Days* hovers over the *Annunciation* – these images may be by a hand other than Goul's, since the *Annunciation* is repeated on the south wall.

Palekhóri: Metamórfosis toú Sotírou

From Agrós (or from Peléndhri), the quickest route to Palekhóri, 13km away, is eastward along the recently upgraded ridge route; from Louvarás and Péfkos junction, you pass slightly south of this, via Áyios Theodhóros.

However you arrive, **PALEKHÓRI** proves to be a sprawling, friendly worka-day place hidden in a gulch at the headwaters of the Peristeróna River – there are a few *kafenía* down by the stream, but no other concessions to tourism. The small fifteenth-to-sixteenth-century chapel of **Metamórfosis toú Sotírou**, signposted from the main bypass road, perches at the east edge of the old quarter, atop the slope up from the river. The very engaging key-keeping priest lives in the apart-ment building two doors north, beside which you should park, but in the evening (a likely arrival time if you've been touring all day) he may be conducting the liturgy down at Panayía Khrysopantánassa, which though contemporaneous has few surviving frescoes.

The frescoes of Metamórfosis toú Sotírou were painted by an unknown artist, sometime between Phillip Goul's heyday and that of Simeon Axenti. They rival those at Áyios Mámas at Louvarás for whimsy, with lions and rivers the main themes. St Mamas appears again, riding a particularly elongated feline; on the south wall, another lion approaches, as tradition holds, to bury *Osia Maria* (Mary the Beatified of Egypt) with his paw, while opposite her Daniel braves the lions in their den. To Daniel's left is portrayed a miracle whereby the angelic diversion of a river saves a monastery; in the *Baptism of Christ*, a crowned-and-sceptred water sprite – personification of the river, derived from pagan portrayals of river-gods – rides a fish in the Jordan. As befits a church dedicated to the Transfiguration (*Metamórfosis* in Greek), the panel of that episode on the south wall is particularly vivid, with two disciples cowering on the ground in fear and awe. Scenes from the life of the Virgin are completely absent, though the apse features an elegant Virgin as Mistress of Angels. Below her to the left, a cow suckling her calf lends an engaging touch to the *Hospitality of Abraham*. In a nearby recess, St George lays a fraternal hand on the shoulder of St Demetrius with whom he rides; their equestrian pairing, common on Crete but unique here to Cyprus, shows these warrior saints' evolution from the ancient Dioscuri, Castor and Pollux, ever ready to rush to the aid of supplicants.

The other two churches visible in the western part of Palekhóri contain noth-ing especially compelling inside; the priest may, however, volunteer to escort you to another pair of local monuments east of the village in an orchard-cloaked valley, including the frescoed sixteenth-century church of **Áyii Anáryiri**, sign-posted off the road to Aplíki.

Mountain villages en route to Makherás

At Aplíki junction, you can turn up towards Farmakás onto a narrow but paved road around a huge reservoir. **FARMAKÁS** and its neighbour **KAMBÍ** are both spectacularly set overlooking the top of the valley draining to the dam, but as with so many communities in rural Cyprus where inhabitants have made good, the visual appeal diminishes on close examination, compromised by tin roofs and shabby brick walls. The two local showcase villages lie a few kilometres north-east along an improved road, better than maps imply, beyond Goúrri.

At **FYKÁRDHOU** the vernacular architecture of stone, mud-straw bricks and tiled roofs is preserved – or rather pickled – in the forty or so houses of this museum-village; the permanent population has dwindled to seven. Two of the dwellings constitute an exhibit (May–Aug Tues–Fri 9am–1pm & 3–6pm, Sat 9.30am–1pm & 3–5pm, Sun 9.30am–3.30pm; Sept–April Mon 9am–1pm, Tues–Fri 9.30am–1pm & 2–4.30pm, Sat 9am–1pm & 2–3.30pm, Sun 9am–3pm; C£0.50), with plans, photos and text in the ticket office giving a full explanation of the project's aims. The **house of Akhilleas Dhimitri**, with its loom and period furnishings, is not too cluttered as ethnographic collections go, since it's the occasional residence of the project's supervising archeologist. The **Katsinioros house** has an olive press, *zivanía* stills and storage urns in its basement, and traditional women's implements such as a spinning wheel and loom in the peaked-roof upper storey.

All in all it's a conscientious restoration job, but ultimately with an obscure purpose – the effect seems a bit lifeless without even the animation of a weekend population (though some of the buildings are reportedly for sale). The only other tourist amenity thus far is the surprisingly authentic *Yiannakos Kafenio*, serving drinks and light meals (mostly to workmen on the project except in high season).

LAZANIÁ, 5km south on the way to Makherás monastery, is more of a going concern, and therefore less twee and perhaps more representative of such hill villages.

Makherás monastery

The **monastery of Makherás** just east of Lazaniá is distinguished by its setting on the north slope of Mount Kiónia, near the headwaters of the Pedhiéos River, and by its associations with **Grigorios Afxentiou**, second in command of EOKA after George "Dhiyenis" Grivas, and by all accounts a more humane, sympathetic figure.

The monastery was established by two hermits in 1148, who arrived from Palestine and, guided by the usual preternatural glow, found an icon of the Virgin attributed to the hand of Luke the Evangelist. Makherás ("The Cutler") is taken variously to mean the sharp-edged, thousand-metre ridge overhead, the biting wind swooping down from it in winter, or the point in the foundation legend when a knife supernaturally materialized and a "voice not of earth" instructed the hermits to use it to free the icon from the underbrush. Soon the community had the support of the Byzantine emperor Manuel Komnenos, and even enjoyed the subsequent patronage of Lusignan rulers – one of whom, Queen Alix d'Ibelin, was rendered mute for three years after sacrilegiously insisting on entering the *ierón* or priestly chambers behind the altar screen. Makherás claims five martyrs (six, counting Afxentiou), commemorated on plaques in the courtyard.

It has also suffered two comprehensive fires (in 1530 and 1892), the later one explaining the rather bleak, echoing stone compound of minimal architectural interest, though the icon miraculously escaped and is the glory of the *katholikón*. There is a one-room museum, with labelling only in Greek, featuring photos of EOKA hero Grigorios Afxentiou disguised as a monk. The monastery is open reasonable hours without midday closure, and there may be a chance of (men only) being put up for the night, except around the November 20–21 and August 14–15 **festivals**. A small restaurant by the car park fortifies you for the drive along the road above or below.

Krysfíyeto toú Afxentíou

When he was not in monk's garb, the brothers of Makherás continued to feed Afxentiou in his hideout, the **Krysfíyeto toú Afxentíou**, 1km below the monastery; a Greek flag, sign and memorial plaque point you down to the (much repaired) bunker in which he met his end in March 1957. Tipped off by a shepherd, British forces surrounded the dugout and called on the occupants to surrender – EOKA members were usually happy to comply in hopeless situations. All of them did except Afxentiou, who, despite being wounded, held off a platoon of sixty for ten hours before being dispatched with a petrol bomb and high explosives.

Approaching the *krysfíyeto* (hideout), completely bare inside without so much as a candle or photo, you pass a huge **statue**, erected just below the monastery at the expense of the diocese, showing a more-than-life-size Afxentiou standing arms akimbo, guarded by an eagle.

Onward routes from Makherás

From Makherás your most obvious course is down to **Nicosia**, 43km distant via the inviting, piney picnic grounds of Mándhra tou Kambioú and the adjacent sites of ancient Tamassos and Áyios Iraklídhios monastery (see pp.211–213). **Towards Larnaca**, a dirt road heads due south through forest and past another picnic ground beside 1423-metre Kiónia peak, last outrider of the Tróödhos range. Áyii Vavatsiniás marks the start of the improved road surface down to Khirokitiá, 33km distant from the monastery (see p.67).

---

travel details

Buses

From **Agrós** to: Limassol on *Agros Bus* (1 daily, except Sun, at about 7am; 1hr 30min).

From **Kakopetriá** to: Nicosia with *Clarios Bus* (Mon–Sat 10 daily, 2 on Sun; 1hr 20min).

From **Plátres** to: Limassol, by both Plátres market bus and *Karydas* service minibus (daily at about 7am; 1hr 15min); Nicosia via Pedhoulás and Kalopanayiótis with *Zingas* (1 daily, except Sun, at 6am; 3hr).

From **Pródhromos** to: Limassol via Tróödhos and Plátres on *KEMEK* (1 daily at dawn; 3hr); Nicosia on *Zingas* (1 daily, except Sun, early morning; 2hr).

From **Tróödhos** to: Nicosia on *Clarios Bus* (1 daily, except Sun, at dawn; 2hr).

Adhélfi	Αδέλφι	ΑΔΕΛΦΙ
Agrós	Αγρός	ΑΓΡΟΣ
Amíandos	Αμίαντος	ΑΜΙΑΝΤΟΣ
Arkhángelos Mihaïl	Αρχάγγελος Μιχαήλ	ΑΡΧΑΓΓΕΛΟΣ ΜΙΧΑΗΛ
Asínou	Ασίνου	ΑΣΙΝΟΥ
Ayía Iríni	Αγία Ειρήνη	ΑΓΙΑ ΕΙΡΗΝΗ
Áyii Anáryiri	Άγιοι Ανάργυροι	ΑΓΙΟΙ ΑΝΑΡΓΥΡΟΙ
Áyios Ioánnis Lambadhistís	Άγιος Ιοάννης Λαμπαδιστής	ΑΓΙΟΣ ΙΟΑΝΝΗΣ ΛΑΜΠΑΔΙΣΤΗΣ
Áyios Mámas	Άγιος Μάμας	ΑΓΙΟΣ ΜΑΜΑΣ
Áyios Nikólaos tís Stéyis	Άγιος Νικόλαος τής Στέγης	ΑΓΙΟΣ ΝΙΚΟΛΑΟΣ ΤΗΣ ΣΤΕΓΗΣ
Áyios Sozómenos	Άγιος Σοζόμενος	ΑΓΙΟΣ ΣΟΖΟΜΕΝΟΣ
Elía	Ελήα	ΕΛΗΑ
Farmakás	Φαρμακάς	ΦΑΡΜΑΚΑΣ
Finí	Φοινί	ΦΟΙΝΙ
Fykárdhou	Φυκάρδου	ΦΥΚΑΡΔΟΥ
Galáta	Γαλάτα	ΓΑΛΑΤΑ
Kakopetriá	Κακοπετριά	ΚΑΚΟΠΕΤΡΙΑ
Kalokhorió	Καλοχωριό	ΚΑΛΟΧΩΡΙΟ
Kalopanayiótis	Καλοπαναγιώτης	ΚΑΛΟΠΑΝΑΓΙΩΤΗΣ
Kambí	Καμπί	ΚΑΜΠΙ
Kámbos	Κάμπος	ΚΑΜΠΟΣ
Kaminária	Καμινάρια	ΚΑΜΙΝΑΡΙΑ
Kannávia	Καννάβια	ΚΑΝΝΑΒΙΑ
Khandhriá	Χανδριά	ΧΑΝΔΡΙΑ
Khionístra	Χιονίστρα	ΧΙΟΝΙΣΤΡΑ
Kímisis tís Panayías	Κοίμησις τής Παναγίας	ΚΟΙΜΗΣΙΣ ΤΗΣ ΠΑΝΑΓΙΑΣ
Koúrdhali	Κούρδαλι	ΚΟΥΡΔΑΛΙ
Kýkko	Κύκκο	ΚΥΚΚΟ
Kyperoúnda	Κυπερούντα	ΚΥΠΕΡΟΥΝΤΑ
Lagoudherá	Λαγουδερά	ΛΑΓΟΥΔΕΡΑ
Lazaniá	Λαζανιά	ΛΑΖΑΝΙΑ
Louvarás	Λουβαράς	ΛΟΥΒΑΡΑΣ
Madhári	Μαδάρι	ΜΑΔΑΡΙ
Makherás	Μαχαιράς	ΜΑΧΑΙΡΑΣ
Makriá Kondárka	Μακριά Κοντάρκα	ΜΑΚΡΙΑ ΚΟΝΤΑΡΚΑ
Marathássa	Μαραθάσα	ΜΑΡΑΘΑΣΑ
Mesapotamós	Μεσαποταμός	ΜΕΣΑΠΟΤΑΜΟΣ
Metamórfosis toú Sotírou	Μεταμόρφωσις τού Σωτήρου	ΜΕΤΑΜΟΡΦΩΣΙΣ ΤΟΥ ΣΩΤΗΡΟΥ
Moutoullás	Μουτουλλάς	ΜΟΥΤΟΥΛΛΑΣ
Nikitári	Νικιτάρι	ΝΙΚΙΤΑΡΙ
Palekhóri	Παλαιχώρι	ΠΑΛΑΙΧΩΡΙ
Panayía Moutoullá	Παναγία Μουτουλλά	ΠΑΝΑΓΙΑ ΜΟΥΤΟΥΛΛΑ
Panayía Podhíthou	Παναγία Ποδίθου	ΠΑΝΑΓΙΑ ΠΟΔΙΘΟΥ
Panayía Theotókou	Παναγία Θεοτόκου	ΠΑΝΑΓΙΑ ΘΕΟΤΟΚΟΥ
Panayía toú Araká	Παναγία τού Αρακά	ΠΑΝΑΓΙΑ ΤΟΥ ΑΡΑΚΑ
Pedhoulás	Πεδουλάς	ΠΕΔΟΥΛΑΣ
Peléndhri	Πελένδρι	ΠΕΛΕΝΔΡΙ

Pitsiliá	Πιτσιλιά	ΠΙΤΣΙΛΙΑ
Platanístassa	Πλατανίστασα	ΠΛΑΤΑΝΙΣΤΑΣΑ
Plátres	Πλάτρες	ΠΛΑΤΡΕΣ
Pródhromos	Πρόδρομος	ΠΡΟΔΡΟΜΟΣ
Soléa	Σολέα	ΣΟΛΕΑ
Spília	Σπήλια	ΣΠΗΛΙΑ
Stavrós	Σταυρός	ΣΤΑΥΡΟΣ
Stavrós toú	Σταυρός τού	ΣΤΑΥΡΟΣ ΤΟΥ
Ayiasmáti	Αγιασμάτη	ΑΓΙΑΣΜΑΤΗ
Thróni	Θρόνοι	ΘΡΟΝΟΙ
Troödhítissa	Τροοδίτισσα	ΤΡΟΟΔΙΤΙΣΣΑ
Tróödhos	Τρόοδος	ΤΡΟΟΔΟΣ

CHAPTER FIVE

SOUTH NICOSIA AND AROUND

The southern sector of divided **Nicosia** (*Lefkosía* in Greek) is the capital and largest town of the internationally recognized Republic of Cyprus. Somewhat gritty and prosaically set, it sees few package tourists apart from groups coached in to visit the Cyprus Museum, simply one of the best archeological collections in the Middle East, and essential viewing. A relative lack of the rampant commercialism found on the coast is refreshing, as is the surviving Gothic and Ottoman domestic and religious architecture of the medieval town. And if you're not averse to mixing politics with your holiday, and interested in getting to grips with what contemporary Cyprus is about, an evening or two in pubs and eateries near the Green Line is well spent.

By comparison, there is little of note in the surrounding countryside under Greek Cypriot control, part of the vast **Mesaoría** ("Between the Mountains"). This is not so much a plain between the Tróödhos range and Kyrenia hills as undulating country, patchworked with green or yellow grain according to season and dotted with large villages, lately become dormitory communities preferred to Nicosia itself. Here you become acutely aware of the island's division: roads close to the boundary are diverted or barred suddenly, and watchtowers of one side or the other dot the horizon. Amidst this bleakness, just a few isolated spots really appeal, and then only if you have time on your hands: the adjacent ruins of **Tamassos** and nunnery of **Áyios Iraklídhios**, a fine church and mosque duo at **Peristeróna**, and another minor church at **Perakhorió**, paired with the scanty nearby remains of **Idalion**.

SOUTH NICOSIA

Great is the contrast between the town and its surroundings, and greater still between the objects within the city. There are Venetian fortifications by the side of Gothic edifices surmounted by the Crescent, on antique Classic soil. Turks, Greeks, and Armenians, dwell intermingled, bitter enemies at heart, and united solely by their love for the land of their birth.

Archduke Louis Salvator of Austria, 1873

SOUTH NICOSIA, depending on whom you ask and how many incorporated suburbs you count, today has between 170,000 and 250,000 inhabitants. Despite the relatively small population, it's a sprawling, amorphous, modern city that makes a poor first impression. The dust and heat – on average 5° higher than on the coast – beginning in April and lasting until October, are prostrating, grit

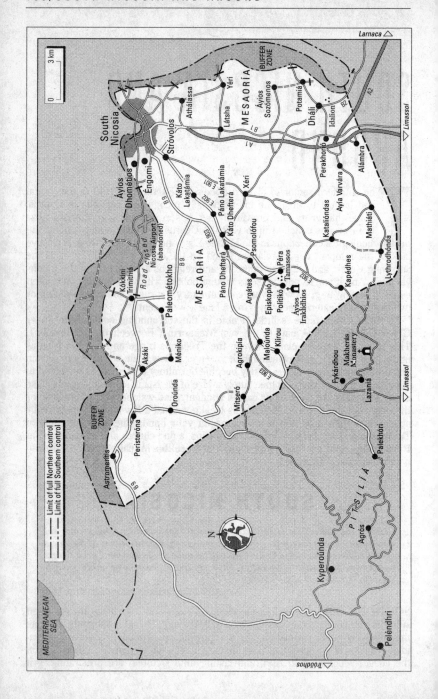

coming in equal measure from the prevailing winds and nearby building sites. Nicosia's inland setting, near the western extreme of the Mesaoría, is prone to earthquakes and flash-flooding from the river Pedhiéos, and otherwise not naturally favoured except in its near-equidistance from the important coastal towns. Since early Byzantine times every ruler has designated the place capital virtually by default, because the island's shore defences were (and are) poor, its harbours exposed to attack.

Medieval Nicosia's profile is owed in varying proportions to the Lusignans, Ottomans and Venetians; the latter endowed the old town with a five-kilometre circuit of walls which largely survives. The map outline of the medieval quarter, still the core of the city, has been compared to a star, a snowflake or a sectioned orange, but in the present, troubled circumstances a better analogy might be a floating mine, the knobbly silhouettes of its eleven bastions the detonators.

Old Nicosia began to outgrow its confines during the 1930s; the British answered this problem with the post-war cantonment-style development just outside the walls, while the post-independence response was to throw up the Los

THE DIVIDED CITY

The **Green Line**, as the ceasefire line is known within the city limits, has existed in some form since the communal troubles of winter 1963–64: first as impromptu barricades of bedframes, upturned cars and other domestic debris, later more sturdily fashioned of oil drums, barbed wire, sandbags and sheet metal. Nicosia is, as the authorities repeatedly remind you on wall signs and in tourist literature, the last hermetically divided city, now that arrangements have been reached one way or another in Berlin, Jerusalem and Beirut.

As such, the barrier exercises a morbid fascination on visitors as well as locals. You find yourself drifting towards it again and again, trying to follow its length, peering through chinks when out of sight of the Greek, Turkish or UN checkpoints. Beyond the boundary stretches the "dead zone", here just a twenty-to-fifty-metre-wide stretch of derelict, rat- and snake-infested houses – and a showroom full of dust-covered Toyotas and Datsuns, rushed in from the Famagusta docks on the day of the invasion to prevent their destruction, which have been irretrievably trapped here ever since. The very existence of the Attila Line (the limit of Turkish Army advance) constitutes a provocation, to which a steady trickle of Greek Cypriots, not all of them certifiably unbalanced, have responded since 1974. Periodically refugee groups stage protest marches towards their home villages in the North, putting their own National Guard in the embarrassing role of trying to prevent them crossing the Attila Line (often they get several hundred metres, or even further, inside northern Cyprus); lone males crash the barriers on foot or in vehicles, only to be imprisoned by the Turks, with attempts every several months on average. A slogan overhead at one Greek checkpoint – "Our frontiers are not these, but the shores of Kyrenia" – hardly argues for self-restraint, and the CTO, riding piggyback on the spirit of the protests, schedules regular walking tours along the Green Line – free, including propaganda dispensed en route.

Finally, then, the rift is the essence of Nicosia and, by extension, of the island. The Greek area of the city is, indeed, mostly Greek in its monumental architecture, the Turkish zone largely Turkish and Gothic, but in the midst of each are marooned traces of the other element: mosques and houses emblazoned with a star and crescent in the south, belfried churches and dwellings with Greek Ottoman inscriptions in the north, reminders of the pre-1974 heterogeneity of Cyprus.

Angeles-style high-rise suburbs beyond. The British, as well as the Cypriots, are to blame for the neglect and even desecration of much in the old city; many monuments, including a Lusignan palace, were senselessly pulled down around the turn of the century, and the Venetian ramparts first pierced by viaducts and later allowed to crumble at the edges. Most streets inside the walls are no longer architecturally homogenous, defaced by thoughtless concrete construction of recent decades.

So the romantic orientalist's town which the Archduke admired on the eve of British rule has vanished forever. Indeed, Nicosia is not an immediately likable city: especially around the Páfos Gate, the old town can be depressing and claustrophobic, qualities made worse by the presence of the Green Line, tensely palpable even when out of sight. Profuse wall graffiti in Hellenic blue concerns itself exclusively with what is delicately termed the National Question, the search for a solution to the island's de facto partition: "Attilas Out", "Federation = Turkification", "The Struggle Continues", or – simply and succinctly – "No". Absent is the Levantine ease of the coastal towns: clusters of men stand or sit about Platía Eleftherías expectantly, and unusually in Cyprus there is some hustle from shop and hotel proprietors. An entire neighbourhood is given over to obvious girlie bars, and there is more discreet, dispersed prostitution near the Ömeriye Mosque; the only other significant industries inside the Venetian fortifications appear to be cabinet-making, metal-working and offset printing.

Lawrence Durrell bemoaned Nicosia's lack of sophistication and infrastructure in the mid-1950s; it's no longer quite so dire, and a small capital that might be expected to be provincial supports a cosmopolitan leavening of Lebanese, Iranians and East Europeans, studying or surviving as refugees. Among the Europeans can also currently be numbered ex-Yugoslav draft-dodgers, and Russian businessmen laundering money – and even less savourily, Romanian and Russian women swelling the ranks of the prostitutes. Taken together, these are hardly foreseen legacies of non-aligned, 1960s Cyprus' diligent cultivation of ties all round. You will also come across journalists monitoring the Middle East from a relatively safe haven, and delegates to the numerous conferences which are a feature of Nicosia's winter calendar.

Some history

Most authorities believe that present-day Nicosia lies on or just north of the site of a Neolithic settlement, subsequently the Archaic town of Ledra. But the city only became prominent in Byzantine times, eclipsing Constantia (Salamis) after the disastrous seventh century, and embarking on a golden age with the arrival of the **Lusignan kings**. Particularly during the fourteenth century, they endowed the place with seven miles of fortifications, palaces, churches and monasteries appropriate to a court of chivalry. Their surviving monuments constitute much of Nicosia's appeal; nowhere else on Cyprus except at Famagusta can you take in the spectacle of Latin-Gothic architecture transplanted to the Levant. The underpinnings of such a hothouse fantasy were by their very nature transient: the Genoese raided Nicosia in 1373, and the Mamelukes sacked the city again in 1426. Following **Venetian** assumption of direct rule in 1489, Nicosia became even more of a stronghold. With an eye to the growing Ottoman threat, the Lusignan circuit of walls shrank between 1567 and 1570 to a more compact, anti-ballistic rampart system designed by the best engineers of the age. Monuments falling outside the new walls were demolished in the interest of a free field of fire.

But it was all unavailing, as the Turks took the city on September 9, 1570 after a seven-week siege, swarming over the Podocataro and Costanza bastions. In a paroxysm of rape, plunder and slaughter graphically described by survivors, the victors dispatched nearly half the 50,000 inhabitants and defenders.

Under **Ottoman rule** the city stagnated, if picturesquely, not to regain such a population level until the 1940s. The three centuries passed quietly, except for riots in 1764, in which a particularly unpleasant governor was killed, and mass executions of prominent Greek Cypriots (including the island's four bishops) in 1821, to preclude an echo of the peninsular uprising. The **British** raised the Union Jack over the town in 1878, but saw their wooden Government House burnt down in the pro-*énosis* riots of 1931.

Colonial authorities moved the administrative apparatus outside the walls in 1946, paralleling the growth of the city. But during the 1950s and 1960s the capital was wracked, first by the EOKA struggle and later by violence between the Christian and Muslim communities. After the events of December 1963 (see "History" in *Contexts*), **factional polarization** proceeded apace: Greeks and Armenians were expelled or fled from mixed neighbourhoods in the north of the city, and any remaining Turks deserted the south, so that Nicosia was already all but partitioned when the Turkish Army reached the northwestern suburbs, and then penetrated the Turkish quarter of the old town, on July 22, 1974.

Since then the runaway growth of the new southern boroughs has been spurred by the necessity of quickly providing housing for tens of thousands of Greek refugees from North Cyprus. By contrast old Nicosia has suffered even where not explicitly damaged by warfare, as shopkeepers and residents close to the Line deserted their premises, leaving often exquisite buildings to decay. Only recently has the trend of neglect been reversed, under the aegis of the **Nicosia Master Plan**, funded by the United Nations Development Programme and the EU. Tentative co-operation between urban planners in the Greek and Turkish sectors, based on the assumption of a reunited city in the future, has resulted in co-ordinated restoration and pedestrianization of the most attractive and vital neighbourhoods on both sides of the Green Line, and even (in 1979) the mundane but necessary completion of a joint sewerage plant, left stranded in the Turkish zone after 1974. The population of "Nicosia within the walls" seems to have stabilized, and it may have some future other than as a depressed, traumatized backwater.

Arrival, orientation and information

Whether approached from the south along the expressway from Larnaca or Limassol, or in a more leisurely fashion from the Tróödhos foothills, **arrival** in Nicosia is not an enticing prospect (the international **airport** has languished in the dead zone, used as UNFICYP headquarters since 1974, its ultimate fate pending a peace settlement). You wind through seemingly interminable suburbs indistinguishable from those of any other Mediterranean or Middle Eastern city, until suddenly thrust into the ring system of streets mirroring the Venetian bulwarks. Most of the **coach terminals** are a short distance from the ramparts, or even on them; see "Listings" and our map for precise locations.

One of the various uses to which the municipality has put the Venetian walls and moat is that of several **car parks**; coming in your own or a hire vehicle, the best areas are the moat between the D'Avila and Costanza bastions, with the top

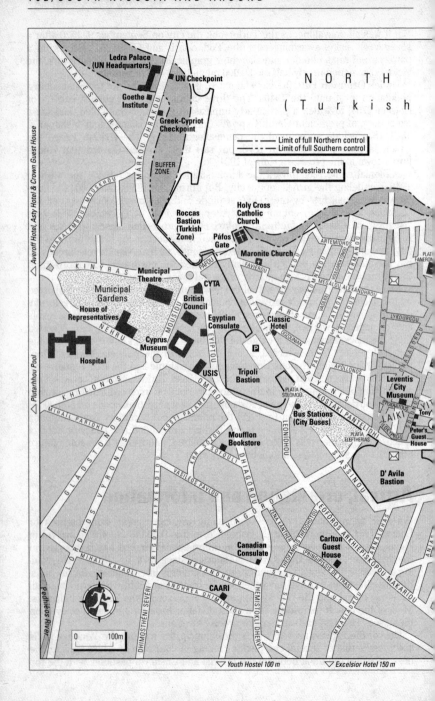

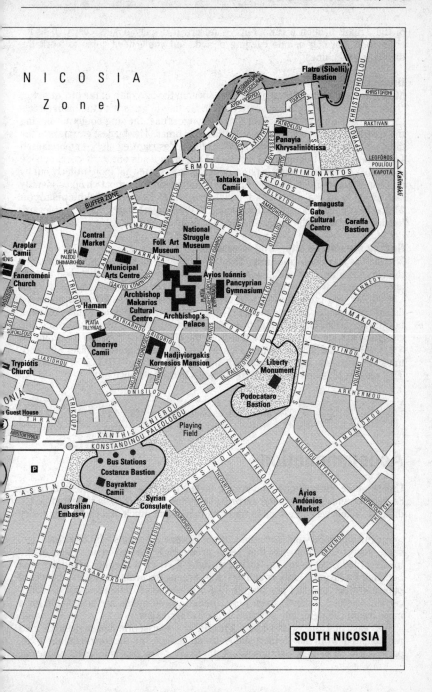

NICOSIA
Zone)

Flatro (Sibelli) Bastion

Panayia Khrysaliniótissa

Tahtakale Camii

Famagusta Gate Cultural Centre

Caraffa Bastion

Central Market

Folk Art Museum

National Struggle Museum

Araplar Camii

Faneroméni Church

Municipal Arts Centre

Ayios Ioánnis Pancyprian Gymnasium

Hamam

Archbishop Makarios Cultural Centre

Archbishop's Palace

Ömeriye Camii

Trypiótis Church

Hadjiyiorgakis Kornesios Mansion

Liberty Monument

Podocataro Bastion

Guest House

Playing Field

Bus Stations

Costanza Bastion

Bayraktar Camii

Australian Embassy

Syrian Consulate

Ayios Andónios Market

SOUTH NICOSIA

of the Tripoli bastion a runner-up. Windscreen display tickets cost C£0.40 for either one morning or one evening period, and you'll need coins to work the dispensing machines.

Orientation

Most of what a visitor will want to see lies within the labyrinth of the **old quarter**, "Nicosia within the walls" as some term it. Getting to grips with the main streets there is made difficult by the fact that the longest one, the ring boulevard linking the bastions, changes names no less than four times. The busiest entrance to the old town is at **Platía Eleftherías**, giving onto pedestrianized and commercialized **Lídhras**, while in the opposite direction **Evagórou** leads out to "Nicosia outside the walls", as the **new town** is often called. This is somewhat more orderly but by no means grid-regular, and the ring road just outside the moat changes identity just as often as its counterpart inside the walls; **Leofóros Arkhiepiskópou Makaríou**, perpendicular to Evagórou, is the longest and glitziest boulevard, headed out towards the Limassol–Larnaca highway.

Getting around the city – and information

Nicosia has an **urban bus network** of about twenty lines, straggling off through the new town into further-flung suburbs at half-hourly intervals between 5.30am and 7 or 8pm, twice as often at peak periods. They're cheap enough at about C£0.30, but you probably won't be using them much unless you want to visit a distant embassy or cultural centre. The **central terminal** is on Platía Solomoú, beside the Tripoli bastion. Full bus information is available there, and route and city maps are sporadically to be had from the **CTO** at Aristokýprou 35 (Mon–Fri 8.30am–4pm, Sat 8.30am–2pm). This is the general enquiries office; for more unusual requests try the world headquarters of the CTO at Theofánous Theodhótou 18, some 600m outside the walls in the new town.

> The south Nicosia phone code is ☎02.

Accommodation

Unless some international conference is being held – most of these between September and April – finding a free bed of some sort in Nicosia shouldn't be too difficult; hotels welcome walk-in trade, as there's not much of a package industry inland.

Appetizing, good-value accommodation, however, presents a bit of a challenge, since many establishments that seem promisingly located at the edge of the medieval town fall inside the main **red-light district**, a roughly triangular area bounded by Riyénis, Lídhras and Arsinóis streets. According to locals, the sleazy pubs and their regulars predate the heavy presence of UN forces, but the latter certainly helped it along. Even here, though, some hotels are acceptable for a mainstream clientele, and indicated in the listings below.

Just east of Lídhras, the **Laïkí Yitoniá** is a tourist-oriented pedestrian area rehabilitated from its former status as an annexe of the disreputable zone; particularly on or near Sólonos street, there are a few passable guest houses or

---

ACCOMMODATION PRICES IN THE SOUTH

All hotel and apartment-hotel prices in the South have been categorized according to the price codes given below. These categories represent the minimum you can expect to pay in the high season for a double room or a two-person self-catering unit. Single rooms will normally cost 50–80 percent of the rates quoted for a double room. Rates for dorm beds in hostels, where guests are charged per person, are given in Cyprus pounds, instead of being indicated by price code. For further details, see p.25.

① under C£12	④ C£20–25	⑦ C£35–40
② C£12–16	⑤ C£25–30	⑧ C£40–50
③ C£16–20	⑥ C£30–35	⑨ over C£50

---

small hotels, though they're all mosquito- and noise-plagued, the commotion starting at about 6.30am and not letting up until midnight. Budget or mid-range hotels in the new town are almost non-existent, though again a couple of exceptions are given below.

Unless otherwise noted, all rooms are with en suite facilities, and breakfast is included in the rates. However, summer water shortages can mean that bathing is out of the question for much of the day in the less expensive hotels.

Guest houses and the youth hostel

Carlton, Zéna Kánther (ex-Pringipíssis de Tyras) 13 (☎442001). Well-located, fairly quiet 1960s building a few minutes' walk south of Platía Solomoú. ②.

Crown, Filellínon 13, 500m west of the Páfos Gate (☎465264, fax 452043). Probably the best value in this category, though scheduled for a revamp at the time of writing so expect rates to climb by 20 percent. ②.

Peter's, Sólonos 5 (☎463153, fax 448519). The most savoury of the ultra-budget options; prices were uncertain at the time of writing, as the place was about to be remodelled.

Tony's, Sólonos 13, corner Ippokrátous (☎466752, fax 454225). Rooms, mostly en suite, in shockingly authentic London B&B style – but floozy-free, friendly and with an unbeatable roof terrace where full English breakfast is served. Rates depend on location in the building and plumbing arrangements (Tony also has longer-term flats for rent in the new city at about C£10 per night for two people). ②–③.

Youth hostel, Ioánni Hadjidháki 5, near Themistoklí Dherví, 700m southwest of Platía Eleftherías (☎444808). C£2.50 per person, plus C£0.50 sheet fee.

Hotels

Asty, Pringípos Karólou 12, 2km west of Platía Eleftherías in the suburb of Áyios Dhométios (☎473021, fax 476344). Rooms at this two-star hotel come with all mod cons such as minibar and air conditioning; there's also an attached restaurant and bicycles for guests' use, and the public pool on Ploutárkhou is ten minutes' walk away. Also available through *Sunvil Holidays*. ⑧.

Averof, Avérof 19, just across the Pedhiéos River west of the Cyprus Museum (☎463447, fax 463411). Old-fashioned two-star standby on a very quiet street, with restaurant and bar. ⑤.

Classic, Riyénis 94 (☎464006, fax 360072). This recently opened and refurbished successor to the *Capital Hotel* offers a pleasant restaurant, sun lounge and TV in the bedrooms; one of the few affordable reputable hotels in or near the red-light district. ⑥.

Excelsior, Fotíou Stávrou 4, corner Ikostipémptis Martíou, about 1km due south of the walled city (☎368585, fax 476740). Relatively luxurious three-star with facilities as you'd expect for the price. ⑧.

The City

The preponderance of interest for a visitor to south Nicosia lies within, on or right outside the Venetian walls, and since their circuit is just less than 2km in diameter, highlights can be toured on foot in a fairly leisurely two full days. After dark the old town (except for the Famagusta Gate area) is essentially deserted, even eerie, and most life shifts outside the walls.

The Venetian walls

Nicosia's **Venetian fortifications** are its most obvious feature, and a good place to start your wanderings. Of the eleven bastions, named for Venetian personalities, five fall into the Greek zone and five, now confusingly renamed, into the Turkish zone; the Flatro bastion, in the no-man's-land between the zones, is under UN control. Three surviving gates, called Páfos, Kyrenia and Famagusta after the towns which they face, breach the walls roughly 120 degrees apart. The Venetians engaged the military engineers Ascanio Savorgnano and Francesco Barbaro to design the ramparts between 1567 and 1570. At the foot of the fortifications they appended a moat, which was never intended to carry water – though the Pedhiéos River, later diverted, managed to fill it sporadically. It was not the fault of the walls themselves that Nicosia failed to withstand the siege of 1570; the Turks took the city mainly because of the incompetence of the pusillanimous commander Nicolo Dandolo, and the exhaustion of the defenders. The Ottomans maintained the ramparts, which were captured more or less intact; it is only since 1878 that substantial alterations have been made. Most of the following monuments are atop, or an integral part of, the bastions which form the most obvious bits of the ramparts. Otherwise it's easy to tread the course of the walls without realizing it, a testimony to how domesticated they've become.

The Páfos Gate area

If you come from the Tróödhos by car, the **Páfos Gate**, which, poised between the Greek and Turkish zones of the town, has been a trouble spot since 1963, will probably be your grim introduction to the old city. Now the flags of the South and the North, plus Greece and Turkey, oppose each other here across a ten-metre airspace, and signs on the Turkish-held Roccas bastion warn against "trespassers". Originally this gate was called Porta San Domenico, after a Lusignan abbey just outside, which the Venetians demolished in 1567 when they contracted the circumference of the walls. The Ottomans had a large barracks and arsenal in and on it; the British made the internal chambers their police headquarters and closed the gate to vehicles, though it reopened to traffic after independence, and there was always a pedestrian tunnel.

Just inside stands one of the many anomalies of the post-1974 situation: the **Holy Cross Catholic church** and papal nuncio's residence, though squarely in the dead zone with its rear in Turkish-occupied territory, was allowed to reopen for business in 1976 on condition that the back door was sealed. The Maronites (see p.259) also have a church, school and clubhouse around the corner.

Moving anti-clockwise, the moats and next two bastions have been put to use as dusty parkland, playing fields, bus terminals or car parks, with D'Avila bastion also supporting a small cluster of public buildings. Three viaducts now compromise the walls and moat, the largest (Platía Eleftherías) scheduled for a face-lift under the Nicosia Master Plan.

Bayraktar Camii and the Liberty Monument

The small **Bayraktar Camii** (Mosque of the Standard-Bearer), in a well-landscaped area beyond the bus stations on the **Costanza fortification**, marks the spot where the Ottoman flag-carrier first scaled the walls in the 1570 siege. Vulnerable as such individuals always were – it was essentially a suicide mission – he was cut down immediately by the defenders, and buried on the subsequently revered site. EOKA activists bombed the mosque and tomb twice in 1962 and 1963, toppling the minaret the second time, but the damage was repaired and the mosque grounds are now kept locked to prevent recurrences. A sign up front, in Turkish and Greek, informs passers-by that while the Greek Cypriots respect the remaining Islamic holy places in the South (occasional EOKA sabotage aside), the Turks have not reciprocated in the matter of churches in the North.

A haven of parkland also surrounds the **Liberty Monument** sculpture, on the **Podocataro bastion**, consisting of fourteen representative Greek Cypriot figures in bronze being released from a white marble jail by two soldiers and being blessed by a cleric. Commissioned and opened to great hoo-hah some years back, the monument is now presumably such an embarrassing obstacle to communal reconciliation that it is absent even from most official tourist literature and maps.

The Famagusta Gate

Tucked into an angle of the **Caraffa bastion**, the **Famagusta Gate** is the most elaborate and best preserved of Nicosia's three gates. Designed by Giulio Savorgnano (brother of Ascanio) as a copy of another such Venetian structure in Iraklion, Crete, the gate is essentially a tunnel through the walls, the inner facade with its six coats of arms and original wooden doors far more aesthetic than the mean outer portal. After more than a century of neglect, the great domed chamber that opens out at the centre of the tunnel was refurbished in 1981 as an **exhibition and concert venue**; the heart of the latter is an acoustically marvellous, gently inclined tunnel surmounted by a dome like a miniature Parisian Pantheon. A side chamber, once either the Ottoman powder magazine or guard house, is now the exhibition hall. Beyond the outer portal stretches a small open-air amphitheatre used during the Nicosia September festival.

The traditional commercial centre

Using Platía Eleftherías as a gateway, you're set at the Y-junction of **Lídhras** and **Onasagórou** streets to explore the time-honoured city centre of Nicosia. A graceless architectural mix of British Raj, Greek Neoclassical and ugly 1950s-and-60s lines these two main shopping streets, which were recently pedestrianized as part of the Master Plan. The Greek Cypriot barricade at the north end of Lídhras, with its little shrine to the lost homelands and a "public relations" booth to one side, is the only point on the Green Line you may photograph; you're supposed to stay a healthy ten metres away from other checkpoints. Businesses, in any case, peter out upon reaching the last three or four premises away from the Line – the uncertainty (and in former years, proclamation battles by the opposing sides using loudhailers) was too nerve-wracking. It is not the first time the street has been embattled; during the late 1950s Lídhras was dubbed "Murder Mile" after EOKA's habit of gunning down its adversaries here.

Platía Faneroménis

The north end of Onasagórou gives onto **Platía Faneroménis**, slated to replace Eleftherías as the official city centre and named after the huge **church** that dominates the square. A hotchpotch of Neoclassical, Byzantine and Latin styles, it was erected during the final Ottoman years to replace an apparently more interesting but derelict medieval basilica. Inside the present structure are the remains of the four clerics murdered by the Ottoman governor in 1821. Behind the apse stands the Neoclassical Girls' Gymnasium, counterpart to the Pancyprian Gymnasium (see below).

More compelling than the Faneroméni church, and virtually filling the adjacent tiny Platía Ikostiogdhóïs Oktovríou, is the **Araplar Camii**, originally the sixteenth-century church of Stavrós toú Missirikoú, a good example of the mixed Byzantine-Gothic style particular to Lusignan times. You're unlikely to gain admission to the mosque, but if you do, the octagonal-drummed dome is supported on magnificent columned arches. Taking advantage of the setting with outdoor sitting is the recommended *Matheos* taverna (see "Eating and drinking").

Laïkí Yitoniá and around

Just east of the Lídhras pedestrianization, and predating it as the first part of the Master Plan to be carried out, the so-called **Laïkí Yitoniá** or "Folk Neighbourhood" forms a showcase district reclaimed from the sin merchants in the late 1980s, with restored premises made available to half a dozen indifferent restaurants and numbers of souvenir shops. Unique and outstanding among the touristy schlock here is *Gallery Dhiakhroniki*, Aristokýprou 2B – see p.208 for a full description.

The south Nicosia municipality is also extremely proud of the nearby **Leventis City Museum** at Ippokrátous 17 (Tues–Sun 10am–4.30pm; admission free, but donation requested), which won the European Museum of the Year award in 1991. This folk-cum-historical collection occupies two floors of a restored mansion, and the collection is arranged in reverse chronological order: ideally you start at the rear of the first floor and work your way forward and down. Unfortunately labelling tends to be in Greek, with occasionally some in English and French. Exhibits include traditional dress, household implements, rare books and prints, with scattered precious metalware or archeological treasures. The best sections are those devoted to the Venetian and Ottoman periods, with the ground floor exhibits dwindling to a disappointment of unlabelled, uncontexted archival photos as the present is reached. There's little on the history of individual monuments, and nothing yet on how the two zones of the city function together now, nor any background on the Laïkí Yitoniá or Khrysaliniótissa renewal projects.

Around the corner on Sólonos, the **Tripiótis church**, dedicated to the Archangel Michael, is the most beautiful of the old town's surviving medieval churches. On the south side, a glassed porch protects a pair of Gothic-arched windows. Over the door between, a fourteenth-century relief shows two lions being subdued by a being sprouting from leafy tracery, clutching hoops; to either side, mermaids and sea monsters gambol. Inside, the brown sandstone masonry has been left unpainted, as has the fine wooden *yinaikonítis* – indeed the whole interior is relatively restrained for a Cypriot church.

The Ömeriye Camii and Hadjiyiorgakis Kornesios mansion

Variously spelled Omerieh, Omerye, and Omeriyeh, the **Ömeriye Camii** on Platía Tillyrías is the only Gothic house of worship converted into a mosque in the Greek zone of Nicosia. Originally it was a church of St Mary, part of a four-teenth-century Augustinian monastery largely destroyed by the Ottoman bombardment in 1570. Many Lusignan nobles were buried here, but as in the case of the Ayía Sofía cathedral in north Nicosia, the victors sacrilegiously "recy-cled" their tombstones to refloor the mosque during reconstruction. The Ottoman conqueror of Cyprus, Lala Mustafa Paşa, got it into his head that the caliph Omar had rested here during the seventh-century Arab raids on Cyprus – hence the name. Today it serves the needs of the city's Arab and Persian popula-tion; you are welcome to shed your shoes inside the ornate west portal and visit the simple, barn-like interior with its shallow pitched roof and series of (post-siege) arches (Mon–Sat 10am–12.30pm & 1.30–3.30pm). At dusk, the Arabic-speaking *muezzin* here vies with the Turkish tropes emanating from the minarets of the Selimiye Camii in north Nicosia, their unsynchronized calls to prayer stir-ring up formations of swallows.

The namesake **baths**, across the square, also still function, worth knowing about in winter or if you're stuck in a bottom-end pension; Wednesday and Thursday are the women-only days, when local prostitutes throng the baths (daily 8am–2.30pm; C£1). Platía Tillyrías itself is now a rather busy street and car park, but there are a few snack and drink cafés to one side where you can rest and admire the mosque.

The Hadjiyiorgakis Kornesios mansion

A few steps down Patriárkhou Grigoríou from the Ömeriye mosque, the delight-ful fifteenth-to-eighteenth-century **Hadjiyiorgakis Kornesios mansion** is a hybrid of Venetian and Ottoman forms – a wooden Turkish lattice balcony perches over a relief coat of arms at the front door – that easily overshadows any of its contents (Mon–Fri 8am–2pm, Sat 9am–1pm; C£0.50). Supposedly home to the Cyprus Ethnographic Museum, only a single room in the back is an authentic recreation of the house in its heyday; most of the others serve as a contemporary antique gallery, rather than featuring medieval furnishings, though several rooms do exhibit assorted metal, glass and ceramic items from various eras.

The house takes its name from one **Hadjiyiorgakis Kornesios**, a native of Térra in Páfos district, who served as the dragoman (multi-lingual liaison between the Ottoman authorities and the Orthodox Christians) of Cyprus from 1779 until 1809. With a fortune accumulated from his vast estates and tax exemp-tion, he was the most wealthy and powerful man on the island, but he met the usual end of Ottoman officials who became too prominent. A peasant revolt of 1804 was aimed at him and the Greek clerics, as much as at the Muslim ruling class; fleeing to Istanbul, he managed to stay alive and nominally kept office by seeking asylum in sympathetic foreign embassies – until beheaded in 1809 as part of the intrigues surrounding the consecutive depositions of the sultans Selim III and Mustafa IV.

Around the archbishop's palace

An alarming concentration of coffin-makers lines the street leading from the Hadjiyiorgakis Kornesios mansion to **Platía Arkhiepiskópou Kypriánou**, which is flanked by a cluster of buildings including the city's diminutive cathedral and three museums. The **archbishop's palace** is the most immediately obvious monument, a grandiose pastiche that has recently replaced its 1950s predecessor, shelled and gutted by EOKA-B in their July 15, 1974 attempt to kill Archbishop Makarios. Except for the "Cultural Centre" wing described on p.202, it is not open to the public. At the southeast corner of the palace precinct, a controversial, not to say downright hideous, statue of Makarios looks (below the waist espe-

---

GEORGE "DHIYENIS" GRIVAS (1898–1974) AND EOKA

Travelling about in the South, you can't help noticing that practically every town has a Griva Dhiyení avenue, sometimes even two. They honour a man as controversial as Makarios – and who, particularly since independence, brought considerable misery, directly or indirectly, to both Greek and Turkish Cypriots.

Born on May 23, 1898, a native of Tríkomo (now renamed İskele) in the North, **George Grivas** attended Nicosia's Pancyprian Gymnasium before enrolling in the officers' academy in Athens. He graduated just in time to see several years' service in Greece's disastrous Asia Minor campaign – which doubtless fuelled his lifelong aversion to Turkey and Turks.

Grivas remained in Greece after the loss of Asia Minor, taking part under General Papagos in the repulsion of the Italians on the Epirot front during the winter of 1940–41. Having idly sat out most of the German occupation of his adopted homeland, in 1944 he formed a far-right-wing guerrilla band of royalist officers known as **Khi** – written "X" in the Greek alphabet – which by all accounts was collaborationist, devoting most of its time to exterminating left-wing bands and leaving the departing Germans alone. When full-scale civil war broke out in 1946, he emerged from retirement as a lieutenant-colonel to help crush the communist-inspired rebellion, again with Papagos as his superior.

A semblance of normal life and elections returned to Greece in 1951. Grivas ran under the banner of Papagos' party but was defeated – his forbidding, abstemious personality, appropriate to the battlefield, did not strike a chord in the Greek electorate. Disgusted, Grivas swore off electoral politics for good, and returned to Cyprus the same year to test the possibility of an uprising there to throw off British rule. It was then that he met Makarios, whom he tried to convince of the necessity of some sort of rebellion. Neither Makarios nor Grivas' Greek sponsors were persuaded until an Athens meeting in early 1953, when Makarios, Grivas and ten others resolved to fight for *énosis* or union with Greece, founding **EOKA**, the *Ethnikí Orgánosis Kypríon Agonistón* or "National Organization of Cypriot Fighters".

At this point Makarios would only assent to violence against property, but during 1954 two caïques loaded with explosives and weapons made their clandestine way from Rhodes to Cyprus, landing on the then-deserted Páfos coast (see p.127). Most of the year was taken up establishing EOKA in Cyprus, with recruits taking oaths of secrecy, obedience and endurance till victory, similar to those of the IRA.

Makarios gave the final go-ahead for the insurrection in March 1955; EOKA made its spectacular public debut on April 1 with bomb explosions across the

cially) more like Lot's wife than a cleric, as he stares down Koráï street towards the Liberty Monument.

Across the way sprawls the imposing Neoclassical facade of the **Pancyprian Gymnasium**, one of the more prestigious secondary academies for Greek Cypriots this century and last. In *Bitter Lemons* Lawrence Durrell described his experiences teaching here in the mid-1950s, when it became a hotbed of pro-*énosis* sentiment.

The church of Áyios Ioánnis

Between the Gymnasium and the palace sits the seventeenth-century **church of Áyios Ioánnis** (Mon–Sat 8am–noon & 2–4pm), which gets some prizes for the

---

island. Self-introductory leaflets were signed **"Dhiyenis"**, Grivas' chosen *nom de guerre*, after Dhiyenis Akritas, hero of a tenth-century Byzantine epic.

The revolt gathered momentum throughout 1955 and early 1956, when Grivas halted a promising round of negotiations between Makarios and Governor Harding with timely explosions which also provoked Makarios' deportation. Thereafter Grivas and EOKA included murder in the scope of their operations, targeting British servicemen, leftist or pro-British Greeks and occasionally Turkish Cypriots as victims. From his movable headquarters in the Tróödhos – at or near Kýkko monastery – Grivas mocked the British with a steady barrage of communiqués and ultimatums. To the British, at their wit's end, he was not "Dhiyenis" but "Egregious" Grivas.

When Makarios returned to Cyprus in 1959, he found himself estranged from Grivas who, furious at the archbishop's acceptance of independence rather than *énosis*, stalked off to self-exile in Greece and a hero's welcome, including promotion to the rank of lieutenant-general. This all apparently went to Grivas' head, and his subsequent paranoid public utterances were deeply embarrassing to all concerned, earning him denunciation by the Greek government.

By 1964, however, Greece, Makarios and Grivas had patched things up to the extent that the Athens government sent Grivas back to Cyprus, ostensibly to impose discipline on irregulars of Greek nationality who had smuggled themselves onto the island. This he did, but he also assumed command of Makarios' new **National Guard** and led several attacks on Turkish enclaves, most notably at Kókkina in 1964 and Kofinou in 1967, pushing Greece, Turkey and Cyprus to the brink of war each time. After the 1967 episode, American diplomacy secured what was hoped would be his permanent removal from the island.

But the 1967–74 Greek junta, in its obsessive machinations to oust Makarios from office, found Grivas useful once again: in 1971 he secretly entered Cyprus disguised as a priest to organize **EOKA-B**, literally "EOKA the Second", whose express intent was the elimination of all enemies of Hellenism – and of the colonels – on the island. This came to include virtually anyone who stood in the junta's way: communists, socialists, centrists, Turkish Cypriots, and eventually Makarios himself. Whether Grivas subscribed to all of this as the junta's willing patsy, or as a royalist shared some of Makarios' disdain for the colonels and remained opposed to any "*énosis*" that would invite the Turks in for a chunk of the island, will never be known; he died in January 1974, still in hiding. Yet had he not left the scene when he did, it is possible to imagine Grivas being persuaded to lead the July 1974 coup against his erstwhile comrade-in-arms, Makarios. With hindsight, it is possible to respect Grivas for his obvious dedication and skill as a guerrilla – but for little else.

quantity (if not always the quality) of its recently cleaned eighteenth-century interior **frescoes**. Among recognizable scenes are the *Last Judgement* and the *Creation* over the south and north doors respectively, and on the south wall a sequence on the rediscovery of the apostle Barnabas' relics. Despite its small size (compared to Faneroméni, for instance), Áyios Ioánnis is the official cathedral of the city; here the archbishops of Nicosia are still consecrated, standing on the floor medallion featuring a Byzantine double-headed eagle.

The Folk Art Museum

Just north, the **Folk Art Museum** (closed indefinitely for "repairs") occupies the surviving wing of a fourteenth-century Benedictine monastery, handed over to the Orthodox and done up as the old archbishop's residence after Latin rule ended. When the collection reshuffling is complete, you should still be able to see chunks of wooden water-wheel in the exterior portico, and a typical assortment of textiles, woodcarving and household implements inside.

The Archbishop Makarios Cultural Centre

Within sight of both Áyios Ioánnis and the Folk Art Museum is the entrance to the **Archbishop Makarios Cultural Centre** (Mon–Fri 9am–1pm & 2–5pm, Sat 9am–1pm; c£1), which owes its grandiose name to the presence of several research libraries and a very audible school of ecclesiastical music, where laymen learn to be *psáltes* or chanters for Orthodox church services. On the upper floor, lit and opened only on request, resides Makarios' private collection of kitschy religious subjects with doubtful attributions, assembled for him by a French Cypriot, Nikolaos Dikeos. The ground floor, however, is another matter, and for most visitors a tour of the Byzantine galleries here will be one of the highlights of a day in Nicosia.

THE KANAKARIÁ MOSAICS

Pride of place, and deservedly so, is given to the recovered **Kanakariá mosaics**, stolen from a church in North Cyprus in the late 1970s but returned to Nicosia in 1991 after a lengthy court battle (see "The Theft of the Kanakariá Mosaics", p.297, for more details). Since late 1992 they have been displayed in the purpose-built, right-rear wing, though their layout here – an artificially flat surface – does not replicate their former positioning in Panayía Kanakariá church, in a curved apse, viewed from below. Originally, the Virgin Enthroned sat between the two archangels, with a band above containing the busts of the apostles. The most famous image is that of Christ clutching a scroll, looking like a young pagan god and adhering to Hellenistic, rather than later, iconographic conventions. Only one archangel, Gabriel, survived into modern times; his eyes, which look strangely averted in the mosaics' present position, would originally have been gazing at the Virgin. The apostles Matthew, James and Bartholomew were recovered more or less intact; all are distinguished by preternaturally large, asymmetrical eyes. Stylistically, all the figures show the marked Hellenistic traits typical for such early Christian mosaics of the sixth century.

THE ICON GALLERY

The mosaics are a hard act to follow, but the **icons** in the adjacent gallery, about 150 in all retrieved from various Cypriot churches, along with a reconstructed apse full of fourteenth-century frescoes rescued from Áyios Nikólaos tis Stéyis (see p.172), acquit themselves commendably. Even when the exhibits are not of the highest artistic standard, they mostly prove unusual in some respect; under the influence of the Lusignans, artists often made astonishingly free with the usual iconographic rules, especially in the variations of the Virgin and Child from the sixteenth century.

To the right, just inside the main door, stands a familiar portrayal of the Prophet Elijah, from the thirteenth century, being fed in the wilderness by the raven, symbol of God's providence; adjacent, an earlier, pensive St John the Baptist is rather more spruced up than his usual shaggy norm. Rarely seen topics include St Anne holding the Virgin and Child; the Burning Bush, as a herald of Christ; and a *Thrinos*, similar to a Latinate *Pietà* with just the dead Christ and the Virgin, whereas Orthodox portrayals of the *Deposition* are usually group scenes. At the rear of the main gallery, a sixteenth-century icon of the *Adoration of the Magi* turns out in practice to be a Renaissance-style family portrait; a *Virgin Orans* of the same period shows the donor family kneeling to either side. Their costumes, and those of other figures, were invaluable in dating these works, and offer an absorbing insight into medieval Cypriot life. Unfortunately, the souvenir stall by the ticket booth disagrees with these assessments, and postcards and books offered are generally disappointing.

The National Struggle Museum

On the north side of the Folk Art Museum, and signed under a small arched alleyway, is tucked the **National Struggle Museum** (Mon–Fri 7.30am–2.30pm & 3–5.30pm; c£0.25), an overwhelming accumulation of memorabilia, mostly photo-archival, on EOKA's 1950s anti-colonial campaign of demonstrations, sabotage and murder. The British reprisals, searches, tortures and detention camps are documented in cartoons and press comment of the time. Also on display are fighters' personal belongings, plus arrays of weapons and gruesomely ingenious bombs. In the middle of the complex, there's a memorial to EOKA's martyrs, plus a mock-up gallows commemorating the nine hanged at the city's Central Prison by the British in 1956. Labelling is minimal, which doesn't help those who can't read Greek; the propaganda impact is visual, and primarily intended for Cypriot schoolchildren. Interestingly, the main emphasis is on opposition to (and from) the British, with little on adverse Turkish Cypriot action – there are even some photos of Turkish Cypriots celebrating independence with their fellow islanders.

Tahtakale and Khrysaliniótissa districts

Heading north from Platía Kypriánou on pedestrianized Ayíou Ioánnou, you shortly reach the small **Tahtakale (Taht-el-Kala) Camii**, the homely focus of the eponymous neighbourhood. Here the Master Plan is in full swing, as dozens of old houses are being renovated for occupation by young families in an effort to revitalize the area. But for a taste of the exotic Ottoman town of the last century, accented with palm trees, arched mud-brick houses and domes, you really need to continue across Ermoú into the **Khrysaliniótissa district**, strolling along Axiothéas, Ayíou Yioryíou and Avtokratóras Theodhóras streets in particular.

Monumentally, this area is anchored by the namesake church of **Panayía Khrysaliniótissa**, a rambling L-shaped building with fine relief carving on its exterior, arches under the two domes, and an overwhelming collection of icons inside. Construction was begun in 1450 by Helena Paleologina, the Greek wife of

Lusignan King John II; the name, "Our Lady of the Golden Linen", is supposed to derive from its vanished original icon's having been found in a flax field.

Perhaps on the heels of the rehabilitation efforts, businesses and residences are used right up to the barriers here, in contrast to elsewhere in town; the dead zone also seems narrower, with North Cypriot/Turkish flags plainly visible over the housetops. This defiant stance gives an extra edge to many of the good *ouzerís* and tavernas (see "Eating and drinking") which have congregated here since the Famagusta Gate was restored. But of the 23 types of exotic bazaars catalogued by Louis Salvator, effectively bisecting the town between the Famagusta and Páfos gates, only traces of the cabinet-making, tin-smithing, cloth and candle-dipping industries remain in the Greek zone, mostly on the few commercial streets between Tahtakale and Khrysaliniótissa.

The Cyprus Museum

Founded early in the British tenure, the **Cyprus Museum** (Mon–Sat 9am–5pm, Sun 10am–1pm; C£1) is easily the best assemblage of archeological artefacts on the island. It stands between the Tripoli bastion and the pleasant **municipal gardens**, Nicosia's largest green space and, with its outdoor café, a worthwhile adjunct to any visit. You should tour the galleries anti-clockwise from the ticket booth for rough chronological order, but the museum is organized thematically as well. Typically for Cyprus, the pre-Classical displays are the most compelling, though every period from Stone Age to early Byzantine is represented. All told, it's an absorbing medium-sized collection that requires at least two hours for a once-over. Individual labelling is often mercifully replaced with hall-by-hall or glass-case explanatory plaques placing the objects in context.

Highlights of the collection

Room 1 is devoted to Neolithic items, in particular andesite ware and shell jewellery from Khirokitiá, and a case of Chalcolithic fertility idols. **Room 2**, the Early Bronze Age gallery, features fantastically zoomorphic or beak-spouted composite red-clay pottery from the Kyrenia coast. The central exhibits illustrate aspects of a pervasive early Cypriot cult: two pairs of ploughing bulls, a rite conducted by priests (wearing bull masks) in a sacred enclosure, and a model sanctuary crowned with bulls' heads.

The pottery of **Room 3** presents the best pictorial evidence of Mycenaean influence in Late Bronze Age Cyprus. A gold inlaid bowl from Enkomi and a faience rhyton from Kition are the richest specimens here, though decorated *kratirs* (wine-mixing bowls) are more revealing in their portrayal of stylized humans in chariots being drawn by equally fantastic horses. Recurrent left- and right-handed swastikas predate any Nazi associations, and merely indicate Asian contacts.

Room 4 is dominated by its startling corner display, a panoply of seventh- and sixth-century votive figurines from a **sanctuary at Ayía Iríni** near Cape Kormakíti, excavated in 1929. The shrine was active after 1200 BC as the focus of a fertility cult, yet few of the two thousand figurines discovered were female. Most of the terracotta men, of various sizes, are helmeted, prompting speculation that the deity was also one of war.

A limestone **Zeus Keraunios** ("Thunderer") from Kition, familiar from the C£10 note, hurls a missing lightning-bolt in **Room 5**. This and other Greek/

Hellenistic statues show marked Assyrian influence in beard, hairdo and dress; an oriental voluptuousness in male or female facial expression decreases as the Hellenistic period is reached, but never entirely vanishes. Among several renderings of the goddess is a first-century AD Roman statuette of **Aphrodite of Soli** – an image reproduced ad infinitum across Cyprus in tourist literature proclaiming it "her" island.

A cast-bronze, large-than-life-size nude of the second-century emperor **Septimius Severus**, unearthed at Kythrea in 1928, forms the centrepiece of **Room 6**. **Room 7A** showcases an intricate **wheeled stand** for a bowl, ranks of animal figures rampant on its four sides, with an account of its rescue by the Cyprus government from Turkish thieves (pre-1974) and German art dealers. Ancient Enkomi, near Famagusta, yielded this and other twelfth-century BC finds like the famous bronze "**Horned God**", one hand downturned in benediction.

Subterranean **Room 8** demonstrates the progression from simple pit-tombs under dwellings, as at Khirokitiá, to rock-cut chamber-tombs, accessed by a *dromos* or "passage". Other steps lead to **Room 11**, the royal Salamis tomb room. Trappings from a hearse, and chariot traces for the horses sacrificed in the *dromos* (see p.372) are overshadowed by the famous **bronze cauldron** on a tripod, with griffon and sphinx heads welded onto its edge. A metal throne was found together with an Egyptian-influenced, finely crafted bed and a throne or chair of wood and ivory.

Room 7B offers a miscellany of objects from around the island, including the famous original mosaic of *Leda and the Swan* from Palea Paphos. Gold specimens include that portion of the Byzantine Lambousa Treasure which escaped the attentions of plunderers and smugglers in the last century (most of the hoard went to US museums, particularly the Metropolitan Museum in New York).

The exhibits are rounded off with **Room 14**'s terracotta figurines from all eras. Among the more whimsical are three humans and a dog in a boat, and a thirteenth-century BC sidesaddle rider, recently recovered from thieves. *Ex votos* of expectant mothers depict midwives delivering babies, and strange bird-headed and earringed women fondling their own breasts. From the Meniko sanctuary dedicated to the Phoenician god Baal Hamman, an outsize, unsettling figure of a bull being led to sacrifice completes a spectrum of taurean worship begun in Room 2.

Kaïmákli

Nearly 2km northeast of the UN-controlled Flatro bastion, the suburb of **Kaïmákli** – until 1968 a separate village – boasts the finest domestic architecture outside the city walls. Local Greek Orthodox architects and stonemasons first came to prominence during the Lusignan period, when the Latin rulers trained and used this workforce in the construction of the massive Gothic monuments of the city centre. Their skills persisted through later changes of regime, and during the late Ottoman years the master masons would often travel abroad for commissions.

With the coming of the British, there was no longer a need to conceal wealth from the powers that were, and the former simple but functional mud-brick houses, with perhaps just a pair of sandstone arches or a lintel, were joined by grandiose stone churches and dwellings sporting pillars, balcony grillwork, and other architectural follies. More recent Kaïmákli history has not been happy. As a mixed district, it was the scene of bitter fighting and EOKA atrocities during December 1963, particularly in the Omórfita neighbourhood (Küçük Kaymaklı to the Turkish Cypriots); this, like much of Kaïmákli proper, now lies in the Turkish zone.

Every Monday the south Nicosia municipality lays on a bus and walking **tour** of Kaïmákli; just show up at 10am at the Laïkí Yitoniá CTO office. The two-hour outing, which involves a coach transfer along the Green Line in addition to the foot itinerary, is free, but patrons are "encouraged" to buy things when stopped at points of interest along the way. If you'd rather go by yourself, **bus** lines #46 and #48 serve Kaïmákli.

CROSSING THE GREEN LINE

There are actually three separate halts at the Ledra Palace crossing, at the Greek Cypriot, UN and Turkish Cypriot posts respectively. The Greek booth, across from the Goethe Institute and Greek embassy, is open daily from 8am to 1pm. You fill in a form (among other things acknowledging the illegality of the Turkish occupation and absolving the South of any responsibility should anything go wrong on your visit) under the baleful shadow of a government placard: "Beyond this checkpoint is an area of Cyprus still occupied by Turkish troops since their invasion of 1974. Turkey expelled 180,000 Cypriots of Greek origin, and brought over colonists from mainland Turkey to replace them. Enjoy yourself in this land of racial purity and apartheid; enjoy the sight of our desecrated churches . . ." and so on in a similar vein. Those with Greek or Armenian surnames, holding any passport, shouldn't bother trying to cross as they won't be let in by the Turks. The Greek Cypriots don't allow overnight luggage to head north, or any shopping sprees while there; only force-majeure-type excuses for coming back later than 5pm are accepted. It appears that rental cars are now allowed over, but if you tell the rental company of your intention to cross, they may void insurance coverage.

Once past the sporadically manned UN barrier and through to the computerized Turkish Cypriot checkpoint, you'll pay c£1 for a **day pass**, but make sure *not* to have your passport itself stamped, since in that case you'll be banned from re-entering south Nicosia – the pass should be issued as a separate, detachable sheet. As a counterpoint to the Greek Cypriot placard, the North has erected its own noticeboard to which are attached archival photos of Greek Orthodox priests shooting at Turkish Cypriots, exhumations of Turkish villagers buried alive by EOKA-B in 1974, and the like. Also occasionally available is an "information sheet" entitled *Northern Cyprus Monthly*, which taps an ever-present vein of *énosis*-phobia in its coverage of the South's secret rearmament and the purportedly imminent arrival of Greek army divisions.

Beyond the Turkish Cypriot checkpoint cluster moneychangers, souvenir stalls and, most importantly, **taxi-drivers**. The latter pitch lightning day trips to one of the North's big attractions (usually you choose between Kyrenia or Famagusta), but some of them are unscrupulous fare-fiddlers and you really can't do the North justice in an eight-hour tour.

The Ledra Palace checkpoint: day trips to the North

From the Páfos Gate area, Márkou Dhrákou winds north towards the Green Line and the UN headquarters in the former Ledra Palace hotel. As you approach, a bizarre sort of parasitic life makes itself felt: a souvenir shop called the *Drop-In* prints commemorative T-shirts for UN forces (as well as archeological excavation teams), who hang the shirts out to dry from balconies of the Ledra Palace; a Karpasian Refugee Association Restaurant dishes up ethnic politics with meals near the checkpoint; and estate-agent signs pitch abandoned properties in the area, presumably at knock-down prices.

If you want to actually pass to **the other side of the Green Line**, this is currently the single legal crossing from southern to northern Cyprus, for day visits only. You cannot stay overnight and then expect to return to the South, since the Greek Cypriot rationale is that all pre-1974 hotels in the North have been expropriated illegally from their rightful owners, and by staying in them you would be using stolen property. The guidelines given in the box are subject to change, as the checkpoint is apt to close without warning when things are going badly.

Eating and drinking

Old Nicosia has numbers of decent, authentic places at which to eat, but they are fairly well hidden – and most emphatically not to be found in the much-touted Laïkí Yitoniá, a twee tourist trap whose nature will be familiar to anyone who's visited Athens' Plaka or Paris' Quartier Latin. Many, though not all, of the better full-on tavernas and less pretentious *ouzerís* are scattered to either side of the Famagusta Gate, lodestar of the city's "alternative" set. Except for listings in the new town, the establishments below are within walking distance of each other.

The commercial centre

Byzantion, Sólonos 2. Virtually the only Laïkí Yitoniá outfit worth a second glance, not least for its wall art and ethnographic exhibits.

Iraklis, Lídhras 110. *The* spot for locally produced quality ice cream; always has customers out front, whatever the hour.

Matheos, Platía Ikostiogdhóïs Oktovríou, behind Faneroméni church and beside the tiny Araplar mosque. Similar idea to *Zanettos* (see below) but nicer setting (outdoor seats by the mosque) and wider menu, featuring quails, rabbit, *óspria*, puddings and walnut cake.

Savvas, Sólonos 65. Zero decor, but tasty and unbelievably cheap homestyle Cypriot dishes. Mon–Sat noon–8pm.

Zanettos, Trikoúpi 65, on the way to the central covered market. Features small *mezé* plates and alcohol, but pitches itself as a "family" establishment. Lunch only.

Between Flatro Bastion and Famagusta Gate

Enotiko Kafenio Egeon, Éktoros 40. An oddball multi-purpose centre, combining record shop, bookshop, culture club and taverna. Run by a one-time anarchist, now fanatically (and belatedly) converted to the cause of *énosis*; his *souvlaki* and cooked casserole dishes are more digestible than his politics. Evenings only; garden seating out back.

No-name grill, Axiothéas, near junction Ayíou Kassianoú, around the corner from *Thermopiles*. From an old house emerges some of the best kebabs to be found in the city, at suppertime only; outdoor seating in this dead-end street smack up against a minor checkpoint.

Thermopiles, Anastasías Toufexís 19, 200m from Flatro. Don't be put off by the dilapidated premises, unmaintained because of its proximity to the dead zone – this is a find, emphasizing cooked vegetable entrees for lunch, leftovers and *mezé* at night, when it's open till after midnight. The clientele is a motley assortment of locals, tourists, expats and UN forces, with intimacy foisted on patrons by the forty-square-metre layout. Hard to pigeonhole, but recommended.

To Steki tis Khrysaliniotissas, Athinás 19, within sight of Flatro. More of a formal, sit-down taverna with both indoor and outdoor tables, serving well-prepared and not too expensive food. Supper only.

The new town

Fytro, Khitrón 11, 600m south of D'Avila bastion. Vegetarian and health fare, in premises next to *L&M Health Food Stores*. Set-price (c£3.50) buffet, plus cakes and herb teas. Lunch Mon–Fri, suppers Tues and Fri only.

Graikos, Menándhrou 3. Somewhat pricy but tasty island specialities – with a large vegetarian range – served (weather permitting) in the front garden of an old villa. Supper only; closed Sun.

Shopping

In general, shopping opportunities in south Nicosia are overrated; only optical goods are very cheap compared to northern Europe, though savings were eroded slightly by the introduction of VAT. Shoes are good quality and reasonably priced, clothes rather less so. The focus for all these types of merchandise is pedestrianized Lídhras, and to a lesser extent Onasagórou. In the new town, most department stores are found along, or just off, Arkhiepiskópou Makaríou.

Art and craft shops

Andhreas Haralambous, Koráï 9 and 21, near the Archbishop's Palace. This artist's paintings and models of his theatre sets fill several lofty rooms in this slightly down-at-heel building. Open 11am–1pm and 6–11pm; ring ☎457280 to confirm days.

Cyprus Handicraft Service, Aristokýprou 6 in Laïkí Yitoniá and Athálassas 186 in the new town.

Gallery Dhiakhroniki, Aristokýprou 2B. Antiquarian and facsimile engravings from Cyprus, the Middle East and Europe, as well as original art by Cypriot and foreign painters. Engravings are partially mounted, and reasonably priced – slight discount on multiple purchases.

Horis Synora/Sans Frontieres, Akhéon 6–8, about 600m west of the Cyprus Museum. Small gallery selling handmade jewellery and other craft objects, as well as hosting painting exhibitions. Sample hours 9.30am–12.30pm and 4.30–9.30pm, but ring ☎369435 to establish current schedule.

Leventis City Museum Giftshop, Ippokrátous 17. Specializes in reproduction Byzantine silverware.

Symvolo, Aristokýprou 20A. Good for contemporary Cypriot ceramic ware.

Nightlife and entertainment

There's actually a bit more **nightlife** in south Nicosia than the naff or dubious pubs in and around Laïkí Yitoniá would suggest, but most of it is out in the new suburbs, and you'll need both a car and local contacts to find it. It's as well to remember also that the concept of a bar or pub is a recent import, and traditionally Cypriots of all ages spent (and still spend) most of the evening lingering over a mix of food and drink in the same establishment.

Exceptions, virtually all of them in or near the trendy Famagusta Gate area, include *Ithaki*, a small outdoor bar at the corner of Nikifórou Foká and Thiséos; *Epea Pteroenda* at Nikifórou Foká 30, with a café-*ouzerí* on the top storey and a taped-music bar downstairs; the durable *bôite* *Bastione*, at Athinás 15, actually within the fortifications; and *Enallax*, on the opposite side of Athinás, closer to the Green Line.

Theatre, music and film

For **theatre and musical events**, south Nicosia has four medium-sized indoor venues: the *Famagusta Gate Centre*, with good acoustics for chamber concerts in its small hall; the 1200-seat *Municipal Theatre* across from the British Council and Cyprus Museum at the edge of the Municipal Gardens; *ENA* at Athinás 4 (though most performances are in Greek); and the *PA.SY.DY Theatre*, for orchestral works, at Dhimosthéni Sevéri 3, the continuation of Leofóros Evagórou.

Film hounds are catered to by numerous commercial cinemas, which include the *Zena Palace* on Theofánous Theodhótou (☎444128); the *Metropol* across the street at no. 3 (☎444840); the *Opera 1 & 2* on the corner of Sofoúlis and Hrístou Sózou; the *Acropole* (winter only; ☎422240); *Pantheon 1 & 2* (☎475787); and *Cine Studio* at Makedhonitíssas 46 (☎358662), featuring art fare. The *Friends of the Film Society* screens weekly movies (usually Monday night) at the Russian Cultural Centre, and the British Council and French Cultural Centre also host films once or twice a month; for these addresses, see the "Listings" below.

For **current schedules** of all events consult the (fairly) useful pamphlet *Nicosia This Month*, published by the municipality and available at CTO, the "Lifestyle" pullout section of the *Cyprus Weekly*, or the Sunday *Cyprus Mail*.

Listings

Airlines *Aeroflot*, Omírou 32B (☎477071); *Air 2000*, c/o *Amathus Navigation*, Omírou 17 (☎462101); *Alitalia*, c/o *Louis Aviation*, Evagórou 52 (☎464500); *British Airways*, Arkhiepiskópou Makaríou 52A (☎442188); *ČSA (Czech Airlines)*, c/o *Alasia Cyprus Cruises*, Gríva Dhiyení 40 (☎442082); *Cyprus Airways*, Arkhiepiskópou Makaríou 50 (☎441996); *Gulf Air*, c/o *R. A. Travelmasters*, Arkhiepiskópou Makaríou 82A (☎447702); *KLM*, Sánta Rósa 13 (☎450921); *Malev (Hungarian Airlines)*, c/o *Alasia Cyprus Cruises*, Gríva Dhiyení 40 (☎442082); *Olympic Airways*, c/o *Amathus Navigation*, Omírou 17 (☎462101); *Royal Jordanian*, Arkhiepiskópou Makaríou 66 (☎452124).

Bicycles If you're suddenly seized with the urge to go mountain-biking in the Tróodhos, try *Dikran Ouzounian & Co* on Gríva Dhiyení for a selection of Raleigh products, or *Micromania* at Ikostiogdhóïs Martíou 72, Makedhonítissa suburb. Prices from C£100.

Bookstores *Bridgehouse*, corner Gríva Dhiyení and Lórdhos Vyronos, on the ground floor of the eponymous high-rise (bus #10 or #15); *MAM*, Aristokýprou 3, Laïkí Yitoniá, specializing in books and maps on Cyprus; and best of all, *Moufflon*, Sofoúli 1, opposite the Chanteclair Building, with an extensive stock of art, literature and general archeology as well as material specific to Cyprus and the Middle East.

Bus terminals *Costas*, on the Tripoli bastion, near Platía Solomoú, to Páfos and Limassol; *Kallenos*, at Leonídhou 34, to Larnaca; *EMAN*, on Konstandínou Paleológou east of the main post office, to Ayía Nápa; *Kemek*, on Leonídhou next to *Kallenos*, to Limassol; *Zingas*, also on Leonídhou by *Kemek* and *Kallenos*, to Plátres via the Marathássa valley; *Clarios*, on the Costanza bastion, to Kakopetriá and Tróödhos summit. Country market-buses for small villages also congregate at Costanza.

Car rental *Andy Spyrou/Europcar*, Armenías 11 (☎497738); *Ansa International*, Platía Eleftherías (☎472352); *Astra*, Iróön 2–4, Áyios Andhréas (☎475800); *Budget/Petsas*, Píndhou 2 (☎462042); *Hertz*, corner Gríva Dhiyení and Sevéri (☎477411).

Cultural centres *British Council*, Mousíou 3 (☎442152); *French Cultural Centre*, Jean Moreas 3–5 (☎443071); *Goethe Institute*, on Márkou Dhrákou across from the Greek Cypriot checkpoint; *Russian Cultural Centre*, Alassías 16, Áyii Omoloyíti (bus #13 or #57; ☎453876); *USIS*, Omírou 33B (☎473143). Most have morning and late-afternoon split shifts, with special events in the evening. The *Cyprus-American Archeological Research Institute* (CAARI), at Andhréa Dhimitríou 11, just off Themistóklí Dherví, has a limited number of publications and a newsletter for sale.

Embassies/high commissions/consulates *UK*, Alexander Pallis, northwest of the old town by the Green Line (☎473131); *Australia*, Ánnis Komnínis 4, corner Stassínou (☎473001); *USA*, corner Metokhíou and Ploutárkhou, Engomí (☎476100); *Canada*, Themistoklí Dherví 15, Margarita House (☎451630); *New Zealand*, Ayíou Nikoláou 35, Engomí (☎444104). Other consulates important for procuring visas include *Egypt*, Éyíptou 3 (near CYTA), and *Syria*, corner Thoukidhídhou and Andhrokléous (across from the Costanza bastion).

Exchange Most banks cluster around Platía Eleftherías, including four with autoteller machines: *Laïki* and *Barclays* for *Visa* customers, *Bank of Cyprus* and *National Bank of Greece* for *Access/Mastercard* holders. Most of these banks open in the afternoon as well as the morning.

Fruit and vegetable markets The old central market, best on Friday and Saturday, is up on Platía Paleoú Dhimarkhíou, at the end of Trikoúpi by the Green Line; two others are the Wednesdays-only street bazaar on Konstandínou Paleológou, by the Costanza bastion, and the daily Áyios Andónios market at the corner of Dhiyení Akritá and Evyenías Theodhótou.

Laundrettes Two, very close to each other on the west bank of the Pedhiéos, at Prodhrómou 121Z and Sína 2B.

Post offices The main branch, with late afternoon and Saturday morning hours plus poste restante service, sits atop the D'Avila bastion, entrance from Konstandínou Paleológou; a secondary branch, with early closure, is at Lídhras 65A.

Service taxis Companies are all on the outer ring road: *Acropolis*, Stassínou 9 (☎472525), to Larnaca; *Karydas*, Omírou 8 (☎462269), to Limassol; *Kyriakos*, Stassínou 27 (☎444114), to Larnaca and Limassol; *Kypros*, Stassínou 9A (☎464811), to Limassol; and *Makris*, Stassínou 11 (☎466201), to Larnaca and Limassol.

Swimming pools The largest and most central indoor public one is on Loúki Akritá, just off this book's map, due west of the old city, across the Pedhiéos riverbed; the most convenient outdoor one is on Ploutárkhou, also west of the Pedhiéos in Engomí.

Telephones CYTA, alarmingly fortified and sandbagged against the Turkish threat, just outside the Páfos Gate on Leofóros Eyíptou, open 7.30am–7.15pm daily for operator-assisted services and indoor card booths.

AROUND SOUTH NICOSIA

The undulating expanses around the capital hold little of compelling interest for a traveller, and access to many sites is complicated by the presence of the Attila Line. Still, certain highlights can be easily taken in while in transit between Nicosia and either the Tróödhos or the coast, and as such make worthwhile stops.

West of Nicosia: Peristeróna

Heading west from Nicosía towards the Soléa or Marathássa districts of the Tróodhos, you've a long diversion round the disused airport in UNFICYP territory; 34km along, the village of **PERISTERÓNA** straddles a usually dry stream.

The church of Áyii Varnávas and Hilárion

The five-domed, tenth-century **church of Áyii Varnávas and Hilárion** on the riverbank is very handsome even just from the outside, but hang about purposefully and the café proprietor next door will appear with the key. The interior architecture is imposing, with its pair of apsed aisles separated from the nave by arches, though there's not much else to see: a surviving sixteenth-century wall painting of King David, the huge contemporary *témblon*, and an antique chest of uncertain date in the narthex depicting the siege of a castle.

The mosque

The CTO makes much of the church's juxtaposition with a **mosque** a couple of hundred metres southwest, one of Cyprus' oldest and finest, as a token of the supposedly long, peaceful co-existence of the two main island communities. Perhaps ironically, then, the Turkish Cypriots accused vengeful Greek Cypriots of setting fire to it in April 1976, though any damage seems to have since been patched up. The square groundplan with its high superstructure and arched, tracery-laden windows is decidedly Lusignan – prompting suspicions that this is in fact a converted church.

The grounds are locked and fenced to prevent vandalism, but the fence is holed, the minaret infested with pigeons, and the front door usually ajar for peeks into the vaulted interior.

Southwest of Nicosia

Ancient Tamassos and Áyios Iraklídhios convent, some 22km **southwest of Nicosia**, can easily be combined with a day visit to the monastery of Makherás, or longer forays into Pitsiliá (see pp.176–184). From central Nicosia, the route out passes through the suburb of Stróvolos, and then the village of Káto Dhefterá.

Ancient Tamassos

One of the oldest-known Cypriot settlements, **ancient Tamassos** owed its existence to extensive local deposits of copper, first exploited in the Early Bronze Age. In Homer's *Odyssey*, Athena went to "Temese" to trade iron for copper; later the revenues from the local mines accrued to the Phoenicians, the kings of Salamis and the biblical Herod, though these beneficiaries fail to give a clear idea of who was actually living, working or ruling at Tamassos itself.

Excavations since 1975 have revealed the foundations of a Classical temple of Aphrodite/Astarte with traces of copper on the floor, implying, as at Kition, that metallurgy was considered sacred and that the priests controlled the deposits. Continuing the metallic and mercenary theme, local farmers dug up a life-size bronze statue of Apollo in 1836 – and hacked it apart, selling the bits to a scrap

THE UN FORCES IN CYPRUS (UNFICYP)

In the wake of the communal disturbances of December 1963, the British announced themselves unable single-handedly to maintain civil peace on Cyprus, and the crisis was referred to the United Nations. A Security Council resolution of March 1964 mandated the dispatch of a 6000-strong UN peacekeeping force, henceforth known as **UNFICYP**. This originally drew its blue-bereted ranks from the armies of the UK, Canada, Austria, Finland, Sweden, Denmark, Australia and Ireland. The initially authorized period was six months, but this has been renewed more or less automatically ever since. What was intended at the outset as a stopgap measure pending a durable solution to Cyprus' ethnic problems showed signs over the years of becoming an apparently permanent island institution.

UNFICYP's brief has always been narrowly defined: to keep physically separate hostile communal factions; to discourage atrocities by their mere presence; and, in their capacity as potential witnesses, to verify the facts of such incidents. However, UN troops have limited means of imposing calm; they cannot launch a pre-emptive strike to nip factional violence in the bud, but are only allowed to return fire if attacked. Nonetheless, UNFICYP was fairly successful in preventing more casualties than actually did occur from 1964 to 1974.

Since the events of summer 1974 the deployment (if not the role) of UNFICYP has changed radically. Instead of policing the boundaries of a number of scattered Turkish Cypriot enclaves, troops now patrol the single, 180-kilometre-long ceasefire line and the buffer zone of varying width straddling it, where 150 watchtowers constitute landmarks. Duties include maintaining utility lines crossing the zone, and ensuring the safety of farmers wishing to cultivate their fields right up to the boundary. UNFICYP has been instrumental in defusing sensitive spots – especially in and around Nicosia where opposing Greek and Turkish troops are close enough to abuse each other verbally. They also provide humanitarian aid to the remaining Greek Cypriots and Maronites in the North, as well as helping to settle disputes between Greek and Turkish Cypriots in the two remaining mixed villages of the South.

Amazingly the ceasefire of August 1974 has substantially held since then, with only the odd (sometimes fatal) potshot in the buffer zone. UNFICYP troops are fairly popular among the populace, though one graffito seen near Famagusta – "UN YOBOS SHIT" – suggests that opinion is not unanimous. Northern officialdom and the Turkish army have occasionally accused UN personnel of leaking strategic information to the Greek Cypriots: hence restrictions on UNFICYP movements in North Cyprus and signs forbidding passage of UN vehicles near sensitive military sites. But however tolerated UN personnel may be individually, many feel that their continued presence merely delays the day of reckoning – non-violent or otherwise – between the two Cypriot communities, and that the islanders should sooner rather than later be left to their own devices.

Such sentiments are increasingly endorsed at the UN Command, no doubt enhanced by the perceived hopelessness of UNFICYP's mission – and the $180 million arrears in maintenance payments by the UN. Until now the troop-contributing countries themselves have been footing most of the bill, which runs to $25 million yearly. The Swedes left Cyprus in 1988, saying they would not serve indefinitely without tangible progress towards a settlement. Denmark withdrew its troops in December 1992, and the Canadian contingent followed in June 1993, leaving the UK with the main burden of peacekeeping – essentially a reversion to pre-1964 conditions. Somewhat ironically, Britain's Falklands adversaries, the Argentines, have replaced the Danes and Canadians, joined also by a few Hungarian troops and civilian police from Australia and Ireland – altogether a force barely 1200 strong.

These departures and reductions make it less probable that a fair system of assessing contributions from UN member states will be devised, an increasingly pressing need in light of the multiplying number of UN expeditions elsewhere since 1992. Yet UNFICYP may continue to be a Cyprus player, perhaps as guarantors of any federal settlement reached by the Cypriots which envisages an otherwise demilitarized island.

dealer. The head was salvaged and eventually found its way into the British Museum, though again it tells us little about Tamassan culture since it was made in Athens during the fifth century.

The **site** exposed to date consists of about half an acre of jumbled foundations (Tues–Fri 9am–3pm, Sat & Sun 10am–3pm; C£0.50), on a slight slope overlooking grain fields at the northeast edge of the modern village of Politikó. The most interesting items are two sixth-century BC **subterranean tombs**, excavated in the 1890s though partially looted before then – in the pitched roof of the larger, double-chambered tomb, you can still see a hole made by the thieves. The sandstone masonry has been cleverly carved in places to imitate wood and bolts appropriate to wooden doors, a style reminiscent of the "house tombs" of Anatolian Lycia.

Áyios Iraklídhios convent

The **convent of Áyios Iraklídhios**, near Tamassos, honours Cyprus' first bishop-saint, a native of the region, who guided the apostles Paul and Barnabas from Larnaca to Tamassos during their missionary journey across Cyprus. They subsequently ordained Iraklidhios (Heracleidius) first bishop of Tamassos, and legend has it he was martyred on this spot at the age of 60. By 400 AD a commemorative monastery of some sort had been established here, to be destroyed and rebuilt a number of times (last in 1773), though the present *katholikón* is dated 300 years earlier. After twice housing monks, it was taken over as a ruin in 1963 by an order of nuns, who transformed it as you see today.

To find the convent, drive through Politikó village until you see the obvious compound on a slight rise to the south. Inside (closed noon–3pm mid-May to mid-Sept), it's a peaceful, domestic, ship-shape world, alive with birdsong: a dozen or so sisters read missals, water the well-tended flowerbeds or doze near sheets of newspaper laid down to catch droppings from the nesting swallows. The nuns sell pickled capers, as well as canaries from an aviary, and one of them may approach you to offer a whirlwind guided tour. In the *katholikón*, you'll be shown a smudged fresco of the two apostles baptizing Iraklidhios; **reliquaries** containing his purported forearm and skull; some icons; and the sole exposed portion of an old **mosaic floor** regrettably covered over by modern tiling. From the side chapel to the south, a narrow stairway descends to a small **catacomb** where it is said the saint lived his last years and was later buried.

South of Nicosia

Heading **south of the capital** towards either Larnaca or Limassol, monuments near the two adjacent villages of Perakhorió and Dháli are worth a short halt if you've time. You wouldn't, however, make a special trip, and both places lie out of reach of the Nicosia urban bus system.

Perakhorió

PERAKHORIÓ village is visited mainly for the sake of the twelfth-century church of **Áyii Apóstoli**, perched evocatively on a hill to the west, surrounded by Perakhorió's churchyard. Inside, the contemporaneous **frescoes** are disappointing – surviving fragments appear to be of the same style as the work at Asínou, and if you've toured the Tróödhos you needn't feel guilty about missing them. Highlight is the troupe of angels lining the drumless dome, just below a badly damaged *Pandokrátor*. The woman keeping the key lives in a house some 300m east, on the north side of the main residential street leading into the heart of Perakhorió. If you need a meal, the *Peristeri* taverna comes recommended.

Dháli and ancient Idalion

Four kilometres east, **DHÁLI** is an altogether busier place, a formerly mixed village perilously close to the Attila Line. (Potamía, 3km down the valley beside the buffer zone, remains bi-communal.) For a night out from Nicosia, the *Romantika* taverna here gets good marks, but again the main interest is not in the village, but a few hundred metres outside, to the south. Here the fortified hillside site of **ancient Idalion** is fairly obvious, though the place is still under sporadic excavation and there is little yet to interest the non-specialist, other than deep pits and courses of masoned wall in various states of exposure. The small city here dated from the Bronze Age and survived almost until the Roman era. American consul-turned-antiquarian Luigi Palma di Cesnola spent several summers here, plundering (according to his boast) 10,000 tombs; yet such was the archeological richness of the area that local farmers subsequently ploughed up many painted votive figurines of Aphrodite, the most important local deity, and an American team continues digging. Legend places the killing of Aphrodite's lover Adonis by a wild boar in the area, and in early spring you can still see red anemones, which supposedly sprang from his blood, poking out among the rocks here.

travel details

Buses

From **Nicosia** to: Kakopetriá (11–12 daily Mon–Sat, 2 on Sun in summer, on *Clarios*; 1hr 20min); Larnaca (6 daily Mon–Fri on *Kallenos*; 1hr); Limassol (6 daily Mon–Fri, 3 on Sat, on *Kemek*, 1–2 daily on *Costas*; 1hr 30min); Páfos (1–2 daily Mon–Sat, via Limassol, on *Costas*; 3hr); Plátres (1 daily Mon–Sat at 12.15pm, via the Marathássa valley, with *Zingas*; 3hr); Tróödhos (1 daily Mon–Sat at 11.30am on *Clarios*; 2hr).

Áyii Omoloyíti	Άγιοι Ομολογίτοι	ΑΓΙΟΙ ΟΜΟΛΟΓΙΤΟΙ
Áyios Dhométios	Άγιος Δομέτιος	ΑΓΙΟΣ ΔΟΜΕΤΙΟΣ
Áyios Iraklídhios	Άγιος Ηρακλείδιος	ΑΓΙΟΣ ΗΡΑΚΛΕΙΔΙΟΣ
Dháli	Δάλι	ΔΑΛΙ
Kaïmákli	Καϊμάκλι	ΚΑΪΜΑΚΛΙ
Laïkí Yitoniá	Λαϊκή Γειτονιά	ΛΑΪΚΗ ΓΕΙΤΟΝΙΑ
Nicosia (Lefkosía)	Λευκωσία	ΛΕΥΚΩΣΙΑ
Perakhorió	Περαχωριό	ΠΕΡΑΧΩΡΙΟ
Peristeróna	Περιστερώνα	ΠΕΡΙΣΤΕΡΩΝΑ
Tamassos	Ταμασσός	ΤΑΜΑΣΣΟΣ

PART THREE

THE NORTH

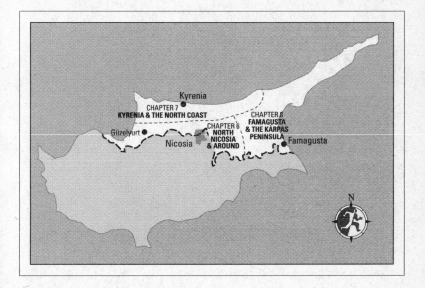

CHAPTER 7
KYRENIA & THE NORTH COAST

Kyrenia

Güzelyurt

Nicosia

CHAPTER 6
**NORTH
NICOSIA
& AROUND**

CHAPTER 8
**FAMAGUSTA
& THE KARPAS
PENINSULA**

Famagusta

N

INTRODUCTION

The **Turkish Republic of Northern Cyprus** (TRNC) came violently into existence in August 1974 as a **refuge** for beleaguered Turkish Cypriots: first as the zone occupied by the Turkish army, later as the interim Turkish Federated State of Cyprus, and finally, by a unilateral declaration of independence in 1983, as the TRNC. Recognized diplomatically by no state except Turkey, its creator and main sponsor, North Cyprus possesses at first glance a Ruritanian charm. Antique Hillmans, Triumphs and Austins tool about (or moulder abandoned in fields); policemen in grey imperial summer twill control intersections; traffic lights still have a colonial "STOP" stencilled over the red disc. While travelling around, however, you'll see a number of conditions contributing to the North's image as a pariah state, and some obvious results of that status.

Public relations problems

The ubiquitousness of the **Turkish army** is immediately off-putting: although there are now fewer no-go areas than previously, barbed-wire-fenced camps and unaesthetic military memorials abound, and an estimated 25,000 mainland conscripts lend a barracks air to Kyrenia and north Nicosia in particular.

Although nearly 20,000 Greek Cypriots chose to stay in the Kırpaşa (Kárpas) peninsula and around Kyrenia in 1974, and approximately 1000 Maronites on the Koruçam (Kormakíti) peninsula, **systematic harassment** by the army and the civil authorities has reduced those numbers to roughly 500 and 200 respectively.

The much-publicized **desecration** of Greek churches and graveyards is largely true, though Southern Cypriot public relations artists occasionally overstate their case: the Byzantine monastery of Akhiropiítos near Kyrenia and the monastery of Khrysostómos near Nicosia, both now occupied by the Turkish army, had already been partly deconsecrated and used by the Cypriot National Guard before 1974. Greek Cypriots are in the main careful to attribute the blame for desecration where it usually belongs – on the invading mainland army – since for many of the Turkish Cypriots, Orthodox shrines, monasteries and catacombs had also been sacred.

Arrested development

Overall there's a feeling of grass growing between the cracks, often literally – this atmosphere of **dereliction** can be attributed partly to the fact that the Turkish army in 1974 bit off rather more than the 120,000 Turkish Cypriots themselves could chew. Much of the North is under-utilized, its rural villages half empty: citrus orchards a couple of kilometres from Kyrenia die of neglect despite abundant water to irrigate them. The public **infrastructure**, too, is starved of improvement funds, one result of keeping the civil service rolls artificially swollen to stem a brain drain. Facilities appear to be kept ticking over, but no more; exceptions include Ercan airport and Kyrenia seaport, while improved, enlarged roads are limited to a single strip west of Kyrenia, another between Nicosia and Güzelyurt (Mórfou) and the vital Nicosia–Famagusta–Kyrenia highway. Except for some Saudi investment, most post-1974 international aid is shunted to the South; there's increasingly less support from Turkey, which lately has been targeting other priorities.

It's widely felt that sufficient aid would materialize, and the place would really take off, following **international recognition**, so far withheld. At various times since 1974 certain pro-Turkish and/or Muslim nations like South Korea, Bangladesh and Pakistan, with turbulent origins similar to North Cyprus, have considered extending recognition – but always backed down in the face of Greek or Greek Cypriot threats in the international arena. Recently the Greek Cypriots have intensified their pressure campaign by convincing the EU to ban any agricultural produce or clothing originating in the North, which now must be sneaked into Europe under the Turkish allotment. This has effectively brought the Northern economy to its knees and made it more dependent on purchases from the Arab world, and on tourism or matriculation fees at its new universities.

Owing to the Greek-orchestrated embargo of the stigmatized North, **tourism** is hardly more developed than in 1974. Unless the situation changes – barely 30,000 English-speaking tourists visit in a typical year – you will enjoy the TRNC's sandy beaches, Crusader monuments and occasionally excellent food in relative solitude, at a leisurely pace so in contrast to that of the busy South. Especially off the beaten track, people's helpfulness and hospitality can be overwhelming.

Native islanders vs Anatolians

The best lands and houses were **allotted** in 1975 to refugees from the South according to a point system; people were credited points for both commercial and residential property according to the value of such assets left behind. This government scheme was, not surprisingly, prone to abuse so that inequities in the distribution of real estate were widespread.

Poorer, isolated spots – fit mainly for goat-grazing – were assigned to **settlers** from Anatolia. Turkey long treated the North as a transportation colony, offloading families of 1974 campaign veterans, surplus urban underclass, landless peasants, and even low-grade criminals and psychiatric cases, until the islanders began to actively oppose the process, and sent the worst elements packing. As no accurate census has been conducted on Cyprus since 1973, estimating current immigrant numbers is an inexact science, with guesses ranging from 30,000 to 80,000 (60,000 seems probable). Their fate is a big sticking point in any potential peace agreement, and their presence has crystallized chronic tension between native Turkish Cypriots and Turks, with the former considering themselves to have a higher standard of living and education. The islanders dub mainlanders *karasakal*, "black beard" (or perhaps a corruption of *karasal*, "continental"). in Turkey a long-standing, patronizing quip characterizes Anatolia as *anavatan* (mother homeland) and North Cyprus as *yavru vatan* (baby homeland).

Since 1974 the Turkish army and nationalist ideologues in local government have acted to dilute the British-ness and Cyprus-ness of the North, not only with settlement programmes, but also by erecting busts of Atatürk and stark monuments commemorating the events of 1974. But a fair amount of pre-1974 *Kıbrıs Türktür* (Cyprus is Turkish) graffiti, scrawled by the TMT, suggests that such sentiments are not completely new; accordingly, the North has indeed been subject to a campaign of **creeping annexation by Turkey**. First the Cypriot pound was replaced by the unstable Turkish lira, next branches or affiliates of Turkish banks replaced island ones, then telephones were completely integrated into the Turkish system, and finally metric measurements were applied to motoring. So far the Northerners have resisted giving up left-hand driving, the most conspicuous remaining token of their separate identity. Those who object to the process say all this is only to be expected, pointing out that, after all, "Mersin 10" – the special post code used to circumvent the International Postal Union's boycott of the North – just means the tenth county of Mersin province, in Turkey.

Obstacles to reconciliation

Currently, the position of more accommodating Turkish Cypriots is that the South must decisively renounce the ideal of *énosis* and make the most of an independent, federal republic. But many adults in the North, not having spoken to a Greek Cypriot in two decades, find it hard to believe that *énosis* has almost no support in the South now. Those born since 1974, who have never met a Greek, are indoctrinated in school to believe that EOKA activists will make kebab out of them should the existing barriers fall. As a gesture of good will prior to establishment of a federal state, progressive Turkish Cypriots would like to see suspected EOKA supporters **purged** from the Southern government. What they got instead was, in 1992, the early release by the South of the protagonist in the 1974 coup, Nikos Sampson, and in 1995 the rehabilitation of 62 coup-supporting civil servants. Both of these actions caused enormous offence in the TRNC and cut the ground from under more conciliatory Northerners.

Such examples of continuing EOKA influence are seen in the North as further evidence of an underlying, unreconstructed Greek Cypriot attitude, summarizable as "You (Turkish Cypriots) are just 400-year guests. Now get lost." At one point the Makarios government offered money and a one-way plane ticket to any Turkish Cypriot willing to resettle overseas, while the Orthodox Church encouraged the Greek Cypriot purchase of Turkish property at double its value, before the violent **coercion** of EOKA spawned open hatred and, ultimately, partition.

Both practices swelled the size of the large **exile** community: while about 100,000 native Turkish Cypriots still reside on the island, almost three times that figure live abroad, mostly in Turkey, Britain, Australia and North America. (Proportionately, there has not been such a diaspora from the Greek side.) Since 1974, not enough Turkish Cypriots abroad have responded to their government's pleas to return and "rebuild the homeland"; instead there's a slow leak outwards of those fed up with the settlers and political and economic stagnation.

Huge flocks of sheep graze the grain-stubble of the central plain, the Mesarya; a steady supply of them, along with market-garden produce and water from underground reservoirs near Güzelyurt, heads clandestinely south across the officially impervious Attila Line, in exchange for tractors and other manufactured goods smuggled in the opposite direction. Until the North's own dynamo came on-line in 1995, the South provided the North with electricity from its plant at Dhekélia, as a "humanitarian" gesture. Almost two thousand Turkish Cypriot workers also shuffle daily through the Dhekélia Sovereign Base, for jobs there or even in the South itself, especially in the construction trades. Cyprus is too small ever to be hermetically divided: its regional economies, if not always its peoples, were too interknit under past unitary administrations. Until the 1950s, intermarriage between the two communities – and attendant religous apostasy in either direction – was more common than generally admitted.

Despite their overwhelming economic and diplomatic advantages, it is the Greek Cypriots who are pressing hardest for a **resolution** of the island's division, whether prior to or part of an EU accession deal. The Northerners feel that they have more to gain than lose from persistence of the status quo; their present "enclave" is more comfortable than the besieged ones of 1963–74, with more ways out. On a human level, many Turkish Cypriots feel sorry for the northern Greeks who were forced from their homes, but consider the Attila Line, guarded by mainland Turks, as the best guarantee of personal safety.

CHAPTER SIX

NORTH NICOSIA AND AROUND

Although most visitors to North Cyprus, as with the South, will be interested in reaching their coastal resort of choice as quickly as possible, it's worth remembering that **north Nicosia** *is* to a great extent North Cyprus, with easily a third of its population. The events of 1974 and North Cyprus' UDI of 1983 resulted in the city's becoming the capital of an as yet unrecognized and perhaps provisional state. What the relatively few day-visitors to north Nicosia are after, though, is a concentration of Gothic and Ottoman monuments; there's little else available for the casual tourist.

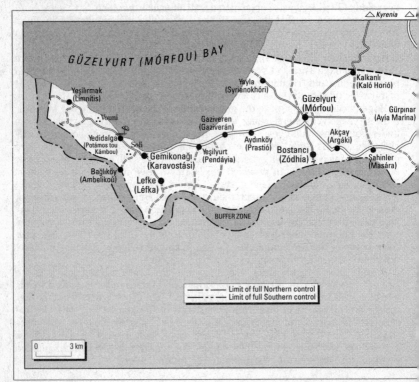

Excursions elsewhere in North Cyprus' patch of Nicosia district head exclusively west past the agricultural centre of **Güzelyurt**, with a museum and former monastery, to the intriguing ancient sites of **Soli** and **Vouni** on the coast. Inland from these, the foothill oasis of **Lefke** makes a relaxing destination, though again with few specific attractions.

NORTH NICOSIA

NORTH NICOSIA (LEFKOŞA in Turkish) is a much sleepier place than the southern portion of the city, with about a quarter as many inhabitants, barely 60,000. Obviously the history of the two sectors, enclosed at their core by the same Venetian wall, was largely shared until 1974; the approaching Turkish Army was quite deliberate in ensuring that all traditionally Turkish districts in the northwest of the city fell under their control.

The justification for north Nicosia's emergence as capital of the North, and indefinite continuance in that role, is epitomized by the story behind the huge Turkish Cypriot flag picked out in white rocks on the foothills of the Kyrenia range, just north of town, placed for maximum provocative effect on south Nicosia. The current inhabitants of the nearest village, Taşkent (Vounó), all came

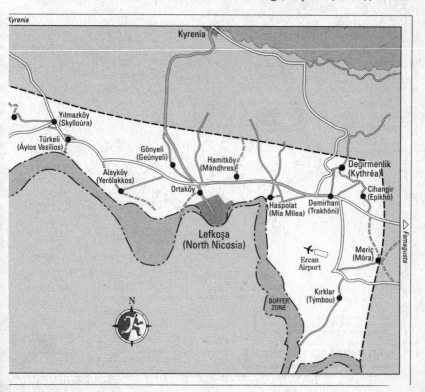

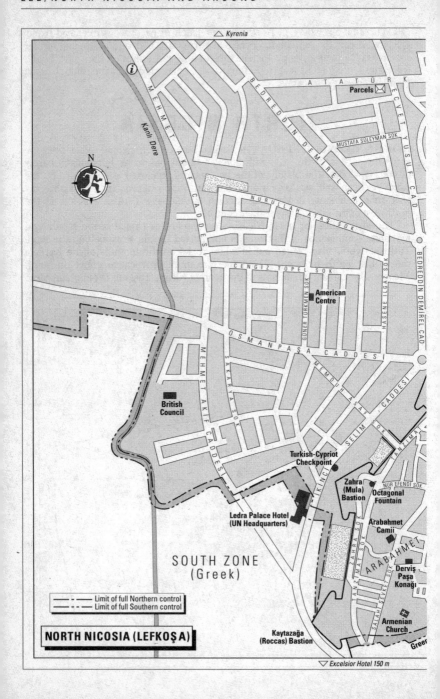

△ Kyrenia

ⓘ

Parcels ⊠

ATATÜRK

BEDREDDIN DEMIREL CAD

RECVET YUSUF CAD

MUSTAFA SULEYMAN SOK

Kanlı Dere

MEHMET AKIF CADDESI

N

NURULLAH ATAS SOK

BEDREDDIN DEMIREL CAD

CENGIZ TOPEL SOK

GÜNER TÜRKMEN SOK

■ American
Centre

HASENE ILGAZ SOK

OSMANPASA CADDESI

MEMDUH ASAF SOK

SAKARYA SOK

■ British
Council

MEHMET AKIF CADDESI

SELIM — CADDESI

TANZIMAT

Turkish-Cypriot
Checkpoint ●

Zahra
(Mula) ● NUR EFENDI SOK
Bastion   Octagonal
           Fountain

IKINCI

Arabahmet
Camii

Ledra Palace Hotel
(UN Headquarters)

TANZIMAT SOK

ARABAHMET

Derviş
Paşa
Konağı

SOUTH ZONE
(Greek)

SALAHI ŞEVKET SOK

✚ Armenian
Church

Limit of full Northern control
Limit of full Southern control

Kaytazağa
(Roccas) Bastion

Green

NORTH NICOSIA (LEFKOŞA)

▽ Excelsior Hotel 150 m

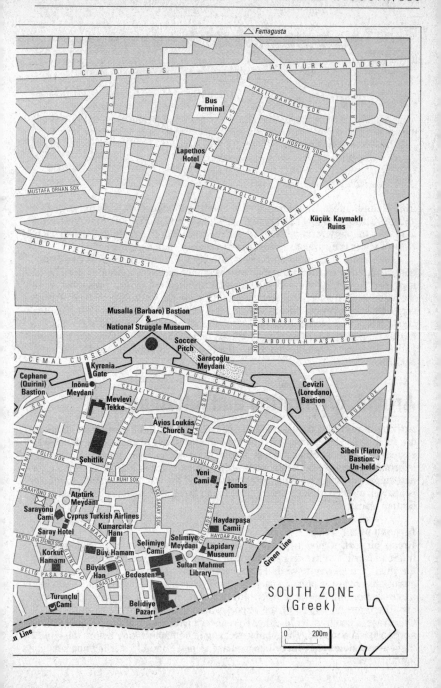

△ *Famagusta*

ATATÜRK CADDESI

CADDESI

Bus Terminal

HALIL BAHÇECİ SOK

BÜLENT HÜSEYİN SOK

Lapethos Hotel

İSTİKAL SOK

KEMAL ASIK CADDESİ

İNSAN GÜVEN SOK

ARİF SALİH SOK

YILMAZ YOLCU SOK

KAHRAMANLAR CAD

MUSTAFA ORHAN SOK

Küçük Kaymaklı Ruins

KIZILAY SOK

ABDİ İPEKÇİ CADDESİ

KAYMAKLI CADDESİ

TAHSİN YAZICI SOK

İBRAHİM ALİ SOK

Musalla (Barbaro) Bastion & National Struggle Museum

SİNASİ SOK

ABDULLAH PAŞA SOK

CEMAL CÜRSEL CAD

Soccer Pitch

Saraçoğlu Meydanı

Kyrenia Gate

İSTANBUL CAD

Cephane (Quirini) Bastion

İnönü Meydanı

CELALİYE SOK

REŞADİYE SOK

Cevizli (Loredano) Bastion

Mevlevî Tekke

KADİ SOK

SOK

Ayios Loukás Church

GİRNE CAD

MAHMUT PAŞA SOK

GİRNE CAD

ALİ ÇAVUŞ SOK

YENİ CAMİ SOK

HÜSEYİN RİZA SOK

POLİS SOK

Şehitlik

FUZULİ SOK

Sibeli (Flatro) Bastion: Un-held

ALİ RUHİ SOK

ATİLLA SOK

Yeni Cami

Tombs

SARAYÖNÜ SOK

Atatürk Meydanı

ESKİ SARAY SOK

ŞEHZADE SOK

Sarayönü Camii

Cyprus Turkish Airlines

Kumarcılar Hanı

Haydarpaşa Camii

Saray Hotel

ASMAALTI SOK

HAYDAR PAŞA SOK

MÜFTÜ ZİYA EFENDİ SOK

Selimiye Camii

Selimiye Meydanı

Lapidary Museum

Korkut Hamamı

Büy. Hamam

GİRNE CAD

Büyük Han

ARASTA SOK

Bedesten

Sultan Mahmut Library

Green Line

BELİG PAŞA SOK

Turunçlu Camii

Belidiye Pazarı

SOUTH ZONE (Greek)

0   200m

n Line

Green Line

from Tókhni (near Khirokitiá) in the South; on August 15, 1974 most of that village's Turkish men of military age were massacred there by an EOKA-B contingent. For the survivors, responsible for the rock-flag, the continued existence of North Cyprus is insurance against a recurrence of such nightmares.

Much more than in south Nicosia, the reality of the old town is desolation: dust-devils eddy on the battered streets, windows are broken even on used buildings, and fine domestic and monumental architecture seems preserved more through inertia than any conscious effort. Outside the walls there is little of interest, with colonial-era brownstones being outstripped by the tatty modern construction that increasingly disfigures the whole island. Within the walls live mostly impoverished Anatolian settlers, enhancing the villagey atmosphere; native Turkish Cypriots who can afford it flee to roomier, more desirable suburbs.

Arrival, orientation and information

Arriving in north Nicosia is relatively painless, owing to its small size; junctions are fairly well signed, though if driving yourself it's easy to get trapped in one-way systems. Like most other aspects of tourist service in town, provision of tourist information tends to be haphazard — the tourist office is hopelessly remote for day-trippers crossing from the South on foot, and the way to individual attractions is not well marked, though once you've found them, they do have bilingual identification placards.

Arriving by air

Ercan airport, a modern terminal just adequate for the current amount of air traffic to North Cyprus, lies southeast of town, 17km by road and well signed off the dual carriageway towards Famagusta. There's no public bus service at the airport; if arriving as part of a package, you'll meet a courier who bundles you into a tour-agency minibus for transfer to your resort, or hands over your pre-reserved car (there are no booths at the airport where you can rent a car on the spot). Otherwise, a taxi transfer to either Kyrenia or Famagusta will run to about £15, to north Nicosia about £5. The money-exchange booth shuts long before the typical flight arrival times of 10pm to 1am, so have some £5 and £10 sterling notes handy for taxi drivers.

About once a year Ercan is closed for maintenance, and flights are diverted to a predominantly military airport, 3km south of **Geçitkale** (Lefkóniko, Lefkonuk), nearer to the Famagusta resort area.

Arriving by land

Approaching Nicosia by road **from Famagusta**, you'll make the acquaintance of a roundabout north of town, currently at the edge of the built-up area, which gives buses the opportunity to barrel south to the **bus terminal** on **Kemal Aşık Caddesi**, near the corner of **Atatürk Caddesi**. If you're **outbound**, the buses are grouped, west to east as you move across the terminal, by towns and villages falling into Kyrenia, Nicosia and Famagusta districts respectively; hunt down your destination accordingly, it's not a big place.

Coming **from Kyrenia**, you'll be caught up in another, even larger roundabout-with-monument at the northwest edge of the city, poised between the suburbs of Ortaköy (Orta Keuy) and Gönyeli (Geunyeli).

Given the town's small population, **parking** presents few problems – as long as you don't do anything rash like trying to leave your car in the congested commercial streets of the old quarter. There are no fee car parks, but spaces are usually available along **İkinci Selim Caddesi**, just outside the old walls and within walking distance of most attractions.

Orientation and information

The northwestern roundabout shunts traffic in every direction, particularly southeast along the road which eventually splits into **Mehmet Akif Caddesi** and **Bedreddin Demirel Caddesi**. Bedreddin Demirel and Kemal Aşık come very close to meeting at the **Kyrenia Gate**, the most historic entrance to north Nicosia's bit of the old town; just inside it, **İnönü Meydanı** marks the north end of **Girne Caddesi**, the main commercial thoroughfare and continuation of Lídhras on the Greek side. Partway along its length is the swelling known as **Atatürk Meydanı**, effectively the city centre.

A **tourist information** branch has long been mooted for the upper guard room of the Kyrenia Gate; until and unless it opens, you'll have to trudge a considerable distance northwest along Mehmet Akif to the ministry headquarters themselves at no. 95 (summer Mon–Fri 8am–2pm; winter Mon–Fri 8am–1pm and 2.30–5pm).

The City

North Nicosia's sights can be seen in a single longish day; as on the other side of the Green Line, you won't need to learn bus routes but should rely on good shoes. Wander the back streets the least bit away from the standard tourist circuit and you're an instant celebrity; stray too far off the main thoroughfares or get too close to the Line, though, and members of the Turkish armed forces may shadow you, particularly if there's any indication that you have a camera.

Urban renewal, in accordance with the Master Plan, has so far been limited to the partial pedestrianization of the bazaar and gradual re-occupation (though not necessarily maintenance) of some stately houses in the Arabahmet district, near the Green Line; you're made painfully aware of what a judicious influx of funding could accomplish.

THE TEACHINGS OF THE MEVLEVI ORDER

A *tekke* is the ceremonial hall of any Islamic mystical *tarikat* or order; the Mevlevî *tarikat* is the outgrowth of the teachings of Celaleddin Rumi, later known as the Mevlâna, whose life spanned most of the thirteenth century and took him from Balkh in Central Asia to Konya in Anatolia. He is most esteemed for the *Mathnawi*, a long devotional poem summarizing his teachings, which emphasized the individual soul's separation from God during earthly existence, and the power of Divine Love to draw it back to the Infinite. Quite scandalously to orthodox Muslims of the time, Rumi stressed music and dance as an expression of this mutual love and yearning, and the Mevlevi order became famous over the centuries for its *sema* or "whirling" ceremony. Musical accompaniment always included at least one *ney* or reed flute, whose plaintive tones have approximately the same range as the human voice. As the *Mathnawi* explains in metaphor, the lonely reed of the instrument has been uprooted from its reedbed as the soul has been separated from the Godhead, and its voice is like the lament of the human soul for reunion with the Infinite.

The ramparts

The five bastions lying wholly within the Turkish zone are not put to as much use as on the Greek side, though the moats are nominally parkland. What used to be the vice-presidential residence in unitary republican days, on the Cephane (Quirini) bastion, is now the North Cypriot presidential palace; on the Musalla (Barbaro) bastion the army has erected a **National Struggle Museum** (free admission when sentry on duty) in response to the one in south Nicosia.

Between these two ramparts stands the **Kyrenia Gate**, the classic entry into the Turkish quarter but looking very useless plopped in the middle of İnönü Meydanı. In 1931, broad swathes were cut through the walls to either side of the gate to allow the passage of motor traffic, isolating it as a sort of pillbox-cum-guardhouse. The Venetians knew it as the Porta de la Proveditore, or "Gate of the Military Governor", and fitted it with a portcullis and still-visible Lion of St Mark; after their victory, the Ottomans added an inscription lauding Allah as the "Opener of Gates".

The Ethnography Museum (Mevlevî Tekke)

Once inside the gate, almost the first thing on your left is the **Ethnography Museum** (Mon–Fri 8am–1pm & 2–5pm; £1, or £1.50 combined ticket, including admission to the Sultan Mahmut Library, the Lapidary Museum and the Derviş Paşa Museum), housed in the former Mevlevî dervish *tekke* of Nicosia. The Mevlevî order survived here as a vital *tarikat* until 1954, long after their proscription in Republican Turkey. As so often in Cyprus, the early seventeenth-century building overshadows most of the exhibits. Centrally there's the fine pine-wood turning floor, just big enough for perhaps ten devotees; the musicians' gallery was perched overhead. The best souvenir on sale here is an archival photo-postcard showing one of the last ceremonies: the *şeyh* or head of the order watches over six dervishes revolving in the confined space, while above in the gallery sit the players of *ney* (reed flute), *oud* (Levantine lute) and *kudum* (paired drums). Display cases offer a motley collection of traditional clothing, musical instruments, archival photos, as well as more arcane items like Rauf Denktaş' wife's Victrola gramophone. In a multiple-domed side hall, whose outline is so distinctive seen from the street, are serried tombs of the sixteen *şeyh*s associated with the *tekke*, including founder Arab Ahmet and the last *şeyh* Selim Dede, who died in 1953.

Girne Caddesi to Atatürk Meydanı

Tucked into a side street south of the *tekke* are more graves – this time arranged as a **Şehitlik** or Martyrs' Memorial created in 1963, and representative of many such in the North. A trilingual sign extolling the hundred-plus "unarmed and defenceless [civilian] victims of Greek thugs" is somewhat undercut by the presence of dozens of headstones for mainland Turkish soldiers who died in the opening days of the July 1974 campaign. In fact more than 1500 casualties were buried here in mass graves between July 24 and 28, often eight bodies to a hole, first with press-ganged local teenagers, later with a captured Greek Cypriot bulldozer. However, the bones were exhumed three years later, and the current, entirely symbolic grave markers installed.

The commercial aspect of Girne Caddesi and the streets immediately around Atatürk Meydanı seems a faint echo of southern Nicosia, and is pitched primarily at soldiers and others from Turkey taking advantage of cheaper North Cyprus clothing prices. In certain photo shops you see a popular ready-frame – intended for mainland conscripts writing home – in which airplanes, paratroopers and artillery pieces swirl around a blank spot for sticking one's mug shot, with overhead the motto *Barış için Savaş* ("War for Peace"). The 1974 Turkish intervention is universally proclaimed the "Peace Action" in North Cyprus, an Orwellian concept if ever there was one.

Atatürk Meydanı itself has been the hub of Turkish life in Nicosia since the Ottoman conquest, and is still surrounded by the British-built post office, law courts and a disproportionate number of banks. In Ottoman days it was called Konak Meydanı, after the governor's mansion (*konak*), more popularly known as the *Saray* (palace), which stood to the southwest, in part the remains of a Lusignan/Venetian palace. Its gatehouse was the remnant of the palace destroyed by the British (see p.190); the name only lives on in the shape of the modern *Saray Hotel*, and the mock-Moorish pastiche of the now-disused Sarayönü Cami. In the centre of the roundabout, a grey **granite column** from Salamis, stuck here by the Venetians after 1489 and so erroneously called after them, was once surmounted by their symbol, the Lion of St Mark. The Ottomans did away with the lion and toppled the column in 1570, which remained prone until 1915 when the British re-erected it, capping it with a neutral globe.

Baths and inns

From Atatürk Meydanı, Asmaaltı Sokağı leads southeast towards the bazaar and the main monumental zone. The **Büyük Hamam**, on a short street of the same name bearing off Asmaaltı, was once part of a fourteenth-century church, of which only the portal remains, slightly below ground level. In its current guise as north Nicosia's largest **public bath**, it's open from 7.30am to 10pm daily. Part of the existing complex is taken up by a souvenir shop specializing in good-quality basketry, but it's expensive – upwards of £20 for something suitable as a laundry hamper – and the proprietor is not much inclined to bargain. Another steambath, the **Korkut Hamamı** (daily 8am–10pm), stands nearby on Beliğ Paşa Sokağı.

RAUF DENKTAŞ (1924–)

President of the Turkish Republic of Northern Cyprus (and its predecessor the Turkish Federated State of Cyprus), **Rauf Denktaş** is a classic example of a big fish in a small pond, simultaneously managing to enjoy a position in the world spotlight far out of proportion to the size of his realm. His non-recognition as a head of state – Denktaş' official title at UN-sponsored negotiations since 1974 is "representative of the Turkish Cypriot community" – has never prevented him from acting like one.

Born in the Soléa valley village of Áyios Epifánios, Denktaş trained as a barrister in London before serving as a protégé of Dr Fazil Küçük, later first vice-president of the unitary republic. Probably with the latter's knowledge, Denktaş in 1957 founded Volkan, the right-wing Turkish nationalist organization modelled on the lines of Sinn Fein to counter the Greek Cypriots' EOKA. This was succeeded by the even more militant and reactionary **TMT** (*Türk Müdafaa Teskilati* or "Turkish Defence Organization"), analogous to the provisional IRA, banned (like EOKA) by the British but revived soon after independence.   Officially, Denktaş had no connection with TMT after 1960, having accepted instead the more respectable chairmanship of the Turkish Communal Chamber. But he was expelled from Cyprus in 1964 for indirect involvement in the December 1963 disturbances, and sought refuge in Turkey. Denktaş was again sent to Anatolia upon being caught trying to land on the Kırpaşa (Kárpas) Peninsula in 1966, but returned under amnesty in 1968 to resume his leadership of the Communal Chamber. As the dominant personality in the Turkish community, overshadowing even his mentor Dr Küçük, he acted as the regular negotiator in the sporadic intercommunal negotiations which took place until the summer of 1974 – a strange role given his life-long conviction that living side by side with Greek Cypriots was undesirable if not impossible.

Even before the establishment of a mono-ethnic North Cyprus in 1974–75, Denktaş was never squeamish about rough-and-tumble politics and (when necessary) resorting to pressure tactics. In 1963 he managed to get Emil Dirvana, the Turkish ambassador to Cyprus, recalled for condemning the TMT murder of two

The Kumarcılar Hanı and Büyük Han

A *han* in medieval Turkey was an inn for both travelling merchants and their horses to spend the night. Such inns were once common across the island, but those in the South have been bulldozed or altered beyond recognition, so the following sites are your best chance to see such buildings in Cyprus.

Within sight of the Büyük Hamam is the seventeenth-century **Kumarcılar Hanı** or "Gamblers' Inn" (Mon–Fri 8.30am–1pm & 2–5pm; free), with shops occupying its outer perimeter. Inside the grassy courtyard, pointed arches on the lower arcade level and square-capitalled columns on the upper one demonstrate more vernacular architectural influence than at the nearby **Büyük Han**. This, at the corner of Asmaaltı and Kurtbaba, was among the first Ottoman public works following the conquest; it became the first city prison under British administration, but reverted in 1893 to a hostel for destitute families, something more like its original role. Finally realizing plans on the drawing boards since before independence, the Büyük Han is now being restored for use as a museum (estimated completion late 1997). Accordingly there's only sporadic admission at present, at the whim of the construction crew: try to get in though, as it's a fine building, where each of the guest rooms in the upper arcade was originally heated by fireplaces. A little *mescit* (the Islamic equivalent of a chapel) balances on six columns leftist barristers who favoured greater intercommunal cooperation. Between 1970 and 1988, outspoken domestic opponents, such as Özker Özgür and Ahmet Berberoğlu, were intimidated or placed under house arrest. Lately, however, the North has acquired more earmarks of a democracy, including multi-party elections.

Denktaş' political machine, the **UBP** (*Ulusal Birlik Partisi* or "National Union Party"), held power uninterruptedly in North Cyprus from 1975 until late 1993, and while, as president, Denktaş is officially non-partisan, the UBP, currently under the leadership of his son Serdar, is still very much a family affair. Little tolerance has been exhibited within the party apparatus towards those who disagree with him; Derviş Eroğlu, a former UBP prime minister considered even more hard-line than Denktaş on the question of a possible settlement, had little choice but to defect with nine others and found the DP (Democratic Party), which held power in a coalition with the CTP (Republican Turkish Party) until mid-1995. Government jobs have historically been much easier to get with UBP membership, and once employed, civil servants were "encouraged" to vote for the party in various ways. Denktaş has periodically (and perhaps tactically, as he always changes his mind) announced his intention to resign from all public offices, news greeted by relief among those fed up with his autocratic manner. However his current presidential term, won in the hard-fought 1995 election against Eroğlu, is indeed probably his last, as Denktaş will be 76 in the year 2000.

Despite (or because of) the unilateral declaration of independence in 1983, more communally conciliatory elements in North Cypriot life regard him as a mere cat's-paw of mainland Turkish policy, not acting in the long-term interest of the Turkish Cypriot community. Denktaş may attract some grudging admiration for a lifetime as a wily, tenacious, and even charming negotiator, but as the years pass most observers are coming to realize that his consistent strategy of teasing the Greek Cypriots with proposals not really made in earnest, together with moving the goalposts when matters look hopeful, is merely a cover for incorrigible intransigence. Thus Denktaş can be currently reckoned the chief obstacle to any federal settlement of the Cyprus issue – sentiments officially reflected in a UN Security Council resolution of November 1992.

over its own *şadırvan* or ablutions fountain, a design seen elsewhere only at the Koza Hanı in Bursa, Turkey.

The bazaars

If you follow Girne Caddesi from Atatürk Meydanı towards the Green Line, you intersect pedestrianized Arasta Sokağı, heart of North Nicosia's **main shopping district**. Cloth and clothing (especially cheap jeans) predominate, with machinists and junk metal depots in surrounding streets, but it's a far cry from the 26 different bazaars the city had a century ago. A section of Girne Caddesi is still called the *Eski Kadanlar Pazarı* or "Former Women's Bazaar": not a female slave market, but rather where female vendors hawked a variety of textiles and household items of interest to other women. *Arasta* means a bazaar either physically built into the ground floor of a mosque, or if separate, one whose revenues go to the upkeep of a religious foundation. In this case the foundation concerned was probably the Selimiye Camii (see below), reached by following Arasta Sokağı east until emerging in front of the covered bazaar and the Bedesten. The **Belediye Pazarı**, or covered municipal market (Mon–Fri 6am–3pm, Sat 6am–1pm), shelters two or three antique and craft stalls in addition to the expected foodstuffs.

The Bedesten

The **Bedesten**, squatting between the Selimiye Camii and the covered market hall, was originally a sixth-century Byzantine church which eight hundred years later had the Roman Catholic St Nicholas church of the English grafted onto it, the whole being made the Greek Orthodox cathedral during the Venetian period. Under the Ottomans it served for a while as a grain store and cloth market (though *bedesten* means a lockable bazaar for precious metals or jewellery), but was later allowed to deteriorate so that only the north vaulting remains intact. Today the building is kept off-limits to protect the collection of medieval tombstones stored here; even from outside the ground plans of two separate churches are apparent, though restoration has begun and more of the complex should become evident as time passes. The magnificent north portal, with six coats of arms above, is a lesser version of the fine Gothic arches of the Selimiye Camii's narthex.

At the northeast corner of the Bedesten, a late medieval, two-roomed structure once served as the local *imam*'s residence; today it is the **Middle Ages Tombstones Museum** (erratic hours; free), the exhibits having been gathered from various places around the island. A painted ceiling is being rather garishly restored, and the rooms are occasionally home to naked, anatomically correct modern statues of medieval torture victims, destined for an exhibit in the dungeon of Kyrenia castle.

The Selimiye Camii (Ayía Sofía)

The **Selimiye Camii**, originally the Roman Catholic cathedral of Ayía Sofía, is the oldest and one of the finest examples of Gothic art in Cyprus, the work of French masons who accompanied the Crusades. Construction began in 1209 during the reign of Lusignan King Henry I and lasted 150 years; it was consecrated in 1326 while still incomplete, and the blunt-roofed bell towers were never finished. The intricate west facade with its triple, sculpted portal and giant window above, seem transplanted directly from the Île de France. Within, Lusignan princes were crowned kings of Cyprus before proceeding to Famagusta for a second, essentially honorary coronation as king of Jerusalem.

When the Ottomans took the city in 1570, they reserved their special fury for the cathedral, chopping up the pulpit and pews for firewood and opening the tombs, scattering the bones within and using the tombstones as flooring; just a few of the stones escaped such treatment, and can be seen stacked in a former side chapel, as well as in the designated museum (see above). The pair of incongruous, fifty-metre-high **minarets**, which constitute an unmissable landmark almost at the exact centre of the old city, were added immediately, but the building was only officially renamed the Selimiye Camii in 1954. You may be able to "tip" the custodian for the privilege of climbing the minarets for unrivalled views over the town.

Since the mosque still serves as a house of worship, there are no set visiting hours; try to coincide with the five prayer times, when you are allowed in shoeless, modestly attired and silent. The sense of internal space is as expected from such a soaring Gothic structure; abominating as good Muslims did all figurative representation, the Turks whitewashed the entire interior as part of their conversion process, so that the Selimiye presents a good example of clutter-free Gothic. But unhappily most of the original window tracery has disappeared over the centuries, replaced by tasteless modern concrete grilles. Other significant adaptations for Muslim worship include a *mihrab* (a niche indicating the direction of Mecca) and *mimber* (a pulpit from where the congregation leader may speak) set into the south transept, plus a women's gallery in the north transept. Outside, high up on the second, southeast flying buttress, hangs a small sundial; the *imam* resident next door could consult it from his doorway to determine the proper hours for prayer.

Other central monuments

Directly behind the apse of the Selimiye Camii, the diminutive **Sultan Mahmut Library** was founded by the Ottoman Governor Ali Ruhi in 1829 on behalf of the reforming Sultan Mahmut II (Mon–Fri 8am–1pm & 2–4.45pm; £1, or £1.50 combined ticket available at the Ethnography Museum – see p.226). The appealing octagonal, domed building, which doubled as a *medrese* or religious academy, houses an array of precious manuscripts and leather-bound books.

However, the main reason to drop in is to recruit the keeper for a visit to the **Lapidary Museum**, across the Selimiye Meydanı, which occupies a Venetian-era house formerly known as the Jeffery Museum, after the colonial official in charge of antiquities early this century. A jumble of unsorted stone relief-work in the building and the garden behind includes a Lusignan sarcophagus, a Venetian Lion of St Mark, lintels with coats of arms, column capitals, Islamic headstones and gargoyles. But more compelling than any of these, and the first thing you see when the keeper opens the door, is the delicate **Gothic tracery window** fitted into the north wall, all that was rescued from the Lusignan gatehouse which stood west of Atatürk Meydanı until being demolished under British rule.

The Haydarpaşa Camii

Walking up Kırlızade Sokağı from Selimiye Meydanı, you can't miss the **Haydarpaşa Camii**. Once the late fourteenth-century Lusignan church of St Catherine, and recently restored as an art gallery (Mon–Fri 9am–1pm & 2–5pm, Sat 9am–1pm; free), it is the most substantial Gothic monument in Nicosia after the Selimiye Camii. Great buttresses arc up to flank its high, slender windows, the roofline rimmed with gargoyles. Over the south door sprouts an ornamental poppy or acanthus bud; the west facade is adorned with (appropriately) a Catherine window, shaped like the wheel of the saint's martyrdom. A purpose-built minaret was tacked awkwardly onto the southwest corner of the structure, rather than adapting the square, keep-like sacristy northeast of the apse. The glorious, airy interior, scarcely altered during the Ottoman centuries, features three ceiling bosses from which sprout fan vaulting, joining eight wall columns.

Yeni Cami

Continuing north along Kırlızade Sokağı, you soon reach the **Yeni Cami** or "New Mosque", the eighteenth-century replacement for a previous one destroyed by a rapacious pasha in his dream-inspired conviction that treasure was concealed underneath. The townspeople complained to the sultan, who executed the impious malefactor, presumably confiscating his assets to build the new mosque. Just the minaret and a Gothic arch of the original building, which must have once been a church, remain marooned in what is now a schoolyard; the successor stands to one side, next to the tomb of the disgraced pasha. There are two more domed **tombs** across the narrow street.

Áyios Loukás

A final item of possible interest east of Girne Caddesi is the former eighteenth-century church of **Áyios Loukás** near Alsancak Sokağı; Greeks hailing from this formerly mixed district claim it was completely wrecked during the disturbances of 1963–64, but since then the church has been meticulously restored to house the municipality's Popular Art Association, with occasional exhibits.

The Arabahmet district

West of Girne Caddesi, the **Arabahmet district** is the counterpart to south Nicosia's Khrysaliniótissa neighbourhood, as you'll see strolling past imposing Ottoman houses on Zahra, Tanzimat and Salahi Şevket streets. But Master Plan or no, there's little sign yet of massive rehabilitation, given scarcer funds for this and lower population pressure than in the South; the Green Line is less obtrusive here, so many houses are still inhabited despite semi-dereliction. Also forlorn is the elaborate, octagonal Ottoman fountain at the Y-junction of Zahra and Tanzimat, which was allowed to run dry some years ago.

Arabahmet was, until the troubles, a mixed neighbourhood, as witnessed by scattered houses with Greek or Armenian inscriptions. The spire of the Roman Catholic church, straddling the Green Line, punctuates the south end of Salahi Şevket Sokağı; east of it, inaccessible within the military zone, stands the four-teenth-century Armenian church of the Virgin, originally a Benedictine monastery but handed over to the Armenians as a reward for siding with the Ottoman invaders. Ironically, then, the Armenian community was expelled from this area at the end of 1963 by the TMT, on the grounds that they had allied themselves with the Greek Cypriots.

The Arabahmet Camii

The unremarkable nineteenth-century **Arabahmet Camii**, named after the founder of the Mevlevî Tekke, serves as the fulcrum of the district. A hair of the Prophet's beard is said to be kept in the mosque, and shown to the faithful once a year; Archduke Salvator saw instead an ostrich egg suspended before the *mihrab*. As at the Selimiye Camii, the courtyard is paved partly with Lusignan tombstones taken from a church formerly on this site; it also shelters the more venerated tomb of Kâmil Paşa, briefly grand vezir of the Ottoman Empire around the turn of the century and the only Cypriot ever so honoured.

The Derviş Paşa Museum

The first street north of the Line on which you can head east without obstruction is Beliğ Paşa Sokağı, with its **Derviş Paşa Konağı** (daily 8am–1pm & 2–5pm; £1, or £1.50 combined ticket available at the Ethnography Museum – see p.226), an ethnographic collection that's the North's version of the Hadjiyiorgakis Kornesios house in south Nicosia. Once again, the well-restored building proves at least as interesting as the embroidery, copperware and basketry adorning the room mock-ups. Original builder and owner Derviş Paşa was the publisher of Cyprus' first Turkish **newspaper**, archival copies of which are also displayed. In the courtyard a **bar** sporadically functions, and behind it certainly the cleanest **toilets** in the city.

Practicalities

North Nicosia has almost no international-standard tourist facilities since few foreigners stay the night. There are just two government-approved **hotels**: the overpriced *Saray* on Atatürk Meydanı (☎22 83 115, fax 22 84 808; ⑤), tallest building in the old quarter, and the slightly more modest *Lapethos* (☎22 87 630, fax 22 87 560; ③), very near the bus terminal at Kemal Aşık Cad 19. It's reasonably comfortable and, considering the location, quiet, as long as you're at least two floors below the roofbar/restaurant.

Only for the sake of completeness might one mention the dozen or so dilapidated **pensions** tucked in various corners of the old city. With nostalgic Anatolian names like *Antalya* and *Bursa Uludağ*, these are intended for off-duty soldiers, shoppers and job-seekers from the mainland, and signs promising low monthly rates, plus the pong of bad drains, do not bespeak Sheraton comfort. Of interest only to compulsive slummers.

Eating and drinking

The choice of **restaurants** is slightly better. Top end of things is *Chinese House*, a branch of the Girne original, out at the *Orient Hotel-Brothel-Casino* on the road to Kyrenia, which charges £5–6 a head for a set Cantonese meal (shut Sun). Other options include the rooftop diner of the *Saray Hotel*, best at lunch, with unbeatable views; *Havuzbaşı*, an attractive open-air bazaar eatery, at the Green Line end of Girne Caddesi; the welcoming, suppertime-only *Zir*, on İstanbul Caddesi across from the National Struggle Museum; and *Anibal*, on the Saraçoğlu Meydanı off İstanbul Caddesi, a long-established kebab grill overlooking a park. For sweet teeth, the *Londra Pastanesi* at İnönü Meydanı dishes up *dondurma* (Turkish ice cream).

The most remarkable nocturnal eatery is *Bizim Ahır*, a bit outside the walls in Küçük Kaymaklı district, on Kahramanlar Caddesi near the corner of Bülent Hüseyin Sokağı. The name, meaning "Our Barn", stems from the fact that the premises were once an abandoned house used as a sheep pen. The *meze* plates – everything from mushrooms to *kağıt kebab* (paper-roasted meat) – are excellent, and the colourful proprietor – a former smuggler into the enclaves, jailed by the Greek Cypriots – can sometimes be persuaded to converse in English. *Bizim Ahır* lies at the edge of a vast area of desolate houses, devastated between December 22 and 25, 1963 by Nikos Sampson and his EOKA irregulars (see p.321); a cenotaph honours the many casualties, and the ruins have been left as a memorial, shown to schoolchildren to keep fear and hatred of the Greek Cypriots alive.

Listings

Airlines *(Cyprus) Turkish Airlines*, Atatürk Meydanı (☎22 73 820); *Akdeniz Airlines*, Girne Cad 144 (☎22 85 827 or 22 88 099); *Istanbul Airlines*, Mirata Apt 3–4, Osman Paşa Caddesi (☎22 83 140).

Airport information ☎23 14 806 for flight schedule confirmation.

Books and newspapers *Kemal Rüstem*, Girne Cad 26 opposite the *Saray Hotel*, looks as if a bomb has hit it, but sift through the mess to find real, and in some cases rare, treasures;

unpredictable hours. *Hazım Remzi*, ground floor of the *Saray Hotel*, is a newsagent with a selection of foreign newpapers and magazines, usually fairly recent.

Car rental Try *Capital*, in the Firko Building on Uluçamgil Sokağı, behind the *Orient Hotel-Brothel-Casino* (☎22 78 172); *Sun*, Abdi İpekçi Cad (☎22 78 787); or *Travelöz*, Muzaffer Paşa Cad, Hacı Ali Apt 50 (☎22 77 147).

Cultural centres/interest offices Because of North Cyprus' international non-recognition, none of the foreign institutions here officially have consulate or embassy status, despite depiction as such on tourist maps. They exist primarily for cultural outreach to the Turkish Cypriots, provision of libraries and events for expatriates, and assistance in dire emergencies for travellers. They are: the *American Centre* on Güner Türkmen Sokak, in Köşklü Çiftlik district northeast of the walled precinct (☎22 72 443); the *British Council*, housed in the former embassy chancellery of the old unified republic, near the Green Line off Mehmet Akif Cad 23 (summer Mon–Fri 7.30am–1.30pm, plus Tues & Thurs 3.30–6pm; no afternoon hours in Aug; earlier afternoon hours in winter; ☎22 83 861); an *Australian Representation Division* in the *Saray Hotel* (Tues & Thurs 9am–12.30pm only; ☎22 77 332); and the *German Cultural Centre*, at Yirmisekiz Kasım Sokak (☎22 75 161). Each publishes lists of forthcoming events.

Exchange The *Kıbrıs Kooperatif Merkez Bankası* on the corner of Nuri Efendi and Mahmut Paşa in the old town has a *Visa/Access*-accepting cashpoint machine. Otherwise, try *Sun* car rental on Abdi İpekçi, also a currency exchange house which claims to accept personal cheques; *Elmaslar*, Girne Cad 89K; or *Merimann Currency Exchange*, İkinci Selim Cad 49E.

Post offices Central branch on Sarayönü Sokağı, just off Atatürk Meydanı (Mon–Fri 7.30am–2pm & 4–6pm, Sat 8.30am–12.30pm); parcels at the Yenişehir branch, Atatürk Cad 6–9, corner Ecvet Yusuf Caddesi.

Public toilets Near the Büyük Hamam, and on the ramparts east of the Kyrenia Gate (middling cleanliness).

Shopping Try antique shops by the Selimiye Camii, or the stalls mentioned above in the Belediye Pazarı.

Travel agency A very helpful one with fluent English-speaking management is *Birinci Turizm*, at Girne Cad 158A (☎22 83 200, fax 22 83 358), which can arrange hotels, air tickets and competitive car rental, as well as currency exchange.

AROUND NORTH NICOSIA

It is actually easier to approach the western salient of North Cyprus from Kyrenia, but since the end of Ottoman rule the attractions in this section have always been part of Nicosia district. With an early start, all the following sites can be toured in a single day. Given the orientation of the Attila Line, use of the pre-1974 main road from Nicosia to the west is not possible; from the northwestern roundabout between Ortaköy and Gönyeli, traffic heads first to Yılmazköy (Skylloúra) and then along a recently upgraded secondary road to Güzelyurt.

Güzelyurt (Mórfou)

Mention **GÜZELYURT** (Mórfou, Omorfo) to even the more moderate among the Greek or Turkish Cypriot communities, and you'll quickly learn just how far apart are their negotiating positions on acceptable minimums. Besides the loss of the tourist infrastructure and the port of Famagusta, the abandonment of the Mórfou plain, with its burgeoning citrus orchards, melon patches and strawberry fields irrigated by vast underground water reserves, was a crushing blow to Greek Cypriot enterprise. Not surprisingly, the South insists on the return of some, preferably all, of the basin as part of any settlement; North Cyprus, with more than ten percent of its population now settled here, and the local *Sunzest* citrus export co-op in the past one of its few dependable hard-currency earners, demurs. However, with the vastly increased acreage of citrus under cultivation since 1974, inefficient irrigation methods have overdrawn the local water table, causing the nearby sea to contaminate it. With Turkish aid, the Northern administration has improved existing reservoirs east of Güzelyurt to recharge aquifers, but progressive salinization of well-water remains a major problem.

Today, as in the past, Güzelyurt serves as a busy market town for the plain around, with little to detain casual tourists. It does, however, boast an excellent **restaurant**, the *Şah*, at the northern roundabout (open daily; ☎71 43 064 for reservations), offering the best *mezé* in the North, including quail and the rare salted lamb. Approaching Güzelyurt from Kyrenia, railway buffs should keep an eye peeled for an isolated section of track east of the road supporting a **Baldwin locomotive** made in Philadelphia in 1924. This is one of two surviving relics (the other is in Famagusta) of the vanished railway across the Mesaoría, which ceased operating in 1951.

The museum

Towards the west end of town, past a nineteenth-century church with its belfry-top shot off, and the double minarets of an enormous new Saudi-financed mosque, you'll find the local **archeological and natural history museum** (vague hours; £1). Specimens of the stuffed-animal collection, including two-headed and eight-legged lambs, are a bit bedraggled, but perusing the bird section is a good way to learn their Turkish names. Upstairs, several galleries contain clay objects from all periods, including one wing devoted to the nearby Late Bronze Age site of Toúmba tou Skoúrou, but it can't compare to any collection in the South. On the roundabout behind the museum, an exceptionally large **monument** honours Turkish Cypriots killed by EOKA in the South between 1950 and 1974 – plus a more recent casualty in 1980.

The church of Áyios Mámas

The museum warden will admit you to the adjacent church of **Áyios Mámas**, long the cult focus of Cyprus' most beloved saint. Originally built in Byzantine times on the site of a pagan temple, it acquired Gothic embellishments in the fifteenth century, and had a dome added three hundred years later. The interior is in reasonable condition, if dusty, and currently functions as a warehouse for icons rescued from around the district. A magnificent *témblon*, where lamps dangle from gargoyles, is the equal of massive columns and imposing masonry; you must stoop under arches to reach the seats of the upstairs *yinaikonítis*, evidence that it was added long after the original construction.

But you have come, as did the faithful pre-1974, mainly to admire the purported **tomb of Mamas**, on the left as you enter the north door; above the marble sarcophagus, undeniably ancient, a dangling curtain is festooned with votive offerings in the shape of ears – a strange image in view of the fact that the saint principally warded off tax collectors. But the story runs that early during Ottoman rule, Turks, convinced that there was treasure hidden in the coffin, bored holes in its side, at which a sort of nectar oozed out, thus terrifying the desecrators into desisting. The stuff, which appeared thereafter at unpredictable intervals, was claimed sovereign against earache, and additionally had the property of calming a stormy sea if poured on the waves. On the exterior west wall, there's a naive relief of Mamas on his lion; the legend behind this iconography is given on p.000.

Lefke and its coast

Soon after Güzelyurt you emerge on the namesake bay, but initially it's a shingly, windswept coast not tempting for a swim. **GEMİKONAĞI** (Karavostási), 17km along, was for decades the port for the busy mines just inland; the 1974 war largely separated the two, but by then most of the open-cast pits inland were played out anyway. Until recently pyrites for shipment to Turkey were still loaded from a conveyor-belted jetty here, but even this activity has ceased. This jetty could easily be adapted for loading Güzelyurt citrus, but Famagusta-based civil servants have allegedly obstructed such a strategy, so the fruit continues to be trucked at considerable extra cost to the latter port.

Gemikonağı practicalities

Gemikonağı is the hub of such tourism as exists west of Nicosia. Halil Bey, former head engineer at the mines, has built the arcaded *Soli Inn* on the site of a former Ottoman *kervansaray* (☎/fax 72 77 575; ③); most people just stop off for lunch at the good-value, chandeliered restaurant, featuring excellent desserts prepared by Halil's English wife. It's open all year, since during term time the inn serves partly as a dorm and canteen for some of Lefke's university students.

Food at the *Mardin Plajı Restaurant*, a bit west of the *Soli Inn*, is pricier, but there's a small artifically strewn beach at the edge of the premises. East of the inn, the characterful beachside *Karyağdı Hotel Bar* contains two yellow fridges for beer, a half-dozen shelves of booze, and an antique collection the envy of many an official ethnographic museum, all presided over by Mehmet Karyağdı, former miners' union organizer.

Lefke

To reach Lefke, turn inland at Gemikonağı, passing a former Danish UN post labelled "Viking Camp" before bumping over the level crossing of a rare surviving section of the Cyprus railway. **LEFKE** (Léfka) itself is an old Turkish Cypriot stronghold at the base of the Tróödhos foothills; abundant water audible in runnels everywhere has fostered lush orchards, forming a stark contrast to the naked hills and slag heaps all around. *Léfka* means "poplar" in Greek but it's predominantly a date-palm and citrus oasis, claiming to have the best oranges on Cyprus, with apricots and plums thrown in for good measure. A single open-cast mine in northern territory worked until the late 1980s, but after the erection of the Attila Line and severance of any connection with the main mines further inland at Skouriótissa, the population fell from over 5000 to under 3000. Of late there's been a modest influx of foreigners: instructors and exchange students (from Brighton) at the local university, and disciples of a charismatic religious leader (see box).

KIBRISLI ŞEYH NAZİM

Lefke has recently achieved some fame as the power base of Naqshbandi Sufi leader **Kıbrıslı Şeyh Nazim**. The Naqshbandi order of Sufism, currently also active in Bulgaria and ex-Yugoslavia, emphasizes the personal authority of the *murshid* or spiritual leader, with teachings that tend towards the reactionary. A trained engineer speaking a half-dozen languages fluently, Şeyh Nazim is a charismatic figure, considered by some to be dangerously persuasive; Dr Küçük, the secularist vice-president under the old republic, saw fit to jail, then exile him to Lebanon. In 1974 he returned, and set up the Turkish Cypriot Islamic Society, to promote greater piety in the notoriously lax religious environment of the North; this is one of several such groups here, whose membership does not much surpass a thousand. Both the late Turkish president Özal and North Cypriot leader Denktaş, who grew up in the same neighbourhood of Nicosia, have ranked among his adherents – as well as numbers of Westerners, including (briefly resident in 1988) pop singer Cat Stevens, or Yusuf Islam as he is now known, and more recently Bob (Mahmut) Geldof.

Should you desire an audience with the great man, Şeyh Nazim is quite accessible, provided he's not at one of his several residences abroad; just ask to be pointed towards the house near the Mahkeme Mescidi, at the northern edge of the town. Of late he spends considerable time in London, either at the Southwark mosque – where followers sleep on the premises just to be near their spiritual leader – or at another mosque on Queen Anne Avenue in Haringey.

Drive through the town – which has no conventional tourist facilities – to catch a glimpse of the unremarkable but pleasing **Piri Osman Paşa** mosque at the edge of the oasis, flanked by palm trees and with the sear mountains as a backdrop. In the courtyard of the little mosque, which is usually locked, stands the ornate marble tomb of Vezir Osman Paşa, an Ottoman worthy supposedly poisoned as part of a political intrigue, and buried here in 1820.

Back in Lefke proper, rambling old houses are scattered among the aqueduct-webbed greenery; up on the main road you'll see some British imperial architecture, a small university campus, and a trilingual plaque marking the graves of the **Gaziveren incident** victims. In 1964 hundreds of EOKA activists attacked the enclaved village of Gaziveren, near Yeşilyurt, whose inhabitants held them off with a dozen hunting rifles, at the cost of these casualties, until Turkey threatened action and a ceasefire was negotiated. On the roundabout just below is a more-extreme-than-usual equestrian statue of Atatürk on a prancing stallion.

Soli

About a kilometre west of the *Soli Inn* in Gemikonağı, the ruins of ancient **Soli** (unenclosed; admission £1 when warden present) are marked inconspicuously on the seaward side of the road – stay alert, as it's easy to miss the "Soli Harabeleri" sign, pointing inland.

Soli was one of the ten ancient city-kingdoms of Cyprus, legendarily founded early in the sixth century BC when the Athenian lawgiver Solon, who supposedly lived here for a while, persuaded King Philocyprus to move the city down from a bluff overhead to its present site. But like Leonardo da Vinci's purported visit to Léfkara, this probably never happened, and there appears to have been a town at this location since the Late Bronze Age, its name more likely a corruption of the Hittite word Sillu. Whatever its origins, it became a hotbed of pro-Hellenic sentiment, and was the last holdout against the Persians in 498 BC. The name in turn engendered that of Soléa, the Tróödhos foothill region inland, whose copper mines near present-day Skouriótissa spurred the growth of Soli, especially during Roman times, from which period most of the surviving ruins date. A Swedish expedition, funded by the archeology-loving Crown Prince of Sweden, excavated the theatre site between 1928 and 1930, while the post-independence government restored it badly with modern materials in 1963 (the original masonry now lines the Suez Canal and the quays of Port Said). A Canadian team uncovered the basilica and part of the agora after 1964.

The site

The ugly concrete **theatre**, originally from the second century AD, looks out over the narrow but lush coastal plain, watered by the streams draining from Lefke. Lower down by the car park are foundations of a large fifth-century **basilica**, whose floor boasts fine **mosaics**, both geometric and animal. The most intact and famous of these show waterfowl flanked by dolphins, and a magnificent swan enclosed in a circular medallion surrounded by floral patterns. The five-aisled basilica was destroyed in the seventh century, and some of the mosaics were built over during construction of a smaller, later church closer to the apse, where a mosaic inscription has been partly obliterated. During the Lusignan period, Soli was apparently the see of the banished Orthodox bishop of Nicosia, who would have mulled over the vagaries of fate amid little but rubble.

Canadian excavations in the **agora**, west of the custodian's hut and below the amphitheatre, were suspended after 1974 (as was all work in the North) and it is now fenced off, but before then a colonnaded paved street leading through the market to a nymphaeum (fountain shrine) had already been uncovered, as had the famous Aphrodite statuette and the bronze boy's head, both now in the Cyprus Museum in south Nicosia.

Yedidalga and the palace of Vouni

Around 1500m northwest of Soli, at **YEDİDALGA** (Potamós tou Kámbou), acceptable **beaches** finally appear; the shore is pebbly but the warm sea shelves gently over a sand bottom, fine for pre- or post-ruin dips.

The mysterious hilltop **palace of Vouni**, three-and-a-half twisty kilometres west towards the nearby Attila Line, occupies a most spectacular setting, with views both over the sea and inland to the Tillyrian ridges. Watch for a "Vouni Sarayı" sign pointing right a kilometre or so after the main road veers inland. Along the side road, you'll notice charcoal burners' pyramids, more vital than ever since wood-burning bread ovens were banned in the interest of air quality and tree preservation.

Vouni's history is controversial and obscure; even the original name is unknown, the modern one merely meaning "mountain" in Greek. It seems probable that the palace was first built around 480 BC by a pro-Persian king of Marion as an outpost to intimidate pro-Athenian Soli in the wake of a failed revolt; a few decades later another insurrection established a pro-Hellenic dynasty, which redesigned the premises. All sources agree that some time after 400 BC the palace was destroyed by agents unknown upon re-establishment of Persian dominion.

The palace site

The site itself is just partially enclosed, with no warden or ticket booth. However, a lockable gate partway along the access drive means you may have to leave vehicles there and walk the remaining distance.

Focus of the palace is a monumental **seven-stepped stairway** leading down into a courtyard, where a guitar-shaped stele, slotted at the top for a windlass, is propped on end before a deep **cistern**. This is one of several collection basins on the bluff top, as the water supply was a problem – and a priority, as suggested by the sophisticated bathing and drainage facilities of the luxury-loving ruling caste in the northwest corner of the palace. At the centre of the **stele** is an unfinished carved face, thought to be a goddess.

The original **Persian entry** to the royal apartments, along a natural stone ramp at the southwest corner of the precinct, is marked by a rusty sign; it was later closed off after the change of rulers and the entry moved to the north side of the central court, the residential quarters subsequently arrayed around this in the Mycenaean style. In the wake of the remodelling, the palace is thought to have grown to 137 rooms on two floors, the upper storey fashioned of mud bricks and thus long vanished.

Between the palace and the access road on its north flank is what appears to be a temple with remains of an obvious **altar** at the centre. On the opposite side of the site, beyond the car park and just below the modern trigonometric point, are the scarcely more articulate traces of a late fifth-century BC **Athena temple**, all but merging into the exposed rock strata here. Yet it must have been popular and revered in its day, for a large cache of votive offerings (now in south Nicosia's Cyprus Museum) was found here.

travel details

Buses

From **Güzelyurt** to: Lefke (every 30min; 30min).

From **Nicosia** to: Famagusta (every 20min; 1hr); Kyrenia (several hourly, departing when full; 30min); Güzelyurt (every 30min; 45min); İskele (5–6 daily; 50min).

CHAPTER SEVEN

KYRENIA AND THE NORTH COAST

K yrenia and its environs have long been considered the most beautiful landscape on Cyprus, thanks to the imposing line of high hills to the south
which temper the climate and separate the area from the rest of the island.
More than one writer has characterized the Kyrenia mountains as the quin-
tessential Gothic range; the limestone crags seem to mimic not only the handful of
castles which stud them, but also suggest the delicate tracery of the Lusignan
cathedrals in Nicosia and Famagusta, towns clearly visible from the heights, and
the pointed arches of the contemporary abbey at Béllapais, in the foothills.

These hills seem remarkably two-dimensional, rising to over a thousand
metres from a very narrow coastal plain and running for some 70km roughly east
to west, but plunging equally swiftly down to the Mesarya (Mesaoría) plain to

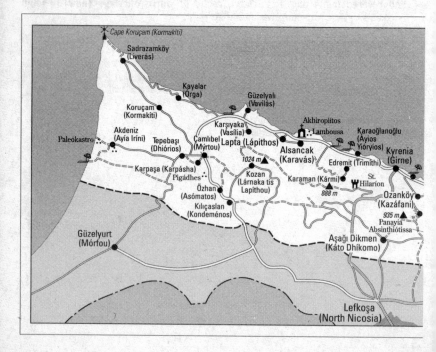

form a veritable wall. In particular they act as an efficient barrier to moisture-laden cloud, with rainfall on the north flank a good fifty percent higher than on the inland side. Springs erupt suddenly partway down the grade on the seaward slopes, keeping things relatively green and cool even in high summer and permitting the irrigation of various orchard and market-garden crops. Under exceptional conditions, Anatolia's Toros mountains are clearly visible across the Karamanian Straits.

Kyrenia, capital of the namesake district, is also lynchpin of tourism here with its compact old quarter arrayed around a nearly circular harbour. When the distractions of the town pall – fairly quickly for most – **Karaman**, **Alsancak** and

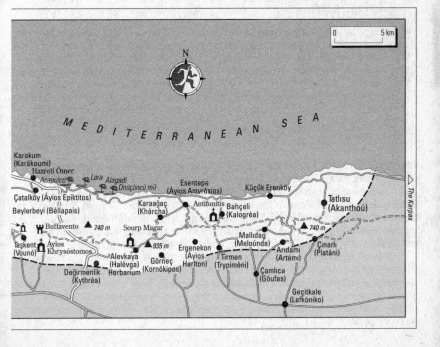

THE INFERNO OF 1995

For three days during late June 1995, the Kyrenia region suffered the worst bush fire in living memory, when nearly seventy square miles of forest and olive groves between Lapta on the west and Beşparmak peak to the east went up in smoke. The blaze, set simultaneously at several points late on a windy afternoon, was almost certainly arson, though the identity of the perpetrators remains a mystery. Paranoid speculation has encompassed Greek Cypriots, Greeks, Israelis and, more likely, PKK (Kurdish separatist) activists from the Turkish mainland; a number of individuals were arrested and swiftly deported to Turkey in a suspiciously hush-hush operation.

Nearly an entire day elapsed before effective fire-fighting measures were undertaken, highlighting glaring deficiencies in staffing, equipment and general funding for North Cyprus' forestry division – the Turkish Cypriots turned down an offer of fire engines from the South, preferring to wait for Turkish helicopters dumping 1000-litre tubs, donated by one of the British Sovereign Bases, filled with seawater. Damage to real estate totalled £3.5 million pounds, with the total value of destroyed wood and crops estimated at roughly £43 million sterling.

Among inland holiday complexes, only the *Hilarion Villas* at Kármi and *Ambelia Village* at Béllapais sustained any structural damage, but several other hillside outfits lost the lush environment which had made them so appealing, and in some instances even their artificial landscaping. The wood-and-plaster sections of St Hilarion castle, including the café, were completely gutted, though this should be repaired by the end of 1996.

During the latter half of 1995, the burn zone was clear-cut by Anatolian woodcutters and the logs shipped by daily barge to paper mills in Turkey, prior to terracing, reseeding and replanting of young trees. Despite the amount of money raised by the sale of timber, logistical and budgetary problems sharply scaled back this programme as well, and it seems that fast-growing mimosa – not the original native vegetation – will be favoured as replacement cover. And while the heavy rains over the winter of 1995–96 have encouraged natural resprouting, this type of Mediterranean forest takes nearly a century to attain any semblance of maturity – in the case of the olive groves, several hundred years – and the seemingly endless scorched hillsides, extending from just above sea level to the watershed of the Pendadákhtylos/Beşparmak barrier range, must now be reckoned a permanent feature of the Kyrenia landscape. If the arsonists intended to strike a blow at North Cypriot tourism, they have probably succeeded beyond their wildest fantasies.

Lapta, spectacularly set foothill villages in what was once the most forested part of the barrier range, beckon to the west. A mixture of Turkish military facilities and hotels co-exist uneasily along the shore below, with the fishing anchorage of **Güzelyalı** marking the end of the strip developed for tourism. Beyond, the thinly populated **Koruçam (Kormakíti) peninsula** with its dwindling Maronite villages makes a good destination for a day's drive, returning via the southwestern slopes of the Kyrenia hills on scenic, if little-travelled, back roads.

Southeast of Kyrenia, the Lusignan abbey of **Béllapais** very much tops the list of things to see, despite its relative commercialization; the surrounding village of **Beylerbeyi** and its neighbours **Ozanköy** and **Çatalköy** have always been elegant dormitory annexes of Kyrenia. Down on the coast, a succession of excellent beaches – in particular **Lara**, **Alagadi** and **Onüçüncü Mil** – remain as yet almost undeveloped.

The **Kyrenia hills** themselves offer satisfying destinations for a few day outings: the celebrated castles of **St Hilarion** and **Buffavento**, and the remote, abandoned **monasteries** of **Absinthiótissa** and **Antifonítis**.

Kyrenia (Girne)

Despite unsightly expansion since 1974, **KYRENIA (GİRNE)** can still easily lay claim to being Cyprus' most attractive coastal town, and the one with the most resonant reputation in foreign circles – helped along by Lawrence Durrell, plus scores of other eulogizing and expatriate Brits. It's certainly the only resort on the island that has anything of the feel of the central Mediterranean; down at the ruthlessly picturesque harbour the Turkish Cypriots have no qualms about playing "Zorba's Dance" on endless loop tapes to impart Aegean "atmosphere". Move away from the kernel of the old town, however, and you could be almost anywhere in coastal Turkey or Cyprus; new three-to-four-storey blocks are redeemed only by the magnificent backdrop of the Kyrenia range. The highlights of Kyrenia, including a trio of very minor museums, can easily be seen on foot in a day – the harbour and its guardian castle are most of what's on offer.

Some history

Kyrenia was founded by refugees from the Greek mainland in the tenth century BC, and figured among the ten city-kingdoms of Classical Cyprus, but little was heard from it until the Byzantines built the castle in the wake of the seventh-century Arab raids which contemptuously swept through the town's rickety outer walls. Thereafter the history of the place more or less parallels its castle (for which see p.246). Like the other ports on the island, Kyrenia only began to grow after the start of British administration, following the construction of roads to the interior and improvements to the harbour.

As the British Empire imploded after World War II, and redundant or retired colonial civil servants drifted homeward from less pleasant postings via Cyprus, many got no further than Kyrenia and its stage-set harbour. Especially those without family ties reckoned correctly that "home" had uncongenially changed beyond recognition, and even after Cypriot independence British expats made up a substantial fraction of the town's population, with hundreds more in the surrounding villages. Foreign numbers plummeted after the events of 1974 as a result of confiscations by the early Turkish administration, and only recently have they again attained three figures, against the town's current population of over 7000.

Arrival, orientation and information

If you've **flown** in, taxis and shuttle coaches take the main road from Ercan airport to Kyrenia via Nicosia; this becomes Ecevit Caddesi as it enters city limits from the south, depositing you at the central roundabout, **Belediye Meydanı**. Under your own steam it's also possible to use the narrower but less crowded bypass road over Beşparmak saddle, which enters Kyrenia to the east.

Ferry boats from Turkey dock at the modern commercial harbour, about 1500m east of the town centre. The main west–east thoroughfare through town doubles as the coast road and changes names a few times: one-way **Ziya Rizki**

KYRENIA (GIRNE)

Famagusta & the Kárpas Peninsula △

△ Bellapais

New Harbour

KTDI
RTDI and
Sidereal Lines

Customs

MEDITERRANEAN SEA

English Cemetery

Abant Cars

Ertürk Agent

Hospital

Laundrette

Yazıcızade Camii

Shipwreck Museum

Castle

Anglican Church

Phone Office

Cafer Paşa Camii

Terra Santa Chapel

Arkhángelos Church (Icon Museum)

Oscar's Car Hire

Dome Hotel & Atlantic Cars

Hotel Bristol

Fine Arts Museum

Military Area

Bus Station

See 'Central Kyrenia' map for detail

DR. FAZIL KÜÇÜK BULVARI

İSKENDERUN CADDESİ

KURTULUŞ CADDESİ

MERSİN CAD

CUMHURİYET CADDESİ

FEVZİ ÇAKMAK SOK

NAMIK KEMAL CADDESİ

ECEVİT CADDESİ

SELDTÜ MEYDANI

HÜRRİYET CADDESİ

CANBULAT SOK

ATATÜRK CAD

KORUTÜRK SOK

FEHMİ ERCAN SOK

KORDON BOYU

ERSIN AV

SOK

ÖZDEMİR ÖZOCAK SOK

ZİYA RIZKİ CAD

FEVZİ SİMAV CADDESİ

HASAN TAHSİN SOK

ASLAN TEKİN SOK

BEDREDDİN DEMİREL CADDESİ

METE ADANIR CADDESİ

ŞEHİTLER CAD

△ Nicosia

△ Bellapais

0   100m

N

△ West Beach Resorts & Green Jacket Bookshop

Caddesi on the far west side, then **Hürriyet Caddesi** just west of Ecevit, **Cumhuriyet Caddesi** (but still shown as Mustafa Cağatay on older maps) on the east side of town, becoming **İskenderun Caddesi** between the turning for Bellapais and the access road to the port.

Despite post-1974 sprawl, Kyrenia is not dauntingly large, though **parking** is a problem in high season; besides the central lot, a limited number of spaces lie along two narrow streets flanking the castle on its south and west. Except for the old harbour area, cars are allowed to circulate along **Kordon Boyu**, the shore road.

There is no longer a public tourist information bureau in Kyrenia, not that it was ever up to much anyway. If you're staying any amount of time, the **Anglo-Cypriot Association noticeboard** in front of the post office, with information on outings, group meetings, real estate and services, is certainly worth a glance.

Accommodation

If you want to savour the atmosphere of the old quarter and aren't sold on the idea of basing yourself in a remote, self-contained holiday complex, there are a number of modest but acceptable **hotels** within a short distance of the harbour, sometimes with views of the water; most offer discounts for stays of a week or more. If you can pay three-star rates however, it probably is best to be out of town somewhere.

Atlantis Hotel, Eftal Akça Sok 4, one lane back from the old harbour (☎81 52 505, fax 81 55 440). Characterless modern building with views, often packed with Germanophone tour groups, but worth a try in the off-season. ②.

Hotel Bristol, Hürriyet Cad 42 (☎81 56 570, fax 81 57 365). Colonial relic, now the most basic no-frills option you'd want to consider; the quieter rooms open onto the neglected back garden and courtyard, behind the bar and common room. ①.

Hotel British, one lane back from the yacht harbour (☎81 52 240, fax 81 52 742). Restored older building, with a lobby bar, air conditioning and partial water views; despite the name, you have to squeeze in between German and Austrian tour groups as well as UK ones (available through *Anatolian Sky*). ④.

Dome Hotel, Kordon Boyu (☎81 52 453, fax 81 52 772). Thanks to its colonial-institution status and Durrellian association, this figures prominently in every package operator's brochures. It's vastly overpriced for rather well-worn facilities (you can stay at the far better-appointed *Olive Tree* near Çatalköy for much the same), though the sea-water pool carved into living rock is a plus.

Ergenekon Hotel, on the yacht harbour just below the *British* (☎81 54 677, fax 81 56 781). Congenial Norwegian management, and better views than its neighbour; just nine simple rooms with air conditioning, named after ancient sites rather than numbered. Available through *Sunquest* and *Cyprus Paradise*. ③.

Harbour Lodge Motel, Kordon Boyu 22 (☎81 57 392, fax 81 53 744). A turn-of-the-century refurbished building just at the edge of the unrestricted traffic pattern, so somewhat noisy; used by German tour operators, but there is a chance of vacancies with advance planning. ③.

Onar Village, at the very top of town on the main road to Nicosia (☎81 55 850, fax 81 55 853). Not the most cheerful setting since the 1995 bush fire, but smallish, newish, well-run and offered by most package outfits. Car hire more or less essential.

Sidelya Hotel, Nasir Güneş Sok 7, downhill from the Belediye Meydanı (☎81 53 951, fax 81 56 052). A newer budget option, convenient and quiet except for occasional broadcasts from the nearby minaret. ①.

Kyrenia castle

An amalgam of different periods and thus irregularly shaped, **Kyrenia castle** (daily 8am–1pm & 2–5pm; £1.50) has only the citadel of Famagusta as a rival for castellated interest on the island. The present Venetian structure represents an adaptation of previous Byzantine and Lusignan castles: much of the walls' present thickness was achieved by simply filling in with rubble the space between the compact Byzantine and overextended Lusignan fortifications, and you can still see a now-superfluous round tower stump up on Hürriyet Caddesi, near Belediye Meydanı, and another remnant – possibly the base of a medieval lighthouse – out in the middle of the old port.

Some history

The Byzantines probably built atop the site of a Roman fort; Guy de Lusignan seized the castle in 1191, finding the Armenian wife and daughter of Isaac Comnenus hiding inside. It subsequently served as an ultimate funk hole during turbulent periods, as in 1426 when the Mamelukes overran the island, and again between 1460 and 1464 by Queen Charlotte, until her deposition by half-brother James. Rebels and disgraced personalities were also incarcerated here throughout the Lusignan period, including the rebellious Ibelin lords during Henry II's rule, and Peter I's mistress, shut up briefly by his wife.

The castle was never taken by force, repelling a fierce Genoese attack in 1374; its defenders always starved under siege or surrendered, as in 1570 when the Ottomans induced the defenders to capitulate by sending as a threat the severed heads of the Venetian commanders of fallen Nicosia. Thus the massive southeast, southwest and northwest towers – all constructed to slightly different specifications by the Venetians according to their military application – were not put to the test as at Famagusta. As elsewhere in the Ottoman empire, non-Muslims were forbidden access to the citadel after dark, when the ruling caste would retire there for the night. The British used it as a prison early in their administration, and again between 1954 and 1960 for EOKA captives.

A tour of the walls and the Shipwreck Museum

Today you enter the castle from the northwest via a bridge over the former moat. The first passage on the left leads to the tiny but perfectly formed **Byzantine chapel**; it stood outside the perimeter walls until the Venetians incorporated it into their circuit. The next ramp left, originally used for wheeling cannon, heads up to the round **northwest tower**, and the start of a partial wall circuit (it's not possible to go all the way around owing to military use). The expected views of the harbour are at your feet, and you can make out St Hilarion castle up on its peak; along the original Byzantine **west wall**, the remains of Lusignan apartments and a chapel are also visible. The **northeast bastion** contains a large vaulted room, its coolness welcome in summer despite its use as a toilet by birds and humans; from here steps descend to a series of chambers and finally the courtyard, which was completely resurfaced in 1995.

This is used for occasional performances, and also gives access to the **Shipwreck Museum** (same hours; included in admission fee). The displays concern a cargo boat which sank just off Kyrenia some 2300 years ago, discovered over a hundred feet down by a local diver in 1967. It is the oldest shipwreck known, and carbon-14 dating indicates it had been in service for nearly eighty

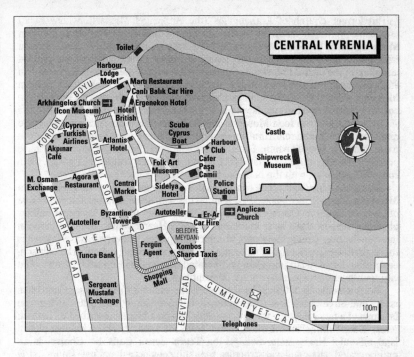

years and much repaired when it foundered. The boat had just plied the coast of Anatolia, judging by freight from Samos, Kos and Rhodes – most of it stone grain-grinders which could double as ballast, and nearly four hundred amphorae of wine. A four- or five-man crew existed mainly on almonds, large quantities of which were found intact, and such fish as they managed to catch.

The upper levels of the exhibit halls show photos of the archeological dive, and lead to the viewing platform over the **wreck** itself, soaked in preservative and kept in a cool, dry, dimly lit environment now that it's out of protecting seabed mud. Curiously, the ship was built in the reverse of modern techniques: the lengthwise planks of Aleppo pine were laid down first, the cross-ribbing later.

Around the old harbour

Although the British closed off its former north entrance and extended the break-water east past the castle after World War II, Kyrenia's little **harbour** had ceased to be a working one even before 1974, despite being by far the safest anchorage on the north coast. Traces of its age-old importance remain in the medieval wall between the *Marabou Restaurant* and the *Corner Bar*, where stone lugs pierced with holes were used as fastening points for mooring ropes. The port is now devoted entirely to pleasure craft touting all-day tours along the coast (for about £15, including a meal and drinks), the rental of speedboats, scuba-dive operations, and berths for several dozen yachts.

The former church of Arkhángelos (the Archangel Michael), whose belfry provides a prominent landmark on the rise west of the water, now houses the **Icon Museum** (daily 9am–1pm & 2–5pm; £1). The large collection offers an assortment of folksy seventeenth-to-nineteenth-century examples, rescued from unspecified churches in the district. Most interesting is a rare icon of the ecumenical council of 843 which restored icon worship after the Iconoclastic period. Inland from the Icon Museum, near the intersection of Canbulat Sokak and Hürriyet Caddesi, the covered **central market** stands very near the relict Byzantine castle tower.

By contrast to the Icon Museum, the **Folk Art Museum**, midway along the quay, contains traditional rural implements and dress in a Venetian-era house (open daily by keeper whim; £1); the best single exhibit is the olive-wood olive press on the ground floor, made partly from unpruned trunks, but it's hardly a compelling display, with the house bidding to overshadow the collection.

Much the same and more can be said for the strictly time-filling **Fine Arts Museum** (daily 8.30am–5pm; £1), installed in a 1930s villa out at the west edge of town on Özdemir Özocak Sokağı, near the military hospital. Its expat builder obviously had Hearst Castle ambitions, if not a Hearst wallet; the fake-baronial interior features grandiosely named kitsch fireplaces in every room. Neither is there anything Cypriot in the collection, which resembles a downmarket auctioneer's sales lot of Asian porcelain and painted screens, and ghastly, unattributed eighteenth- and nineteenth-century oil paintings.

More specifically Ottoman and Cypriot, the chunky **Cafer Paşa Camii** has stood one street back from the water since 1589; sometimes you can't get in because of a funeral, when the municipality lays on a hearse inscribed in Turkish "Only God is Immortal". A block inland from the *Dome Hotel* on its own plot of land off quiet Ersin Aydın Sokağı, the **Terra Santa Catholic Chapel** is an undesecrated, late-medieval structure that still sees occasional use (Mass 1st & 3rd Sun of the month) in tourist season.

Eating and drinking

It's difficult to resist eating or at least drinking in the old port at least once, where nearly a dozen restaurants and bars shamelessly exploit their position. Prices aren't much lower inland, but food variety and quality – plus atmosphere – are occasionally superior. If you have your own transport, consider driving out to Karaoğlanoğlu, with its fine clutch of restaurants (see p.250).

The seafront

Akpınar Café, 200m east of the *Dome Hotel*. Sticky cakes, with a view of the sea across the road; indoor and outdoor seating.

Harbour Club Downstairs, east end of the quay. Unexceptional but pleasant establishment with a full local-food menu, serving continuously through the afternoon when most places are shut; count on £7 per person for the set *meze*, a main course, a beer and service. (The flashy *Upstairs* banks on its reputation as a pre-1974 watering-hole of assorted nobs.)

Martı Restaurant, far end of the harbourfront, adjoining the *Harbour Lodge Motel*. Perhaps the most no-nonsense and reasonably priced of several fish restaurants on the quay.

Niazi's, opposite the *Dome Hotel*. Long-established mecca for carnivores, doing up their grills on a central hooded fire; the £5 "bistro lunch" menu (though minutely portioned) is less expensive than supper, for which you should expect to pay £7 a head.

Inland

Agora, Canbulat Sokak, opposite *Şah Supermarket*. Foreign-run, but does creditable "nouvelle" versions of local dishes. Open only April–Oct; about £5 a head.

Chinese House, well signposted up in the pre-1974 Turkish quarter on Namik Kemal Caddesi, near the Yazıcızade Camii. Sister branch to the namesake restaurant in north Nicosia, offering the usual Cantonese standards (Chinese chef, local management). Mon–Sat supper only, Sun lunch and supper; £5–6 for a set meal.

The Grapevine, on Ecevit Caddesi next to the *Esso* filling station. Pre-1974 institution, now run by "Jimmy" (Keço), offering ingenious *objet trouvé* decor and generously portioned international cuisine. About £8 for a meal; shut Sun.

The Melting Pot, inside the *Chinese House* premises. Pub lunches secondary to the patter dispensed by local character and stand-up-comic-in-disguise Allan Cavinder. Mon–Sat 10am–5pm.

Nightlife

Organized **nightlife** – or rather the lack of it – conforms very much to the tenor of family tourism hereabouts. Certain hotels, such as the *Dome*, *Mare Monte* and the *Celebrity* (the latter two well west of town), have sporadically functioning **discos** attached, open to non-guests.

   Casinos are a big thing in North Cyprus; no fewer than eight hotels in the Kyrenia area – the *Dome*, *Oscar*, *Jasmine Court*, *Club Lapethos*, *Acapulco*, *Grand Rock*, *Liman* and *Celebrity* – have one, equipped with slot machines and roulette tables. These are pitched to a fair extent at visitors from Turkey, whose citizens – in particular the numerous public employees – are forbidden to patronize their own gambling dens.

   Out on the coast road west of Kyrenia, the *Zakkum* and *Avşar* nightclubs contain a good proportion of the North's hookers and are worth avoiding unless that's your style.

Listings

Airline *(Cyprus) Turkish Airlines*, Philecia Court Suite 3, Kordon Boyu (☎81 52 513).

Bookstore *Green Jacket Bookshop*, Yirmi Temmuz Caddesi, at the extreme west end of Kyrenia; open Mon–Fri 9am–5pm, Sat 9am–1pm. Friendly English management and a large stock of Cyprus-related books and maps, most published by Eothen or Kemal Rüstem (see "Books" in *Contexts*) and difficult to get elsewhere. Also a small second-hand stock, plus quality cards and gift stationery.

Car rental *Abant*, next to *Oscar's Petrol* on İskendurun Caddesi (☎81 54 524); *Atlantic*, in the *Dome Hotel* (☎81 53 053, fax 81 52 772); *Canlı Balık*, on the old harbour (☎81 51 123); *Er-Ar*, Hürriyet Cad 6 (☎81 52 907); for *Interrent* (no connection with the eponymous international chain), enquire at either the *Altınkaya I* or *II* restaurants (☎81 55 001); *Oscar*, on Kordon Boyu opposite the *Dome Hotel* (☎81 52 272, fax 81 53 858).

Exchange *Sergeant Mustafa*, on Atatürk Caddesi south of Hürriyet Caddesi, and *M. Osman & Son*, on Atatürk north of Hürriyet, are two of several agencies swapping foreign currency notes instantly, travellers' cheques with a bit more bother (and a lower rate). The cashpoint machines of the *Kıbrıs Türk Kooperatif Merkez Bankası* on the central square, and the *İş Bankası* on the corner of Hürriyet and Atatürk, are the only two that will accept foreign plastic. *Tuncabank* on Hürriyet Caddesi is, unusually, open all day until 4.45pm.

Ferry boat agents *Ertürk*, corner of Cumhuriyet Caddesi and the Béllapais road (☎81 52 308); *Fergün*, on the west side of Belediye Meydanı (☎81 52 344); *KTML*, just before the port gate, on the right (☎81 57 885); *Sidereal Lines (Hydrofoils)*, next to *KTML* in same building (☎81 57 787).

Laundrette *Wash and Go*, two doors down from the *Ertürk* agency on Cumhuriyet Caddesi; cheap snacks and drinks served while you wait.

Post office Just off Belediye Meydanı (Mon–Fri 8am–1pm & 2–5pm, Sat 8.30am–12.30pm); parcel post in the basement (Mon, Wed & Fri 9–11.30am).

Public toilets At the base of the north jetty, on the old harbour, sparklingly clean and wardened; 25p for the privilege.

Scuba diving *Scuba Cyprus*, whose boat is conspicuous in the old port, have their offices out on the coastal highway just east of Alsancak – see the box on p.255 for full details.

Telephones Across from the post office, daily 9am–1pm & 2–6pm; sole vendors of telecards for the one booth inside here, the two outside in front of the post office, and the three on Belediye Meydanı. All of these tend to have queues of soldiers and students, so it may be better to make calls from your accommodation (though all calls from hotels, particularly overseas ones, attract ridiculous surcharges).

West of Kyrenia

The stretch of coast **west of Kyrenia** is the district's hotel strip, with a good two-thirds of the North's tourism facilities either on the sea or just inland. Beaches are not brilliant, often merely functional, but the character of the foothill villages with their eyrie-like situations redresses the balance.

Karaoğlanoğlu (Áyios Yióryios)

The first separate municipality west of Kyrenia on the coast, **KARAOĞLANOĞLU (ÁYIOS YIÓRYIOS)** is remarkable only as the site of the Turkish landing at dawn on July 20, 1974; the village has been renamed in honour of a Turkish colonel who was killed as he came ashore. A higher density than usual of grotesque monuments, including a cement abstract vaguely suggestive of an artillery piece (dubbed the "Turkish erection" by local residents), marks the spot some 8km west of Kyrenia. There's also a "Peace and Freedom Museum" consisting mostly of disabled Greek Cypriot military vehicles in an open-air display, a chronicle of EOKA atrocities against Turkish Cypriots, and general glorification of the Turkish intervention.

The **beach** itself, the first decent strand this side of Kyrenia and sheltered by a large offshore rock, was "Five-Mile Beach" in British times, but is now known as Yavuz Çıkarma ("Resolute Outbreak" in Turkish) or Altınkaya, after the rock and a recommended namesake restaurant which overlooks it – though **Beşinci Mil** (Fifth Mile) is still widely understood.

Practicalities

Topset Hotel Bungalows (☎82 22 204, fax 82 22 478; package holidays only) has its own small beach, and nearby also is one of the only official **campsites** in the North: the *Riviera Mocamp*, charging about £3 a day for caravans.

The **restaurant** that shares its name with the beach, *Altınkaya I*, is deservedly well thought of by its partly local clientele. The excellent-value set meal of unusual *meze* such as *molehiya*, calamari rings and *tatar böreği*, plus fish main courses, costs about £6, with drinks and service charge extra. On the whole, Karaoğlanoğlu is well stocked with locally flavoured restaurants, though it's advisable to make reservations in high season. The best restaurant in the area after *Altınkaya I* is *Yama*, at the seaward end of Ömer Kurt Sokak in Kervansaray neighbourhood (☎82 22 888; follow more conspicuous signs for *Güler Hotel-Restaurant* and the *Savarona* complex). Open daily for lunch and dinner most of the year, this small, tastefully decorated eatery has some of the most original *meze* in the Kyrenia area, as well as such specialities as *laz böreği* (essentially a meat-stuffed crepe) and *mantı* (similar to ravioli); count on £6.50–9 a head, with wine and dessert.

Some unpretentious, good-value kebab-and-*meze* houses congregate around the turning up to Karaman. The doyen of these seems to be *Olgun* (☎82 22 497), which operates all year on a winning formula of *meze*, meat grills, and complementary fruit plate and brandy; budget for about £7 per person with wine. A few hundred metres west of the junction, on the north side of the road, sits *Dünya*, a tiny, shack-like *meyhane* (supper only; ☎82 22 392) that's immensely popular with islanders and discerning tourists. A fixed-price menu of £6.50 per person includes *meze* such as home-style sausages and unusual meatballs, sometimes grilled quail, as well as drinks. The place is often known by its alias of *döşeme evi*, "upholstery house", after proprietor Hasan's daytime profession.

Finally, for a nightcap in congenial surroundings, or even a good bistro-style meal, *The Veranda Bar* at the very east edge of Karaoğlanoğlu can be recommended (☎82 22 053), with an enclosed sunporch overlooking the sea, outside seating, and a woodstove going in winter. Drinks are normally priced, though a full meal –mostly continental dishes with added Cypriot flair – will set you back about £8, including service and drinks.

Karaman (Kármi)

With its whitewashed houses scattered along a webbing of arcaded, cobbled lanes, **KARAMAN** is arguably the most beautiful of the Kyrenia hill villages. Still referred to even by officialdom as **KÁRMI**, it has in recent years acquired a reputation as something of a bohemian outpost. After lying abandoned since 1974 (it was too marginal agriculturally to appeal to either Turkish Cypriots or Anatolians), the place was in 1982 designated a special category of the tourism development concessions. Only Europeans – except for two Turkish Cypriot war heroes, one married to a foreigner – were allowed to renovate the hundred or so derelict properties on 25-year leases; tenants bore all costs of restoration and continue to pay a yearly ground rent. As a social experiment and architectural showcase, it is more successful than many such, though inevitably twee (lots of plaque-named cottages), and a bit of an ingrown and bitchy scene, where recently there seemed little better to do than count heads to see whether English- or German-speakers predominated. If you're interested, about ten percent of the cottages are up for grabs at any given time, at startlingly high prices considering that only ten to twelve years may be left on the lease-term.

The "villagers", who at certain times have included such high-powered personalities as two present/former British MPs, are generally strong supporters of the North's position (the very act of settling here is a political statement), and consider that their predecessors got their just deserts. Greek Cypriot Kármi was an EOKA-B stronghold, and thus was heavily damaged in the 1974 fighting; for many years any heavy rain would leach the blue paint of "ENOSIS" slogans through the covering of new whitewash.

ASİL NADİR (1943–)

Travelling in North Cyprus, it's difficult to avoid encountering traces of the business holdings of **Asil Nadir**. This secretive entrepreneur made UK headlines in late 1990 when his vast financial empire spectacularly crashed, sending shock waves across both the City and North Cyprus, and again in May 1993 when, facing multiple indictments for £155 million in fraudulent transactions, Nadir jumped bail and flew back to Cyprus, declaring that he had no chance for a fair trial under prevailing conditions.

Born in the traditional Turkish Cypriot stronghold of Lefke (Léfka) and the son of a prominent businessman, Nadir studied briefly in Istanbul before moving to London during the early 1970s. Having made his first bundle in the East End clothing industry, he used it in 1980 to acquire a controlling interest in a small company called Polly Peck. It provided a handy umbrella when Nadir began diversifying into electronics (the Japanese brand Sansui and Turkish Vestel), fruit-packing (Del Monte of California, plus Sunzest Citrus and Unipac in North Cyprus), plus an array of newspapers and magazines in Turkey and North Cyprus too numerous to list. Large numbers of hotels were also purchased or constructed in Turkey and North Cyprus. His sister, Bilge Nevzat, was placed in charge of Noble Hotels, a London outfit with two divisions devoted exclusively to tourism: Mosaic Holidays for packages to Turkey and North Cyprus, and Noble Air to fly the customers there. The name "Polly Peck" was to be seen only on the large fleet of cargo ships plying between Famagusta and northern Europe, trading North Cyprus' agricultural produce for manufactured goods. The Nadir family empire, worth £2 billion on paper, became, after the public sector, the largest single employer in the North, keeping nine thousand adults in work at its peak.

Despite occasional murmurs of discontent from lending agencies, everything seemed to go smoothly until September 1990, when a prejudicial Inland Revenue investigation, coupled with sudden, severe cash flow problems at Polly Peck, triggered a sharp dive in its share value on the London stock market. Several subsidiaries were compelled to cease trading immediately, and by mid-1991 Nadir had been declared personally bankrupt, with debts of over £1.3 billion. Court-appointed administrators spent much of 1991 and 1992 filing civil suits to retrieve £378 million in funds improperly removed from Polly Peck and subsidiaries, on behalf of former shareholders. Unfortunately many of the more valuable assets, such as hotels, warehouses and ships, lay out of reach in unrecognized North Cyprus, where court orders would have no effect; the selling off of other, more accessible, holdings – in particular the Turkish media titles – produced very little.

Following Serious Fraud Office investigations, multiple indictments were drawn up in 1991 charging Nadir with fraud, embezzlement and false accounting, and his two passports were confiscated. A friend, Ramadan Güney, and Nadir's ex-wife Ayşegül acted as partial sureties for his bail, set at £3.5 million; he repaid their trust, and outwitted the Home Office, by sneaking out of Britain on May 5, 1993 on his private jet. The Serious Fraud Office, which had always urged that bail should not be granted to Nadir, was furious, but little could – and can – be done; there is no extradition treaty between Britain and unrecognized North Cyprus, which claimed that he had broken no local laws. It has been suggested in some circles that the UK Conservative Party was secretly glad to have Nadir out of the way, since this would ensure a dully quiet trial rather than a boisterous and potentially embarrassing one, now proceeding after its postponement from an original September 1993 date.

In retrospect it appears the root causes of the crash were in part similar to the BCCI scandal: Nadir's pre-emptory and highly personalized management style relied heavily on largesse to friends and purchase of favours, preferably with other people's money. Recipients included the Conservative Party, as embarrassingly revealed by a letter, leaked in late 1990, of effusive gratitude for Nadir's generous contribution of £440,000, signed by then-Prime Minister Thatcher. By early 1995, the Conservatives were under strong pressure from the administrators to return the donation, convincingly shown to be part of the stolen funds. The "fraudulent accounting" portions of the various indictments stem from the Nadir practice of citing profits and assets based on the Turkish lira exchange rate at the beginning, rather than the end, of a statement period, which disregarded its dizzying devaluation rate; thus his various companies tended to be overvalued by as much as 35 percent. Many North Cypriots, aware of his dubious reputation all along, derived a grim sort of told-you-so satisfaction out of the whole affair, noting that Nadir's backers were exclusively foreign and that no Turkish Cypriot had been gullible enough to invest in his harebrained schemes (which have included, at various moments, bringing giant polythene sacks of water from Turkey by helicopter; drilling for oil at Alagadi beach; and setting up three heavy industrial plants in the North).

As noted, a substantial fraction of the family fortune remains intact in North Cyprus, for the moment out of reach of investigators and administrators (though in April 1995, administrators Coopers and Lybrand were granted the right by local courts to access Nadir's companies in North Cyprus). Nadir's influence in the North is still pervasive: the newly completed *Crystal Cove*, *The Olive Tree* and *Jasmine Court* resorts near Kyrenia, and the *Palm Beach Hotel* in Famagusta, all continue as affiliates of Noble Hotels; the high-tech, four-colour newspaper *Kıbrıs*, essentially a mouthpiece of the long-dominant UBP party, as well as the English-language *Cyprus Today*, have also survived. If all else fails Nadir can certainly live indefinitely on the more than £1 billion he is alleged to have spirited out of the UK in the years prior to 1993 – money which he has dispersed among his relatives and surviving companies. Currently he hides out in a villa at Lapta, venturing forth only in a cocoon of twenty bodyguards, as a precaution against being kidnapped by British agents.

From the standpoint of civic health, the greatest lingering cause for concern is not Asil Nadir's long-running financial antics but the near-identity between Polly Peck and the UBP (National Unity Party), which ruled the North uninterruptedly from 1975 to 1993. The Nadir-controlled local media have always been completely at the disposal of the UBP regime, especially at polling time, and the numerous employees of Polly Peck and its subsidiaries were allegedly threatened with the sack during the hard-fought 1990 elections if they did not vote for UBP lists. In return Rauf Denktaş – a personal friend of the Nadir family – long ensured that no legal harm befell them, at least within the confines of North Cyprus. Lately, however, the government has tried to distance itself, and even collect back taxes, from its embarrassing friend. The fleet of Polly Peck freighters formerly based in Famagusta has been sold to overseas buyers, and the Sunzest citrus processing plant at Güzelyurt was nationalized in lieu of a large tax debt.

In such a small society – perhaps 90,000 adults at present, including Anatolian settlers – it seems unlikely that more than one such prodigy as Asil Nadir would emerge in a generation, but at the same time it's an unhealthy sign that the most internationally famous Turkish Cypriot should have run the North for years almost as his private fiefdom.

The foreign community here views the possibility of any peace settlement with almost as much ambivalence as the native islanders. Some expats are elated at the possibility of longer-term leases and the opportunity to go for trips to the South; others are apprehensive about the steamroller of mass tourism – the backwater quality of the North was usually an important factor in their coming here – and the theoretical return, one fine morning, of irate Greek Cypriot owners demanding their homes back.

If you're here on a Sunday between 11am and 1pm, it's worth stopping in at the old church to view the **icon collection** which the residents have assembled from other abandoned churches in the area. Near the *Duckworth House* restaurant, a small sign points towards some Bronze Age **chamber-tombs**, though they're hardly essential viewing. The most substantial of a dozen holes in the ground has a stone shelter built atop it, and incised slabs flanking the subterranean entry. In one of these tombs was found the so-called "Kármi Cup" (now in the Cyprus Museum in south Nicosia), a specimen of Minoan Kamares ware, important evidence of Middle Bronze Age contacts between Crete and Cyprus.

Practicalities

Whatever their attitudes towards each other, the Greek Cypriots or the Northern authorities, the "villagers" welcome visitors, who might make their first stop at the pair of **pubs**, especially the *Crow's Nest* (closed Sun night and Mon), which has a small bistro attached. It's probably better to **eat** at *Duckworth House* on the village outskirts (closed Thurs; reserve on ☎82 22 513), a very English place right down to the afternoon cream teas, but offering excellent, sustaining value for about £8 a head.

If you fancy **staying short-term** – though not between November and March, when the north-facing setting is extremely dank and sunless – this needs to be arranged beforehand through the *Karmi Service Center* (☎/fax 82 22 568, fax only 82 22 670), which manages 24 houses of various sizes, whose leaseholders when absent make a little pocket money on the side in this fashion. Many of these properties can also be booked through *Tapestry* or *Cyprus Paradise* (see p.5).

Going up to Kármi you'll pass through the much smaller village of **EDREMİT (TRIMÍTHI)** 2km below, where you'll find an excellent **basketry** specialist – best in the North – across from the church, and two notable **restaurants**: *Jashan's* is North Cyprus' only Indian restaurant, though pretentiously expensive, at £15–17 a head; the *Mulberry Tree* (reserve on ☎82 22 625) has excellent Belgian/Cypriot cuisine – calamari in wine sauce featured – but there have been reports of misunderstandings owing to the absence of a written menu, so verify all prices first.

Alsancak (Karavás) and ancient Lambousa

Some 5km west of Karaoğlanoğlu, the main district of **ALSANCAK (KARAVÁS, KARAVA)** lines a single ravine, with runnels and aqueducts everywhere irrigating the lemon orchards. Fire-damaged carob and olive groves are interspersed with abandoned houses higher up the slopes. It was founded after the first Turkish conquest as an overflow of Lapta (see below), and most of its present inhabitants are refugees from Páfos, who have converted the huge church into a mosque; the carved *témblon* is still there, though the icons have vanished.

Directly north of Alsancak, out on a promontory, stands the twelfth-century **monastery of Akhiropíítos**, which can only be glimpsed from a distance as it falls squarely within a Turkish army camp, the buildings being used as storage depots. The monastery takes its name ("Made Without Hands" in Greek) from a foundation legend asserting that the central church was teleported whole from Anatolia to save it from marauding infidels. Adjacent to seaward stands the emphatically made-with-hands **chapel of Áyios Evlálios** (also off-limits), supposedly hewn from a single monolith. Both share the peninsula with the scant ruins of **ancient Lambousa**, of which the most famous evidence is the so-called "Lambousa Treasure", quantities of sixth-century Byzantine silver and gold items dug up beside Áyios Evlálios in 1905 and presently distributed among the Cyprus Museum in south Nicosia, the Medieval Museum in Limassol, the Metropolitan Museum in New York, and the British Museum in London.

The only portions of ancient Lambousa now open to the public lie on the east side of the promontory. To reach them, take the turning for the *Mare Monte* hotel, bear left onto a dirt track when you reach the resort gate, and continue around the perimeter fence towards the shore; four-wheel-drives can get within five minutes' walk of the site. The main things to see, just before the army-base barbed wire, are a series of **rectangular tanks** carved into the soft rock, the largest about the size of an Olympic swimming pool. These were fashioned by Roman-era fishermen to keep their catch alive prior to sale, and feature a pair of ingenious, diagonal sluices leading to the sea for water to flow in and out. Just inland, fairly obvious behind intermittent chains and stanchions, is a complex of similarly rock-cut **cliff tombs**.

SCUBA IN NORTH CYPRUS

Scuba Cyprus, a fully accredited diving school that offers both PADI and BSAC certifications, has its main local office (☎82 18 432, fax 82 18 075) on the coast highway at Alsancak, next to the *King's Court Apartments* and opposite the *Deniz Kızı Hotel*. You can also sometimes find staff, particularly operations head Asım Uygur, on their sixteen-metre wooden caique anchored in Kyrenia's old harbour.

A basic, PADI open-water course costs £225 over five days, the BSAC sports diver certification £185 over four days. For those already qualified, a ten-dive package runs to £115 with tanks and weight belt supplied, £150 for full gear. *Scuba Cyprus*' London office (see p.5 for details) can arrange full packages, with accommodation at either the *Deniz Kızı*, *Espri* or *Villa Club*. The sea is at its warmest from May to November (21–28°C), with just long-john suit feasible in July and August for shallower dives.

There are more than a dozen local dive sites to choose from, ranging in depth from 12 to 45 metres and accessible by the company's three Zodiac-type rubber boats. These operate twice daily (except January) from the small beaches of either the *Deniz Kızı* or *Mare Monte* hotels, with one additional night dive offered weekly. Even shallow day-divers will see huge groupers and enormous shoals of banded bream, with luckier sightings of scorpion fish, moray or even sea turtle.

All-day trips to a wreck site off the Kárpas peninsula are undertaken on alternate days in high season, in the wooden boat. This craft serves on the "off" days for pleasure cruises, which cost about £20 per person, with food, drink and snorkelling equipment included. Non-divers may also partake of *Scuba Cyprus*' shore-based watersports programme, including banana rides, boogie boarding and water skiing.

Practicalities

Most local tourist facilities are along or north of the coast road, around the *Deniz Kızı Hotel*. Available through most package-tour operators are the well-landscaped *Riverside*, at the east edge of town south of the main road, with indoor and outdoor pools, sauna, gym, water-gardens and aviaries (☎82 18 906, fax 82 18 908); and *The Villa Club* self-catering bungalows, east of Alsancak in Yeşiltepe district, which is small and attractively set in a citrus grove (☎82 18 400, fax 82 18 047).

On the inland side of the highway, the *Allahkerim* is a very simple family-run **restaurant** with *meze* and fish on weekend nights, meat otherwise, and outdoor seating. Small and inconspicuous on the seaward side of the road, beside the *Deniz Kızı* access drive, the *Bamboo* – so named for its interior decor – serves *meze* and seafood for about £7 per person, drinks inclusive.

Lapta (Lápithos)

A sprawling community draped over several spurs separated by canyons, its houses scattered in spring-fed greenery or perched on bluffs, **LAPTA (LÁPITHOS)** seems a more elaborate, shaggy version of Alsancak, completely unscathed by the 1995 fire and so your only chance to see what the Kyrenia escarpment once looked like. Its abundant water supply has attracted settlers since the twelfth century BC, who lived however mostly down at Lambousa until the turbulence of the seventh century AD compelled retreat inland. Lápithos was one of the original city-kingdoms of Cyprus, and during the Roman era served as a regional capital.

Lapta was famous in former times for its silk, carved chests, potters and water-powered corn mills – and lately for a strange **snake-charmer** who lives in a houseful of serpents, some poisonous. He has not only tamed them, but is apparently able to neutralize their venomous bites, and once appeared on Turkish TV to demonstrate his talents to 1980–84 junta leader Kenan Evren.

Lapta was formerly a bicommunal village; the pair of mosques and seven churches or monasteries correspond to the nine separate historical districts, but the minaret of the seventeenth-century Mehmet Ağa Camii was vandalized during the 1963–64 troubles and the Turkish Cypriots "encouraged" to leave. It's still mixed after a fashion: Turkish Cypriots, Anatolians and a handful of foreigners occupying a few properties on 25-year leases from the tourism authorities.

Practicalities

The *Club Lapethos*, just off the coast road and featured in virtually all package catalogues, has both hotel-type and self-catering units, with a private beach, sauna, gym and a submarine restaurant viewing one of two pools (☎82 18 961, fax 82 18 966).

For independent travellers, accommodation is available at the admirably well-signposted *Başpınar* ("Headspring") **taverna**, a wonderful eyrie under plane trees at the very top of the village, near where the fountain-water in question emerges after a long trip down the mountain. Recently reinvigorated, the taverna offers basic dishes on spec, or local specialities with advance notice, as well as several bungalows and car hire (☎82 18 661, fax 82 12 237; ①). *Başpınar* is also the start of a three-hour hike along the waymarked "Red Track" up to the prominent radio mast.

Another authentic local restaurant, below the Lapta town hall on the main shopping street, is *Süleyman's*, featuring a special vegetarian buffet on Wednesday evenings. *Ingo's*, at Şehit İbrahim Nidai Cad 75, west of *Süleyman's* near the police station, also comes recommended for German-slanted European cuisine (closed Wed).

Karşıyaka (Vasília) and Güzelyalı (Vavilás)

Some 18km west of Kyrenia, you reach an unmarked crossroads, though to the seaward side of the road there's an Atatürk bust at the middle of a plaza ringed with coffee houses. The inland turning leads shortly to **KARŞIYAKA (VASÍLIA, VASILYA)**, whose gushing fountain contrasts with a barren, sunbaked setting near the western end of the Kyrenia range. The abundant water allows for the irrigation of farmland in the plain below, but the village is about as far west as expats – and more casual tourists – are inclined to settle, and thus far there are few takers. Above Karşıyaka stand the shattered remains of the **monastery of Sinai**.

If you instead follow restaurant signs to seaward from the plaza with the Atatürk bust, **GÜZELYALI (VAVILÁS, VAVILLA)** soon appears. Formerly a functional port for the shipping out of carob pods, beautiful (*güzel* in Turkish) it ain't – nor are there any beaches worth mentioning – but it is an authentic outpost of Cypriot fishing culture.

Practicalities

The **Şirinyalı** **restaurant** in Güzelyalı, run by the Üçok family (closed Thurs), is an inexpensive seafood place with indoor and outdoor seating overlooking the water, and makes an excellent halt while touring. Equally good and unbelievably reasonable – about £6 a head for a main-course-plus-*meze* meal, including wine – is the adjacent *Birka Motel/Restaurant* (☎82 52 015 or 82 52 016; ①). Provided you have your own transport, their self-catering **flats**, suitable for up to four and with advantageous weekly rates (£80), would be a peaceful base, with only the sound of the sea after dark.

Your other local accommodation choice is the recently built *Club Güzelyalı* (☎82 52 017, fax 82 52 020; ⑤), 1km west of the Güzelyalı turning, the westernmost bit of development on this coast. A medium-sized, if lonely **hotel**, it's popular with both locals and foreigners, and just across the road from its own (slightly reefy) beach; several tour operators offer it.

The Koruçam (Kormakíti) peninsula

The western reaches of Kyrenia district terminate in the **Kormakíti peninsula** (**Koruçam Burnu** to the Turks), a rolling expanse of farmland and sparsely vegetated hills. Like the Akámas and the Kárpas, the other great promontories of Cyprus, it has a back-of-beyond feel and an interesting demographic history, in this case as the last stronghold of the island's thousand-year-old Maronite community.

Once past the turnings for Güzelyalı and Karşıyaka, and the *Club Güzelyalı*, the previously generous road dwindles somewhat as it bears inland on its long, indirect way towards Nicosia; the entire route is heavily militarized from here on, as it's the easiest way around the Kyrenia hills.

Less than a kilometre inland, an unmarked but paved, narrow road heads west back towards the coast, and the half-empty village of **KAYALAR (ÓRGA)**, where a handful of foreigners' villas perch incongruously above crumbling dwellings occupied by settlers from Turkey. Just before reaching Kayalar, a few coves look appealing from afar, but up close prove to be rocky and filthy – barely fit as a platform for jumping in.

The next settlement, **SADRAZAMKÖY (LIVERÁS)**, is too poorly sited to have attracted more than a handful of Anatolian settlers, who in 1992 were forbidden to graze goats in the surrounding scrub – it's been declared a "forestry region" in a possible ploy to discourage their continued residence. You can bump further along dirt tracks to the unmanned beacon out on bleak **Cape Koruçam** (Kormakíti) itself; this is Cyprus' nearest point to Turkey, some forty nautical miles from the promontory to Cape Anamur in Anatolia.

Koruçam (Kormakíti) village

The road hairpins on itself from Sadrazamköy to head back southeast, passing a tiny medieval chapel of the Virgin just before arriving at the formerly prosperous Maronite "capital" of **KORUÇAM (KORMAKÍTI)**. Its permanent population, about 1100 in 1960, has dwindled to 150 mostly elderly residents, and just seven children, taught by two nuns from a small convent in the village centre, keep the primary school going. A priest is still resident, with mass celebrated daily in the enormous modern church of Áyios Yióryios; you can visit the interior at other times by applying to the convent. There is no doctor and no means of summoning one since the authorities ripped out the pre-1974 telephone apparatus next to the municipal **coffee house**; inside this, Beirut football pennants hang next to portraits of various Maronite patriarchs.

Despite their obviously straitened circumstances, the people are overwhelmingly hospitable and cheerful, even by the standards of Cyprus. Wandering the streets between crumbling, unmaintained houses, you may be invited in if you speak any Greek, only to feel embarrassed at accepting generosity from those who have so little to spare. The watchword in conversation is *apó ekí* – "over there", that is, the South – where the only viable future is seen to lie.

South and east from Koruçam

ÇAMLIBEL (MÝRTOU), near the high point of the road to Nicosia, has become a major Turkish army depot; the direct road from here to Koruçam is often closed (at a checkpoint just north of the Çamlıbel–Tepebaşı road) at the whim of the sentries, who may ask to see a special pass. Consequently it's best to get to Koruçam via Kayalar and Sadrazamköy, and save the tricky checkpoint for the return leg; presented with a *fait accompli*, the sentry may merely request a handful of imported cigarettes (*Rothmans* will do) as "toll".

From just south of Tepebaşı (Dhiórios), another road leads west towards **AKDENİZ (AYÍA IRÍNI)**, near the important eponymous Late Bronze Age site excavated in 1929; since the place yielded up its treasures, it's of strictly specialist interest, and anyway falls squarely within Turkish Army territory, whose conscripts will insist on accompanying you around, if indeed they let you in at all.

Most visitors head this way for a patch of serviceable beach recently ceded by the military, and indeed the turning just south of Tepebaşı towards Akdeniz is

THE MARONITES OF KORMAKÍTI

The **Maronites** are an ancient Middle Eastern sect, whose identity arose out of a seventh-century theological dispute between the Monophysites, who postulated a single, divine nature for Christ, and the Orthodox, who believed Christ simultaneously God and Man. When asked their opinion by the Emperor Heraclius, the monks of the the Monastery of St Maron in Syria proposed that Christ had a dual nature but a single divine will. For a time this was championed as an ideal compromise, but later the doctrine was deemed heretical and its adherents had to seek safety in the mountains of the Lebanon.

Supposedly, the Maronites first came to Cyprus in the twelfth century with the Crusaders, whom they had served in Palestine as archers and guides, settling primarily in the Kárpas and Kormakíti areas. A contending theory asserts that these merely supplemented an existing Maronite colony which had existed on the island since the seventh century.

Although Uniate Christians – they acknowledge the supremacy of the pope, and still call themselves *Katholikí* (Catholics) – the Maronites have always been culturally similar to the Greek Orthodox majority, being bilingual in modern Greek as well as their own medieval Syriac, and using Greek personal names. The Kárpas community assimilated some time ago through intermarriage, and like the island's Latin Catholics, the Maronites have for some years celebrated Easter on the same date as the Orthodox, not least so that children at university can visit parents during a uniform week of holiday.

Despite all this, the Maronites attempted to remain neutral in the struggle between the Greek Orthodox and Turkish Muslim communities, taking no part in EOKA excesses either before or after independence. In their opinion the current situation in Cyprus is largely the result of pre-1974 government policy, and they bear little animosity towards Turkish Cypriots, thinking it best that the two main Cypriot ethnic groups continue to live separated.

Accordingly the Maronites of Kormakíti were among the enclaved Christians theoretically allowed to remain in the North after 1974, though in practice Turkish military and civil administration has been every bit as hard on them as on the Greeks of the Kárpas. Houses, public buildings and farmland (including rich citrus groves and corn fields) have been expropriated without compensation, and secondary schools shut down, making the continued existence of a viable community virtually impossible. Almost everyone between the ages of 12 and 45 in the four traditional Maronite villages has elected to emigrate, either to the South or abroad: rarely to ancestral but troubled Lebanon, more usually to Italy and England, where intermarriage with other Catholics is common.

The remaining older Maronites are allowed to visit the South for five days at a time on a pass costing about £1 (though it is alleged that their economically more active children, making the reverse journey, are charged exorbitant fees). If they overstay their "visa", they can lose the right to return to the North. Their status as some of the few individuals allowed relatively free movement between the two sides of the island makes them useful business intermediaries – for instance in the smuggling back and forth of title deeds for Greek Cypriot properties whose refugee owners, despairing of a settlement providing for the right of return, have elected to sell land or ruins to foreigners.

Most of what's left of the Kormakíti Maronite community now lives in the eponymous village, officially renamed Koruçam. Of the other three settlements, Karpaşa (Karpásha) can muster just a dozen households, Özhan (Asómatos) even fewer, and Gürpınar (Ayía Marína) has been completely deserted by the Maronites, despite the fact that their main monastery, Profítis Ilías, was nearby. For the ones choosing to stay behind, it's now mostly a matter of clinging grimly on, hoping to see an improvement in their lives if and when some sort of federal reunification settlement is reached.

helpfully signposted "Beach/Plaj". At the Akdeniz village mosque, 5km along, bear left, and then again onto a dirt track, following more "Beach/Plaj" signs. It's just over 7km in total to the beach, trash-strewn like the other public beaches around Kyrenia and equipped only with toilets, showers and a seasonal drinks stall. The shore itself is gravel on hard-packed sand, best for jogging on a calm day; dunes behind and the sweeping views along the arc of the bay lend what beauty there is.

You can also proceed unhindered a couple of kilometres south from Çamlıbel to **KIRPAŞA (KARPÁSHA)**, where the Maronite church at the east edge of the village stands locked except for the Friday mass, and only a dozen elderly Maronite couples soldier on. There is no longer a functioning Maronite primary school here; the teacher was tried on cooked-up espionage charges and then expelled a few years back. Some hay in spring, barley in summer and pasture for a few sheep are all that the land here affords to the inhabitants.

The Pigádhes sanctuary

Returning to the main road and heading towards north Nicosia, you sense the beginnings of the Mesarya; corn fields become increasingly common, and all open water disappears. Exactly 2km southeast of the junction at Çamlıbel, keep an eye out on the right for a narrow but paved track running between cypresses; the start is obliterated by a ditch, and there is no sign. After about 250m, you end up at the fenced enclosure (unlocked gate) containing the Bronze Age shrine known as **Pigádhes**. The most prominent structure is a stepped **altar** of rough ashlar masonry, carved with geometrical reliefs and crowned by a pair of stone "horns of consecration" reminiscent of, and contemporary with, Creto-Minoan sacred art of the same period. Around this sprawl the foundations of the courtyard sanctuary, plus some more trees which make the site fairly easy to spot from the road. Though not dazzling in impact, it's an intriguing antiquity, well worth the short detour and the slight risk to your undercarriage involved in crossing the roadside ditch.

An alternative return to Kyrenia

For an interesting return route to the Kyrenia coast, bear north at Kılıçaslan (Kondeménos) towards **KOZAN (LÁRNAKA TÍS LAPÍTHOU)**, beautifully set on the southern slopes of Selvilidağ (Kiparissóvouno), at 1024m the summit of the Kyrenia range. A few grapevines are coaxed from the sunny terraces here, but nothing like the profusion south of the Tróödhos. The main church here is now a mosque, though the monastery of Panayía ton Katháron visible to the west was thoroughly sacked after 1974.

The onward road over a 500-metre-high saddle in the ridge ahead is steep and single-lane, but also paved and scenic; near the top debouches a colonial-vintage dirt-track system, blazed in the early 1950s at a purported cost of £300 per mile. This can be followed, preferably with a four-wheel-drive or mountain bike, past the highest summits all the way to St Hilarion castle (see p.265). Once beyond this junction the tarmac route descends to Karşıyaka to pick up the coast highway.

Southeast of Kyrenia

Immediately **southeast of Kyrenia** cluster several inland villages which, perhaps even more than those to the west of town, have been particularly favoured by foreigners since the start of British administration. The coastal plain seems wider and more gently pitched; the hills are further in the background, permitting more winter sun than at Kármi or Lapta. Even the laziest tourist manages to make it up here, if only to see one of the crown jewels of North-Cypriot tourism, the romantically half-ruined abbey of Béllapais.

Beylerbeyi (Béllapais)

The village of **BEYLERBEYİ (Béllapais, Bellabayıs)** occupies a sloping natural terrace overlooking the sea, a ravine to the east providing some definition. **Lawrence Durrell's** sojourn here during the mid-1950s put it on the literary and touristic map, and his former house – more or less in the centre of the village – sports an ornamental ceramic plate over the door, reading: "Bitter Lemons: Lawrence Durrell lived here 1953–56". Here he finished the *Justine* volume of the *Alexandria Quartet*, and entertained a succession of British literati who before or subsequently made their mark as travel writers or chroniclers of the east Mediterranean. Since his time the large house's exterior has been somewhat taste-lessly revamped, but out front the mains-water standpipe which figured so promi-nently in the drama of Durrell's purchase of the property still protrudes from the pavement.

Frankly there are more attractive villages in the Kyrenia hills than Beylerbeyi: there's little greenery (especially since the bush fire) and open space compared to Kármi or Lapta, and cobbles have long since vanished from the lanes. The glory of the place resides definitively in the Lusignan **abbey of Béllapais**, at the north edge of the village.

The history of the abbey

Béllapais abbey was originally founded as St Mary of the Mountain just after 1200 by Augustinian canons fleeing Palestine. Almost immediately the brethren changed their affiliation to the Premonstratensian order under Thierry, the man behind the construction of Ayía Sofía cathedral in Nicosia, and adopted the white habits which gave the place its nickname of the "White Abbey".

Lusignan King Hugh III richly endowed it later the same century; he also conferred on the abbot the right to wear a mitre, sword and golden spurs, which only puffed up the abbey's pretensions in its frequent squabbles with the archbish-opric of Nicosia – as did a gift of a supposed fragment of the True Cross in 1246.

Succeeding Lusignan kings were benefactors and even lived in the abbey, but it provided a tempting target for the Genoese plunderings of 1373, after which it spun into both moral and physical decline, when the friars' reputation became scandalous for their concubines and the fact that they would only accept their own children as novices. The Venetians corrupted the long-standing name, *Abbaye de la Pais* (Abbey of Peace), to *De la Pais*, from which it was an easy elision to *Bellapais*.

The Turks dispersed the community in 1570 and handed the abbey over to the Orthodox church, while a village – apparently populated by descendants of the monks – grew up around the monastery. The site subsequently suffered from being used as a quarry by villagers and even the British, who despoiled the build-ings in various ways before their embryonic antiquities department began repairs under George Jeffrey, first curator of the Lapidary Museum in north Nicosia, early this century.

Visits to the abbey

You approach through a promenade of palm trees that lend an exotic fillip to the Gothic ambience, though the cloister's courtyard is still garnished with the robust cypresses planted by Durrell's Mr Kollis in the 1940s. Admission policies are somewhat flexible (nominally daily 8am–5pm, until 6pm in high season; £1.25), since the *Kybele* restaurant operates within the grounds after hours, so in practice you should be able to see much of the complex by patronizing it.

Except for its western arcade, where the vaulting is gone, the graceful fourteenth-century **cloister** is intact and enlivened by carvings of human and monster heads on the corbels. Just south of this the thirteenth-century **church**, used by the Greek Orthodox community here until its last members were forced out in 1976, is now open for visits. The interior is much as the Greeks left it, with intricately carved pulpit, *témblon* and bishop's throne still intact in the dim glow of five fairly restrained chandeliers. Over the entrance, a horseshoe-shaped wooden *yinaikonítis* seems to defy gravity; the groin-vaulted ceiling is rather more substantially supported by four massive columns. Underfoot, several Lusignan kings are thought to be entombed beneath the floor pavement. A stairway outside leads to a rooftop parapet that's the best vantage point for the ruined **chapter house** to the east of the cloister, and leads also to a small treasury, atop the church's north aisle, and the upper-storey **dormitory**, of which only one wall survives.

On the north side of the cloister, a Roman **sarcophagus** once served the monks as a wash basin before they trooped into the magnificent **refectory** (now open only in high season, and as an occasional performance venue). Six bay windows frame the sea, with a thirty-metre drop below them along the edge of the escarpment on which Béllapais was built. A raised **pulpit** in the north wall, from where scriptural selections would be read during meals, is accessible by a narrow spiral stairway. Late last century British forces used the refectory as a shooting range – hence the bullet holes in the east wall, where a higher **rose window** admits more light. A stairway leads from the ruins of the kitchen at the refectory's west end down to a pillared **undercroft** or storage basement.

Practicalities

Lest he accomplish nothing all day, Durrell was warned away from the "Tree of Idleness" (a now-sickly mulberry) shading its attendant café on the square southwest of the abbey. Across the street, a bogus *Huzur Ağaç* ("Tree of Repose" in Turkish) **restaurant** is a modern full-service outfit, tackily souvenir-festooned and tour-orientated, part of a general local pattern – besides Kyrenia harbour, the abbey's surroundings are the only place in the North that could be deemed rampantly commercialized. Of the handful of eateries and cafés arrayed in a half-circle around the abbey, the *Abbey Bell Tower* with its decor of hanging gourds is the simplest; the aforementioned *Kybele* inside the abbey grounds trades largely on its incomparable position.

Among **accommodation** options in Beylerbeyi, the *Bellapais Gardens*, just below the abbey, is a well-executed, human-scale bungalow cluster with its own view restaurant (☎81 56 066); rather less expensive, but equally appealing, are the three cottages of the *Gardens of Irini*, in the ravine at the east end of the village. Both of these properties are exclusively represented by *Cyprus Paradise*.

Ozanköy (Kazáfani) and Çatalköy (Áyios Epíktitos)

Both of these attractive settlements are linked with Beylerbeyi by a secondary road. **OZANKÖY (KAZÁFANI)**, before the troubles began a mixed village famous for its carob syrup and olive oil, is home to one of the less expensive and more characterful restaurants in the Kyrenia area: *Şenol's* (aka *The Old Mill*), formerly an olive press, open only for supper – and erratically at that. Ozanköy can also boast the faded-frescoed medieval church of **Panayía Potamítissa**, now the village mosque, where a fourteenth-century tomb in one corner sports a bas-relief of the occupant in period dress.

Above **ÇATALKÖY (ÁYIOS EPÍKTITOS)** lies *The Olive Tree* (☎82 44 200, fax 82 44 290), one of the more luxurious privately run hotel-apartment complexes in the North and represented by most package companies. The village itself, built atop a peculiar low escarpment riddled with **caves**, is attractive; in one of these lived the hermit Epiktitos during the twelfth century.

East of Kyrenia: the coast

In contrast to the shoreline west of Kyrenia, the coast to the east is largely unde-veloped and even deserted, any villages being built some way inland, out of reach of pirates. Yet tucked between rocky headlands are the best (if exposed) beaches in the district, lonely except on summer weekends.

Karakum (Karákoumi) and around

The first beach of any significance east of town is at **KARAKUM (KARÁKOUMI)**, accessible by a side road past the *Isola Celesta* restaurant and then another right turn once the initially rocky shore is reached. Just inland from this junction, the *Courtyard Inn*, longest established of the area's international-cuisine gourmet restaurants, is worth a special splurge but not surprisingly requires advance reservations (☎81 53 343). A bit further east, about halfway to the turning for Çatalköy, a seaward driveway leads a few hundred metres to the *Paradise*, a not-too-hyperbolic name for the poolside restaurant run by the amia-ble Ahmet Derviş and family. A large mixed *meze*, including *bumbar* (skinny sausages) and calamari rings, plus a portion of fish will run to about £7. Friday and Saturday nights feature live music, when the place tends to be packed (☎82 44 397 for reservations).

Tomb of Hazreti Ömer

A bit east of the Çatalköy turning, the **tomb of Hazreti Ömer**, another Durrellian locale extensively renovated since the 1950s (see "Beylerbeyi" above), is signposted as "Hazreti Ömer Türbesi" from the coast road. The tomb is reputed to be the final resting place of not one but seven warriors or holy men, and possibly dates from the Arab raids of the seventh century, though there was almost certainly a local pagan shrine before then. In the Cypriot fashion, the *tekke* or dervish convent which grew up around the tombs was venerated by both Greek and Turkish communities (as "Áyii Fanóndes" in the former case) before 1974. Its setting on a sea-lashed rocky promontory is the thing, with views back towards the mountains. Posted visiting hours (daily except Fri 9am–4pm) should not be trusted implicitly, but if you coincide with the keeper, you'll be treated to a glimpse of the dazzlingly kitsch interior: day-glo wall tapestries of Mecca, gaudy rugs in all shapes and sizes, piled books (not all of them religious) obscuring the tomb of the seven.

One cove to the west, **Fortuna** – the house originally built by Durrell's friend Marie – still stands among greenery, but inaccessible today as it falls within a fenced-off military area. Signposted from the main highway as "Villa Fırtına", it's now the local Turkish commander's residence.

The main eastern beaches

Unless you're staying there, it's best to skip **"Acapulco"** beach with its hotel resort complex, completely surrounded by barbed-wire army installations and incorporating the Neolithic site of Vrysi. **Lara** beach, 3km east, is nearly as well maintained and has a single café-restaurant; startling rock formations at its west end, repeated in various forms throughout this coast, give you something to sunbathe on or snorkel round.

Beyond Lara the coast road, though paved, is far narrower and curvier than maps imply, and progress is quite slow. A Siemens-designed power plant, the subject of considerable controversy hinging on its obsolete and polluting technology, was completed just east of Lara in 1993 to eliminate the North's dependence on electricity from the Dhekélia generator in the South. In the event it has been an ill-thought-out gesture of defiance, since consumers have not been paying their bills, turbine-fuel reserves have been exhausted, and accordingly the North now spends a fair number of weekly hours in the dark owing to frequent power cuts.

Alagadi ("Turtle Bay")

Two **restaurants**, the popular *Hodja's* and the *St Kathleen's,* along with a small villa complex, signal your arrival at the sand and shingle Esenyalı Halk Plajı.

THE PAY BEACH SCANDAL OF 1991

You may find, if you're not staying at shorefront hotels, that you will be charged a fee (£1–1.50 per person) for use of many beaches either side of Kyrenia, artificially strewn or otherwise. This is a legacy of what has gone down in local history as the **Pay Beach Scandal** of 1991, when the government, in an effort to keep "riff-raff" (meaning mainland Turkish conscripts and local picnickers) off beaches frequented by tourists, instituted the charges along with a ban on bringing one's own food and drink onto the sand. While the fees may not seem excessive to a foreigner, they are well beyond the means of the miserably paid soldiers, and represent a considerable hardship for a typically large family of mainland settlers, intent as well on doing its own barbecuing and not giving the beach-side snack bars much custom.

The local uproar was so great that the tourism ministry was forced to concede three sandy but virtually undeveloped bays east of Lara as *Halk Plajları* or "Public Beaches". They are accordingly very popular on weekends in season when large groups of Cypriots descend on them, though you should have the water almost to yourself as they're not especially keen swimmers. The main advantages of patronizing the fee beaches will be guaranteed presence of certain amenities (umbrellas, snack bar) and a much higher degree of cleanliness owing to regular raking and rubbish collection.

Better to continue a kilometre to **Alagadi (Alakáti)** beach, well marked at a sharp curve where a sign for the "Green Turtles Beach Bar" points to a 500-metre dirt sidetrack; this ends at a vast sandy bay about a kilometre long, with no facilities aside from toilets and the aforementioned bar, sporadically operated by the state tourism corporation. Unfortunately, because of the lack of development there is no clean-up of the enormous amount of rubbish – predominantly from Arab shipping, judging from product labels – that washes up here, but swimming is otherwise enjoyable. The cove here is best known to expats as **'Turtle Bay'**, after its status as a loggerhead turtle egg-laying site, but between the rubbish, the new power plant whose stacks jab the horizon, the firepits of weekend barbecuers and the manoeuvring jeeps (despite signs prohibiting the practice), the hatchlings' life expectancy must be rated as low.

Onüçüncü Mil

The headland to the east of "Turtle Bay" is possibly the site of ancient Alakati; beyond this promontory is yet another bay, also accessible by a track from the main road signed "Halk Plajları", known as **Onüçüncü Mil** or "Thirteenth Mile" after its distance from Kyrenia. If anything it is even more attractive than Alagadi, despite an abandoned, half-completed holiday village up in the trees, testimony to Asil Nadir's financial troubles. Only the bravest of drivers make it down off the wooded bluff via the tracks that fizzle out in the dunes here, one turning leading back in fact to the east end of "Turtle Bay". To either end of Onüçüncü Mil's sandy crescent, eerie jumbles of eroded limestone rear up like ruined fortifications, making it difficult to distinguish between them and man-made ancient masonry.

Inland: castles and monasteries

Along the watershed of the Kyrenia hills are scattered a handful of **castles and monasteries**, evocatively set on rock spires or down in wooded valleys. They're justifiably some of the biggest tourist attractions in the North, and all are served by roads of passable standard taking off from the two main Kyrenia–Nicosia routes, or from villages at the east end of the Kyrenia coastal strip.

The castles were built so as to be in visual communication with each other, Kyrenia and Nicosia – a Byzantine/Crusader early-warning system for pirate raids on the north coast. At the start of the Venetian era, all of them were partly dismantled to prevent further mischievous use, though warfare in general had changed and ballistics technology in particular had made them obsolete.

St Hilarion castle

Westernmost and best preserved of the three redoubts in these hills, **St Hilarion castle** (summer daily 8.30am–5pm; winter daily 8.30am–4.30pm; £1.25) does justice to the much-quoted passage of Rose Macaulay's ("a picture-book castle for elf-kings"), and the rumour that Walt Disney used it as a model for the castle in *Snow White and the Seven Dwarfs*. Indeed it has a fairy-tale quality, walls and towers sprouting out of the rocks almost at random.

Local legend once credited St Hilarion with 101 rooms, of which 100 could easily be found; the last, an enchanted garden, contained a fabulous treasure belonging to an elusive "queen" of Cypriot folklore, probably a holdover of Aphrodite worship. Shepherds or hunters stumbling through the magic doorway of the treasury had a tendency to awaken years later, Rip Van Winkle-like, empty-handed among the bare rocks.

Some history

The castle's verifiable history is almost as intricate as its battlements, with occasional valiant or grisly episodes belying its ethereal appearance. The saint of the name was a little-known hermit who fled Palestine during the seventh century to live and die up here, purging the mountain of still-lurking pagan demons; a Byzantine monastery, and later a fort, sprang up around his tomb.

Owing to its near-impregnability, it was one of the last castles taken by the Lusignans in 1191, who improved its fortifications throughout the early thirteenth century and rendered *Didhimi*, the Greek name for the twin peaks overhead, as *Dieu d'Amour*. St Hilarion was the focus of a four-year struggle between Holy Roman Emperor Frederick II and regent John d'Ibelin for control of the island, won by John's forces at the battle of nearby Agírda (today Ağırda) in 1232. During the subsequent 140 years of peace, sumptuous royal apartments were added, so that the castle doubled as a summer palace and, during 1349–50, as a refuge from the plague.

In 1373, during the Genoese invasion, the castle again acquired military importance as the retreat of the under-age King Peter II. His uncle and regent John of Antioch, misled by his hostile sister-in-law Eleanor of Aragon into believing his bodyguard of Bulgarian mercenaries treasonous, had them thrown one at a time from the highest tower of the castle; miraculously somebody survived the several-hundred-foot drop to tell the tale. Without his loyal retinue, John – implicated in the murder of Eleanor's late husband, Peter I – was easy prey for the vengeful queen and her followers.

The Venetians rendered the castle useless, they thought, for modern warfare. But in 1964 the beleaguered Turkish Cypriots found the castle not so militarily obsolete after all, using it as headquarters of their main enclave which included several Turkish communities on the main Kyrenia–Nicosia road. A small garrison of teenage TMT activists was able to fend off EOKA attacks on the castle, and the Turks remained in control of the place thereafter. With passage on the traditional main highway denied to Greek vehicles, or possible only in slow, UN-escorted convoy, the central government was forced to construct a bypass via Beşparmak/Pendadháktylos (see below). In 1974 St Hilarion and its surrounding enclave were a primary goal of Turkish paratroop landings early on July 20.

The site

Although St Hilarion is now very much open to visits, the twisty but well-marked approach road from the main highway still passes through a Turkish army base, with signs forbidding stopping or walking, let alone photography. Partway along, the restricted zone ends just past a clearing where the Crusaders held their jousting tournaments, and suddenly the castle appears, draped over the bristling pinnacles before you.

Once up in it, you'll spend a good hour scrambling over the crags to see it all. It's hot work: come early or late in the day, and bring stout shoes – beach- or pool-wear won't do on the often uneven ground.

First you cross the vast **lower ward** beyond the ticket booth, where medieval garrisons kept their horses; the now-charred, wood-and-plaster work of the lower towers must have appeared during the period of the TMT occupation. Once through the hulking **gatehouse and tunnel** into the middle enceinte (the name given to the defended area enclosed by the castle walls), your first detour is to the half-intact **Byzantine chapel**, earliest structure in the castle. You continue through a myriad rooms on a variety of levels; these include the monastic **refectory**, later the royal banqueting hall, up some stairs north of the chapel, and the handsome vaulted **belvedere** just beyond it.

Occasional modern roofing that survived the 1995 bush fire dates from the colonial era; almost everything else became a casualty of the blaze, including the drinks café with its unbeatable views over the Kyrenian coast, and it will be late 1996 or early 1997 before a new structure emerges.

An **arched gate** allows entry to the upper enceinte; you can scramble immediately up south to the **highest towers** (elevation 732m), the more outrageously placed called "Prince John's" and venue for the massacre of his Bulgarian auxiliaries – not a spot for acrophobics to linger. Alternatively, climbing the stony stair-paths towards the west end of the complex, you'll pass the **aqueduct** and **cistern** (the latter now just a dangerously deep mud puddle), which supplied the otherwise waterless garrisons here. Excursions end at the **royal apartments**, whose windows afforded the TMT garrison a good view of their mortal enemies in Kármi before 1974.

Panayía Absinthiótissa monastery

The **monastery of Panayía Absinthiótissa** enjoys a grand setting amidst juniper forest on the south flank of the range, gazing out across the Mesarya. Founded in late Byzantine times, it was taken over by Latin monks during the fifteenth century, and well restored during the 1960s – only to suffer comprehensive vandalization since 1974.

Despite its condition, Absinthiótissa still merits a visit, perhaps as a detour on the way between Kyrenia and north Nicosia. **Getting there** is fairly easy: from the new road linking those towns, turn east towards Aşaği Dikmen (Káto Dhíkomo) and Taşkent (Vounó); after about twenty minutes of mostly single-lane driving, you'll reach the latter village, just after the giant Turkish Cypriot flag and Atatürk slogan painted on the hillside. At the junction opposite the central shop, head north uphill along an initially paved lane, which forks after 500m; take a right, away from the gravel pit, and another right at a water tank. The monastery is in sight most of the way, so there's little chance of getting badly lost, but you'll be more comfortable with a 4WD vehicle to skirt the yawning quarry pits.

The enormous, twelve-windowed drum and dome of the **church** are visible from afar, but as you approach you'll notice the peculiar narthex which the Catholic monks added, with apses at each end and marvellous Gothic rib vaulting inside. Any frescoes have been defaced or stolen since 1974; the only other thing to admire is the **refectory**, north across the courtyard, with shallow ceiling vaulting and unusual lancet windows outlined in 1960s brickwork.

Buffavento castle

Buffavento (access permitted only Wed & Sat 9am–1pm, with military escort from roadside checkpoint), the least well preserved but most dramatically sited – and at 940m the highest – of the Kyrenian hill castles, requires considerable effort to reach, but will appeal to those who like their ruins wild and sinister.

Getting there

To **get there**, first take the inland turning, following the signs for Ercan airport and Famagusta, just past Çatalköy; the excellent surfacing is a legacy of the Greek Cypriots having bulldozed this route in 1969–70 to get around the Turkish Cypriot enclave at St Hilarion.

The only local village, reached by a side road partway along, is **ARAPKÖY (KLEPÍNI, KLEBİNİ)**. A curious legend once held that no more than forty families could reside in the place, or the Angel of Death would cull the surplus within the year; there are still only about 150 people here, a mix of native Turkish Cypriots, Anatolian settlers and foreigners attracted by the views. The countryside itself is bleak, doubly so after the recent fire, and east of here few outsiders wish to live, with most amenities lacking.

At the very top of the grade, when the Mesarya comes into view, take the rough track heading west, opposite the signed Alevkaya (Halévga) forest road. The first 400m are fortunately the worst; thereafter the surface improves along the total 6km to a circular area where vehicles without four-wheel drive must park. A jeep track, indicated by a rusty sign apt to be uprooted, continues a few zigzags further up to the true trailhead, where an olive tree grows in a stone planter ring next to a trilingual marble memorial to victims of a 1988 air crash: a small aircraft, approaching Ercan in misty conditions, failed to clear the ridge above and disintegrated nearby.

From the lower parking area, it's a full 45-minute walk up to the castle, which blends well into the rock on which it's built; though the path is in good condition, there's a consistent southern exposure, so you'll bake to death in summer unless you go early on the allowed visiting days.

Incidentally, don't believe maps – either the internationally published ones or that issued by the North Cyprus tourist office – which imply that the easiest way up to the castle is from the south, via Güngör (Koutsovéndis) and the tempting-looking monastery of Áyios Ioánnis Khrysóstomos. Beyond the village all tracks are unmarked, and a giant army camp blocks the way, placing the deconsecrated monastery off-limits as well. (In all fairness, the Greek Cypriot National Guard was using the grounds as a barracks before 1974, though you could still visit the main church.)

The site

Buffavento began life as a Byzantine watchtower in the tenth century and was surrendered to Guy de Lusignan in 1191. The Lusignan kings used it as a political prison, in particular Peter I who, warned by his friend John Visconti of Queen Eleanor's infidelity, repaid the favour by locking Visconti up here to starve to death.

The buildings themselves, almost all fitted with cisterns, are in poor-to-fair condition since their decommissioning by the Venetians, and home now only to bats; they're a pretext, really, for a nice walk in the hills. You can follow the stair-path from the graffitoed **gatehouse** up through the jumble of walls to the highest tower, where a natural terrace affords superb views, and would have been the site of signal fires to communicate with St Hilarion and Kantara castles.

Up top here, you'll usually learn how the place got its name (*Buffavento* means "wind gust"), and be treated to the best views on Cyprus: Kyrenia, Nicosia and Famagusta are all visible in the right conditions, as are the Tróödhos mountains and indeed half the island.

Around Beşparmak (Pendadháktylos)

Coming up from the north coast, you can't help noticing the sculpted bulk of **Beşparmak (Pendadháktylos)**, the "Five-Finger Mountain", just to the east of the Kyrenia–Nicosia bypass road. Although of modest elevation at 740m, its suggestive shape has engendered legend: the Greeks say the Byzantine hero Dhiyenis Akritas left the imprint of his hand here after leaping across the sea from Anatolia.

Sourp Magar Monastery

You can get a good view of the peak's south flank by turning left at the watershed along the signed Alevkaya (Halévga) forest road (away from the marked Buffavento turning). Downhill to the north after 7km, you'll glimpse the roofless, thoroughly vandalized remains of the **Armenian monastery of Sourp Magar** or St Makarios of Egypt. Founded by Copts in the eleventh century, it became the property of the island's Armenian community four hundred years later, and hosted an important festival every May until 1974.

Driving in this direction, the side track down to Sourp Magar is a hairpin left from a shady clearing with two round picnic tables, a water spout and a blank green placard. Just under a kilometre's bumpy, rutted driving brings you to the gate of the irregularly shaped monastery enclosure. Beside a withered orchard stands the tiny church, with pilgrims' cells lining the east and south perimeter walls. Absolutely nothing has been left intact by the Turkish army, venting its rage on a shrine of its historic enemies, and it's only worth visiting for the setting amidst dense, unscathed forest.

The North Cyprus Herbarium

Just 100m east of the turning for Sourp Magar, the forestry track emerges onto a secondary paved road up from the Nicosia–Ercan Airport expressway; turn right to reach, after 300m, the vast picnic grounds around the forestry station at **Alevkaya (Halévga)**. In 1989 the main building here was refurbished and opened as the **North Cyprus Herbarium** (daily 8am–4pm; free) under the direction of Dr Deryck Viney of Kármi. With nearly a thousand preserved specimens of plants endemic to the island, pressed in folders or pickled in spirit, this is really more of a library or research facility than tourist attraction; however, it is a handy place to pick up a number of flora guides offered for sale, including Dr Viney's manual of Cypriot plant life. The keeper of the small snack bar in the middle of the picnic grounds is very keen for custom, and will sell you a guide or fizzy drink with equal alacrity.

Antifonítis monastery

The twelfth-century **monastery church of Antifonítis**, tucked into a piney valley northeast of Alevkaya, was once the premier Byzantine monument of the Kyrenia hills. It takes its name – "He Who Answers" – from the foundation legend, in which a rich man and a poor man met at the place. The pauper asked for a loan from the grandee, who retorted, "Who will act as witness that I have loaned you the money?", to which the penniless one replied, "God". At once a celestial voice was heard sanctifying the transaction, and the monastery grew up around the miracle.

Getting there

There are two usual approaches. From the herbarium and recreation area, proceed northeast on the paved road, shunning the turn down to Karaağaç (Khárcha) and leaving the tarmac above Esentepe in favour of a dirt track contouring along just north of the watershed. Some 14km from Alevkaya, at an X-shaped junction, a sign points back against you, giving the distance to Alevkaya (9 miles), and another down and hairpin left to Esentepe (3.5 miles). Bear left ahead onto a steep, unmarked track – best to have a four-wheel-drive vehicle – and at the foot of this valley look out for the dome of the monastery church peeking above dense foliage.

From the coast road east of Kyrenia, turn off at the large village of **ESENTEPE (ÁYIOS AMVRÓSIOS, AYKURUŞ)**, once known for its apricots and crafts, and now resettled partly by natives of Áyios Nikólaos village in the Páfos hills. Traverse to the high end of Esentepe, following signposting to Alevkaya and Lefkoşa, but at the next junction, marked by a derelict forestry placard, go straight onto the dirt surface, rather than right with the pavement. The tiny monastic **church of Apáti**, not to be confused with Antifonítis and not worth the trouble getting up to, is soon seen above and to the right among pines. Shortly you'll reach the crossroads described above.

The site

The final couple of hundred metres of approach must be made on foot. A neglected, overgrown courtyard surrounds the twelfth-century *katholikón* which, while appealing, wins no prizes for architectural purity: the vaulted Lusignan narthex on the west side dates from the fourteenth century, and the Venetians added an arched loggia to the south in the following century.

Since 1974 the church's interior has been heartbreakingly vandalized, and is currently used as a goat pen. Of its once-vivid and notable **frescoes**, only the magnificent *Pandokrátor* survives undamaged in the huge irregularly shaped dome – supported by eight columns and covering the entire nave – plus the occasional saint or apostle out of reach on arches and columns. The tracery has been knocked out of the dome windows, allowing nesting swallows free passage.

Leaving Antifonítis, you can continue eastward on the forestry track system, though signposting has been allowed to deteriorate since 1974. Within a minute or two there's another major junction at a pass: down to the south leads towards Gönendere (Knodhára), straight keeps following the crest, and down and left goes to the rather poor village of Bahçeli (Kalogréa), just above the coast road.

travel details

Buses

From **Kyrenia** to: Famagusta (hourly; 1hr 30min); Güzelyurt (several daily; 1hr); Nicosia (every 15min; 30min). Daily out-and-back minibus services exist for most villages between Bahçeli in the east and Tepebaşı on the Kormakíti peninsula, but usefully frequent schedules only for Çatalköy, Ozanköy, Beylerbeyi and Lapta.

Ferries and hydrofoils

From **Kyrenia** to: Taşucu (Turkey), 2–3 car ferries daily except Sat & Sun, between 11.30am and 1pm (4–5hr); passenger-only catamarans or hydrofoils to Taşucu, 2–3 daily, summer only; catamaran to Alanya (Turkey), 3–4 weekly, summer only. See *Basics* for a complete discussion of companies and fares.

CHAPTER EIGHT

FAMAGUSTA AND THE KÁRPAS PENINSULA

The Mesarya (Turkish for Mesaoría) plain, hummocky and relatively confined around Nicosia, opens out to steppe-like dimensions as it approaches the long gradual arc of Famagusta Bay. This coast has been advancing slowly east over millennia, courtesy of silt brought down by the Kanlıdere River (the Pedhiéos in Greek), in recent centuries flowing intermittently at best.

At the southeast corner of the Mesarya, just as the land begins to rise appreciably to bluffs beyond the Attila Line, the town of **Famagusta** rears up, a Turko-Gothic chimera with no equal on Cyprus. It's the successor to ancient **Salamis**, a few miles north on the far side of bird-haunted wetlands fed by the sluggish Kanlıdere and fringed by beaches. Salamis in turn replaced older **Enkomi-Alasia** as the main port of the region; the narrow strip of plain between the two is peppered with **tombs** of various eras, one – supposedly that of the Apostle Barnabas – Christianized and until recently venerated. A **monastery** which honoured him now serves as the North's newest archeological museum.

The sandy shoreline here and at Varósha, south of Famagusta, saw the first mass tourism in Cyprus after independence, but now that Varósha is off-limits, the little fishing port of Boğaz anchors the otherwise functional row of resorts extending north of Salamis. It's also the gateway to the long, narrow **Kırpaşa (Kárpas)** peninsula, the island's panhandle and likened by more than one demagogic Turkish politician to a "dagger aimed at the underbelly of Anatolia". Today it is in fact almost insignificant militarily – depopulated, remote, and sprinkled

---

ACCOMMODATION PRICES IN THE NORTH

The hotels and apartment-hotels in the North which can offer rooms to independent travellers (ie those which are not monopolized by package-tour operators) have been categorized according to the price codes given below. These categories represent the minimum you can expect to pay in the high season for a double room or a two-person self-catering unit. As prices quoted in the unstable Turkish lira are fairly meaningless, the codes are based on the pound sterling, the most widely recognized foreign currency in the North, which can often be used to pay hotel bills. For further details, see p.26.

① £10–15	③ £20–25	⑤ over £30
② £15–20	④ £25–30	

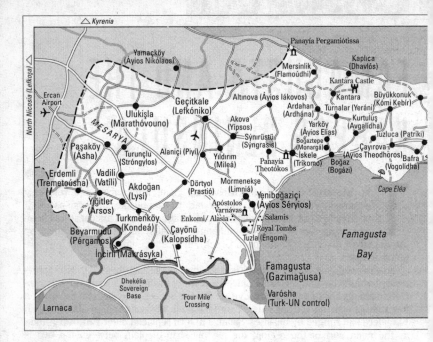

with traces of past importance, especially at the early Christian sites of **Ayía Triás**, **Áyios Fílon** and **Aféndrika**. The **castle of Kantara** effectively marks the base of the peninsula; the barely functioning **monastery of Apóstolos Andhréas** sits near the far end, between the finest beach on Cyprus and the desolate cape itself.

THE FAMAGUSTAN MESARYA

The de facto capital of Cyprus has always been in the immediate environs of Famagusta, with a combination of geology and military history determining its current location. Famagusta town presents a stark contrast to its featureless surroundings, which, particularly at twilight, take on a sinister aspect, perhaps from the numerous ancient dead in the graves of the Bronze Age and Roman cities.

Famagusta (Gazimağusa)

Its Venetian walls now enclosing almost nothing, the tracery of its exotic Gothic churches colliding in your field of vision with palm trees and upturned fishing boats, **FAMAGUSTA** (Gazimağusa, Mağosa, Ammókhostos) is the architectural equivalent of a well-behaved houseplant gone to seed in its native jungle. *Ammókhostos* means "sunken in sand" in Greek: its ramparts and deep harbour

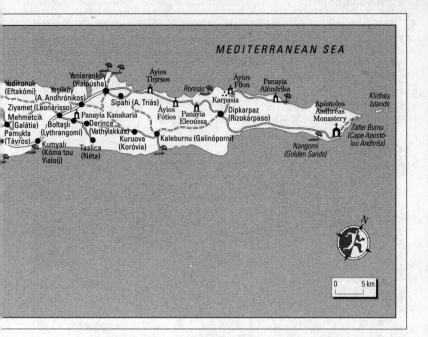

protect the old town from such a fate, but to the north, sand piles up in dunes, while offshore Maymun Adası (Monkey Island) is essentially a shifting spit. The climate is nearly subtropical, the sea air eating away metal and stone alike; in the years before swamp drainage, malarial mosquitoes had a similar effect on the people. All told, not much of a prospect for greatness.

Yet this was, briefly during the thirteenth century, the wealthiest city on earth, of sufficient romance for Shakespeare to make it purportedly part of the setting for *Othello*, a theory based on the brief stage instruction "a seaport in Cyprus".* Today Famagusta is a double city: the compact, ghostly walled town, a crumbling Lusignan-Venetian legacy, and the sprawling, amorphous new town, similarly derelict since 1974. If conditions do not change on Cyprus, it is easy to imagine both portions living up to the epithet of "sunken in sand" within decades.

Some history

By Cypriot standards Famagusta is a young settlement, though not quite so new as Limassol. Some historians derive the name from "Fama Augusta" after the Emperor Augustus, implying an imperial Roman foundation, but the place is really first heard from only after the seventh century, when the survivors of Arab-

---

*The character of **Othello** appears to be based on a historical Venetian soldier serving in Cyprus, most probably Francesco de Sessa, known as *Il Moro* for his dark complexion and banished in 1544 for an unspecified offence – along with two subordinates, possibly the models for Iago and Cassio.

sacked Salamis drifted here. It pottered along as a Byzantine fishing port, taking advantage of the only natural deep-water harbour on the island.

Boom

All that changed suddenly in 1291, after Palestinian Acre fell to the Saracens; Christian merchants poured in as refugees from a dozen entrepots on the Middle Eastern mainland. The pope forbade any trafficking with the infidel on pain of excommunication, thus guaranteeing Famagusta's monopoly – and spectacular growth. Every commodity of East and West, no matter how exotic, changed hands here; the city became a Babel of creeds, tongues and nationalities, reducing the native residents to a minority. Fortunes were literally made overnight, engendering spectacular exhibitionism and vulgarity: merchants' daughters wore more jewels at their weddings than certain European monarchs, and the prostitutes were as wealthy as the merchants, one of whom legendarily ground up a diamond to season a dish at table in full view of his guests.

Foreigners were fascinated and horrified in equal measure; Saint Bridget of Sweden, preaching in front of the cathedral (to a doubtless cynical audience), railed against the immorality of the city. The multiplicity of sects and perhaps guilty consciences resulted in scores of churches being built, supposedly one for every day of the year – many of them still standing.

Decline

But Famagusta's heyday lasted less than a century, for in 1372 a diplomatic contretemps triggered its decline. At the coronation of the Lusignan boy-king Peter II, a tussle between the Genoese and Venetian envoys as to the protocol of leading the royal horse degenerated into a brawl with massive loss of Genoese life and property. In revenge a Genoese expedition ravaged Cyprus over the next year, occupying Famagusta and inducing its traders to leave for Nicosia. James II expelled the Genoese in 1464, but it was already too late, and his Venetian widow, Queen Caterina Cornaro, presided over a diminished town before abdicating at the behest of her Venetian handlers in 1489.

Anticipating the growing Ottoman threat, the Venetian military governors busied themselves improving Famagusta's fortifications just as they had at Nicosia and Kyrenia, thickening the Lusignan walls to make them withstand the most powerful ordnance of the day. So when the Turks appeared in October 1570, having taken the rest of the island with relatively little resistance, it required a ten-month siege to reduce the city, where the Venetian garrison put up a heroic defence, though outnumbered twenty to one.

Turkish Famagusta

Under Ottoman rule, walled Famagusta became an emblem of decay; the bombardment needed to subdue it levelled or severely damaged almost every building, and for centuries the space within the walls lay desolate and weed-choked, inhabited only by garrisons under the command of soldiers disgraced elsewhere. Ottoman sultans favoured it as a place of exile for political prisoners, most famously (both during the nineteenth century) the Turkish nationalist poet Namik Kemal, and Suphi Ezel, founder of the Ezeli sect, an offshoot and rival of Bahaism. Christians were forbidden entry to, let alone residence in, *Kaleiçi* (the area within the ramparts), so that the predominantly Greek Orthodox town of Varósha (Maraş in Turkish) sprang up just south.

With independence and the subsequent communal troubles, old Famagusta again acquired significance as a Turkish stronghold. Greek Cypriots who had early this century ventured into Kaleiçi to live were expelled in 1964, while Turkish Cypriot refugees streamed into the town from vulnerable villages on the Mesarya. This trend accelerated during the tense weeks between July 20 and August 15, 1974, when the EOKA-B-dominated National Guard attacked any Turkish Cypriot they found outside the walls; the luckier ones entered Kaleiçi via a network of predug tunnels, joining both besieged civilians and the small TMT garrison holding down the port and walled town. Old Famagusta was relieved by the advancing Turkish Army on August 15, after the Greek Cypriots abandoned Varósha in the face of intense Turkish air raids. After the ceasefire went into effect the next day, the Turkish army pushed forward into Varósha, which, except for a few UN observation posts, they now effectively control (see box on p.283).

Arrival, information and accommodation

Coming **by boat** from Mersin, Turkey, you'll dock at the customs and passenger terminal, conveniently just east of the Sea Gate leading into the heart of the old town and open only for ferry arrivals. Arrival **by land** is equally uncomplicated; both the road from Salamis (**İsmet İnönü Caddesi** once within city limits) and the Nicosia highway (**Gazi Mustafa Kemal Bulvarı**, where the **bus terminal** is) converge on **Yirmisekiz Ocak Meydanı**, the roundabout directly opposite the Land Gate of the old city. Generally, **parking** within the old town presents no problems; if necessary drive to the thinly populated areas around the Canbulat Gate or Othello's Tower.

The **tourist information** bureau (nominally Mon–Fri 7.30am–2pm, plus Mon 3.30–6pm) is on **Fevzi Çakmak Bulvarı**, east of the main roundabout; as in Nicosia, don't expect much.

Accommodation

Since virtually all of the pre-1974 hotels were in now-inaccessible Varósha, there are few accommodation options in or around Kaleiçi – the overwhelming majority of visitors stay out on the beaches near Salamis. Of **in-town hotels**, both the *Panorama* on İlker Karter Caddesi, Maraş (☎36 65 880; ①), and the *Altın Tabya* at Kızıl Küle 9, inside the old city (☎36 65 363; ①), have lost their tourism ministry certifications and are lugubrious, if safe enough, places, patronized by travelling salesmen and long-term residents. On the shoreline next to the dead zone, the pastel-pink, five-star *Palm Beach Hotel* has a small private beach and boasts everything you'd expect for its star rating, including a casino, several bars, water sports, tennis courts and a gym (☎36 62 000, fax 36 62 002; offered by all the package-tour operators).

The City

Famagusta is usually visited as a full day trip or two shorter outings from a beachfront base further north. Interest is confined almost entirely to the Kaleiçi, but don't raise your expectations too high. What you get are the walls, built to last by the Venetians, and such churches as escaped Turkish ordnance and British vandalism. It's claimed that the Ottomans bombarded the town with more than 100,000 cannonballs during their siege, and many of these are still to be seen lying about. The devastated neighbourhoods were mostly never rebuilt, leaving vast expanses of desolate ground that can have changed little since the day the Ottomans entered the city.

The city walls

> *More complete than Istanbul or Antioch, stronger than Fez, Jerusalem and even Avila, [a] prince of walled cities . . .*

So enthused Colin Thubron in 1972 – and well he might, given the **walls'** average height of fifteen metres, thickness of eight metres, their fifteen bastions and five gates. Yet they were ultimately an exercise in futility, considering the Ottoman victory, though structurally they mostly withstood the test of the siege. The Venetians had gradually raised them atop existing Lusignan fortifications between 1489 and 1540, according to the latest precepts of engineering and ballistics.

The ramparts are still dry-moated on their three landward sides, overgrown with prickly bushes on top, and impossible to walk around owing to partial occupation by the Turkish Army. Content yourself instead with a stroll up the ramp near the southwestern **Land Gate** to the most spectacular bit, the **Ravelin** or **Rivettina Bastion**. This vast complex of guardhouses and galleries was protected by a double moat, the main one now crossed by an alarmingly rotten wooden bridge. The Ottomans knew it as the *Akkule* or "White Tower", from the Venetians' waving of the white flag of surrender from this point.

At the southeast corner of the perimeter, the **Canbulat Bastion** (sometimes Canpolat or Cambulat) takes its name from an Anatolian bey who, confronted by a spinning wheel studded with knives which the Venetians had mounted in the gate here, charged it with his horse. Both were cut to ribbons, but the infernal machine was also destroyed and for years Turkish women used to come to his tomb in the bastion to pray for sons as valiant as Canbulat.

Today the interior is home to a small **museum** (hours in constant flux, sample schedule winter daily 8am–4pm; summer daily 8.30am–1pm & 2.30–5pm; £1), not money terribly well spent as it's merely an assemblage of mediocre pottery, traditional dress, Ottoman weaponry, amphorae and Iznik tiles. On the wall, a famous engraving by Stephano Givellino of the siege, its text translated into English, somewhat redeems the collection.

Heading northwest on Canbulat Yolu from the namesake bastion, most of the buildings facing the wall are devoted to warehousing and customs brokerage – the harbour is just the other side of the ramparts, formerly accessible by the now-boarded-up Sea Gate, which along with the Citadel (see below) was one of the earliest Venetian improvements. Beside it squats a more naturalistic than usual **Venetian lion**: a legend says that once a year the mouth opens, and anyone lucky enough to be there at the unpredictable moment can stick their hand down its throat and extract a valuable object.

Around Namik Kemal Meydanı

Entering Kaleiçi through the Land Gate and along İstiklal Caddesi, you pass a concentration of basic tradesmen's restaurants and jewellery shops before seeing the fourteenth-century church of **Saints Peter and Paul** (later the Sinan Paşa Camii) on the left. Supposedly built by a merchant from the profits of a single business transaction, it's a rather inelegant, workaday building, its good condition assured by its former use as a mosque and current role as a venue for the state theatre.

Just north across the street, the Venetian governor's palace is little more than a shell, most of the site ignominiously cleared for use as a car park. The remaining east facade is admittedly impressive, facing **Namik Kemal Meydanı**, the town centre named after a dissident Ottoman writer of the late nineteenth century; a bust of the man stands outside, near the Kaleiçi's main taxi ranks. His **dungeon** (open sporadically as a museum), where he spent 38 months at the sultan's pleasure for writing a seditious play, incorporates a surviving bit of palace. North of the palace precinct, the equally ruined church of St Francis abuts a set of **Turkish baths**, now disused and formerly home to a disco.

Lala Mustafa Paşa Camii (St Nicholas Cathedral)

Dominating the eastern side of the square, the **Lala Mustafa Paşa Camii** (10p donation suggested; headscarves and leg-coverings provided) is the most

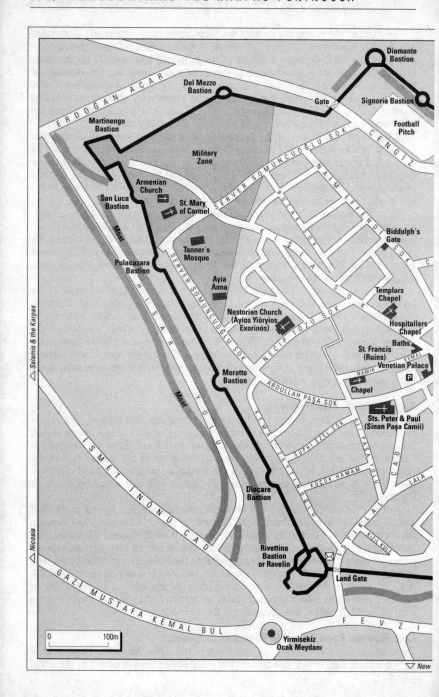

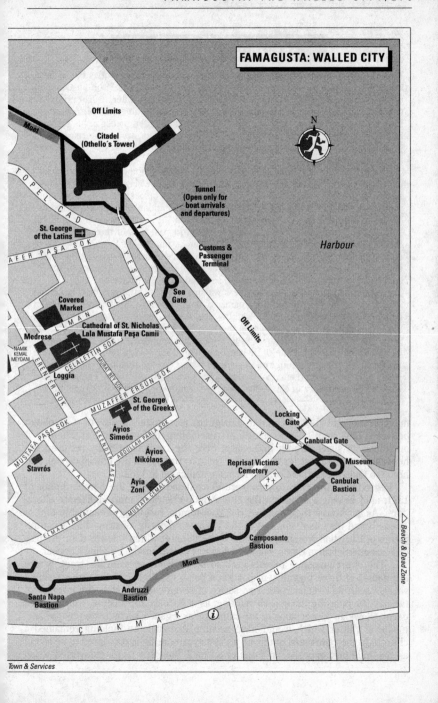

FAMAGUSTA: WALLED CITY

Off Limits

Moat

Citadel
(Othello's Tower)

TOPEL CAD

St. George
of the Latins

Tunnel
(Open only for
boat arrivals
and departures)

AFER PAŞA SOK

Customs &
Passenger
Terminal

Harbour

Covered
Market

Sea
Gate

LIMAN YOLU

Medrese

Cathedral of St. Nicholas
Lala Mustafa Paşa Camii

NAMIK
KEMAL
MEYDANI

CELALETTIN SOK

Off Limits

ERENLER SOK

Loggia

MURAT BEY SOK

MUZAFFER ERSUN SOK

St. George
of the Greeks

CANBULAT YOLU

Locking
Gate

MUSTAFA PAŞA SOK

İSKENDER PAŞA

Áyios
Simeón

ABDULLAH PAŞA SOK

Canbulat Gate

Stavrós

Áyios
Nikólaos

PIYALE PAŞA

Reprisal Victims
Cemetery

Museum

Canbulat
Bastion

Ayia
Zoní

MUSTAFA CEMAL SOK

ELMAS TABYA

ALTIN TABYA SOK

Camposanto
Bastion

Moat

BUL

Beach & Dead Zone

Santa Napa
Bastion

Andruzzi
Bastion

ÇAKMAK

ⓘ

Town & Services

THE SIEGE OF FAMAGUSTA AND BRAGADINO'S MARTYRDOM

The **1570–71 siege of Famagusta** ranks as one of the great battles of medieval times: for ten months a force of 8000 Greeks and Venetians held off an Ottoman army of almost 200,000, and the outcome might have been different had promised relief from Venice and Crete ever arrived. The Venetian commander, **Marcantonio Bragadino**, was brilliant and as resourceful with the limited means at his disposal as could be expected; Lala (Mentor) Mustafa Paşa, his Ottoman counterpart, was a seasoned if unimaginative campaign veteran whose main weakness of character was an explosive temper.

The entrance of Famagusta harbour could be chained shut, starting from a salient of the Othello Tower; the opening at the south end of Maymun Adası (Monkey Island) didn't then exist. Thus the Turks concentrated on assaults of the south and west land walls, avoiding the north and west with its formidable Martinengo Bastion. Armenian sappers dug coils of trenches towards the ramparts deep enough to completely conceal the Turkish soldiery except for the tops of their turbans; the main evidence of their presence on the plain around the city was a forest of campaign tents, three miles wide. The sappers also burrowed under the walls, setting off mines, while the Ottoman artillery of 150 guns (as opposed to the 90 small-bore weapons of their adversaries) reduced the walls from afar.

Despite this pounding, little progress was made by the attackers over the initial winter of siege, with Bragadino organizing bold sorties to create the impression that he had manpower to spare – and also to raid for necessary food. On July 7, 1571 the Turks gained a foothold on the Rivettina bastion, and started to scale the walls. Seeing how the structure was useless for its intended purpose, the Venetian command detonated a mine of their own prepared for such a moment, burying a thousand Turks (and a hundred of their own men) in the resulting rubble, which partly blocked further enemy advance. The defenders fell back behind hastily improvised barricades of earth-filled carts and sandbags; with the relief fleet having

magnificent and best-preserved Lusignan monument in town. Completed between 1298 and 1326 to a design resembling the cathedral at Rheims, it outshines its sister church in Nicosia; here the Lusignan royalty received the honorary crown of lost Jerusalem after their coronation in the official capital, and here too Queen Caterina Cornaro formally abdicated in 1489.

Regrettably, the twin towers were decapitated during the bombardment of 1571; after seizing Famagusta the Ottomans perpetrated more deliberate alterations. As at Nicosia they emptied the floor-tombs, including presumably that of James II and his infant son, last of the Lusignan dynasty; destroyed all accoutrements of Christian worship; and added the minaret which – lower than the pair on Nicosia's Selimiye Camii – happily detracts little from the building's appeal.

The church-mosque reveals itself to best advantage from the **west**, where the gables of three magnificent porticoes point still higher to the fine six-paned window with its circular rose. Two series of seven columns stalk the **interior** of the nave, supporting the superb vaulting; as at Nicosia, the austere, whitewashed decor allows an appreciation of the cathedral's elegance, undistracted by the late-medieval clutter which would have accumulated had the building remained a church. In the **courtyard** out front, a giant sycamore fig is rumoured to be as old as the building; opposite, in front of a small Venetian loggia converted to an failed to materialize, the situation inside the city became increasingly desperate, with plague spreading and rats or cats figuring in the diet. On August 1, having lost nearly three-quarters of his forces, Bragandino ran up the white flag, and negotiated a surrender whereby civilians were to be unmolested and he and his men were to be given safe conduct to Crete in Turkish ships.

When the remnant of the garrison emerged from the smoking ruins and staggered over to the Turkish lines, the besiegers were amazed that so few men had been able to mount such courageous resistance against hopeless odds, and were moved to pity by their woebegone appearance. At first the defeated were received with kindness and all courtesy, even by the volatile Lala Mustafa himself, but the flouting of Turkish might for so long – and his own casualties of over 50,000 – must have preyed on the general's mind, for Bragadino's audience with him suddenly turned sour.

Lala Mustafa abruptly demanded retention of the Venetian officer Quirini as security against the safe return of the Turkish fleet from Crete; when Bragadino protested that this hadn't been part of the agreed surrender, Lala Mustafa accused him of murdering fifty civilian prisoners in the last weeks of the siege. Working himself up into one of the towering rages he was known for, the Turk summoned his executioner and before Bragadino's horrified eyes Quirini and two other assistant commanders were hacked to bits. Then came Bragadino's turn: his nose and ears were sliced off, and he was thrown into a dungeon for ten days before being retrieved, publicly humiliated in various ways, and finally chained between two pillars in front of the cathedral and flayed alive. Eyewitness accounts agree that Bragadino bore all these torments in dignity and silence, and that even many Turks disapproved of these and other atrocities perpetrated by their frenzied leader.

But Lala Mustafa Paşa was not to be mollified: he gutted the body, stuffed Bragadino's skin with straw, and paraded it around the city on a cow, under the red parasol which the Venetian had jauntily used when marching out to give himself up. The stuffed skin was later ransomed from Istanbul at considerable cost by Bragadino's descendants, and it now rests in an urn at the Venetian church of SS Giovanni e Paolo.

Islamic ablutions fountain, stand a pair of granite columns from Salamis, between which the hapless Bragadino was flayed. The *Faisal Islamic Bank*, across the courtyard from the loggia, occupies what was formerly a *medrese* or Koranic academy, while across Liman Yolu, unsung in most tourist literature, the **covered market** occupies a building at least partly Venetian.

The Citadel (Othello's Tower)

The treasure-lion in front of the Sea Gate, at the seaward end of Liman Yolu, is complemented by a larger relief lion of St Mark above the entry to the **Citadel** (daily 8am–1pm & 2–5pm; £1.50), 100m north across the oval roundabout. Originally a Lusignan fort, which was extensively remodelled between 1489 and 1492, this Venetian strongpoint is popularly known as **"Othello's Tower"**, after Famagusta's Shakespearean connections. On the far side of the courtyard, partly taken up by a stage used for folkloric performances, the **Great Hall**, 28m long, boast fine vaults whose limestone groin ribbing is, however, mostly eaten away by the all-corroding sea air.

From the **northeast tower**, you can peer over the industrial harbour; you'll get no closer, as the protruding citadel mole is as militarily important today as in medieval times. Up on the perimeter parapet, **ventilation shafts** or cistern mouths alternate with rooms whose roofs were stove in by the bombardment. Some of these shafts lead down to Lusignan passages and chambers which the Venetians either filled up or simply sealed at one end, giving rise to the persistent theory that somewhere in this citadel is hidden the fortune of the Venetian merchants, who were only allowed to leave the city empty-handed by the victorious Ottomans. This legend has exercised the Turkish imagination ever since, with investigations conducted periodically; similar hollows in the Martinengo bastion served as a bomb shelter for two thousand civilians during August 1974.

Minor churches: the north of town

Just southwest of Othello's Tower, **St George of the Latins** is one of the oldest Famagustan churches, originally part of a fortified monastery which may predate the Lusignan ramparts. Today it's merely a shell, but a romantic one; on the surviving apse and north wall, a group of carved bats peer out of a column capital. Nearby on Naim Effendi Sokağı, **Biddulph's Gate** is a remnant doorway of a vanished mansion and named in honour of an early high commissioner who made it an exception to the pattern of British destructiveness.

Naim Effendi leads towards the northwest corner of Kaleiçi, a military zone since 1974; the Martinengo bastion in the wall was never stormed by the Turks in their first campaign, and the returning modern Turkish army seems to have taken the hint of impregnability. Access to the churches of **Ayía Ánna**, **St Mary of Carmel**, and the **Armenians**, or the (converted) **Tanners Mosque**, is therefore restricted at present, with photography out of the question.

One church which you can at least approach is the fourteenth-century Nestorian church of **Áyios Yióryios Exorinós**, usually locked but used as an occasional cultural centre by the local university. Built by one of the fabulously wealthy Lakhas brothers, he of the jewel-sprinkling incident (see p.274), it was before 1964 the parish church of the small Greek Orthodox community. The epithet *exorinós* means "the exiler", after a strange legend, reminiscent of the one pertaining to Áyios Misitikós in Páfos (see p.115): dust gathered from the floor and tossed in an enemy's house would cause them to die or leave the island within a year.

Nearby on Kışla Sokağı, on the way back to Namik Kemal Meydanı, the adjacent box-like churches of the **Knights Templar** and **Knights Hospitaller**, both fourteenth-century, enjoy a proximity which those rival orders never had in their day. The chapel of the Templars is distinguished by a pretty rose window out front, and is now used as a theatre and art gallery; the Hospitallers' chapel serves as music rehearsal hall.

More churches: the south

The otherwise unremarkable Lusignan church of Stavrós, two blocks south of Namik Kemal Meydanı, marks a small concentration of **arched lanes and medieval houses** on Lala Mustafa Paşa Sokağı, all that survived the siege and later developers. A few steps east, half-demolished **St George of the Greeks**, an uneasy Byzantine-Gothic hybrid whose three rounded apses clash with the two rows of column stumps, stands cheek-by-jowl with the purer Byzantine but equally ruinous **Áyios Simeón**, tacked onto its south wall.

VAROSHA GHOST TOWN

Only a small fraction of the new town, called Maraş by the Turks, is currently inhabited; the rest, by the terms of the 1974 ceasefire, is technically UN territory but effectively under Turkish Army control, a ghost town entered only occasionally by UNFICYP forces since then. Their patrols, and specially escorted journalists, reported light bulbs burning for years, washing in tatters on the line, and uncleared breakfast dishes, so precipitous was the Greek Cypriots' departure.

Behind the barricade of wire and oil drums, weeds have attained tree-like dimensions on the streets and inside buildings, while cats, rats and snakes prowl as in Nicosia's dead zone. The fate of the Famagusta Archeological Museum's contents is unknown, but unlikely to be happy in light of how the magnificent, private Hadjiprodhromou archeological collection was looted and dispersed for sale quite openly on the international market. In contrast to the automotive "time capsule" in Nicosia, the Turks here helped themselves to the contents of an automobile showroom, with the exception of a single Alfa Romeo that remains inside to this day.

The disposition of Varósha has figured high on the agenda of nearly every intercommunal negotiating session since 1974. Greek Cypriots see its return to use as an initial gesture of good faith for progress on any other issue: the town has practical as well as symbolic significance, since with 40,000 former Greek inhabitants its **resettlement** could solve a goodly fraction of the South's refugee problem.

With Northern tourism at its current modest level, the Turkish Cypriots have little need for the row of 33 mouldering, not-quite-state-of-the-art **hotels** which line Varósha's long, narrow beach, but they have periodically proposed that a limited number of Greek Cypriots return to manage the 3000-bed resort. The South has refused, objecting that these offers are always couched in such a way as to make it clear that the hotels would be run largely for the financial benefit of the North.

Meanwhile, fully exposed to the elements, most of Varósha has attained write-off condition, and it's hard to avoid the suspicion that the Turkish side is maintaining Varósha in its present status for use as a **bargaining chip** at some crucial stage of negotiations.

Two more tiny but exquisite late Byzantine chapels stand to the south amid palm-tree greenery: battered **Áyios Nikólaos**, and intact **Ayía Zoní**, which make a satisfying duo seen juxtaposed.

Maraş

Polat Paşa, the commercial main street of inhabited **Maraş**, currently parades grandiosely to nowhere – behind the oil-drum-and-sand-bag barricades at its south end, where it detours abruptly, rusty street and shop signs in Greek and the dome of a church are visible. About halfway down, in front of the courthouse, a parked **locomotive**, built in 1904 by a Leeds company, seems far less derelict than anything in the dead zone. It plied the now-vanished Lefke–Famagusta railway from 1907 until 1951: the tracks were to have been extended to Larnaca, but the mayor vetoed the plan to protect local camel drivers from the competition. At the time he was roundly jeered for the decision, but in the event the camel caravans outlasted the trains by over a decade.

Out on the shore, the *Palm Beach Hotel* is virtually the last occupied building in Maraş before the dead zone; beyond sheet-metal barricades, emblazoned with no-photography signs, begins the long, Benidorm-like row of abandoned 1960s hotels, many bearing marks of shelling, and the northernmost one partly bull-dozed to form a clear zone.

Eating, drinking and nightlife

Given the dearth of accommodation within the actual city limits, eating and drinking options are similarly limited – you can count the **restaurants** of distinction on one hand, and simple affairs for local tradesmen on the other.

Just inside the Land Gate on Elmaz Tabya 17, *Agora* specializes in *fırın kebab* (meat baked in a clay oven) and is open for lunch and supper daily except Sunday; order a double portion, however, as this dish contains a high proportion of bone and gristle. You can get further carniverous platters at the *Viyana*, with seating in a garden setting near the apse of Lala Mustafa Paşa Camii on Liman Yolu. Diagonally across the street from the *Viyana*, the diminutive *Esra* does *pide* as well as chicken kebabs.

Opposite the telephone office on Polat Paşa Bulvarı in accessible Maraş, *Cyprus House* serves lunch and supper daily except Sunday amidst an interesting antique decor, with a more varied menu and occasional evening floor shows.

The *Petek Pastanesi* on the corner of Liman Yolu and Yeşildeniz Sokağı is an oasis of glitz in the otherwise down-at-heel old town; enjoy your sweet or ice cream at seating arrayed around an indoor fountain. As for consistent nightlife, you're pretty much restricted to the nightclub, casino and discotheque inside the *Palm Beach Hotel*.

Listings

Airline *(Cyprus) Turkish Airlines*, İlker Karter Caddesi, Maraş (☎36 67 799).

Car rental *Atlantic*, c/o *Adataş*, Sinan Paşa Sokağı (☎36 63 277); *Benzincioğlu* (☎36 65 479); *Sur*, İsmet İnönü Cad (☎36 65 600).

Exchange The *Kıbrıs Türk Kooperatif Merkez Bankası* has a free-standing cashpoint machine 3km out on İsmet İnönü Caddesi on the way to Salamis, at the university gate, while the *İş Bankası* has a more central one opposite the Lala Mustafa Paşa Camii. Otherwise use the *Batu* agency, across from Saints Peter and Paul in the old town, or *Şehzade*, opposite Lala Mustafa.

Ferry agency *KTML* has its well-signposted sales office on Ecevit Caddesi (☎36 64 557), southeast of the Venetian walls near the naval base; you might also try in the passenger terminal itself a few hours before sailing.

Post offices Main branch on İlker Karter Cad, Maraş (Mon–Fri 8am–1pm & 2–5pm), with a more convenient branch in the Ravelin.

Public toilets Easiest to find are those behind the *Erin Fırını* on İstiklal Caddesi in Kaleiçi, or a set by the parking lot behind the Templars' chapel.

Telephones The *Telekomünikasyon Dairesi* on Polat Paşa Bulvarı (daily 8am–1pm & 2–8pm) sells cards for its three cardphones, and also has a rare metered counter phone.

Salamis

The most famous and important ancient city of Cyprus, **SALAMIS** remains the island's most prominent archeological site, for once living up to the tourist-brochure hype. Even if your interest is casual, you'll need a few hours to see the best-preserved highlights; a full day can easily be spent on the site, especially if you allow for periodic intermissions at the wonderful beach that fringes Salamis

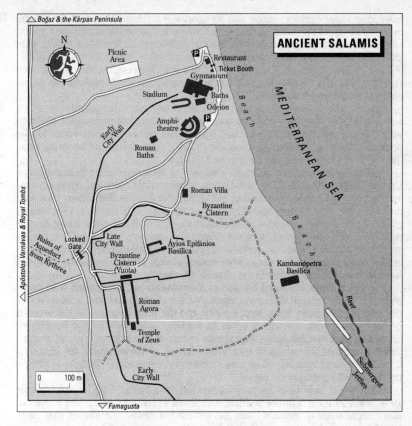

Boğaz & the Kárpas Peninsula

ANCIENT SALAMIS

N

Picnic Area

Restaurant
Ticket Booth
Gymnasium

Stadium

Baths

Odeion

Early City Wall

Amphi-theatre

Roman Baths

MEDITERRANEAN SEA

Beach

Beach

Roman Villa

Byzantine Cistern

Apóstolos Varnávas & Royal Tombs

Ruins of Aqueduct from Kythrea

Locked Gate

Late City Wall

Byzantine Cistern (Vuota)

Áyios Epifánios Basilica

Kambanópetra Basilica

Reef

Roman Agora

Temple of Zeus

Early City Wall

Submerged Jetties

0   100 m

Famagusta

to the east. Various, mostly Roman and Byzantine monuments are widely scattered – it's well over a kilometre from the entrance to the ancient harbour, for example – so if you have a vehicle, bring it along on the site, as well as stout footwear, sun protection and drinking water.

Some history

To Salamis are ascribed quasi-mythical foundations in the twelfth century BC by the Trojan war hero **Teucer** (Tefkros), exiled by his father King Telamon from the **Greek isle of Salamis**. The young city shared not only the name but the Mycenaean culture of its parent – borne out spectacularly by the finds in the nearby royal tombs (p.288) – and quickly replaced nearby Enkomi-Alasia as the chief settlement on the coastal bight here. By the eighth century it was already the greatest of the ten Cypriot city-kingdoms, and within two hundred years Salamis was the first place on the island to mint coinage.

The city was the leader in the first fifth-century revolt against the Persians; **Onesilos** temporarily deposed his brother King Gorgos, a Persian collaborator, and commanded a hastily thrown-together Hellenic confederacy at the Battle of Salamis – lost mostly because of treachery on the part of the Kourion faction.

Later that same century, native son **Evagoras** – a remarkable man for whom every other street seems to be named in the South – shrewdly united the Cypriot city-kingdoms in another, somewhat more durable, pro-Hellenic federation, with culture as well as politics orientated towards peninsular Greece. Despite his political and military ingenuity Evagoras could not actually prevail against Persia, but over a period of a decade fought the oriental empire to a standstill, finally negotiating a vassalage relationship.

Salamis actively assisted Alexander the Great and was subsequently rewarded with the copper revenues of Tamassos. But under the Ptolemaic kings, the city briefly fell on evil times. Its last king, **Nicocreon**, rather than surrender to the besieging Ptolemy I, committed suicide in 295 BC, as did all his surviving relatives, who torched the royal palace before doing so.

During the **Roman era**, although Paphos was designated the official capital of Cyprus, Salamis remained the island's main commercial centre and figured prominently in early Christianity: another native son, the Apostle **Barnabas**, lived and died here (for the full story see "The monastery-museum of Apóstolos Varnávas", p.289). In the Jewish revolt of 116 AD, it is thought that the city's entire gentile population was slaughtered; after the Romans had put down the rebellion, Jewish residence on the island was forbidden, an edict not effectively countermanded until a small colony of European Jews settled nearby at the Mesaorian village of Koúklia (today Köprülü) late in the nineteenth century.

The **Byzantines** renamed Salamis as **Constantia** and designated it an archbishopric and capital of the island again, but the earthquakes and tidal waves of the mid-fourth century badly hurt the city, and the Arab invasions of the seventh century, along with the silting up of its harbour, administered the final blow. From this time neighbouring Famagusta began its ascendancy. Bits of ancient Salamis, used as a convenient quarry throughout medieval times, are scattered throughout contemporary villages and towns of the Kanlıdere (Pedhiéos) River's flood plain which drains the region.

Salamis had only been partially **excavated** by a Franco-Cypriot team before 1974, and assuming a future political settlement which permits further research, more archeological treasures can be anticipated under the dunes that have largely covered the city since its abandonment.

The main site

The ruins lie eight to nine kilometres north of Famagusta between the main highway and the beach, served in theory by any bus heading for Boğaz or beyond. More effectively than the small official "Salamis" signs, a placard for the *Bedi Restaurant* marks the one-kilometre side turning off the coast road, passing a piney picnic area to the north and the **site entrance** (daily sunrise–sunset; £2), flanked by an "improved" beach and the aforementioned restaurant.

The gymnasium

A rusty arrow directs you towards the walkway of the **gymnasium's east portico**, probably once covered over and still mosaic-paved in variegated Byzantine-era marble, with two rectangular plunge-pools at either end. The northerly one is ringed by a gallery of headless statues, decapitated by Christian zealots in a fury against pagan idolatry; some are now in the Cyprus Museum in south Nicosia, others have allegedly disappeared since 1974.

To the west, an impressive, photogenic **colonnade**, re-erected during the 1950s after being tumbled by earthquakes, stakes out the quad of the gymnasium's **palaestra**. The eastern series is taller, and the whole mismatched and hotch-potchy, because the Byzantines recycled Hellenistic and Roman columns from the theatre and another building without too much regard for symmetry or which capitals belonged where. The semicircular structure at the southwest corner of the palaestra is a **latrine**, capacity 44; the flush pipe and tank are still visible at the rear, as are armrests to one side – privacy was not a concern, elimination being considered by the Romans as another social event.

The baths

East of the palaestra and portico loom the **baths**, like the gymnasium a Byzantine reworking of Hellenistic and Roman predecessors. Just off the portico another set of cool-water pools – one nearly circular, one octagonal – sandwich the giant **west-central hall** (reckoned the *tepidarium* or mildly steamy anteroom) whose under-floor heating cavity is exposed. Over the south entry, a Christian **fresco fragment** shows two faces, one angelic, executed in a naturalistic, almost Buddhist style.

At the seaward end of the **east-central hall** (probably the *caldarium* or hot-plunge room) another, elevated, pool has been partially restored, and a dank, crypt-like cavity under its floor can be entered. This hall contains further mosaics: a patch of abstracts in a niche of the north wall, and another one of an orange on its tree in the northerly semi-dome of the **north hall**, probably a hot-steam "sauna" chamber.

The best, most complete **mosaics** in the entire complex, however, are found in the south bays of the **south hall**, possibly an alternative entry way. The smaller one shows the river god Evrotas – part of a damaged version of Leda and the Swan – while the other displays the shield and quiver of a fragmentary warrior, part of a scene whose identity is disputed: either Apollo and Artemis slaying the Niobids, or a battle between men and Amazons.

The amphitheatre

Another paved and partly colonnaded way leads south from the palaestra, between a vaulted structure with banks of seats against its south wall – probably an **odeion** (concert venue) – and an unexcavated area to the west, thought to be a small **stadium**. Both are overshadowed by the fine Roman **amphitheatre**, dating from the reign of Augustus and not over-restored as these things go. From the top eighteen surviving rows of seats you have excellent perspectives over the site. Occasional performances still take place during tourist season, though not attracting anything like the original capacity of 15,000.

Áyios Epifánios basilica

Continuing southwest from the amphitheatre along the paved drive, there seems little left at first glance of the six-aisled **basilica of Áyios Epifánios** other than the stumps of four rows of fourteen columns, but at the rear (east) of the southern-most naves, mosaic flooring covers a **crypt**, the presumed tomb of the patron saint, emptied by Byzantine Emperor Leo for the sake of its holy relics. In the manner of so many post-Arab-raid churches on Cyprus, this shrunken area around the crypt was refurbished for use after the rest of the basilica was destroyed.

Nearby, an aqueduct bringing water from Kythrea ended at the giant **Byzantine cistern** or *Vuota* beside the **Roman agora**, at the far end of which are the negligible remains of a **Zeus temple**.

Kambanópetra basilica

Most recently excavated, and perhaps more interesting, the romantically set fourth-century **Kambanópetra basilica** overlooks the sea from one curve of a dirt track leading towards the southeast corner of the archeological zone. Its western forecourt, with small rooms giving onto it, may have been a colonnaded agora or an early monastic cloister. The central apse of the three-aisled nave was provided with a *synthronon* or seats for church dignitaries, while a fourth aisle to the south contains a half-dozen marble sarcophagi.

A handful of standing columns to the east belong to yet another set of **baths**, as suggested by some tumbled-over hypocaust bricks and a tank with a fill-hole. The highlight here is a magnificent **opus sectile floor** (see p.373), consisting of concentric rings of alternating light and dark triangles, the most elaborate mosaic at Salamis.

The beach

The **beach** fringing the entire site is particularly accessible just below Kambanópetra. A reef encloses a small lagoon, extending all the way south past a cape before subsiding; snorkelling in the metre-deep water, you see not only fish but long courses of man-made stone – the **jetty** or breakwater of the **ancient port** – on the sea floor. The wind is often brisk here, and the ancient harbour facilities were distributed to either side of the point, for use according to the weather. But there has been so much quake-generated subsidence, and silting-up courtesy of the river, that it's difficult to envisage the ancient shore profile.

The Royal Tombs

Just 100m south of the disused, locked Salamis west gate, a side road heads off west for 500m to a yet smaller turning, signposted for the **Royal Tombs** (partially fenced; £1 fee when warden present). Two of the nearly 150 eighth- and seventh-century burial sites and graves here caused a sensation when discovered in 1957, because they confirmed Homer's descriptions of Late Bronze Age funerary rites, and their observance five centuries after the original Mycenaean homeland on the Greek Peloponnese had passed its zenith.

Most of the tombs had already been looted in antiquity, but others, in particular **Tombs 47 and 79** east of the access drive, yielded the elaborate remains of several royal funerals. Hoards of precious metal or ivory objects, pottery, weapons and food containers were all intended to serve the dead in the underworld, and included the famous ivory inlaid throne and bed – showing profound Phoenician/Egyptian influence – now in the Cyprus Museum.

All of the tombs save one opened to the east, and were approached by gently slanting *dromoi* or ramps – on which the most telling artefacts were unearthed. Over the years at least four ceremonial chariots bearing a king's bier had been drawn by pony-like horses to a certain point on the ramps, where the deceased was cremated after the horse (and frequently favourite human servants) were ritually sacrificed. East of three of the tombs the preserved, paired skeletons of the slaughtered horses have been left rather gruesomely in situ, protected by glass plates. A few of the terrified horses broke their own necks at the deadly moment by lunging in their tackle, and at least some of the attendants did not willingly follow their masters in death, as can be gathered by human remains in the *dromoi* discovered bound hand and foot.

Officially **Tomb 50**, the so-called "St Catherine's prison" became associated with the Alexandrian saint through a Cypriot legend proposing her as a native of Salamis, briefly imprisoned here by her father the Roman governor for refusing an arranged marriage. That this tomb didn't start life as a Christian place of worship is dramatically borne out by the well-preserved pair of fossilized horses found adjacent; the T-shaped subterranean interior, with a vaulted antechamber and tiny tunnel-like room that was the tomb, still bears some ecclesiastical trappings. The upper courses of masonry date from the Roman/Byzantine era, when they were built atop the tomb itself, hidden from Christian worshippers until the excavations.

Three tombs to the west of the access drive include a prominent tumulus concealing a mud-brick **"beehive" chamber** nearly identical in design to those at Greek Mycenae. South of these, less exalted citizens were interred in the Kellarka complex, apparently used well into Christian times.

The small adjacent **museum** (daily 8am–sunset, same ticket) displays plans and photographs of the tombs and excavations, plus a reconstruction of one chariot used to transport the dead kings to the necropolis: the brass fittings and horse ornamentations are original, remounted on facsimiles of the long-decayed wooden structures.

Salamis area practicalities

In the immediate environs of Salamis various tourist amenities beckon. South of the ruins, once past a soldiers' beach, **Glapsides** and **"Silver" beaches** tout camping as well as swimming, though in this case "camping" seems merely to mean the pitching of sun-flaps for day use. The only organized **campsite**, *Onur* (☎37 65 314), with an attached restaurant, lies a couple of kilometres north of the archeological site.

Between Salamis and Boğaz, the shoreline features intermittent sandy patches, occasionally ballooning out into respectably wide beaches; eucalyptus, planted by the British to drain the local marshes, thrive just inland, though there are still plenty of mosquitoes about on summer nights.

The chalet-like *Park Hotel* (☎37 88 213, fax 36 65 113; available through tour operators *President*, *Celebrity* and *CTA*) stands slightly to the north of the ruins, right on the beach like all of the **accommodation** on this stretch. The self-contained luxury complex *Salamis Bay* is a bit of an overwhelming behemoth; the adjacent *Mimoza* (☎37 88 219, fax 37 88 209; available through *President*) is more intimate, while sharing most of the *Salamis Bay*'s facilities, such as the tennis courts. More or less halfway between Salamis and Boğaz, the recently built *Cyprus Gardens* (☎37 12 567, fax 37 12 722; available through *President*, *Celebrity*, *Mosaic*, *Imperial* and *CTA*) is a well-designed self-catering complex with tennis and pony-riding on offer.

Monastery-museum of Apóstolos Varnávas

Continuing 500m further on the same minor road that serves the Royal Tombs, you soon approach the former **monastery of Apóstolos Varnávas** (daily 8am–sunset; £1.50), recently refurbished as a museum. A monastic community first grew up here in the fifth century following the discovery of the purported tomb of the Apostle Barnabas, with funds provided for its construction by the Byzantine emperor himself. The Arab raiders destroyed this foundation during their seventh-century pillagings; the present church and cloister date from 1756, though some columns from Salamis are incorporated into the church.

Until 1974 Apóstolos Varnávas was a favourite goal of pilgrimage among Famagustans, with sequential baptisms being conducted by one of three look-alike, Santa-Claus-bearded monks: Barnabas, Stefanos and Khariton. Since 1917 these three (biological) brothers had presided over the monastery, supporting it through sales of honey and mass-produced icons popular with the nearby villagers, but of rather limited artistic merit. Somehow they contrived to stay after August 1974, but finally, too weak and old to combat Turkish harassment, gave up and moved to the South in 1976, living out their days at Stavrovoúni monastery near Larnaca.

The museum

It's certainly not the **icon collection**, housed in the former *katholikón*, that justifies the entrance fee; the oldest and most artistically worthy is an unusual *Herod's*

BARNABAS AND THE AUTOCEPHALOUS CHURCH OF CYPRUS

Barnabas (*Varnávas* in Greek), a native of Salamis, was the companion of the Apostle Paul on missionary voyages around Cyprus and Asia Minor before their falling-out over whether or not Barnabas' cousin Mark was to accompany them overseas. He is generally credited with being the apostle most influential in introducing Christianity to the island, and – long after his demise – with perpetuating its independent status through a miraculous intervention.

His activities having aroused the ire of the Salamis Jewish community into which he had been born, Barnabas was martyred by stoning in about 75 AD; thereafter matters become apocryphal, with most accounts having Mark interring the corpse at an undisclosed location. There things would have rested had it not been for an ecclesiastical squabble four hundred years later.

Late in the fifth century the Church of Antioch, having been founded by Peter and thus an Apostolic See, claimed precedence over that of Cyprus, which retorted, initially unsuccessfully, that as a foundation of the Apostle Barnabas the island's Church was also apostolic and of equal rank. Subordination to the Syrian archbishopric was only avoided through the supernatural intervention of Barnabas himself, who appeared in a dream to Anthemios, Archbishop of Salamis, and bade him unearth the apostle's remains from a lonely spot on the Mesaoría marked by a carob tree. Following these instructions, the cleric indeed found a catacomb matching the description and containing what could well have been the bones of Barnabas, clasping a mildewed copy (in Hebrew) of the Gospel of St Matthew to his breast. Armed with these incontrovertible relics, the Cypriots went to Constantinople, where a synod convened by the Emperor Zeno was sufficiently impressed to grant special privileges to the island's Church.

Foremost it was to remain autocephalous (autonomous), deferring only to the sees of Constantinople, Alexandria, Antioch and Jerusalem in importance, and in later centuries pre-eminent over larger autocephalous churches, such as those in Russia. Cypriot bishops retained the right to elect their own archbishop, who was permitted to sign his name in red ink in imitation of the Byzantine emperor's custom, wear imperial purple, and wield a sceptre instead of a pastoral staff.

When Cyprus fell to the Ottomans, these hitherto symbolic privileges acquired practical import inasmuch as the churchmen were charged with the civil as well as the spiritual administration of their Orthodox flock. Following independence, Archbishop Makarios revived the medieval term "ethnarch", further blurring the lines between secular and ecclesiastical power, with ultimately catastrophic consequences for the island.

Banquet (1858), with John the Baptist being beheaded in the lower frame. Most seem scrabbled-together replacements for 35 more valuable ones which went mysteriously missing from the lightly guarded premises in 1982.

The former cells around the appealingly landscaped court have been converted into what is at present the North's best **archeological museum**; how much, if any of it, is based on the looted Hadjiprodhromou collection or the holdings of the inaccessible Famagusta Archeological Museum (see box on p.283) is uncertain. Eras are presented slightly out of order, proceeding clockwise from the Bronze Age to the Venetian period, with a strangely mixed Ottoman/Classical Greek wing at the end. Labelling gives only dates, with few indications of provenance.

The Bronze Age room features incised red polished and white slip pottery, as well as bronze items. A model house and set of miniature plates appear in the Geometric room; Archaic jugs exhibit Mycenaean influence in their depiction of an archer and birds. Among terracotta votive figurines and chariots stands an unusual wheel-footed horse – definitely not a chariot – on which a lyre player entertains two other riders.

Star of the Classical section is a woman in a head-dress – possibly the goddess Demeter – holding a poppy; Cyprus was one of the earliest centres of opium production. Two stone lions squat, haunch to haunch, with their tongues out, near a perfectly formed sphinx; continuing the animal theme, some Hellenistic child's rattles have the shape of wild boars.

The tomb of Barnabas

To one side of the monastery car park stands a small, undesecrated little mausoleum-chapel, shaded by a carob tree and erected during the 1950s over a catacomb that is the presumed **tomb of Barnabas**. A light-switch at the top illuminates stairs leading down to two rock-cut chambers with room for half-a-dozen dead, similar to the crypt of St Lazarus in Larnaca – and far older than Christianity. Occasional fresh candle drippings and flower offerings would suggest that the local Turks continue to revere the cave regardless of the departure of its Orthodox custodians. The stratum of simple, fervent belief runs deep in Cyprus, predating the monotheistic religions and not respecting their fine distinctions.

Enkomi-Alasia

From the monastery-museum it's a short drive southwest to a T-junction, just beyond which, reached by making a right turn, lies the inconspicuously signed entry to the Bronze Age town of **ENKOMI-ALASIA** (unenclosed, but £1 admission when warden present), opposite a water tank. Founded in about 2000 BC, it first appeared historically four hundred years later on some Pharaonic tablets, referred to as "Alashya" (Engomí is the modern Greek name of the nearest village). Alasia figured in Egyptian trade documents because from the sixteenth century BC onwards it acted as a thriving copper-exporting harbour, in an age when the coast was much closer and the river Pedhiéos more navigable than it is today. Mycenaean immigration had swelled the population to 15,000 by the twelfth century, but fire and earthquake mortally weakened the city during the eleventh century, after which it was abandoned in favour of Salamis.

The site

Excavations sponsored by the British Museum began in 1896, revealing the most complete Late Bronze Age town on Cyprus, and continued at intervals by French, Swedish and Cypriot missions until 1974. The town plan was a grid of narrow, perpendicular streets and low houses, surrounded by a wall; Alasia was initially thought to be a necropolis for Salamis, since human skeletons were discovered under each dwelling as at Khirokitiá (see p.67).

Also found here was an as-yet-undeciphered tablet in Cypro-Minoan script; the famous "Horned God", possibly an avatar of Apollo whose worship was imported from Arcadia in the Peloponnese; and an exquisite silver bowl inlaid with ox-head and floral designs, whose only known equal also came from the same region. These and other treasures are distributed between the British Museum and the Cyprus Museum.

Notwithstanding these glories, the site, west of the eucalypt-tufted hill where the excavation warehouses sit, is today of essentially specialist interest. Little remains above waist level, and there's absolutely no labelling; problems of inter-pretation are made more difficult by the fact that survivors of the eleventh-century earthquakes divided up damaged open-plan houses with crude rubble barriers. The walled precinct was originally entered via a north gate; west of the main longi-tudinal street, the **"Horned God"** was found in a namesake sanctuary marked by stone horns similar to those at Pigádhes, surrounded by the skulls of animals presumably worn as masks during the celebration of his cult. At the south edge of the exposed grid stands the so-called **House of Bronzes**, where many such objects were discovered in 1934.

The cenotaph of Nicocreon

If you turn left at the T-junction towards Famagusta, you'll pass through the modern village of **TUZLA (ÉNGOMI)**, at the far side of which stands the cut-open tumulus known as the **cenotaph of Nicocreon**. Excavations revealed an elevated platform on which an ancient mock cremation had taken place; among the limited number of items recovered were various clay dummies, thought to represent the actual family of Nicocreon, who had killed themselves in their palace rather than surrender to Ptolemy I. Its burning, collapsing beams were their real pyre; another unsolved mystery here is who conducted the memorial ceremony honouring the recently defeated dynasty.

Boğaz and around

BOĞAZ (BOGÁZI) makes a pleasant base with its fishing anchorage and small beach, though oil storage tanks and a cement plant across the bay, built a stone's throw from the almost vanished Templars' castle of Stronglyos, are a bit disconcerting.

Of the half-dozen seafood **restaurants** on either side of the road here, *George's* is about the simplest, *Kocatepe* the fanciest, with others like *Çarlı* and *Karsel* filling various niches in between. All are rather cheaper than their equivalents in Kyrenia, and you can be fairly sure that the fish really is fresh and locally caught. At locally popular *Karsel*, also known as *Hamdi'nin Yeri* (Hamdi's Place), a meal of *mercan* fish, *meze*, beer and some of the freshest chips in the North will work out at £7.50.

Either of the two local three-star **hotels**, represented by most tour operators, are acceptable choices. The sea-level *Boğaz* (☎37 12 659, fax 37 12 559) has the advantages and disadvantages of its setting: a beach just across the road, but some noise from cement trucks in the morning. At the co-managed *(Sea) View* (☎37 12 651, fax 37 12 559), actually closer to the hilltop village of Boğaztepe (Monagrá), most of the rooms live up to the name (including those in a new bungalow annexe), and there's a pool as well as tennis courts to compensate for the slight distance inland.

İskele (Tríkomo)

Approaching Boğaz from Nicosia or Kyrenia, you'll almost certainly pass through **İSKELE (TRÍKOMO)**, notable as the birthplace of notorious EOKA leader George Grivas, and less controversially that of Vassos Karageorghis, Cyprus' foremost archeologist. In the central square and roundabout, the diminutive fifteenth-century Dominican chapel of **Áyios Iákovos** (locked) seems plunked down like a jewel-box; supposedly Queen Marie of Romania was so taken with it that she had an exact replica built on the Black Sea coast as a royal chapel.

The "Icon Museum" (Panayía Theotókos)

At the western edge of the village, on the way to Geçitkale (Lefkóniko), stands the double-aisled, twelfth-to-fifteenth-century church of the **Panayía Theotókos**, functioning and identified as a so-called "Icon Museum" (daily 9am–7pm, closes earlier in practice; £1) – though there have been allegations that at least one of the exhibits was spirited away from another, still-functioning church. In any case, the entirely modern icon collection is of negligible artistic merit; what makes the admission charge justifiable are the best surviving **frescoes** in the North, strongly related in style to those at Asínou in the Tróödhos (see p.175).

The oldest are found in the south aisle, where scenes from the **life of Joachim and Anna**, the Virgin's parents, predominate, appropriately so for a church dedicated to the Virgin. In the arch of the south recess, below the dome, the *Prayer of Joachim in the Wilderness* faces the *Meeting of Joachim and Anna*, where the couple embrace while a maidservant looks on; the north recess arch features the *Prayer of Anna* (for offspring; the couple had been childless) and the pair's *Presentation of Gifts to the Temple*. In the apse, over the altar, a *Virgin Orans* presides below a fine *Ascension*, with Christ borne heavenward by four angels, while an archangel and six awed disciples look up from either side.

But the most arresting image is the severe **Pandokrátor** in the dome itself, where the frowning Christ averts His gaze towards a surrounding inscription, identifying him as "Overseer of All" who searches hearts and souls, concluding with the injunction: "Mortals, Fear the Judge!" Angels on bended knee worship all around, while below the bust of Christ flanked by the Virgin and John the Baptist, awaits the Throne of Judgement, with the instruments of the Passion.

THE KIRPAŞA (KÁRPAS) PENINSULA

The remote "panhandle" of Cyprus, known variously as the **Kırpaşa**, **Kárpas**, **Karpasia** or **Karpaz peninsula**, presents a landscape of rolling hills and grain fields, partly domesticated with vineyards, tobacco fields or olive and carob trees, and fringed by some of the loneliest beaches on the island. In ancient times it was much more densely inhabited, something attested to by a surprising concentration of small archeological sites and early Christian churches which, taken together, are considerably more interesting than the celebrated monastery of Apóstolos Andhréas near the far cape. The inhabitants were once noted for relict traditions which had died out elsewhere, for their craftwork and for a smattering of blue or green eyes – and more finely chiselled features – that hinted at Frankish or Arab settlement.

Until 1974 the peninsula was an ethnic mosaic, Turkish villages such as Áyios Simeón, Koróvia and Galinóporni alternating with Greek ones like Rizokárpaso, Ayía Triás and Yialoússa. However only a handful, like Kómi Kebír and Áyios Andhrónikos, were actually mixed; Denktaş reportedly came through in 1964 to urge its Turks to segregate themselves. They refused then, though the small Turkish Cypriot minority of Áyios Theódhoros moved to ethnically homogeneous Galátia when the troubles started, and a fortified enclave eventually formed around the kernel of Áyios Simeón, Koróvia and Galinóporni.

Today the crumbling villages seem at least fifty percent resettled by mainland Turks. But the peninsula is no longer heavily garrisoned by the Turkish army, superfluous as it is to the argument of who controls the North.

Kantara castle and around

Poised at the spot where the Kyrenia range subsides into rolling hills, **Kantara castle**, the easternmost and lowest of the Byzantine/Crusader trio, is as good a spot as any to call the base of the peninsula. Even here the Kárpas is so narrow that the castle simultaneously surveys impressive arcs of shoreline along both the north coast and the Bay of Famagusta. The name is thought to derive from the Arabic *qantara*, "arch" or "bridge", though it's difficult to pinpoint such a structure in the surrounding landscape.

Traditionally the castle is reckoned to be where Isaac Komnenos surrendered to Richard the Lionheart in 1191. Like St Hilarion castle, it figured prominently in the 1229–30 war between the supporters of the Holy Roman Emperor Frederick II and the Lusignan–Ibelin cartel, and again during the Genoese invasion, when the regent John of Antioch was smuggled out of prison in Famagusta to this hide-out disguised as a pot-tinner. Kantara shared the fate of the other Kyrenia hill-castles at the hands of the Venetians early in the sixteenth century, but it is still the best preserved of the three.

Getting there

From Boğaz you'll need the better part of 45 minutes driving to get to the castle, climbing via dilapidated Yarköy (Áyios Elías); Turnalar (Yeráni) with a conspicuous desecrated church; and finally pine-swathed **KANTARA** village, the closest thing to a hill station in the Kyrenia range.

Among the boarded-up Greek summer villas and dried-up fountains, there's a fitfully operating restaurant and an apparently abandoned hotel. Nobody has bothered to obliterate some of the more extreme EOKA-B graffiti near the church: "Greeks, listen to the voice of your hearts, énosis or death" and "Dhiyenis [ie Grivas] didn't die, he lives in our souls" – the latter precisely every Turkish Cypriot's misgiving about their erstwhile countrymen. Pray for no oncoming traffic on the one-lane surface between Turnalar and Kantára – it's a long way back to the next lay-by – and bear right once in the hill station, following signs for "Piknik yeri" (picnic grounds) once on the watershed. The tarmac gives out shortly before the castle's car park, 4km east of the village.

The site

Seven hundred metres above sea level, most of the complex faces east, the only direction from which it is easily accessible. You enter the outer enceinte through a **barbican** flanked by a pair of towers, then climb steps to the inner ward. First stop here will probably be the massive **southeast tower**, its lower part a cistern which occasionally doubled as a dungeon. Further along the southeast wall are the **barracks**, a trio of rooms fitted with loopholes; adjacent, an obvious latrine was flushed by the castle's sophisticated plumbing system. Thus far the buildings are in good condition, down to the woodwork and groin-vaulted ceilings, and could be used tomorrow. Beyond this point, however, Kantara is quite ruinous until the southwest corner of the battlements, where one chamber contains a hidden **postern gate** for surprising besiegers.

Crossing the rubble of the inner bailey, or returning to the southeast tower, you can attain the militarily remarkable **northern towers**, where two long galleries equipped with arrow slits are joined by a square chamber. Just one wall and a Gothic window survive of the highest watchtower, used for communicating with Buffavento to the west; the **northeast bastion**, by contrast, is impressively complete.

North of Kantara: Kaplıca (Dhavlós) and around

From either the castle or village of Kantára, you can plainly see **KAPLICA (DHAVLÓS)** and its bays just below on the north coast. To get there, return to the four-way junction in Kantára village for the sharp but brief descent. The village, resettled by mainlanders, is actually 1km inland from the main, rather average, beach and drinks stand, popular with islanders; just east there's an anchorage and a small fish-fry shack, and another sandy patch lies about 3km west, but frankly neither beach would be worth the bother of travelling all the way from Kyrenia.

Ten kilometres west, near the boundary between Famagusta and Kyrenia districts, the lonely late Byzantine church of **Panayía Pergamiótissa** sits about 400m inland from the road. Once completely frescoed and the seat of a monastery, it's now bricked up to prevent further vandalism, and more evocative seen from afar.

Beaches and churches: the route to the cape

The most obvious excursion from Boğaz goes northeast, towards Zafer Burnu (Cape Apostólou Andhréa). You can see the most interesting sights in a single, long day, but to really savour the area you'd want two.

For very private, sandy **beaches** relatively near Boğaz, two nameless strands to either side of Zeytin Burnu (Cape Eléa) fit the bill well. For the first one, head southeast out of the central crossroads in the village of Çayırova (Áyios Theodhóros) on the most prominent dirt track, always turning towards the sea when given the choice. Soon you emerge at an impromptu car park/turnaround area very near

Zeytin Burnu; the shore below can be rubbishy and seaweed-strewn, but walk to the far end of the 400-metre beach and the litter thins out. Up on the headland closing off the cove are supposed to be the sparse remains of an ancient town, Knidos.

For the other local beach, bypass Çayırova in favour of Bafra (Vogolídha), from where another, briefer dirt road continues to a decent beach deposited by a rather stagnant stream. A holiday village under construction here seems to have run out of steam, testimony to the collapse of the Asil Nadir empire; instead there is just a single, summertime "restaurant-camping" (really a day-use area).

Your next opportunity for a swim will be the small, reefy beach below Kumyali (Kóma tou Yialoú), encroached on somewhat by another "restaurant/camping", the *Pelican*, and a fishing port.

Panayía Kanakariá church and Kaleburnu

The intriguing fifth-to-twelfth-century monastic church of **Panayía Kanakariá** stands at the very western edge of Boltaşli (Lythrangomí), just east of the main Kárpas trunk route at Ziyamet (Leonárisso). Today it is locked – rather a case of bolting the stable door after the horse has fled (see box opposite) – but enough can be seen of the design from outside to convince you of the building's merit. Nave and aisles represent an eleventh-century revamping of the original fifth-century structure, of which only the apse (former home of the mosaics) remains. The domed narthex was added shortly afterwards, while the high, drummed central cupola followed in the 1700s.

The narrow but paved side road beyond the village passes through the former Turkish Cypriot enclave before ending at **KALEBURNU (GALINÓPORNI)**, a remarkable semi-troglodytic village wedged in between two hills. Both slopes and the surrounding areas are rife with rock-cut **tombs**. A seaward track just before reaching the village leads to **Üsküdar beach**, not utterly wonderful but acceptable for a dip. Dirt tracks shown on virtually all maps, heading northwest to Yenierenköy and east to Dipkarpaz from here, are negotiable only with a 4WD vehicle with high clearance, and even then at speeds hardly exceeding walking pace.

Yenierenköy and around

YENIERENKÖY (YIALOÚSSA, YALUSA), the second largest village on the peninsula and centre of the local tobacco industry, has been resettled by the inhabitants of the Kókkina (Erenköy) enclave in Tillyría (see p.137) since 1975. Just northeast, the small **beaches** and boat jetties of "Yeni" and "Malibu" lie almost within sight of the main coast road, to either side of **Yassi Burnu (Cape Plakotí)**, but except for the namesake *Malibu* **restaurant** there seems no compelling reason to take advantage of them unless the south wind is up, when these coves will be more sheltered than usual.

The basilica of Ayía Triás

The inland turning from the southern edge of Yenierenköy leads to **SİPAHİ (AYÍA TRIÁS)**, noted for the handsome mosaic floor of an **early Christian basilica**. The site (fenced but always open; free) lies at the northerly exit of the village going downhill towards the sea, just west of the road.

The fifth-century, three-aisled basilica seems far too large for the needs of the modest early village partly excavated here. From their similar style, it seems likely

THE THEFT OF THE KANAKARIA MOSAICS

The sixth-century **mosaics** which formerly graced the apse of Panayía Kanakariá are contemporary with those at Ravenna; in situ, they consisted of a Virgin and precociously aged Child flanked by the archangels, while above the Virgin busts of various evangelists and apostles, particularly Matthew, Andrew, Bartholomew and James, ran in a band. Art historians disagree on their merit, but the expressiveness of the figures compensates somewhat for the crudeness of the tesserae (the pigmented or gilded glass cubes used to compose the mosaic).

Even before independence, the mosaics had suffered at the hands of superstitious villagers who believed that the tesserae were efficacious against skin disease. Much worse was to follow, however, at some undetermined moment between 1974 and 1979, when thieves broke in through the windows of the drum, hacked four sections of mosaic off the wall, and spirited them off the island.

The whereabouts of the fragments were unknown until the late 1980s, when American art dealer Peg Goldberg purchased them for $1.8 million from a Swiss intermediary who claimed to have an export permit from the North Cyprus government. They were then offered for sale to the Getty Museum in California for ten times that amount, but by now Cyprus' Autocephalous Orthodox Church and Department of Antiquities had got wind of the dealings.

Acting jointly with the Church, the government of the South sued for the return of the mosaics in the US District Court of Indianapolis, finally winning their case in August 1989; the presiding judge essentially agreed with the Greek Cypriot contention that an export licence granted by an internationally unrecognized state was invalid, and that the artwork remained the property of the Orthodox Church. Following a failed appeal by the dealers, the mosaics returned to the South in the summer of 1991, and are now displayed in a special wing of the Archbishop Makarios Cultural Centre (see p.202). Whether this is a precedent that can be used in other instances of antiquities theft remains to be seen; a similar recent judgement in Texas concerning frescoes romoved from the fourteenth-century church of Áyios Efimianós on the Mesarya increases the possibility.

that the same craftsmen who decorated the annexe of Eustolios at Kourion (see p.98) are responsible for the **nave mosaics** here, which are entirely but engagingly geometric. An inscription at the west entry relates that three men contributed to the cost of the decoration in honour of a vow, while up by the apse another inscription informs that Iraklios the deacon paid for that section of the floor.

In the **north aisle mosaics**, there are several exceptions to the pattern of abstract imagery, including a cluster of pomegranates, diagonally opposite one of two pairs of sandals. This curious symbol, common in the early Christian Middle East but found nowhere else in Cyprus, may represent the pilgrimage through this world to the next. The **baptistry**, just southeast of the basilica, has a deep, marble-lined cruciform font, largest on the island.

Other local churches

The inland detour to Sipahi and the coastal route join up again well before **Áyios Thýrsos**, a tiny resort grouped around two namesake churches: the desecrated modern one up on the road is of little interest, but the older one down at sea level contains a crypt at the rear in which a healing spring once trickled. One or the other is still actually used for the saint's commemorative mass on July 23 by the remaining local Greeks.

THE GREEKS OF THE KÁRPAS

The 1974 war effectively bypassed the peninsula, so that there was no panicky exodus of civilians in the path of the oncoming Turkish army. Thus of the nearly 20,000 **Greeks** who chose to stay in the North, most of them lived on the Kárpas. But since 1975, systematic harassment by the Turkish army and the North Cypriot government has reduced this population to a handful of middle-aged and older individuals. There have been forcible expulsions to the South when property was coveted by settlers or Turkish Cypriot refugees, and the remaining Greek Cypriots require permits to travel outside their home village. Secondary education is no longer allowed, with only two Greek primary schools still functioning, so any children over the age of eleven must go to the South for continued education, without any right of return. Similarly, no Greek Cypriot doctor practises anywhere in the North.

Not surprisingly, then, only about 520 stubborn Greeks continue to live on the peninsula: about 400 in Dípkarpaz (Rizokárpaso), 120 in Sipahi (Ayía Triás) and perhaps half-a-dozen in Yeşilköy (Áyios Andhrónikos). The UN post in Ziyamet (Leonárisso), staffed by Austrians, exists to protect their interests; primarily they bring food from the South at regular intervals, as their lack of facility in Turkish and their restricted participation in the local economy mean the Greeks can't or won't shop locally. The Greeks are allowed to visit doctors and relatives in the South on one-week, Friday-to-Friday visas, but are shuttled to the Ledra Palace crossing in Nicosia by the UN, since they're not permitted to take their own vehicles. Very occasionally, relatives from the South are allowed to make reciprocal visits, though

Minuscule, tenth-century **Áyios Fótios**, the next church passed, is accessible by a non-motorable, 300-metre track some 5km past Áyios Thýrsos; after 3km more, another bumpy drive leads up through the pines to the medieval monastery church of **Panayía Eleoússa**, romantically overlooking the broad sweep of Ronnás Bay. Here dunes give way to a fine beach possibly favoured by egg-laying turtles, but the prevailing north wind brings a lot of garbage, and you've a bit of a hike in over the tyre-confounding sand.

Dipkarpaz – and more churches

From Ronnás the road turns inland to **DİPKARPAZ (RIZOKÁRPASO)**, the remotest and yet largest village on the peninsula, with a population of around 3000. Here a huge new mosque overshadows the church of the remaining Greeks; there's a single hotel-restaurant, though you'd be hard pressed to find a reason to patronize it. Once a prosperous place, Dipkarpaz has been reduced to the status of an Anatolian village, with added poignancy in the use of once-imposing arcaded houses as poultry pens and hay barns.

Áyios Fílon and Aféndrika

Both of these early Christian sites are well worth the slight detour north from Dipkarpaz; once up on the northerly of the two ridges enclosing the village ask for the road to the fisherman's anchorage (*balıkçının barınağı* in Turkish, *psarádhiko limáni* in Greek).

The basilicas of **Áyios Fílon**, 3km along this, are the most obvious remains of ancient Karpasia – even from the ridge you can easily spot the seven bedraggled in these cases it seems that Turkish Army vehicles effect the transfer, charging passengers £5 for the privilege.

Relations between the Greek Cypriots and goat-grazing Anatolian settlers are strained, somewhat better with Turkish Cypriots or Bulgarian-Turkish immigrants used to farming, though the coffee houses in Sipahi and Dipkarpaz are ethnically segregated. The conditions of the Greeks' continued residence here are undeniably humiliating: "We live like animals" can be an unsolicited comment on the state of affairs. This is often voiced in tandem with the fatalistic, almost Byzantine belief that the invasion and its aftermath were God's punishment for their sins – sentiments expressed by Greeks at regular intervals since the Turks first appeared in Anatolia during the tenth century. Medieval harassment extends even to religious observance: the church bell in Dipkarpaz may not be rung lest it offend the Muslims, although the bells in Sipahi – with a proportionately higher Greek population – may be sounded. The icon of the Sipahi village church went missing in December 1991, allegedly appearing thereafter among the exhibits of the museum in İskele (Trikomo).

Despite their troubles, the Greek Cypriots of the Kárpas are a friendly, hospitable lot when approached, though some caution is in order to avoid compromising them: their pleasure at having someone new to talk with is well dampened by awareness that being seen in unsupervised conversations with outsiders can later result in unpleasant interrogations by the police. One definitely does not go banging on doors or barging through coffee houses asking after Greeks; if someone gives you a knowing nod or searching look in the fields or on the street or addresses you in English, odds are they are Greek Cypriot. It's really best to have a name and address to call on in advance; at any rate, be discreet.

washingtonia palms and ruined resort buildings surrounding them. Typically, the half-ruined tenth-century chapel, of which only the apse and south wall are intact, sits amid foundations of a far larger, earlier basilica and baptistry, perhaps the seat of the saintly Fílon, first bishop of Christian Karpasia. Its extensive *opus sectile* flooring includes an abstract ring design similar to that of Kambanópetra at Salamis. Just north of the two churches, you can find the ancient jetty sticking 100m out to sea, its masonry furrowed where long-vanished iron pins held the stones together. The rest of Hellenistic and Roman Karpasia, which supplied building stone for both churches, lies scattered to the west of the road in, but it's a long slog through thornbushes to never-excavated walls and a necropolis.

Beyond Áyios Fílon the paved but narrow road swings east to follow the coast 8km more to **Aféndrika**, another important ancient town on an even larger scale than Karpasia, with three contiguous ruined churches: Panayía Khrysiótissa, a twelfth-century ruin inside which is a smaller chapel two hundred years younger; partly domed, double-apsed Áyios Yióryios; and three-aisled Panayía Asómatos, in much better condition. West of the group of churches is a necropolis, while in the opposite direction the rooms of the citadel were partly cut into the outcrop on which it was built. By now you may be craving a swim; there is a decent sand beach some 1500m east of the church complex, accessible across fields.

The cape environs

The main road, bearing south from the central junction in Dipkarpaz, soon narrows to one (paved) lane; pines of the Kárpas forest, centred round the village, subside to terebinth as you change sides of the narrowing peninsula and emerge on its south shore.

Some 5km east of Dipkarpaz, the road passes the *Blue Sea* **restaurant**, an ideal lunch stop if touring these parts, offering fresh fish from the adjacent anchorage. The proprietors, refugees from Páfos district, also let several **rooms** upstairs – tidy but rather basic, with no electricity and no contact phone (①).

Nangomí ("Golden Sands") beach

Continuing, the road bears inland again for a while, passing through fields and pastures surprisingly well tended for such a deserted region. Some 14km beyond the *Blue Sea* begins the best **beach** in the North, if not the entire island, initially hidden behind a straight line of scrub-covered knolls halting the advance of vast dunes. Known officially in pre-1974 days as **Nangomí**, it has lately been dubbed "**Golden Sands**", though the strand is of a distinctly reddish tint.

Westerly access is provided by a dirt lane starting by some old stone foundations at the roadside; this track threads through a conspicuous gap in the barrier hillocks, leaving you with a ten-minute walk across the sand to the water. Alternatively, you can proceed until the road skirts the edge of the hard-packed dunes themselves, and the beach extends obviously southwest, though the walk in from several lay-bys here is no shorter.

The five-plus kilometres of sand could easily accommodate most of the North's population on a summer weekend, and probably does on occasion, though there are no facilities. There's some hope for its preservation, as the tip of the peninsula has been declared a protected area – good news for the quail and other birds living in the dunes, and the turtles who reportedly lay eggs on this wild, spectacular beach.

Apóstolos Andhréas monastery

The downed phone lines which have shadowed the road for miles end at the sprawling, barracks-like **monastery of Apóstolos Andhréas**, until 1974 a lodestone for Cypriot pilgrims. The spot has been revered since legend credited the Apostle Andrew with summoning forth a miraculous spring on the shore during a journey from Palestine, and using the water to effect cures. By Byzantine times there was a fortified abbey here, long since disappeared but a debatable alternative to Kantara as the site of Isaac Komnenos' capture by Richard the Lionheart.

The tradition of mass pilgrimage and popularity, however, only dates from the well-documented experience of one **Maria Georgiou**, an Anatolian Greek whose small son was kidnapped by brigands in 1895; seventeen years later the apostle appeared in a dream and commanded her to pray for the boy's return at the monastery. Crossing the straits from Turkey in a crowded boat, Georgiou happened to tell the story to a young dervish among the passengers, who grew more and more agitated as the narrative progressed. He asked the woman if her lost son had any distinguishing signs, and upon hearing a pair of birthmarks described, cast off his robes to reveal them and embraced her. The son – for he it was – had been raised a Muslim in Istanbul, but upon docking on Cyprus was rebaptized, to the general acclaim of the population.

Subsequent **miracles** – mostly cures of epilepsy, paralysis and blindness – at the monastery further enhanced its prestige and rendered it enormously wealthy in votive donations. But the faithful never missed the opportunity for a fun day out as well, eventually scandalizing the church into censuring the weekend carnival atmosphere.

All that came to an abrupt end **after 1974**, since when the pilgrims' hostel has been occupied by the army, and the monastery shrunk to a pathetic ghost of its former self. In a reversal of policy from the years when the place was off-limits to outsiders, it is now signposted by yellow-and-black placards (*Manastır*) as a tourist attraction, run like a sort of zoo by the authorities to prove North Cyprus' religious tolerance. "Zoo" is not such an arbitrary characterization, with about fifty cats far outnumbering the human population, plus an enormous sow – presumably kept to annoy the majority Muslim population in the North. Amazingly, the major November 30 and August 15 festivals are still observed after a fashion, and the priest comes from Dipkarpaz to conduct liturgies at other times.

Visits begin with a check-in at a small police post, where your personal details (bring your passport) and time of arrival are logged in a giant notebook. Then one of five remaining Greek caretakers, too dispirited or intimidated to talk much, will show you the nineteenth-century **katholikón**, of little intrinsic interest except for the giant wax votive candles which keep coming from the South to judge by their wrapping; you might be generous at the donations box, as the monastery is plainly in reduced circumstances nowadays. Finally, an old woman will take you down to the fifteenth-century seaside **chapel**, now essentially a crypt below the main church, where the **holy well** of the apostle flows audibly below a heavy stone cover; both Turkish and Greek Cypriots still esteem and collect the water for its therapeutic properties.

Zafer Burnu (Cape Apostólou Andhréa)

From the monastery, 7km of rough track brings you to Cyprus' John O'Groats, **Zafer Burnu**, the definitive, if somewhat anti-climactic northeastern tip. A cave-riddled rock, the Neolithic village known as Kastros, was later the site of an ancient Aphrodite temple, of which nothing remains; the goddess was by most accounts in a savage aspect here, a siren-like devourer of men in the sea below. Beyond an abandoned guardhouse and around the offshore **Klidhés Islets** (the "Keys"), beloved of seabirds, many a ship has been wrecked; *Scuba Cyprus* visits one as part of its programme (see box p.255). Even modern shipping, often evident on the horizon, gives the cape a wide berth as it plies the sea lanes between Syria, Lebanon, Turkey and Cyprus.

travel details

Buses

From **Famagusta** to: Kyrenia (every 30min; 1hr); Nicosia (every 30min; 1hr); Yenierenköy (several daily; 1hr 15min).

Ferries

From **Famagusta** to: Mersin, Turkey (10hr), 3 weekly (currently Tues, Thurs, Fri afternoon); details of fare structures in "Getting There" in *Basics*.

PART FOUR

THE
CONTEXTS

THE HISTORICAL FRAMEWORK

With its critical location on the way to the Middle East, the history of Cyprus can't help being long and chequered. The following summary is heavily biased towards antiquity and events of this century, enabling a reader to grasp what they are most likely to see in a museum – and on the street.

BEGINNINGS

Settlements of **round stone dwellings**, particularly along the north coast and at Khirokitía near Larnaca, indicate habitation in Cyprus as early as 7000 BC; the origins of these first **Neolithic** settlers are uncertain, but items in obsidian, a material unknown on the island, suggest the Middle Eastern mainland opposite. The first Cypriots engaged in hunting, farming and fishing, but were ignorant of pottery, fashioning instead rough vessels, idols and jewellery from stone. Religious observance seems to have been limited to **burial practices** – the dead were interred under or near dwellings in a fetal position, with their chests crushed by boulders to prevent them from haunting the living.

After this initial colonization, a 1500-year-long hiatus in archeological evidence, so far unexplained, ensued until the so-called **Neolithic II** culture appeared after 4500 BC.

Sites near Áyios Epíktitos on the north coast and Sotíra in the south yielded quantities of so-called "red combed" and abstractly painted ware, the first indigenous **ceramics**.

The **Chalcolithic** period, whose cultures emerged after 4000 BC in a gradual transition from the late Neolithic, was distinguished by the settlement of the previously neglected western portion of Cyprus. The era takes its name from the discovery of copper (*chalkos* in Greek) implements, but more important, as indications of developing **fertility cults**, are the limestone female idols at Lémba and Kissónerga, and cruciform grey-green picrolite pendants at Yialiá, reminiscent of similar work in the west Aegean.

With the advent of the **Early Bronze Age** (reckoned 2500 BC and onwards), the focus of Cypriot life shifted to the Mesaoría and its perimeter, conveniently near the first **copper mines**, where the importation of tin permitted the smelting of bronze. Curiously, no confirmed habitation has yet been excavated, but settlement has been inferred from the distribution of elaborate subterranean chamber **tombs or shrines** and their contents, especially at Vounous near Kyrenia. Ceramics executed in red clay seem to have spread across the island from north to south; deeply incised, whimsical zoomorphic or composite ware, imaginatively combining humorous aesthetics with function, appeared along with cruder models of schematic figures engaged in elaborate religious ceremonies pertaining to a bull-centred fertility cult. The **bull**, imported from Asia, permitted for the first time the ploughing of hitherto unusable land, and models show this also.

Well into the second millennium BC, during the so-called **Middle Bronze Age** period, settlements appear on the south and east coasts of Cyprus, facing probable **overseas trading** partners; commerce with immediate neighbours, fuelled by the copper deposits, would by now have been well developed. The most important eastern port was Enkomi-Alasia, the second name soon to be synonymous with the island. Rectangular or L-shaped **dwellings** with flat roofs completely supplanted round ones, and, ominously, **forts** – their inland positioning indicative of civil conflict over the copper trade, rather than of threats from outside – sprang up at various sites around the

Mesaoría. Both transport and warfare were facilitated by the recent importation of **horses**. In religious life, female **plank idols**, alone or nursing infants, and bird-headed, earringed figurines were important – the latter probably intended as symbolic companions for interred men, or manifestations of an earth goddess reclaiming one of her children.

THE LATE BRONZE AGE AND ARRIVAL OF THE MYCENAEANS

As Cypriot political and commercial transactions became more complicated, a **writing script** became necessary: the earliest known Cypriot document, from the **Late Bronze Age**, is an incised clay sixteenth-century tablet unearthed at Enkomi-Alasia. Called **Cypro-Minoan** after its supposed derivation from Cretan Linear A, the origins or language of the eighty still-undeciphered characters have not been proved, though pottery finds at Toúmba toú Skoúrou and Ayía Iríni on the bay of Mórfou indicate the necessary contacts with Minoan culture. Fragmentary passages were inscribed frequently on cups, cylinder seals and loom-weights, implying that the language was common throughout Cyprus, though the Enkomi-Alasia tablet remains the only known complete text. Variations of this script remained in use long after the arrival of the Mycenaeans, who did not impose the use of their own presumed form of Linear B.

Other people's records, especially those of the Egyptians, suggest that the island was consistently referred to as **Alashiya** (or Asy, or Alasia) by the fifteenth and fourteenth centuries BC and also imply that for the first time Cyprus formed a loosely united **confederation** of towns. Of these, **Kition** and **Enkomi-Alasia** came to the fore, their high standard of living reflected in elaborate **sanitary facilities**, including bathtubs and sewers. Two new ceramic styles emerged: so-called "base ring", shiny and thin-walled in imitation of metal, usually with a basal ring; and "white slip", provided with a primer coat of white slurry on which brown or black patterns were executed.

THE MYCENAEANS

But the most dramatic change in island culture was fostered by the first **arrival of the Mycenaeans** from the Greek Peloponnese,

who replaced the Minoans as the main Hellenic influence in the east Mediterranean after 1400 BC. Their immediate influence was most obvious in **pottery** of that era – "rude style" pictorial *kratirs*, showing mythological scenes and bestiaries (including the octopus, a Minoan favourite) – though it's still uncertain whether such items were brought by the Mycenaeans to trade for copper, or whether their production techniques were taught to local potters using wheels for the first time. From the same period date the notable enamelled *rhyton* (a horn-shaped drinking vessel; now in the Cyprus Museum in south Nicosia) from Kition, with three series of hunters and animals, and the famous silver bowl of Enkomi-Alasia, inlaid with a floral and bull's-head design.

Around 1200 BC, Mycenaean civilization in its Peloponnesian homeland collapsed when confronted with invasion by the Dorian peoples, events which had a profound knock-on effect on Cyprus. Rogue Mycenaean survivors fled Greece via Anatolia, where others joined them to become the raiding "sea peoples" mentioned in Egyptian chronicles of the time. They established an initial Cypriot foothold at **Maa** in the west of the island, choosing a headland easily defensible from both land and sea, and proceeded to destroy Enkomi-Alasia and Kition. Both were soon rebuilt with fortification walls reminiscent of the Mycenaean Argolid, with ashlar blocks used for these and individual buildings.

Religious shrines were closely associated with the **copper industry**; in separate temple niches at Enkomi-Alasia the famous "Horned God" was discovered, possibly a version of Apollo melded with aspects of the indigenous bull cult, and the so-called "Ingot God", a spear-wielding figure poised atop an ingot shaped like an oxhide, then the standard form of copper export. While Kition was not so spectacularly rewarding in artefacts, the sanctuaries here formed a huge complex of multiple temples with more Middle Eastern characteristics, though again in intimate association with copper forges. Large numbers of **bull skulls** have been found on the floors of all these shrines, implying their use as ceremonial masks – and the retention of bull worship and sacrifice.

At this time the **Aphrodite** shrine at Palea Paphos first attained prominence. Her cult and that of the smithing deity were not so disparate as might seem at first: in mainstream Greek culture, Aphrodite was the consort of Hephaistos, the god of fire and metal-working. A voluptuous female statuette in bronze found at Enkomi-Alasia is thought to be the consort of the martial ingot deity, and terracotta figurines of the Great Goddess with uplifted arms were among archeological finds at the Kition temples.

In general, Mycenaean influence was in the ascendant on Cyprus even as the same culture died out in its Aegean birthplace. But the immigrants introduced few of their religious practices and conventions wholesale, instead adapting their beliefs to local usage. Mycenaean technology did, however, invigorate local **metallurgy**, permitting the fashioning of such exquisite objects as the square, often wheeled stands for libation bowls found at Enkomi and Kourion, their sides intricately decorated in relief figures. The concept of kingship and **city-states**, along with Hellenic foundation-legends, became institutionalized after another wave of Mycenaean-Anatolian settlement around 1200 BC, at the seven "capitals" of Salamis, Lapithos, Marion, Soli, Palea Paphos, Kourion and Tamassos; pure or "Eteo"-Cypriot culture retreated to Amathus.

A violent earthquake finished off Mycenaean Enkomi-Alasia and Kition around 1050 BC; Palea Paphos continued to be inhabited, but effectively the Bronze Age was over. Not, however, before the Mycenaean-tutored island smelters had apparently mastered the working of **iron**, as borne out by large numbers of iron weapons appearing in excavated sites of the early eleventh century.

THE GEOMETRIC ERA

The beginning of the **Geometric Era** in Cyprus was an echo of the "Dark Ages" in surrounding realms: the Mycenaean homeland was now thoroughly overrun by the Dorians; the Hittite empire of Anatolia had collapsed; Egypt was stagnant. Cyprus was essentially **isolated** for around two centuries. Most Cypriots, now a mix of settlers and indigenous islanders, gravitated toward the Mycenaean-founded city-kingdoms, such as Salamis; nearby Enkomi-Alasia was gradually abandoned after a mid-eleventh-century earthquake, which, along with silting up, rendered its harbour unusable.

Despite the cultural doldrums, early Geometric **pottery** is quite startling; cups and shallow dishes were popular, painted boldly in black rings, very occasionally with human or animal figures. **Funerary customs** show Mycenaean habits, especially among the population descended from immigrants: chamber tombs were approached by long *dromoi* or passages, and slaves were occasionally sacrificed to serve their deceased master; cremations took place at Kourion, as did the use of ossuary urns for old bones when reusing a tomb – an increasingly common strategy. In one grave at Palea Paphos, **syllabic Greek script** was found for the first time on a meat skewer, spelling the name of the deceased in Arcadian dialect – partial confirmation of the foundation myth of Palea Paphos by Agapinor, leader of the Arcadian contingent in the Trojan war.

Following stabilization in the west Aegean around 800 BC, trade and other **contacts resumed** between Greece – particularly Euboia – and the indigenous or "Eteo-Cypriot" centre of Amathus, more extroverted than the Myceno-Cypriot centres. Further fresh input was provided by the peaceful **Phoenician** resettlement of Kition, whose temples had never been completely abandoned even after the natural disaster of the eleventh century. The Phoenicians, an up-and-coming mercantile empire of the Middle East, rededicated these shrines to Astarte, the oriental version of Aphrodite; the **multiple sanctuary**, rebuilt after a fire in 800, was the fulcrum of Phoenician culture on Cyprus, with worship continuing until 312 BC. Not surprisingly, bichrome pottery of the eighth century BC throughout the island shows Phoenician characteristics of dress style and activities.

These exceptions aside, the Geometric culture of Cyprus was **deeply conservative** – Mycenaean observances, whether or not melded with Eteo-Cypriot expression, maintained static or even retrospective forms, a trend accentuated by the two-century gap in communication with most of the outside world. The seven city-states were ruled by despotic monarchies, unmindful of the recent experiments in constitutional government in Greece; the Arcadian dialect continued to be written in syllabic script, rather than a true alphabet, until the fourth century BC.

No better demonstration of this traditionalism can be found than the **royal tombs** at Salamis of just before 700 BC, where the details of several burials seem to have been taken from public readings of Homer. The grave artefacts themselves are manifestly oriental, in a blend of Phoenician and Egyptian styles, reflecting the royal taste of the time; but the numerous roasting spits – similar to the inscribed one at Palea Paphos – the skeletons of sacrificed chariot-horses at the entrance to tombs, and great bronze cauldrons containing the ashes of cremated royalty can only be accounted for in the light of the Homeric epics. Here was a perhaps politically motivated revival of the presumed funerary customs of the Trojan War character Teukros, the reputed Mycenaean founder of Salamis.

ANCIENT ZENITH: THE ARCHAIC ERA

Some consider the start (750 BC) of the **Archaic Era** on Cyprus to overlap the end of Geometric by half a century, but the signal event was the island's domination by the **Assyrians** between 708 and 669 BC; however, Cypriot kings were merely required to forward tribute regularly, and this episode left little trace on island life other than some suggestive beards and hairstyles in later sculpture. Upon the departure of the Assyrians, a century of **flourishing independence** followed, producing some of the finest ancient Cypriot art. Its genius was an innate inventiveness combined with a receptivity to surrounding influences and their skilful assimilation into styles that were more than the sum of their component elements.

ART

Archaic Cyprus excelled for the first time in large-scale **sculpture** in limestone, which exhibited strong similarity to the art of Ionia in Asia Minor. Figures were nearly always robed in the Ionian manner, rarely nude, with the great attention paid to facial expression contrasting with an often cursory rendering of body anatomy. Large almond-shaped eyes, prominent eyebrows and more than a trace of the celebrated "Archaic smile" were often surmounted by Asiatic hair-and-beard styles, bound by head bands or, later, elaborate headdresses. A famous example is the **statue of Zeus Keraunios** (Thunderbolt-Hurler) from Kition. Female statue-heads were adorned with suggestions of **jewellery** matching in all respects some exquisitely worked gold and precious-stone originals which have been found. **Pottery** advanced from the abstract to bichrome figurative ware, especially the so-called "free-field" style, where single, well-detailed animal or human figures are rampant on a bare background.

RELIGION

Religious observance in Archaic Cyprus varied considerably, a function of the increasing number of foreigners visiting or living on the island. In contrast to cosmopolitan ports where the Greek Olympian deities and other more exotic foreign gods like the Egyptian Bes or Phoenician Astarte competed for admirers, the important **rural shrines** of the seventh and sixth centuries were more conservative in their adoration of old chthonic gods, or localized variants of imported divinities. The Phoenicians had their own rural cult, in addition to the Kition temples: that of Baal Hamman at Méniko, in the middle of the island near the copper mines they controlled, though it displayed many elements – such as bull sacrifice – of native Cypriot religion. The other most important sanctuaries were that of Apollo Hylates near Kourion and the long-venerated shrine at Ayía Iríni, where two thousand terracotta figurines were discovered.

Such **figurines** were typically arranged as ex votos around the altar of the usually simple courtyard shrines; in accord with Cypriot belief that the deity often resided in the temple, these clay figures served as permanent worshippers, ready for the divine presence. Some of the terracottas were realistically modelled for individual detail, and so have been taken to be gifts of a particular worshipper, made to order at workshops adjacent to the shrines. Figurines of musicians and women in various attitudes (including childbirth) accumulated logically enough at Aphrodite or mother-goddess shrines, while the preferred offerings to male deities were bulls, horse-drawn chariots or helmeted warriors such as formed the bulk of the finds at Ayía Iríni.

THE PERSIAN INFLUENCE

The sixth century BC saw a very brief interval of direct Egyptian rule which, while stricter than the Assyrian era, left a similarly subtle legacy in the form of more outlandish beards or headdresses on statues. Monumentally, this time is characterized by the strange subterranean "house" tombs at Tamassos, possibly built by itinerant Anatolian masons. The newest Asian power on the horizon, the **Persians**, assumed control over Egypt in 545 BC; with their existing ties to the Middle East through the Phoenicians, and relatively weak military resources, it was easy enough for the Cypriot kingdoms to reach a vassalage arrangement with King Cyrus in 545 BC. Yet for a while a measure of autonomy was preserved, and Evelthon, the late sixth-century king of Salamis, minted his own coinage.

In 499 BC, however, this modus vivendi dissolved as Persian rule under Darius became harsher and the non-Phoenician Cypriots joined the **revolt** of the Ionian cities. **Onesilos of Salamis** mutinied against his brother the Persian puppet-king and attempted to rally the other Myceno-Cypriot city-kingdoms, but this hastily patched-together confederation, despite land and sea reinforcements from the Ionians, was defeated in a major battle at Salamis, largely due to the treachery of the Kourion contingent. Onesilos' head was stuck on the city gate of pro-Persian Amathus as a warning, though after it filled with honeycomb an oracle advised the townspeople to bury it and revere his memory. After the battle, each of the remaining Cypriot city-kingdoms except Kition was besieged and reduced one by one, Soli and Palea Paphos being the last to capitulate in 498. Such prolonged resistance against the mighty Persian empire was made possible by vastly improved stone and mud-brick fortifications, which dwarfed the original designs of the Mycenaean settlers. The **pro-Persian Phoenicians** took the opportunity to extend their influence northward, placing their kings on the throne at Marion and Lapethos; in the aftermath of the revolt the hilltop palace of Vouni was also built by the king of Marion to intimidate nearby pro-Hellenic Soli. Never again, until this century, would Cyprus be both independent and united.

TURMOIL AND DECLINE: CLASSICAL CYPRUS

By the start of the fifth century, Cyprus had ten **city-kingdoms**: Kyrenia, Idalion, Amathus and Kition were added to the Myceno-Cypriot seven, with Soli now subservient to Marion. The island now became thoroughly embroiled in the struggle between Greece and Persia; **Athens** repeatedly sent forces to "liberate" Cyprus, but the distance involved, plus pro-Persian factions on the island, made any victories transient. Athenian general **Kimon** led three of these expeditions to various parts of Cyprus, especially the pro-Persian strongholds of Marion, Salamis and Kition, dying at the hour of victory in his last attempt in 449 BC, outside the walls of Kition. Deprived of leadership, the Greeks sailed home, and the next year the Athenians signed a treaty with the Persians agreeing to drop the matter.

But if the political results of these campaigns were minuscule – the palace at Vouni was rebuilt to a nostalgic Mycenaean plan, though oligarchic, dynastic rule continued at most city-kingdoms whether pro-Greek or not – profound **cultural effects** attended the five decades of contact with Greece. A craze for Attic art swept the island in everything from pottery – imported via Marion and Salamis – to coinage, to the marked detriment of local creativity. Sarcophagi and Attic-style memorial *stelae* began to rival rock-cut tombs in popularity; the worship of Heracles and Athena as deities came into vogue, and many Phoenician divinities acquired a Hellenic veneer.

Before the truce, however, the Phoenician regime at Kition, perennial allies of the Persians, had again struck northwards, taking Idalion in 470 BC. The Persians took the peace itself as a cue to tighten their control yet again on the island, and the stage was set for the emergence of a great Cypriot patriot and political genius, **Evagoras I of Salamis**. Born in 435, at the age of 24 he overthrew the Phoenician puppet-king of the city, but skilful diplomatic spadework and judicious payment of tribute to the Persians ensured no repercussions then or for a long time after, giving him the necessary breathing space to build up his defences and elaborate his sophisticated intrigues. Though fiercely pro-Hellenic, he was able to act simultaneously as a mediator between the Athenians and the Persians, even convincing the latter to lend him a fleet for use against the Spartans on behalf of Athens, which duly honoured him after the victory was accomplished. Evagoras' court became a haven for Attic artists or soldiers in exile, voluntary or otherwise, and he vigorously promoted Greek culture throughout his expanding dominions, including the introduction of the **Greek alphabet**, which slowly replaced the Cypriot syllabic script over the next century.

His conduct of domestic statecraft, however, tended towards the megalomaniac; in attempting to forcibly **unite** all the Cypriot city-kingdoms into one state, Evagoras alienated Kition, Amathus and Soli sufficiently that they appealed for help to the Persians. Evagoras had finally overreached himself; despite some aid from the Athenians, he failed to depose the king of Kition, and another treaty in 386 between Greeks and Persians, acknowledging the latter's hegemony over the island, left him to confront the eastern empire effectively alone. But with some support from Anatolian Greek city-states he managed to carry the fight to the enemy's home court, causing confusion by landing on the Syrian coast. Though the Persians returned to Cyprus in force in 381, sacking Salamis, Evagoras battled them to a stalemate, and negotiated relatively favourable surrender terms, keeping his throne.

He and his eldest son were apparently murdered in a domestic plot at Salamis in 374 BC; he was a hard act to follow, and Evagoras' descendants were insignificant in comparison, not having his touch in handling the Persians — least of all in another abortive revolt of 351. Of his **successors** only Pytagoras salvaged a shred of dignity as a vassal king of the Persians, though pro-Hellenic in culture, ushering in the Hellenistic era.

RECOVERY: HELLENISTIC AND ROMAN CYPRUS

When **Alexander the Great** appeared on the scene in 333, the Cypriot city-kingdoms responded unequivocally, furnishing 120 ships for his successful siege of Persian Tyre. But following his general victory in the east Mediterranean it soon became clear that, while finally rid of the Persians, Cyprus was now a subordinated part of the Hellenistic empire, without even the minimal freedoms pertaining under their old masters.

When Alexander died in 323, the island became a battleground for his successors **Ptolemy** and **Antigonus**, with the city-kingdoms split in their support and **civil war** the result. Ptolemy's forces initially prevailed, and the losing cities — Kition, Marion, Lapithos and

Kyrenia — were razed or severely punished. **Nicocreon**, the pro-Hellenic king of Salamis, was promoted for his loyalty, but in 311 he was denounced for plotting with Antigonus, and Ptolemy sent an army under his deputy Menelaos to besiege Salamis. Rather than surrender, Nicocreon and his family set their palace alight and committed suicide, and the truth of the accusations remains uncertain; in any event the dynasty founded by Teukros died with them.

Antigonus' adherents were still very much in the picture, though, and the dynastic war continued in the person of his son **Demetrios Polyorketes**, who defeated both Ptolemy and Menelaos and single-handedly ruled the island from 306 to 294. The pendulum swung back one final time, however, for in an unguarded moment Ptolemy I Soter of Egypt — as he now styled himself — retook Cyprus, commencing two and a half centuries of relatively peaceful and prosperous **Ptolemaic, Egyptian-based rule**.

Cyprus became essentially a province of the Alexandria-based kingdom, exploited for its copper, timber, corn and wine, and administered by a military governor based first at Salamis, later at Nea Paphos. All city-kingdoms were now defunct, replaced by four **administrative districts** and uniform coinage for the whole island; its cultural life was now thoroughly Hellenized, with the usual range of athletic, dramatic and musical events. To existing religious life were added the cult of deified Ptolemaic royalty and a fresh infusion of Egyptian gods. Art was largely derived from Alexandrian models, with little in the way of originality. Portraits in the soft local limestone or terracotta made up the majority of statuary, with the marble work common elsewhere in the Greek world relatively rare. The only idiosyncratic expressions were in funereal architecture, especially at Nea Paphos, where the subterranean "Tombs of the Kings" were a blend of Macedonian and Middle Eastern styles.

During the first century BC, the decline in the Ptolemies' fortunes was matched by the growing power of republican **Rome**, which annexed Cyprus in 58 BC; with the see-sawing of events the island reverted to Egyptian control twice, but Roman rule was consolidated in the imperial period after 31 BC. The *Koinon Kyprion* or civic league of the Ptolemies continued under the Romans, charged with coordinating religious festivals, including emperor-worship. The four Ptolemaic districts were also retained but Cyprus as a whole was administered as a senatorial province, through a proconsul (one of the first was the orator Cicero), still based at Nea Paphos. Salamis, however, remained the most important town on the island, its commercial centre with a population of over a quarter of a million.

The Hellenistic pattern of **stability and prosperity** continued, permitting massive public works, some redone several times in the wake of earthquakes; Roman roads, bridges and aqueducts have long since vanished, but gymnasia, theatres and baths constitute most of the archeological heritage visible on Cyprus today. Wealthier private citizens too commissioned major projects, as borne out by the sophisticated villa-floor **mosaics** at Nea Paphos. Otherwise, however, not much effort was expended to Latinize the island – Greek, for example, continued to be used as the official language – and as a largely self-sufficient backwater, Cyprus took little part in the larger affairs of the Roman empire.

CHRISTIANITY

Christianity came early (45 AD) to Cyprus, which was evangelized by the apostles Paul and Barnabas, the latter a native of Salamis. The pair ordained Iraklidhios of Tamassos as the island's first bishop, and supposedly converted Sergius Paulus, proconsul at Nea Paphos. Barnabas was subsequently martyred by the Jews of Salamis, who participated in the major **Jewish rebellion** which swept across all of the Middle East in 116 AD. Cyprus was particularly hard hit since, given its scant political and military importance, it was lightly garrisoned; some estimated that virtually the entire gentile population of Salamis was slaughtered by the rebels. The insurrection was finally put down by Hadrian, and a decree promulgated which expelled all Jews from Cyprus. Despite this removal of an obstacle to proselytizing, Christianity spread slowly on the island, as suggested by the enthusiastically pagan Paphos mosaics – executed on the eve of Emperor Constantine's designation of Christianity as the official religion of the eastern empire in 323.

The Roman empire had been divided into **western and eastern portions** in 284, and

local Cypriot administration transferred to Antioch in Syria – a situation which would last until the fifth century, when the opportune discovery of Barnabas' relics (see p.290) provided the justification for Cyprus' **ecclesiastic and civic autonomy**, answerable only to the capital of the eastern empire, Constantinople. Cyprus' prestige in the Christian world was further enhanced by the 324 visit of Helena, Constantine's mother, who left fragments of the True Cross and the cross of the Penitent Thief.

THE BYZANTINE ERA

The break with antiquity was punctuated not only by a new faith and governmental order, but by two cataclysmic **earthquakes** – in 332 and 365 – which destroyed most Cypriot towns. Rebuilt Salamis was renamed Constantia, and designated again the capital of the island. As elsewhere in **Byzantium** – that portion of the empire centred on Constantinople – some of the more inhumane pagan-Roman laws were repealed, and mass conversion to Christianity proceeded apace, as evidenced by the huge fifth- and sixth-century basilica-type cathedrals erected in all cities. Foundations and **mosaic floors** for many of these are the most attractive early Byzantine remains on Cyprus; little else survives, however, owing to the repeated, devastating **raids of the Arab caliphate**, beginning in the seventh century AD. Their intent was not to conquer outright but to pillage, and to neutralize Cyprus as a Byzantine strongpoint; the Arabs' only significant legacy is the Hala Sultan *tekke* near Larnaca.

An immediate result of the raids was the **abandonment** of most coastal cities, which were far too vulnerable, and also plague- and drought-ridden at this time. By the terms of an **Arab-Byzantine treaty**, the island was to accept Muslim settlers, remain demilitarized except for naval bases of each side, and pay taxes equally to both the caliphate and the Byzantine empire. Except for occasional skirmishes, this strange agreement of condominium endured for three centuries, while Cyprus thrived on its silk trade and food exports, and served as a convenient place to exile dissidents from both Constantinople and the caliphate.

Only in 963 did Byzantine Emperor **Nikiphoros Phokas** permanently end Arab co-rule on Cyprus, and the Muslim colonists left or converted to Christianity. For another two centuries Cyprus had a peaceful, if heavily taxed, respite as a fully-fledged province of Byzantium, during which most of its **existing towns** – Kyrenia, Famagusta, Nicosia, Limassol – were **founded** or grew suddenly, with formidable **castles** raised against the threat of further attacks. At the same time, in the Tróödhos mountains, the first **frescoed chapels** were endowed by wealthy private donors.

WESTERN RULE: THE LUSIGNANS AND VENETIANS

Trouble loomed again in the eleventh century, however; the **schism** between the Catholic and Orthodox churches in 1054 fostered political antagonism between the Byzantine empire and most Latin principalities, and after their defeat of the Byzantines at the Battle of Manzikert in 1073, the **Seljuk Turks** were able to spread south and occupy the Holy Land. In response, the **First Crusade** was organized in western Europe during 1095, and Cyprus lay near or on the Latin knights' path towards the infidels. Although the first two Crusades bypassed the island, the knights soon established mini-kingdoms in Palestine, and the Seljuks also occupied most of Anatolia, allowing a capricious, despotic Byzantine prince, **Isaac Komnenos**, to declare Cypriot independence from a fatally weakened Constantinople in 1184 and rule for seven years. Greedy, cruel and consequently unpopular, he was hardly an improvement on the succession of incompetent and unstable emperors in the capital; this misrule made Cyprus a ripe plum for the Crusaders.

In the spring of 1191 a small fleet bearing the sister and fiancée of **Richard the Lionheart of England** hove to off Limassol. Isaac, realizing their value as hostages, tried to inveigle them ashore, but they wisely declined; he then refused them provisions. When the English king himself appeared, he landed in some force, considering his kinswomen to have been gravely insulted. After an unsuccessful attempt to secure Isaac's cooperation in the Third Crusade, Richard and his allies pursued the Byzantine forces across the island, defeating them at the battle of Tremetoushá on the Mesaoría; Isaac surrendered at the end of May,

sent away in silver chains upon his insistence that he not be put in irons.

Richard had never intended to acquire Cyprus, and was still keen to resume crusading; having plundered the island, he quickly sold it to the **Knights Templar** to raise more funds for his army. The Templars put forty percent of the purchase price down and had to raise the balance by confiscatory taxation; the Cypriots not unnaturally rebelled, with the knights quelling the revolt viciously to save their skins.

Having received more than they bargained for, the Templars returned Cyprus to Richard, who quickly resold it to **Guy de Lusignan**, a minor French noble who had been the last Crusader king of Jerusalem before having lost the city to Saladdin in 1187. Cyprus was essentially his consolation prize; Guy recreated the feudal system of his lost realm, parcelling out fiefs to more than five hundred supporters – principally landless allies without future prospects in what remained of Crusader Syria – and the Knights Hospitaller of St John, who soon displaced the Templars. Guy's brother and successor **Aimery** styled himself **king of Cyprus and Jerusalem**, the latter an honorific title used by all subsequent Lusignan rulers, though the Holy City went permanently back to Muslim control after 1244.

THE LUSIGNANS

Under the **Lusignans**, Cyprus acquired a **significance** far out of proportion to its size. European sovereigns, including **Holy Roman Emperor Frederick II Hohenstaufen**, stopped off obligatorily on their way to subsequent Crusades, and the Lusignans – and their deputies the **Ibelins** – married into all the royal houses of Europe. **Regencies** for underage princes were common, owing to the short life-expectancy of Crusader kings; an unusually long regency for Henry I in the early thirteenth century caused complications, obliging the Ibelin regents to defend Henry's title to the throne in a prolonged war against counterclaimant Frederick II Hohenstaufen.

Monumentally, the Byzantine **castles** of the Kyrenia range were refurbished, and new ones built around the capital Nicosia and the eastern port of Famagusta, which after the **1291 loss** of Acre, Sidon and Tyre, the last Crusader toeholds in the Holy Land, saw an influx of Christian refugees from all over the Near East.

For barely a century **Famagusta** served as the easternmost outpost of Christendom, and became one of the wealthiest cities on earth owing to a papal prohibition on direct European trade with the nearby infidel. No longer having to siphon off resources to defend their slender Syrian coastal strip also improved the military and financial health of the Cypriot kingdom. The Lusignan royalty were crowned in two massive Gothic **cathedrals** at Nicosia and Famagusta: coronations for the Kingdom of Cyprus were conducted at Nicosia; at Famagusta, facing the Holy Land across the water, the honorary ceremony for Jerusalem took place. All major **monastic orders** were represented, though the sole surviving foundation is the abbey of Béllapais.

The **everyday life** of the nobility was notorious for its luxury and ostentation, a privilege definitely not shared by the common people. The Greek Orthodox population, which had initially welcomed the Crusaders, soon discovered that they were effectively shut out from power or material security. Most of them lived as **serfs** of the Catholic overlords, and by a papal edict of 1260 the Orthodox archbishops were effectively **subordinated** to a Catholic metropolitan and furthermore exiled to rural sees. Orthodoxy was constrained to a rearguard holding action, awaiting a change in its fortunes; yet during this time many of the finest frescoes were painted in rural chapels of the Tróödhos Mountains.

In general, the Lusignan **kings** were a visibly overweight, mediocre bunch, probably resulting from a combination of hereditary thyroid problems and "riotous and unclean living", as one historian of the time put it. The most extravagant and activist sovereign was **Peter I** (1358–69), who in contrast to the live-and-let-live attitude of his lethargic predecessors canvassed Europe for support of his mini-Crusades along the neighbouring Muslim coasts, culminating in a thorough sacking of Alexandria in 1365. Also an inveterate womanizer, he was in the arms of one of his two mistresses when certain nobles, tired of his increasingly erratic behaviour and disregard for feudal law, burst into the bedchamber and murdered him.

Decline followed Peter's murder, though it was more the last straw than the root cause. If the Lusignans ran the Cypriot kingdom, the Venetians and Genoese were rivals for supremacy in its commercial life; at the 1373 Famagusta coronation of Peter II, a dispute between the two factions as to who would have the honour of leading the young king's horse escalated into destructive anti-Genoese riots. Incensed, **Genoa** sent a punitive expedition to ravage the island. For a year a virtual civil war raged, ending with the return of the throne to the Lusignans only upon payment of a huge indemnity – though the royal family was actually held prisoner in Genoa for 18 years – and the retention of Famagusta by the Genoese. But the damage had been done; both Cyprus and the Lusignans were in a disastrously weakened condition economically and politically.

A harbinger of worse "infidel" attacks to come took place in 1425–26, when the **Mamelukes** of Egypt, still smarting from Peter I's attack, landed on the south coast to plunder Limassol and Larnaca. **King Janus** met them near Stavrovoúni monastery, was roundly defeated and taken prisoner; the Mamelukes marched inland to sack Nicosia before returning with their treasure to Egypt. Janus was only released three years later after payment of a crippling ransom and a humiliating promise of a perpetual annual tribute to the Mamelukes.

With Janus' dissolute successor **John II**, the Lusignan saga entered its last chapters. He complicated matters by favouring his bastard son, **James II**, over his legitimate daughter **Charlotte**, and the two strong-willed offspring spent six years disputing the succession after John died in 1458. Securing Mameluke aid – which in effect meant an extension of the onerous tribute – James returned from Egypt and deposed his sister; he matched this success by finally evicting the Genoese from Famagusta, though it was far too late to restore that town to its former importance. A roistering, athletic man, James was relatively popular with his subjects both for his daring exploits and his fluency in **Greek**; indeed the language had recently begun to replace French in public use.

James did not run true to family form in his own choice of consort, contracting marriage with a Venetian noblewoman, **Caterina Cornaro**. Both the king and his infant son died mysteriously within a year of each other (1473 and 1474) – a Venetian poisoning plot has been suggested – leaving Queen Caterina to reign precariously in her own right. Charlotte, in exile, intrigued ceaselessly against Caterina until Charlotte died in 1485. Besides her foiled plot to assassinate Caterina, there was a Catalan-fomented rebellion in 1473. All this, and the growing **Ottoman threat**, convinced the Venetians that Caterina was better out of the way, and she was persuaded to **abdicate** in 1489, given as a sop the town and hinterland of Asolo in the Veneto, where she continued to keep a court of some splendour.

THE VENETIANS

Three centuries of Lusignan rule were over and the **Venetians** now governed the island directly through a *provéditore* or **military governor**. Their tenure was even more oppressive than the Lusignan one from the point of view of ordinary people; Cyprus was seen simply as a frontier fortress and money-spinner, with the island otherwise neglected and inefficiently administered. The Lusignan nobility retained their estates but were excluded from political power. The Venetians devoted most of their energy to overhauling the fortifications of Kyrenia, Nicosia and Famagusta in anticipation of the inevitable Ottoman attack. In the end, however, the undermanned Venetian forces were no match for the Turkish hordes, especially when relief failed to arrive from Venice: Nicosia fell after a seven-week **siege** in 1570, with almost half its population subsequently massacred, while Famagusta held out for ten months until July 1571 in one of the celebrated battles of the age (see p.280). The victor, **Lala Mustafa Paşa**, perhaps irked at having been so valiantly defied by the tiny garrison, went back on his promises of clemency, flaying commander **Marcantonio Bragadino** alive after butchering his lieutenants.

Surrounded on three sides by Ottoman territory, it was almost certain that Cyprus should eventually fall to the Muslim power, but the specific impetus for the 1570–71 campaign is interesting. The incumbent sultan, **Selim the Sot**, had a particular fondness for Cypriot Commandaria wine; his chief adviser, **Joseph Nasi**, was a Spanish Jew whose family had suffered at the hands of the Venetians during their long exile after the 1492 expulsion, and who longed to take revenge on the Serene Republic – and perhaps secure a haven for Jewry. In fact the invasion plan was hatched

over the objections of the grand vizier and others, who considered it unfeasible, and feared the wrath of the European powers. Selim died just three years later, fracturing his skull by slipping in his bath – while drunk on Commandaria.

STAGNATION: OTTOMAN RULE

Because the Lusignans had never made any attempt to bridge the gap between ruler and ruled, they remained an upper crust, all trace of which was swept away by the Turkish conquest. By 1573 most of the monasteries and Latin churches had been destroyed, and most surviving **Catholics** had departed or converted to Islam; the tiny "Latin" minority on the island today is all that survives. Other ancestors of the present **Turkish population** date from the year of the conquest, when Ottoman soldiers and their families formed the nucleus, some 20,000 strong, of initial settlement, later supplemented by civilians from Anatolia (see box opposite). Their relations with the native Greek population were, if not always close, usually cordial.

The Greek Orthodox peasantry, perhaps surprisingly in the light of later events, actually **welcomed** the Ottomans at first; both were united in their hatred of the Franks, whose feudal system was abolished and lands distributed to the freed serfs. The Greeks also appreciated Ottoman **recognition of their church**: not only were certain Catholic ecclesiastical properties made over to Orthodoxy, but in 1660 the archbishop was officially acknowledged as the head of the Greek community in accord with prevailing Ottoman administrative practice, with the right of direct petition to the sultan. This was followed in 1754 by the revival of the role of **ethnarch**, with comprehensive civil powers, and in 1779 by the stipulation for a **dragoman**, a Greek appointed by the ethnarch to liaise with the island's Turkish governor. The most powerful and famous dragoman was **Hadjiyorgakis Kornesios**.

None of this, however, was done in a spirit of disinterested religious tolerance; the Ottomans used the ecclesiastical apparatus principally to collect **onerous taxes**, and the clerics, who eventually all but ran the island together with the dragoman, made themselves every bit as unpopular as the Turkish governors. In fairness the clergy often attempted to protect their flock from the more rapacious exactions of the various governors, who – minimally salaried and having paid huge bribes to secure their short-term appointments – were expected to recoup their expenses with extractions from the populace. People unable to meet assessments forfeited **land** in lieu of payment, the source of the Orthodox church's still-extensive real-estate holdings.

If the Greeks had hoped for a definitive improvement in their lot with the end of Frankish rule, they were thoroughly disillusioned, as Cyprus became one of the **worst-governed and neglected** Ottoman provinces. Almost all tax revenues went to Istanbul, with next to nothing being spent to abate the drought, plagues and locusts which lashed the island, or on other local improvements; Turkish medieval monuments are rare on Cyprus, with most large mosques merely churches adapted for Muslim use. Between 1571 and the late 1700s the population dropped sharply, with many Greeks **emigrating** to Anatolia or the Balkans despite administrative reshuffles aimed at staunching the outflow.

Such conditions ensured that the three Ottoman centuries were punctuated by regular **rebellions** which often united the Muslim and Christian peasantry against their overlords. The first occurred in 1680; in 1764 the excesses of the worst governor, **Çil Osman**, precipitated a longer and bloodier revolt in which he was killed, the Turkish commander of Kyrenia mutinied, and the Greek bishops appealed to Istanbul for the restoration of order. With the rise of Balkan nationalism later that century, the *Filikí Etería* (Friendly Society), the Greek revolutionary fifth column, was active on Cyprus after 1810. To forestall any echo of the mainland Greek rebellion, Governor **Küçük Mehmet** got permission from the sultan in 1821 to execute the unusually popular **Archbishop Kyprianos**, his three bishops and hundreds of leading Greek Orthodox islanders in Nicosia, not so coincidentally confiscating their considerable property and

---

WHO ARE THE TURKISH CYPRIOTS?

The number of Muslims on Cyprus, even during the most vigorous periods of Ottoman rule, has never exceeded about one-third of the population, and had already declined to about one-quarter when the British arrived in 1878. The word "Muslim" is used deliberately since religious affiliation, and not race, was the determining civic factor in the Ottoman empire; the present-day Turkish Cypriots are in fact descended from a variety of sources.

At the time of the 1571 conquest, Ottoman civil servants arrived with their families, whose descendants tend to preserve their aristocratic consciousness to this day. Some twenty thousand janissaries, by definition of Anatolian or Balkan Christian origins, took as wives the widows of the defeated Venetians, as well as a number of Orthodox Christian virgins. Turkmen nomads were brought over from Turkey for the sake of their reed- and textile-weaving skills, and various Ottoman prisons were emptied, with the convicts transported to a more comfortable exile on Cyprus. Blacks from Sudan also arrived, mostly working as porters in and around Larnaca and Limassol, and obliged by local colour consciousness to marry less desirable, "low-class" women.

The so-called **Linovamváki** (Cotton-Linens) sect, which practised Islam outwardly but maintained Christian beliefs in private, arose mainly among Venetian civilians (names like Mehmet Valentino occur on old archives); curiously, they spoke Greek in preference to Turkish, and many areas such as Louroujína (today Akıncılar), Vrécha, and most of Tillyría were once almost exclusively *Linovamváki*. After 1878, evangelization of this group by both Muslim and Christian clerics, and the resulting assimilative marriages, resulted in a hitherto unknown polarization in island society; in the North today, many of the more fanatical nationalists are of *Linovamváki* background.

Another more recent development is the **Ba'hai** sect with its approximately five hundred adherents. It was founded by the adoptive son of the holy man Babi, who was hanged as a troublemaker by the Iranian shah towards the end of the last century. Babi's biological son, Süphi Ezel, was exiled to Famagusta, and while the Ezeli rite is no longer a vital religion in the North, his tomb is still a focus of pilgrimage for Iranian believers.

Given these motley, often "heretical" origins of the Turkish Cypriots, it's hardly surprising that observance of Islam on Cyprus has always been famously lax – despite recent Saudi input – and that fervent Turkish nationalism has had to be whipped up by outsiders in the past century.

inaugurating another spell of unrest on the island, which ended in the revolt of 1833.

Such incidents were not repeated after European powers established more trading posts and watchful consulates at Larnaca, and the Church's power **waned** with the suspension of its right to collect taxes and the emergence of an educated, westernized class of Greek Cypriot. As the nineteenth century wore on, **Britain** found itself repeatedly guaranteeing the Ottoman empire's territorial integrity in the path of Russian expansionism; in 1878, this relationship was formalized by the **Anglo-Turkish Convention**, whereby the Ottomans ceded occupation and administrative rights of Cyprus – though technically not sovereignty – to Britain in return for having halted the Russian advance outside Istanbul during the 1877–78 Russo-Turkish war, and for a continued undertaking to help defend what was left of Turkish domains. Curiously, retention of Cyprus was **linked** to Russia's occupation of Ardahan, Kars and Batumi, three strongpoints on Turkey's Caucasian frontier; Kars and Ardahan were returned to republican Turkey in 1921, but in the NATO era Turkey's and Britain's continued alliance against the Russian threat still served as justification for occupation of Cyprus.

BRITISH RULE

British forces landed peacefully at Larnaca in July 1878, assuming control of the island without incident; ironically, the British acquisition of Egypt and the Suez Canal in 1882 made Cyprus of distinctly secondary importance as a **military base**, with civilian high commissioners soon replacing military ones.

The Greek Orthodox population, remembering Britain's cession of the Ionian islands to Greece in 1864, hoped for the same generosity here, and the bishop of Kition (Larnaca)'s greeting speech to the landing party alluded directly to this. Free of the threat of Ottoman-style repression, the demand for **énosis** or union with Greece was to be reiterated regularly by the Greek Cypriots until 1960 – and beyond. From the very outset of the colonial period the Turkish Cypriots expressed their satisfaction with the status quo and their horror at the prospect of being Greek citizens.

What the Cypriots got instead, aside from separate Greek- and Turkish-language education, was a modicum of **better government** – reaffor-

estation, an end to banditry and extralegal extortion, an English legal system, water supplies, roads and a stamping out of disease and locusts – combined with a continuance of **crushing taxes**, which militated against any striking economic growth. An obscure clause of the Anglo-Turkish Convention mandated that the excess of tax revenues (appreciable) over local expenditures (almost nil) during the last five years of Ottoman rule was theoretically to be paid to the Turks, a rule which pressured colonial administrators to keep programmes modest so as to have some sum to forward – or to squeeze the Cypriots for more taxes. The practice was widely condemned by Cypriophiles and Turkophobes in England, including Gladstone and Churchill, but continued until 1927. Worse still, the monies went not to Istanbul, but to bond holders of an 1855 loan to Turkey on which the Ottoman rulers had defaulted. So while Cyprus recovered much of its population, the British-promised prosperity never appeared, the islanders in effect being required to **service an Ottoman debt**. The only apparatus of self-government was a very rudimentary **legislative council**, numerically weighted towards colonial civil servants and with limited powers in any case.

CYPRUS AS COLONY

Following Ottoman Turkey's 1914 entry into World War I as one of the Central Powers, Britain declared most provisions of the Anglo-Turkish Convention void, and formally **annexed** Cyprus. The next year she secretly offered the island to Greece as a territorial inducement to join the war on the Allied side, but Greece, then ruled by pro-German King Constantine I, declined, to the Greek Cypriots' infinite later regret. In the 1923 Treaty of Lausanne, republican Turkey renounced all claims to Cyprus, but the island did not officially become a British Crown Colony until 1925, by which time calls for *énosis* were again been heard; these increased in stridency, leading in **1931** to the first serious **civil disturbances**: the Greek Cypriot members of the legislative council resigned, and rioters burned down the Government House, a rambling bungalow diverted from use in Ceylon. The Cypriots' anger was not only sparked by the *énosis* issue, but derived from disappointment at the thus-far modest level of material progress under British rule, especially the woebegone state of agriculture.

ADVENT OF THE LEFT

The British **response** to the mini-rebellion was predictably harsh: reparations assessments for damages, bans on publications and flying the Greek flag, proscriptions of existing political parties (especially the KKK or Communists, who had organized strikes in 1929 at the asbestos mines), and imprisonment or deportation of activists – including two bishops. The legislative council was abolished, and Cyprus came under the nearest thing to martial law; only the **PEO** or Pancyprian Federation of Labour, though driven underground until 1936, remained as a pole of opposition to the colonial regime, and a haven for both left-wing Turks and Greeks. **AKEL**, the new **communist party**, grew out of it in 1941, and has remained an important faction in the Greek Cypriot community to this day. Municipal elections were finally held in 1943, and served as a barometer of public sentiment through the balance of the colonial period; the British could not very well profess to be fighting fascism while simultaneously withholding basic political freedoms.

During **World War II**, Cyprus belied its supposed strategic value by escaping much involvement other than as an important supply depot and staging post. The island suffered just a few stray Italian raids from Rhodes – after the German difficulties on Crete, Hitler had forbidden another paratroop action to seize Cyprus. Both Greek and Turkish Cypriots fought with British forces in Europe and North Africa, and the Greeks at least expected some political reward for this at the war's end.

The extent of this was the 1947 offer by Governor Lord Winster of a **limited constitution** of self-rule, similar to that tendered in other colonies at the time. It was summarily rejected by the enosist elements, principally the Orthodox Church, who proclaimed that anything less than *énosis* or at least provision for its implementation was unacceptable – a stance which probably guaranteed later bloodshed. AKEL was lukewarm on the idea; they were busy mounting the inconclusive but distinguished 1947–48 **strike** in the American-run copper mines of Soléa district.

THE POSTWAR YEARS

By 1950 demands for *énosis* had returned to the fore, in a **referendum** campaign organized by newly elected Archbishop and Ethnarch **Makarios III**, with results showing 96 percent support for *énosis* among Greek Cypriots. They seemed to ignore the fact that Greece, dominated by far-right-wing governments and still a stretcher case after the rigours of German occupation and a civil war, was a poor candidate as a partner for association; yet so great was the groundswell for union that even the PEO and AKEL subscribed to it after 1950, though they could both expect a fairly unpleasant fate in a rightist "Greater Greece". In general outsiders did, and still do, have trouble understanding the enormous emotional and historical appeal of *énosis*, whose advocates readily admitted that Cypriot living standards would drop sharply once the island was out of the sterling zone and yoked to chaotic, impoverished Greece.

Soon the at least theoretical possibility of *énosis* dawned on the island's **Turkish minority** – some 18 percent of the population – who began agitation in opposition, advocating either the status quo or some sort of affiliation with Turkey rather than becoming a truly insignificant minority in a greater Greece. As the Turkish Cypriots were scattered almost uniformly throughout the island, forming nowhere a majority, the option of a separate Turkish Cypriot province did not seem available without painful population transfers.

Many Greek Cypriots retrospectively accused the British (and to a lesser extent the Americans) of **stirring up** Turkey and the Turkish Cypriots against them, and while there is some truth to this – divide and rule was very much a colonial strategy – mainland Turkey itself would probably have eventually become involved without cues from Britain, and the Turkish Cypriots were certainly not quiescent. Greek Cypriots saw the situation as a non-colonial problem of the island's wishing to transfer its allegiance to the "mother country"; Britain, in their view, transformed matters into a general Greco-Turkish dispute under the guise of "harmony in the southeast flank of NATO", ensuring that Turkey would forcefully block any move towards *énosis*.

After Egyptian independence in 1954, **British Mid-East Military HQ** was moved to Cyprus over a period of twenty months, making self-determination far less likely, and the British position increasingly inflexible – thanks to such intemperate Tory personalities as Anthony Eden, and murmurs of support for such policy by the Americans. In July of that year, the minister of state for the colonies declared that "certain Commonwealth territories, owing to their particular circumstances, can never expect to be fully independent" – and went on to express fears of AKEL dominating an independent Cyprus. To the Greek Cypriots this utterance seemed ludicrous in the light of independence being granted to far less developed parts of Asia and Africa. That "never" closed off all avenues of communication with more moderate Greek Cypriots, and came back repeatedly to haunt the British over the next five years.

In **Greece** the government encouraged a shrill, anti-British media barrage in support of *énosis*, accessible to any radio on Cyprus. For the first time Greece also tried to internationalize the Cyprus issue at the **UN**, where it failed to get a full hearing, though Turkey bared its teeth in the preliminary discussions, a promise of trouble in the future. Only the Greek ambassador to London had astutely seen that the mainland Turks were now an interested party and would have to be included in any solution.

THE EOKA REBELLION

In conjunction with **General George Grivas** (see also p.200), codenamed "Dhiyenis" after the hero of a Byzantine epic, Archbishop Makarios in 1954 secretly founded **EOKA**, *Ethnikí Orgánosis Kypríon Agonistón* or "National Organization of Cypriot Fighters", as an IRA-type movement to throw off British rule. Late that year several clandestine shipments of arms and explosives were transferred from Rhodes to the deserted Páfos coast, though the archbishop initially shrank back from advocating lethal force against persons, restricting Grivas to sabotage of property. EOKA's campaign of violence on Cyprus began spectacularly on April 1, 1955 with the destruction of the Government radio transmitter, among other targets.

Overseas, a hastily scheduled **trilateral conference** in July 1955, convening representatives of Greece, Turkey and Britain, flopped miserably; Makarios remarked that Greece's attendance at it had merely legitimized Turkish involvement in the Cyprus issue. Two months

later, massive, Turkish-government-inspired **rioting** in Istanbul caused staggering loss to Greek property and effectively dashed any hope of a reasonable future for the Greek Orthodox community there. Greek government recourse to the UN was again futile.

Newly appointed **High Commissioner John Harding**, a former field marshal, pursued a hard line against EOKA; ongoing negotiations with Makarios, who distanced himself at least publicly from the armed struggle, were approaching a breakthrough when Grivas set off more strategically timed bombs. Talks were broken off and the archbishop and two associates **deported** in March 1956 to comfortable house arrest in the Seychelles. Deprived of its ablest spokesman, EOKA now graduated to murderous **attacks** on Greeks who disagreed with them, as well as on British soldiers and civilians. The island terrain was ideal for such an insurgency; despite massive searches, internments, collective punishments for aiding EOKA, and other now-familiar curtailments of civil liberties in such emergencies, the uprising couldn't be squelched. An estimated three hundred guerrillas, based primarily in the Tróödhos, tied up twenty thousand regular British Army troops and 4500 special constables. The latter were overwhelmingly composed of Turkish Cypriot auxiliaries – who often applied **torture** to captured EOKA suspects under the supervision of British officers, an assigned task which perceptibly increased intercommunal tensions. Spring and summer of 1956 also saw the **hangings** of nine convicted EOKA men, touching off violent protests in Greece and plunging British–Greek relations to an all-time low.

International pressure in **1957** – and Britain's realization that no other Greek Cypriot negotiating partner existed – brought about Makarios' release, just after Greece finally managed to get Cyprus on the UN agenda, resulting in a resolution accepting independence "in principle". Harding was replaced with the more conciliatory civilian **Governor Hugh Foot**, and a constitutional commissioner, Lord Radcliffe, was dispatched to make more generous proposals for limited self-government than those of 1947. These were again rejected by the Greek Cypriots, because they didn't envision *énosis*, and by the Turkish Cypriots – represented by the **Turkish National Party**, headed by future vice-president **Fazil Küçük** – since it didn't specifically exclude that possibility.

TMT

After isolated intercommunal incidents since 1956, the **TMT** or *Turk Müdafaa Teskilati*, (Turkish Defence Organization) was founded early in **1958** to counter EOKA's goals and work for *taksim* or partition of the island between Greece and Turkey. TMT's cell structure was modelled on EOKA, and it also duplicated EOKA's rabid **anti-communism**, killing various left-wing Turkish personalities, and pressurizing Turkish Cypriots to leave PEO and AKEL, virtually the last unsegregated institutions on the island. TMT also organized a boycott of Greek products, just as EOKA was presiding over a Greek Cypriot boycott of British products.

INTERCOMMUNAL CLASHES

A June 1958 bomb explosion outside the Turkish press office in Nicosia – later shown to have been planted by TMT provocateurs – set off the first serious **intercommunal clashes** on the island. In Nicosia, Turkish gangs expelled Greeks from some mixed neighbourhoods, and induced some of their own to abandon villages in the south of the island in favour of the north – a forerunner of events in 1974. Shortly after, in what became known as the **Gönyeli incident**, seven EOKA suspects were released from British custody to walk home through a Turkish area, where they were duly stabbed to death – as was presumably the English intent. EOKA retaliated by targeting Turkish policemen, and also stepping up assaults on the British after a year's lull. The **death toll** for the whole insurrection climbed to nearly 600, of these almost half left-wing or pro-British Greek Cypriots killed by EOKA. **Truces** were declared in late summer by both TMT and EOKA, with many displaced Cypriots returning to their homes in mixed areas. The EOKA truce did not, however, extend to members of AKEL, which now favoured independence again – and continued to suffer fatal consequences.

One last mainland Greece-sponsored UN resolution for Cypriot "self-determination " (by now a code word for *énosis*) failed in 1958 to muster the necessary two-thirds majority in the General Assembly, so Makarios began to accept the wisdom of independence especially as both the British, in the person of Prime Minister Harold Macmillan, and the Turkish Cypriots were threatening to renew the option of partition and massive population movements.

Throughout the later 1950s, EOKA, Greece and most Greek Cypriots had failed to take seriously the **mainland Turkish position**: that Turkey would take steps to prevent strategically vital Cyprus becoming Greek territory, as Crete had after a 15-year period of supposed independence at the start of the century. Less genuine, perhaps, was Turkey's new-found concern for its "brothers" on the island – programmes broadcast regularly over Radio Ankara agitating feelings in its communal audience just as mainland Greek programmes did. The British, now faced with hostility from the Turkish Cypriots as well as from the Greeks, and contemplating the soaring costs of containing the rebellion, desperately sought a way out.

THE GRANTING OF INDEPENDENCE

In February 1959, the foreign ministers of Greece and Turkey met in **Zurich** to hammer out some compromise settlement, with a supplementary meeting including the British and Cypriots in **London** a few days later. The participants agreed on the establishment of an independent Cypriot republic, its **constitution** to be prepared by an impartial Swiss expert. Of its 199 clauses, 48 were unalterable, with *énosis* or *taksim* expressly forbidden. The two ethnic communities were essentially to be co-founders, running the republic on a 70:30 Greek:Turk **proportional basis** that slightly favoured the Turkish minority. A single fifty-seat House of Representatives – with fifteen seats reserved for the Turks – two separate communal chambers funded partly by Greece and Turkey, and a Greek Cypriot president plus a Turkish Cypriot vice-president elected by their respective communities was also envisioned. With some misgivings Makarios gave his assent to the constitution.

The meetings also produced three interrelated **treaties**, which in turn were incorporated as articles of the constitution. Britain, Turkey and Greece simultaneously entered into a **Treaty of Guarantee**, by which they acted as guarantors to safeguard Cypriot independence. A **Treaty of Establishment** stipulated the existence of two British military bases, their extent to be determined, and other training areas. The **Treaty of Alliance** provided for the stationing of Greek and Turkish military forces on the island and the training of a Cypriot army, presumably as an arm of NATO; this provision was roundly denounced by AKEL, and indeed in the long run this treaty was to prove the most destabilizing element of the package.

Makarios, who had been in Greece since 1957, was finally permitted to **return to Cyprus**, where an amnesty was declared for most EOKA offenders. Grivas and the more hard-line enosists, excoriating Makarios for his supposed betrayal of the cause, flew off to self-imposed exile in Greece, while certain supporters stayed behind to punctuate most of 1959 with fulminations against the independence deal. More moderate individuals personally opposed to Makarios' personality cult, such as **Mayor Themistoklis Dhervis of Nicosia**, formed the first opposition party, the **Democratic Union**, to contest the presidential elections of December 1959 with the archbishop's **Popular Front**. Makarios won handily with two-thirds of the vote, while Fazil Küçük ran unopposed for the vice-presidential seat.

Elections for the **House of Representatives** in February 1960 were poorly attended, with absenteeism and abstention rates of up to sixty percent in some districts reflecting popular disgust at the civic arrangements – and a poor omen for the future. The Popular Front took thirty seats, its coalition partners AKEL five, while Küçük's National Party got all fifteen Turkish seats. Polling for the powerful **communal chambers**, charged with overseeing education, religion, culture and consumer credit co-ops, showed a similar profile, though in the Greek chamber one seat each was reserved for the Armenian, Maronite and "Latin" communities.

Final independence, which had been set for no later than February 1960, was postponed until **16 August 1960**, as the Cypriots and the British haggled over the exact size of the two sovereign bases. By coincidence, Venetian and British rule lasted exactly the same time: 82 years.

THE UNITARY REPUBLIC: 1960–1964

The Republic of Cyprus seemed doomed from the start, with EOKA and TMT **ideologues** appointed to cabinet positions. Neither organization completely disbanded, but maintained shadowy existences, waiting for the right moment to re-emerge. They and others made Makarios' life difficult: the enosists considered that he'd sold them out, the Turks were convinced that he was biding his time for an opportunity to impose it, and many of the communists felt he was too accommodating to the West.

On a **symbolic** level, communal iconography, street names, etc, all continued referring to persons and events in the "mother" countries; the respective national flags and national days were celebrated by each community, and while there was (and still is) a Cypriot flag, there never was a national anthem. Such institutionalized separatism was inimical to fostering a national consciousness. The **constitution**, an improbably intricate one for a population of just over half a million, proved unworkable in application. The Greek Cypriots chafed at it for having been imposed from outside, while the Turkish Cypriots took every opportunity to exploit its numerous clauses benefiting them. It was, as several outside observers remarked, the only democracy where majority rule was explicitly denied by its founding charter.

The **70:30 ratio**, running through all civil service institutions, could not be reached within the five months prescribed, and the **army**, supposed to be set up on a 60:40 ratio with ethnic mix at all levels, never materialized, since the Turks insisted on segregated companies; instead Makarios eventually authorized the establishment of an all-Greek **National Guard**. Both the president and the vice-president had **veto power** over foreign affairs, defence or internal matters, exercised frequently by Küçük. Laws had to clear the House of Representatives by a majority of votes from **both communal factions**: thus eight of the fifteen Turkish MPs could defeat any bill. When agreement could not be reached in the first two years of the republic's life, colonial rules were often extended as **stopgaps**.

For much of 1962 Cyprus had no uniform income tax or customs excise laws, the Turks having obstructed them in retaliation for Greek foot-dragging on implementation of separate municipalities for the five largest towns; another concession to the Turkish Cypriots was the maintenance of **separate municipalities**, first set up in the 1950s, for each community in those five towns – an incredibly wasteful and time-consuming duplication from the Greek point of view. Yet they did not hesitate to pass **revenue** laws through their own communal chamber when frustrated in the parliament, thus perpetuating the apartheid by providing services only to the Greek Cypriot community and those Turks choosing to acknowledge its jurisdiction.

Among the hardline elements, the TMT struck first, against its own community: on 23 April 1962 gunmen murdered **Ahmet Gurkan and Ayhan Hikmet**, leaders of the only Turkish Cypriot political party to oppose Küçük's National Party, promoting closer co-operation between two communities. It was an echo of numerous such actions in 1958, and now as then no action was taken against TMT or its backers; **Rauf Denktaş**, protégé of Küçük, even managed to get Emil Dirvana, Turkish ambassador to Nicosia and one of many to condemn the murders, recalled. There would be no other significant Turkish opposition group until the 1970s.

In late November 1963, Makarios proposed to Küçük **thirteen amendments** to the constitution for make bicommunal public life possible. These included the abolition of both the presidential and vice-presidential right of veto, the introduction of simply majority rule in the legislature, the unification of the municipalities and justice system, and an adjustment of communal ratios in civil service and the still-theoretical army. Apparently, this proposal had been drafted with the advice of the British High Commissioner; the mainland Greeks subsequently deemed the bundle incredibly tactless, even if such reforms were worth introducing gradually. Turkey was sent the suggestions and denounced them, threatening military action if introduced unilaterally, even before Küçük had finished reading them, leaving him little room to manoeuvre.

FURTHER INTERCOMMUNAL FIGHTING

Reaction to the Turkish refusal was swift: on **December 21, 1963** shots were exchanged between a Greek Cypriot police patrol and a Turkish motorist, and within hours EOKA and TMT took to the field again. EOKA struck at Turkish neighbourhoods in Larnaca, and also in the mixed Nicosia district of Omórfita (Küçük Kaymaklı), with an EOKA detachment under one **Nikos Sampson** rampaging through, seizing 700 hostages. In retaliation the Armenian community, accused of siding with the Greek Cypriots, was expelled by the Turks from north Nicosia on 23 December, and mainland Turkish troops left their barracks next day to take up positions along the Nicosia–Kyrenia road, with more forces concentrated on the Turkish mainland opposite; the mainland Greek force also deployed itself. Barriers, known as the **Green Line** after an English officer's crayon mark on a map, were set up to separate Greek and Turkish quarters in Nicosia after a UK-brokered ceasefire was effected on Christmas Day.

Already, all Turkish Cypriots had **resigned** from the government and police forces, to begin setting up a parallel administration in north Nicosia and in the rapidly growing number of **enclaves**. Any Turkish Cypriot who might have thought to continue at his post in south Nicosia would have to run a gauntlet of both his own co-religionists, enforcing the sequestration, and Greeks who might shoot first and ask questions later. The enclaves in fact constituted a semi-deliberate policy of laying the physical basis for later partition, and the Turkish Cypriot position from now on asserted that the 1960 constitution was **defunct**, and there were merely two provisional regimes on the island pending the establishment of a new arrangement. Makarios agreed that the 1960 constitution was hopeless – but differed in his conclusions: namely that majority rule would prevail as per his suggested amendments, with minority guarantees, whether the Turks liked it or not.

INTERNATIONAL REPERCUSSIONS

Because of the superpower interests involved, the Cyprus intercommunal dispute again took on **international** dimensions. The Greek Cypriots preferred, as they always had done, the UN as a forum; the US, UK, and both mainland Turkey and the Turkish Cypriots pressed for **NATO intervention**. Turkish opinion, expressed by Küçük's and Denktaş' rightist Turkish National Party, helped plant the seeds of implacable American hostility to Makarios by successfully painting him with a pink (if not red) brush, calling attention to his forthright espousal of the **non-aligned movement**, and purchase of arms from the USSR and Czechoslovakia. In the event the Cypriot government, with the support of the Soviets and Greek Premier George Papandreou, had its way: in February 1964, a UN resolution dispatched **UNFICYP** (UN Forces in Cyprus) for an initial three-month peace-keeping assignment – extended later to six months and renewed since then without a break. A mediator was also sent. George Ball, the US under-secretary of state who had unsuccessfully tried to persuade Makarios to accept occupation by a NATO landing force, was later overheard to say "that son of a bitch [ie Makarios] will have to be killed before anything happens in Cyprus."

Little was accomplished immediately by UNFICYP; the death toll in the communal disturbances in the six months after December 1963 reached nearly six hundred, with the Turkish Cypriots suffering disproportionately. Unfortunately ten thousand **mainland Greek troops** also landed on the island, which gave EOKA and Greek Cypriots a false sense of being able to act with impunity. After TMT occupied St Hilarion castle and the Kyrenia–Nicosia road to form a core enclave, US President Lyndon Johnson sent Turkish Premier İnönü a letter, in his inimitably crude style, warning him off plans to invade. At the same time the US administration pressurized Greece to follow its prescription or possibly face Turkey alone on the battlefield; heads were to be knocked together, if necessary, to preserve NATO's southeast flank.

The UN mediator having reached a dead end (and himself soon dying anyway), the **Acheson Plan** – named after the incumbent US secretary of state – was unveiled in mid-1964. It amounted to double *énosis*: the bulk of the island to Greece, the rest, plus the cession of the tiny but strategic Greek isle of Kastellórizo, to Turkey – effectively partition and the disappearance of Cyprus as an independent entity. After initial mulling over by both Greece and Turkey, the Greeks rejected the idea because of vociferous objections from Nicosia.

THE TURKISH CYPRIOT ENCLAVES

The **Kókkina incident** made world headlines in August 1964, when the newly formed National Guard, commanded by a returned Grivas, attacked this coastal enclave in an effort to halt the landing of supplies and weapons from Turkey. Guarantors Greece and Turkey were again brought to the brink of war as Turkey extensively bombed and strafed the Pólis area, causing numerous casualties, and Makarios threatened to sanction attacks on Turkish Cypriots throughout the island unless Turkey ceased its air strikes. It was the first, but not the last, time that US-supplied NATO weapons were used in contravention of their ostensible purpose.

Any residual trust between the two island communities was destroyed by the end of 1964: the Turkish Cypriots were well **barricaded** in their enclaves, the central government retaliating by placing a ban on their acquisition of a wide range of essential materials deemed militarily strategic. The enclave inmates, numbers swelled by Turkish army personnel, retaliated by keeping all Greeks out, setting up a TMT-run state-within-a-state with its own police, radio station and other services, which provocation EOKA could not resist on numerous occasions.

Despite all this, Cypriot **economic progress** post-independence was considerable – though heavily weighted towards the Greek community, whose attitude towards the Turkish Cypriots at best resembled sending naughty children to bed without supper. The first of many **irrigation dams** to ease chronic water problems began to appear on the slopes of the Tróödhos range and Kyrenia hills. Tourism became important for the first time, primarily on the sandy coast to either side of Famagusta and to a lesser extent around Kyrenia.

A TWILIGHT ZONE: 1965–1974

The new UN mediator **Galo Plaza** submitted his report in March 1965; it astutely diagnosed the shortcomings of the 1960 constitution and made forthright suggestions for a new one, principally that the Greek Cypriots must decisively renounce *énosis* and that the Turkish Cypriots must acquiesce to majority rule, with guarantees for certain rights. This did not go over well with them or the mainland Turks, who arranged to send Plaza packing.

After April 1967 Greece had been taken over by a **military junta**, anxious – with American approval – to remove the "Cyprus problem"

GREEK CYPRIOT POLITICAL ORGANIZATIONS

AKEL *Anorthotikón Kómma tou Ergazómenou Laoú* or "Regenerative Party of the Working People" – in plain English, the Communist Party of Cyprus; historically enemies of EOKA and conciliatory towards the Turkish Cypriots, though unreconstructed as opposed to Euro-communist.

ADISOK *Ananeótiko Dhimikratikó Sosialistikó Kómma* or "Renovating Democratic Socialist Party", a recent Euro-splinter off AKEL.

DIKO *Dhimokratikó Kómma* or "Democratic Party", headed by ex-President Spyros Kyprianou; pursues a relatively tough line in negotiations with the North.

DISY *Dhimokratikós Synayermós* or the "Democratic Rally", headed by former communal

negotiator, President Glafkos Clerides; despite a right-wing domestic and foreign policy, advocates sweeping concessions to the North.

EDEK *Enoméni Dhimokratikí Énosis tou Kéndrou* or "United Democratic Union of the Centre" – despite the name this is a socialist party, perennial also-rans and coalition partners in national elections.

EOKA *Ethnikí Orgánosis Kypríon Agonistón* or "National Organization of Cypriot Fighters", right-wing, IRA-type group co-founded by Makarios and Grivas to effect *énosis* or union of Cyprus with Greece. Continued to exist after independence, metamorphosing into the virulently anti-Makarios, pro-junta **EOKA-B**.

from the global agenda. However, secret summer meetings with Turkey, exploring variations of the Acheson Plan, came to nothing. In November, Grivas' National Guard attacked **Kofínou**, another enclave between Limassol and Larnaca, with considerable loss of Turkish life; Greece and Turkey both mobilized, Ankara again tendered an ultimatum to Athens, and American diplomats got little sleep as they shuttled between the two capitals. Despite its soldierly composition the Greek regime meekly complied with Turkish demands; **Grivas** and most of the 10,000 smuggled-in mainland soldiers were shipped **back to Greece**. The National Guard, however, remained in place, an ideal Trojan horse for future plots.

In 1968 the UN sponsored direct **intercommunal negotiations**, which sputtered along until 1974, with **Glafkos Clerides**, president of the House of Representatives, and Rauf Denktaş as interlocutors. Substantial agreement on many points was actually reached, despite the Turks pressing for implementation of a high degree of local communal power in place of a spoiler role at the national level, and the Greek side holding out for more comprehensive central control. But Makarios never made the necessarily dramatic, generous concessions, and Clerides repeatedly offered to resign in the absence of what he saw was a lack of consistent support from Makarios.

The Turkish enclaves were, though, finally **opened** to the extent of supplies going in and Turks coming out; with UN mediation, local

arrangements – such as joint police patrols – were reached for a semblance of normal life in less tense areas of island. But in most details the leaders of the Turkish Cypriot community still enforced a policy of **self-segregation** as a basis for a federal state. But whether they meant a federation as most outsiders understood it, or merely federation masquerading as partition, was highly moot. The Turkish Cypriots, biding their time in cramped and impoverished quarters, perhaps knew something that the Greek islanders didn't or wouldn't realize: that the mainland Turks were in earnest about **supporting** their cause materially and militarily as well as morally.

Both Makarios and Küçük were overwhelmingly re-elected early in 1968, though Makarios' three bishops had repudiated him for dropping *énosis* as a realistic strategy. This was just one aspect of his **deteriorating relations** with the Greek colonels, who – with the approval of the CIA – began **plotting** repeatedly to eliminate him, through the medium of the Greek regular army officers who by now controlled most of the National Guard.

A bizarre **counterplot** of the same year deserves mention: **Polycarpos Yiorgadjis**, a former EOKA operative and minister of interior, provided one Alekos Panagoulis in Greece with the explosives for an abortive attempt on the life of junta chief Papadopoulos. Exactly why Yiorgadjis would do this – considering that EOKA and junta aims were now identical – remains a mystery; he was also implicated in a later attempt on Makarios' life, and was himself assassinated, either by junta operatives or forces loyal to the archbishop, in March 1970.

Grivas slipped back into Cyprus during 1971 and founded **EOKA-B** with the express intent of resuming the struggle for *énosis*; the old trouble-maker, now in his seventies, died in January 1974, still in hiding. EOKA-B and its allies set in motion various devices to destabilize the elected government of Cyprus, reserving – as had its predecessor – special venom for AKEL. Publically, the Greek junta demanded, and eventually got, the resignation of **Spyros Kyprianou**, long-time foreign minister and future president. The three dissident bishops of 1968, still acting as junta placemen, claimed at one point to have defrocked Makarios, reducing him to lay status. Makarios retaliated by getting the **three bishops dismissed** with the help of other Middle Eastern prelates, and was re-elected in 1973 unopposed. By this time Küçük had been replaced as nominal vice-president by Rauf Denktaş.

1974: COUP AND INVASION

The Greek junta, by early 1974 tottering and devoid of any popular support at home, now tried a Falklands-type diversion. Makarios, well aware of the intrigues of the junta's cadres in his National Guard, had proscribed EOKA-B in April 1974, and wrote to the Greek president on July 2 demanding that these officers be withdrawn. The junta's response was to give the go-ahead for the **archbishop's overthrow**, which, despite advance knowledge, Makarios' primarily left-wing and poorly armed supporters proved powerless to prevent.

Early on **July 15**, National Guard troops attacked the presidential palace, gutted it and announced the archbishop's demise. But Makarios miraculously escaped to loyalist strongpoints in Páfos district and, with British help, left the island for Britain, which offered lukewarm support, and then the US, where he was refused recognition as head of state by Henry Kissinger, a man who had done as much as anyone to depose him. He got a warmer reception, as usual, at the UN.

Unfazed, the coup protagonists proclaimed as president **Nikos Sampson**, long-time EOKA activist, Turkophobe and head of the (anything but) Progressive Party. A contemporary foreign correspondent characterized him as "an absolute idiot, though not quite illiterate – a playboy gunman. He spends every night in cabarets getting drunk, dancing on tables, pulling off his shirt to show his scars." A widely circulated photo showed him in full battle regalia, one foot atop the corpse of a Turkish Cypriot he'd killed as a "hunting trophy". Small wonder, then, that his term of office and EOKA-B's direct rule would last exactly one week.

On reflection, the EOKA-B people might have realized that their coup would give Turkey a perfect **pretext** to do what it had long contemplated: partition the island, claiming as guarantor to be acting as protectors of the threatened minority. Indeed many Turkish Cypriot fighters resident in the North pre-1974 recall receiving coded messages weeks before the coup, telling them to prepare for action. Post-coup international opinion initially favoured Turkey, whose prime minister **Bülent Ecevit** went through the proper legalistic motions on July 16–17 of flying to Britain to propose joint action for protecting the Turkish minority, restoring Cypriot independence and demanding that Athens withdraw its officers. While Sampson was indeed quoted as saying "Now that we've finished with Makarios' people, let's start on the Turks," EOKA-B in the end killed more Greek opponents – estimates run to several hundred interred in mass, unmarked graves, including many wounded buried alive – than the 200–300 Turkish Cypriots slaughtered at Tókhni and three villages around Famagusta.

"PHASE I"

Just before dawn on July 20, Ecevit authorized the **Turkish invasion** of Cyprus, entailing amphibious armoured landings, napalm strikes, bombing raids on many towns and paratroop drops around Kyrenia. **"Phase I"** of the campaign lasted from **July 20 to July 30**: despite the demoralizing coup, and being outnumbered four to one, the Greek Cypriots managed to confine Turkish forces to a lozenge-shaped bridgehead straddling the Nicosia–Kyrenia road. The initial Turkish landing west of Kyrenia, the first time its forces had fought since the Korean War, was a near-fiasco. For starters, Turkey was expecting little or no resistance from the Greek Cypriots, and threw poorly equipped, trained and disciplined soldiers into the opening battles. Soldiers disembarked without water bottles in the July heat, and tanks rolled ashore with no ammunition and insufficient fuel. Turkish air-force jets managed to sink two of their own landing craft, while completely missing the contents of a Cypriot National Guard tank camp (though the Greek Cypriots also mistakenly shot down two Hercules transports bringing reinforcements from Greece). The brigadier general in charge of operations was killed as he came ashore, with the next-highest-ranking officer, for some days, being a captain. UN observers subsequently estimated a ratio of seven Turkish to every Greek casualty over the entire war; much of this can be attributed to pre-landing lectures by Turkish religious leaders, who assured the raw recruits that death in battle with the infidels ensured a direct path to Paradise. To such pep talks – and not (as often alleged) the ingestion of drugs – was owed the repeated and oft-corroborated spectacle of human wave attacks by wild-eyed Turkish canon fodder, marching zombie-like into Greek Cypriot machine-gun fire, until the latter ran out of ammunition and had to retreat.

In Greece, the junta chiefs ordered the Greek army to attack Turkey; its officers refused, precipitating the collapse of the junta on **23 July**, the same day Sampson fell from power. Glafkos Clerides replaced him as acting head of state in Makarios' absence, as a civilian government took power in Athens. The first round of hastily arranged **negotiations** between the Greek, Turkish and British foreign ministers convened in **Geneva**, resulting in the ceasefire of July 30. On August 8, talks resumed, with Clerides and Denktaş additionally present. The Turkish military, with little to show for the heavy casualties sustained during Phase I, and with their forces increasingly vulnerable as the Greek Cypriots began to comprehensively mine the perimeter of their toehold, began to pressurize their civilian leaders to be given a freer hand. Accordingly, on the night of August 13–14, the Turkish foreign minister gave Clerides an effective **ultimatum** demanding approval of one or the other Turkish plans for "federation": either six dispersed cantons or a single amalgamated one under Turkish Cypriot control, adding up to 34 percent of Cyprus. Clerides asked for 36 hours to consult his superiors, which was refused at 3am on August 14; ninety minutes later, the Turkish army resumed its offensive.

"PHASE II"

"Phase II" was a two-day rout of the Greek Cypriots, who had insufficient armour and no air support to stop the Turkish juggernaut, this time manned by crack troops. The Greek Cypriots – as opposed to the Greek officers, whom the Turks regarded with contempt from the start – had acquitted themselves splendidly during "Phase I", far exceeding their brief to hold the line for 36 hours until massive aid came from Greece, which never arrived; come "Phase II", they were completely exhausted, demoralized and literally out of gas and ammunition.

The behaviour of the Turkish infantry in both phases of the war featured sporadic, **gratuitous violence** against Greek Cypriot civilians unlucky enough to lie in their path; word of the rapes, murders and widespread looting which marked their advance was enough to convince approximately 165,000 Greek Cypriots to flee for their safety; had they in fact not done so, the entire purpose of the campaign to create an ethnically cleansed sanctuary for the Turkish Cypriots would have been confounded.

At a second ceasefire on August 16, the areas occupied by the Turkish Army totalled 38 percent of the island's area – slightly more than had been demanded at Geneva – abutting a scalloped boundary, henceforth the **Attila Line**, extending from Káto Pyrgos in Soléa to Famagusta. The Greek Cypriot **death toll**, including combatants and civilians, rose to 3850. The **missing** numbered 1619, though now it seems likely that many of these were leftists killed by EOKA-B activists and Greek junta officers, as noted above, or – as Turkish Army units often found them – chained to their gun emplacements or shot in the back. Turkish Cypriots living in the South were put in an untenable position by the Turkish "peace action", as it was termed; EOKA-B units occupied or cleared out most of their enclaves, with reprisal killings at several points.

Since July 15, a flurry of **UN Security Council resolutions**, calling on all concerned to desist from warlike actions and respect Cypriot independence, had been piling up, blithely disregarded then and in the years since. With the benefit of hindsight, UK parliamentary and US congressional committees duly condemned the timidity, lack of imagination and simple shamefulness of their governments' respective past policies towards Cyprus, specifically the absence of any meaningful initiative to stop the Turkish war machine. The **British** claimed that with just over five thousand men on the sovereign bases, there was (despite their role as guarantor) little they could have done – other than what they actually did, which was to ferry tourists to safety out of the North, and take in Turkish Cypriots fleeing EOKA-B gunmen in the South. In retrospect, though, it seems the UK had been content to follow American dictates rather than pursue an independent course.

On the part of the **US**, there was more of a failure of will than inability to do something. President Nixon, on the point of resigning over Watergate, had deferred to the archpriest of *realpolitik*, **Henry Kissinger**, who made no secret of his "tilt" towards Turkey rather than Greece as the more valuable ally in the Aegean, or of his distaste for Makarios. Thus the integrity of Cyprus was sacrificed to NATO power politics; the only substantive American congressional action, over Kissinger's objections, was the temporary **suspension of military aid** to Turkey as a wrist-slap punishment.

During anti-American riots in Nicosia on **August 19**, the **US Ambassador Rodger Davies** and a Cypriot embassy employee were gunned down by EOKA-B hitmen aiming deliberately from an unfinished building opposite. Periodic assertions that Davies was the CIA paymaster and handler for the EOKA-B coup do not hold water, as he was an Arabist by train-ing and had been on the job for less than two months – though this does not rule out "conduct incompatible with diplomatic status" on the part of his predecessor, for whom the gunmen may have mistaken him. Eleven days later **Vassos Lyssarides**, head of the socialist **EDEK** party supporting Makarios, narrowly escaped death at the hands of the same bunch. These lurid events demonstrated that clapping Sampson in jail – where he remained until 1992 – wouldn't cause his associates to simply disappear.

DE FACTO PARTITION: CYPRUS SINCE 1974

While still acting head of state, Clerides acknowledged that the Greeks and Greek Cypriots had been acting for years as if Turkey did not exist, and that some sort of **federal republic** was the best Cyprus could hope for. Makarios returned on December 7, 1974 to a diminished realm, and contradicted Clerides: the Greek Cypriots should embark on a "long-term struggle", using their favourite method of **internationalization**, to induce the Turkish army to leave and get optimum terms from the Turkish Cypriots. This prefigured a final break between the two men the following year. In his homecoming speech in Nicosia, with half the South turned out to welcome him, Makarios also forgave his opponents – not that he had much choice, with EOKA-B operatives still swaggering about in full battle dress. But others, especially those who had lost relatives

TURKISH CYPRIOT POLITICAL ORGANIZATIONS

CTP *Cumhuriyetçi Türk Partisi* or "Republican Turkish Party", headed by Özker Özgür until late 1995; cast in the image of the namesake secularist Anatolian party; formerly conciliatory towards the South, but has become less accommodating as a participant in recent coalitions.

DP *Demokrat Partisi*, a hiving-off from the UBP and leading component of recent coalition govern-ments, run by Serdar Denktaş and Hakki Atun.

TKP *Toplumcu Kurtuluş Partisi* or "Communal Liberation Party", headed by Mustafa Akancı, a centre-left grouping favouring rapprochement with the South.

TMT *Türk Müdafaa Teskilati* or "Turkish Defence Organization", formed in 1958 to counter EOKA's activities; its ideology still guides the North's government to a great extent.

UBP *Ulusal Birlik Partisi* or "National Union Party", centre-right party established by Rauf Denktaş in 1974 and governing the North until 1993; now headed by Derviş Eroğlu. Pro-Anatolian, nationalist and against significant accommodation with the South.

YDP *Yeni Doğuş Partisi* or "New Birth Party", representing the interests of Anatolian settlers.

YKP *Yeni Kıbrıs Partisi* or "New Cyprus Party", centre-left faction headed by Alpay Durduran; anti-settler and anti-Turkish army in platform.

at the hands of either the rebels or the Turks, were not in such a lenient mood; two decades on, assessing blame for the fiasco of 1974 still occupies a certain amount of the South's agenda.

Top priority was given to **rehousing the refugees** from both communities: the Turkish Cypriots simply occupied abundant abandoned Greek property in the North, but it took the South more than a decade to adequately house those who had fled the North. The international community, so disgracefully sluggish at the time the problem was created, was reasonably generous and prompt with **aid** to help reconstruct the island — aid which, however, went primarily to the South.

Strangely, **intercommunal negotiations resumed** almost immediately, though at first they centred almost entirely on the fate of Cypriots caught on the "wrong" side. Greeks in the South separated from relatives and homes in the North were at first allowed to rejoin them; the government initially attempted to prevent southern Turks from **trekking north**, but by early 1975 this too had happened. This departure was not entirely voluntary, especially in the case of Turkish Cypriots with extensive properties or businesses in the South, or with Orthodox Christian spouses; accounts abound, especially in the Páfos area, of Turkish and British army trucks virtually rounding up Turkish Cypriots, with their neighbours compelled to rescue those — usually non-observant Muslims or converts to Orthodoxy — who wished to stay behind. Once these Turks were safely on the "right" side of the Attila Line, most northern Greeks were expelled and the North pronounced, over the South's protests, that an equitable exchange of populations had been carried out.

The North declared itself the **Turkish Federated State of Cyprus** (TFSC) in February 1975, though as always what the Turkish Cypriots meant by federation, and with whom, was quite different from what the South had in mind. Clerides and Denktaş, brought together again by UN Secretary General **Kurt Waldheim**, made hopeful noises of peacemaking intent through much of 1975, but no substantive progress was registered. In 1977, Makarios and Denktaş met for the first time in fourteen years at the latter's request, agreeing on various **general guidelines** for a bi-communal, federal republic, the details of territorial jurisdiction to be determined later but envisioning a reduction in the amount of land held by the Turkish Cypriots.

After **Makarios died** in August 1977, **Spyros Kyprianou** replaced him as president and Greek Cypriot representative at the on-again, off-again talks. As an initial goodwill measure, it was first suggested in 1978 that the empty **ghost town of Varosha** be resettled by its former Greek Cypriot inhabitants: the Greeks wanted this to precede any other steps, while the Turks would only countenance it under limited conditions and as part of an overall settlement. The reopening of Nicosia international airport has also been also mooted periodically, though it is now obsolete and virtually unusable owing to post-1974 urban growth, with symbolic flight schedules envisioned at best. In 1981, Waldheim seized the initiative by presenting an "evaluation" of the talks thus far, and generating for the first time **detailed proposals** for the mechanics of a federal republic, which came to nothing.

In the international arena, the South increasingly protested Turkish and Turkish Cypriot practices in the North — specifically the **expulsion** of most Greek Cypriots and denial of human rights to those remaining, the **settlement** of numerous Anatolian Turks to alter the demographic balance of the island, and vandalism against Greek religious property. Well-orchestrated boycotts of the North ensure — among other things — that **archeological sites** are thoroughly neglected, since no archeologists would be permitted to work in a Greek-speaking country again if they were known to have visited the North, even just to inspect their old digs.

The North put a spanner in the works by unilaterally declaring full independence on November 15, 1983 as the **Turkish Republic of Northern Cyprus** (TRNC), generating the usual storm of pious UN resolutions of condemnation and widespread overseas support for the Greek Cypriot position. To date no other state besides Turkey has recognized the TRNC. Yet talks towards a peaceful island-wide solution continued: early 1984 saw more proposals by Kyprianou to the UN, not significantly different from those before or since. **Perez de Cuellar**, the new Secretary General, presented successively refined draft frameworks for a federal settlement between 1985 and 1986; first the South said yes, but the North no; then the Turks agreed, but Kyprianou wavered until the **opportunity was lost** – behaviour for which he was roundly pilloried, and which contributed to his loss of office in 1988.

POLITICS IN THE SOUTH

Coalitions have long been a fact of life among the Greek Cypriots, since no one party is strong enough to govern alone – though AKEL has historically mustered about a third of the votes in any contest. And in such a small society, horse-trading and flexibility are essential, for if ideology is taken too seriously, public life becomes rapidly unliveable, as it did briefly in 1974; stances or declarations of one campaign are cheerfully eaten in the presence of new coalition partners in the next elections. Small parties such as EDEK often control swing votes, and are assiduously courted as partners in the ever-changing parliamentary constellations. The South has a **presidential** system, with no prime minister, and considerable power – more so than in France, for example – resides in the executive office. Both presidential and **parliamentary** elections occur every five years but are at present out of sync: the former in years ending in 8 and 3, the latter in years ending in 6 and 1.

Tóh Kypriakó or the **"National Question"** – the most appropriate response to Cyprus' de facto partition – is theoretically the paramount electoral issue. In general, Kyprianou's centre-right party **DIKO** (*Dhimokratikó Kómma* or "Democratic Party") has stood for an idealistic solution over the long haul, relying on cumulative international pressures from various quarters to get the Turkish army to depart and the Turkish Cypriots to come to terms. Clerides' **DISY** (*Dhimokratikós Synayermós* or the "Democratic Rally"), eschewing excessive reliance on the UN, and preferring a pro-NATO/EU alignment, has stressed pragmatic deal-cutting directly with the Turkish Cypriots to get as many of the refugees home as quickly as possible. **AKEL** and **EDEK** can point to their track record of never having systematically harassed the Turkish minority as a valuable asset for bridge-building in a theoretical federal republic. Left unarticulated is the possibility of a partial solution necessitating massive concessions, with some politician allotted the unenviable

task of indicating which refugee constituents can go home to the North, and who will have to stay in the South.

After 1974, the leftist parties were in a position to exert additional pressure, with many **social-welfare measures** introduced for the first time by 1983 to alleviate some of the misery caused by the refugee influx. Despite US misgivings, a "dictatorship of the proletariat" was never on the cards; Cyprus is far too bourgeois for that, the (until recently) unreconstructed Brezhnevism of AKEL notwithstanding.

In the House of Representatives elections of **1976**, AKEL, EDEK and Makarios' Popular Front combined to shut out Clerides' rightist DISY party, owing this sweep to a first-past-the-post system. After Makarios' death in 1977, his groomed successor Kyprianou was designated to serve out the remainder of the archbishop's presidential term, then re-elected unopposed in **1978** in his own right.

By **1981**, the parliamentary system had been changed to one of proportional representation; AKEL and DISY finished in a dead heat, with Kyprianou's DIKO and EDEK holding the balance of power in the 35-seat House of Representatives; the **1983** presidential voting returned Kyprianou to office with AKEL backing, again shutting out Clerides.

In the **1988** presidential contest **George Vassiliou**, a professional businessman and political outsider, was elected, backed by the strange bedfellows of AKEL and DISY who, despite their wide differences on domestic issues, agreed that the timely resolution of the National Question was imperative and that Kyprianou had been repeatedly tried and found wanting.

The **1991** parliamentary polls showed a slight rightward swing in the House, now expanded to 56 seats: a DISY–Liberal coalition won 20, AKEL 18, DIKO 11 and EDEK 7.

On his fourth try for the presidency in February **1993**, DISY candidate **Clerides** upset AKEL-supported incumbent Vassiliou by less than two thousand votes in run-off polling – a margin garnered, it is claimed, by numbers of hunters seduced by Clerides' (unfulfilled) promise to reinstate the controversial springtime bird-shoot. The result was regarded as a rejection of the UN-sponsored negotiations to date – Clerides proposed to renegotiate "unacceptable" clauses of a proposed draft treaty – and an endorsement of his intent to pursue EU membership more strongly.

The 1996 parliamentary elections may well show a continuation of the recent rightward tilt in Southern politics over which Clerides has presided. One particularly conspicuous instance of this, early in 1995, was the reinstatement with back pay of 62 coup supporters – educators, civil servants and police officers who'd been cashiered some years back – and the exiling of their opponents to minor posts. This was done unilaterally by the Clerides administration, over the objections of parliament.

Spates of terror **bombings** and **gangland crimes** have hit the South since early 1995. The campaign of the terrorist group EKAS, the "Greek Cypriot Liberation Army", to extort donations from wealthy businessmen for ostensibly patriotic purposes was cut short by its suppression in late April, but their abortive attempts were overshadowed by a long series of car bombings, arson attacks and eight fatal shootings, all apparently part of a battle to control the lucrative trade in cabaret girls, gambling dens and drugs. None of the crimes has been solved to date, and in December President Clerides made the sensational announcement that this was hardly surprising, given the **police** force's deeply corrupting involvement in the underworld, and demanded the resignations of the national police chief and his deputy. The national police had already been in bad odour following an exposé of systematic **torture** of suspects (including foreigners) at Limassol since 1990, with twelve officers sacked. All this severely dented the South's overseas image of savouriness and safety, and constituted a propaganda windfall for the North, which was not slow to exploit it after years of being on the receiving end of a Southern slander campaign implying that North Cyprus was a dark, dangerous place heaving with Anatolian barbarians.

POLITICS IN THE NORTH

As borne out by the record of murderous suppression by TMT of its opponents, multiple parties or even factions were not actively encouraged in the Turkish Cypriot community until after the founding of the Turkish Federated State of Cyprus in 1975. Even since then Denktaş on a number of occasions has used questionable tactics to nip budding opposition – specifically against unsuccessful presidential candidate Ahmet Berberoğlu in 1975, and important opposition party chief Özker Özgür in 1988 – though lately there has been more genuine **pluralism**.

North Cyprus has a tiny electorate, with a high degree of **overlap** between government figures, business bigwigs, the usual ruling parties and President Denktaş' personal acquaintances. The description of the shifting coalition kaleidoscopes in the South applies doubly here, with politicking inevitably personalized in the prevailing village atmosphere: in 1990, for example, one out of every 670 registered voters was a candidate. Though the North's system provides for both a **president and a prime minister**, Denktaş as president has always been the dominant figure. Presidential and parliamentary elections are held more or less together every five years, formerly in years ending in 6 and 1 but lately 5 and 0.

The first elections in the North were held in **1976**: Denktaş won easily, with 75 percent of the vote and the same percentage of seats for his **UBP** (National Unity Party) in the forty-seat legislative assembly. In **1981** the UBP margin of victory diminished: Denktaş squeaked by with just over half the votes, and while the UBP remained the largest party in the assembly, it no longer enjoyed an absolute majority, losing seats in a hung parliament to both Alpay Durduran's left-wing **TBP** (Communal Liberation Party), and Özker Özgür's **CTP** (Republican Turkish Party), with two minor parties holding the balance. Following an unstable period, and the 1983 UDI, the assembly was expanded to fifty seats, allowing Denktaş to pack the new ranks with compliant appointees so that he could get on with the business of governing.

In the **1985** elections, only parties breaching the eight-percent barrier were awarded seats, which forced splinter factions to disappear or join with others. A previous constitutional clause prohibiting more than two consecutive presidential terms was eliminated, and Denktaş ran again as an **independent**. Although he stayed in office in an "above-party" role, the UBP's share of votes declined to just over a third of the electorate, reflecting disillusionment with its handling of affairs. Yet because of the various "reforms", its proportion of seats in the expanded assembly remained the same – about half.

Denktaş was re-elected yet again in the early **1990** presidential polls, and prior to the hard-fought May parliamentary elections, more **changes in the election laws** were introduced. These included a bonus-seat system for high-vote parties, a more-than-usually-enhanced system of proportional representation; and prohibitions against voting across party lists and, most importantly, against coalition governments. The opposition's response to this last condition was to combine into a single unit, the **DMP** (Democratic Struggle Party). Composed of the CTP, TKP and YDP, it ran on a platform of anti-corruption, better economic management and liberalization of the official electronic media – which not surprisingly gave little air time to opposition parties. But its lack of detailed proposals addressing the National Question and the economic doldrums, compared to the equally insubstantial but slick, nationalist-emotive campaign of the UBP, netted surprisingly disappointing results. With a bit under half the votes, the DMP received less than one-third of the available seats – mostly because of the bonus-seat rule. Alpay Durduran's new left-wing **YKP** (New Cyprus Party), running alone, gained no seats. Despite a disturbing number of polling irregularities – allegations of voters intimidated to vote UBP, the biased electronic media, etc – they were not decisive, and it appears that the UBP victory was genuine: DMP simply hadn't convinced enough voters that the UBP's shortcomings overrode its promises of continued national security in the face of the Greek Cypriot "threat".

In late 1992, the first major cracks in the UBP edifice appeared: Denktaş had a major falling out with his prime minister Eroğlu, who accused the president of being (of all things) too "flexible" on the issue of a settlement. Ten MPs loyal to Denktaş defected, forming the *Demokrat Partisi* (**DP**), under the leadership of Hakki Atun and Serdar Denktaş. Snap elections in December 1993 resulted in virtually a dead heat between the UBP, now headed by Eroğlu, and the DP, a deadlock broken by the latter's entry during 1994 into an unprecedented coalition with Özker Özgür's CTP. Greek Cypriot hopes that the new government would broker a settlement were disappointed, as the CTP's actual power – or desire – to do so proved illusory.

In March 1995, this coalition crumbled, leaving the North in a rudderless state – which doubtless contributed to Denktaş' decision to run yet again in presidential elections of the following month, despite his repeated, publically expressed intention to resign in 1995. In the event, Denktaş suffered the minor humiliation of being forced into a run-off by his rival Eroğlu, which he won mainly through the support of CLP and RTP members convinced he was the lesser of two evils. Shortly thereafter, the RTP–DP coalition was revived under Prime Minister Atun, only to collapse amidst recriminations in November, and be dusted off yet again within a few weeks. But in January 1996 Deputy Prime Minister Özgür threw in the towel, exasperated by what he saw as Denktaş' continued obstructionism in negotiations with the South, and was replaced in all his offices by Mehmet Ali Talat.

It's as well to remember that in North Cyprus, the political designations "Left" and "Right" often mean the **opposite** of what they do elsewhere: leftist parties advocate economic liberalism and free trade, along with an unfettered press and a more open-minded position on the "National Question", whilst the conservative parties stand for heavy state intervention in commerce, protectionism for the North's infant industries, a swollen civil service and a more hardline stance in negotiations with the South.

1991–1995: MORE FRUITLESS TALK

Late in 1991, Cyprus returned to the global picture as it periodically does; President Bush, needing another foreign-policy feather in his cap prior to the 1992 US elections, called for a **new peace conference**, and visited both Turkey and Greece canvassing support for one – the first American presidential junket to either country in decades.

Intercommunal meetings did not actually materialize until mid-1992, with **Boutros Boutros-Ghali** now UN Secretary General. His "Set of Ideas" was similar in most respects to all proposals of preceding years: Varosha and some or all of the Mórfou plain would revert to Greek Cypriot control, and Turkish Cypriot-administered territory would shrink overall to 28 or 29 percent of the island's surface area. Left discussable was the degree of Greek refugees' return to the North; by juggling the boundaries of the Turkish-administered zone, a profile could be reached such that most Greek Cypriots could go home without complications – Varosha taking a big percentage of the total – and even if all Greeks formerly resident in the agreed Turkish zone decided to go back, they would still be in a minority there.

Politically, a joint foreign ministry and finance ministry was foreseen, with the Cyprus pound reintroduced throughout the island. Either a rotating or ethnically stipulated presidency was suggested, plus a supreme court equally weighted ethnically, and a bicameral legislature, with upper house biased towards the Turkish Cypriots in the sense that each federal unit would be represented equally rather than proportionately, as the states are in the US Senate.

July sessions between Vassiliou and Denktaş at the UN were inconclusive; Boutros-Ghali had circulated to all interested parties a **tentative map** showing proposed adjustments of territory in a bizonal federation. When details of this were leaked, the North reacted strongly: "We won't be refugees a third time" was a typical newspaper headline, referring to the previous compulsory shifts of 1964 and 1974. Visits of high-level US envoys to Güzelyurt (Mórfou) in particular seemed to be testing the waters for just such an eventuality.

October sessions in New York were again a washout; the Security Council passed yet another **resolution** late in November 1992, the most strongly worded in years, laying most of the blame for their failure on Denktaş for his intransigence in refusing to accept the Boutros-Ghali guidelines for a settlement. Denktaş' reaction was to threaten immediate resignation rather than sign any agreement under duress which he deemed unfavourable. As the years go by it is hard to avoid the lurking suspicion that he is content with the status quo, and has merely been humouring world opinion by his attendance at successive conferences.

There has been no significant progress since then, and Cyprus virtually disappeared from the international agenda during 1993 and 1994, except for the UN's recycling of the "Set of Ideas" as the so-called "**Confidence Building Measures**" (CBMs), in particular the rehabilitation of Nicosia airport and Varosha, and five "informal talks" between Denktaş and Clerides

in the presence of a UN mediator during November 1994. But 1996 is once again an American election year, and President Clinton, fresh from his success in brokering Haitian, Bosnian and Israeli settlements, probably senses a chance for another quick foreign-policy victory in Cyprus, so a visit by US special envoy Holbrooke will probably be in the offing.

1996 AND BEYOND: LAST CHANCE FOR SETTLEMENT?

Over two decades of UN-sponsored negotiations have repeatedly foundered on the same reefs: the Greek Cypriot vision of a well-integrated federal republic with relatively strong central powers, versus a Turkish Cypriot ideal of vast devolution of power to local and communal entities and a token structure at the top. More concretely, the Greeks' demands for Turkish withdrawal (including settlers), demilitarization of the island, significant territorial adjustments, and the right of return of most if not all refugees remains incompatible with Turkish Cypriot insistence on a mainland Turkish presence of all sorts, Turkey's perennial right of unilateral intervention, minimal territorial adjustments, and very restricted return of Greeks to the Turkish zone. It has, for instance, been suggested that there could be an 18-year delay in implementation of full freedom of movement for Greek Cypriots in the North, enough time, presumably, for all those personally involved in EOKA and EOKA-B atrocities to pass away.

If it is decided that certain people cannot go home, there is the additional matter of devising a just formula for assessment of **abandoned property** – Greek and Turkish estimates differ wildly as to its extent and value, with the Turkish Cypriots claiming that their real estate in the South is vastly underassessed – and who would foot the bill for **compensation**. The position of Denktaş on Greek Cypriot refugees is that, rather than be allowed to return to their old homes, they should be compensated financially for their lost value; in this he has the support of most Northerners, who do not want Greek Cypriots to live among them again. There is still appreciable support for the persistence of a fully independent TRNC, and widespread apprehension that, following a lenient settlement, the Northern economy would be completely swamped by Greek Cypriot entre-preneurs. Token representation and forced buyouts of Turkish Cypriot businessmen remains a potential danger in any future federation; the number of major tourist enterprises owned or managed by Turkish Cypriots before 1974, for example, could be counted on one hand, and it seems undeniable that they faced de facto discrimination in the unitary republic.

In an agrarian culture like Cyprus, where real property is paramount, both Greek and Turkish Cypriots have pursued their feud with **court litigation** and other legal maneouvres centred on said property. 1995, for example, saw Denktaş threaten to distribute full title deeds of Greek Cypriot properties to Turkish Cypriots and Anatolian settlers, a ploy that figured largely in the two collapses of the coalition, and the early 1996 departure of Özker Özgur from Northern politics. At the same time, a refugee from Kyrenia took Turkey to the European Court, asserting that her human rights were being violated by her inability to return to her home, while a Turkish Cypriot family from the South, long resident in the UK but retaining Cypriot citizenship, sued to regain possession of their land near Limassol which had been allotted as refugee housing after 1974.

As part of the South's disengagement from excessive reliance on the UN to oversee a settlement, full **membership of the European Union** is now being vigorously pursued as a way of forcing the issue. The Turkish army would legally be put in the position of occupying the territory of an EU member state, and denying universally accepted, pan-European rights of residence and commerce to its former Greek Cypriot inhabitants. However, this supposed catalyst to a solution risks backfiring badly, as Turkey periodically threatens to formally annex the North if the formal accession mechanism now set to begin in 1997 proceeds. The Turks view EU membership, for either the South alone or the entire island, as back-door *énosis*, since Greece is a member and Turkey for the foreseeable future is not. For its part, the TRNC has little affection for the EU, notwithstanding the fact that thousands of its residents hold British – or even South Cypriot – passports, since the July 1994 decision by the European Court to ban all direct exports from the North to the EU. This ruling is deeply resented locally, and thus far has provoked

defiance rather than knuckling under; the following month, the Northern parliament in retaliation repealed previous resolutions endorsing federation as the preferred mode of settlement, and declared that there was little point to further discussion of the CBMs.

Following the decision in recent years to greatly **scale down the UNFICYP presence** and leave the islanders more or less to themselves, there is now a regular pattern of border incidents involving demonstrations by Southern refugee groups, counter-representations by Northerners, and pitched battles on each side with their own police. Every few weeks, it seems, a young (invariably male) Greek Cypriot motorist rams barriers at a checkpoint and leads soldiers in the North on a merry chase before the invariable long prison term. For its part, the Northern regime has taken to abducting or even killing Greek Cypriot fishermen off Famagusta whom it claims stray into its territorial waters, as well as apprehending unarmed Greek Cypriots who stray too far into the buffer zone. Alarmist scenarios of renewed fighting on Cyprus cannot be completely dismissed, given how each side is busily **stockpiling heavy weapons**: the Greek Cypriots supplied by France, the Czech Republic and Russia, the Turkish Cypriots (of course) by Turkey. Although the South still commands appreciable international sympathy and has notched up an impressive number of UN resolutions in its favour, they would still probably come off worse in world opinion – not to mention militarily – if they used this arms build-up to force the Turkish army off the island. Amidst the resurgent jingoism in the South, a hard-learned lesson of 1974 is in danger of being forgotten: that Cyprus is essentially indefensible from Greece. Without a significant air force of its own, the only offensive strategy for the South would be to have massive, Greek-equipped air bases on its territory – a possibility which continues to preoccupy the Turks as it did during the 1960s.

It is difficult to overestimate the degree of **bitterness** that divides the two main island communities, and which persists unabated as the years pass – as well as a certain apathy and resignation in the South among those not actually displaced by the events of 1974. In the short run, perhaps the best that can be hoped for are more conciliatory victors in the upcoming Southern parliamentary election, the retirement of Denktaş from politics in the North, and relegation of right-wing ideologues on both sides of the line for long enough to broker a peaceful settlement. But with memorials to those killed by whomever between 1954 and 1975 lovingly tended in every village of the island, a spate of new, grandiose monuments glorifying EOKA as part of a generally intensified Hellenic climate in the South, and children on each side raised to believe that their counterparts come equipped with horns and a curly tail, it is likely to be another generation before any **significant rapprochement** takes place. It can be said that for the Greek Cypriots, 1974 was the beginning of history, with a curiously selective memory enveloping the preceding years, while for the Turkish Cypriots 1974 marks the end of history. Establishing a mutually agreed-upon version of the truth, complete with shared symbols and institutions, would be as much a part of any settlement as territorial and economic arrangements.

THE EVENTS OF SUMMER 1974: PERSONAL ACCOUNTS

The following two accounts are intended mainly to illustrate the personal impact of events during July and August 1974. Their authorship – a Turkish Cypriot and an American expatriate – in no way constitutes an endorsement of any position, nor do they imply that any group suffered more than another. Strenuous attempts were made to recruit a Greek Cypriot viewpoint from within the South, but were unsuccessful. Such accounts for use in future editions are most welcome.

DANA DAVIES' STORY

Dana Davies is the daughter of the late American ambassador to Cyprus, Rodger Paul Davies. She now lives in California, where she is preparing a book on her experiences during the summer of 1974.

I was a twenty-year-old sophomore at Mills College in Oakland, California, in March 1974 when I first learned that we would be moving to Cyprus; I was also attending a Middle East history seminar at UC Berkeley, where by coincidence we were actually studying Cyprus. My father was considered an Arab specialist and had spent most of his 28-year foreign service career working in the Bureau of Near Eastern and South Asian Affairs, having been stationed in Saudi Arabia, Syria, Libya and Iraq. A Mediterranean island seemed spectacular by comparison, so when Dad asked me if I could take time off from school and serve as his hostess, I jumped at the chance. I returned to Washington, DC three weeks before our departure date to pack up twelve years of life there, and also to attend a day-long crash course on how to run an ambassadorial residence: how to set a table, how to plan a meal that would not offend any of the religious dietary restrictions I might encounter, the proper protocol for

determining seating. Nothing, however, prepared me for what actually lay ahead.

By the time July 15 came, I had lived in Nicosia for just sixteen days. The summer stretched before me with promises of new friends, diplomatic functions and learning to speak Greek. All that changed at 8.30am that day, when dull thumps accompanied by fire-cracker-like pops roused me from sleep in the embassy residence. I wondered briefly if I was hearing gunfire from the Green Line; during the past two weeks we had heard several brief bursts. This cacophony, however, continued, and sounded much closer than downtown. I had just about convinced myself that the sounds were coming from a building under construction across the street when the phone rang. In short, gruff phrases Dad informed me that a coup was under way. I was to get my brother John and move quickly to the den, which was the only room with no windows facing the street, and wait for further instructions. He answered my pleas for more information with "We just don't know anything. I'll call when we do."

For the next several hours we were alone in that room with little contact with the outside world. The television was useless: loud military music played over a frozen image of the Cypriot flag, broadcast continuously. The BBC and British Armed Forces stations were equally frustrating; news of the coup had not reached the rest of the world, judging from continuous talk of dreary London fog and ongoing reports on the Watergate scandal. From now until our evacuation on July 22, I was able to leave the embassy compound only twice, so my understanding of events relied heavily on what Cypriot embassy employees, foreign service officers and Marine guards told me.

My initial worry was for our household staff. Andreas lived in a village south of Nicosia and drove into town every Monday morning, stopping downtown to do our shopping; I was certain he must be trapped by the fighting. We also had two housekeepers who lived in Nicosia, whom we imagined must be in some danger out on the streets. We called downstairs and were told that they hadn't heard from anyone who wasn't actually in the building before 8.30. Shortly before noon Antoinette Varnava, a Maronite Cypriot from Kormakíti village who was an administrative assistant for the embassy, came upstairs to help us prepare a tray of sandwiches and fruit for embassy personnel on the floors below. John and I had been obediently avoiding windows all morning, but Toni – already one of our favourite people there – was determined to view the city from our living room, so of course we joined her. This was the largest room in the residence, running the full length of the building. From the waist up, three walls were actually windows, from which we could see most of Nicosia and the Pendadháktylos range to the north. To our horror, the eastern window revealed a mushroom cloud rising from the skeleteon of the presidential palace's domed roof. I heard Toni swallow a sob and followed her gaze to the archbishop's residence; its majestic arcade had jagged black bites in the stonework and we could see flames licking at the yellow-and-white masonry. "How could they!" she cried. "Not a man of the cloth! He didn't have a chance." I clumsily tried to comfort her: "But Toni, I thought you were a Maronite Christian, not Orthodox." "Orthodox, Maronite, it makes no difference. Even if one does not agree with the politics, it is not right to kill a man of the cloth!" Later that night, when we learned that Makarios had escaped to Páfos, even those embassy staff who had voiced opposition to some of his policies expressed relief that he had not been killed.

Later that afternoon both Andreas and our housekeeper Anna made it to the residence. Andreas had been taking his two children to summer school when he found himself trapped for hours in a road-block line near the presidential palace, watching pillars of smoke pour from the building. After settling his children in a small room off the kitchen, Andreas sprang into action, whipping up meals for the 45 employees and embassy dependants we would be feeding three times daily for the next week. Embassy officers defied the curfew to check on other Americans trapped across the city, taking the opportunity to accumulate cooked chickens from the Hilton, bread from a favourite restaurant and a freezer full of meat from one of their own houses, defrosting since the power had been cut. Nicos, another assistant, also managed to run regular errands; much to our alarm, he drove Dad out to Béllapais to meet with the UN forces commander – which let us know that most of the trouble was confined to the capital. They also managed to find an open market selling fish and fresh vegetables.

Our other housekeeper, Anna, lived close by and so was able to go home sooner than other employees; it wasn't until she returned to work on Thursday that we learned she hadn't seen her son, a young National Guardsman, since breakfast time on Monday morning. From her we had our first accounts of trucks full of bodies driving out of the city. Also trapped in the embassy on Monday were two men – one a Turkish Cypriot, the other a member of Makarios' palace guard – who often travelled with my father as bodyguards. As John and I brought food to the buffet table in the living room, we saw these two huddled together, talking in low tones about their families and events outside; only later did I understand that these men in particular would both have been in extreme danger had they left the embassy before Wednesday or Thursday and been caught by EOKA-B members.

Dad stood by his promise of keeping us informed on developments; shortly after lunch he rang and told me to turn on the television. The coup leaders were expected to make an announcement naming their leader and declaring the status of their military exercise. The onscreen visuals had not changed from the static flag, but the martial music was now punctuated every thirty seconds with a brusque announcement. Dad and two of his officers who spoke fluent Greek arrived shortly, and translated the announcement as a reiteration of one on the radio instructing the public to stand by for important information. It was nearly half an hour before the big announcement came, but during that time these three gave me a good outline of the morning's events, learned in turn from an American staff member who was still at home a few blocks from the palace when the coup erupted. He had a portable two-way radio, and despite repeated orders to take cover, had spent the morning on his apartment building roof, relaying detailed reports of the attack on the palace, thus giving the embassy much-needed information about possible open roadways and enabling foreign service officers to reach Americans and embassy dependants stranded elsewhere in the city.

As time wore on, conversation turned to jokes about the coup leaders, and their lack of forethought as to who would assume leadership; someone even wondered if they were trying to bribe someone to take the position, and who might actually become the interim head of state. Their jokes halted when the blaring music stopped and a new voice filled the room with angry sounds. All three men leaned towards the set, and I watched my father straining to catch the rapid words in his newest language. Periodically the Greek statements were punctuated with American curses; finally the broadcast ended, and the quiet was interrupted only by a groaned "Oh, God!" from within the room and sporadic sounds of fighting from outside. Once the men had collected themselves, they gave us a quick summary of the broadcast and let us know that Nikos Sampson – the designated leader – would never be acceptable to anyone concerned. Also mentioned for the first time was their fear that this would guarantee Turkish intervention.

As it soon became evident that the coup against Makarios was not going to finish swiftly or neatly, our residence became an extension of the embassy itself. A strong sense of solidarity developed among this community of people who had been virtual strangers a week before. Over our daily group meals for up to 45, we learned of life beyond our compound. Pairs of foreign service officers ventured in cars out into Nicosia and beyond, asking, pleading or even demanding at the various curfew checkpoints for permission to pass. They made the rounds of hotels to check on American citizens, called on the two Americans wounded during the second day of fighting, and moved their own family members to safer lodgings.

When Dad managed to get away from his downstairs office, he would settle into the study just off the living room, usually with two or three other officers, for informal discussions. He always invited me and my brother to join them, as part of a lifelong habit of discussing his work in front of us, tolerating our interruptions and always answering our questions. With constant talk about the shuttle diplomacy that American envoy Joseph Sisco undertook between Greece, Turkey and Great Britain during the week after the coup, it seemed natural for us to discuss possible American involvement in the current crisis. Dad said bluntly that, except for diplomatic efforts aimed at influencing these three guarantors of

Cypriot independence, America had no legitimate role at present. From watching the actions of my father and others, I firmly believe that the US took what diplomatic measures possible to prevent a Turkish intervention during the week after the coup. Relations between the US and Turkey were at low ebb during summer 1974, owing partly to a Turkish decision to resume growing opium poppies, and in the waning days of America's involvement in Vietnam, there would have been little political support for military action on Cyprus to stop the Turks.

I remember clearing dishes from that study long after midnight on the morning of Friday, July 19. Dad and several others were loudly discussing the best possible wording for a radio announcement. Nicosia airport was scheduled to reopen at 6am for the first time that week, and they were desperately trying to phrase the message in such a way that would encourage American visitors to leave the island without creating panic, while simultaneously ensuring that any public utterance would not in any way influence – or be interpreted as influencing – Cypriot politics.

I don't think I fully understood the sensitive nature of diplomatic statements or gestures until a number of years later, when I read in Christopher Hitchen's *Cyprus* that "In Nicosia, Ambassador Rodger Davies received [coup participant] Dimis Dimitriou as 'Foreign Minister' – the only envoy to do so." I can't be sure if it was that same night or the preceding one, but it was during the only supper that Dad managed to have with John and me. We had just sat down when someone rang Dad from downstairs. I had never seen him so angry before; he was yelling at the person on the other end of the phone. Finally he calmed down and said he would go downstairs, but to have whomever was waiting to remain in the lobby, at the Marine guard's desk – he did not want him received in the office. The visitor standing at the front gate was Dimis Dimitriou, demanding to see the ambassador. Most of us at the table were acquainted with Dimitriou, whose brother was the Cypriot ambassador to Washington, and by showing up he had put all the foreign service officers present, including the deputy chief of mission, in a compromising position. Dimitriou had just been appointed foreign minister of the EOKA-B regime, which no country had recognized. After several minutes of discussion, Dad felt he had no choice but to go down to the lobby and speak to him as briefly and informally as possible, without inviting Dimitriou to official premises. Unfortunately his actions were misconstrued.

***

I was not actually present on August 19, 1974, when at least two men fired into the embassy from the building site across the street, killing my father and our friend Toni Varnava, but I have had extensive interviews with those who were actually there, and possess photographs of the bullet holes. So it amazes me to still hear – from Glafkos Clerides, among others – the theory that their deaths were accidental, a result of random shots from the ground-level riot. The only two locations to be struck by gunfire were my father's second-floor office, and his third-floor bedroom, precisely where he would most likely have been. The one random aspect of the deed was that Ambassador Davies chose to step into the hallway and phone Clerides to demand protection as the fighting outside escalated; the fatal bullets passed through the thick wooden shutters and glass of the office window, cleared the official reception room, and out into the hallway. One struck my father in the heart, and shortly after another hit Toni in the head as she ran to his aid. The identity of the assassins is in fact known; one actually served time in prison for a token charge of illegal firearms possession, and is now a security guard at a Cypriot race track.

KÜFI BIRINCI'S STORY

Küfi Birinci, a travel agent, hotelier and TKP politician in North Cyprus, was 16 at the time of the Turkish invasion of Cyprus. While he was experiencing the events described below, his future business partner and his twin brother both narrowly escaped death before an EOKA-B firing squad in their home village, only through the intervention of a widely respected Turkish Cypriot policeman.

On the night of July 19, 1974, I heard on the BBC 7pm news that the Turkish fleet had "sailed towards an unknown destination". I didn't know exactly why, but this time I was sure that Turkey was really coming. Early next morning, my uncle came by, in a really excited state, and woke us up: "Wake up, they came!" I didn't even have to ask who "they" were. Within a few minutes we were all in the streets, singing and dancing, as we watched the Turkish parachutists landing on the fields of Hamitköy [an area just north of Nicosia]. It crossed nobody's mind that this was the start of a fierce war; we only came back to our senses after the shooting started, and our great joy gave way to panic as people started thinking about the safety of their loved ones. (I myself had no news of my twin brother, trapped in our home village of Áyios Nikólaos, until after August 1.)

Caught up in the general excitement, I was nearly half a mile from home when I decided to go back, but it was too late. A police Land Rover stopped next to me, and a police sergeant told me to jump in; I replied that I had to go home, but he said that he knew better where I should be going. So we went around the streets of Turkish Nicosia, collecting some other young lads who were not old enough to fight, but fit for other services.

On the first day our job was easy; we filled potato-sacks with sand for use as cover for Turkish Cypriot fighters against gunfire from the Greek Cypriot National Guard. But on the second day we were taken to Tekke Bahçesi, site of a Turkish martyr's cemetery, given the necessary hand tools and ordered to start digging. There were about twelve of us, all teenagers except for one older, partly disabled man unfit for military service. Over the next two days and nights, we dug countless graves; we weren't given proper food, and had to sleep rough in the building site of what is now called the Vakıflar Çarşısı. There was another sergeant in charge of us, who was very rude and cruel; perhaps he had to be like that in order to keep us under control.

On July 23, while we were having a bit of a rest at lunchtime, an open lorry pulled into the cemetery and turned around; with it came a horrible, unbearable stench. I could see that the back payload area was covered with a white sheet, now stained a dirty mud-and-blood colour. On top of the sheet was somebody we all easily recognized: Hami the sandwich-maker, who sold sandwiches next to the Zafer cinema. Sitting with his legs crossed, he had cigarettes in each hand, which he was chain-smoking, looking really nervous. When he jumped off the lorry and pulled the dirty sheet off, immediately a huge swarm of flies and a horrible smell spread around. I'd never smelt anything worse, anywhere, in my entire life, but the stink was nothing compared to the scene before my eyes. The lorry was full of dead soldiers who had been killed during the landing [near Kyrenia]; the driver used the lorry dumper to sling them off as if the corpses were sand or pebbles at a building site. The bodies were in an awful state: three days old, and all blown up like balloons in the July heat. Some of them were without heads, or sometimes the head was lying separate next to the body; others had hands missing, and some were badly burned.

Hami the sandwich man sat by the pile of corpses and started to take their boots off with a huge knife; since then I've never been able to buy a sandwich from him, thinking he still uses the same knife. According to Muslim belief, war martyrs (*şehitler*) go directly to heaven and so can be buried with their clothes on; however their shoes must be removed to make them more comfortable. After removing their boots, Hami checked the soldiers' pockets, collected their personal belongings and put them each in a nylon bag together with their *künye* [ID dogtag worn around the neck]. We just watched him, astonished, holding our breath; we couldn't breathe that stinking air anyway. Hami and everyone else who'd arrived with the lorry had cologne-drenched handkerchiefs to hold over their noses – we didn't. We just stood there terrified and shocked, not knowing what to do next; I was praying to God to get out of there, without knowing how I might do that. While we waited there with these feelings, the sergeant ordered us to go and bury the soldiers. He shouted at us but we still wouldn't move, so he came over and hit us one at a time. Those whom he hit snapped out of it and ran to bury the bodies. I thought to myself, "We'll have to do it anyway, better to do it before the bastard hits you", so I ran off to bury them before he got to me.

There was a *hodja* [Islamic prayer leader] present, reciting the necessary last rites for the dead soldiers and ensuring that they were buried in accordance with Islamic rules. My first body was the most difficult; I tried, together with another boy, to carry and bury it, but since we were both so disgusted, not want-

ing to touch the corpses, we couldn't get a proper grip. I was trying to grab him by the end of his trousers, while my companion was trying to hold the soldier by his shirtsleeves; it was a difficult task because the swollen body weighed much more that it would have when alive. We just managed to bring it to a ready-dug grave, and threw him inside. The *hodja* saw us and shouted angrily: "You must not *throw* him in, you must *put* him in gently." He then came and inspected the body in the grave and said: "You laid him out in the wrong direction. His head is not facing the *kible* [the direction of Mecca]. Jump in and do it right." So I had no choice but to jump into the grave and turn the corpse to the right orientation. Neither Turkish nor English is adequate to explain in words my feelings at that moment.

Lorries and transit vans arrived one after the other that day; the pile of dead bodies got bigger and bigger. We hadn't dug enough graves to bury them all, so on the advice of the *hodja* we started putting three corpses to a hole. Soon this wasn't enough either, so the *hodja* gave us permission to make it five in each grave. In the end I recall being allowed to bury them eight to a grave, and still we didn't have enough space bury them all. We spent that night next to a pile of unburied corpses, plus those in the many open graves which we hadn't had time to cover with soil.

The next morning someone brought a bulldozer abandoned by the Greek Cypriots. We were very happy to see it, because we were really at our physical and psychological limits. The 'dozer made things much faster, and helped us finish the job – I would guess that by that second afternoon, we boys had buried almost 1500 corpses.

My grandmother had a house with one door opening onto this cemetery, and another looking towards Girne Caddesi [the main commercial street of north Nicosia]. I pointed out her house to the sergeant, and got permission to go and get a handkerchief for the smell; he gave me fifteen minutes' leave. So I entered my grandma's house through the back door, and immediately ran out the front door to my own house, which was about a mile away. When I got home, I went straight to our basement toilet, where I hid for 48 hours until I was convinced that the sergeant was not following me.

I write of this terrible experience to show everybody how war and nationalism are the worst enemy of mankind. Why do we Cypriots have to distinguish ourselves as Turkish or Greek? Cyprus our homeland has more than enough for both communities; all we have to do is recognize that it's our country and that we can share everything it offers us. We must stop running after other countries as our motherland; if we deny our real home in favour of other nations, then the day will come when we won't have a motherland of our own. Didn't the Turkish Cypriots already lose one part of it and the Greek Cypriots the other? If we don't come back to our senses, one day soon we will lose all of it.

WILDLIFE

Cyprus' location has made it a "collecting basket" for wildlife from Asia Minor, Africa and the Mediterranean countries, and the island offers a rare chance to see plants and animals which could only be found by making separate journeys further afield.

Cyprus escaped the ravages of the Ice Ages which wiped out so many species in northern Europe, so within its territory there's a staggering diversity of rock types and natural habitats. The island supports a varied **flora** with some 1350 different species of flowering plants – comparable to the total number of wild species listed in Britain, but concentrated within an area about the size of Wales.

The current political division of Cyprus has parallels in the island's **geological history**. Until the Pleistocene period around one million years ago, the Tróödhos to the south and Kyrenia mountains to the north stood as the hearts of separate islands, with the primordial Athalas Sea in between. This became silted up to form the central plain (Mesaoría) at a time coinciding with the "dawn of man" and the most recent Ice Age in much of mainland Europe. Today, wherever winter streams cut through the plain, they expose fossil shells from that era which look like scallops, mussels and oysters.

Long-term isolation from neighbouring land masses such as Turkey has meant that some plants have had time to evolve into **distinct species**; there are currently over ninety endemic plants – species found only in Cyprus. To a lesser extent this is true for animals, and there are insects, birds and even races of shrews and mice that the island can claim as its own. Even the separation of the southern and northern mountain ranges has been long enough for plants in the Tróödhos to have relatives in the Kyrenia hills which evolved separately from a common ancestor – for example, purple rock cress (*Arabis purpurea*) is abundant on volcanic rocks in the south, while the similar Cypriot rock cress (*Arabis cypria*) grows on the northern limestones.

Away from intensive cultivation and over-enthusiastic use of insecticides, the **insect fauna** is as diverse as the flora: butterflies, hawkmoths, beetles and mantids are abundant. The impact of **human activity** has changed Cyprus in the same way that much of the rest of the Mediterranean has been changed. Eratosthenes (275–195 BC) writes of a very different Cyprus, an island where innumerable streams flowed year round and even the Mesaoría was thickly forested. The Phoenicians and other traders up until the Venetians were attracted to the island by an abundance of timber suitable for ship-building; the destruction of the forests has contributed to drastic local climatic change since antiquity.

From the early days of British administration through to the present, forestry departments in Cyprus have been enlightened enough to manage and establish new forests throughout the island. Thus, about 18 percent of the island's territory is covered with "forest", although it's a much more open, park-like woodland than northern Europeans associate with the word. It is easy to remember only the negative side of human impact on the vegetation, but the commercial history of Cyprus has resulted in horticultural benefits such as the palms, agaves, cacti, mimosas, eucalyptus and citrus trees which are a familiar part of today's landscape. Even the olive (*Olea europaea*) originated in the Middle East and today its range is taken to broadly define the "limits" of Mediterranean vegetation and climate in Europe.

Birdlife is diverse, especially in the mountains, and the island lies astride spring and autumn migration routes. Though having comparatively few **mammals** (sixteen species, including eight kinds of bat), Cyprus has a surprising range of **reptiles and amphibians** – in spite of the age-old association of snakes with evil, which seems to require that every snake crossing a road be crushed by car tyres.

WHEN TO COME

To sample the wildlife at its most varied, the **hot summer** months should be avoided: the ground is baked in the lowlands, sensible life-forms are hidden well away from the sun, and there's no birdsong – crickets and cicadas make up loudly for the absence. However, many native flowers persist in the mountains through June and July, and plants on the coast go on blooming throughout the year. In Cyprus bulbs start to flower with the first rains in October and November, anemones are in flower by Christmas, while orchids appear in abundance in the lowlands from February (even December in some years) through to early April. **Springtime** sees the real explosion of colour on the plains and lower hills.

In the winter months **weather** is unpredictable: until late March, days can change quickly from pleasantly warm to cloudy and windy in the space of a few hours. In recent years, a serious shortage of winter rains has left water levels in mountain reservoirs way below what is needed to cope with the summer tourist influx. By the end of April the plains are getting hot (summer temperatures in Nicosia reach 40°C and above, with a more tolerable 35°C or so on the coast). In May, June and again in late September and October the mountains are a delight for the walker: warm, sunny and not another soul for miles.

HABITAT TYPES

Geographically, the island can be split into three broad regions: the **northern mountains**, which are mainly limestone; the **southern mountains** of igneous rocks which have erupted volcanically from deep in the earth through younger sedimentary rocks to leave volcanic mountain heights with flanks of chalks and limestone; and the **central plain** of comparatively recent deposits with schists forming conical hills at its edges. This geological diversity creates added interest in the **four main habitat types**: coastal habitats, cultivated land, low hillsides less than 1000m, and mountains above 1000m.

COASTAL HABITATS

Coastal scenery is varied. Some **plains**, such as those in the north around Güzelyurt (Mórfou) which continue along the coast to Cape Koruçam (Kormakíti) and those in the south stretching westwards from Limassol, are kept moist much of the year. Water reaches them from the mountains in seasonal streams, or from deep wells. This enables them to support vast citrus orchards and, more recently, avocado groves. Reedy river mouths are rare nowadays, since reservoirs in the mountains hold back much of the winter rainfall, reducing some water courses to little more than a trickle. The wide, stone-strewn bed of the Xeropótamos between Páfos and Koúklia shows that river's former extent.

Undeveloped **coastal wetlands** are found north of Famagusta, in pockets in the Mórfou and Pólis hinterland, and in a limited area east of Xylofágou, near Ayía Nápa. Little of the once-extensive marshland at Asómatos, north of the Akrotíri saltlake, remains untouched and what is left can be hard to find because of drainage for vast fruit orchards.

Most resorts boast so-called "beaches", but some are just shingle or dirt-grey sand and hardly deserve the status. Naturalists and connoisseurs should try the west coast from Coral Bay to Lára and beyond, which takes in some interesting fossil-rich chalk (shark's teeth and sea urchins), which the sea has eroded into a stark lunar landscape. Further to the north-west, there are small **sandy beaches** on the Akámas peninsula. In the north, excellent beaches run from Famagusta to İskele (Tríkomo) on the east coast and on the north coast to the east of Kyrenia and on the Kárpas (Kırpaşa) peninsula.

Much of the coastline, however, consists of **low cliffs** of clay or limestone with rocks plummeting down to the sea; high cliffs occur between Episkopí and Pétra toú Romíou. Coastal plantations of eucalyptus date from attempts to control mosquitoes by draining swamps; those of funeral cypress or Aleppo pine are more recent and form extensive **open woodlands** – near Hala Sultan Tekke and the Péyia forest, for example. These plantations provide essential shelter and are rapidly colonized by all sorts of insects, birds and plants (orchids in particular, though the latter take some years to actually flower).

CULTIVATED LAND

Large areas of **cultivated land** are maintained clinically free of weeds and insect pests by drastic measures such as deep ploughing, insecticides and fertilizers. But smaller areas on the Mesaoría – orchards near villages, olive groves (even in Nicosia) or carob orchards – can be very colourful in the spring with numerous annuals. A direct consequence of the diverse plant life is that it supports rich populations of insects, lizards and occasional snakes – in the early morning orchards are good places to wander with binoculars and see small migrant birds.

Numerous species of flowering plants thrive in badly tended mountain vineyards and even at the edges of well-tended ones. One family of plants, always well represented, is the *Leguminosae* (vetches and peaflowers) – which also includes many commercially important food plants such as peas, chickpeas, beans of all types and lentils. In Cyprus, these crops often play host to another family of plants, the parasitic broomrapes (*Orobanchaceae*) and when present in large numbers these are a highly damaging pest.

LOW HILLSIDES

Low hillsides (slopes up to 1000m) occur over much of Cyprus away from the central and coastal plains. They take on a markedly different character according to whether the underlying soil is limestone (alkaline) or volcanic (neutral to slightly acidic). Over-grazing by **goats** is another factor affecting large areas of the island. These voracious animals leave pastures with few flowering plants other than the tall spikes of white asphodels, one of the surprisingly few plants they find distasteful in a diet which can include woody and spiny shrubs. Government policy in the North has allowed settlers from the Turkish mainland to bring in their flocks, so that meadows which a few years ago were ablaze with flowers now have the goat-grazed look of their Southern counterparts.

In the Mediterranean region, low hills are extensively covered with a dense, low scrub composed of spiny, often aromatic shrubs. It forms a type of vegetation widely known as **garigue** – in the Greek-speaking world it's called *frigana* (sometimes written "phrygana"), literally "toasted". Left to grow, it may well become maquis, with bushes and low trees a few metres high. The final, or "climax", stage is

the evergreen forest which once covered the island. In general, garigue and maquis often blend into one another on the same hillside.

On limestone or chalk, shrubby thymes, sages and a wickedly spined member of the rose family, *Sarcopoterium spinosum*, form an often impenetrable scrub. Numerous bulbous plants grow between and below the bushes, sheltered from the full glare of the sun and protected from all but the most determined goats. As you climb higher in the Tróödhos foothills the soil changes quite dramatically in nature from white chalks to a range of browns due to underlying serpentines and pillow lavas. A noticeable shift in vegetation accompanies the change in geology, with acres of **French lavender** (*Lavandula stoechas*), its flowers sticky to the touch, and various **rock roses** (*Cistus* spp.) – a magnificent sight in late April and May when bushes are covered with large pink or white flowers.

Whatever the underlying rock types, garigue can slowly evolve into a dense **maquis** – look over any hillside covered in dense bushes and the range of shades of green will show the sheer variety of species. In a limited area you can find **lentisk** (*Pistacia lentiscus*), **terebinth** (*Pistacia terebinthus*), **storax** (*Styrax officinalis*), **myrtle** (*Myrtus communis*), the red-barked **strawberry tree** (*Arbutus andrachne*) and several kinds of evergreen oaks, more like holly bushes than the stately oaks of Britain.

Many of the plants in the garigue are **aromatic** and, on a hot day, their oils vaporize to scent the air. In spring, after a few days outdoors, you may well find yourself almost absent-mindedly picking a leaf and gently crushing it before smelling it. Anyone venturing off paths and brushing shrubs will find their clothing has taken on the scent of the island where tiny amounts of fragrant essences – thyme, oregano or lavender – have rubbed off. Some of the plant oils are highly volatile and, on a really hot day, have been known to ignite spontaneously: the origin of Moses' burning bush, perhaps.

Aspect – the direction a slope faces – can make a great difference to the vegetation supported there because it determines how much sun and, on higher hills, how much rain the land will get. In Cyprus, there is an obvious change when you cross either mountain range and leave behind the rich, almost lush vegetation of the north-facing slopes to find the dry southern slopes, with their xerophytic (drought-adapted) species clinging to life in the "rain shadow".

Woodlands on the northern limestone hills are largely composed of **funeral cypress** and **Calabrian pine** (*Pinus brutia*) grading into maquis, a pattern also repeated in the far west on the Akámas peninsula. In the Tróödhos, woodlands in the low and middle regions are mainly extensive open pine forest, with less lofty specimens of **strawberry tree**: the wood has an attractive natural sheen and is used for making village chairs. Another characteristic small tree is the endemic evergreen **golden oak** (*Quercus alnifolia*) – the leaves have a leathery, dark-green upper surface but are golden-brown on the lower side. Beneath the trees, a dense **understorey** of assorted shrubs – cistus, lavender, thyme and honeysuckle – completes the picture.

THE HIGH TRÓÖDHOS

The **High Tróödhos** – land over 1000m – is extensively forested and much reafforestation has been done using native species. Lower woods of **Calabrian pine** yield to **black pine** (*Pinus nigra* sp. *pallasiana*) mixed with **stinking juniper** (*Juniperus foetidissima*) and, near the summit of Khionístra, trees of both species appear gnarled as a consequence of their age, attained in a rigorous climate of long, dry summers and cold, snowy winters. On Khionístra you will also see trees where the trunk is violently twisted or split – the cause is lightning strikes which boil the sap almost explosively to vapour. Under these tremendous pressures the trunks split, but such incidents are seldom fatal to resilient trees and they continue to grow, albeit with an unexpected change of direction. In open areas there are low bushes of ankle-tearing **gorse** (*Genista fasselata*), a spiny **vetch** (*Astragalus echinus*) and a **barberry** (*Berberis cretica*). The native **cedar** (*Cedrus libani* sp. *brevifolia*) is being extensively propagated after becoming largely confined to the so-called "Cedar Valley" in the course of this century, especially after destructive fire-bombing of the forests by the Turkish air force during the invasion of 1974.

FLOWERS

Even though something, somewhere, is in bloom throughout the year, things begin in earnest when the first rains of autumn relieve the summer drought and moisten the hard-baked soil. It only seems to take a few drops percolating into the parched soils of the plains to activate the bulbs of a tiny, light-blue **grape hyacinth** known locally as "Baby's Breath" (*Muscari parviflorum*), or the delicate, white **autumn narcissus** (*Narcissus serotinus*). In the mountains, under bushes of golden oak, you can find the **Cyprus cyclamen** (*Cyclamen cyprium*), with distinctive pink "teeth" to its otherwise white flowers. The flowering sequence continues with **friar's cowl** (*Arisarum vulgare*), a curious candy-striped arum. The first of the **crown anemones** (*Anemone coronaria*) appears at Christmas time near the coast, followed by pink, then red varieties. Growing close by will be the highly scented **polyanthus narcissus** (*Narcissus tazetta*) and the royal purple stars of the **eastern sand crocus** (*Romulea tempskyana*).

Cyprus is justifiably famous among orchid enthusiasts for its unique assemblage of species – a good example of the "collecting basket" role mentioned earlier. The first **orchids** to appear are the robust, metre-high spikes of the **giant orchids** (*Barlia robertiana*). Look closely and you see flowers like tiny "Darth Vader" figures and perhaps catch a hint of its iris-like scent. Even by late December these orchids are blooming near Hala Sultan Tekke, close to Larnaca airport, along with the fleshy-stemmed **fan-lipped orchid** (*Orchis collina*). By late February to early March the season is in full swing, with an abundance of bee orchids including the remarkable endemic **Cyprus bee orchid** (*Ophrys kotschyi*), the pick of a fascinating bunch of insect mimics – this one has a fat black and white lip forming the insect "body". It occurs in scattered populations in the South near Larnaca, but is more common in the North.

In the **lowlands**, especially on the limestone soils of the northern slopes of the Kyrenia mountains, the Akámas peninsula and the southern Tróödhos, the early **spring wildflower** display is staggering, with a profusion of **turban buttercups** (*Ranunculus asiaticus*) in white, yellow, various shades of pink, scarlet and even occasional bi-coloured forms. Less obvious to the eye, but equally diverse in colour, are the small pea and vetch family members with over 170 species listed in the island's flora, many of them endemic to Cyprus.

Two, in particular, stand out: the **veined vetch** (*Onobrychis venosa*), with white flowers and marbled leaves which spread over dry limestone, and the yellow and violet **crescent vetch** (*Vicia lunata*) which flourishes on volcanic soils – around Asínou church, for example.

Snow melting on the heights of Tróödhos reawakens one of the island's three endemic species of **crocus**, the **Cyprus crocus** (*Crocus cyprius*), followed by a pink **corydalis** (*Corydalis rutifolia*), an endemic **golden drop** (*Onosma troodi*) and numerous other local flora from **dandelions** to **garlics** and **deadnettles**. Cyprus has two other species of crocus: the winter-flowering **late crocus** (*Crocus veneris*), especially frequent on the northern slopes of the Kyrenia range, and **Hartmann's crocus** (*Crocus hartmannianus*), usually encountered in early spring if you happen to be walking on peaks near Makherás.

By mid-March, many of the bulbous plants will already be dying back. The **annuals**, however, more than make up for the loss by providing sheets of colour, often created from surprisingly few species: scarlet **poppies**, the golden yellow of **crown marigolds** (*Chrysanthemum coronarium*), pink **Egyptian catchfly** (*Silene aegyptiaca*), perhaps tempered with white **camomile** (*Anthemis chia*). In the days before intensive cultivation and deep ploughing, **field gladiolus** (*Gladiolus italicus*) made cornfields magenta with its stately spikes, and people still talk of looking down on a Mesaoría scarlet with tulips. Today, in the South, **wild tulips** (*Tulipa agenensis*) still survive under fruit trees near Stroumbí, north of Páfos, but to see the endemic **Cyprus tulip** (*Tulipa cypria*), with its dark red, almost purple flowers, you either have to visit bean fields and orchards around Çamlıbel (Mýrtou) or chance upon it in the wilder parts of the Akámas peninsula.

Two **coastal displays** of wildflowers are not to be missed. First appearing in late January and February, the **Persian cyclamen** (*Cyclamen persicum*) cascades over rocks on the north slopes of the Kyrenia mountains. You will also find them forcing their way through cracks and crevices around the Tombs of the Kings in Páfos, but the most spectacular display is on the natural rockery of the Akámas peninsula where they grow in white, pink and

magenta shades waiting to be photographed with an azure blue sea below. A couple of months later, towards the beginning of April, there's another display: the **three-leaved gladiolus** (*Gladiolus triphyllus*) with scented pink and white flowers, growing in countless thousands, virtually all around the coast of the island.

In the **Tróödhos mountains** things are slower off the mark. As you travel north from the coast, however, two new orchids – the yellow **Roman orchid** (*Dactylorhiza romana*) and the pink **Anatolian orchid** (*Orchis anatolica* sp. *troodi*) – become noticeable as soon as the soil changes from chalk to volcanic. From late May onwards, an unusual saprophytic orchid, the **violet limodore** (*Limodorum abortivum*), with purple stems and large purple flowers, is a common plant of the woodlands, usually growing beneath pines or close to them. It occurs in some abundance not far from Tróödhos resort itself, with three other orchid companions: **Cyprus helleborine** (*Epipactis troodi*), **Holmboe's butterfly orchid** (*Platanthera holmboei*) and **red helleborine** (*Cephalanthera rubra*).

When the **plains** are burnt dry, **pink oleander** (*Nerium oleander*) brings a welcome touch of colour to dried streambeds. It has been widely planted as a flowering "hedge", and at the right season you can travel the Nicosia–Tróödhos road flanked by the colourful flowers of these bushes. Few other species of plant, in flower now, relieve the grey and brown shades of a dessicated landscape. There are **thistles** – the **cardoon** (*Cynara cardunculus*), a wild artichoke growing several metres tall, is quite spectacular – and also a yellow dandelion relative forming sticky-leaved bushes, often covered in dust. This plant is one of those you see everywhere but rarely find in field guides: it's called **aromatic inula** (*Dittrichia viscosa*) and this is one of those cases where "aromatic" does not mean pleasant.

In the **middle heights** of the Tróödhos massif, where the road climbs up to Pródhromos, May is the time to see the white, lupin-like flowers of **Lusitanian milk vetch** (*Astragalus lusitanicus*), with **purple rock cress** (*Arabis purpurea*) in pink cushions hanging over rock faces above. Late in the day, shafts of sunlight on an open glade might illuminate scarlet **peonies** (*Paeonia mascula*), almost making the flowers glow. This is the time of year when the **French lavender** (*Lavandula stoechas*) flowers on the pillow lavas, and whole hillsides can seem to be in bloom with a variety of **cistus**: white (*Cistus salviifolius* and *C. monspeliensis*), pale pink (*C. parviflorus*) and deep pink (*C. creticus*).

In only a few places in the Tróödhos does **water** run all the year round, but locate it and there, in early summer, you can find the rare **eastern marsh helleborine** (*Epipactis veratrifolia*), the **marsh orchid** (*Dactylorhiza iberica*) and an indigenous **butterwort** (*Pinguicula crystallina*), a plant that traps insects on its sticky leaves. By July, even plants in the mountains find it too hot, and only spiny things such as various gorses, brooms and barberry provide a bit of colour.

Surprisingly, it's only when the sand gets too hot to stand on in the day that delicate white **sea daffodils** (*Pancratium maritimum*) bloom: they were once so numerous on the east coast that they were called Famagusta lilies. Under these same "desert" conditions, in coastal and other lowlands all over the island, you find tall spikes of starry-white flowers, emerging leafless straight out of hard-baked ground. These are **sea squills** (*Drimia maritima*) and are what becomes of the huge bulbs you might have wondered about, in spring, when you saw them half-pushed out of the ground, topped by long, strap-like, leathery leaves. The bulbs were once used as the source of both a rat poison and a cough remedy.

When little else is left in flower near the sea, you will find **carline thistles**, favourites of flower arrangers for their long-lasting flower heads. The tiny one with scarlet, daisy-like flowers found near Southern beaches is yet another Cypriot endemic – the **dwarf carline thistle** (*Carlina pygmaea*).

EXOTIC AND EDIBLE PLANTS

Introduced exotic plants, noted in the introductory section, now play an important part in the island's **food production**. The climate has favoured the introduction of subtropical species which are now widely cultivated: palms (from North Africa, Asia and the Americas), agave, avocado, prickly pear, tomatoes, potatoes, peppers and aubergine (the Americas), mimosa and eucalyptus (Australasia), citrus (originating in Asia) and pomegranate (Iran). The British administration introduced flowering trees from other colonies which, in maturity, have become a colourful feature of the parks and gardens in towns and cities: orchid tree (*Bauhinia variegata*), bougainvillea (*Bougainvillea spectabilis*) and silk oak (*Grevillea robusta*).

Cypriots north and south of the Attila Line are essentially pragmatic people when it comes to natural resources, readily recognizing **edible "weeds"** while remaining indifferent to or disparaging of less "useful" plants. Even town-dwellers will head for the countryside in spring, perhaps to gather shoots of woody-stemmed **wild asparagus** (*Asparagus acutifolius*) or of the **bladder campion** (*Silene vulgaris*), called *strouthkiá* – "little sparrows". Both are fried with eggs to make a kind of omelette. In the Pólis region it's still possible to ask for *spatziá* (pronounced "spajá") or *faskómilo* – a tea made from the leaves of a bitter-tasting **wild sage** (*Salvia cypria*). In autumn, the slightest of bumps in woodland leaf-litter can lead the sharp-eyed and knowledgeable villager to edible wild fungi. Outside private gatherings with Cypriot families, it is almost impossible to try most of these foods: only *kápari*, whole, spiny **caper stems** softened by pickling, are readily available.

Over the centuries, Cypriots have employed many plants as natural remedies for every imaginable ill; with increasing Westernization much of this lore has been forgotten. If you're interested in further study, some of the botanical field guides listed in the bibliography at the end of this article will be useful.

BIRDS

Cyprus no longer has the large numbers of birds of prey it once had – thanks to the mania, North and South, for the gun, along with the use of poisoned carcasses by misguided goatherds, anxious to protect their flocks and their meagre income.

Fortunately **griffon vultures** still nest in colonies in the gorges of the Akámas peninsula as well as on the high cliffs to the west of Episkopí and in the Kyrenia hills. Although the days are long gone when up to a hundred of these scavengers might gather round a suitably "ripe" carcass, the sight of a few, wheeling on thermal updraughts over the Akámas, is still a sight to quicken the heartbeat. **Kestrels** are still common, but nesting **peregrine** only survive in remote strongholds in the Kyrenia range and offshore on the Klídhes islands at the tip of the Kırpaşa (Kárpas) peninsula. **Bonelli's eagle** is far from common nowadays in either northern or southern mountain ranges, whereas in the past it was even known to have nested in the walls of Buffavénto castle.

Other raptors seen over the island are usually migrants, transient visitors on passage to nesting grounds in spring, returning in autumn. They tend to be seen as they hunt over reservoirs and at the salt lakes for prey to sustain them on their journey, or when flying over the peninsulas of Akámas and Kırpaşa (Kárpas). Species regularly observed include the **red-footed falcon** and the **hobby**, a small falcon which looks like a large swift in flight and which has the turn of speed and agility in the air to take swallows, martins and even swifts on the wing. There are also broad-winged raptors such as **marsh harrier**, **common buzzard** and **black kite**, for example, which can be seen soaring above scrub-covered hills or hunting low over reedbeds.

Eleonora's falcons breed late in the year in colonies on the cliffs at Akrotíri, safely protected within the Episkopí Sovereign Base. They favour Cape Gáta at the tip of the peninsula and nest late, timing the hatching of their chicks to coincide with the autumn migration of exhausted hoopoes, orioles, swifts and sandmartins, exploiting the passerines' misfortunes. Once you have witnessed their mastery of flight, as they scythe through the air, you may forgive their opportunism.

In the Tróödhos massif there are permanent nesting populations of familiar species such as **raven**, **jackdaw**, **rock dove** and **wood pigeon**. Less familiar to those used to watching birds in northern Europe will be **crag martin**, **Cretschmar's bunting** and the colourful **hoopoe** with pink body, black and white crest and a call which can be heard from afar. In the northern range, Kantára has always been a favourite place for birdwatchers in spring and, in the course of a couple of hours you might see **blue rock thrush**, **alpine swift**, **black-headed bunting** and **spectacled warbler**.

The **chukar**, an attractive rock partridge, manages to survive as a ground nester in dense scrub, in spite of its being the favourite target of hunters North and South: just enough seem to escape the hunters to maintain the population in a fragile equilibrium. The **black francolin**, exterminated in much of southern Europe by thoughtless hunting, just managed to recover from the brink of extinction in Cyprus when the British administration revoked gun licences during the EOKA troubles of the 1950s. Sadly, it's still hunted in one of its main strongholds in the Kárpas, to the east of Dipkarpaz (Rizokárpaso).

Rollers and **bee-eaters** are the most colourful of the spring migrants seen each year on passage through the island. Both species are known to breed locally, choosing suitable holes in sandy riverbanks or soft cliffs for the purpose. Being vividly coloured they attract the attention of hunters and have been regarded as articles of food. Cyprus suffered habitually in the past from depredation by **locusts** – government reports for the years 1878 and 1879 record how villagers were expected to catch locusts to be bagged up and weighed. Failure to comply with the directive or even to collect minimum weights brought fines and sometimes imprisonment. Ironically, locusts form part of a roller's diet – if these insects are around then they will eat nothing else.

Salt lakes provide both food (tiny brine shrimps siphoned up in their millions) and a resting place for the **greater flamingoes** which winter at Akrotíri and Larnaca. Together with reservoirs, the salt lakes and marshes constitute the main areas of open water on the island and regular visitors have a chance to observe a changing variety of **water birds** in the course of a year. There are various species of duck (**mallard**, **shoveler**, **teal** and **wigeon**), **black-necked grebe** and larger birds such as several members of the heron family (**squacco heron**, **night heron**, **little bittern**, **little** and **cattle egrets**). Shallow waters at the edges of reservoirs and salt lakes provide the mud in which waders probe incessantly for their food. Occasionally, one can be lucky and see **glossy ibis**, **black-winged stilt** or **black-tailed godwit**. The migratory routes of storks do not pass over the island but, occasionally, individuals of both **black** and **white stork** and even **pelican** can be blown off course and spend a few days in the island, before resuming their journey.

Cyprus has several endemic bird species, distinct enough from their nearest relatives that they can be properly thought of as species; others are only regarded as distinct "races". The best known of the endemics is the **Cyprus warbler**, with a wide distribution in scrubby areas throughout the island. It closely resembles the Sardinian warbler but differs in having underparts marked with black – it also lacks the red ring around the eye and the red iris which are the trademarks of the Sardinian species. Only one other endemic is widespread and that is the **Cyprus scops owl**: the others – **pied wheatear**, **coal tit**, **jay**, **crossbill** and the **short-toed treecreeper** – are confined to the Hígh Tróödhos pine forest.

Both **demoiselle** and **common cranes** spend the winter months in the Sudan but migrate via Cyprus – en route to the demoiselle's breeding sites in Asia Minor and southern Russia in March and April, while the common crane flies in the opposite direction, leaving the Balkans, Turkestan, Asia Minor and northern Europe in August and September. They are often seen following the line of the Akámas peninsula in spring, but particularly evocative are hot, late-August nights over Nicosia: the birds are far out of sight, only the wing beats and trumpeting metallic calls identifying their passage.

MAMMALS – PAST AND PRESENT

The Mediterranean Sea has had a chequered history, and geological evidence shows that it has even dried out on several occasions, enabling plants and animals to migrate to mountain peaks which have since become islands. The basic shape of the **Mediterranean basin** was formed about 40 million years ago, but until around 20 million years ago it was open at either end to the Atlantic and Indian oceans respectively. First the eastern channel closed up, isolating sea life but still allowing land animals to cross between continents, and then the western outlet closed, effectively sealing it off.

Some six million years ago the land-locked sea **evaporated** almost completely; the Mediterranean became an arid, inhospitable basin with a few shallow salt lakes on its floor and some of today's islands standing as **forested oases**, in which animals congregated

and developed. Drilling has revealed salt deposits which show that the Atlantic breached the debris dam at the present-day Straits of Gibraltar on several occasions over a 700,000-year period. Finally, the "dam" gave way and the basin was filled in about a century by a gigantic cascade of Atlantic water, isolating the forested hilltops and their inhabitants.

Excavations on the Mesaoría have revealed **fossil bones** showing that Cyprus, in Pleistocene times, was the home of mammals such as pygmy elephants, pygmy hippopotamus, ibex, genet and wild boar. Today the largest mammal on the island is the **Cyprus mouflon** (*Ovis musimon*), possibly a survivor from those times. Although hunted almost to the point of extinction, it has been saved by a captive breeding programme in the forests of the southern mountains, and is widely used as a symbol of the island – visitors first meet it as the symbol of *Cyprus Airways* (see also p.352).

Although **foxes** are rarely seen in the open, they are not uncommon in the Akámas and Kárpas peninsulas. They have paler coats than north European races and blend easily with the browns and greys of the landscape. **Cyprian hares** (*Lepus cyprius*) can sometimes be seen as they break cover, but they are shy creatures – justifiably – barely able to sustain small populations between successive hunting seasons. Other small animals include the **Cyprian shrew**, a race of **spiny mouse** and **long-eared hedgehogs** – which look like the animal equivalent of an old Renault 4, with their long back legs keeping their rear end higher than the front. For years, hedgehogs were persecuted because of a reputation for climbing into chicken coops and trying to have their spiny way with the inhabitants. As laughable as it's physically impossible, the strongly held superstition did the welfare of these creatures no good at all.

Of the eight species of bat recorded in Cyprus, the **fruit-eating bat** (*Rousettus aegyptiacus*) is the most spectacular, with a powerful bird-like flight. They can sometimes be seen on the outskirts of Pólis and in villages along the northern coast, when they come in the evening to feed on ripe fruit. They live and breed in limestone caves and so are confined to the Akámas (where they were filmed for David Attenborough's TV series on the Mediterranean) and the Kyrenia mountains.

Their visits to orchards have made them the target of hunters, but in the wild they have an important role to play because hard-coated fruit seeds pass undamaged through their digestive systems. Thus fruit-eating bats have played an unwitting but essential role in the propagation of trees by spreading seeds in their droppings.

REPTILES AND AMPHIBIANS

Saint Helena, mother of the Byzantine emperor Constantine, apparently visited Cyprus on her return voyage from Jerusalem to Constantinople after a successful venture to discover the Holy Cross. She found an island gripped by the ravages of drought, but what really perturbed her was that it seemed to be infested with snakes and lizards. Her answer to the problem was to return with a shipload of cats to hunt them down, and these were landed at the tip of the Akrotíri peninsula, henceforth known as Cape Gáta (*gáta* means cat). Although feral cats in cities still take an enormous toll of lizards (and small birds), **reptiles and amphibians** still occur in numbers sufficient to interest those who want to see them.

Spring and autumn are the times to see the island's eight endemic species of snakes: in winter they hibernate and in summer they are hidden, virtually comatose, from the unremitting heat. Looking like a glossy earthworm, the **worm snake** is the smallest; at a length which can easily exceed two metres; the large **whip snake** just qualifies as the longest, edging out its cousin the **Cyprus whip snake**. The former is easily recognized by its almost black back – it wriggles away when disturbed in vineyards or at field edges and will also climb trees. The **coin snake** has distinctive lozenge markings on its back; it and the recently rediscovered **grass snake** are harmless. The **cat snake** and **Montpellier snake** feed on small lizards and produce venom which can paralyse or kill their prey in a matter of minutes. Humans fare better if bitten by either, since the inward-pointing fangs are set far back in the throat, but a large Montpellier snake can still inflict a wound which is slow to heal, with local swelling and headache as an accompaniment. The **blunt-nosed viper**, fortunately quite rare, is the only really dangerous serpent on Cyprus. Called *koúfi* locally, it has a distinctive yellow, horn-like tail and can inflict a bite which is highly **poisonous**: its fangs remain embedded in the tissue and the venom is pumped into the wound by movements of the jaws.

During the years of the British administration, problematically large numbers of rodents led to the idea of importing more Montpellier snakes from southern France as a biological control. Some were undoubtedly brought in to bolster the local population, but as to numbers involved, the period of time and the ultimate success of the venture, nobody seems certain. In Cyprus all snakes have a bad press, based almost entirely upon superstition – none of the island's species is aggressive and individuals will only bite in a desperate move to defend themselves.

Small **lizards** seem to be everywhere. You will see tiny **geckos** coming out at night to feed on insects attracted to wall lights, or agile **sand lizards** racing over rocks or even dashing suicidally across roads. The largest lizard in Cyprus is the **starred agama** (*Agama stelio*) which grows up to 30cm long. It has a disproportionately large head, and if you see one at close quarters it's like looking back in time to the age of dinosaurs. They are shy creatures, often seen scuttling into cracks in walls or the trunks of ancient olive and carob trees. In Cyprus, the politest of the local names means "nosebiter", inspired by the oversized head.

In summer, **tree frogs** (*Hyla arborea*) are usually heard rather than seen when they call, often at night and far away from water, with a volume out of all proportion to their small size. In winter, they return to water to breed and lay eggs and can be found on bushes or reeds close to streams, ponds and rivers, where you might be lucky enough see their acrobatic climbing. **Marsh frogs** and **green toads** are considerably larger and, thus, correspondingly easier to find.

Stripe-necked terrapins can still be found, even in surprisingly murky pools, although they have suffered badly from the effects of pollution – mainly from agricultural chemicals. A plop into a muddy pool as you approach will usually be a large frog – occasionally it might be a terrapin, which will surface several metres away to survey you, the intruder, with quiet confidence.

SEA TURTLES

Cyprus is one of the few places in the Mediterranean where **sea turtles** still come ashore to breed, on the sandy beaches of the

Kárpas and Akámas peninsulas. Tourism has driven them from the sands of the south coast, where they once nested on Governor's Beach to the east of Limassol. Since the early 1980s, the Fisheries Department has run a camp at Lára, near Páfos, with the express purpose of protecting nests and collecting hatchlings in order to transfer them to the water, safe from predation by crows and foxes. Simultaneously, a running battle has been fought between conservationists and the developers who see the obvious tourist potential of this superb, sandy beach.

Both **loggerhead turtles** (*Caretta caretta*) and **green turtles** (*Chelonia mydas*) haul themselves ashore at night, landing from June onwards on beaches to the northwest of Páfos. In the north mainly loggerheads come ashore to lay eggs on sandy beaches east of Kyrenia and also on the Kárpas peninsula. Both species mate at sea.

The green turtle is the larger of the two species, with mature adults attaining a length of some 100–140cm, while the loggerhead grows from 75 to 100cm in length. They are smooth-shelled herbivores, feeding on sea grasses and seaweeds and, in the nesting season, a female can produce several clutches of eggs at two-week intervals – they tend to breed every two to three years. Loggerheads have a tapered shell or carapace, a short muscular neck and powerful jaws which can crush the shells of the molluscs – one part of the varied diet, along with jellyfish, crabs, sponges and aquatic plants. Numbers of them die yearly from mistaking plastic carry-bags floating at sea for edible jellyfish. They breed every other year and will lay three or four clutches in a season.

A popular local belief maintains that turtles will only lay on the two or three nights to either side of the full moon. What is certainly true, however, is that turtles the world over prefer to emerge on bright, **moonlight nights**. The laborious journey up the beach, the digging of a nest, followed by egg-laying and then covering with sand, is an exhausting business which takes several hours. Turtles disturbed as they come ashore will simply return to the sea, but when laying has started they carry on until virtually drained of energy – behaviour that has made them extremely vulnerable to hunters.

Temperature plays a very important part in the development of the embryo within the parchment-skinned turtle egg, as it not only controls the incubation rate, but also determines the sex of the offspring. Instinctively, the female selects a place on the beach and lays her eggs at such a depth (about 40cm) that the ambient temperature will stay fairly constant during the incubation period. Since sea turtles have evolved from land-based ancestors, their eggs will not develop in water; to survive, they need the air trapped between the grains of sand that surround them in the "nest".

Hatchlings appear some six to ten weeks after the white, ping-pong-ballish eggs are laid in batches of 75–120; in Cyprus most nests are established in June, and hatchlings emerge throughout August into September. The lower in the sand an egg is placed, the cooler it is and hence the slower the development. Thus hatchlings emerge at different rates, a batch each day from the same nest. Immediately after biting and wriggling their way out from the egg, they still have part of the yolk-sac attached and will have to wait beneath the sand until that has been absorbed into the body. The young struggle the final few centimetres to the surface and make directly for the sea around dawn or in the evening when it's cool. Occasionally, their internal clocks can go wrong and they try to emerge in the hot sand with fatal consequences.

In some countries, hatchlings have to run a gauntlet of seabirds to reach the sea; in Cyprus, foxes have been the major **predators**. The hope is that the immediate danger of predation at Lára is removed by placing wire cages over nests, ensuring one less peril in the seven or eight years it will take them to reach maturity. It is very difficult to assess the success of conservation ventures with sea turtles because of other hazards they have to face: predation from other sea creatures when small, deliberate killing by fishermen, or being left to die, trapped in drift nets. The good news is that numbers have certainly not decreased in Cyprus in the fifteen years that a conservation programme has been operational.

INSECTS

As soon as the sun comes out, butterflies are in evidence as they fly over patches of open ground in scrub or hotel gardens. Here, often for the first time, visitors see the glorious

swallowtail butterfly (*Papilio machaon*), rare in Britain yet common here, where its larvae thrive on fennel plants. Strawberry trees along the south and north coasts are the food-plant of the magnificent **two-tailed pasha** (*Charaxes jasius*), a powerful flier which defends its territory against infiltrators by flying at them. When seen at close quarters a complex and beautiful striping of the under-wings is revealed.

Cyprus has several unique species of butter-fly, including the **Paphos blue** (*Glaucopsyche paphia*) and **Cyprus festoon** (*Zerynthia cerisyi* sp. *cypria*), a swallowtail relative with scalloped margins to the wings. It has curiously spiked caterpillars which feed on a plant with a simi-larly bizarre appearance, the Dutchman's pipes (*Aristolochia* species), found thoughout the island's hills on chalk and volcanic soils. **Cleopatras** (*Gonepteryx cleopatra*) fly through sunny glades in the mountain woods, heralding the arrival of spring; the males are a deep sulphur yellow, with a splash of orange just visi-ble on the forewings in flight.

In summer, numerous species usually referred to collectively as "browns" (*Satyrids*) and "blues" (*Lycaenids*) are found all over the island wherever weeds grow. In spite of heavy use of insecticides, enough weeds are left to enable caterpillars to thrive. Some larvae are very particular and restrict their diet to one species of plant, while others are virtually omnivorous, even resorting to cannibalism if there is nothing else to eat.

One of the things you notice in pine trees are the hanging nests of gossamer, spun by **caterpillars** after they hatch from their eggs. They feed on pine needles within the nest and then drop to the ground in a wriggling mass until one sets off and the others attach them-selves in a "follow my leader" arrangement. So successful are these processionary caterpillars of **pine beauty** and **gypsy moths** that they have become a forest pest, causing serious damage to trees.

Many moths could be grouped under the heading "small, brown and boring", but the **hawkmoths** rival butterflies in terms of colour, and are superbly equipped for fast, powerful flight with strong forewings and small hind-wings. Their caterpillars are often more gaudily coloured than the parents and can assume a curious posture to frighten off predators – a

habit which has given them the common name of **sphinx moths**. In Cyprus, the most common member of the family is the **hummingbird hawk** (*Macroglossum stellatarum*), which can be cheeky enough to approach on whirring wings and, with long, thin tongue, sample the liquid from the edges of your drink glass as you enjoy an evening meal outdoors. Less frequently seen are the beautiful **oleander hawk** (*Daphnis nerii*) with olive-shaded wings and the **death's-head hawk** (*Acherontia atro-pos*) whose large yellow- and violet-striped caterpillars feed on potato plants and were quite common crop pests before the use of insecticides. **Praying mantids** are curious creatures and, in Cyprus, range from the small brown species to the larger **crested mantid** or *empúsa*, named after a Greek demi-goddess who visited men in their beds and made love with them until they expired: the insect males have to be fast to avoid becoming the main item in the post-coital breakfast.

Not strictly insects, but coming into the general category of "crawlies", most Cypriot **spiders** are small except for the **European tarantula** which lives in burrows on open hill-sides venturing out to catch any suitable prey passing its way. **Scorpions** are not as common as they once were, primarily due to destruction of habitat and to the use of agricul-tural chemicals. By carefully turning up stones in chalky areas or looking in the cracks in old limestone walls you can still find them. They are shy, pale-coloured creatures, but in defence of their brood they will inflict a very painful sting. The large black **millipedes** are harm-less, but orange **centipedes** pack a nasty, venomous bite: if camping in the wild shake out your sleeping bag carefully.

MARINE LIFE

The sea turtles mentioned above are the most spectacular of the marine creatures regularly seen in the waters around the island. Although **dolphins** are infrequently sighted off the north coast, their true haunts are much closer to Turkey's southern shore where there are more fish. The lack of tidal movement, coupled with very few streams providing nutrients to enrich the coastal water, keep plankton levels on the low side. Also, the building of Egypt's Aswan Dam has drastically reduced the outflow of nutrient-rich Nile water into the southeastern end of the Mediterranean. Consequently, fish numbers around the coasts are not as high as might be expected, but there is still a surprising diversity of colourful species – scuba-diving is a very popular activity because the absence of plankton makes the waters very clear.

A visit to a quay when a fishing boat comes in is also a recommended experience. As the catch is unloaded you see a great mixture of fish, including **peacock** and **rainbow wrasse**, **parrot fish**, **red soldier fish** and **red** or **grey mullet**. Many of these are visible from the surface if you're lazily snorkelling, in addition to the ubiquitous **sea urchins**, **starfish**, **anemones** and the occasional **octopus**. Further out to sea are small, harmless **sharks** and several species of **ray** (including electric and thornback), making a total of around two hundred species of fish recorded in the seas off the island. However, due to overfishing and high tourist levels in the south, the squid you dine on probably came in boxes from Taiwan, and nowadays boats have to sail almost to the Libyan coast in order to catch swordfish.

SITES

THE SALT LAKES: LARNACA AND AKROTÍRI

If you arrive in Cyprus in winter or spring and collect a hire car at Larnaca airport, the first taste of the island's wildlife is only a short drive away at the **Larnaca salt lake**, right next to Hala Sultan Tekke, burial place of Muhammad's aunt. From the tourist pavilion, you can see rafts of pink flamingoes and from January onwards contemplate a walk under the pines to the west in pursuit of orchids. Luck might allow for the flamingoes, feeding on brine shrimp, to be near the road when you visit. They're here all winter in thousands, adults arriving first, with juveniles following later from Turkey, Iran and even further afield. They start to leave by late March, with small flocks flying at low levels; the last stragglers quit in June for their nesting areas.

Near Limassol, **Akrotíri** is a reed-fringed lake which, with crossed fingers and a good map, you can try to approach on small roads from the north, but it's easier to take the road to the RAF base and turn left before reaching the gates. To prevent problems, always carry your passport when in this area, and avoid

pointing cameras at any obvious installations. On a good day in spring, it's possible to find scorpions, green toads, tree frogs and Cyprus bee orchids in the scrub around the lake. Throughout the year, it's a magnet for migrating birds and thus a favourite bird-watching site for off-duty military personnel, visiting ornithological tour parties and increasing numbers of local enthusiasts.

On maps, another salt lake is marked **near Paralímni**, but it only fills after heavy rains. It has always been a good area in which to observe migrant birds but, distressingly, has also long been a centre for the trade in tiny pickled birds caught on lime sticks (see "Conservation", p.356).

THE AKÁMAS PENINSULA

The **Akámas peninsula** was the first area in Cyprus to have been proposed as a national park, intensifying ongoing controversy as to its fate. The peninsula forms the northwestern tip of the island and its geology is varied, with outcrops, cliffs and deep gorges of limestone in addition to serpentine and other igneous rocks. This allows for a diversity of soil types and a rich plant life as a direct consequence – there is even an endemic alyssum (*Alyssum akamasicum*), for example, as well as the endemic tongue orchid, *Serapias aphroditae*.

Although once an inhabited area, as extensive remains of ancient settlements show, its separation from present concentrations of population, plus its long-time use as a practice range by the British Forces, means it has remained largely unspoiled. Scattered pine groves constitute the nearest thing to virgin forest the island can offer, but considerable tracts of land have suffered the depredations of feral goats. Where grazing has been controlled, the plant life is rich and, now under protected status, the whole peninsula should eventually be the same.

In February and March, coastal walks here take you over hillsides of cascading cyclamen, and you might see the first rollers and beeeaters to have arrived on the spring migration. **Gorges** hidden from view provide nesting sites for lammergeiers and cave roosts – especially near **Faslí** and **Andhrolíkou** – where you might discover some of the island's fruit bats. Green and loggerhead turtles use the beaches such as Lára for breeding, as discussed previously. There are orchids too, although these have suffered as much as other plant species because of grazing. Encouragingly, numbers increase by the year and include the rare yellow flowered punctate orchid (*Orchis punctulata*).

From Káthikas, at the more populated southern base of the Akámas, a road descends through Péyia to the coast and is worth travelling for the views alone. As a bonus, you pass through an area planted with pines – the **Péyia forest** – where orchids grow in both abundance and astonishing variety. High above the sea, it is a cool place that has become something of a haven for small birds.

THE HIGH TRÓÖDHOS

High on the mountains, snow can remain in pockets until April – in fact the name of the summit **Khionístra** means "snow-pit". Thus, spring starts late but with a choice series of plants: crocus, corydalis, various vetches, an endemic buttercup (*Ranunculus cyprius* var. *cadmicus*) – no large-scale displays, more like a huge rock garden with many plants unique to the island. In colonial times the British established a network of paths, mostly on a contour, so that walks around Mount Olympus can be as long or as short as you like. Wherever the paths pass through the open forests of black pine you can look for the endemic coal tits, pied wheatear, jay, crossbill and short-toed treecreeper.

Another nature trail follows the Krýos river past **Caledonian Falls**, just southwest from and below Tróödhos resort, and numbered posts indicate plants of interest; both Greek and scientific names are given. In early summer there are various endemic plants – many of them with *troodi* as part of the Latin name. Look out for groups of marsh orchids (*Dactylorhiza iberica*), near the streams, and eastern marsh helleborines (*Epipactis veratrifolia*) around the Caledonian Falls near the end of the trail. Here, well out of reach on wet rocks behind the falls grows the rare Cyprus butterwort (*Pinguicula crystallina*).

The extensive forests to the northwest below Khionístra offer peonies (*Paeonia mascula*) in May near Pródhromos; a curious red parasite, the Cyprus broomrape (*Orobanche cypria*) and a seemingly endless network of dirt roads, usually well maintained, which take you far from other visitors. Better roads run to Kýkko Monastery (the area has its very own buttercup – *Ranunculus kykkoënsis*) and beyond, leading to **Stavrós tis Psókas**, a forestry station where it's possible to stay by prior arrangement, falling asleep to the sound of nightingales and waking to the scent of pines.

Several rather dejected-looking **mouflon** are kept penned here and, for most visitors to the island, they will be the only ones seen, even though the Páfos forest is their stronghold. The exact origins of this wild sheep are uncertain but remains have been found in Neolithic settlements, dating to around 8000 years ago. It could well have been a domesticated animal then, either brought to the island by settlers, or the direct descendant of creatures trapped when the Mediterranean filled for the last time. In Greco-Roman times, mouflon were plentiful throughout the Tróödhos and in the Kyrenia mountains, but hunting, especially during the Middle Ages, reduced the population drastically. In 1878, the first year of British rule, only twenty animals were counted, a situation which pertained until 1939 when game laws were strengthened and the Páfos forest became a game reserve. At the same time goat-grazing was banned in the reserve, removing competition for the available food; subsequently, numbers began to increase steadily, with counts of 100 animals in 1949, 200 in 1966 and 800 in 1982.

The mouflon is a very agile animal, but shy and not readily seen – let alone approached. Its closest relatives are island races of wild sheep *Ovis musimon* in Sardinia and Corsica, which tend to live in open, rocky territory. The Cypriot race, however, has found its "niche" as a forest-dweller, although for fodder it prefers grasses to bush or tree shoots. When the uplands are snow-covered, it descends to lowland valleys, always relying on the cover provided by the forest. Mating takes place in November when competitive males become aggressive: the dominant male in a group sires the lambs, and the gestation period is five months. In both males and females the summer coat is short and pale brown, becoming white on the underparts; in winter they grow a coat of dense brown hair.

The "**Cedar Valley**" is much advertised as a tourist attraction. It is certainly pleasant woodland with a rich flora and some attractive birds – Cyprus cyclamen (*Cyclamen cyprium*), various orchids and hoopoes for example – but not quite deserving its hype in tourist brochures. The particular attraction, for naturalists who like to wander, is the ease with which you can get off the beaten track – dirt roads from here to the coast are tortuous but negotiable. Allow time to linger as you travel from volcanic to limestone soils and pass interesting collections of roadside plants, see butterflies or notice birds. Cultivated fields in the area still sport collections of colourful cornfield weeds such as field gladiolus, corn marigold and a royal-purple poppy (*Roemeria hybrida*), so delicate that its petals seem to fall as soon as a camera is pointed its way.

Near Agrós looms **Mount Adhélfi**, at 1612m the second highest peak in the island. On its slopes and also on nearby hills grow some of the rare endemic bulbs of Cyprus, such as Hartmann's crocus (*Crocus hartmannianus*) and chionodoxa (*Scilla lochiae*). From Agrós you can explore the Pitsiliá region which is known for its fruit and nut trees, but little explored by tourists. The roadsides and field edges are particularly interesting for a rich assortment of "weeds" – "candlesticks" of *Sedum lampusae*, various parasitic broomrapes and whole banks of purple vetch, for example.

Mount Adhélfi can also be approached from **Kakopetriá** where one of the few **permanent streams** in Cyprus is located. It runs close to the famous church of Áyios Nikólaos tís Steyís through a wild valley with abundant flowers (Cyprus broomrape, orchids, Cyprus butterwort). This wealth of flora inevitably attracts butterflies such as Cleopatras and the southern white admiral (*Limenitis reducta*) – as the latter sups nectar from tree honeysuckle you will see its open wings, and two rows of large white spots relieving the jet-black surface. Dutchman's pipe (*Aristolochia sempervirens*), food-plant of the larvae of the Cyprus festoon butterfly, straggles over ancient vines near here with its hanging rows of striking brown and yellow flowers – close by will be the butterflies themselves.

This little river is also the home of a curious, olive-green, freshwater crab (*Potamon fluviatilis*) which was once common around the island, especially in brackish streams near the coast. Sadly, numbers have dwindled as a direct consequence of pollution caused by agricultural chemicals running off into streams. In this, one of its last strongholds, it survives hiding under stones but will come out at night on to the bank to feed. Locals regret the disappearance since it was regarded as a good *mezé* or taverna snack.

THE TRÓÖDHOS FOOTHILLS

Although the core of the Tróödhos range is igneous, overlying chalks were deposited much later than the volcanic rocks, when seas covered the land. Upheavals have pushed the underlying serpentines and pillow lavas through the chalk, and you can move confusingly between the two types of strata, noticing the dramatic changes in plant life. The road from Áyios Iraklídhios (southwest of Nicosia) to Makherás monastery epitomizes these transitions. The route first takes in a cultivated area with great telegraph-pole spikes of agave, then a dry chalk valley with orchids and grape hyacinths wherever the slightest humus builds up from fallen needles beneath the pines. Where the rocks change, the cistus and lavender bushes form a roadside scrub, with yellow Roman and pink Anatolian orchids protected beneath them.

Around Makherás itself, the woods are worth exploring since they are typical forest of the lower Tróödhos with their eastern strawberry trees and golden oak. Early in the year, you find an occasional Hartmann's crocus and in autumn the Cyprus cyclamen. Birdlife is varied, with scops owl frequently heard but seldom seen; chukars prefer to run for cover through the bushes rather than fly.

From Limassol, journeys to Yermasóyia and its dam, to Léfkara and further west through Páhkna to Malliá and Vouní cut through country with dry, chalky soils which have proved good for viticulture. Even with abundant vines there are still pockets of scrub rich in the shrubby herbs that make up the *frígana*, giving protection to numerous plants such as yellow Star of Bethlehem, grape hyacinths, "naked man" orchid, and giant and dense-flowered orchids, as well as turban buttercups in whites, creams, yellows or even with a reddish tinge. You can see and hear stonechats and the Cyprus warbler standing sentinel on bushes, while dry chalk, with its high reflectance of light and heat, always seems particularly attractive to numerous small lizards and the occasional snake lazily sunning itself. If your eyesight is particularly acute you might spot a chameleon:

they are fairly common but stay well hidden from view, camouflaged by their ability to match the varied browns and greens of their surroundings.

RIVERMOUTHS AND RESERVOIRS

Extensive natural wetlands near Güzelyurt (Mórfou) in the North and near Limassol in the South proved ideal for establishment of the extensive citrus groves that now occupy them, being fed by mountain waters and kept moist all year round. Death from malaria was common until early in the British period, when malarial swamps were drained by planting thirsty eucalyptus. In recent years, diversion of streams to fill the newly built and much-needed reservoirs is another factor which has cut down water flow. Thus reedbeds – other than those planted as windbreaks – are a rarity in Cyprus.

In the South, try **east** and **west of Pólis** or **north of Akrotíri salt lake;** in the North, for the birdwatcher, there is **Glapsides** just to the north of Famagusta, where a popular beach is backed by a freshwater lake and wetland vegetation.

Also in the North are large **reservoirs** at **Köprülü** (Koúklia) and at **Gönyeli** on the northern perimeter of Nicosia, which are important sites for over-wintering wildfowl (ducks, grebe and heron). They are also attractive to smaller lowland and mountain birds throughout the year, since insects always hover near water. Consequently, indigenous and migrating raptors patrol the reservoirs and their immediate environs, regarding these smaller birds as a readily available "in-flight meal". Areas of open water are attracting growing numbers of people, both visitors and locals, interested in the changing variety of birds throughout the year.

THE COAST AROUND CAPE KORUÇAM (KORMAKÍTI)

Although **Cape Koruçam** (Kormakíti) itself can be bleak in the winter months, being openly exposed to the prevailing winds, its spring wildflowers – anemones in particular – are delightful. Coastal rocks at first sight seem to provide an inhospitable environment, but fleshy-leaved stonecrops grow in the crevices with another succulent – *Mesembryanthemum crystallinum* – a relative of the colourful Livingstone daisies grown in gardens.

In Cyprus, dunes – however modest in size – will probably reveal flowering sea daffodils during the hotter months. They survive their arid environment by having a bulb buried so deeply that it would need an excavator to get to it. Even where the sand meets low cliffs, and debris washed down by winter rains bakes dry to form a rock-like surface, these resilient plants are able to grow. Butterflies always seem to be abundant on Cape Koruçam and it's a good place to visit with binoculars and observe the arrival of spring migrants, which might include the occasional kingfisher providing an iridescent diversion as it darts over the rocks below you.

Between Güzelyurt (Mórfou) and Lapta (Lápithos), the road passes through cultivated fields, always tinted with splashes of colourful annuals, especially at their edges. However, the loveliest of the island's "weeds" of cultivation must be the native Cyprus tulip (*Tulipa cypria*). It has blackish-purple flowers and is abundant enough to colour cornfields on the road from Mýrtou to Nicosia; it also grows among the broad-bean plants in fields around the Maronite village of Koruçam (Kormakíti).

Sadly the best **beaches** along Mórfou Bay are now off-limits because of the Turkish military presence. You can get to Akdeniz (Ayía Iríni), where pygmy hippo fossils have been found, but no further; as a consolation prize, try exploring **near Yayla** (Syrianokhóri).

THE KYRENIA MOUNTAINS (BEŞPARMAK OR PENDADHÁKTYLOS RANGE)

The sculpted limestone pinnacles of the **Kyrenia range**, whose Greek and Turkish names both mean "Five Fingers", have an appropriately "Gothic" look, mimicking the three medieval castles tucked among them. Their northerly and southerly aspects are quite different: the northern slopes are much lusher, receiving more rain and less of a baking, so that in spring there are cyclamen, anemones and turban buttercups everywhere. Vegetation is mainly Aleppo pine with funeral cypress and dense maquis; the southern slopes have sparse, xerophytic (drought-tolerant) vegetation.

A mountain road built during the colonial period runs from **St Hilarion** westwards along the range for 18 miles (29km) via the highest peak Kyparrisóvouno – at 1023m, offering stupendous views right and left plus birds, butterflies, lizards and flowers in abundance. Avoid detours because of the heavy military presence on the south side of the route.

Only the eastern approach to **Buffavento** is open to the public; here you can see lammergeiers wheeling and a host of mountain birds mentioned earlier, such as the blue rock thrush. Around St Hilarion, Buffavento and Alevkaya, shaded limestone cliffs are the places to look for endemic plants of the northern range, such as Cypriot rock cress (*Arabis cypria*), Cypriot sage (*Phlomis cypria*) and St Hilarion cabbage (*Brassica hilarionis*), an ancestor of the cultivated cauliflower.

At **Alevkaya** (Halévga), the old forest station is the site of the North Cyprus Herbarium, open since 1989 (daily 8am–4pm) and housing a collection of more than 800 preserved plant specimens plus line drawings. This offers an opportunity to identify what you have seen and also to find out what more there is to spot. The area around Alevkaya has long been known for its orchids, especially the tiny insect-mimicking bee orchids (*Ophrys* sp.) which have a lifestyle as bizarre as their appearance. They produce scents which are chemical cocktails with the power to fool tiny male solitary wasps into thinking they have found a female – each orchid produces a subtly different blend to delude a particular species of wasp. When they land they try to mate with the flower, eventually get frustrated and fly off in disgust, carrying pollen to the next orchid flower; fortunately memory is not an insect's strong point. The Cyprus bee orchid (*Ophrys kotschyi*) and Lapithos bee orchid (*Ophrys lapetheca*), both found growing here, are exclusive to the island.

THE KIRPAŞA (KÁRPAS) PENINSULA

Long, sparsely populated, but well cultivated in parts, the **Kırpaşa (Kárpas) peninsula** is a continuation of the limestone ridge of the Kyrenia range, which makes its final Cypriot appearance as the Klídhes islands before re-emerging as the Amanus range in southeast Turkey. Its spine is gently hilly, rising to 364m at Pámboulos. You can approach the peninsula from the northern side of the Kyrenia mountains by heading east from Kyrenia along the coast road, then turning south via Kantára, or by turning off further along, through Büyükkonuk (Komí

Kebír). Alternatively, south of the hills, you can travel the coast road north from Famagusta with giant fennel lining your route. Whatever the choice, take your time – the roads are good but the wayside flowers in spring are superb and well worth lingering over.

In springtime, on reaching the peninsula itself, you will find multicoloured displays of anemones, turban buttercups, poppies and gladioli. Here, the "terra rossa" soil derived from limestone is often a rich red thanks to traces of iron compounds; although it has long proved excellent for cultivating tomatoes, fruit trees and bananas, you can find numerous uncultivated pockets on the peninsula, where orchids and other lime-loving plants thrive on it. The long "panhandle" of the Kárpas provides a flight path into the island for numerous colourful migrants such as rollers, golden orioles and bee-eaters. Rollers are a familiar sight, perching on telegraph wires before taking off across country with a distinctive buoyant flight; they get their name from the way they somersault on the wing as part of their courtship displays.

Turtles – mainly loggerheads – come ashore to lay eggs on sandy beaches to the east of **Yası Burnu (Cape Plakotí)**, not far from the sixteenth-century monastery church of Panayía Eleoússa. All along this coast, where rocks gently shelve to the sands, grow white sea daffodils in the height of the summer. At **Dipkarpaz (Rizokárpaso)** the land is well cultivated by the remaining Greek Cypriot population, but a choice of roads beyond the village leads into wilder country, close to the shore. Along the north coast, the road leads to ancient Karpasia: by travelling across the fertile plains you reach Khelónes (meaning "turtles" in Greek) and an amazingly **long beach**, stretching nearly to Zafer Burnu (Cape Apostólou Andhréa), where loggerheads have been known to breed.

The **Klidhés islands** mark the last outpost of Cyprus to the east and are one of the few places where sea birds such as shag and Audoin's gull can nest undisturbed. The cliffs also provide one of the last strongholds for nesting peregrine falcons, which breed in March or April and are both fast and strong enough to make doves and pigeons a favourite prey for themselves and their ever-hungry nestlings.

Incidentally, the **Cyprus Ornithological Society** (South) is always pleased to hear from visiting birders; contact the Honorary Secretary at Yiángou Souroullá 6, Larnaca.

CONSERVATION

After the trauma of the 1974 invasion, when over 200,000 islanders lost homes and (often) family, and the Cypriot sense of security was shattered, many on the island felt that they could not afford the luxury of being Green. Thanks to the joint efforts of comparatively few Cypriots and resident "foreigners" however, people are becoming conscious of what has been lost environmentally by unbridled development since 1974 and, moreover, that remedial action has to be immediate and drastic. Dedicated **conservationists** in the Cyprus Biological Society, Cyprus Wildlife Society, Friends of the Earth, Green Movement and the Ornithological Society, as well as individuals in governmental departments such as education, fisheries and forestry, have all fought an at-times-difficult battle to alert people to what is in imminent danger of being lost for ever.

There have been exhibitions, lectures, sets of stamps and avidly followed broadcasts of David Attenborough's TV series, all part of the exercise to **increase public awareness**. Although still not officially a national park, such publicity has saved the Akámas peninsula – for the moment at least – from an unholy alliance of the Orthodox Church and big business which foresaw its potential for development. Extensive coverage of the Akámas in the media awakened more and more people to the frightening rate at which other areas in the Cyprus countryside are being changed in the name of development. One of the strongest cries from opponents to the Akámas conservation venture was that the Pafiot villagers, like their counterparts in Ayía Nápa, had an inalienable right to make money. To try and ensure the prosperity of the area but simultaneously avoid the seemingly inevitable destruction of the last wilderness in the South, the **Laona Project** was set up to encourage **sustainable** or **"agro"-tourism** (see p.131).

The impact of **hunting** on birds, particularly migrants, is devastating. In Cyprus North or South, hunting is a national pastime, the "kill" definitely secondary to the social aspect of getting out into the country with the boys. The right to have a hunting licence is passionately defended, and although the Southern government ratified the Berne Treaty on endangered species, two weekly days of shooting are allowed during the autumn migratory season (the traditional spring shoot was banned in 1995). Another little-considered factor is that the weight of lead shot, falling annually on the land, presents a tangible pollution hazard.

Cypriots sometimes claim that it was the Western Europeans, personified by Templars, who introduced **bird-liming** to the island. Cyprus is certainly not alone among Mediterranean countries as an offender, and has at least passed legislation to outlaw lime sticks and the import and use of fine-filament "mist" nets. It is now far less socially acceptable than it was, but there is still a market in the Middle East, and during the 1980s conservative estimates claimed that millions of small passerines were taken annually in mist nets and on sticks coated with the sticky "lime". Exhausted migrants were trapped and their necks wrung, the pickled carcasses regarded as a delicacy in the Arab Middle East as well. At well over C£1 per bird, there's a ready cash incentive, and villages like Paralímni grew wealthy on the trade. Friends of the Earth (PO Box 3411, Limassol; ☎05/347042) have mounted a valiant and tireless campaign to make people on and outside the island take note, by getting concerned organizations worldwide to besiege the government and tourist bodies with complaints.

Conservationists in Britain, particularly those concerned with ornithology, have often called upon naturalists to **boycott** the island. When tourism is as important to the economy as it is in Cyprus, considerable pressure can indeed be brought to bear by the threat of lost revenue. However, national pride over "outside intervention" – a justifiably touchy subject, given the history of Cyprus – will merely provoke a stubbornly defiant reaction. Perhaps the worst thing that armchair activists unwittingly manage to achieve is the effective isolation of those people on Cyprus working at the cutting edge. However, local campaigns are considerably strengthened by support for their efforts from visiting outsiders – sabotage methods include ripping mist nets and urinating on lime sticks (a technique which renders them useless). And if you see things you don't like while in Cyprus, complain in writing to the Cyprus Tourism Organization and the government: it counts if enough people do it.

In the North there is now an active North Cyprus Society for the Protection of Birds (its initials KKKKD in Turkish) – and President Rauf Denktaş apparently has a keen interest in his country's wild flowers. **Hunting** is as much a problem in the North as in the South, with a large number of gun licences for the size of the population. Another pressing concern is the level of **grazing** permitted by the enormous herds of goats brought in by Anatolian settlers. Visiting botanists, especially Germans working on a detailed mapping of the orchid flora, have voiced great concern over changes seen over a two- or three-year period: once flower-filled hillsides now host little but grass, thistles and white asphodels. There is talk, but so far only that, of making the Kırpaşa (Kárpas) peninsula a protected area.

WILDLIFE BOOKS

Cyprus falls just outside the loose definition of Europe used in field guides other than those for birds. Thus, it's not easy to find good illustrations of its special plants or butterflies, and a well-nigh impossible task for many of the insects, snails and other creatures which have a lower rating in the popularity stakes. Since a significant proportion of the Cypriot flora and fauna is found around much of the Mediterranean, you can make considerable headway with popular guides, but identifying endemic species is often difficult.

Perhaps the **best-value single purchase** specifically for the island is *Nature of Cyprus: Environment, Flora, Fauna* (South Nicosia, Cyprus) by Christos Georgiades. Widely available in bookshops in the South, this is a very useful introduction to local ecology by one of the island's top naturalists: it includes checklists of birds, butterflies, reptiles, indigenous plants, fish and mammals that are almost impossible to find anywhere else.

Some of the better natural history works are now **out of print**, but appear fairly regularly in catalogues of specialist secondhand and antiquarian booksellers dealing in natural history titles, who advertise in the natural history press. One in particular to aim for is A. C. Campbell's very useful *The Hamlyn Guide to the Flora and Fauna of the Mediterranean* (Hamlyn/Country Life, UK); this was also published as *The Larousse Guide to the Flora and Fauna of the Mediterranean* (Larousse).

FLOWERS AND PLANTS

Marjorie Blainey and Christopher Grey-Wilson *Mediterranean Wild Flowers* (HarperCollins, UK). Comprehensive field guide that includes the lowlands of Cyprus; recent and thus up to date.

K. P. Buttler *Fieldguide to the Orchids of Europe* (Crowood Press, UK); consultant editor Paul H. Davies. A wealth of colour pictures and modern nomenclature.

E. F. Chapman *Cyprus Trees and Shrubs*. The only guide for the larger flora.

Lance Chilton *Plant Checklist: Akamas* (Marengo Publications, Retford, Notts, UK). Personal and literature records for this peninsula.

Paul H. Davies, Jenne Davies and Anthony J. Huxley *Wild Orchids of Britain and Europe* (Chatto & Windus/The Hogarth Press, UK). Written while the authors lived in Cyprus, this includes all the island's orchids and where to find them.

Pierre Delforge *Orchids of Britain and Europe* (HarperCollins, UK). The most up-to-date orchid guide, covering Cyprus; however the author has disavowed HarperCollins' translation owing to numerous errors.

Christos Georgiades *Trees and Shrubs of Cyprus; Flowers of Cyprus; Plants of Medicine* (Nicosia, South Cyprus). Widely available in Cyprus; useful for endemic plants.

Sonia Halliday and Laura Lushington *Flowers of Northern Cyprus* (Kemal Rüstem, Nicosia, North Cyprus). As much a close-up photo-essay as field guide.

Anthony J. Huxley *Flowers of Greece and the Aegean* (Chatto & Windus/The Hogarth Press, UK). Helpful in conjunction with other general works – but does not specifically cover Cyprus. See also his *Flowers of the Mediterranean* (Chatto & Windus/The Hogarth Press, UK), a classic book on Mediterranean flowers; coverage is general but surprisingly useful.

R. Desmond Meikle *Flora of Cyprus* (Bentham Trust; available from the Royal Botanic Gardens, Kew, Richmond, Surrey). Two-volume work for the serious plant freak who jettisons clothes from the luggage in favour of books. Whatever you'll find is in here: no colour pictures but plenty of line drawings. A model of clarity and erudition as far as this sort of work goes.

V. Pantelas, T. Papachristophorou and P. Christodoulou *Cyprus Flora in Colour: The Endemics.* Good photos of endemic plants; cheaper in Cyprus than in Britain.

Oleg Polunin *Flowers of Greece and the Balkans* (Oxford University Press, UK/US). Useful for plants generally distributed in the eastern Mediterranean.

I. and P. Schoenfelder *Wildflowers of the Mediterranean* (HarperCollins, UK). General but includes many of the ordinary Mediterranean species in Cyprus.

George Sfikas *Wild Flowers of Cyprus.* Covers about 150 species, including endemics.

BIRDS

David and Mary Bannerman *Handbook of the Birds of Cyprus* (Kemal Rüstem, Nicosia, North Cyprus). Though recently reissued, this warhorse is several decades old, pricy and well out of date.

Peter Flint and Peter Stewart *The Birds of Cyprus* (British Ornithological Union). Available from the BOU, British Museum, Tring, Herts. A thorough checklist with details of good sites for birdwatching.

Heinzel, Fitter and Parslow *The Birds of Britain and Europe with North Africa and the Middle East* (Collins). Another useful item in your bags.

Hollom, Porter, Christensen and Willis *Birds of the Middle East and North Africa* (Poyser, UK). Very thorough, with good illustrations and distribution maps.

Petersen, Mountfort and Hollom *Field Guide to the Birds of Britain and Europe* (HarperCollins, UK/Stephen Green Press, US). Provides complete coverage of Cyprus when used in conjunction with the preceding title.

Lars Jonsson *Birds of Europe with North Africa and the Middle East* (Helm, UK). Very good coverage and excellent illustrations.

INSECTS

Michael Chinery *Collins Guide to the Insects of Britain and Western Europe* (HarperCollins, UK/Stephen Green Press, US). A lovely book which excludes the Mediterranean but is still very useful for getting the genus, and also for things like hawkmoths and mantids.

Lionel Higgins and Norman Riley *A Field Guide to the Butterflies of Britain and Europe* (HarperCollins, UK/Stephen Green Press, US). A very detailed classic which contains most of the Cyprus butterflies except the handful of indigenes.

Paul Whalley *The Mitchell Beazley Pocket Guide to Butterflies* (Mitchell Beazley). Marvellously illustrated guide which stops just short of Cyprus but has most species except the few natives.

REPTILES AND AMPHIBIANS

Arnold, Burton and Ovenden *A Field Guide to the Reptiles of Britain and Europe* (HarperCollins, UK) Most, but not all, species – again stops short of the Middle East.

Jiri Cihar *Amphibians and Reptiles* (Conran Octopus, UK). Selective in coverage, but has many species from Asia Minor and is useful for Cyprus.

MARINE LIFE

B. Luther and K. Fiedler *A Field Guide to the Mediterranean Seashore* (HarperCollins, UK). Very thorough and includes much of what occurs around the Cyprus coast.

**Paul H. Davies,
with contributions by
Lance Chilton and David Whaley**

BOOKS

As befits a former Crown Colony, there are a fair amount of books on Cyprus in English. Many worthwhile classics have been reissued recently, and others are often available in university libraries or rare-book dealers. Publishers are detailed below, where applicable, in the format British/American, with "UK" or "US" specified when a volume is available in one country only. Often a title is published, and most easily obtainable, in Cyprus.

Other abbreviations include O/P, for an out-of-print but still worthwhile book, and UP, for University Press.

ARCHEOLOGY AND PRE-INDEPENDENCE HISTORY

There are a vast number of scholarly works on Cyprus, but most are expensive, hard to find, drily academic, or all three. The following titles are more accessible in every sense.

Porphyrios Dikaios *Khirokitia* (Oxford UP, UK, O/P). By the long-time excavator of the site. See also his *Enkomi Excavations 1948–1958* (Mainz, O/P) and *A Guide to the Cyprus Museum* (Nicosia, reissued regularly).

Ahmet C. Gazioğlu *The Turks in Cyprus: A Province of the Ottoman Empire (1571–1878)* (Kemal Rüstem, Nicosia, North Cyprus). Useful, if rather tendentious history, in which one of the main thrusts is how beneficent and tolerant the sultan's rule was.

Einar Gjerstad et al. *The Swedish Cyprus Expeditions, 1927–1931* (Stockholm, The Swedish Cyprus Expedition, 8 vols 1934–56). More anecdotal is his *Ages and Days in Cyprus* (Paul Åströms Förlag, Göteborg), a record of travels, personal encounters and life on site digs.

Vassos Karageorghis *Cyprus, from the Stone Age to the Romans* (Thames and Hudson, UK/US). Definitive, well-written introduction by one of the foremost Cypriot archaeologists, long director of the island's Antiquities Department. Other titles by the same author and publisher, though long O/P, are *Salamis in Cyprus: Homeric, Hellenistic and Roman* and *Kition, Mycenaean and Phoenician Discoveries in Cyprus*; also, with F. G. Maier, *Paphos, History and Archaeology* (Nicosia, 1984) – all lavishly illustrated.

Demetrios Michaelides and W. A. Daszewski *Mosaic Floors in Cyprus* (Ravenna, Edizioni del Girazole, 1988). More precisely, Part I covers the magnificent Roman mosaics of Paphos; Part II describes the mosaic floors of Christian basilicas across the island. Michaelides' *Cypriot Mosaics* (Cyprus Department of Antiquities) is a lot cheaper, and easier to find, and is adequate for most levels of interest.

Louis Palma di Cesnola *Cyprus: Its Cities, Tombs and Temples* (Star Graphics, South Cyprus). A reprinted classic – the diplomat and archeologist/plunderer in his own shameless words, including fascinating vignettes of everyday life on the eve of British rule.

David Soren and Jamie James *Kourion, the Search for a Lost Roman City* (Anchor/Doubleday, US). Despite its American-pop style, a valuable account of the most recent finds at Kourion, particularly evidence of the mid-fourth-century earthquake.

Veronica Tatton-Brown *Ancient Cyprus* (British Museum Press, UK). Good introduction to the island's past, from Neolithic to late Roman times, by a distinguished archeologist with years of dig experience on Cyprus.

PRE-1955 HISTORY

Doros Alastos *Cyprus in History* (Zeno, UK). Two massive tomes covering all periods to 1955; unfortunately the author died before finishing Volume III.

Peter W. Edbury *The Kingdom of Cyprus and the Crusades, 1191–1374* (Cambridge UP, UK/US). Plumbs the intricate power struggles of the relatively little-known Lusignan period, but frustratingly stops short of the Venetian tenure.

Sir George Hill *A History of Cyprus* (Cambridge UP, UK, 4 vols, O/P). The standard, if sometimes flawed, pre-independence reference work – rare and pricy.

David and Iro Hunt *Caterina Cornaro, Queen of Cyprus* (Trigraph, UK). Picks up more or less where the preceding volume left off, but concentrates mostly on the life and times of the last sovereign of the island, a Venetian married into the Lusignan line.

Sir David Hunt, ed. *Footprints in Cyprus, an Illustrated History* (Trigraph, UK). Lavishly illustrated anthology covering all eras, more literate than the usual coffee-table book – available in paperback.

Sir Harry Luke *Cyprus Under the Turks, 1571– 1878* (Kemal Rüstem, Nicosia, North Cyprus; Hurst, UK). Extensive quotations from documents of the era, not as expository or interesting as it could be – but virtually the only source in English.

GUIDES, MONUMENTAL ART AND PHOTO PORTFOLIOS

Camille Enlart *Gothic Art and the Renaissance in Cyprus* (Trigraph, UK). Recently translated from the French, this highlights the magnificent architecture and exterior decoration left behind by the Lusignan rulers.

Rupert Gunnis *Historic Cyprus, A Guide to its Towns and Villages, Monasteries and Castles* (Kemal Rüstem, Nicosia, North Cyprus). Gunnis visited every site on the island over a five-year period in the 1930s; this is the result, good for the legends accruing to various spots, but a little uncritical in its evaluations.

George Jeffrey *A Description of the Historic Monuments of Cyprus* (Zeno, UK). Just that, by the founder of the eponymous museum. Exhaustive, and rather less dry than the *Blue Guide*.

Andreas and Judith Stylianou *The Painted Churches of Cyprus* (Trigraph, UK). The last word on the Tróödhos country churches especially, by a couple who have made this subject their life's work; only to be faulted for the scanty number of colour reproductions. Much less expensive in Cyprus.

John Thomson *Through Cyprus with the Camera in the Autumn of 1878* (Trigraph, UK). First-ever photos of the island – showing how exotic it was just over a century ago.

Reno Wideson *Cyprus: Images of a Lifetime* (Demetra Publications, Limassol and UK) and *Portrait of Cyprus* (O/P; rare and expensive). Forty-two years of stunning pictures by the top Cypriot photographer, the former a recently published colour study.

TRAVELOGUES AND MEMOIRS

Sir Samuel Baker *Cyprus as I Saw it in 1879* (Macmillan, UK, O/P). By turns scathing and rapturous, with plenty of white-man's-burden stuff – including proposals to raze what remained of old Famagusta – from the first year of British administration.

Patrick Balfour *The Orphaned Realm* (Percival Marshall, UK, O/P; rare). Impressionistic and anecdote-laden account from the late 1940s; the title is taken from a famous passage by Leontios Makhairas.

Oliver Burch *The Infidel Sea* (Ashford, Buchanan and Enright, UK). North Cyprus as it was in the mid-1980s, before tourism had revived; heavily reliant on *Excerpta Cypria* for background filler, but excellent as a portrait of the Northern community.

Anne Cavendish, ed. *Cyprus 1878: The Journal of Sir Garnet Wolseley* (Academic and General, Larnaca). The memoirs of the first British High Commissioner, recently published at a modest price.

Claude Delaval Cobham *Excerpta Cypria, Materials for a History of Cyprus* (Kraus Reprint, Millwood, New York). An engaging, landmark endeavour: pithy snippets from travellers' and local protagonists' views of Cyprus from biblical times to the last century, diligently mined by all subsequent writers on Cyprus. But with the price-tag at well over £100, you'd have to be a rather dedicated researcher.

Lawrence Durrell *Bitter Lemons* (Faber and Faber, UK/US). Durrell's lyrically told experiences as an English teacher, minor colonial official and bohemian resident of the Kyrenia hills in the EOKA-shadowed mid-1950s have worn remarkably well despite the intervening years.

Leontios Makhairas *Recital Concerning the Sweet Land of Cyprus* (Clarendon, UK). Another rare and expensive medieval classic, translated by R. M. Dawkins.

Giovanni Mariti *Travels in the Island of Cyprus* (Zeno, UK). A wonderful eighteenth-century account, translated by Cobham; this edition includes Umberto Foglietta's seventeenth-century *The Sieges of Nicosia and Famagusta*.

Kyriacos Markides *The Magus of Strovolos; Homage to the Sun; Fire in the Heart* (Penguin Arkana, UK/US). Hard to classify: Markides, author of *The Rise and Fall of the Cyprus Republic* (see below), becomes involved in the circle of mystic and spirtiual healer "Daskalos", resident in the Nicosia suburb of Stróvolos; the resulting, late 1980s trilogy is rather sounder than the *Castaneda* series to which it's been compared. His more recent *Riding the Lion* may also be of interest.

David Matthews *The Cyprus Tapes* (Kemal Rüstem, Nicosia, North Cyprus). Unashamedly pro-North memoirs by a former BBC freelancer; intimations of Greek Cypriot skulduggery, and good detail on UN operations.

Ludwig Salvator, Archduke of Austria *Levkosia, The Capital of Cyprus* (Trigraph, UK). Nicosia as it was in 1873, delightfully described by one of the Belle Epoque's great eccentrics – though his command of Greek and Turkish terminology was shaky at best, which can make identifying monuments difficult.

Sir Ronald Storrs and B. J. O'Brien *The Handbook of Cyprus* (London, 1930, O/P). Detailed volume intended for colonial officials, co-written by one of the first high commissioners (Storrs); the last two chapters of his career memoirs *Orientations* (Nicholson and Watson, UK, O/P but easy to find) concern Cyprus.

Colin Thubron *Journey into Cyprus* (Penguin/Viking Penguin, UK/US). Account of a three-month trek round the island during 1972 – and in terms of history in context, and a finger on the pulse of contemporary Cyprus, arguably the single best book on the place ever written. Widely available in southern Cyprus.

INDEPENDENCE AND AFTER

It is unfortunately very difficult to find anything more current than the mid-1980s – observers of the Cypriot scene, perhaps despairing of any substantive changes in the situation, seem reluctant to set down between hard covers the latest rumour or trend in intercommunal negotiations.

Nancy Cranshaw *The Cyprus Revolt: An Account of the Struggle for Union with Greece* (Allen and Unwin, UK, O/P). Factual but highly readable, this is the standard reference work on the rebellion.

Clement H. Dodd, ed. *The Political, Social and Economic Development of Northern Cyprus* (Eothen Press). Collection of scholarly articles on everything you could possible want to know about the "non-existent" TRNC. Objective, and frank about the North's problems.

Michael Harbottle *The Impartial Soldier* (Oxford UP, UK, O/P). Worthwhile memoirs of the first (1964–68) UNFICYP commander.

Keith Kyle *Cyprus, Minority Rights Group Report No. 30* (MRG, UK/Cultural Survival, US). One of the excellent series of pamphlets by this organization, though the summary ceases in 1984 and has not been updated since.

Stanley Mayes *Makarios* (Macmillan, UK, O/P). The best biography of the man.

Laurence Stern *The Wrong Horse* (Times Books, New York, O/P). Reveals America's involvement in the 1974 coup and the alleged "tilt" towards the Turks; most of the press run was supposedly bought up and destroyed by villain of the piece Henry Kissinger.

THE GREEK CYPRIOT VIEWPOINT

Especially in the aftermath of 1974, Greek Cypriots were quite successful in monopolizing historiography; the following are some of the more durable and objective sources.

Michael Attalides *Cyprus: Nationalism and International Politics* (Q Press, UK, O/P). A wide-ranging and readable, if dated, discussion of all aspects of the problem.

Peter Loizos *The Heart Grown Bitter: A Chronicle of Cypriot War Refugees* (Cambridge UP, UK). Describes Argáki (lately Akçay), a village on the Mórfou plain, and the fate of its inhabitants after the Turkish invasion; moreover an excellent introduction to the complexities of Cypriot communalism and politics, by a London professor with roots in Argáki.

Kyriacos Markides *The Rise and Fall of the Cyprus Republic* (Yale UP, UK/US, O/P but findable). The excellent standard history.

Stavros Panteli *A New History of Cyprus, from the Earliest Times to the Present Day* (East-West Publications, UK, O/P). Choppy and partisan, this is nevertheless one of the best sources for the colonial period; coverage unfortunately stops at 1984. His slightly more recent *The Making of*

Modern Cyprus (Interworld, UK) may also be of interest; certainly it's less expensive, illustrated and easily available.

Polyvios Polyviou *Cyprus, Conflict and Negotiation 1960–80* (Duckworth, UK, O/P). Dry but detailed – and relatively objective.

P. N. Vanezis *Cyprus: The Unfinished Agony*, and *Makarios: Life and Leadership* (Abelard-Schuman, UK, O/P). These two relatively balanced works are preferable to his Makarian hagiographies *Faith and Power* or *Pragmatism versus Idealism*.

THE TURKISH CYPRIOT VIEWPOINT

For decades, the North's position got less of a hearing in the international arena, but since the early 1990s there has been a veritable flood of material, most of it generated by two publishers: Kemal Rüstem in North Nicosia or London, and The Eothen Press, Huntingdon, Cambs PE18 9BX (☎01480/466106), who should be contacted directly in case of difficulty in ordering.

Mehmet Ali Birand *30 Hot Days* (Kemal Rüstem). Hour-by-hour, fairly objective account of the 1974 war by a top Turkish journalist; especially revealing on why the Geneva peace talks failed.

Rauf Denktaş *The Cyprus Triangle* (Allen and Unwin, UK, O/P; Kemal Rüstem). Point of view from one of the main protagonists, the triangle in question formed by Athens, Ankara and Nicosia.

Clement H. Dodd *The Cyprus Issue: A Current Perspective* (Eothen Press). Regularly updated pamphlet concisely describing the background to the de facto partition, and present obstacles to a settlement, by a faculty member of the School of Oriental and African Studies, London, and head of Eothen Press.

Necati Ertekün *The Cyprus Dispute and the Birth of the Turkish Republic of Northern Cyprus* (Kemal Rüstem). Somewhat dated (1984) legalistic analysis of the situation by a former foreign minister of the TRNC.

Zaim Necatigil *The Cyprus Question and the Turkish Position in International Law* (Oxford UP, UK). Sets forth the official TRNC position, as of 1990.

Pierre Oberling *The Road to Bellapais: The Turkish Cypriot Exodus to Northern Cyprus* (Columbia UP, US). Objective and useful study, written just before the UDI.

Metin Tamkoç *The Turkish Cypriot State* (Kemal Rüstem). Ideological justification for the UDI of 1983.

Vamik Volkan *Cyprus – War and Adaptation; A Psychoanalytic History of Two Ethnic Groups in Conflict* (UP of Virginia, US, O/P). Heavy going through the Freudian jargon, but the Turkish Cypriot/American author does outline the stresses and adaptive neuroses of the island's beleaguered Turks, pre- and post-1974. His more recent *Turks and Greeks: Neighbours in Conflict* (Eothen Press), co-authored with Norman Itzkowitz, is a needed first step in putting both island cultures on the shrink's couch, but proves ultimately disappointing.

SPECIFIC GUIDES

Adrian Akers-Douglas *Discover Laona: Walks, Strolls and Drives in "Undiscovered" North-western Cyprus* (The Laona Project, Limassol). As the title says: a delightful small booklet covering villages, monuments and legends of the Akámas in great detail.

Lance Chilton *Walks in Western Cyprus* (Marengo Publications, Retford, Notts, UK). Brand-new guide focusing on the best of the Akámas.

Gwynneth der Parthog *Byzantine and Medieval Cyprus: A Guide to the Monuments* (Interworld, UK/Cyprus). Newish (1995) and obsessively detailed guide to churches, castles and other monuments in the South; excellent plans and sketches, far superior to the *Blue Guide* for its chosen period.

BOOKSTORES

The best **UK sources** for English-language books on Cyprus are *The Hellenic Bookservice* (91 Fortess Rd, London NW5, near Kentish Town tube; ☎0171/267 9499), run by an Anglo-Greek Cypriot family, or *Zeno's* (6 Denmark St, London W1, near *Foyles*; ☎0171/836 2522), which also does many reissues of old classics. Both are knowledgeable and well stocked with new, used and out-of-print titles. For materials with a specifically Turkish Cypriot slant, *Daunt Books* (83 Marylebone High St, London W1; ☎0171/224 2295) makes an effort to stock products of Kemal Rüstem and Eothen Press.

Useful **bookstores in Cyprus** are detailed in the town listings for Larnaca, Limassol, Páfos, Kyrenia and Nicosia south and north.

LANGUAGE

I asked in Greek and was answered in English. I asked again in Greek and was once again answered in English. It was a long moment before I recollected why. I was in the presence not, as I thought, of Turks who either knew no Greek, or would not condescend to speak it: no, I was in the presence of babus. To lapse into Greek with anyone who was not a peasant would involve a loss of face. It was rather sad.

Lawrence Durrell

Durrell's experience still applies, and to a great extent in the Turkish Cypriot community as well. Speaking English in Cyprus is

a badge of sophistication, the road to advancement and civil service employment. In touristed areas, your Greek or Turkish will have to be nearly perfect to get a reply in kind. Most tourists can and will get by on the island without learning a word of either local language; leave the beaten track, in the North, however, and you'll be surrounded by a monolingual culture.

Both Cypriot **Greek** and Cypriot **Turkish** are strong dialects, some might say almost separate languages, from the standard phrasebook fare, and familiarity with the latter is not as much of an advantage as you'd think. You will be understood if you utter Athens or Istanbul pleasantries, but you may not catch the reply the first time round – and you won't be alone, since before the homogenizing effect of continental Greek and Turkish television, islanders could carry on conversations virtually incomprehensible to visitors from the "mother" country. About fifteen percent of the vocabulary of each community is still peculiar to Cyprus, and the distinctive island accent tends to make Cypriot Greek and Turkish sound almost identical to the untrained ear.

GREEK

So many Greek Cypriots have lived or worked abroad in Britain, and, to a lesser extent,

GREEK LANGUAGE-LEARNING MATERIALS

TEACH-YOURSELF GREEK COURSES

Breakthrough Greece (Pan Macmillan; book and two cassettes). Excellent, basic teach-yourself course – completely outclasses the competition.

Greek Language and People (BBC Publications, UK; book and cassette available). More limited in scope but good for acquiring the essentials, and the confidence to try them.

Anne Farmakides *A Manual of Modern Greek* (Yale UP/McGill UP; 3 vols). If you have the discipline and motivation, this is one of the best for learning proper, grammatical Greek; indeed, mastery of just the first volume will get you a long way.

PHRASEBOOKS

Greek, A Rough Guide Phrasebook (Rough Guides). For an up-to-date, accurate pocket phrasebook not full of "plume de ma tante"-type

expressions, look no further than Rough Guide's very own; English-to-Greek is sensibly phonetic, but the Greek-to-English section, while transliterated, requires mastery of the Greek alphabet.

DICTIONARIES

The Oxford Dictionary of Modern Greek (Oxford University Press). A bit bulky but generally considered the best Greek–English, English–Greek dictionary.

Collins Pocket Greek Dictionary (HarperCollins). Very nearly as complete as the *Oxford* and probably better value for money.

Oxford Learner's Dictionary (Oxford University Press). If you're planning a prolonged stay, this pricey two-volume set is unbeatable for usage and vocabulary. There's also a more portable one-volume *Learner's Pocket Dictionary*.

THE GREEK ALPHABET: TRANSLITERATION

Set out below is the Greek alphabet, the system of transliteration used in this book, and a brief aid to pronunciation.

Greek	Transliteration	Pronounced
A, α	a	a as in father
B, β	v	v as in vet
Γ, γ	y/g	y as in yes, except before consonants and a, o or long i, when it's a breathy, throaty version of the g in gap
Δ, δ	dh	th as in then
E, ε	e	e as in get
Z, ζ	z	z sound
H, η	i	i as in ski
Θ, θ	th	th as in theme
I, ι	i	i as in ski
K, κ	k	nominally k sound, often "tch" if medial, "g" when initial
Λ, λ	l	l sound
M, μ	m	m sound
N, ν	n	n sound
Ξ, ξ	ks (initial; x medial)	ks sound
O, o	o	o as in toad
Π, π	p	p sound, but often more like b
P, ρ	r	r sound
Σ, σ, ς	s	s sound
T, τ	t	t sound, but often more like d
Y, υ	i or y	indistinguishable from η
Φ, φ	f	f sound
X, χ	kh (h if initial before vowel; often sh if medial)	harsh h sound, like the ch in loch
Ψ, ψ	ps	ps as in lips
Ω, ω	o	o as in toad, indistinguishable from o

Combinations and dipthongs

AI, αι	e	e as in get
AY, αυ	av/af	av or af depending on following consonant
EI, οι	i	long i, exactly like η
OI, οι	i	long i, identical again
EY, ευ	ev/ef	ev or ef, depending on following consonant
OY, ου	ou	ou as in tourist
ΓΓ, γγ	ng	ng as in angle; always medial
ΓΥ, γυ	g/ng	g as in goat at the beginning of a word; ng in the middle
ΜΠ, μπ	b	b as in bar, but effectively p in Cypriot Greek
NT, ντ	d/nd	d at the beginning of a word, nd in the middle
ΤΣ, τσ	ts	ts as in hits
ΣΙ, σι	sh	sh as in shame
ΤΖ, τζ	tz	j as in jam

North America and Australia, that you will find numbers of people speaking English in the remotest village. Add to this the fact that most adults grew up under British administration, that English is all but compulsory at school, and the overriding importance of the tourist industry, and it's easy to see how many British visitors never bother to learn a word of Greek.

You can certainly get by this way, but it isn't very satisfying, and the willingness and ability to say even a few words will transform your status from that of dumb *tourístas* to the honourable one of *ksénos*, a word which can

GREEK WORDS AND PHRASES

Essentials

Yes	*Néh*	Now	*Tóra*	Big	*Megálo*
Certainly	*Málista*	Later	*Argótera*	Small	*Mikró*
No	*Óhi*	Open	*Aniktó*	More	*Perisótero*
Please	*Parakaló*	Closed	*Klistó*	Less	*Ligótero*
Okay, agreed	*Endáksi*	Day	*Méra*	A little	*Lígo*
Thank you	*Efharistó (polí)*	Night	*Níkhta*	A lot	*Polí*
(very much)		In the morning	*Tóh proḯ*	Cheap	*Ftinó*
I (don't)	*(Dhen)*	In the	*Tóh apóyevma*	Expensive	*Akrivó*
understand	*Katalavéno*	afternoon		Hot	*Zestó*
Excuse me, do	*Parakaló, mípos*	In the evening	*Tóh vrádhi*	Cold	*Krío*
you speak	*miláteh*	Here	*Edhó*	With	*Mazí*
English?	*angliká?*	There	*Ekí*	Without	*Horís*
Sorry/excuse me	*Signómi*	This one	*Aftó*	Quickly	*Grígora*
Today	*Símera*	That one	*Ekíno*	Slowly	*Sigá*
Tomorrow	*Ávrio*	Good	*Kaló*	Mr/Mrs	*Kírios/Kiría*
Yesterday	*Khthés*	Bad	*Kakó*	Miss	*Dhespinís*

Other Needs

To eat/drink	*Trógo/Píno*	Stamp	*Gramatósima*	Toilet	*Toualéta*
Bakery	*Foúrnos, psomádhiko*	Petrol station	*Venzinádhiko*	Police	*Astinomía*
Pharmacy	*Farmakío*	Bank	*Trápeza*	Doctor	*Iatrós*
Post office	*Tahidhromío*	Money	*Leftá/Hrímata*	Hospital	*Nosokomío*

Requests and Questions

To ask a question, it's simplest to start with *parakaló*, then name the thing you want in an interrogative tone.

Where is the bakery?	*Parakaló, o foúrnos?*	How many?	*Póssi* or *pósses?*
Can you show me the	*Parakaló, o dhrómos*	How much?	*Póso?*
road to . . . ?	*ya . . ?*	When?	*Póteh?*
We'd like a room for	*Parakaló, éna dhomátio*	Why?	*Yatí?*
two	*ya dhío átoma?*	At what time . . . ?	*Tí óra . . . ?*
May I have a kilo of	*Parakaló, éna kiló*	What is/Which is . . . ?	*Tí íneh/pió íneh..?*
oranges?	*portokália?*	How much (does it cost)?	*Póso káni?*
Where?	*Poú?*	What time does it open?	*Ti óra aníyi?*
How?	*Pós?*	What time does it close?	*Tí óra klíni?*

Talking to People

Greek makes the distinction between the informal (*esí*) and formal (*esís*) second person, as French does with *tu* and *vous*. Young people, older people and country people nearly always use *esí* even with total strangers. In any event, no one will be too bothered if you get it wrong. By far the most common greeting, on meeting and parting, is *yá sou/yá sas* – literally "health to you".

Hello	*Khérete*	My name is . . .	*Meh léneh . . .*
Good morning	*Kalí méra*	Speak slower, please	*Parakaló, miláte pió sigá*
Good evening	*Kalí spéra*	How do you say it in Greek?	*Pos léyeteh sta Eliniká?*
Good night	*Kalí níkhta*	I don't know	*Dhén kséro*
Goodbye	*Adío*	See you tomorrow	*Tha se dhó ávrio*
How are you?	*Ti kánis/Ti káneteh?*	See you soon	*Kalí andámosi*
I'm fine	*Kalá ímeh*	Let's go!	*Pámeh!*
And you?	*Keh esís?*	Please help me	*Parakaló, na me*
What's your name?	*Pos se léneh?*		*voithísteh*

Continues overleaf...

Greek Words and Phrases continued

Greek's Greek

There are numerous words and phrases which you will hear constantly, even if you rarely have the chance to use them. These are a few of the most common.

Éla!	Come (literally) but also Speak to me! You don't say! etc.	*Pó-pó-pó!*	Expression of dismay or concern, like French "O la la!"
Orísteh?	What can I do for you?	*Maláka(s)*	Literally "wanker", not often heard in Cyprus, and best not used by foreigners.
Embrós! or *Léyeteh!*	Standard phone responses		
Ti néa?	What's new?		
Ti yíneteh?	What's going on here (here)?	*Sigá sigá*	Take your time, slow down
Étsi k'étsi	So-so	*Kaló taxídhi*	Bon voyage
Pedhí moú	My boy/girl, sonny, friend, etc.	*Ópa!*	Whoops! Watch it!

Accommodation

Hotel	*Ksenodhohío*	Cold water	*Krío neró*
A room . . .	*Éna dhomátio . . .*	Can I see it?	*Boró ná tóh dho?*
for one/two/three people	*yía éna/dhío/tría átoma*	Can we camp here?	*Boróume na váloumeh tín skiní edhó?*
for one/two/three nights	*yía mía/dhío/tris vradhiés*		
with a double bed	*méh megálo kreváti*	Campsite	*Kámping/Kataskínosi*
with a shower	*méh doús*	Tent	*Skiní*
Hot water	*Zestó neró*	Youth hostel	*Ksenón neótitos*

On the Move

Aeroplane	*Aeropláno*	Where are you going?	*Pou pas?*
Bus	*Leoforío*	I'm going to . . .	*Páo sto . . .*
Car	*Aftokínito*	I want to get off at . . .	*Thélo ná katévo stó . . .*
Motorbike, moped	*Mihanáki, papáki*	The road to . . .	*Ó dhrómos yía . . .*
Taxi	*Taksí*	Near	*Kondá*
Ship	*Plío/Vapóri/Karávi*	Far	*Makriá*
Bicycle	*Podhílato*	Left	*Aristerá*
Hitching	*Otostóp*	Right	*Dheksiá*
On foot	*Méh tá pódhia*	Straight ahead	*Katefthía*
Trail	*Monopáti*	A ticket to . . .	*Éna isitírio ya . . .*
Bus station	*Praktorío leoforíon*	A return ticket	*Éna isitirio me epistrofí*
Bus stop	*Stássi*	Beach	*Paralía*
Harbour	*Limáni*	Cave	*Spiliá*
What time does it leave?	*Tí óra févyi?*	Centre (of town)	*Kéndro*
What time does it arrive?	*Tí óra ftháni?*	Church	*Eklissía*
How many kilometres?	*Pósa hiliómetra?*	Sea	*Thálassa*
How many hours?	*Pósses óres?*	Village	*Horió*

Numbers

1	*énos éna/mía*	12	*dhódheka*	90	*enenínda*
2	*dhío*	13	*dhekatrís*	100	*ekató*
3	*trís/tría*	14	*dhekatésseres*	150	*ekatón penínda*
4	*tésseres/téssera*	20	*íkosi*	200	*dhiakóssies/ia*
5	*pénde*	21	*íkosi éna*	500	*pendakóssies/ia*
6	*éksi*	30	*triánda*	1000	*hílies/hília*
7	*eftá*	40	*saránda*	2000	*dhío hiliádhes*
8	*okhtó*	50	*penínda*	1,000,000	*éna ekatomírio*
9	*enyá*	60	*eksínda*	first	*próto*
10	*dhéka*	70	*evdhomínda*	second	*dhéftero*
11	*éndheka*	80	*ogdhónda*	third	*tríto*

Months and seasonal terms

January	*Yennári*	June	*Ioúnios*	November	*Noémvris*
February	*Fleváris*	July	*Ioúlios*	December	*Dhekémvris*
March	*Mártis*	August	*Avgoustos*	Summer schedule	*Therinó dhromolóyio*
April	*Aprílis*	September	*Septémvris*	Winter schedule	*Himerinó*
May	*Maïos*	October	*Októvris*		*dhromolóyio*

The time and days of the week

Sunday	*Kiriakí*	What time is it?	*Tí óra ínheh?*
Monday	*Dheftéra*	One/two/three o'clock	*Mía íy óra, dhío/trís íy óra*
Tuesday	*Tríti*	Twenty to four	*Tésseres parà íkosi*
Wednesday	*Tetárti*	Five minutes past eight	*Októ kéh pénde*
Thursday	*Pémpti*	Half past eleven	*Éndheka kéh misí*
Friday	*Paraskeví*	In half an hour	*Séh misí óra*
Saturday	*Sávato*	In a quarter-hour	*S'éna tétarto*

mean foreigner, traveller and guest all rolled into one.

LEARNING BASIC GREEK

Greek is not an easy language for English-speakers but it is a very beautiful one and even a brief acquaintance will give you some idea of the debt owed to it by Western European languages. On top of the usual difficulties of learning a new language, Greek presents the additional problem of an entirely separate **alphabet**. Despite initial appearances, this is in practice fairly easily mastered – a skill that will help enormously if you are going to get around independently (see the alphabet box on p.364, and the Greek-alphabet lists of place names at the end of each chapter of Southern Cyprus). In addition, certain combinations of letters have unexpected results. This book's transliteration system should help you make intelligible noises but you have to remember that the correct **stress** (marked throughout the book with an acute accent) is crucial. With the right sounds but the wrong stress people will either fail to understand you, or else understand something quite different from what you intended.

Greek **grammar** is more complicated still: nouns are divided into three genders, all with different case endings in the singular and in the plural, and all adjectives and articles have to agree with these in gender, number and case. (All adjectives are arbitrarily cited in the neuter form in the lists on p.365.) Verbs are even worse, with active ones in several conjugations, passive verbs, and passive verbs used

actively. To begin with at least, the best thing is simply to say what you know the way you know it, and never mind the niceties. "Eat meat hungry" should get a result, however grammatically incorrect.

IDIOSYNCRASIES OF CYPRIOT GREEK

The "b" sound of standard Greek is largely absent on Cyprus, with a simple "p" replacing it: thus *parpoúni* for the tasty reddish fish, not *barboúni*; *tapélla* for "sign, placard", not *tabélla*. Strong sibilants, lacking to most peninsular Greek-speakers, are also a feature of the dialect: the letter combination sigma-iota (s-i) is pronounced, and transliterated, as sh. The letter khi, when medial, is often pronounced the same way – *éshi*, not *ékhi*, for "there is" or "he/she/it/ has". Medial kappa or "k" will sound like the "tch" of Crete, as in *Yerostchípou* for the village near Páfos (Yeroskípou). When initial, "k" sounds more like "g"; the letter tau or "t" often sounds more like "d"; thus, *káto* comes out more like *gádo*. The letter pi or "p" is in turn rendered more like "b", as in *baboútsia* (shoes) rather than *papoútsia*. Especially in Páfos district, Turkisms in the vocabulary abound: examples include *chaki* instead of the standard *souyiás* for "pocketknife", *chatália* (literally, "forks") for "pantaloons".

TURKISH

It's worth learning as much Turkish as you can while you're in North Cyprus; if you travel far from the tourist centres you may well need it, and Cypriots will always appreciate foreigners who show enough interest and courtesy to learn at least basic greetings. The main advantages of the language from the learner's point of view are that it's phonetically spelt, and grammatically regular. The disadvantages are that the vocabulary is completely unrelated to any language you're likely to have encountered at a European school, and the grammar, relying heavily on suffixes, gets more alien the further you delve into it. Concepts like vowel harmony, beyond the scope of this brief primer, further complicate matters. Trying to grasp at least the basics, though, is well worth the effort.

TURKISH PRONUNCIATION

Pronunciation in Turkish is worth mastering, since once you've got it, the phonetic spelling and regularity helps you progress fast. The following letters differ significantly from English pronunciation.

Aa	short a, similar to that in far.
Ââ	softly aspirated a, can sound as if preceded by a faint y or h.
İi	as in pit.
Iı	unstressed vowel similar to the a in probable.
Oo	as in mole.
Öö	like ur in burn.
Uu	as in blue.
Üü	like ew in few.
Cc	like j in jelly.
Çç	like ch in chat.
Gg	hard g as in get.
Ğğ	generally silent, but lengthens the preceding vowel and between two vowels can be a y sound.
Hh	as in hen, never silent.
Jj	like the s in pleasure.
Şş	like sh in shape.
Vv	soft, between a v and a w.

DICTIONARIES AND PHRASEBOOKS

For a straightforward **phrasebook**, look no further than *Turkish: A Rough Guide Phrasebook* (Rough Guides) though based on the mainland dialect, it has useful two-way glossaries and a brief and simple grammar section. If you want to **learn** more, Geoffrey L. Lewis's *Teach Yourself Turkish* (Hodder) still probably has a slight edge over Yusuf Mardin's *Colloquial Turkish* (Routledge); or buy both, since they complement each other well. Alternatively, there's Geoffrey Lewis's *Turkish Grammar* (OUP), a one-volume solution.

Among widely available Turkish **dictionaries**, the best are probably those produced by Langenscheidt in miniature or coat-pocket sizes, or the *Concise Oxford Turkish Dictionary*, a hardback suitable for serious students. The Redhouse dictionaries produced in Turkey are the best value: the four-and-a-half-inch *Mini Sözlük* has the same number of entries as the seven-and-a-half-inch desk edition and is adequate for most demands; the definitive, two-tome version even gives Ottoman Turkish script and etymologies for each word, but it costs the earth and isn't exactly portable.

IDIOSYNCRACIES OF CYPRIOT TURKISH

Pafiot Turkish in particular, as long as it lasts as a separate sub-dialect, shows the effects of long cohabitation with Cypriot Greek. There is no indicative tense as in standard Turkish, the indefinite mood being used on most occasions; nor are there interrogative particles as in Turkey, a question being indicated by voice inflection as in Greek.

Moreover, refugees from Páfos (*Baf* in Turkish, incidentally) frequently use *etmek*, normally only an auxiliary verb in Anatolian Turkish, in place of *yapmak* for "to do, to make". Slurred pronoun constructions are common and confusing: *ba* for *bana* (to/for me), *sa* for *sana* (to/for you), *gen* for *kendin'e* (to/for oneself). *Na'pan*, the standard colloquial greeting, is an elision of *Ne yaparsın* (approximately, "Whaddya up to?" or "Whatcha doin'?")

That translation gives a fairly accurate idea of the casualness of Cypriot linguistic mores; the islanders derive some amusement from the painfully polite diction of Istanbul people, who in turn consider the island dialect just plain slovenly. However, Turkish television plus nearly two decades of army occupation and refugee status are steadily eroding these peculiarities, which will probably disappear over the next generation.

TURKISH WORDS AND PHRASES

Basics

Mr; follows first name	*Bey*
Miss; precedes first name	*Bayan*
Mrs (literally lady) polite	*Hanım*
Ottoman title; follows first name	
Half-humorous honorific title bestowed on any tradesman; means "master craftsman"	*Usta*
Honorific of someone who has made the pilgrimage to Mecca	*Hacı*
Good morning	*Günaydın*
Good afternoon	*İyi Günler*
Good evening	*İyi Akşamlar*
Good night	*İyi Geceler*
Hello	*Merhaba*
Goodbye	*Allahaısmarladık*
Yes	*Evet*
No	*Hayır*
No (there isn't any)	*Yok*
Please	*Lütfen*
Thank you	*Teşekkür ederim/Mersi/ Sağol*
You're welcome, that's OK	*Bir şey değil*
How are you?	*Nasılsınız? Nasılsın? Ne haber?*
I'm fine (thank you)	*(Sağol) İyiyim/İyilik Sağlık*
Do you speak English?	*İngilizce biliyormusunuz?*
I don't understand	*Anlamadım/Anlamıyorum*

I don't know	*Bilmiyorum*
I beg your pardon, sorry	*Affedersiniz*
Excuse me (in a crowd)	*Pardon*
I'm sightseeing	*Geziyorum/Dolaşiyorum*
I'm English/Scottish/ Irish/Australian	*İngilizim/İskoçyalım/ İrlandalıyım/ Avustralyalım*
I live in . . .	*. . .'de/da oturuyorum*
Today	*Bugün*
Tomorrow	*Yarın*
The day after tomorrow	*Öbür gün/Ertesi gün*
Yesterday	*Dün*
Now	*Şimdi*
Later	*Sonra*
Wait a minute!	*Bir dakika!*
In the morning	*Sabahleyin*
In the afternoon	*Öğleden sonra*
In the evening	*Akşamleyin*
Here/there/over there	*Burda/Şurda/Orda*
Good/bad	*İyi/Kötü, Fena*
Big/small	*Büyük/Küçük*
Cheap/expensive	*Ucuz/Pahalı*
Early/late	*Erken/Geç*
Hot/cold	*Sıcak/Soğuk*
Near/far	*Yakın/Uzak*
Vacant/occupied	*Boş/Dolu*
Quickly/slowly	*Hızlı/Yavaş*
With/without (milk)	*(Süt)lu/(Süt)suz*
. . . (meat)	*(Et)li/(Et)siz*
Enough	*Yeter*

Driving

Left	*Sol*
Right	*Sağ*
Straight ahead	*Doğru*
Turn left/right	*Sola dön/Sağa dön*
Parking/No parking	*Park yapılır/Park yapılmaz*
One-way street	*Tek yön*

No entry	*Araç giremez*
No through road	*Çıkmaz sokak*
Slow down	*Yavaşla*
Road closed	*Yol kapalı*
Crossroads	*Dörtyol*
Pedestrian crossing	*Yaya geçidi*

Some Signs

Entrance/exit	*Giriş/Çıkış*
Free/paid entrance	*Giriş ücretsiz/Ücretlidir*
Gentlemen	*Baylar*
Ladies	*Bayanlar*
WC	*WC/Tuvalet/Umumî*
Open/closed	*Açık/Kapalı*
Arrivals/departures	*Varış/Kalkış*
Pull/push	*Çekiniz/İtiniz*
Out of order	*Arızalı*
Drinking water	*İçilebilir su*
To let/for hire	*Kiralık*

Foreign exchange	*Kambiyo*
Beware	*Dikkat*
First aid	*İlk yardım*
No Smoking	*Sigara İçilmez*
Don't tread on the grass	*Çimenlere Basmayınız*
Stop/halt	*Dur*
Military Area	*Askeri bölge*
Entry Forbidden	*Girmek Yasaktır*
Please take off your shoes	*Lütfen ayakkabılarınızı çıkartınız*
No entry on foot	*Yaya giremez*

Continues overleaf...

Turkish Words and Phrases continued

Accommodation

Hotel	*Hotel/Otel*	For one/two weeks	*Bir/İki haftalık*
Pension, Boarding house	*Pansiyon*	With an extra bed	*İlave yataklı*
Campsite	*Kamping*	With a double bed	*Çift kişilik yataklı*
Hostel	*Yurt*	With a shower	*Duşlu*
Tent	*Çadır*	Hot water	*Sıcak su*
Is there a hotel nearby?	*Yakinda otel var mı?*	Cold water	*Soğuk su*
Do you have a room?	*Boş odanız var mı?*	Can I see it?	*Bakabilirmiyim?*
Single/double/triple	*Tek/Çift/Üç kişilik*	I have a booking	*Reservasyonim var*
Do you have a double room for one/two/three nights?	*Bir/İki/Üç gecelik çift yataklı odanız var mı?*	Can we camp here?	*Burda kamp edebilirmiyiz?*

Travelling

Aeroplane	*Uçak*	When is the next bus/ferry?	*Bir sonraki otobus/vapur kaçta kalkıyor?*
Bus	*Otobus*		
Car	*Araba*	Where does it leave from?	*Nereden kalkıyor?*
Taxi	*Taksi*		
Bicycle	*Bisiklet*	How many miles is it?	*Kaç mildir?*
Ferry	*Vapur/Feribot*	How long does it take?	*Ne kadar sürerbilir?*
Hitch-hiking	*Otostop*	Which bus goes to . . . ?	*Hangi otobus . . . 'a gider?*
On foot	*Yaya*		
Bus station	*Otogar*	Which road leads to . . . ?	*A hangi yol . . . 'a çıkar?*
Ferry terminal/jetty	*İskele*		
Harbour	*Liman*	Can I get out at a convenient place?	*Müsait bir yerde inebilirmiyim?*
A ticket to . . .	*. . . 'a bir bilet*		
What time does it leave?	*Kaçta kalkıyor?*		

Days of the week, months and seasons

Sunday	*Pazar*	January	*Ocak*	September	*Eylül*
Monday	*Pazartesi*	February	*Subat*	October	*Ekim*
Tuesday	*Salı*	March	*Mart*	November	*Kasım*
Wednesday	*Çarşamba*	April	*Nisan*	December	*Aralık*
Thursday	*Perşembe*	May	*Mais*	Spring	*İlkbahar*
Friday	*Cuma*	June	*Haziran*	Summer	*Yaz*
Saturday	*Cumartesi*	July	*Temmuz*	Autumn	*Sonbahar*
		August	*Ağustos*	Winter	*Kış*

Time Conventions

(At) 3 o'clock	*Saat üç(ta)*	It's 8.10	*Sekizi on geçiyor*
2 hours (duration)	*İki saat*	It's 10.45	*On bire çeyrek var*
Half hour (duration)	*Yarım saat*	At 8.10	*Sekizi on geçe*
Five-thirty	*Beş büçük*	At 10.45	*On bire çeyrek kala*

Numbers

1	*Bir*	7	*Yedi*	13	*On üç*	70	*Yetmiş*
2	*İki*	8	*Sekiz*	20	*Yirmi*	80	*Seksen*
3	*Üç*	9	*Dokuz*	30	*Otuz*	90	*Doksan*
4	*Dört*	10	*On*	40	*Kırk*	100	*Yüz*
5	*Beş*	11	*On bir*	50	*Elli*	140	*Yüz kırk*
6	*Altı*	12	*On iki*	60	*Altmış*	200	*İki yüz*

700	*Yedi yüz*
1000	*Bin*
9000	*Dokuz bin*
1,000,000	*Bir milyon*

Compounded numbers tend to be run together in spelling: 50,784 *Ellibinyediyüzseksendört*

Questions and Directions

Where is the . . . ?	. . . *Nerede?*	How far is it to . . . ?	. . . *'a/e ne kadar uzakta?*
When?	*Ne zaman?*	Can you give me a lift	*Beni . . . 'a/e*
What (what is it?)	*Ne (ne dir?)*	to . . . ?	*götürebilirmisiniz?*
How much (does it cost?)	*Ne kadar/Kaça?*	What time does it	*Kaçta açılıcak?*
How many?	*Kaç tane?*	open?	
Why?	*Niye?*	What time does it	*Kaçta kapanacak?*
What time is it?	*(polite) Saatınız var mı?*	close?	
	(informal) Saat kaç?	What's it called in	*Türkcesi ne dir? Turkçe*
How do I get to . . . ?	. . . *'a/e nasıl giderim?*	Turkish?	*nasıl söylersiniz?*

GLOSSARY

For glossaries of acronyms of political parties, see p.321 and p.325.

ARCHEOLOGICAL, ARTISTIC AND ARCHITECTURAL TERMS

ACROPOLIS Ancient fortified hilltop.

AGORA Market and meeting place of an ancient Greek city.

AMPHORA Tall, narrow-necked jar for oil or wine.

ANICONIC Abstract, non-figurative, dating from the Iconoclast Period (eighth–ninth century AD).

APSE Polygonal or curved recess at the altar end of a church.

ARCHAIC PERIOD An era (750–475 BC) when Cypriot artistic expressiveness was most developed in its own right, though heavily influenced by the Middle East.

ASHLAR Dressed, squared masonry in an ancient structure, either free-standing or facing a rubble wall.

ATRIUM Open, inner courtyard of a house.

BASILICA Colonnaded, hall- or barn-type church, common in Cyprus.

BETYL Bullet-shaped stone, sacred object of the Aphrodite cult and anointed like a Hindu Shiva *lingam*.

BRONZE AGE Early (2500–1900 BC) to Late (1650–1050 BC); the latter eras show marked cultural influence of the Mycenaean migration from the Greek Peloponnese.

BYZANTINE EMPIRE Created by the division of the Roman Empire in 395 AD, this, the eastern half, was ruled from Constantinople (modern Istanbul). Byzantine rule ended in 1191 on Cyprus.

CAPITAL The top, often ornamented, of a column.

CHALCOLITHIC PERIOD Cultures (3900–2500 BC) distinguished by advanced ceramic and worked-stone artefacts, and by the first smelting of copper – from which Cyprus probably takes its name.

CLASSICAL ERA In Cyprus, from the start of the fifth century BC to the rule of the Macedonian kings late in the next century; a period of destruction at the hands of the Persians, and thus poor in home-grown artefacts.

CONCH Curved wall surface at the top of an apse.

DROMOS Ramp leading to the subterranean entrance of a Bronze Age tomb.

FORUM Market and meeting place of a Roman-era city.

FRIGIDARIUM Cold plunge-pool room of a Roman or Byzantine bath.

GEOMETRIC Archeological epoch (1050–750 BC) so named for the abstract designs of its pottery.

GROIN VAULTING Series of projecting curved stone ribs marking the junction of ceiling vaults; common feature of Lusignan monastic and military architecture.

HELLENISTIC ERA Extending from 325 to 50 BC, this meant for Cyprus rule by the Ptolemaic kings, based in Alexandria.

HYPOCAUST Hollow space, with round-brick struts, for hot-air circulation below the floor of an ancient bath.

ICONOCLASM Eighth- and ninth-century Byzantine movement whereby the veneration of icons was forbidden as idolatrous; during this time many figurative frescoes were destroyed as well.

IERÁRKHI The Fathers of Christianity, a common fresco subject.

IERÓN Literally, "sacred" – the sanctuary between the altar screen and the apse of a church, reserved for the priest's activities.

KATHOLIKÓN Central church of a monastery.

KRATIR Large, usually two-handled ancient wine goblet.

LUSIGNAN DYNASTY Mostly French, Catholic nobility which ruled Cyprus from 1191 until 1489, a time typified by monumental Gothic architecture, the introduction of feudalism and the suppression of the Orthodox Church.

MACHICOLATIONS Openings at the edge of a castle's parapet or above its doorway, usually between corbels, for dumping noxious substances on invaders.

MITRÓPOLIS Cathedral of a large town.

NAOS The inner sanctum of an ancient temple; also, any Orthodox Christian shrine.

NARTHEX Vestibule or entrance hall of a church; also *exonarthex*, the outer vestibule when there is more than one.

NAVE Principal lengthwise aisle of a church.

NECROPOLIS Concentration of above-ground tombs, always outside the walls of an ancient city.

NEOLITHIC PERIOD Earliest era of settlement on Cyprus, divided into Neolithic I (7000–6000 BC), as at Khirokitiá, and Neolithic II (4500–3800 BC).

ODEION Small amphitheatre, Hellenistic or Roman, used for musical performances, minor dramatic productions, or municipal councils.

OPUS SECTILE Roman technique for wall or floor mosaics, using thin, translucent sections of marble, mother-of-pearl or glass set in adhesive, framed when necessary by metal clamps.

ORANS Term for depiction of the Virgin with both arms aloft in an attitude of blessing.

PANDOKRÁTOR Literally "The Almighty", but generally refers to the stern portrayal of Christ in Majesty frescoed or in mosaic in the dome of many Byzantine churches.

PEDIMENT Triangular wall space between roof and wall of a chapel.

RHYTON Vessel, often horn-shaped, for libations or offerings.

STELE Upright stone slab or column, usually inscribed; an ancient tombstone.

STOA Colonnaded walkway in ancient marketplaces.

SYNTHRONON Semicircular seating for clergy, usually in the apse of a Byzantine church.

TÉMBLON Wooden altar screen of an Orthodox church, usually ornately carved and painted and studded with icons.

TEMENOS Sacred precinct, often used to refer to the sanctuary itself.

TEPIDARIUM Warm anteroom of a Roman or Byzantine bath.

TESSERAE Cubes used to compose a mosaic, either naturally coloured rock or painted or gilded glass.

THOLOS Conical or beehive-shaped building, especially a Bronze Age tomb.

TRANSEPT The "arms" of a church, perpendicular to the nave.

TYMPANUM In Orthodox use, the semicircular space over a church side door reserved for dedicatory inscriptions, dates, frescoes, etc.

XENON Hostel for pilgrims at an ancient shrine; the tradition continues at modern Cypriot Orthodox monasteries, though such inns are more accurately rendered *ksenónas* in modern Greek.

YINAIKONÍTIS Women's gallery in an Orthodox church, almost always at the rear.

COMMON GREEK CYPRIOT TERMS

ÁNO Upper; as in upper town or village.

ÁYIOS/AYÍA/ÁYII Saint or holy (m/f/pl). Common place name prefix (abbreviated Ag or Ay.), often spelt AGIOS or AGHIOS.

EXOKHIKÓ KÉNDRO Rural taverna, often functioning only at summer weekends.

KAFENÍO Coffee house or café; in a small village the centre of communal life and probably serving as the bus stop, too.

KÁTO Lower; as in lower town or village.

KINOTÁRKHIS See *múkhtar*, below.

LOUKOÚMI Turkish delight – a sweet made primarily from powdered sugar, rosewater or citrus extract, and gelatin.

MESAORÍA The broad plain between the Tróödhos and Kyrenia mountains; site of Nicosia.

MONÍ Monastery or convent.

MÚKHTAR Village headman.

NÉOS, NÉA, NÉO "New" – a common part of a town or village name.

PALEÓS, PALEÁ, PALEÓ "Old" – again, common in town and village names.

PANAYÍA Virgin Mary.

PANIYÍRI Festival or feast – the local celebration of a holy day.

PLATÍA Square, plaza; KENDRIKÍ PLATÍA, central square.

COMMON TURKISH CYPRIOT TERMS

AĞA A minor rank of nobility in the Ottoman Empire, and still a term of respect applied to a local worthy – follows the name (eg Ismail Ağa).

BAHÇE(Sİ) Garden.

BEDESTEN Covered market hall for textiles, often lockable.

BEKÇİ Caretaker at an archeological site or monument.

BEY Another minor Ottoman title, like *Ağa,* still in use.

CAMİ(İ) Mosque.

ÇARŞI(SI) Bazaar, market.

DAĞI, DAĞLARI "Mount" and "mountains", respectively.

DOLMUŞ Literally "filled" – the shared taxi system operating in larger North Cyprus towns; some confusing overlap with "minibus", since not all of the latter are *dolmuşes,* and vice versa.

ESKİ "Old" – frequent modifier of place names.

EZAN The Muslim call to prayer.

HALK PLAJI/PLAJLARI Free-of-charge public beach(es).

HAMAM(I) Turkish sauna-bath.

HASTANE(Sİ) Hospital.

HOCA Teacher in charge of religious instruction of children.

İMAM Usually just the prayer leader at a mosque, though it can mean a more important spiritual authority.

KALE(Sİ) Castle, fort.

KAPI(SI) Gate, door.

KİLİSE(Sİ) Church.

KONAK Large private residence, also the main government building of a province or city; genitive form *konağı.*

KULE(Sİ) Tower, turret.

MABET Temple, common signpost at ancient sites; genitive *mabedi.*

MAHALLE(Sİ) District or neighbourhood of a larger municipality.

MESARYA Turkish for the Mesaoría; officially renamed *İçova.*

MEYDAN(I) Public square or plaza.

MEYHANE Tavern serving alcohol and food.

MEZAR(I) Grave, tomb; thus *mezarlık,* cemetery.

MİHRAB Niche in mosque indicating the direction of Mecca, and prayer.

MİMBER Pulpit in a mosque, from where the *imam* delivers homilies.

MİNARE Turkish for "minaret", the tower from which the call to prayer is delivered.

MÜEZZİN Man who pronounces call to prayer from the minaret of a mosque; the call is often taped these days.

MUHTAR Village headman; *muhtarlık* is the office, both in the abstract and concrete sense.

NAMAZ The Muslim rite of prayer, performed five times daily.

PAŞA Ottoman honorific, approximately equivalent to "Lord"; follows the name.

SUFİ Dervish – more properly an adherent of one of the heterodox mystical branches of Islam.

TABYA Bastion (on walls of north Nicosia or Famagusta).

TAPINAK Alternative term for "temple" at archeological sites; genitive *tapınağı.*

TARIKAT Any one of the various Sufi orders.

TEKKE(Sİ) Gathering place of a Sufi order.

VAKIF Islamic religious trust, responsible for social welfare and religious buildings; holds extensive property, often donated by believers, in North Cyprus.

VIZIER The principal Ottoman minister of state, responsible for the day-to-day running of the empire.

YENİ "New" – common component of Turkish Cypriot place names.

INDEX

A

"Acapulco" beach 264
Accommodation 25–27
ADISOK 323
Admission charges 40
Aféndrika 299
Afxentiou, Grigorios 183
Agrós 180
Akámas Firing Range 141
Akámas peninsula 131–133, 139–143
Akapnoú 92
Akdeniz 258
AKEL 317, 323, 328
Akhiropiítos monastery 255
Akrotíri peninsula 94
Akrotíri village 95
Aktí Kivernítou, see Governor's Beach
Alagadi beach 264
Alevkaya 269
Alsancak 254–256
Amathoúnda, see Amathus
Amathus 93
Ammókhostos, see Famagusta
Andhrolíkou 139
Angelóktisti church 65
Antifonítis monastery 269
Aphrodite, cult of 123
Apollo Hylates sanctuary 101
Apóstolos Andhréas monastery 300
Apóstolos Varnávas monastery-museum 289–291
Arakapás 92
Arapköy 268
Archbishop Makarios III 144, 146–147, 319–327
Arkhángelos church, Galáta 173
Arkhángelos church, Pedhoulás 165
Aródhes, Páno/Káto 132
Ársos 91
Asínou church 175
Attila Line 212, 325
Autocephalous Church of Cyprus 290
Avgás gorge 129
Ayía Ekateríni church 134
Ayía Iríni, see Akdeniz

Ayía Mávra chapel 90
Ayía Moní monastery 145
Ayía Nápa 74–76
Ayía Nápa monastery 74
Ayía Paraskeví church 122
Ayía Triás basilica 296
Áyii Anáryiri Milioú 134
Áyios Amvrósios, see Esentepe
Áyios Epíktitos, see Çatalköy
Áyios Fílon basilicas 298
Áyios Fótios church 298
Áyios Ioánnis Lambadhistís monastery 169
Áyios Iraklídhios convent 213
Áyios Mámas chapel, Louvarás 181
Áyios Neófitos monastery 125
Áyios Nikólaos 151
Áyios Nikólaos tis Steyís church 172
Áyios Sávvas tis Karónos 150
Áyios Sozómenos church 174
Áyios Thýrsos 297
Áyios Yióryios (North), see Karaoğlanoğlu
Áyios Yióryios 128
Áyios Yióryios museum 127
Ayíou Nikoláou ton Gáton convent 95

B

Banks 18
Bargaining 46
Baths of Aphrodite, see Loutrá Afrodhítis
Beer 33
Béllapais abbey 261
Béllapais village, see Beylerbeyi
Beşinci Mil beach 250
Beşparmak summit 269
Beylerbeyi 261
Boğaz 292
Bogázi, see Boğaz
British Sovereign Bases 73, 96
Buffavento castle 267
Bureaux de change 18
Buses 20

C

Caledonian falls 159
Çamlıbel 258
Campsites 27

Cape Apostólou Andhréa, see Zafer Burnu
Cape Eléa, see Zeytin Burnu
Cape Gréko 77
Cape Kíti 66
Cape Lára 129
Car rental 23
Çatalköy 263
Caterina Cornaro 280, 313
Cedar Valley 148
Cenotaph of Nicocreon 292
"Chapelle Royale", see Pýrga
Children 45
Churches 41
Cinema 37
Clerides, Glafcos 323, 328
Coffee 34
Contraceptives 45
Coral Bay 127
Crafts 44
Crime 42
CTP 326
Curium, see Kourion
Currency 18
Cycling 24

D

Denktaş, Rauf 228, 321, 329–333, 362
Departure tax 45
Dháli 214
Dhassoúdhi 93
Dhavlós, see Kaplıca
Dhekélia Sovereign Base 73
Dherínia 76
Dhiárizos valley 150
Dhiyenis' Landing 127
Dhorá 91
Dhroúsha 132
DIKO 323, 328
Dipkarpaz 298
DISY 323, 328
DMP 330
Dolmuşes 21
DP 326, 330
Drinking 32–34
Driving 22–24
Durrell, Lawrence 201, 261–264, 360

E

EDEK 323, 326–328
Edremit 254
Electric current 46

Émba 125
Emergencies 45
Éngomi, see Enkomi-Alasia and Cenotaph of Nicocreon
Enkomi-Alasia 291
EOKA 200, 318
EOKA-B 201, 224, 294, 324–326
Eptagónia 92
Esentepe 270
Evagoras of Salamis 286, 309
Evdhímou 102
Exchange facilities 18

F

FAMAGUSTA 272–284
  Accommodation 276
  Arrival 276
  Canbulat Bastion museum 277
  City walls 276
  Eating and drinking 284
  Lala Mustafa Paşa Camii 277
  Listings 284
  Maraş 283
  Namik Kemal Meydanı 277
  Nightlife 284
  Othello's Tower 281
  Saints Peter and Paul church 277
  Siege of Famagusta 280–281
Farmakás 183
Faslí 139
Ferries 6–8
Festivals 38–40
Fíni 163
Flights
  from Australasia 10
  from Britain 3–6
  from neighbouring countries 3
  from North America 8–10
Flights from Turkey 6
Flória beach 121
Fontána Amorósa 143
Food 27–32
Frescoed churches of the Tróödhos 166
Fykárdhou 183
Fýti 144

G

Galáta 173
Galinóporni, see Kaleburnu
Gay life 45
Gazimağusa, see Famagusta
Gaziveran incident 237
Gemikonağı 199
Girne, see Kyrenia

Governor's Beach 94
Greeks of the Kárpas 298
Green Line, The 189, 206
Grivas, George "Dhiyenis" 200, 293
Guest houses 26
Güzelyalı 257
Güzelyurt 234–236

H

Hala Sultan Tekke 64
Halévga, see Alevkaya
Hazreti Ömer tomb 263
Health 12
Hiking in the Akámas peninsula 128–131, 141–143
Hiking in the Tróödhos range 148–149, 159–163, 178–179
Hitching 21
Hostels 26
Hotels 25, 26

I

Idalion 214
Ínia 132
Insurance 14
İskele 293

K

Kakopetriá 171
Kalavassós 67
Kaleburnu 296
Kalokhorió 181
Kalopanayiótis 168
Kambí 183
Kámbos 171
Kaminária 164
Kanakariá mosaics theft 202, 297
Kantara 294
Kaplıca 295
Karákoumi, see Karakum
Karakum 263
Karaman 251
Karaoğlanoğlu 250
Karavás, see Alsancak
Karavostási, see Gemikonağı
Kármi, see Karaman
Kárpas peninsula 293–301
Karpásha, see Karpaşa village
Karpasia 299
Karpaşa 260

Karşıyaka 257
Káthikas 132
Káto Akourdhália 134
Káto Léfkara 70
Káto Pýrgos 137
Káto Páfos 110–116
Kayalar 258
Kazáfani, see Ozanköy
Kelláki 92
Kelliá 72
Kıbrıslı Şeyh Nazim 237
Khionístra peak, see Mount Olympus
Khirokhitiá 67
Khóli 135
Khrysfíyeto toú Afxentíou 184
Khrysokhoú 135
Khrysorroyiátissa monastery 145
Kiláni 90
King James II 313
King Janus 72, 313
King Peter I 313
Kırpaşa peninsula 293–301
Kíti, see Angelóktisti church
Klepíni, see Arapköy
Klonári 92
Knights Hospitaller of Saint John 93, 97, 282, 313
Knights Templar 282, 312
Kofínou 70
Kókkina enclave 137, 296
Kokkinokhoriá 76
Kolossi 97
Kormakíti peninsula 257–260
Kormakíti village, see Koruçam
Kórnos 70
Koruçam 258
Koruçam Burnu, see Kormakíti peninsula
Koufón gorge 129
Koúklia (South) 122
Kourdhalí 179
Kourion 98–102
Kozan 260
Krassokhoriá 89
Krítou Térra 133
Kséros valley 149
Ktíma Páfos 116–118
Küçük, Dr Fazil 319–321
Kýkko monastery 170
Kyperoúnda 178
Kyprianou, Spyros 324, 327
Kyrenia 243–250

L

La Cavocle manor 124
Lady's Mile Beach 94
Lagoudherá 176
Lánia 92
Laona Project 131, 356
Lápithos, see Lapta
Lapta 256
Lara beach (North) 264
LARNACA 54–64
  Accommodation 58
  Ancient Kition 61
  Archeological Museum 60
  Arrival 56
  Áyios Lázaros 58
  Bazaar 59
  Eating and drinking 62
  Listings 63
  Nightlife 63
  Orientation 56
  Pierides Museum 60
  Shopping 63
  Turkish Quarter 59
Lárnaka tis Lapíthou, see Kozan
Látchi 138
Lazaniá 183
Lazarus, patron saint of Larnaca
  55, 58, 65
Léfka, see Lefke
Lefke 236
Lefkosía, see Nicosia, South
Lémba 126
Lemesós, see Limassol
LIMASSOL 80–89
  Accommodation 82
  Archeological Museum 86
  Arrival 82
  Bazaar 83
  Castle 83
  Drinking and nightlife 88
  Eating 87
  Folk Art Museum 86
  Listings 88
  Orientation 82
  Wineries 85
Limassol foothills 89
Liverás, see Sadrazamköy
Loutrá Afrodhítis 141
Louvarás 181
Lusignans 312–314

M

Máa, see Coral Bay
Madhári ridge 178
Magazines 36
Mail 34
Makherás monastery 183

Malliá 91
Mamónia 150
Mansoúra 137
Maps 14–17
Marathássa 165–171
Maróni 66
Maronites of Kormakíti 259
Melíni 92
Mesaoría (South) 187
Mesarya (North) 240, 271
Mesopótamos monastery 159
Metamórfosi tou Sotírou church
  182
Mevleví Sufi order 226
Monágri 91
Monastery accommodation 27
Money 18
Mopeds 24
Mórfou, see Güzelyurt
Mosque etiquette 41
Mount Adhélfi, see Madhári ridge
Mount Olympus 159–163
Moúsere 91
Moutoullás, see Panayía
  Moutoullá
Museums 40
Mycenaeans 306
Mýrtou, see Çamlıbel

N

Nadir, Asil 252, 265
Neokhorió 138
Newspapers 36
Nicocreon of Salamis 310
NICOSIA, NORTH 221–234
  Accommodation 233
  Arabahmet district 232
  Arrival 224
  Atatürk Meydanı 227
  Bazaars 229
  Bedesten 230
  Derviş Paşa Konaği 232
  Eating and drinking 233
  Ethnography Museum 226
  Listings 233
  Orientation 225
  Ottoman baths and inns 227
  Ramparts 226
  Selimiye Camii 230
NICOSIA, SOUTH 187–210
  Accommodation 194
  Archbishop Makarios Cultural
    Centre 202
  Arrival 191
  Commercial centre 197
  Cyprus Museum 204
  Eating and drinking 207

  Entertainment 209
  Famagusta gate 197, 207
  Folk Art Museum 202
  Hadjiyiorgakis Kornesios mansion
    199
  Kaïmákli suburb 205
  Khrysaliniótissa district 203
  Laïkí Yitoniá 198
  Ledra Palace checkpoint 207
  Listings 209
  Nightlife 208
  Ömeriye Camii 199
  Orientation 194
  Platía Faneroménis 198
  Shopping 208
  Tahtakale district 203
  Venetian walls 196
Nikóklia 150
Nissí beach 76
North Cyprus Herbarium 269

O

Odhoú 92
Ómodhos 90
Onüçüncü Mil beach 265
Opening hours 38
Órga, see Kayalar
Ottomans 314–316
Ozanköy 263
Özgür, Özker 229, 329

P

Package holidays from Britain
  6
PÁFOS 108–121
  Accommodation 110
  Arrival and information 109
  Ayía Kyriakí 114
  Ayía Solomóni 115
  Buses 109
  Castle 112
  Eating 118
  Drinking and nightlife 120
  Harbour 111
  Listings 120
  Moúttalos 116
  Museums 116–118
  Roman mosaics 112–114
  Saránda Kolónes 114
  Tombs of the Kings 115
Pakhýammos 137
Palea Paphos 122–124
Palekhóri 182
Panayía 144
Panayía Absinthiótissa
  monastery 267
Panayía Eleoússa church 298
Panayía Eleoússa Síndi 150

Panayía Forviótissa, see Asínou church

Panayía Kanakariá church 296

Panayía Khryseléoussa church 125

Panayía Moutoullá church 168

Panayía Pergamiótissa church 295

Panayía Podíthou church 173

Panayía Theotókou church, Galáta 174

Panayía tou Araká church 176

Páno Akourdhália 134

Páno Léfkara 69

Paphos, see Páfos

Paralímni 77

Pay beach scandal 264

Pedhoulás 165–167

Peléndhri 180

Pendadháktylos, see Beşparmak

Perakhorió 213

Peristeróna 211

Perivólia 66

Pernéra 77

Pétra tou Romíou 103

Péyia 131

Pharmacies 13

Pissoúri 102

Pitsiliá 176–184

Platanistássa 177

Plátres 155–158

Police 42

Pólis 135

Pomós 137

Post 34

Potamioú 90

Potamós Liopetríou 74

Potamós tou Kámbou, see Yedidalga

Prastió 150

Pródhromos 165

Protarás 77

Pýla 73

Pýrga 72

R

Radio 37

Restaurants 29

Richard the Lionheart 81, 312

Rimbaud, Arthur 74, 159

Rizokárpaso, see Dipkarpaz

Royal Tombs 288

S

Sadrazamköy 258

St Barnabas 290

St Hilarion castle 265–267

St Mamas 181, 235

Salamis 284–288

Sampson, Nikos 321, 324

Sea turtles 130

Seferis, George 95

Self-catering 26

Sexual harassment 42

Shopping 44

Sipahi 296

Skiing Mount Olympus 162

Skoúlli 134

Smoking 45

Soléa 171–176

Soli 237

Sourp Magar monastery 269

Sport 43

Stavrós church 180

Stavrós tis Psókas 148

Stavrós tou Ayiasmáti church 177

Stavrovoúni monastery 71

T

Tamassos 211–213

Taxis 21

Telephones 34–36

Television 37

Thróni hill 170

Tillyría 148

Time 46

Tipping 46

TKP 326

TMT 228, 319–322, 326

Tour operators 5, 10, 11

Tourist offices 14, 15

Tríkomo, see İskele

Trimíthi, see Edremit

Troödhítissa monastery 163

Tróödhos resort 160

Ttákas Bay 139

"Turtle Bay" 264

Tuzla, see Cenotaph of Nicocreon

U

UBP 326, 329

Umm Haram, see Hala Sultan Tekke

UN-sponsored negotiations 327, 328, 330–333

UNFICYP 212, 322, 332

V

Varósha ghost town 76, 283

Vasília, see Karşıyaka

Vássa 90

Vassiliou, George 328

VAT 46

Vavatsiniá 69

Vavilás, see Güzelyalı

Vávla 69

Vegetarian food 29

Venetians 314

Víkla 92

Visas 12

Vouni (North) 238

Vouní (South) 89

Vrécha 149

W

Wine 32

Wish-trees 115, 170

Work 46

Y

YDP 326

Yedidalga 238

Yenierenköy 296

Yeroskípou 122

Yialoússa, see Yenierenköy

YKP 326

Z

Zafer Burnu 301

Zeytin Burnu beaches 295

Zíyi 66

THANK YOU

This second edition of the *Rough Guide to Cyprus* was considerably improved by letters from: S. A. Ashton, Rick Aspen, Jack & Barbara Barker, Jim Blythe, Jenny Boff, Stephen Brown, Alison Chilton, Diana Chitty, Mike Chivers, Deirdre Clark, Pam Cochrane, Norman & Diana Coward, Fritz & Joanna Curzon, Eric Davey, Carol Fletcher, Rebecca Foster, Brian Goodey (twice), Mary Alice Hayward, Jan Hewson & Alfy Lucas, Richard Jeremy, Joe Lembo, Mr A. G. Lloyd, Mark Mascall, Dave Martin, M. E. Millar, Duncan J. Moore, Gerald Noeske, Su Schechter, Simon Sparrow, Roger Teagle, Tim Thornton, Peter Tomlinson, Margaret Waller, David Webb, Joyce Whyte, Brian Williams, Paul Williams, Anita & Tony Woods, S. Wray, the Robbins-Zust Permanent Floating Marionette Theatre (!), and a regrettably unsigned writer from Wotton-under-Edge, Gloucestershire.

HELP US UPDATE

We've endeavoured to make this guide as up-to-date as possible, but it's inevitable that some of the information will become inaccurate between now and the preparation of the next edition. Readers' updates and suggestions are very welcome – please mark letters "Rough Guide Cyprus Update" and send to:

Rough Guides, 1 Mercer Street, London WC2H 9QJ
  or
Rough Guides, 375 Hudson Street, 9th Floor, New York NY10014
  or
cyprus@roughtravl.co.uk

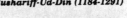

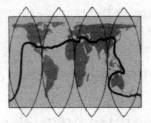

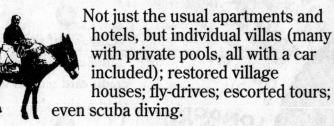

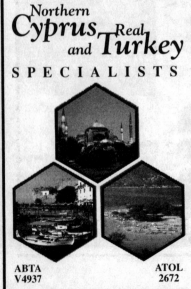

NORTH CYPRUS & TURKEY

North Cyprus is possibly the only Mediterranean holiday destination, which remains unspoilt, indeed little has changed over the past thirty years. In fact those who have been lucky enough to discover the unspoilt resorts of Kyrenia and Famagusta, like to keep their discovery a closely guarded secret.

North Cyprus offers the historical enthusiast a treasure trove of medieval castles, abbeys, mosques and ancient amphitheatres, bearing witness to the wealth of its chequered past. The nature-lover too cannot fail to be impressed by the stunning mountain scenery, the variety of wildlife and the beautiful beaches.

President Holidays is also a leading specialist tour operator for ISTANBUL CITY BREAKS, and SUMMER SUN in TURKEY's beautiful resorts. From the golden sandy beaches to some of the best reserved ancient monuments in the world; from the sophistication of Kusadasi's famed nightlife to the simplicity of unspoilt, secluded coves such as Turunç Bay...
we have exactly what you are looking for!

PRESIDENT HOLIDAYS
The true specialist for NORTH CYPRUS & TURKEY

0181 688 7555

24 hr. Brochure Line: 0181 667 1313
92 Park Lane, Croydon, Surrey, CRO 1JF

ABTA
V057X

ATOL
2 4 8 3

Registered in England No. 2270512. A member of The President Group PLC.